A HISTORY OF
THE CHRISTIAN CHURCH.

A HISTORY

OF THE

CHRISTIAN CHURCH

Since the Reformation.

BY

S. CHEETHAM, D.D.

ARCHDEACON AND CANON OF ROCHESTER;
HONORARY FELLOW OF CHRIST'S COLLEGE, CAMBRIDGE;
FELLOW AND EMERITUS PROFESSOR OF KING'S COLLEGE, LONDON.

WIPF & STOCK · Eugene, Oregon

Wipf and Stock Publishers
199 W 8th Ave, Suite 3
Eugene, OR 97401

A History of The Christian Church Since the Reformation
By Cheetham, Samuel
Softcover ISBN-13: 978-1-6667-6115-3
Hardcover ISBN-13: 978-1-6667-6116-0
eBook ISBN-13: 978-1-6667-6117-7
Publication date 10/4/2022
Previously published by Macmillan and Co., Limited, 1907

This edition is a scanned facsimile of the original edition published in 1907.

TO MY WIFE

MY FAITHFUL HELPER AND CRITIC.

PREFACE.

THIS book is founded on many years' study of the period over which it extends. It was indeed soon after the death of Archdeacon Hardwick that I formed the project of completing his work, and imparted it to the late Mr Alexander Macmillan. Other occupations and failure of health prevented me from carrying out this design, as I had hoped, within a few years, but it has never been long absent from my mind and is now at last completed. My History of the Early Church, Archdeacon Hardwick's Histories of the Middle Age and of the Reformation, together with that of the Modern Period now published, form a complete History of the Christian Church, on a small scale indeed, but written with constant reference to original authorities, and including, it is hoped, all the more important events and movements which have made the Church what it now is. More than this could not be attempted in so brief a narrative, and the difficulty of deciding what to give and what to reject is of course great, especially in regard to the complex streams of thought which have pervaded the seventeenth, eighteenth, and nineteenth centuries. The history is brought down, so far as the leading events are concerned, to our own time, but, with few exceptions, no reference is made to living persons.

I have to acknowledge my obligations, for general guidance, to the historical works of Schröckh, Gieseler, Kurtz, Hase, Alzog, Krauss, Funk, D. K. Müller, and, in the most recent portion, to F. Nippold's excellent *Handbuch der Neuesten Kirchengeschichte*. For the account of the English Freethinkers I am indebted to Miss Beatrice A. Lees, History Tutor of Somerville College, Oxford. The index is the work of my wife. And I have to express my gratitude to my old friend the Rev. G. C. Bell, late Master of Marlborough College, who has read the proofs and given me many valuable corrections and suggestions.

S. CHEETHAM.

ROCHESTER, 16 *Oct.* 1907.

TABLE OF CONTENTS.

	PAGE
INTRODUCTION	1

CHAPTER I.

LAST STRUGGLES OF THE REFORMATION.

1.	The Struggle in France.	7
2.	Switzerland and Piedmont	11
3.	Hungary, Transylvania and Poland	13
4.	The Thirty-Years' War.	15
5.	The Sequel of the Treaty of Westphalia	22
6.	The Struggle in England	27
7.	In Scotland	43
8.	In Ireland	49

CHAPTER II.

THE ENGLISH CHURCH.

1.	Anglican Theology and Theologians	54
2.	English Sects.	65
3.	Extension of the English Church.	68

CHAPTER III.

THE ROMAN CHURCH.

1.	General Characteristics.	74
2.	The Papacy	82
3.	New Orders and Societies	93
4.	Jansenism and Port-Royal	99
5.	The Gallican Church and its Liberties	106
6.	Mysticism and Quietism	109
7.	Missions.	112

CHAPTER IV.

THE DEVELOPMENT OF PROTESTANTISM.

		PAGE
1.	Lutheran Orthodoxy	118
2.	The Revival of Religious Life	121
	A. Pietism	121
	B. The Moravian Brotherhood	127
3.	Mystics and Theosophists	132
4.	Literary Activity of the Reformed	139
5.	The Arminians	142
6.	Projects for Religious Unity.	148
7.	Protestant Missions	154

CHAPTER V.

THE EASTERN CHURCH . . . 159

CHAPTER VI.

THE AGE OF REASON.

1.	English Free-thinking	167
2.	Methodism and Evangelicalism	185
3.	French Scepticism	194
4.	German Enlightenment	199
5.	The Popes and the Princes	218

CHAPTER VII.

THE SHAKING OF THE NATIONS.

1.	The French Revolution	233
2.	Napoleon and the French Conquests	238
3.	The Churches and the Revolution	245
4.	Religious Romanticism	247
5.	Sects of the Revolutionary Period	251

CHAPTER VIII.

THE ENGLISH-SPEAKING CHURCHES.

		PAGE
1.	The Oxford Movement	255
2.	Liberal Tendencies	271
3.	Life of the Church	282
4.	Church and State	286
5.	Non-Anglican Religious Bodies	292
6.	Scotland	309
7.	Ireland	319
8.	North America	326

CHAPTER IX.

THE PAPACY AND THE VATICAN COUNCIL.

1.	The Pope's return to Rome	346
2.	The Jesuits restored	347
3.	Pope Leo XII.	350
4.	Pope Pius VIII.	351
5.	Pope Pius IX.	353
6.	Reforms in Piedmont	356
7.	The Vatican Council	359
8.	Old-Catholicism	367
9.	Pope Leo XIII.	372

CHAPTER X.

FRANCE AND THE LATIN NATIONS.

1.	The Roman Catholic Church in France	375
2.	Protestantism in France	391
3.	Socialistic Movements	395
4.	Belgium	397
5.	Spain and Portugal	398
6.	The South-American Republics	402

CHAPTER XI.

THE TEUTONIC AND SCANDINAVIAN NATIONS.

I. *The Roman-Catholic Church.*

		PAGE
1.	Church and State	407
2.	Literature and Life	416
3.	The Contest for Culture	423

II. *Protestantism.*

4.	The Evangelical Union	427
5.	Theology and Biblical Criticism	436

CHAPTER XII.

THE EASTERN CHURCH.

1.	In Turkey	453
2.	In Greece	454
3.	In Armenia	456
4.	In Russia	457
5.	In Poland	458

INTRODUCTION.

THE ecclesiastical history of the seventeenth, eighteenth and nineteenth centuries is the history of the development of principles brought into prominence in the Reformation of the sixteenth. We generally understand by the Reformation a religious outburst which in the end separated from the spiritual dominion of the Papacy a large part of Europe, and set up the Bible alone as the highest authority in matters of faith, in place of ecclesiastical tradition expounded by the See of Rome. And this is its most obvious aspect, but this great religious change was in fact but part of a wider movement which affected the whole political, moral, intellectual, and social life of Europe.

During the Middle Ages, though there were not wanting indications that human thought desired to break the heavy bonds of tradition and authority, the Western branch of the Catholic Church was the only recognized form of religion from the British Isles to the Mediterranean, and from the frontier of Russia to the shores of the Atlantic. Every citizen of a state of Western Europe was, as a matter of course, in outward profession at least, a Christian and a Catholic. No Church stood alone; from every Church the last court of appeal in spiritual matters was the Roman Curia. There were frequent differences between Church and State, but no one went the length of denying the right of the Church in any state to exercise spiritual jurisdiction unhindered by the secular power, unless, it might be, in certain cases agreed upon between the several authorities.

When a large portion of Northern Europe rejected the authority of the Papal See and new religious communities

Marginalia: INTRODUCTION. — *The Reformation and its consequences.* — *Mediæval Church.* — *Political Problems.*

C.   1

were formed, certain political problems of great importance presented themselves for solution. Where the whole of a state, with its ruler, adopted one of the new forms of faith, whether Lutheran or Calvinist, the matter was comparatively simple. The Reforming leaders generally accepted the maxim, "cujus regio ejus religio," "lord of region, lord of religion"; they recognized the right of the sovereign to determine the form of religion in his own state. But there was often controversy and political strife as to the extent of the prince's power and the manner in which it should be exercised, and where a sovereign was converted from one form of faith to another serious perplexity, and often persecution, arose.

But when a nation was not agreed on the subject of religion, how were the relations of dissident communities to be regulated? In a country, for instance, which was still mainly Roman Catholic, were communities of Protestants, whom the bulk of the population regarded as mere infidels, to be tolerated? In France, where the Protestants were strong and had able leaders, they were actually permitted to hold certain fortified towns, and formed a kind of state within a state. This however was an arrangement which could not long endure. It was put an end to by the vigorous policy of Richelieu, but Protestants continued to enjoy most of the rights of citizenship until the intolerant folly of Louis XIV. made their position intolerable and drove into exile a large number of the best citizens of France. In the Swiss Confederation the quarrels of Romanists and Protestants frequently broke out into open hostilities, and sometimes into hideous massacre. But nowhere were the political complications arising out of the change of religion so great as in the Empire. The Holy Roman Empire had been for many generations regarded as a kind of secular counterpart of the Papacy. It was before all things Catholic; all its component parts were Catholic. What was to be done when some of the Princes of the Empire, with their subjects, fell away from their ancient faith? Could a Protestant continue to be an Elector? Supposing that an Elector who was actually a spiritual person ceased to hold his ecclesiastical office, could he still retain his temporal power? Was it consistent with allegiance to the Emperor for a Prince of the Empire to grant toleration within his dominions to non-Catholics? All these questions were imperfectly solved at the end of the sixteenth century, and were at last fought out in the terrible struggle of the Thirty-years' War, though even after that war was ended by the Peace of Westphalia there were still sporadic cases of persecution and oppression. In England a large and powerful section of the people, commonly called Puritans, were discontented with the Elizabethan settlement which retained—though with many reforms—the old Church order and ritual, and during the war between King and Parliament managed to possess themselves of the status and the benefices of the Church, and to change the services of the Church in accordance with their own views. When, at the Restoration, this state of things came to an end, separatist congregations were formed, which were severely persecuted, and religious peace was not permanently established until the Toleration Act of 1689, which may be regarded as the end of the Reformation-struggle in England. In Scotland, the Presbyterian system established under Knox, after many conflicts, and after being more than once put down and restored, was finally adopted by the Scottish Parliament in 1690. In Ireland, the Reformed Church which had the support of the English Government, and was put into possession of all the benefices, obtained but a small number of adherents, while the great majority of the population clung to their old faith, and provided out of their poverty for the continuance of their old worship. The massacre of Protestants in 1641 is however a terrible blot on their history. To speak generally, we may say that the hostilities which were the consequence of the Reformation came to an end with the seventeenth century.

Introduction.

England.

Scotland.

Ireland.

While the political struggle was going on, theological controversy continued, and the recognized doctrines of various religious bodies were in some cases reformed and extended. As the Reforming leaders had no mind to give to others the liberty which they claimed for themselves, of taking the Bible for a guide and teaching for doctrines the propositions which they believed they found there, they were willing to concede to a sovereign prince

Protestant Dogma.

INTRODUC-TION. — the power of maintaining orthodoxy within his dominions. Otherwise they were helpless in the face of heterodoxy, however extravagant. The methods of Protestant theologians in the seventeenth century differed little from those of their Catholic predecessors. Their authorities were different; citations of canons of councils, sentences of Fathers and Papal decrees dropped into the background or vanished altogether; only Scripture was regarded as of the first importance; but their philosophy, and consequently the form of their theology, differed little from that prevalent before their time. But meanwhile there was quietly growing up a school of thought which was to subvert it.

Philosophic Movement. — The renewed study of the classics, and especially of Greek, brought with it a knowledge of ancient philosophy, with its characteristic desire to follow reason whithersoever it might lead, which was soon seen to be in contrast with the barren disputations which occupied the mediæval divines. The revived philosophy found indeed no favour with the leading Protestant teachers, but it nevertheless gradually leavened the mass of ecclesiastical teaching. And when the first shock of the Reformation was dying away, philosophy received a new and vigorous impulse. Bacon taught that all true science must be derived from open-eyed investigation of the world around us; Descartes endeavoured to sweep away all preconceptions, and to accept no assumption but that of personal existence; and somewhat later Locke propounded his theory that all knowledge is derived from experience, and proclaimed that if Christianity was to be accepted it must be on reasonable grounds. In the eighteenth century these philosophies, or systems derived from them, became dominant, and were not found to be favourable to faith. And it was not only among Protestants that the prevalent philosophy influenced theology.

Roman Church. — The leading men of the Roman Church in the early days of the sixteenth century were much more moved by ancient philosophy than the Protestant divines, and their successors in the eighteenth could not withdraw themselves wholly from the influence of the "philosophes" of France and the "enlightened" of Germany. It was in the air, and they breathed, whether they would or not, the stimulating atmosphere. Many symptoms shewed that, however strictly the traditional formularies might be maintained, intellectual life in the Church had acquired a new and more liberal—not to say sceptical—tone. Before the end of the century by far the greater number of the brilliant men of letters who adorn it, both in France and Germany, were either hostile to Christianity, or regarded it merely as one—perhaps the best—of the various imperfect religions of the world. And the advance of liberal ways of thinking had also very important effects in the political world. As the spiritual powers claimed by the Pope and the hierarchy came to be brought in doubt, almost all the European powers sought to prevent the intrusion of the Papacy into their domestic affairs, and to increase their own authority and the independency of their clergy. This tendency shewed itself before the French Revolution. After that terrible explosion, in which an attempt was made to abolish Christianity altogether, there was a great reaction. Both in England and on the Continent it was felt by great numbers of tender and ardent spirits that the rationalistic teaching did not supply food for the soul, and that a system hallowed by the love and reverence of many generations could not lightly be set aside. There ensued everywhere a revival of Church feeling and Church practice in the midst of which we still live. But with this revival of a warmer and more earnest Christian feeling went a great extension of a freer and bolder criticism and interpretation of Holy Scripture, and it is one of the marked characteristics of the latter part of the nineteenth century that the leading principles of the critical school are accepted by many who are, beyond all doubt, true servants of Christ.

When Erasmus in 1516 published a text of the Greek New Testament in which the passage relating to the Three Heavenly Witnesses was not found, because it appeared in no Greek manuscript known to him, he began the long series of those who have laboured to produce, using all available testimony, a text which shall as nearly as possible represent the original. And when he subjoined to this text a translation in Classical Latin which in many places varied from the Vulgate, he became the forerunner of those who have endeavoured to interpret

INTRODUC-TION. — the text on scholarly principles without dogmatic prepossession. In this direction however human thought advanced but slowly. Theologians in general were favourable neither to textual criticism nor to frank interpretation, and it was not until the eighteenth century that the general movement of thought rendered such studies acceptable to the learned, while the thorough and scientific investigation and classification of manuscripts belongs almost wholly to the nineteenth.

Physical Science. — When Copernicus in the middle of the sixteenth century produced his modest work on the Revolutions of the Heavenly Bodies, his voice was little heard amid the strife of tongues. Yet in fact he had not only made an immense advance in physical science, but his demonstration, that the phenomena of the heavens were best explained by the hypothesis that the earth moves round the sun, produced in the end an immense revolution in man's conception of the world and of his own station in it. Man was no longer in the centre of the universe, but the inhabitant of an insignificant orb moving in infinite space. This changed conception was one with which theology had to deal, and which for some generations it regarded with little favour. Even to the present day, to reconcile Science with Revelation, the scientific conception of man and his dwelling-place with that derived—or thought to be derived—from Scripture, is a task which occupies some of the ablest among the servants of the Church.

CHAPTER I.

LAST STRUGGLES OF THE REFORMATION.

1. THE STRUGGLE IN FRANCE.

THE Calvinists in France, no less than elsewhere, struggled to maintain their freedom of worship, and the Edict of Nantes[2] did in effect constitute them a state within a state. They had their own fortified towns, their own seminaries, which soon became famous, and took in common such measures as they thought necessary for the protection of their rights and liberties. These measures, natural as they were in a people living in the midst of a bitterly hostile nation, soon drew on the Huguenots the suspicion of the government.

In 1605, it required all the address of the Protestant Sully, the King's minister, to apologise for the precautions which his co-religionists thought it needful to take for the preservation of their fortresses and their liberties. During the minority of Louis XIII., however, they remained quiet and peaceable, until at length Louis himself gave the signal for disturbance, by attacking the civil and religious privileges of the Protestant province of Béarn. The Assembly of Loudun remonstrated in vain. Two years later, the General Assembly at Rochelle divided their seven-hundred Churches into eight "circles," and drew up a kind of constitution, in which, "subject to the authority of the King," they provided for the raising of

French Protestantism[1].

1605.

Assembly of Loudun, 1619. 1621.

---

[1] Soulier, *Hist. du Calvinisme en France* (Paris, 1686); G. von Polenz, *Gesch. d. Franz. Calvinismus* (to 1629); W. S. Browning, *Hist. of the Huguenots*; E. Smedley, *Hist. of the Reformed Religion in France*; G. de Felice, *Hist. des Protestants de France* (Eng. trans., Lond. 1853); E. Benoît, *Hist. de l'Édit de Nantes* (1693, 5 vols.); Haag, *La France Protestante.*

[2] See Hardwick's *Reformation*, p. 130.

revenue and the discipline of troops; they set up, in fact, a government distinct from the supreme authority in the state. France was once more the scene of a religious war, which was terminated by the Peace of Montpellier. This treaty confirmed the Edict of Nantes, and left the Protestants in possession of all their privileges, but forbade them to unite for political purposes.

Peace of Montpellier, 1622.

Peace was, however, not long maintained; the Huguenots had many annoyances and injuries to endure, and the court was no longer influenced by the tolerant spirit of Henry IV. Above all, Richelieu, who in 1626 became almost absolute ruler of France, was bent upon making that country one great, united, and well-organised nation subject to an almost despotic king; and to effect this, he was ready to trample under foot the independence, whether of provinces, nobles, or Protestants. War again broke out, and in 1627 the hopes of French Protestantism centred in La Rochelle[1], which was besieged by the troops of the king; it held out with extraordinary gallantry (though very ill supported by the English[2], who were nominally its allies) for more than a year, when it fell (Oct. 28, 1628) before the energy of Richelieu, who directed in person the operations of the siege, after its inhabitants had endured sufferings which have been compared to those of the people of Jerusalem in its last struggle with the Romans.

Richelieu, 1626.

La Rochelle falls, 1628.

But the war was not ended by the fall of the great fortress of the Huguenots; the Duc de Rohan, encouraged by Spain, continued the campaign in the South. He too was, however, compelled to submit, and conclude a Peace at Alais. The Protestants formed no longer an independent state in France, but by the "Edict of Grace" they were assured in the possession of all the religious privileges they had hitherto enjoyed[3]. They were no longer the powerful party they had been in the sixteenth century; the great nobles who had once led them to victory, converted by Jesuits, drawn away by the temptations of the court, and perhaps disgusted by the democratic turbulence of their companions, had mostly gone over to the Roman

Peace of Alais, June,1629.

Edict of Grace, July,1629.

---

[1] See Barbot's *Hist. de la Rochelle*, ed. Denys d'Aussy (1886—1891).
[2] On this see S. R. Gardiner's *Hist. of England*, vols. v. and vi.
[3] De Felice, 319; Gieseler, III. i. 550.

Catholic Church[1], leaving behind them a society of religious citizens, distinguished by their loyalty to their king, their intelligence, and their manufacturing industry[2].

 The Edict of Nantes still remained unrepealed, but the loss of the fortified towns which they had hitherto retained in their hands materially changed the position of the Protestant party in France. Richelieu, however, Cardinal as he was, set his mind much more on bringing about the political unity of the kingdom than on converting heretics, and he led the Protestants to hope that, now that they could no longer be dealt with as a separate and often hostile power, they might trust their rights and privileges in the hands of the sovereign. Nor had the Protestants much reason to complain of the civil government when it was directed by Mazarin. Under his influence, one of the first acts of the young King Louis XIV., when he came of age, was to declare the Edict of Nantes to be still in full force, and any Acts of a Parliament, or even of the King's Council, which contravened it, invalid. In the year 1659 Mazarin gave them the permission, which had been for many years withheld, to hold provincial synods. But the Catholic majority never relinquished the hope of bringing the Huguenots back into their Church, and when at the synod of Charenton the more rigorous Protestants refused to entertain a proposal to this end, the king took it very ill, and the thought thenceforth constantly rankled in his mind, that a large body of his subjects held his own Church to be in damnable error. In a state in which no assertion of independence was tolerated, this appeared mere obstinacy and self-will, and the king inclined more and more to give ear to the representations of the Catholics against the Protestants. The latter were consequently systematically oppressed; the mixed tribunals which had been created for their benefit were abolished, and conversions from Catholicism absolutely forbidden. The king in 1680 communicated to a synod of the Clergy the edict against conversions, the transgression of which was to be punished with the utmost rigour of the law. Other vexatious restrictions and withdrawals of privileges followed, and every pretext was seized to close or destroy

Margin notes: Ch. I. — Richelieu. — Mazarin, 1659. Louis XIV., 1661. — Synod of Charenton, 1673. — Oppression of Protestants.

[1] Gieseler, III. i. 549, note 7. Gieseler, III. i. 551, note 10.
[2] See Mazarin's testimony, in

Protestant places of worship. No Calvinist could hope for employment in the king's service. Girls of seven years old and boys of twelve might be taken from their parents on the pretext that they had become Catholic. Missionaries with sermons and missionaries with swords were actively employed. Troops were quartered on the unfortunate Protestants in the most unfair and oppressive manner. By such means thousands of "conversions" were brought about and the number of avowed Protestants very seriously diminished. Why, asked the Jesuits and the courtiers, should the Edict of Nantes be maintained when the number of those whom it concerned was so insignificant? It was on this ostensible ground that its revocation was determined on[1]. The Edict for that purpose was registered by the Parliament of Paris on 22 October, 1685. The Reformed religion was not, as such, proscribed, but its assemblies for worship were forbidden, its churches destroyed, and even meetings in private houses declared illegal. Ministers of Reformed communities were banished, while emigration of the lay people was forbidden under the severest penalties. Nevertheless, in spite of all precautions and penalties, France lost within a short time from the Revocation some five or six hundred thousand of her best, most industrious, and most skilful citizens, who were readily welcomed in Switzerland, in England, in Holland, in some countries of Germany, and in America, where they found the freedom in matters of religion for which they had sacrificed their homes[2]. The king and the Jesuits rejoiced that France was purged from the stain of tolerated heresy.

But all trouble was not at an end when the Edict of Nantes was revoked. In the district of which the Cevennes mountains form the centre, in Languedoc, were found steadfast and courageous Evangelicals who made an obstinate resistance to the oppressors. Under the pressure of the most barbarous cruelty a kind of madness seized

---

[1] J. Michelet, Louis XIV. et la Revocation de l'Édit de Nantes (Hist. de France, vol. XIII).
[2] Weiss, Hist. des Réfugiés Protestants de France (trans. New York, 1854); Mrs H. F. Lee, The Huguenots in France and America (Camb. Mass. 1843); S. Smiles, The Huguenots, their Settlements, Churches, and Industries, in England and Ireland; R. Lane Poole, Hist. of the Huguenots of the Dispersion (Lond. 1880).

these unfortunate people; prophets and miracle-workers arose among them and encouraged them in acts of violence; many Catholics were put to death and many churches burnt. In the guerilla warfare which was long maintained the king's troops were not unfrequently driven back. At last Louis XIV., involved in a disastrous war and anxious at all costs to have peace at home, sent to them the celebrated Marshal Villars, who by skilful strategy and offers of pardon to those who surrendered did at length bring the war of these "Camisards," as they were called from the smock-frocks which they wore, to an end[1]. Meantime, one of the most fertile and flourishing provinces of France had been desolated.

Ch. I.

put down, 1704.

2. SWITZERLAND AND PIEDMONT.

Switzerland[2], surrounded as it was by Roman-Catholic powers, and itself divided in matters of religion, could scarcely escape attack in the anti-Evangelical reaction. It suffered in fact from the ill-will of the Spaniards, then powerful in Italy, the Austrians, and the Savoyards.

Switzerland.

The Grisons, though mainly Protestant, contained many Romanists, and in the Valteline the latter constituted the great majority. Their animosity against the Calvinists who dwelt among them was encouraged by emissaries from the neighbouring Milan, and at last broke out in a fearful massacre[3]. At the sound of a tocsin in the early dawn of morning the conspirators burst into the houses of the Protestants, murdering all whom they found

The Grisons.

---

[1] Authorities for the troubles in the Cevennes are M. Misson, *Le Théâtre Sacré des Cévennes* (Lond. 1707); Cavalier, *Memoirs of the Wars of the Cevennes* (Lond. 1712); *Le Camp des Enfants de Dieu* and the *Mémoires de Monbonnoux*, printed in the *Bulletin de la Société de l'Histoire du Protest. Franç.*, 1867, p. 273, and 1873, p. 272; the *Mémoires de Rossel d'Aigaliers* in the *Bibliothèque Universelle*, March—May, 1866; C. J. de la Baume, *Relation Hist. de la Revolte des Camisards*, ed. Goiffon (Nismes, 1874).—A. Court, *Hist. des Troubles de Cévennes*; N. Peyrat, *Hist. des Pasteurs du Désert* (said to be inaccurate); Ch. Coquerel, *Hist. des Églises du Désert*; J. C. K. Hofmann, *Geschichte des Aufruhrs in den Sevennen*; Mrs Bray, *Revolt of the Protestants of the Cevennes* (Lond. 1870).

[2] Hottinger, *Helvetische K.-G.*, vol. IV.; J. von Müller, *Schweiz. Geschichte*, continued by Vuillemin x. 482 f. (Zürich, 1845).

[3] [C. Waser] *Das Veltlinische Blutbad* (Zürich, 1621); De Porta, *Hist. Eccl. Reformatæ Rhæt.* II. 286 ff.

Valais.
1626.

Persecution of Waldensians in Piedmont,
1655.

even to the babe in the cradle (July, 1620). The Italian districts of the Grisons were then seized by the Spaniards, while Austrian troops took possession of those which border on the Tyrol. France and Venice attempted to put an end to the Spanish-Austrian occupation, and so arose one of the minor wars which complicated the great contemporary struggle in Germany. The German Grisons recovered at last their old freedom; the Italian districts were restored to the Swiss confederation at the Peace of Milan (1639) only on condition that Catholic worship should alone be permitted within their territory. From the Valais, too, the Reformed were completely expelled, after severe persecution, as early as 1626[1]. Nor was this all that Switzerland had to suffer. The French-speaking cantons were constantly threatened by their Roman-Catholic neighbour, the Duke of Savoy, whose power was seconded by the great spiritual influence of Francis of Sales, from 1602 Bishop of Geneva, but residing at Annécy. Francis at first used only spiritual weapons, but, finding that method slow, in 1596 he consented to the Duke's proceeding, in violation of the treaty by which he was bound, to suppress the Protestant religion by force[2]. It is said to have been at his suggestion that the Duke in 1602 made an attempt to storm Geneva by a sudden attack with a band of fanatics allured by a promise of indulgences. The attempt however failed disastrously, and Geneva thenceforth was protected partly by Bern, partly by the dissensions which prevented France from coöperating with Spain and Savoy for her destruction. The frustrated attempt was long commemorated at Geneva by the festival of the Escalade[3]. But the persecuting spirit of the princes of Savoy was not extinct. In Piedmont, though the Duke had ratified the privileges of the Waldensians in 1654, at Easter-tide in the following year a furious persecution began. A Piedmontese army, accompanied by a number of Irish—refugees from Cromwell's tyranny—to whom the Duke had promised the habitations of the Protestants, devastated the Waldensian villages with circumstances of the most horrible atrocity.

[1] Hottinger's *Helvetische Kirchengeschichten*, III. 1039.
[2] Marsollier, *La Vie de S. François de Sales*, I. 252.
[3] "Journée des Escalades." See Spon, *Hist. de Genève*, III. 371.

A cry rang through Europe. Then it was that Milton gave vent to his indignation in the well-known lines:

"Avenge, O Lord, Thy slaughtered saints, whose bones
Lie scattered on the Alpine mountains cold."

Cromwell sent Samuel Morland[1] with a message to the Duke beseeching him to rescind his persecuting edicts, and in August, 1655, the emissary was authorized to announce that the Duke, at the request of the King of France, had granted an amnesty to the Waldensians and restored their ancient privileges. In 1685 however, at the instigation of Louis XIV., bands of soldiers invaded their valleys and dragged many thousands into fortresses or gaols. But the remaining Waldensians, fighting with the energy of desperation, inflicted severe defeats upon their butchers, and compelled the rulers to release the captives and give them liberty to emigrate. Some found refuge in Germany, some in Switzerland. Those however who settled in the latter, supported by Swiss troops, in 1689 invaded Piedmont and reconquered their old dwelling-places, where they have ever since remained.

3. HUNGARY, TRANSYLVANIA AND POLAND.

In the latter part of the sixteenth century, the Protestants in Hungary[2], however disquieted by the fierce animosities of Lutherans and Calvinists, suffered little molestation from the civil government. It is even said that the greater part of the Hungarian population became Protestant, and that only three of the magnates remained Catholic. But here, as elsewhere, the Jesuits ardently promoted the Counter-Reformation. As under their influence the imperial governor of Upper-Hungary, the Count of Belgiojoso, began in 1603 to persecute the Protestants in Kaschau, and openly declared his intention

---

[1] Morland published (1658) *The History of the Evangelical Churches of the Valleys of Piedmont*. The supposed ancient MSS. which he brought to England turned out to be forgeries. W. Willis, *Oliver Cromwell and the Vaudois*, 1895.

[2] *Geschichte der Protestanten in Ungarn*, in *Archiv für K.-G.*, vol. I. part ii. See also Armin Vambery, *The Story of Hungary* (London, 1887), and L. Léger, *Hist. of Austro-Hungary*, trans. by Mrs Birkbeck Hill, with preface by E. A. Freeman (London, 1889).

14 Hungary, Transylvania and Poland

Ch. I.

Peace of Vienna, 1606.

Atrocities at Eperies, 1687.

Protestants outlawed, 1715.

Poland.

of exterminating them, and as this seemed to have the sanction of the Emperor Rudolf, the Hungarian Protestants rose in arms, together with the Transylvanians, under the guidance of the magnate Stephen Botskai, and extorted from the archduke Matthias the Peace of Vienna (1606), which granted freedom of religion and recognized Botskai as prince of Transylvania. But in spite of all imperial protestations, the activity of the Jesuits and the persecution of the Protestants were unchecked. Gabriel Bethlen (known to Hungarians as Bethlen Gabor) attempted during the troubles of 1619 to possess himself of the country, but only obtained from the emperor a renewal of the old promise of religious freedom (1621), a promise again and again broken. Meantime, the tactics of the court and the clergy had been so successful, that in 1634 the Roman Catholics, who thirty years before had been a small minority, had an actual majority in the Diet. They used their power to oppress the Protestants, but help again came from the Transylvanians, whose prince, George Rakoczy, obtained in 1645 a confirmation of the Peace of Vienna. It was however to little purpose that right struggled against might. When Count Caraffa came as governor, he declared that he cared no more for the Hungarian constitution than for a rotten egg, and set himself to persecute the Protestant nobles. A veritable reign of terror was set up at Eperies. A tribunal was constituted composed wholly of Roman Catholics, and some of the noblest blood of Hungary was shed upon the scaffold. And great inducements were offered to draw men to the Roman Church, offers of high positions both in Church and State, which few of the magnates in the end resisted. When finally in 1715 the Diet decided to receive no more complaints from Evangelicals, they lost all protection of law. Protestant ministers were sent to prison or to the galleys for no crime but that of their religion.

In Poland[1], the Swedish king Sigismund III. (1587–1632) promoted the interests of Rome with the zeal of a

---

[1] *Jura et Libertates Dissidentium in Regno Pol.* (Berlin, 1707); C. von Friese, *Reformations-geschichte von Polen* (Breslau, 1786); W. S. Krasinski, *Rise and Decline of the Reformation in Poland* (London, 1838 ff.).

convert. All the influence of the court was employed to draw over the nobility, and the Jesuits in their excellent colleges gained a firm hold on the younger nobles, who, in their juvenile intolerance, pulled down a Protestant Church in Cracow under the very eyes of the king. In many places Protestant worship ceased, and it was only on the estates of the nobles who remained attached to their party that the Protestants were protected. Wladislav IV. (1632–1648), more tolerant than his father, did his best to prevent the persecution of dissidents from the dominant form of faith, and in 1645 caused a Conference to be held at Thorn[1] with the view of promoting concord and unity in religion. His benevolent intentions had however but little result. When in 1724 the popular hatred broke out in an attack on the Jesuit college at Thorn, the Jesuits took a bloody revenge. The Protestants were in the end deprived of their churches and their civil rights, being declared in 1733 incapable of sitting in the Diet and of holding office in the state. Despairing of other help, they at last appealed to Russia, and gave the Empress Catharine the opportunity of intervening in the affairs of Poland with a considerable shew of Christian feeling and magnanimity. They were restored to civil rights, but the unpopularity of the step which they had taken rendered their position almost unendurable, and it was not until Poland ceased to be an independent kingdom that they found peace under a foreign government, which was on the whole more favourable to Protestants than to the adherents of the Pope, whom it regarded as an unfriendly power.

Jesuit influence.

Conference at Thorn, 1645.

Riot at Thorn, 1724.

Edict of 1733.

Intervention of Russia, 1767.

Partition of Poland, 1772.

4. THIRTY-YEARS' WAR[2].

The Pacification of Augsburg[3] had recognized the principle that the rights of a prince of the Empire should be in no way lessened by his adherence to the Evangelical

Augsburg Peace, 1555.

---

[1] The *Professio* which resulted from this discussion is in Niemeyer's *Collectio*, p. 669.
[2] Khevenhiller, *Annales Ferdinand. II.* 1578—1637 (Leipzig, 1716 ff.); M. Ritter, *Briefe u. Acten zur Geschichte des Dreissigjähr. Krieges* (München, 1870); Schiller, *Geschichte d. Dreissig. Kr.* (1791), continuation by Woltmann (1809); Eng. translation by A. J. W. Morrison and others; R. Menzel, *Gesch. d. Dreiss. Kr.* (Breslau, 1835 ff.); A. Gindely, *Gesch. d. D. K.* (Prag. 1869 ff.), trans. New York (1884); S. R. Gardiner, *The Thirty-years' War* in *Epochs of Modern History*.
[3] Gieseler, *K.-G.* III. i. 372 ff.

party. In the same instrument it was provided that any prince might introduce into his states either of the allowed forms of worship, the Roman Catholic or Lutheran, without interference from the imperial power; only, in the interest of the subjects, it was provided that the right of emigration should in all cases be granted to those whose religion differed from that of their sovereign. But by a proviso, the famous "reservatum ecclesiasticum," this right of reform was withheld from the spiritual princes, lest they should be placed under too strong a temptation to marry and declare their states hereditary. No provision was made for the Free-Cities of the Empire, nor for " mediate[1]" princes.

This was probably the best compromise which could be devised in the then state of Germany. It evidently could not fully satisfy the struggling parties; yet, under the impartial management of Ferdinand I. (1556–1564) and Maximilian (1564–1576), it gave peace to Germany for many years. But various causes of discontent were at work, which became more manifest under Rudolf II. (1576–1612), who was much under Papal and Spanish influence, and his successor Matthias (1612–1619).

Every successive Diet brought new discussions and fresh irritation; Jesuits intrigued at the Courts, while Protestant preachers thundered before the people against the idolatry and superstition of Rome. Nor were more solid subjects of complaint wanting. The Roman Catholics saw with indignation that, in spite of the Proviso of Augsburg, many of the sees of Northern Germany had fallen into the hands of Protestant princes or Protestant bishops. When, however, Gebhard, Elector-Archbishop of Cologne, who had fallen in love with the fair Agnes von Mansfield, went over to the Reformed Church, and wished to retain the sovereignty and the income of the see, his conduct was thought outrageous. The Chapter of Cologne elected the Bishop of Liege, a Bavarian prince, who was forcibly installed, the Pope having pronounced the deposition of the reformed Archbishop. He had virtually deprived a Prince of the Empire of his Electorate.

---

[1] Princes, that is, who did not hold their territories as feudatories of the Empire, but of some prince who was himself an imperial feudatory.

The Protestants, too, had their grievances. Rudolf attempted to suppress Protestantism in the Austrian cities; Bishop Julius of Würzburg banished all Protestants from his dominions, and several bishops and Catholic free-cities followed his example. In 1590, James, Marquis of Baden-Hochberg, joined the Church of Rome, and at once threatened to exterminate Protestantism in his territories. This was prevented by his death. The Archduke Ferdinand, however, did actually suppress Protestant worship in his states of Styria, Carinthia, and Carniola. But nothing caused so much agitation and alarm among the Protestants as the affair of Donauwerth.

In this free-city, which was almost wholly Protestant, a mob had attacked a Romish procession which displayed unusual pomp and splendour. The city was laid under ban of the Empire; Maximilian of Bavaria undertook the execution of it, and not only suppressed Protestant worship, but retained possession of the city on the plea that the costs of the execution of the ban were not paid. In Aix-la-Chapelle also and Strasburg the Protestants were put down by imperial authority. The Evangelical party were now thoroughly alarmed; the greater part of the Protestant States entered into an "Evangelical Union," at the head of which was Frederick IV., the Elector-Palatine. To oppose it the "Catholic League" was formed in Munich (July 10, 1609) under Maximilian of Bavaria. Germany was now divided into two hostile camps; and war would probably have broken out forthwith had not Henry IV. of France, the real head of the Union, fallen by the dagger of Ravaillac. This deferred the outbreak for a time; but everything was ready for a devastating conflict. The spark which sprang the mine came at last from Bohemia.

Bohemia[1] had been a stronghold of Protestantism since the days of John Huss. The Protestants there had suffered considerable oppression in the days of the Emperor

CH. I.

Protestantism assailed in Austria, 1578, 1586,

in Styria, 1598.

Donauwerth under ban, 1607.

Evangelical Union, 1608. *Catholic League,* 1609.

Bohemia.

---

[1] See J. Richter, *Des Böhmen-Aufruhr's Ursachen u. Beginn.* (Erfurt, 1844); C. Pescheck, *Gesch. d. Gegenreformation in Böhmen* (Dresden, 1844); Rod. Reuss, *La Destruction du Protestantisme en Bohème* (Strasburg, 1867).

Matthias. When they embodied their complaints in a petition to the Emperor, the threatening tone of his answer caused fresh irritation, and the two imperial commissioners Martinetz and Slawata, who were thought to have prompted this reply, were thrown from the windows of the castle at Prague. It was a "custom of their country," the Bohemians said, thus to punish traitors. The Protestant nobles placed the government in the hands of thirty "Directors," under the presidency of the Count of Thurn, rose in arms, drove out the Jesuits, and invaded Austria. When, on the death of Matthias, Ferdinand II., a man thoroughly devoted to the Catholic faith, and already distinguished by his persecution of Protestants in his Archduchy, was crowned Emperor, the Bohemians refused to receive him as their king, and raised the young Frederick V., the Elector-Palatine, to the throne of Bohemia. The League took arms for Ferdinand, who also received powerful assistance from Spain; while Frederick, who belonged to the "Calvinistic Antichrist," received but little help from the Lutheran Union, and from his father-in-law, James I. of England, nothing but ambassadors[1]. Poor Frederick was but a "winter-king," for the battle of the White Mountain, near Prague, speedily put an end to his reign. Bohemia was converted by an army of Jesuits and dragoons. A period of cruel oppression followed, in which there was no safety but in flight for the wretched Protestants. This "conversion" is said to have reduced the number of the inhabitants of Bohemia from nearly four millions to one million. The Commission for restoring Romanism destroyed Bohemian literature as heretical, and nothing was allowed to appear in Slavonic but translations of Romish prayer-books and legends. Great pains were taken to root out the memory of John Huss from the minds of the people, and John Nepomuk, a former Vicar-general, who had been thrown from the Moldau-bridge in a fit of rage by King Wenzel (1393), was made the national saint of the now Catholic Bohemia; it is even said that his name was given to the pictures and statues of Huss[2].

---

[1] James's conduct in this matter was very unpopular in England. See S. R. Gardiner, *Hist. Eng.*, vol. III.

[2] A. H. Wratislaw, *Life and Legend of St John Nepomucen* (1873).

The brave Count Mansfeldt, Christian of Brunswick, and others carried on the struggle on behalf of Frederick in the Palatinate, but in vain. He was driven from his ancestral states; the Emperor seized the Lower Palatinate, while the Upper Palatinate, with the Electorate of the conquered prince, was given to the Emperor's firm ally, Maximilian of Bavaria. *Frederick deposed, 1623.*

Many lands besides the Palatinate were overrun by the Imperialists in pursuit of their flying foes, and the whole of Northern Germany seemed in danger. In this extremity, Christian IV. of Denmark, with some support from England, took up arms on behalf of oppressed Protestantism, but being defeated by Tilly and Wallenstein, was compelled to accept the Peace of Lubeck, and withdrew from German affairs. *Christian of Denmark, 1625. Peace of Lubeck, 1629.*

So far, the Imperial and Romish party was triumphant, nor was it slow to use its power against Protestantism. It was already almost suppressed in the Austrian territory, but now the proceedings of the imperial government and the publications of the Jesuits left little doubt that the Emperor intended the complete extermination of the Protestants in Germany. He felt himself strong enough to issue an "Edict of Restitution," which was set forth as an authentic explanation of the Pacification of Augsburg. By the provisions of this Edict the endowments of the Catholic Church confiscated since the Treaty of Passau were to be restored, Calvinists excluded from the Peace of Religion, and Catholic princes to be free to convert their subjects in their own way. This Edict, if not in itself unjust, was certainly impolitic, as it gave the Protestant princes a powerful motive for resistance. *Edict of Restitution, 1629. 1552.*

Just when German Protestantism seemed lost, help presented itself from a Catholic power. Richelieu, who then governed France, looked with great jealousy on the rising power of the House of Hapsburg, and determined to counteract it. France was already, in the contest for the Mantuan succession, allied with Italian princes against the power of Spain and the German Emperor; nay, even Pope Urban himself was brought through the political perplexities of the time into alliance with France, and so indirectly with the German Protestants. Richelieu now turned his thoughts to Gustavus Adolphus, the heroic *Intervention of France. Gustavus Adolphus*

2—2

Ch. I.

lands in Germany, June 24, 1630.

Tilly defeated, 1631.

Death of Gustavus, Nov. 6, 1632.

Peace of Prague, 1635.

Negotiations for peace, 1645.

Peace of Westphalia, Oct. 24, 1648.

king of Sweden; set him free from his Polish war, and enabled him to land with a considerable force in Germany. The capture and horrible treatment of the Protestant city of Magdeburg by Tilly decided the wavering Protestant princes; Hesse, Brandenburg, and Saxony joined Sweden; Tilly was defeated at Leipzig; Gustavus marched through the Rhineland, invaded Bavaria, freed the oppressed Protestants, and added them to the number of his adherents. He fell on the field of Lützen, victorious over Wallenstein; but the war was not yet over. Supported still by Richelieu, the famous Swedish Chancellor Oxenstierna, the brave Bernard of Weimar, and other pupils of Gustavus, succeeded not unworthily to the conduct of affairs. The war dragged on with various fortune. Saxony concluded a separate peace with the Emperor at Prague, May 30, 1635. Still, on the whole the Protestants, supported by Sweden, France, and the Netherlands, were decidedly victorious over the Spanish and Imperialist armies. Meantime, the desolation of Germany was inconceivable; a great part of that rich country was almost depopulated; it was said that corpses had been found with their mouths full of grass, and even that men had been driven to prey upon the corpses of their fellows. The state of a country where such stories could be told and believed must have been horrible indeed.

At last, after many vain attempts, negotiations were entered into for peace. The business lingered, but the victories of Turenne and Wrangel over the Imperialists quickened the movements of the negotiators, and three years later the Peace of Westphalia, or of Osnaburg and Münster[1], was concluded; the most important diplomatic transaction of the seventeenth century.

France and Sweden acquired important accessions of territory. Alsace, the key of Germany on its western frontier, was given to France; maritime Pomerania, the isle of Rügen, Wismar, Bremen and Verden to Sweden, with five million thalers for the costs of the war. In Northern Germany, many ecclesiastical properties were

---

[1] *Instrumentum Pacis Westphalicæ*, ed. Berninger (Münster, 1648), often reprinted. The most essential portions of it are given by Gieseler, *K.-G.* III. i. 425 ff. See also Pfister, *Gesch. der Teutschen*, IV. 646 ff.

secularized in favour of Protestant princes. Of the Catholic powers, Bavaria alone retained the acquisitions which it had made, the sovereignty of the Upper Palatinate with the Electorate; while for the Palsgrave, restored to the Lower Palatinate, an eighth Electorate was created. The right of any state of the Empire to conclude treaties with foreign powers, only not against Empire or Emperor, was admitted.

With regard to the all-important matter of religion, the Pacification of Augsburg was in the main established, but with additions and definitions intended to preclude a repetition of the former controversies.

In all imperial councils and tribunals, the two great religious parties were to have equal rights.

The right of each state to reform itself, unhindered by the authority of the empire, was fully recognized. The possession of ecclesiastical property of all kinds was regulated by the standard of actual possession on Jan. 1, 1624, henceforward spoken of as the "normal year." With regard to the exercise of a form of worship differing from that established in any state, the privileges of 1624 were to be maintained; but in no case was a subject to be deprived of civil rights on account of his religion. The right of emigration was also maintained, with provisions designed to prevent princes from oppressing or plundering emigrants or exiles for religion.

Normal Year, 1624.

The Reformed (*i.e.* Calvinistic) body was to enjoy, in relation to the Roman Catholics, precisely the same privileges as the Lutherans or "adherents of the Augsburg Confession."

With regard to the relation of Lutherans and Calvinists to each other, it was enacted that a prince who passed from one communion to the other should have full license for the personal exercise of that form of religion which he preferred; but he must abstain from all interference with the already established religion of his subjects, and from diverting the funds belonging to churches, schools, hospitals, and the like.

This treaty extended to the whole German empire, except that the Emperor refused to admit it into his hereditary states; saving, however, the rights of certain Lutherans in Silesia.

The Pope protested against these provisions, but in vain; means had already been taken to deprive the Papal protestation of all force.

Thus, at the cost of much blood and infinite misery, the religious dissensions of the Empire were closed. Protestants had still, in some parts, to endure oppression or annoyance; but they had acquired, within certain limits, a legally unassailable position, and sufficient means to enforce and defend their rights. The Counter-reformation had failed.

On the 24th Oct., 1648, three salvos of cannon from the bastions of Münster announced the conclusion of the momentous treaty. It was not until the 2nd March in the following year that, ratifications having been exchanged and the Emperor's fiat issued, the messengers of peace sped forth from Osnaburg.

From the Lake of Constance to the Baltic Sea; through the desolated lands by the Rhine, in Saxony and in Bohemia, went forth the cry of peace; peace to a whole generation which had known no peace. The bells rang, the people streamed into the re-opened churches, and poured forth their gratitude in thanksgivings and songs of praise.

5. SEQUEL OF THE TREATY OF WESTPHALIA.

Relations of Church and State.

It was hoped that the Treaty of Westphalia had provided a compromise under which Roman Catholics and Protestants should at any rate be free from persecution on the part of the State, but this result was by no means always attained. During the negotiations which led to the treaty the Evangelical members of the Imperial Diet which met at Ratisbon had naturally been led to act together for their common interests, and in 1653 they formed themselves into a regularly organized body, called the *Corpus Evangelicorum*, to defend the rights conferred on Protestants by the new constitution. In opposition to this, the Roman-Catholic representatives in the Diet formed a union, the *Corpus Catholicorum*. Both these bodies continued to exist until the dissolution of the Empire in 1806.

Corpus Evangelicorum, 1653.

Corpus Catholicorum.

But there were forms of oppression against which such a body as the *Corpus Evangelicorum* was powerless. In the Protestant states the course of the Reformation had tended to throw great power in matters of religion into the hands of the temporal princes. In the German Lutheran churches the jurisdiction once exercised by the bishops was claimed by the territorial princes, and this was exercised through boards, called Consistories, under the control of the civil government, and even the Superintendents became little more than officials of the state. The sovereign was recognized as chief bishop in his territory. This was called the Territorial system[1]. Such a power had never been conferred on the princes by any ecclesiastical authority; it simply fell into their hands because when its ancient holders were removed no one else took possession of it. The princes did not however claim the right to teach or to confer the grace of Holy Orders. The right of princes to be supreme heads in matters ecclesiastical as well as civil was vigorously maintained in the seventeenth century by Hugo Grotius and Thomas Hobbes; but the man who did most to give it currency among Lutherans was Christian Thomasius. According to these teachers supremacy over the Church is inherent in the very conception of royalty. Thus the king became a pope with almost unlimited temporal power; the tiara was added to the crown. Such a system, it is evident, gave abundant opportunity for oppression in matters of conscience, and so naturally called forth opposition. The leader of this was Christopher Matthew Pfaff[2], Chancellor of the University of Tübingen, who was followed by the well-known historian J. L. Mosheim and many others. In his system—called the collegial system—the Church stands to the State in precisely the same relation as other corporations (*collegia*) recognized by law. The state has the right to exercise a general superintendence over such corporations, and to take care that they make no enactments prejudicial to itself, to which end it has a right to require that all their canons and resolutions be submitted to it for confirmation before

Episcopal power of princes.

Territorial System.

Collegial System.

---

[1] S. Pufendorf, *De habitu Rel. Christ. ad Vitam Civilem* (Bremen, 1687).

[2] *De Originibus Juris Ecclesiastici* (Tübingen, 1719).

they are put in force—a system which gives the state an indefinite power of restraint but none of initiation. It would leave the Church the power, in the first instance, of legislating for itself, while leaving to the state what was called the *jus circa sacra*. This system naturally involves the free holding of synods, consisting of persons chosen by the Church itself, for the purpose of legislation; and with this is associated the right of appointing the officials through whom its decrees are to be carried into effect.

This system was in fact never established in Germany; almost everywhere the Church was governed by the territorial lord through consistories not chosen by itself but by the civil government. It was however in practice mitigated by recognized custom, which prescribed that a consistory must include clerical as well as lay members, and that when any considerable change was contemplated other clergy should be taken into council and opinions obtained from theologians of repute. In Würtemberg the consistorial and the synodal system existed side by side, but the latter obtained little real authority or importance. In the Duchy of Cleves the reigning family was Roman Catholic, and did not claim direct authority over Protestant Churches, so that in this territory both the Lutheran and the Calvinistic bodies governed themselves through synods. When on the failure of the royal line in 1609 the duchy was divided between Brandenburg and the Palatinate, the former allowed the synodal constitution to remain unimpaired, although in the Brandenburg dominions generally the consistorial system was maintained. But that portion which fell to the Palatinate was less fortunate. On the accession of the Roman-Catholic house of Pfalz-Neuburg an attempt was made to deprive the Protestants of their independence under a clause in the Treaty of Ryswick which provided that ecclesiastical institutions should remain in the state into which they had been brought during the French occupation. Some alleviation was brought about by the intervention of Brandenburg (now become the kingdom of Prussia) in 1705, when the Elector Palatine promised complete freedom of religion to his subjects. This promise was however soon disregarded, nor were the remonstrances of the Protestant princes, or even those of the Emperor himself, productive of lasting benefit. The Protestants always found themselves hampered and thwarted.

In Electoral Saxony the Elector Frederick Augustus on becoming a candidate for the crown of Poland was convinced of the validity of the Papal claims, so that a Roman-Catholic prince became ruler of a people almost wholly Protestant, and of the early home of Lutheranism. Here however, through the zeal of the estates heartily supported by the people, the Protestant Church lost none of its rights. Saxony of course ceased to be the leader of the German Protestant powers and Brandenburg took its place. The influence of the court naturally tended to bring about conversions to Romanism, but non-Catholics were not unfairly dealt with.

Saxony. Elector becomes Roman Catholic, 1697.

In Brunswick-Wolfenbüttel, Christina Elizabeth, granddaughter of the reigning duke, not without reluctance, deserted the faith of her fathers to become the wife of Charles III. King of Spain (afterwards the Emperor Charles VI.) and the mother of a lineage of emperors. A few years later the Duke Anton Ulrich himself, more than seventy years old, followed her, but without diminishing the privileges of his Protestant subjects. In Würtemberg, when Charles Alexander, who had been converted to Romanism while in the Imperial service, became heir-apparent, the Würtemberg assembly required of him a solemn engagement to maintain intact the existing constitution in matters of religion; an engagement which he ratified on his actual accession to the throne, and which the Evangelical members of the Diet confirmed. In Hesse-Cassel also the landgrave William VIII., when he received convincing evidence that his son and heir had gone over to the Roman Church, convened the Council, and strongly insisted that the heir should take a solemn oath that, except for the services in one private chapel, he should do nothing to favour Romanism or to prejudice the Lutheran form of worship. In these cases the Roman Church gained nothing by the conversion of princes.

Brunswick. 1707.

1710.

1733.

The most signal instance in the eighteenth century of the persecution of Protestants by a Roman-Catholic ruler

CH. I.

Salzburg Exiles, 1731.

was that in Salzburg[1], where however the Protestants had no definite rights under the Treaty except that of emigration. From the days of the Hussites, and still more from the time of the Lutheran Reform, there had existed in Salzburg a considerable number of persons who at heart desired a simpler and purer worship than that which prevailed around them. They do not seem to have held any peculiar dogmas, but secretly read the Bible and Protestant books of devotion, while still attending the services of the Church. Such secret Protestants had occasionally been detected and banished both before and after the Thirty-years' War. These expulsions were comparatively unimportant, but in 1729 Count Firmian, who was Prince-Archbishop, began a more systematic and rigorous inquisition. A number of Jesuits were set to work, and when those whom they denounced were required to give up their devotional books and to forswear their principles, disturbances arose in several places. These enabled the archbishop to deal with the Protestants as insurgents and to request the assistance of an armed force from the Emperor. The Evangelical party in the Diet in vain made counter-representations and insisted that the charges of rebellion should be investigated. The result was that on Oct. 31, 1731 an ordinance[2] was published which required, under severe penalties, all Protestants at once to quit the country. These unfortunate people, to the number of about twenty-two thousand, were consequently driven out in inclement weather, selling their property for the pittance which it would bring under forced sale, and with very inadequate provision for their journey. Their hard case however excited great compassion. The King of Prussia (Frederick William I.) in particular settled a large portion of them—about 17,000—in Prussian Lithuania and other districts of his kingdom. Others went to South Carolina in

---

[1] Schelhorn, *De Relig. Evan. in Prov. Salisb. ortu et fatis* (Leipzig, 1732); Clarus, *Die Auswand. der Protest. gesinnten Salzbürger* (Innsbruck, 1864); Erdmann in Herzog, XIII. 323 ff. This forced emigration of the Salzburgers supplied the framework for Goethe's *Hermann u. Dorothea*.

[2] This violated the provisions of the Treaty of Westphalia, which gave three years to those who left their homes on account of religion to prepare for emigration. See the text in Gieseler, III. i. 429.

America, where, with the support of the King of England, they formed a settlement called Ebenezer. A similar expulsion of Protestants from Berchtesgaden took place two years later. Several of these found homes in Berlin and in some of the Hanoverian towns, where they were valued as skilled artificers. *Berchtesgaden, 1733.*

The hereditary dominions of the house of Austria had not been included in the provisions of the Treaty of Westphalia, and in them Protestants had no legal toleration. The expulsion of the Salzburgers in 1731 caused some sympathetic agitation in the Austrian states. Here however the Protestants were not permitted to emigrate whither they would, but bodies of them were from time to time deported to Transylvania, where most of the inhabitants were already Protestant. It was not until the time of Joseph II. that the Austrian Protestants acquired the right to exist and to build for themselves places of worship. *Austria.* *Toleration, 1781.*

In Silesia the Reformation had made much progress, especially in Lower Silesia. Here the Treaty of Westphalia had expressly stipulated for freedom of religion, but it was not long before the Protestants found themselves unequally dealt with. Most of their churches were taken from them and other measures were taken to their prejudice. Charles XII. of Sweden for a time put an end to this persecution by binding the Emperor in the Treaty of Altranstadt to restore the status given by the Treaty of Westphalia; but oppression soon began anew, nor did it cease until by the Peace of Breslau the whole of Lower Silesia became Prussian. *Silesia.* *1707.* *1742.*

6. THE STRUGGLE IN ENGLAND[1].

The Reformation of the Church of England had never wholly satisfied the nation. That those who still acknow- *Discontent with the Church.*

---

[1] On the reign of James I., besides the general histories of the Church of England by Fuller, Collier, Perry, Wakeman, and others, see S. R. Gardiner's *Hist. of England*, vols. I.—IV., and his *First two Stuarts and Puritan Revolution*, 1603—1660. Earlier works are Camden's *Annals of James I.*, Winwood's *Memorials of State*, Hacket's *Life of Williams*, and Harrington's *Nugæ Antiquæ*. The *Calendars of State Papers* for the period contain a great store of original information.

ledged the authority of the Pope were ill at ease goes without saying; but it was not Romanists only who were discontented. During the later years of Elizabeth the High Commission Court wielded the immense power of the Crown in matters ecclesiastical. This was presided over by the archbishop, and gave to the successive holders of the see of Canterbury the means of imposing tests of doctrine without much regard to those created by law. By the help of this court Whitgift had produced a considerable measure of outward conformity. But there was still a large number of Englishmen to whom the Anglican compromise was by no means acceptable. Not only tradesmen and mechanics, but men of good station and education thought that too much of the ritual of the old Church had been retained. They disliked ceremonies, however innocent in themselves, which were popularly identified with the Roman use. Many, who had no objection to the government of the Church by bishops, still regarded as superstitious the use of the surplice, the sign of the cross in baptism, the posture of kneeling at the reception of Holy Communion, and wished for greater freedom for the minister to exercise the gift of prayer in the services generally. Whether these scruples were reasonable need not here be discussed. It is a fact that they seemed very important to the Puritans, as they were called, and that the Puritans were powerful enough to influence the fortunes of the kingdom. But an extreme party among them went still further, and wished to substitute for the ancient Church of the realm one modelled on that of Geneva, without bishops, ruled by a hierarchy of elders or presbyters. This was, they maintained, the only form of Church government sanctioned by the New Testament, and was alone to be tolerated.

During the later years of Elizabeth religious feuds raged less violently, for all eyes were bent on her successor. The Romanists hoped for at least tolerance from the son of Mary Stuart; the Puritans looked to have on their side the pupil of George Buchanan; while the great body of the nation believed that the new king would not venture to change the system of the great Elizabeth. James on his accession soon shewed that he was at least not inclined to favour that Calvinistic party which had hampered and sometimes insulted him in his native land.

Soon after the king's arrival in his new dominions, a large number of Puritan ministers presented a petition [1] to him praying to be relieved from their "common burden of human rites and ceremonies." They did not attack the episcopal government of the Church, but they prayed "that the cross in baptism, interrogatories ministered to infants, confirmation, as superfluous, may be taken away.... The cap and surplice not urged.... That examination may go before the communion; that it be ministered with a sermon. That divers terms of priests, and absolution, and some other used, with the ring in marriage, and other such-like in the book, may be corrected. The longsomeness of service abridged. Church songs and music moderated to better edification. That the Lord's day be not profaned. The rest upon holy days not so strictly urged.... No ministers charged to teach their people to bow at the name of Jesus. That the canonical scriptures only be read in the church." Further, they prayed that measures might be taken for the supply of more able ministers, from whom no subscription should be required but such as were sanctioned by law; that their maintenance should be improved and pluralities diminished; and that the reckless use of excommunications "for trifles and twelve-penny matters" by the officials of bishops' courts should cease.

This petition led to the king's appointing a meeting for the settlement of religious differences at Hampton Court[2]. There assembled the king, his council, and "divers of the bishops and other learned men." On the second day of their sitting, they called before them four well-known Puritan ministers who might state the case of the objectors to the liturgy; and on the third day certain civilians who should aid by their professional knowledge in the discussion concerning the High Commission Court.

Ch. I.

Millenary Petition.

Hampton Court Conference, Jan. 14, 1604.
Jan. 16.
Jan. 18.

---

[1] Printed in Fuller's *Ch. Hist.* v. 305 ff. (ed. Brewer); Collier's *Eccl. Hist.* II. 672; Gee and Hardy's *Documents*, 508 ff.; part in Cardwell's *Conferences*, 130 ff.

[2] The principal documents relating to this Conference are in Cardwell's *Conferences*, 147—228. The accounts in Fuller and Collier are taken mainly from Barlow's *Sum and Substance of the Conference at Hampton Court* (London, 1604).

The Puritans obtained no concession likely to satisfy their friends. The alteration of a few rubrics and the addition of a few prayers to the liturgy were very far from satisfying their wishes. The objectionable rites remained, and the king declared that "he would make the Puritans conform themselves, or else harry them out of the land." The disappointment of the Puritans vented itself in complaints against the king and the prelates.

But at least one very important work sprang from the Conference. The king disliked the then popular Geneva version of the Scriptures; the Puritans found fault with the "Bishops' Bible." With the view of superseding both, the king nominated fifty-four learned men, who, adhering as closely as might be to the Bishops' Bible, but adopting the expressions of other well-known translations when they agreed better with the original text, should produce a work worthy to be used in the services of the Church of England and the devotions of its members[1].

The "Authorized Version," 1611.

The work, begun in 1607 and published in 1611, was extraordinarily successful. The time had not yet come for a critical revision of the text, or even for exact scholarship, but, combining as it does the copious vocabulary of an age of learning with idiomatic raciness of speech, this "Authorized Version" is loved and admired wherever the English tongue is known. It was for some generations the one book known to all Englishmen, and it influenced their thoughts and their language to an extent which it is difficult to over-estimate.

Canons of 1604.

The Convocation of Canterbury in 1604 codified a number of Orders and Injunctions relating to the Church. These "Constitutions and Canons" were ratified by the king, and—though not binding in themselves on the laity—are still a part of the ecclesiastical law as regards the clergy[2]. The Parliament which sat at the same

---

[1] See the King's Letter to the Bishop of London, July 31, 1604, in Cardwell's *Doc. Ann.* II. 65. His rules to be observed in the translation, and lists of the translators, are given in *Doc. Ann.* II. 106 ff., and in Lewis's *Hist. of Translations*, 310, 317 (ed. 1818).

[2] These Canons were accepted by the Convocation of York in 1606. See Fuller, *Ch. Hist.* v. 324; Cardwell's *Synodalia*, I. 164, II. 583, with the notes. In the case of Croft *v.* Middleton (1736) it was decided by a unanimous judgment of the Court of King's Bench that these canons do not *proprio vigore* bind the laity. See Phillimore's *Eccl. Law*, 1959.

time passed an Act permitting the marriage of the clergy, which had been only connived at in the preceding reign[1].

In the reign of James, Puritanism acquired new intensity from a new form of opposition. There sprang up under the fostering care of the king[2] a school of divines who brought again into prominence the Catholic conception of the Church. The king was to them not merely the chief whom the great barons consented to obey; he held the crown by a divine and indefeasible right. The episcopal constitution was to them not merely an ancient and allowable form of Church government; bishops of a true succession were essential to the completeness of a Christian Church. They attached great importance to the decency, and even splendour, of divine worship, and made the central point of their service not—as the Puritans did—the sermon, but the Eucharist. Many of them held the Lord's Day to be rather a solemn feast-day of the Church than a scriptural sabbath. The man who did most to give effect to these principles was William Laud, who was the leader in matters ecclesiastical from the accession of Charles I.[3], though he did not become Archbishop until eight years later.

James I.[4] said of him with great shrewdness, "he hath a restless spirit which cannot see when things are well, but loves to toss and change, and to bring matters to a pitch of reformation floating in his own brain." This was so; he had before him an ideal of the Church which he set himself to realize with the steadfastness and courage which distinguished him. But his training had been mainly academic, and he had not the tact and knowledge of mankind which were so needful for a man in high

Marriage of Clergy.

High Church Movement.

W. Laud, b. 1573, Abp. 1633, d. 1645.
Charles I. acc. 1625.

---

[1] I. James, I. c. 25. See Hallam, *Const. Hist.* I. 173.

[2] See his instructions for the study of divinity in Collier's *Ch. Hist.* II. 708, Wilkins' *Concilia*, IV. 459; and for preachers in Cardwell's *Doc. Ann.* II. 149 and in Gee and Hardy's *Documents*, 516.

[3] For the reign of Charles I. we have abundant contemporary authorities. The *Calendar of State Papers for the reign of Charles I.* supplies a great mass of valuable documents. Clarendon's *Rebellion* and *Life* are the best known of contemporary narratives. D. Neal, *Hist. of the Puritans*, 1517—1688 (1732 ff.) gives the opposite side, not always accurately. Nalson (*Impartial Collection*, 1682) and Rushworth (*Historical Collections*, 1659—1701) supply documents; also S. R. Gardiner, *Constit. Doc. of the Puritan Revol.* (Oxf. 1889). S. R. Gardiner's *History* is the principal modern guide up to 1660.

[4] Quoted by J. R. Green, *Hist. Engl.* c. 8, sec. 4.

place in those dangerous days. Clarendon[1] says of him that "he was a man of great parts and very exemplary virtues"; but "he believed innocence of heart and integrity of manners was a guard strong enough to secure any man in his voyage through this world"; and "he had usually about him an uncourtly quickness, if not sharpness, and did not sufficiently value what men said or thought of him." And Thomas May[2], who belonged to the opposite party, says that Laud was "a man not altogether so bad, as unfit for the state of England." Such was the man who set himself not only to reform the slovenliness and indecorum which too often pervaded the English churches and services, but to place the Church of this realm in what he considered its right position of dignity and authority. This involved of course collisions with many, often powerful, persons.

Under his influence, preachers were restrained from "curious search" into those differences which have for so many years exercised the Church of Christ[3]. Certain Puritan feoffees, who had purchased impropriate tithes and employed them in the maintenance of preachers, were put down by a decree of the Exchequer Chamber[4]. The Declaration of James I., permitting his subjects to indulge in "lawful recreations upon Sundays after evening prayers ended," was republished by his son[5]. New churches were consecrated with unusual pomp[6], and old ones cleansed and beautified[7]. The Holy Table was set "altar-wise" at the East end of the chancel, and preserved by a rail from profane intrusion[8]. Surplices

---

[1] *Rebellion*, I. 90, 150 (ed. 1705).
[2] *Hist. of Long Parliament*, p. 28 (ed. 1854). See also Carte, *Hist. Eng.* IV. 314.
[3] See the King's *Declaration* in Cardwell's *Doc. Ann.* II. 169 ff.
[4] Rushworth, *Collections Abridged*, II. 122.
[5] In Cardwell's *Doc. Ann.* II. 188.
[6] See the account of the consecration of St Catharine Creed in Rushworth, *Abr.* II. 69.
[7] Laud's *Troubles*, &c., pp. 156, 224.
[8] Elizabeth's *Injunction* of 1559 (Cardwell, *Doc. Ann.* I. 201) orders the Tables to be set altar-wise, when not used for Communion. An Order in Council of Nov. 3, 1633 (in Cardwell, *Doc. Ann.* II. 185) leaves the position of the Table to the judgment of the Ordinary. As to the views of Laud and his party, see *Statutes of Canterbury* (Laud's *Works*, v. 536); Wren's *Orders* for Norwich (Cardwell, *Doc. Ann.* II. 201) and Canons of 1640, Canon VII. (Cardwell's *Synodalia*, I. 404). Compare Fuller, VI. 110.

were insisted upon in all parish churches, and copes in cathedrals, where also lights were frequently set on the decorated altar¹. If a minister refused to conform, there was the High Commission to compel or deprive him; if he gave vent to his grievance in a pamphlet or even a hasty expression, there was the dreaded Star Chamber to punish him; and in both courts he met the ever-active Archbishop. In 1640, when the Convocation over which Laud presided enacted Canons² embodying the views of his party on the Royal Prerogative and the Ceremonies of the Church, he might seem to have attained the goal of his hopes. But the cloud, which years before he had seen rising³, now covered the sky; the storm was at hand which was to sweep away for a time the old landmarks both in Church and State.

Ch. I.

Canons of 1640.

In the "Long Parliament" of 1640 the proceedings of the Primate and his suffragans were especially attacked. Their doctrines, their ceremonies, their persecution of Puritans, their mixing in state affairs, their newly made Canons⁴, were alike offensive to the majority of the House of Commons. Nor were the Peers altogether favourable to the prelates; many Lords inclined to Puritan opinions; probably more were indignant at being elbowed in Court and Council by ecclesiastics, men of mere academic fame, not trained in courts and embassies like the splendid prelates of an earlier time⁵.

Long Parliament met, Nov. 3, 1640.

The progress of events in Parliament was rapid. The Commons in particular soon claimed an authority far greater than had ever been conceded to that assembly. Laud was impeached of treason and committed to the custody of the Black Rod, whence he was in a few weeks removed to the Tower⁶. The Commons, by their own

Laud impeached, Dec. 18, 1640.

---

¹ E.g. at Durham; see Dr Cosin's Case, in Fuller, VI. 182, and Appendix B. Nalson's *Coll.* I. 518.
² In Wilkins, IV. 543; Cardwell, *Synod.* I. 380. W. A. Shaw, *Hist. of the English Church*, 1640—1660, is a good authority for this period.
³ Laud's *Diary*, Jan. 29, 162⅚ (*Works*, III. 180).
⁴ Nalson's *Coll.* I. 666.
⁵ Lord Brooke complained that the Bishops were "in respect of their studies no way fit for government, or to be Barons in Parliament." Fuller, VI. 212. "The largest part of the Lords were fermentated with an Anti-episcopal sourness." Hacket's *Williams*, Pt. II. p. 179. Compare Selden, *Table Talk*, Art. 'Bishops in the Parliament,' 8 (p. 15, ed. Singer, 1856).
⁶ See his *Diary*, Dec. 18, 1640; March 1, 1641.

Commission, Jan. 23, 1641.

sole authority sent forth a commission for removing images and such like from churches. In vain the Lords appointed a 'Committee of Religion,' presided over by shrewd Bishop Williams, to devise a compromise; the more fiery spirits had now the upper hand[1], and the voices of moderate men, even of the Puritan party, were unheard.

July 5, 1641.

The Star Chamber and High Commission were swept away, with general approbation[2]. In February, 1642, Charles, won over by the entreaties of his terrified queen, gave a reluctant assent to a Bill depriving the Bishops of their votes in the House of Lords[3]. By this great concession he hoped to put an end to the differences between himself and the Parliament: but the event was far otherwise. Before many months had passed, King and Parliament were at open war, and destruction of the ancient Church of England proceeded with unabated speed. The very institution of episcopacy itself was voted needless by the House of Commons[4]; that body desired a new form of Presbyterian government, which should be common to the Northern and the Southern kingdom.

Assembly of Divines, 1643.

To this end an 'Assembly of Divines,' comprising Anglican clergy, Presbyterian ministers, 'dissenting brethren[5],' lay lords and gentlemen, and Scotch commissioners, was summoned by Parliament, and met for the first time in Henry VII.'s Chapel at Westminster, on July 1, 1643[6]. For more than five years they pursued their labour of settling the doctrine, the government, and the worship of the future Church.

Solemn League and Covenant, 1643.

On September 25, 1643, the members of the House of Commons and the Assembly of Divines publicly subscribed a "Solemn League and Covenant," slightly altered from the "Covenant" to which the Scots had already pledged themselves. This famous instrument bound the

---

[1] Laud's *Diary*, Mar. 1, 1641; and *Troubles*, p. 174; Hacket's *Williams*, pt. II. 146.

[2] Rushworth, *Abr.* IV. 112, 115; Fuller, VI. 207.

[3] Fuller, VI. 239; Hacket's *Williams*, pt. II. 179, 181.

[4] Rushworth, *Abr.* VI. 68.

[5] This was the name then given to the few 'Independents,' such as Goodwin and Nye, who were members of the Assembly. Fuller, VI. 249, 310.

[6] An outline of the Ordinance constituting the Assembly, with a complete list of members, in Rushworth, *Abr.* V. 123–6. Also in A. F. Mitchell's *History of the Westminster Assembly* (London, 1883).

subscribers to "endeavour the preservation of the Reformed Religion in the Church of Scotland," and "the Reformation of Religion in the kingdoms of England and Ireland, according to the Word of God, and the example of the best Reformed Churches," and to "the extirpation of Popery, Prelacy, and whatsoever shall be found to be contrary to sound doctrine and the power of godliness." Subscription to this Covenant was afterwards required from all ministers and official persons throughout the kingdom[1].

In 1645, Archbishop Laud, long imprisoned, was condemned by Ordinance of Attainder, which passed a thin House of Lords, January 4. On the 10th of the same month he went undaunted to the scaffold[2]. A week before that event the use of the Common Prayer had been forbidden in all the churches, and a "Directory for Public Worship," the work of the Westminster Assembly, substituted[3]. The Presbyterian majority in the Commons and the Assembly proceeded further to decree a complete "Presbyterian platform" of Church government, with due subordination of congregations to classical, provincial, and national assemblies, and of assemblies to Parliament, throughout the whole kingdom[4]. But to give this scheme a vigorous and exclusive establishment was beyond their power; the direction of affairs was passing into other hands.

Laud executed, Jan. 10, 1645.

Directory for Public Worship, 1645.

The sectaries, the philosophers, and the libertines had never looked with favour upon Presbyterian rigour; they hated prelates indeed, but they were by no means inclined to tolerate a "new presbyter" who was "but old priest writ large." This "independent" party had gradually gained ground in Parliament, and even in the Assembly

---

[1] A full account of this transaction, with a copy of the document itself, is to be found in Fuller, VI. 254 ff.; Clarendon, *Rebellion*, II. 369 ff.; Rushworth, *Abr.* v. 208 ff.

[2] See Laud's *Troubles*, &c., with the Supplement from Rushworth and Heylin, in Laud's *Works*, IV.

[3] Ordinance of Jan. 4, 1645; enforced by another, Aug. 23, 1645. Fuller, VI. 311. Rushworth, *Abr.*

v. 449, 576, gives Jan. 3 for the first Ordinance.

[4] By a series of Ordinances of Aug. 19, Oct. 20, 1645; Mar. 14, June 5, Aug. 28, 1646; Jan. 29, 1648. Fuller, VI. 329; Rushworth, *Abr.* v. 584, VI. 336. In the Debate of Oct. 13, 1647, both Houses consented to tolerate Nonconformity, with certain exceptions, as "Prelacy and Popery." Rushworth, *Abr.* VI. 276.

itself, when, after the great victory of Naseby (June 14, 1645), and the complete destruction of the King's power, it acquired irresistible strength from the adhesion of the victorious troops of Cromwell. They had amongst themselves representatives of almost all sects, and for these they naturally demanded toleration. This wonderful army, strong at once in enthusiasm and discipline, put their King to death under forms of law, and bore their own chiefs into the highest offices of State. By their support Oliver Cromwell became virtually King under the title of "Lord Protector" (December 16, 1653)[1].

Cromwell Protector, 1653.

He found the affairs of religion utterly disorganized. The restraints of ecclesiastical government being removed, the pent-up currents of opinion rushed over the land in a thousand devious streams. Of the old parish priests, some were dead; many had been ejected as "scandalous ministers" or "malignants," many for refusing the Covenant[2]; into their places had been thrust half-educated youths, mechanics, troopers, and the like[3]. To this state of things the Protector applied a rough soldier-like remedy. He nominated (March 20, 1654) a "Commission for the Trial of Public Preachers," with sub-committees in the several counties[4]. To them it was committed to remove scandalous ministers, and to prevent the intrusion of unfit persons for the future. These "Triers," however unconstitutional a body, are believed to have brought about a considerable amendment[5]. During the short remainder of Cromwell's reign the ministers of the parishes were for the most part Presbyterian[6]. All sects were tolerated, so long as they did not interfere with the civil power; but Papists were proscribed, and the use of the Anglican Liturgy was still forbidden.

The 'Triers,' 1654.

---

[1] Carlyle's *Cromwell*, II. 370 (ed. 1857).
[2] The number of ejected ministers is stated by Walker at 8,000 (*Sufferings of the Clergy*, pp. 299 ff. ed. 1862), but he gives less than 2,000 names. Neal (*Puritans*, p. 93) states the number at 1,600. See Hallam, *Const. Hist.* I. 585. Among them Hales, Walton, and Pococke, perhaps the three most learned men in England, were deprived as "ignorant and scandalous ministers."
[3] Fuller, VI. 273.
[4] Carlyle's *Cromwell*, III. 6.
[5] Baxter's *Life and Times*, pt. I. p. 72. Baxter was very unfriendly to Cromwell; his favourable testimony is therefore above suspicion.
[6] Neal, *Puritans*, 228; Hallam, *Const. Hist.* I. 619 note.

The Struggle in England

The Protector died in 1658, on his "fortunate day," September 3. His power soon fell from the slack grasp of his son Richard, and Charles II., the son of the late King, was restored to his native kingdom, in the midst of almost universal joy (May 29, 1660). The Bishops again took their seats in the House of Lords, and the ejected clergy were at once restored to their privileges and their property, without compensation for their long exclusion. The unauthorized intruders were ejected. But there were many moderate Presbyterians in possession of benefices which had become legally vacant; how were they to be treated? They had been active in the restoration of the King, and Charles had given them reason to expect some concessions[1]. A Conference was held at the Savoy[2] (1661), between twelve Bishops and as many Puritan ministers, with nine "Coadjutors" on each side, all appointed by the King. Nothing, however, could be done; the Puritan objections differed little from those which had been current in the days of Elizabeth, while the party in power were naturally less than ever inclined to concede; indeed, to have conceded the demands of the Puritans would have been to destroy the ancient Church. The Conference degenerated into a wit-combat, which amused the idlers of the town[3]. Convocation revised the Prayer-Book[4], bringing it into the form in which it is still used. A new Act of Uniformity (13 and 14 Car. II. c. 4) required all beneficed persons to declare their "unfeigned assent and consent" to everything contained in this book before St Bartholomew's Day (August 24) in the same year. On that day many hundreds[5] of nonconforming ministers passed, as many hundreds of loyal Churchmen had done but a few years before, from their benefices into poverty

Ch. I.
Cromwell's death, 1658.
The Restoration, 1660.
Savoy Conference, 1661.
Act of Uniformity, 1662.

---

[1] See his declaration from Breda (Clarendon, III. 743), and that of Oct. 25, 1660 (Wilkins, IV. 560; Cardwell, *Doc. Ann.* II. 234). It must be remembered, however, that the King was not independent of Parliament.

[2] The principal documents relating to this matter are brought together by Cardwell, *Conferences*, 238 ff. See also Procter and Frere, *On the Common Prayer*, 170 ff.; Tulloch's *English Puritanism*, &c., 357 ff.

[3] Burnet's *Own Time*, I. 181.

[4] Cardwell, *Conf.* 369 ff.; Procter and Frere, *C. P.* 194 ff.

[5] The exact number cannot be determined. Baxter (*Life*, pt. II. p. 380) says 1,800 or 2,000 were deprived; while Bishop White Kennet states the number at about 2,000 (*Register*, p. 748).

and suffering for conscience' sake[1]. The Long Parliament had allowed to the families of those who were ejected a fifth part of the income they had lost, but this precedent was not followed by the royalist Parliament of 1662.

'Conventicle' and 'Five-mile' Acts. 1664, 1665.

Poverty, however, was soon to be the least part of the sufferings of the deprived ministers. The "Conventicle Act" forbade, under severe penalties, any religious meeting where more than five persons were present besides the household; and by another Act all ministers deprived for Nonconformity were required to declare, among other things, that they would attempt no alteration in the government of Church and State. Anyone who refused was prohibited from coming within five miles of any corporate town, or any place where he had himself officiated. The gaols were soon filled with dissenters; and unfortunately the most earnest and conscientious suffered most from this kind of persecution.

Indulgence, 1672.

In 1672 some hope of better times seemed to dawn. The King published a "Declaration of Indulgence[2]," by which the penal laws against Roman Catholics and Nonconformists were at once set aside; but this arbitrary proceeding excited so violent an opposition in Parliament (1673) that it was withdrawn. Nay more; in their fear of the advancing power of the Romanists the Houses passed a Bill, providing that all persons holding any office, civil or military, should take the oath of supremacy, subscribe a declaration against transubstantiation, and receive the Communion according to the ritual of the Church of England; an Act which pressed, as was intended, most hardly upon Papists, yet frequently occasioned the exclusion of Puritans also[3].

'Test' Act, 1673.

James II. acc. 1685.

Charles was a Romanist, so far as he was of any religion. His brother James, who succeeded him, was an avowed and earnest advocate of the claims of Rome. Nor was it long before the effects of this change were seen and felt. The King went openly to Mass[4]; a Papal nuncio was received; Romish chapels were opened in the City; the unaccustomed habits of Romish religious orders

---

[1] Many, however, were able to work at the trades which they had relinquished to become preachers; and some found wealthy patrons.

[2] Cardwell, *Doc. Ann.* II. 282.
[3] Macaulay's *Hist. Eng.* I. 223.
[4] Burnet, *Own Time,* I. 623.

The Struggle in England

were seen in the streets, and Romish ecclesiastics held English benefices by dispensation from the King. In July, 1686, James entrusted the regulation of the Church to seven Commissioners, who had all the powers, and even the seal, of the hated "High Commission" of former days[1]. On the 4th of April, 1687, was published the famous "Declaration of Indulgence," by which the King suspended the penal laws against all classes of separatists. The intent of this clearly was, to ally the Protestant dissenters with the Roman Catholics in support of the arbitrary pretensions of the Crown. It met with little success, for few Protestants at that time were ready to accept a toleration which they must share with Papists. This "Declaration" was republished in the following year, and an Order in Council enjoined all officiating ministers to read it in their churches on two successive Sundays[2]. The Bishops were to distribute copies through their dioceses. Of the clergy scarcely one complied.

The Archbishop (Sancroft) and six of his suffragans, Lloyd of St Asaph, Ken of Bath and Wells, Turner of Ely, Lake of Chichester, White of Peterborough, and Trelawney of Bristol, presented a petition to the King[3] that they might be excused from distributing and reading in public a document which they looked upon as illegal. For this they were sent to the Tower, and soon after brought before the Court of King's Bench, on a charge of having "written or published a false, malicious, and seditious libel[4]." The excitement during the trial ran high; and when, on the morning of the thirtieth of June, it was known that the jury acquitted the prelates, there burst forth a tumult of joy throughout the land. Even the very troops on whom James counted to overawe the capital shouted with their countrymen. In fact, the country was weary of the constant attempts of the King to make his power absolute and introduce Popery into the kingdom. Almost all classes were alienated; and when the Prince of Orange, James's son-in-law, landed at Torbay, he was welcomed as a deliverer; courtiers and country gentlemen flocked to his standard; a "Convention" of

Ch. I.

High Commission, 1686.

Declaration of Indulgence, 1687.

Order in Council, May 24, 1688.

Bishops' Petition.

Their trial, 29 June, 1688.

William of Orange lands, 5 Nov., 1688.

---
[1] Burnet, *Own Time*, I. 675.
[2] *Ib.* I. 736 ff.
[3] Given (with facsimile) in Cardwell's *Doc. Ann.* II. 316.
[4] Burnet, *Own Time*, I. 742; Macaulay's *Hist. Eng.* II. 370 ff.

William and Mary, 12 Feb. 1689.

Lords and Commons agreed that the Prince and Princess of Orange (William and Mary) should be King and Queen of England. The regal power was in fact vested in the King[1].

Toleration Act, 18 Apr. 1689.

In this reign the Nonconformists at last enjoyed freedom of worship. A "Toleration Act[2]," without repealing any of the existing Acts against separatists, permitted loyal and peaceable dissenters to attend meetings of their own body unmolested. Their ministers received immunity in the exercise of their vocation on condition that they subscribed thirty-four of the Thirty-nine Articles of the Church of England. Preachers and people alike were to take the oaths of Allegiance and Supremacy, and subscribe the Declaration against Transubstantiation. A separate form was provided for Quakers, whose principles forbade their taking any oath whatever. This famous Act, with all its imperfections, "put an end, at once and for ever in England, to a persecution which had raged during four generations, which had broken innumerable hearts, which had made innumerable firesides desolate[3]."

Comprehension.

The present time was thought suitable for an attempt at a "Comprehension" of some of the moderate dissidents in the Church. The King favoured it; and the late common fear of Popery had drawn together the leaders of the Church and of Dissent. A "Comprehension Bill," however, introduced into Parliament, merely resulted in an address to the King, begging him to summon a Convocation of the Clergy. This was done. Meanwhile, the King constituted a Commission to prepare such a scheme for alterations of the Liturgy and Canons as might conciliate Protestant dissenters. But nothing could be passed; the lower House of Convocation refused even to discuss the scheme prepared by the Commissioners; nor was it long before all friends of the Church saw that it was well that the "Comprehension" had been rejected[4].

Sancroft and the Nonjurors.

The Convocation was presided over by Compton, Bishop of London, for Archbishop Sancroft was under suspension. He, with several of his suffragans (including

---

[1] Burnet, *Own Time*, I. 819.
[2] 1 William and Mary, c. 18; Burnet, *O. T.* II. 10.
[3] Macaulay's *Hist. Eng.* III. 86.
[4] *Ibid.* III. 475, 491.

five of the famous six who had joined their Primate in resisting the Indulgence), felt that he could not in conscience take the oath of allegiance to the new government, and about four hundred of the clergy were of the same mind. They were deprived after six months' suspension, on the 1st of February, 1690. This was the origin of the schism of the "Nonjurors," a schism which carried with it few of the laity, and died out in the course of the following century. They are not to be too harshly blamed for their schism. Their refusal to acknowledge a *de facto* government accepted by the nation may indeed seem over-scrupulous; but it must be remembered that several bishops had been driven from their sees by the mere fiat of the civil government, infringing what earnest Churchmen believed to be the rights of the Church. And as in the small body of Nonjurors we find devotional writers like Ken, Kettlewell, R. Nelson, and W. Law; liturgiologists like Brett and Spinckes; controversialists like C. Leslie; antiquaries like T. Baker, Hearne and Rawlinson; philologists like Hickes; historians like Carte and Collier, we may be sure that it was something more than a mere idle fancy which led them to secede[1].

The Church of 1690 differed little, in its outward and legal form, from that of the days of Charles I.; but its spirit was greatly changed. The Puritan humours, which then convulsed the body of the Church, had found vent in tolerated dissent, and the school of Laud was hardly to be found, except among the Nonjurors. Henceforward, for about a century the most active and learned members of the Church were "Latitudinarian." The age of Andrewes and Bacon had given place to that of Tillotson and Locke.

The toleration brought in by William III. did not benefit the Roman Catholics, who from the time of Elizabeth had been oppressed and persecuted. James I. was averse to harsh dealing with them, and even in the early days of his reign entered into secret negotiations with the Pope[2], and in his speech to his first Parliament spoke of the Roman Church as the mother Church of the

Roman Catholic disabilities.

1604.

---

[1] On the Nonjurors see T. Lathbury, *Hist. of the Nonjurors* (London, 1845); J. H. Overton, *The Nonjurors, their Lives, &c.* (London, 1903).
[2] Ranke's *Popes*, Bk. 7, c. 3, § 5.

West[1]. But he was nevertheless compelled to assent to the execution of the existing penal statutes, and even to reinforce them by harsher measures[2], so that they had to endure much suffering. Gunpowder Plot, the work of a few fanatics, of course very much heightened the antipapal feeling. The King himself deprecated violent measures[3], but he spoke to regardless ears. More oppressive statutes were passed[4]. To the King himself is due the Oath of Allegiance, devised, says Fuller[5], "to discriminate the pernicious from the peaceable Papists." This was at first accepted by several loyal Romanists, but the Pope, Paul V., published two Briefs[6] against it, which occasioned much suffering to perfectly loyal subjects of the Crown, as well as to many disaffected. When, in 1622, the prospect of a Spanish match for the Prince of Wales induced the King to discharge a few Popish Recusants[7], complaints were heard in the House of Commons[8]. Charles II. attempted in vain to mitigate their lot. In 1678 the abominable perjuries of Titus Oates as to a "Popish Plot" occasioned a new outbreak of hostility against Romanists. An Act was passed for disabling Papists from sitting in either House of Parliament, and also for requiring members to make a declaration against certain Romanist doctrines, as well as to take the oath of supremacy. In 1687, James II., an avowed Romanist, attempted to suspend the penal statutes against Roman Catholics and others[9], with the result that he was driven from his kingdom. The conduct of James raised the antipapal feeling to fever heat. But even without this, Papists were not regarded in the same light as adherents of other forms of faith; Puritans looked upon their

---

[1] King James's *Works*, 491.
[2] 1 James I. c. 4. See also the Proclamation of Feb. 22, 1604, in Wilkins, *Conc.* IV. 376; and the Commission of Sept. 5, 1604, in Rymer's *Fœdera*, XVI. 597.
[3] King James's *Works*, 503.
[4] 3 James I. cc. 4 and 5.
[5] *Ch. Hist.* v. 365; the oath in full, *ib.* 364; also Wilkins, *Conc.* IV. 425, and in Collier's *Ch. Hist.* II. 696.
[6] Dated 22 Sep. 1606 and 23 Aug. 1607. (King James's *Works*, 250, 258; Wilkins, IV. 430.) These Briefs drew from the King an *Apologie for the Oath of Allegiance* (*Works*, 247). Matthæus Tortus (Bellarmine) replied in an *Apologia*, which Andrewes met with *Tortura Torti*. Bellarmine rejoined and Andrewes sur-rejoined. See A. T. Russell, *Life of Andrewes*, p. 205 ff.
[7] Fuller, v. 533; Hacket's *Life of Williams*, pt. I. p. 91.
[8] Collier, *Ch. Hist.* II. 729; Rushworth, *Abr.* I. 92.
[9] See p. 38.

worship as idolatrous, while politicians distrusted men who owned allegiance to a foreign potentate. For many generations Roman Catholic priests were forbidden to teach the doctrines or perform the services of the Church to which they belonged, and lay Romanists were deprived of almost all the rights of citizenship[1].

7. SCOTLAND.

Nothing is more characteristic of the Kirk of Scotland than the vigour with which it struggled to become entirely independent of the State; and no monarch experienced more of this tendency than James I.[2] In the early part of his reign he submitted to see his authority slighted and his person sometimes insulted by turbulent leaders of the Presbyterian party; but he never relinquished his views as to the due subjection of ecclesiastics, and no sooner did he feel himself firmly seated on the throne of England than he set himself to curb those whom he had long disliked. He forbade the meeting of the General Assembly which was to have been held in 1605; some hardy Presbyterians met in spite of his prohibition and were arrested as rebels, and six of their number banished (1606). The famous Andrew Melville was first confined in the Tower, then exiled. James then proceeded, bearing in mind his favourite maxim, "no bishop, no King," to reestablish Episcopacy in Scotland. A shadow of Episcopacy subsisted, indeed, already; and since 1598 certain titular bishops sat in the Scottish Parliament[3]; but they had neither consecration nor authority in the Church; the King wished to give them both.

He proceeded in this matter with his characteristic caution and address. In 1606 he desired that the bishop might be perpetual moderator of the Presbytery within the limits of which he resided. This proposition, with much demur and many precautions (for the Presbyterians saw the horns of the mitre, however carefully covered)

Scottish Ecclesiastical independence.

Titular Bishops, 1606;

---

[1] See W. J. Amherst, *Hist. of Catholic Emancipation* (1886).
[2] J. Spotswood's *History of the Church of Scotland* (to the end of James VI.'s reign); David Calderwood's *Hist. of the Kirk of Scotland* —a great storehouse of information—also extends to the death of James VI.
[3] Spotswood, 448 ff.

was assented to by the General Assembly[1]. It was not, however, until 1610 that these prelates received episcopal consecration. In that year, the power of the bishops having been enlarged by the Assembly held at Glasgow, John Spotswood, titular Archbishop of Glasgow, together with the Bishop of Brechin and Galloway, was consecrated in London. Henceforth, for some thirty years, the bishops of the Church of Scotland exercised both the jurisdiction and the power of ordination belonging to their office; and their hands were strengthened by a High Commission, on the English model, for the managing of ecclesiastical causes[2]. This Commission was not well received by many, though there was no overt opposition; but much louder murmurs greeted the "Articles of Perth," which enjoined kneeling at the reception of the Eucharist, Confirmation of children, and the observance of certain festival days; permitting also, in certain cases, Private Baptism and Communion[3].

King James procured an Act "For the Restitution of the Estate of Bishops[4]," which was, however, so clogged with exceptions that it left many bishops in poverty; and his successor was able to induce the Parliament to pass an Act, "For the Commission of Surrenders and Teinds," which was of great and permanent benefit to the Church[5]. This was a kind of "Tithe-commutation" Act, which relieved both clergy and "heritors" from much oppression and annoyance on the part of the "lords of erections" or impropriators, and seems to have been received with sincere gratitude. It still forms the basis of a system which provides for the support of parochial ministers in Scotland.

But, though the Scottish Church suffered no convulsion, and her affairs were ably administered by shrewd Archbishop Spotswood, there was in it a lurking disquiet which needed but some unusual provocation to break forth into open violence. It was not long before this provocation arose.

The Church had hitherto been without a Liturgy; it was determined by the King and his English advisers

---

[1] Spotswood, 501 ff.
[2] Spotswood, 512, 514.
[3] Spotswood, 538. Ratified by Parliament, 1621. *Ib.* 542.
[4] Spotswood, 496. The Act is James VI., Parl. 18, c. 2.
[5] Charles I., Parl. 1, c. 8. Collier, II. 756.

to supply this defect. As a preliminary, Canons were set forth by royal authority, which were not only in many ways vexatious and inquisitorial, but required assent to the Liturgy which was not yet published. The Liturgy itself, which was drawn up on the English model by certain Scottish bishops, but so revised by Laud that it may be considered his work[1], was authorised by Royal Proclamation, December 20, 1636[2]. Thus, on an ancient and high-spirited nation, disliking liturgies and hating Popery, jealous of its independence, jealous, above all, of its independence in spiritual things, it was attempted to force a liturgy of foreign origin, thought to savour of Romanism, which had received the assent of no synod of the Scottish Church. The event could not be doubtful. It was not until the 23rd July, 1637, that the Dean of Edinburgh attempted to read the service from the new book in St Giles's Church in that city; he was interrupted by cries and missiles, and the whole place was soon in an uproar[3]. The agitation spread; similar scenes took place in other churches where the liturgy was introduced; everywhere Scotchmen were ready to defend their ancient rights and their Presbyterian church-government; several bishops fled, and the episcopal party was for the time scattered to the winds. Committees—"Tables," as they were called—were formed at Edinburgh to organize and direct the movement; and in 1638 was drawn up at Edinburgh the "Confession of Faith of the Kirk of Scotland, and General Band for the maintenance of the True Religion and the King's Person," afterwards known as "the Covenant[4]." It sped through the country like the fiery cross, and in a few months almost all Scotland, except the placemen and a few earnest episcopalians and Romanists, was united in the bond[5]. The Marquis of

CH. I.

Canons, 1635.

Liturgy, Dec. 20, 1636.

Tumult in Edinburgh, 1637.

The Covenant, 1638.

---

[1] A. Stevenson, *Hist. of Church of Scotland*, I. 154. Kirkton (*Hist.* p. 30) says that he saw the original with corrections in the handwriting of Laud. See Cunningham, *Ch. Hist. of Scotland*, II. 68.
[2] In Collier, *Ch. Hist.*, II. 769.
[3] H. Guthrie's *Memoirs of Scottish Affairs*, p. 20; J. Row's *History*, p. 408; R. Baillie's *Letters*, etc., I. 18; G. Crawfurd's *Lives*, p. 181; Clarendon's *Rebellion*, I. 109; Burnet's *Lives of the Dukes of Hamilton*, p. 31.
[4] Baillie's *Letters*, II. 91; Collier, II. 779.
[5] Spalding (*Troubles in Scotland*, II. 132) describes the coercion used by the Covenanters at Aberdeen to obtain signatures; and probably this was not a solitary instance.

Hamilton was sent into Scotland as royal commissioner, and obtained with some difficulty several concessions from the King. The High Commission, Canons, and Liturgy were to be withdrawn; the Five Articles of Perth no longer to be insisted upon; a General Assembly to be convened; subscription to the Covenant of 1580 enjoined[1]. Everything was here granted which the Scots could reasonably ask; but in the excited state of public feeling even concession seemed to augment their suspicions. The national synod met at Glasgow, but proved so intractable that Hamilton pronounced its dissolution after a week's session[2]. It continued to meet, however, in spite of him, and (says Burnet)[3] "went on at a great rate, now that there was none to curb them." They condemned all the assemblies of the previous forty years, as not free; Episcopacy, Articles of Perth, Canons, Service-book, and High Commission were declared unlawful; the Covenant, in its new and offensive form, was ordered to be taken by all on pain of excommunication. The bishops were deposed, and eight of them excommunicated. All the institutions of Presbytery were revived. This done, the Assembly separated. Until the vigorous hand of Cromwell restored the ascendancy of the civil power, the Kirk reigned almost uncontrolled, not only in the pulpit and the synod, but in the council and the camp, and no government ever exercised a sterner despotism.

Synod at Glasgow, Nov. 21, 1638.

The King's proceedings.

Meanwhile, the King was preparing to reduce Scotland by force. The Scots raised an army to oppose him, which was placed under the command of Alexander Lesley, a veteran of the Thirty Years' War. Neither party, however, was anxious to put the contest to the issue of a battle, and a "Pacification[4]" was concluded at Berwick, which probably both parties felt to be but a hollow truce; the inevitable decision was but adjourned. Accordingly in the following year a Scottish army entered England and won the battle of Newburn. This army was disbanded, but in 1643 Parliament made an agreement with the Scots for assistance, and signed the Solemn

Pacification of Berwick, June 18, 1639.
1640.

---

[1] The King's instructions to Hamilton, Burnet's *Hamiltons*, 72; his offers to the Assembly, *ib.* 96.
[2] Burnet's *Hamiltons*, 106.
[3] *Hamiltons*, 110.

[4] The Articles of this Treaty—about which there was afterwards much dispute—are given in Burnet's *Hamiltons*, 142. Cf. May, *Hist. of Long Parliament*, p. 52 (ed. 1854).

Scotland

League and Covenant[1], in which they bound themselves to endeavour the preservation of the Reformed religion in Scotland, and the reformation of religion in England and Ireland according to the Word of God and the example of the best Reformed Churches. The intention was to establish a uniform system in the three kingdoms. Shortly afterwards a strong Scottish force crossed the Border. In 1645 the General Assembly gave its sanction to the Form of Church Government and Directory for Public Worship; in 1647 it accepted the Westminster Confession of Faith, and in 1648 the Longer and Shorter Catechisms[2]. These formularies, especially the Shorter Catechism, have had an immense influence in moulding the Scottish character.

When Cromwell became master in Scotland the uncontrolled power of the Kirk came to an end. Neither he nor Monk, who took his place when he returned to England, would endure that the Kirk should rule despotically by means of censures and excommunications, so as to "overtop the civil power[3]"; and in 1653, Colonel Coterel dispersed the General Assembly, forbidding them to sit without authority from the Parliament of England[4]. It was long before the Kirk recovered even a shadow of its former authority.

In 1660 Charles II. was restored to the throne of his forefathers. The Scottish Presbyterians, who had never consented to the death of Charles I., and had shown conspicuous loyalty to his son, deserved some consideration; but the restored King had no sympathy with a religion which "was not a religion for gentlemen[5]." Episcopacy, without the hated Liturgy, was restored[6], and Sharp, a convert from Presbyterianism, was made Archbishop of St Andrews. Other bishops were consecrated at the same time, among them the saintly Robert Leighton to the see of Dumblane, almost the only man in the Scottish

CH. I.
Solemn League and Covenant, Sept. 25, 1643.
Scottish Army, Jan. 19, 1644.
Westminster Confession, 1647. Catechisms, 1648.
Cromwell in Scotland, 1650.
Charles II. restored, 1660.
Bishops restored, 1661.

---

[1] In Clarendon, Bk. VII. (II. 372).
[2] Cunningham's *Ch. Hist. of Scotland*, II. 154.
[3] See Cromwell's letters to the Edinburgh ministers, Sept. 9 and 12, 1650, in Carlyle's *Cromwell*, II. 204 ff.; Collier, II. 866.
[4] Baillie's *Letters*, II. 370; Collier, II. 867.
[5] Burnet, *Own Time*, I. 107.
[6] Cunningham's *Ch. Hist.* II. 183 ff. The bishops of 1661 enjoyed much more extensive powers than those of 1610; see Kirkton's *History*, ed. C. K. Sharpe, pp. 141, 142.

episcopate of this period whose name is associated with Christian gentleness and holiness[1]. They were received in Scotland generally with gloomy acquiescence; the country which had done battle so valiantly for the Covenant was now so far cowed and exhausted that few thought of resisting the powerful government of the Restoration. But the 'Whigs[2]' of the south-western counties would not so readily resign their Presbyterian government and Calvinistic doctrine; many pastors left their churches; many of their flocks refused to attend the ministry of the hirelings who succeeded them; they met their favourite preachers in the glens, on the moors, or on the mountainside. Dispersed, persecuted, hunted down, tortured, slain, they held still to their faith; but their fanaticism rose to frenzy; they regarded themselves as Israelites in the midst of an idolatrous Canaan, and thought it a merit to destroy the worshippers of Baal. A party of these zealots murdered Archbishop Sharp, on Magus Muir, and gave thanks to God for the glorious work which they had been permitted to accomplish[3]. A serious insurrection which followed was crushed by the Duke of Monmouth at the battle of Bothwell-Brigg[4]. It was in the persecution of these western Covenanters that Graham of Claverhouse, a soldier who carried out the orders of the Council but too faithfully, earned an evil immortality.

The Revolution at last brought quiet to the distracted country. The great majority of the Scots accepted the sovereignty of William and Mary, and the Convention made the abolition of prelacy one of the Articles of their 'Claim of Right[5]'. After a year of anarchy the Scottish Parliament of 1690 adopted the Westminster Confession as the standard of doctrine for the Kirk, and reestablished the synodical polity[6]. The delicate point, whether the

---

[1] Burnet, who knew him well, had a hearty admiration for Leighton; see *Own Time*, I. 134 ff.

[2] The west-country farmers were called Whiggamors, or Whigs, according to Burnet (*Own Time*, I. 43), from a word 'whiggam,' used in driving their horses. An account of the persecutions of this time is in Wodrow's *History*, vol. IV.

[3] An account of this horrible deed, by James Russell, one of the murderers, was printed by Mr C. Kirkpatrick Sharpe with his edition of Kirkton's *History*.

[4] Burnet's *Own Time*, I. 472.

[5] Burnet, II. 22.

[6] Macaulay's *Hist. Eng.* II. 690. On the violence with which this reestablishment was conducted see Burnet, II. 64.

sovereign should have power to convoke and dissolve ecclesiastical assemblies, was left in an ambiguity which is not removed to this day[1]. This settlement satisfied the Presbyterians, with the exception of the most furious Covenanters, whom perhaps no scheme of human polity could content. The Episcopalians became, in their turn, a persecuted remnant, devoted, for the most part, to the exiled House of Stuart. Thus, after a struggle of more than a century, was established that Scottish Presbytery, which, if somewhat wanting in breadth and dignity[2], has retained the affection and penetrated the life of the nation more than any other Calvinistic system in Europe.

8. IRELAND[3].

There are few more dismal pages in Church history than that of the so-called Reformation in Ireland. After 1534 Henry VIII. lost no time in causing every part of his dominions to recognize his own ecclesiastical supremacy, which was acknowledged by the Irish Parliament in 1537, but was rejected by the greater part of the clergy. Instead, however, of attempting to teach the Irish through their own language, the Government directed that preferment should be given only to such as could speak English, and that English should be taught in the schools. In fact, English ascendancy was the Government motto. The phrase "Church of England and Ireland" began to be used in 1538. In 1560 the English formularies were synodically accepted, so that the two Churches became, in form at least, one. The state of things which ensued was disastrous. In 1562 the Earl of Sussex, Lord Deputy, wrote to Cecil, "The people without discipline, utterly void of religion, come to divine service as to a May-game. The ministers for disability and greediness be had in

---

[1] "The Moderator dissolves the assembly in the name of the Lord Jesus Christ, the head of the Church; and, by the same authority, appoints another to meet on a certain day of the ensuing year. The Lord High Commissioner then dissolves the assembly in the name of the King, and appoints another to meet on the same day." Arnot's *Hist. of Edinburgh*, p. 269; quoted by Hallam, *Const. Hist.* II. 495.

[2] According to Burnet, Leighton found that the Presbyterians of his time 'were not capable of large thoughts.' *Own Time*, I. 135.

[3] R. Mant's *History of the Church of Ireland from the Reformation to the Revolution* is a good summary of the events of this period.

contempt; and the wise fear more the impiety of the licentious professors (*i.e.* of Protestantism) than the superstition of the erroneous Papists[1]." Many of the ultra-papists did not hesitate to negotiate a union with Spain. The general tone of the Anglo-Irish Church was Calvinistic, and its test of orthodoxy was the set of eleven Articles put forth by Parker in 1559, which was imposed upon all Irish incumbents by the Lord Deputy and the bishops in 1566. In 1615 the Dublin convocation put forth a body of Articles independent of the English.

State of Irish Church.

When James I. came to the throne Ireland was still seething from the late rebellion. Many benefices were vacant and many churches waste and desolate, but the people almost everywhere adhered to their old communion. The English service-books were as unintelligible to the Irish as the Latin had been. An Irish translation of the Prayer-Book had indeed been made, but it received no public sanction and was rarely used, while the vernacular translation of the New Testament did not appear until 1602[2]. When the Lord Deputy in 1607 visited a part of Ulster he found in county Cavan "the churches for the most part in ruins; such as were presented to be in reparation are covered only with thatch. But the incumbents, both parsons and vicars, did appear to be such poor, ragged, ignorant creatures...as we could not esteem them worthy of the meanest of those livings, albeit many of them are not worth above 40*s.* per annum[3]." About fifteen years later Bishop Ussher reports that in his diocese of Meath out of two hundred and thirty-two churches one hundred and fifty were ruinous, and that the incomes of the benefices were utterly insufficient to maintain a minister in every cure[4]. When Bishop Bedell entered on his diocese of Kilmore and Ardagh he found "the parish churches all in a manner ruined and unroofed and unrepaired. The people, save for a few British planters here and there,...obstinate recusants. A Popish clergy, more numerous by far than we, in full exercise of all jurisdiction ecclesiastical by their vicar-

Ussher, 1622.

Bedell, 1630.

---

[1] Hardwick's *Reformation*, 246.
[2] *Ib.* 249.
[3] Sir John Davies' Letter, in his *Tracts*, p. 227; quoted by Mant, 354.
[4] Mant, 398.

general and officials; who are so confident that they excommunicate those who come to our courts even in matrimonial causes.... Every parish has its priest and... mass-houses also; in some places mass is said in the churches.... For our own, there are seven or eight ministers in each diocese of good sufficiency, and (which is no small cause of the continuance of the people in Popery still) English, which have not the tongue of the people, nor can perform any divine office, or converse with them; and which hold, many of them, two, three, four, or more vicarages apiece[1]." This picture of the utter insufficiency of the Anglican ministry in Ireland, and of the dominance of Romanism, was probably true of other dioceses besides those of Kilmore and Ardagh[2]. It is confirmed and amplified in Strafford's letter to Laud of January 31, 1634[3].

Meanwhile, though the Church of Ireland had, in theory at least, adopted the Prayer-Book of the Church of England, it still retained the Articles of 1615[4], differing in several points from the English, especially in embodying Whitgift's Nine Articles, and in attempting to define certain speculative questions which in England had more wisely been left undetermined. In the Convocation of 1635, under severe pressure from the Viceroy, Lord Strafford, the English Articles of Religion were adopted, and a body of Canons drawn up which, though not identical with the English, satisfied Archbishop Laud[5]. In 1641 there burst out, quite unexpectedly, a rising of the Papists which seemed to aim at the extermination of the Protestants. Vast numbers of them were murdered in cold blood. In the first year of the rebellion it seems probable that nearly forty thousand[6] were put to death, often with circumstances of great atrocity. The Romanist clergy assembled in synods and assumed spiritual authority

Irish Articles, 1615.

1635.

Articles; Canons.

Irish Rebellion, 1641.

---

[1] In Mant, 436.
[2] See R. Cox, *Hibernia Anglicana* (1689), II. 53.
[3] *Strafford Letters*, I. 187 f.
[4] Hardwick's *Reformation*, 248.
[5] See the letters of Laud and Strafford in Mant, 485 ff.
[6] Sir W. Petty, an excellent authority, calculated that 37,000 perished in the first year of the outbreak. Carte accepts this. Clarendon says above 40,000. Sir John Temple (*Irish Rebellion*) states that from Oct. 23, 1641, to Sept. 15, 1643, above 30,000 were destroyed or driven from their homes.

Ireland

Glamorgan's Treaty, 1645.

over the country, and in 1645 the Earl of Glamorgan, acting on behalf of the King[1], made a secret treaty with the confederates by which the Romanists were granted possession of all the churches and church-revenues which they had seized since October 23, 1641, on condition of their providing an army of 10,000 men for the service of the King in England—a condition which was never fulfilled.

1645.

Meanwhile, the events in England influenced Ireland. The Solemn League and Covenant[2] was pressed upon the inhabitants of Ulster, who were largely Scottish settlers drawn thither by the inducements offered by King James, and was accepted by large numbers. In 1647 the supreme power in Ireland passed into the hands of the English Parliamentary party. The commissioners who exercised jurisdiction by its authority issued injunctions requiring the discontinuance of the use of the Prayer-Book and the adoption of the Directory for Public Worship.

Parliamentary Commissioners' Injunctions, June 24, 1647.
King proclaimed in Dublin, May 14, 1660.

On the Restoration, the Duke of Ormonde[3], a steady friend of the Church, became Lord Steward of the Household, and the principal adviser of the Crown in matters ecclesiastical. Efforts were made without effect by a considerable party to have the existing state of things, under which the benefices of the Church were held by Presbyterians, maintained. The King restored to the Anglo-Irish Church all its temporalities as they existed in 1641, and proceeded to fill the vacant sees. John Bramhall, an able man both as a theologian and a man of affairs, was made Primate, and shewed moderation and sound judgment in the exercise of his office. An Irish Act of Uniformity was passed in 1667, superseding that of 1560 which enjoined the use of Elizabeth's Prayer-Book. But the Church was little more than a skeleton, since the mass of the people in the South and West adhered to Rome, and in the North to some form of Protestant dissent. With the accession of James II. a cloud naturally came

Act of Uniformity, 1667.

James II., 1685.

---

[1] Few points in English history have been more hotly debated than the genuineness and intention of the commission given to Glamorgan. The most probable opinion is that it was genuine, though irregular. See J. H. Round in *Academy*, 8 Dec. 1883, and S. R. Gardiner in *Eng. Hist. Review*, II. 687 ff.

[2] See p. 45.

[3] T. Carte's *Life of James, Duke of Ormonde, from 1610 to 1688* contains many valuable documents for this period.

over the Anglo-Irish Church. Henry Hyde, Earl of Clarendon, a Churchman, became Lord Lieutenant, but the real power was exercised by Richard Talbot, Earl of Tyrconnel, a Romanist, who in 1687 was placed at the head of the Irish administration, with the revived title of Lord Deputy. Such was the terror inspired by his name that many Protestants sold their possessions in Ireland and left the kingdom, while those who remained often found it difficult to obtain the protection of the law. After the victory of William at the Boyne the Church of Ireland was restored to the position which she had occupied before the accession of James. Under William were enacted the penal statutes against Roman Catholics which remained as a proof of Orange ascendancy for many generations. This code "denied to the persecuted sect the power of educating their children at home, and at the same time...prohibited them from seeking education abroad. It disabled them from acquiring freehold property. It subjected their estates to an exceptional rule of succession...with a view to break them into fragments.... It excluded them from the liberal and influential professions. It took from them the guardianship of their own children. It [enabled] the son of a Papist, on turning Protestant, to dispossess his father of the fee-simple of his estate.... In the case of the Roman Catholic priesthood, persecution, legally at least, did not stop short of blood.... It would not be difficult to point to persecuting laws more sanguinary than these—Spain, France, and Austria will supply signal examples. But it would be difficult to point to any more insulting to the best feelings of man or more degrading to religion[1]."

[1] Goldwin Smith, *Irish History and Irish Character*, p. 126 f.

Battle of the Boyne, 1690.

CHAPTER II.

THE ENGLISH CHURCH.

1. ANGLICAN THEOLOGY AND THEOLOGIANS.

Reformation.

IN the days of James I. and his son the Reformation was still going on. Its aim was to remedy abuses which had grown up in the Church without breaking with its history and its traditions; to give to the Crown, acting within the limits of law, new powers of correction and control, without trenching on the inherent privileges of the spiritual body. The English leaders never propounded a clear and definite theory of Church reform as the Roman Church did at Trent, or as Calvin did for the bodies which owned his sway. In England measures were devised to meet the emergencies which from time to time arose. But through all the clouds of prejudice and controversy, we can see that the idea present to the best spirits of the Reformation was to take the Church of Augustine and Becket and Warham as the representative in England of that great Society which is traceable through the ages to Apostolic times. They accepted the Bible, as the primitive Church had accepted it, as the test by which all Christian teaching must be tried, but not so as to exclude the authority of the Church Universal. They maintained the due succession of bishops, they put the Bible into the hands of the people in their mother tongue, and turned the Latin Offices, not without many changes, into the language which all understood. They defined their position on disputed points in Articles of Religion. But such matters as canons and tribunals were adjourned to a more convenient season, and even now remain in an unfinished condition which has been productive of difficulty and danger.

Its characteristics.

During the sixteenth century Roman controversialists became much more powerful than they had been when Luther's theses first appeared. The Jesuits placed at the service of the Pope not only enthusiasm but learning and literary skill. Systems of theology appeared written in full view of the movements of the time. It was difficult for Protestants to find a match for the learning and subtlety of such men as Bellarmine. At the beginning of the seventeenth century it had become evident that the Church of Rome lacked neither defenders nor arguments.

Roman Controversy.

On the other hand, Calvin was entirely uninfluenced by any respect for existing institutions, and his system had for many minds the charm of being unflinchingly logical. It had no hesitations or reservations. It won the favour of many able men in England, both among the clergy and the laity. These men steadily endeavoured to impose the Calvinistic theology in its severest form on Anglican teaching, and denounced any deviation from its tenets as disloyalty to Christian truth. In truth, this sombre teaching was so congenial to grave and rigid minds in England and Scotland that it flourished in our island with a vigour which it soon lost in its native seats. When Whitgift put forth the Lambeth Articles in 1595 it came perilously near to making itself master in the English Church.

Calvinism.

Such were the forces which pressed upon and moulded English theologians of the seventeenth century. In the early stages of the Reformation men had acted and written somewhat hurriedly to meet immediate necessities. Now there came a period of wider knowledge and steadier judgment. The later years of Elizabeth, being settled and quiet compared with an earlier time, gave to the larger and more powerful minds time to think, to learn, to weigh and follow out arguments. It was seen that something more was needed than mere invectives against Roman corruptions and pretensions; "it was necessary to find some positive ground on which to rest the claim that England was better and more primitive than Rome." And "something was wanted as fervent, but more true, more noble, more Catholic than [the Calvinists'] devotion and self-discipline. The higher spirits of the time wanted to breathe more freely and in a purer air.

Anglicanism.

Anglican Theology and Theologians

Ch. II.

They found what they wanted in the language, the ideas, the tone and temper of the best early Christian literature. That turned their thoughts from words to a Person. It raised them from the disputes of local cliques to the ideas which have made the Universal Church. It recalled them from arguments that revolved round a certain number of traditional formulæ about justification, freewill, and faith, to a truer and worthier idea both of man and God, to the overwhelming revelation of the Word Incarnate and the result of it on the moral standard and behaviour of real and living men. It led them from a theology which ended in cross-grained and perverse conscientiousness, to a theology which ended in adoration, self-surrender, and blessing, and in the awe and joy of welcoming the Presence of the Eternal Beauty, the Eternal Sanctity, and the Eternal Love, the Sacrifice and Reconciliation of the World[1]." Such were the influences which presided over the formation of the theology which has come to be known distinctively as Anglican.

Hooker, 1553(?)—1600.

At the head of Anglican theology must be placed Richard Hooker[2], to whom, more than to any other man, its characteristics are due. Where others had been content to meet particular assertions by special arguments, he goes back at once to the first principles from which the phenomena spring. If the Puritans held that no law was universally binding which was not found in Scripture, and that laws written in Scripture must abide for ever; he points out that laws of God are found in the very constitution of the physical and moral world—laws to which man cannot refuse obedience[3]. To discuss the question rightly we must enter into "consideration of law in general, and of that law which giveth life to the rest,

On Law.

---

[1] R. W. Church, in *Masters in English Theology* (ed. A. Barry, 1877), p. 89 f.

[2] *Life*, by Isaac Walton, reprinted in Wordsworth's *Eccles. Biog.* III. 433 ff., and the edition of Hooker's *Works* by J. Keble, whose Introduction, with the corrections of R. W. Church and F. Paget in the edition of 1888, is valuable. See also R. W. Church's essay prefixed to his edition of *Eccl. Polity*, Bk. I. (Oxford, 1876); A. Barry in *Masters in English Theology* (1877); F. D. Maurice, *Moral and Metaphysical Philosophy*, II. 189 ff. (ed. 1873); J. Hunt, *Religious Thought in England*, I. 56 ff.; C. de Rémusat, *La Philosophie en Angleterre*, I. 125 ff.; Sidney Lee in *Dict. Nat. Biog.* XXVII. 287.

[3] *Ecclesiastical Polity*, Bk. I.

namely, the law by which the Eternal Himself doth work." Even in Scripture itself some laws were given to men, as men; some to men in particular circumstances, which "may perhaps be clean otherwise a while after." When he treats of the great question, so hotly disputed, of the Presence of Christ in the Eucharist, he bases his arguments on the fundamental truth of the Incarnation itself[1]. And in the doctrine so deduced he finds a large agreement of Christian men, so far as they consent to leave mysteries unexplained; "let disputes and questions, enemies to piety, abatements of true devotion...take their rest." He was the first to defend the organization and the worship of the Church in England in a strain worthy of so high a theme. And all this was set forth in a stately, measured, and yet flexible style, of which before him English theology had no example. It cannot be said that Hooker founded a school, but he gave to Anglican theology a tone which it has never lost.

On the Eucharist.

Style.

By the side of Hooker may be placed his friend, Richard Field[2], who wrote a very learned and able treatise, *Of the Church*, "to meet the assaults," he says, "of the Romanists rather than the Puritans." It does, however, more than any other work of that age, define the position of the Church of England as it was understood by her most orthodox and learned divines. Two points are especially noteworthy in it. Field does not hold episcopal succession to be of absolute necessity, for it may devolve on the presbyters remaining Catholic to perpetuate a Church; and he was probably the first to note the agreement in many points of the Anglican with the Greek Church, and to urge the desirableness of intercommunion.

R. Field, 1551—1616. "Of the Church," 1606.

Among the creative spirits of English theology we may place Lancelot Andrewes[3]. Only two years younger than Hooker, he survived him by more than a quarter of a century. Born in the reign of Mary, dying in that of Charles I., he links the age of the Tudors with that of the Stuarts. Like Bacon, his contemporary and friend, he

Andrewes, 1555—1626.

---

[1] *Eccl. Pol.*, Bk. v. c. 51 ff.
[2] Wood's *Athenæ Oxon.* II. 181 ff. (ed. Bliss); *Memorials of R. Field*, by N. Field (Lond. 1716); Life in *Dict. Nat. Biog.* XVIII. 410 ff., by R. Hooper.
[3] *Life* by H. Isaacson (1650), A. T. Russell (1863); *Classic Preachers*, ed. J. E. Kempe (1877), Lect. 3.

Tortura Torti, 1609.

loved to observe the works of Nature, their orders, qualities, and uses. But he was no naturalist; he was, both by natural bent and by training, a theologian. When King James, not very wisely, published a defence of the oath of allegiance which had been imposed on Papists after Gunpowder Plot, and was in consequence attacked by Bellarmine, Andrewes defended his royal master with much vigour and learning. But his great fame, both in his lifetime and in after ages, was won as a preacher. "No

Sermons.

sermons like his had yet been preached in the English Church. If the stupendous facts of the Christian Creed are true, no attention, no thought, is too great for them; and their greatness, their connexion, their harmony, their infinite relations to the system of God's government and discipline of mankind, and to the hopes and certainties of human life, are here set forth with a breadth, a subtlety, a firmness of touch, a sense of their reality, a fervour and reverence of conviction, which have made the sermons worthy and fruitful subjects of study to English theologians.... But the style is like the notes of the unceremonious discourse of a very animated and varied talker rather than the composition of a preacher.... It is of the same kind as the style of much of Bacon's writings, especially his speeches.... But students of English thought and literature are not deterred by the harsh fashion of Bacon's writings, and students of English theology will find under the quaint form of Andrewes' sermons enough to justify his reputation as a divine both in his own day and since[1]."

Donne, 1573—1631.

Merely as a preacher John Donne[2] must have a higher place than Andrewes; for while his matter is hardly inferior, he has a quickness of fancy, an aptness of illustration, and a felicity of language worthy of a contemporary, perhaps a friend, of Shakspere. Few men have been so fitted by natural gifts and by the circumstances of their life to win the attention of cultivated men of the world. Poet, lawyer, courtier, diplomatist, learned

---

[1] R. W. Church, in *Masters in Eng. Theol.* p. 70 f.

[2] *Life* by Isaac Walton, reprinted in Wordsworth's *Eccl. Biography*, III. 623; best edition by H. K. Causton (1855); sketch by H. Alford, prefixed to his edition of Donne's *Works*; *Life* by A. Jessopp in *Dict. Nat. Biog.* xv. 223 ff.

theologian and well-bred gentleman, he presents an assemblage of qualities which no contemporary could rival. Having had in his youth to "blot out certain impressions of the Roman religion" which he had received from his mother and his tutors, he was well acquainted with the Roman controversy. He wrote his treatise *Pseudo-Martyr*, while still a layman, by command of the King, "wherein this conclusion is evicted, that those which are of the Roman religion in this kingdom may and ought to take the oath of allegiance." He was ordained, there is reason to think, on January 25, 1615, in his forty-second year, and from this time he poured forth a constant succession of sermons which, eloquent in themselves, were made more impressive by his striking presence and manner.

"Such was thy carriage and thy gesture such
As could divide the heart and conscience touch[1]."

He seems in fact, during the sixteen years which elapsed between his ordination and his death to have been the most popular preacher in England.

Of Laud's political and administrative activity, which absorbed the greater part of his energy, some account has already been given[2]. But if he had been less occupied with practical matters he might have been notable as a theologian. With regard to matters of ritual, he was indignant with the dirt and dilapidation of many churches and the slovenliness of many services; he hated dirt and disorder; but with regard to dogmatic teaching his views were at any rate much more liberal than those of the Puritan. He was "the intellectual successor of the men of the new learning who had attempted, with the King at their back, to reform the Church under the influence of constituted authorities and learned inquiry[3]," and was not for placing human reason in bondage. In his controversy with Fisher the Jesuit he strove against the proposition

---

[1] Jasper Mayne, quoted by Alford (Donne's *Works*, I. xviii.).
[2] p. 31. Laud's life has been written by his contemporaries W. Prynne (scurrilous) and Peter Heylin (laudatory). Also by J. Parker Lawson (1829), C. W. Le Bas (1836), J. Baines (1855), A. C. Benson (1887), and S. R. Gardiner in *Dict. Nat. Biogr.* XXXII. 185 ff. An *Autobiography*, collected from his Remains, was published at Oxford in 1839.
[3] S. R. Gardiner, *l.c.*, p. 188.

that "all points defined by the Church are fundamental," being anxious to recognize the fewest Articles possible as necessary for "soul-saving faith." The foundations of faith were to him the Scriptures and the Creeds; doubtful points as to the meaning of these should be determined by a lawful and free General Council. The Church of England, he said, "would not be too busy with every particular school-point"; men were not to be "forced to subscribe to curious particulars disputed in schools[1]." The enmity which he brought on himself by his rigidity in ritual and order have caused one of the broadest-minded men of his time to be regarded as a narrow bigot.

W. Chillingworth, 1602—1644.

Next to Laud we may name his godson William Chillingworth[2], a man who, driven to Rome by the desire of rest from the acrid controversies of his time, returned to the Church of his baptism when he found that even the Roman Church was turbulent and divided. He acquiesced in Laud's views of ritual without being an eager advocate of them. But his great distinction is his earnest advocacy of Protestantism—which he did not regard as sectarian dogmatism—as a means of salvation. "The Bible," he said, "the Bible only is the religion of Protestants[3]." From the Bible he believed that any honest man, who earnestly sought the help of the Holy Spirit, could learn the truth sufficiently to guide him to eternal life. Dogmatic Articles, such as the Protestantism of his day delighted in, he greatly distrusted.

H. Hammond, 1605—1660.

Among the other able men who supported Anglican views, a few may be specially mentioned. Henry Hammond[4], who in time of trouble had steadfastly adhered to the royal cause while reproving the excesses of royalists, may be regarded as the founder in England of a new and better school of New Testament interpretation.

---

[1] See Laud's *Works* (Oxford, 1847 ff.), VI. 265; II. 31, 144, 402, 428, cited by Gardiner, *D. N. B.*, p. 186.

[2] *Life* by P. Desmaizeaux (1725); T. Birch in C.'s *Works* (1742); E. H. Plumptre in *Masters in Theology* (1877), p. 113; Mandell Creighton in *Dict. Nat. Biog.* X. 252.

[3] *Religion of Protestants*, I. vi. 56.

[4] *Life* by Bishop Fell (1661), reprinted in Wordsworth's *Eccl. Biog.* IV. 313 ff.; by R. B. Hone (1833); by G. G. Perry (S.P.C.K.); by W. H. Teale (1846); and by R. Hooper, in *Dict. Nat. Biog.* XXIV. 242, with a full list of his works.

Robert Sanderson[1], another steadfast Royalist and churchman, wrote a treatise on the binding force of conscience which is distinguished among English books on moral theology by its clearness and logical cogency. Jeremy Taylor[2] preached toleration to an intolerant age; dissuaded from Popery men who, in a time of endless and heated discussion were drawn to an authority which claimed, as by a commission from Heaven, to decide all moral and spiritual questions; attempted to guide those who were troubled in conscience and to point out the way to Holy Living and Holy Dying; and in his sermons taught the great truths of Christianity in a strain of florid eloquence rarely equalled. Isaac Barrow[3], great in almost all learning, but especially in mathematics and theology, expounded the Christian Creed, contended against the Pope's Supremacy, and enforced moral duties with a vigour of reasoning and a dignity of language which often rise into eloquence. John Pearson deliberately and avowedly adhered to the scholastic method in theology[4], and the system which he most admired and followed was that of Thomas Aquinas. But if he admired the great schoolmen for their orderly logic, he was very far from rejecting the light of contemporary scholarship. The schoolmen had their defects, of which the first is, that they knew not how to criticise authorities. He himself gave a signal example of the kind of inquiry by which the age and authenticity of an ancient document may be determined, in his *Vindiciæ Ignatianæ*, written to prove the genuineness of the seven Letters attributed to Ignatius, which remained the standard work on the subject up to our own time. Pearson was, in short, a schoolman with the scholarship

Ch. II.
R. Sanderson, 1587—1663.
Jeremy Taylor, 1613—1667.
Isaac Barrow, 1630—1677.
John Pearson, 1613—1686.
Vindiciæ Ignatianæ, 1672.

---

[1] *Life* by Isaac Walton (1678), reprinted in Wordsworth's *Eccl. Biog.* IV. 395 and elsewhere; by J. H. Lupton in *Dict. Nat. Biog.* l. 265.

[2] *Life* by H. K. Bonney (1815), Hughes (1831); Reg. Heber (1822), revised by C. P. Eden (1854), prefixed to *Works*; R. A. Willmot (1847); [S. Cheetham] in *Quarterly Review*, no. 261, p. 113 ff. (July, 1871); A. Gordon in *Dict. Nat. Biog.* lv. 422.

[3] *Life* by T. S. Hughes, prefixed to his edition of *Works* (1830); notice, mainly of his academic and mathematical work, by W. Whewell, in vol. 9 of Napier's ed. of *Works*; [S. Cheetham] in *Quarterly R.*, Oct. 1869; *Life* by J. H. Overton in *Dict. Nat. Biog.* III. 299, who refers to the Davy mss. in British Museum.

[4] *Life* by E. Churton, prefixed to Pearson's *Minor Theol. Works* (Oxford, 1844); S. Cheetham in *Masters in Eng. Theol.* p. 213; J. H. Overton in *Dict. Chr. Biog.* XLIV. 168.

of the Renaissance. The citations in the notes to his great work on the Creed are almost always the best for his purpose and almost always fairly interpreted. George Bull[1] contended for the primitive antiquity of the Catholic doctrine of the Holy Trinity in a work so clear and convincing as to win the applause of Bossuet. This book remains one of the classic treatises of the English Church. A remarkable man, Robert South[2], bridges over the interval between the age of Milton and the age of Pope. He was a schoolboy at Westminster when Charles I. was beheaded, and when he died Atterbury was Dean. His admirable style and keen invective delighted the Cavaliers, whose faults, however, he did not forget to reprove. The Anglicanism of this time has never wanted adherents in the English Church, though for a time it was overshadowed by a teaching more in harmony with an age which did not much regard ancient landmarks.

There were of course among the clergy who conformed many who held Puritan opinions. Such were, for instance, John Lightfoot, the learned Hebraist, and Edward Reynolds, Bishop of Norwich. But the best of the Presbyterians and Independents who had held offices and benefices in the Church during the Commonwealth resigned their places rather than make the declaration required by the Act of Uniformity. Such were John Owen, the author of a once well-known commentary on the Epistle to the Hebrews; and Richard Baxter, now known principally as the author of the *Saints' Everlasting Rest*, but once famous for more than a hundred tracts and treatises. There has from this epoch never been a time in which the Puritan spirit has not been represented both within the Church and without it; but the influence of Presbyterianism, once dominant in England, has steadily diminished.

In the excited discussions of the seventeenth century the basis of morality was attacked from opposite camps.

---

[1] *Life* by R. Nelson (1714), reprinted, with additions by E. Burton, in vol. 7 of *Works* (Oxford, 1827); *Classic Preachers*, ed. J. E. Kempe, 2nd Series; W. Hunt in *Dict. Nat. Biog.* VII. 236.

[2] A *Memoir* with South's *Post-* humous *Works* (London, 1717). See also Wood's *Athenæ Oxon.* (ed. Bliss), IV. 631; [S. Cheetham] in *Quarterly Review*, no. 248 (Apr. 1868); A. Gordon in *Dict. Nat. Biog.* LIII. 275.

The Puritans generally held that the natural man is utterly alienated from God, so that all his words and deeds are equally evil; it rested with God only to choose arbitrarily whom He would. This view logically, if not practically, cut at the root of all morality. On the other hand, Thomas Hobbes[1], one of the most vigorous writers of his time, without denying that there are certain immutable and eternal laws of nature, maintained that the commands of the sovereign power are the final measure of right and wrong for the conduct of its subjects, and ought to be absolutely obeyed, since to dispute its dictates would be the first step towards anarchy. Religion is with him fear of invisible powers. The fear of those invisible powers which the State recognizes is religion; the fear of powers not thus recognized is superstition. Religion and morality have thus no basis beyond the will of the supreme power in the State, whatever it may be.

Hobbes, 1588—1679.

Leviathan, 1651.

These phenomena of a troublous time caused thoughtful and peace-loving men to turn from the ceaseless war of tongues and pens in search of eternal principles. The leaders of these thinkers were found at Cambridge[2]. Against the Puritans they contended that "the spirit of man is the candle of the Lord," that reason is "lighted by God, and lighting us to God"; they regarded Christianity as sent to elevate and sweeten human nature. God is to be sought within us, not only in books or writings "where His truth is too often not so much enshrined as entombed." Holding such views, they were very ready to seek truth in such authors as Plato and Plotinus, and they did not, like too many of the High Church clergy, set themselves against the investigations of physical science; they thought it the duty of those who were "learned and able, to search into the freest theories of nature, and not rashly or unskilfully to condemn anything that may be innocent

New School at Cambridge.

---

[1] Two *Lives* were published in 1681 by R. Blackburne, two (in prose and in verse) by Hobbes himself, one by R. B. from Aubrey's notes. These are prefixed to the Latin *Works* in Molesworth's ed. (1839–46). There is a good article on H. in Bayle's *Dictionary*. See also F. D. Maurice, *Moral and Metaph. Philosophy*, II. 235 ff. (ed. 1873); Ueberweg, *Hist. Phil.* II. 38 ff. (Morris's Trans.); H. Sidgwick, *Hist. of Ethics*, 160 ff.; G. Croom Robertson, *Hobbes*, in Blackwood's *Phil. Classics* (1886); Leslie Stephen in *Dict. Nat. Biog.* XXVII. 37.

[2] Burnet's *Own Time*, I. 186; J. Tulloch's *Rational Theology* (1872).

and true." Against the notion that morality depends merely on a compact among men or the command of a sovereign power, they contended that the principles of justice and goodness are eternal and immutable, forming part of the very essence of God. Man is capable of obeying or breaking these laws, and is therefore responsible for his actions. The most prominent members of this school were Benjamin Whichcote[1] who, though he published nothing, exercised a great influence by his teaching and preaching, his life and conversation; his pupil John Smith[2], who in his short life made a singular impression on his friends as a truly devout, learned and able man; Henry More[3], who even as a boy "could never swallow down that hard doctrine concerning fate," and passed more than fifty years studying and meditating and writing in the quiet shades of Christ's College, because he believed that he could serve God better in the contemplative than in the active life. But the greatest of the party, the only one indeed who attained European fame, was Ralph Cudworth[4], whose 'Intellectual System of the Universe' was put forth (1678) as a refutation of all forms of materialistic atheism. His 'Eternal and Immutable Morality' was not published until long after his death (1731). To the same school belonged John Wilkins[5], Bishop of Chester, a man of science and one of the founders of the Royal Society, who was especially anxious to make the national Church comprehensive of all who had true faith in Christ. John Tillotson[6], afterwards Archbishop of Canterbury, diffused in London the principles which he had learned under Cudworth at Cambridge, in a style which pleased courtiers and citizens alike, and won the admiration of Dryden and Addison. This school

---

[1] B. F. Westcott in *Masters in Theology*, p. 147; J. B. Mullinger in *Dict. Nat. Biog.* LXI. 1.

[2] *Memoir* prefixed to Smith's *Select Discourses* by H. G. Williams (Camb. 1859); J. B. Mullinger in *Dict. Nat. Biog.* LIII. 74.

[3] Some particulars of More's life are in the *Præfatio* to his *Opera Omnia* (1679). *Life* by Richard Ward (1710); J. H. Overton in *Dict. Nat. Biog.* XXXVIII. 421.

[4] *Life* by T. Birch, prefixed to C.'s *Intellectual System* (London, 1820); by Leslie Stephen in *Dict. Nat. Biog.* XIII. 271.

[5] *Life* by F. Sanders in *Dict. Nat. Biog.* LXI. 264.

[6] *Life* by F[rancis] H[utchinson] (1717), reprinted in Wordsworth's *Eccl. Biog.* IV. 655; by T. Birch (1752); Alexander Gordon in *Dict. Nat. Biog.* LVI. 392.

took too little account of the Church and its Sacraments, but on the whole it met the wants of men wearied with scholastic disputations, and it dominated English theology for fully a hundred years. The warmth and gentle mysticism of the early Platonists no doubt died away, but their recognition of the natural powers of man, their tendency to regard the Gospel mainly as enhancing man's natural inclination to the worship of God, their resolute defence of freewill and man's consequent responsibility for his actions—these traits appear in almost all the leading divines of the eighteenth century, including the greatest of them, Joseph Butler. We may say too that their manner of regarding the Gospel as life rather than theory, and their insistance on the necessity of personal experience of the love of Christ, came again into view in the Wesleyans with whom began the revival of evangelical teaching in the English Church.

2. ENGLISH SECTS.

As was natural, in a period of intellectual ferment and ecclesiastical anarchy, many sects appeared. Opinions held in secret were proclaimed when the old restraints were removed. Presbyterians and Independents have already been mentioned[1]. Shortly before the outbreak of the civil war, those Independents who were opposed to the baptism of infants, and held that it should be administered only to such as could give an account of their faith, and that by immersion of the whole body, began to form separate congregations, and to be known as Baptists[2]. They seem to have been to some extent influenced by the continental Mennonites[3], but are to be carefully distinguished from the fanatical Anabaptists[4] of an earlier time.

Baptists, c. 1633.

Some of the sects of this period arose out of the circumstances of the time and vanished with them. The "Fifth-Monarchy Men," ardent republicans, believed that Christ would speedily appear and establish a new Kingdom, according to the words of the prophet Daniel[5].

[1] See pp. 34 ff.
[2] G. H. Curteis, *Bampton Lectures*, 1871.
[3] Hardwick's *Reformation*, 258.
[4] *Ibid.* 182.
[5] vii. 18, 22.

Ch. II.

Seekers,
1645.

Ranters,
1645.

Familists.

Behmenists,
c. 1644.

George Fox, 1621
—1691.

1643.

Society of Friends, or 'Quakers.'

Meantime, the saints were to rule the earth, and every earthly king invaded the prerogatives of Christ. The "Seekers" derived their name from their seeking the true Church, which in their opinion was lost. The "Ranters" claim to have Christ within themselves, and are said to have declared themselves incapable of sinning. Like some other exalted sects, they are believed to have degenerated into lewdness. The "Family of Love[1]" still dragged on an obscure existence. The innocent and interesting mysticism of Jacob Boehme or Behmen found, from the middle of the seventeenth century onward, many disciples in England, but these can scarcely be considered as forming a sect.

In the turmoil of the Civil War a peasant of genius, George Fox[2], set himself to proclaim truths which might bring peace. In his early days when he tended sheep he meditated on sacred things, until, in obedience to the divine voice within him, he went forth to preach the Word. He taught that men should guide their lives by the inward light which is given to every man, but which is commonly obscured by self-will and self-indulgence. The Kingdom of God was within them, if they would but have faith in it. The Sacraments of the Church he regarded as merely outward ordinances, unnecessary and unprofitable for the spiritual life; nor did he admit any order of ministers or any set form of service, holding that when two or three were gathered together in Christ's name, the Spirit would give them utterance as need might be. He travelled widely both in England and abroad, and drew to himself a little band of ardent followers, who called themselves "Friends," and were called by scoffers "Quakers" from the nervous trembling which often accompanied their utterances. As Fox and his early followers often interrupted public worship, especially in "steeple-houses," and refused to comply with the ordinary usages

---

[1] Hardwick's *Reformation*, 271.
[2] G. Fox's *Journal* (1691, often reprinted) gives a full account of his journeyings and experiences. See also W. Sewel's *Hist. of Quakers*. There are *Lives* by H. Tuke (1813), Josiah Marsh (1847), J. S. Watson (1860), A. C. Bickley (1884), and A. Gordon in *Dict. Nat. Biog.* xx. 117. An Essay on *G. Fox, His Character, Doctrine, and Work* [by Edward Ash] (1873), and Robert Barclay's *Inner Life of the Religious Societies of the Commonwealth* (1876), give a clear account of Fox's tenets and aims.

of good-breeding, it is hardly to be wondered at that they were the most persecuted of sects under the government of the Restoration.

Fox was unlettered and had not the gift of style which distinguished his equally unlettered contemporary Bunyan, but among his disciples were men of high standing both intellectually and socially. Robert Barclay[1], a cultivated man of an old Scottish family, finding in Puritans and Papists alike a "straitness of doctrine" and an absence of love which shocked his kindly and generous nature, in 1667 joined the Friends, among whom he believed that love of God and simplicity of life were taught and practised. A few years afterwards he published his famous defence[2] of the principles which he adopted, the teaching of the inner light and its consequences. This work, which—unlike George Fox's writings—is both learned and lucid, from this time to the present day has always been appealed to as the best statement of the views of Friends, and has had an influence far beyond their rather narrow circle. Barclay also protested against the warfare[3] in which Christian nations too readily engaged.

Another early convert was William Penn[4], son of the admiral of the same name, who, converted while an undergraduate at Oxford, was not content to hold his own faith without interfering with that of others. His rudeness brought him into trouble, and even into the Tower, where he wrote the most famous of his works, *No Cross, No Crown*. In 1681 however he obtained from the King a grant of land in North America, of which he obtained peaceable possession from the Indians and called "Sylvania." Charles II. prefixed "Penn" in honour of the admiral. There Quakerism was dominant, and there was established that toleration of other forms of faith for which both Barclay and Penn had pleaded. He died in England in 1718.

R. Barclay, 1648—1690.

W. Penn, 1644—1718.

Pennsylvania, 1681.

---

[1] *Life* by Wilson Armistead (1850); Leslie Stephen in *Dict. Nat. Biog.* III. 167.
[2] *An Apology for the True Christian Divinity as the same is held forth and preached by the People* called in scorn *Quakers* (1678).
[3] In his *Treatise on Universal Love* (1677).
[4] *Life* by Joseph Besse, prefixed to Penn's *Works* (1726); J. M. Rigg in *Dict. Nat. Biog.* XLIV. 311.

3. EXTENSION OF THE ENGLISH CHURCH.

Care for Colonies.

In the midst of controversy and unbelief the great duty of spreading the Gospel of Christ was never wholly lost sight of in England[1]. Our country, sending out her children to the ends of the earth, has commonly recognized the duty of caring for the maintenance of the faith among them and for the spread of it among the heathen. Thomas Harriot, the great mathematician, who went out to America with Sir Richard Grenville's expedition in 1585 as surveyor, has some claim to be called the first English missionary to the New World; for "many times," he says, "in every town where I came, according as I was able, I made declaration of the contents of the Bible, that therein was set forth the true and only God and His mighty works, [and] the true doctrine of salvation through Christ...as I was able then to utter and thought fit for the time." And a little later his pupil Walter Raleigh gave £100 to a merchant-company to be employed specially in "planting the Christian religion in those barbarous countries" of North America. That most high and mighty prince James I. shewed in an ordinance of 1606 that he did not regard English colonies as mere trading outposts, for he desires "that the true word and service of God be preached, planted, and used not only in the colonies, but also, as much as might be, among the savages bordering upon them, and this according to the rites and doctrines of the Church of England." This ordinance accompanied the charter for Virginia, and the English clergyman who accompanied the earliest colonists to that country deserves to have his name commemorated. This was Robert Hunt[2], who, under very heavy discouragement, built a church and maintained the services in the town which the colonists named after their King, Jamestown. Another noble pioneer in Virginia was Alexander

Harriot, 1585.

Raleigh's Gift, 1589.

---

[1] On the Church in the American Colonies see S. Wilberforce, *Hist. of the Church in America* (1844); J. S. M. Anderson, *Hist. of the Church of England in the Colonies* (2nd ed. 1856); Ernest Hawkins, *Historical Notices of the Missions of the Church of England* (1845); J. A. Doyle in the *Cambridge Modern History*, VII. 57 ff.

[2] Bancroft, *Hist. U.S.A.* (I. 118), testifies to Hunt's "modest worth."

Whitaker, a son of the well-known William Whitaker, Master of St John's College, Cambridge, who, seeing the abundant harvest to be reaped among the American Indians, lamented that so many of his brethren wasted their energies in foolish disputes about the surplice and such like, when they might be profitably employed in ministering to the heathen. It may be noted that Nicholas Ferrar, the founder of the "Protestant nunnery," as it was called, at Little Gidding, was for some years the principal manager in England of the Virginia Company. At its dissolution in 1623 he paid over £300 to the Bermuda Company for the education in Bermuda of native Virginian children, who might be sent back to their own country to convert their brethren. The King had already issued letters directing a collection in all parish churches for the same object, by which about £4,000 was raised. We may see from this narrative that those who first undertook what Bacon calls "the heroical work of plantations" took thought for the maintenance of God's honour in the sight of the heathen.

CH. II.

N. Ferrar.

The charter granted by Charles I. to the Massachusetts Company in 1628 expressed the hope that "the colony would win the natives of the country to the knowledge and obedience of the true God and Saviour of mankind;" and the colonial seal bore an Indian with a label issuing from his mouth bearing the words " Come over and help us." In 1646 the Massachusetts Legislature passed an Act for the encouragement of missions among the Indians, and in the same year the excellent John Eliot began the work to which he devoted his life. Eliot[1] was an Englishman, born in Hertfordshire, and graduated at Cambridge in 1622. After taking Holy Orders in the Church of England he left his native land for conscience' sake, and landed at Boston in New England in 1631, where for some time he "exercised"—according to the current phrase—and then settled at Roxbury, where some of his friends had preceded him. After two years' study of their language he began to preach to the Indians in 1646. His maxim was, that it was "necessary to carry on civility

Charter of Massachusetts, 1628.

John Eliot, 1604 (?)— 1690,

at Boston, 1631;

preaches to Indians, 1646.

---

[1] The earliest *Life* is by Cotton Mather (1691), the most complete by C. Francis (Boston, U.S.A., 1836). See also H. R. Tedder in *Dict. Nat. Biog.* XVII. 189 ff.

with religion," and with this view he established his converts in regular settlements where the whole society was Christian. His work was approved both in the colony and at home, and in England a corporation was formed under the auspices of Cromwell in 1649 "for the promoting and propagating the Gospel among the Indians of New England," which defrayed the expenses of the preachers and the cost of printing the translations which were made. At one time there were more than a dozen townships of "praying Indians" within the bounds of Massachusetts, and many outside those limits. But though the organization survived until the death of the last native pastor in 1716, the "praying towns" decayed after an unlucky war in 1675, in which it is said that the converts suffered equal cruelties at the hands of their heathen countrymen and of the English, whose allies they were and whom they served faithfully. Eliot died at Roxbury in 1690, leaving a singularly stainless memory, honoured as among the greatest in New England history. But the great work and noblest monument of his devoted life was the translation of the Bible into the tongue of the Indians of Massachusetts, Algonquin, which was completed in 1663. "Since the death of the Apostle Paul," says the American orator Everett, "a nobler, truer, and warmer spirit than John Eliot never lived"; and his own contemporaries speak of him as a man personally most attractive. He united love of learning to fervent piety and enthusiasm for the spread of the Gospel, which were guided by excellent good sense. He was of the true saintly type, without fanaticism, spiritual pride, or ambition.

It must not be supposed that Eliot's was distinctively Church teaching. He was indeed an ordained clergyman, but in sentiment he was an Independent. In fact, of the important colonies sent forth from our shores to America in the seventeenth century, Massachusetts was controlled by Independents, Maryland by Romanists, and Pennsylvania by Quakers. The constitution of Maryland was, however, tolerant. In the New England States not a single Anglican church existed until 1679, when Compton, Bishop of London, prevailed on King Charles II to give orders for the erection of one in Boston. In 1698 the excellent Dr Bray, who was commissary for Maryland, where the legislature had made provision for a body of parochial clergy, set about forming a society for the promotion of Christian knowledge at home and abroad. The labours of this Society were to be devoted to (1) the education of the poor; (2) the care of the Church in the colonies; (3) the printing and circulating of books of sound Christian principles. But after about two years' experience of the working of this Society it was thought expedient to form a new Society which should devote itself exclusively to mission work abroad. Not without difficulty Dr Bray and his friends, aided by Archbishop Tenison, Bishop Compton of London, and many others, succeeded in procuring a Charter under the seal of William III, constituting as a corporation the Society for the Propagation of the Gospel in Foreign Parts. The objects of this Society, as defined in its charter, were (1) the care and instruction of our own people settled in the colonies; (2) the conversion of the Indian natives; (3) the conversion of negro slaves. Its first missionaries landed at Boston on June 11, 1702. Since that time the Society has continued to work not only for the spiritual welfare of the great host of English colonists, but for the spread of the Gospel among the heathen.

In America the Church continued for several generations to struggle against great difficulties, of which one was the want of organization. A missionary of the Society[1], writing from Rhode Island in 1709, says, "You can neither well believe, nor I express, what excellent service for the cause of religion a bishop would do in these parts;—these infant settlements languish for want of a father to oversee and bless them." The American colonies however remained without a bishop until Dr Seabury was consecrated as Bishop of Connecticut by three Scottish prelates in 1784. Meantime many excellent men had worked among them, among whom one ought to be especially commemorated. This is George Berkeley, afterwards Bishop of Cloyne, and famous as a philosopher, who at the height of fame, fortune, and social distinction, offered to resign his rich preferment and devote himself to the education of American Indians for the rest of his

[1] James Honyman, in Hawkins, p. 166.

Margin notes: Ch. II. | S.P.C.K., 1698. | S.P.G., June 16, 1701. | Hawkins. | Seabury bishop, 1784. | Berkeley in America, 1728.

72 *Extension of the English Church*

Ch. II.

life on a stipend of £100 a year, reviving Ferrar's scheme for a college in Bermuda. This actually received a charter in 1726, but the money which was promised by the minister, Sir R. Walpole, for its foundation was never paid, and Berkeley, who had landed on Rhode Island in 1728, was obliged to return to England, and abandon a scheme on which "he had expended much of his private fortune and more than seven years of the prime of his life." John Wesley visited Georgia (1736–7), where he ministered with great assiduity to the settlers for a year and nine months; and George Whitfield reached the same State (to which he had paid a brief visit in the previous year) in 1739, after a tour of preaching in the northern States which occasioned great excitement. In consequence, many illiterate persons of both sexes took upon themselves to become "exhorters," as their own term was, but notwithstanding this fanaticism it is believed that Whitfield's preaching had the effect of directing attention to the liturgy of the Church, and of bringing many considerable families within its pale. But the Church in the United States has never attained to the numbers of the Independent communities.

Wesley in Georgia, 1736.

West Indies. Barbadoes.

Of the West Indian possessions of the British Crown Barbadoes soon became rich and prosperous[1]. The early settlers do not seem to have been altogether unmindful of their duty towards God, but it was not until 1629 that any definite provision was made for the Church. In that year six parishes were formed in the island, and to these five were added under the beneficent rule of Philip Bell. Lands appear to have been granted for their maintenance, and Acts[2] were passed by the local authority forbidding conventicles and enjoining attendance on divine worship in the churches in the same spirit as was manifested in similar ordinances in England. Jamaica[3] became an English possession under the Commonwealth, when a desire to spread the Gospel among the heathen was alleged as one of the motives for this conquest[4]. It was not however until after the Restoration that churches were

Governor Bell, 1642 —1650.

Jamaica taken, 1655.

---

[1] R. Ligon, *History of Barbadoes* (London, 1657). See Clarendon's *Rebellion*, III. 466.
[2] In Anderson's *History*, II. 57 ff.
[3] E. Long, *Hist. of Jamaica* (London, 1774).
[4] Documents in Anderson, II. 70 ff.

built for the Anglican services and land given for their maintenance. Among the Acts confirmed by the King in Council in 1684 is one "for the maintenance of Ministers and the Poor, and erecting and repairing of Churches." The same Act also assigns stipends to ministers, but they seem to have been but few in number. Among the Englishmen who have taken a keen interest in Jamaica may be mentioned Charles Selwyn[1], a son of the William Selwyn who had been for a few months Governor of the island, and of the same family as the famous Bishop of New Zealand.

As in America, so also in India[2], the English traders were anxious that their agents should lead Christian lives. The merchants of London trading to the East Indies, who were incorporated as a Company at the end of the year 1600, sent out chaplains in their ships, and were anxious to maintain in their settlements the forms of divine worship. In 1640 we learn that prayers were said at the chief factory in the President's house twice on every week-day and thrice on Sunday; in 1669 the Deputy-Governor of Bombay was tried and found guilty for giving drinking-parties during church-time on Sundays; at one time every servant of the Company was expected to attend divine service at least eight times a week, and if he failed in this he was fined[3]. But with all this there were constant complaints that the evil lives of professing Christians discredited their religion, and little or nothing was done for the conversion of the natives of the country. Ziegenbalg from Tranquebar paid occasional visits to Madras, where he was received in the most friendly manner both by the civil authorities and the chaplains, one of whom, George Lewis, wrote to the Christian Knowledge Society that the Tranquebar mission ought to be encouraged; and his successor, Stevenson, gave it practical help. It was mainly owing to the encouragement of these worthy men that in 1726, under the auspices of the S.P.C.K., Danish missions began to work in Madras and Cuddalore. In the latter part of the century one of the greatest and most revered of the missionaries, Christian Frederick Schwartz[4],

Ch. II.

W. Selwyn, Governor, 1702.

1712.

---

[1] Anderson, III. 544.
[2] James Hough, *Hist. of Christianity in India* (1839—45); J. W. Kaye, *Christianity in India* (1859).
[3] Kaye, p. 59.
[4] H. N. Pearson, *Life of C. F. Schwartz* (London, 1834).

was employed by the S.P.G., but on the whole we must confess with shame that up to the end of the eighteenth century England had done very little towards the conversion of the vast heathen population of Hindustan. Then, under the influence of the Evangelical movement, men who earnestly desired the spread of Christ's Gospel, feeling how little had been done for the Eastern nations which had fallen under our influence, founded a Society especially for sending missionaries to the heathen, which, under the now well-known name of the Church Missionary Society for Africa and the East, has done a great and admirable work. Even still the Church of England is perhaps not sufficiently conscious of the obligations laid upon it by the position of Great Britain as the great naval and colonizing power of the world.

Church Missionary Society, April 12, 1799.

CHAPTER III.

THE ROMAN CHURCH.

1. GENERAL CHARACTERISTICS.

IN the period with which we have now to deal it came to be generally recognized that if the Church was to be defended it must first be cleansed. The most glaring abuses were therefore done away, indulgences were no longer common articles of traffic, the ban of the Church was comparatively seldom inflicted, though in Rome itself excommunication sometimes came in aid of the police. The decrees of Trent were gradually put into force to bring the clergy to a more decent and orderly life. Piety and devotion took a more sentimental turn which, it must be confessed, sometimes has an air of being self-conscious and artificial. The teaching of the young in the upper classes fell largely into the hands of the Jesuits, who, while they successfully taught classics, mathematics, and formal logic, carefully avoided everything which might give an impulse to independent thought. The higher ecclesiastics, distrusting the universities, where in spite of all precautions a freer breath blew in from the world without, insisted more and more on training candidates for Orders in episcopal seminaries. The putting-down of opposition to the dominant opinions was now attempted rather by the burning of books than of men, though as late as 1619 Vanini[1] was burnt, with cruel preliminary tortures, by the parliament of Toulouse, on a charge of atheism. The censure was guided by the Index of Prohibited Books[2] drawn up by a Congregation instituted for

[1] M. Carriere, *Die Philosophische Weltanschauung der Reformationszeit*, p. 495 ff. (Stuttgart, 1847).

[2] Hardwick, *Reformation*, 299, 302.

the purpose by Pius V. in 1571. No pantheistic dreamer, like Giordano Bruno[1], was burnt at Rome by the Inquisition in the seventeenth century, though Galileo[2] was terrified into abjuring the heretical theory that the earth moves round the sun, no doubt retaining his faith in Copernicus in spite of Roman orthodoxy. And generally we may say that the clergy gave an inquisitive attention to the opinions of their flocks which went far beyond what had been usual in the Middle Ages, and tended to produce a certain littleness of thought both in clergy and people.

When auricular confession is constantly resorted to, casuistry[3], the consideration of cases which present themselves to a perplexed conscience, soon becomes necessary as a guide for confessors. The precepts of Christ and His Church have to be adapted to the requirements of men living the ordinary life of the world, an adaptation in which they sometimes suffer much violence. The Jesuits especially devoted themselves to the task of suiting the yoke of Christ to the necks of the worldly. Sanchez, Suarez, Laymann, and Escobar published works which had a large circulation and great influence. But the German Busenbaum in his *Marrow of Moral Theology* furnished a manual which supplied the wants of many generations, and passed through more than seventy editions, ranging in date from 1645 to 1848. After the attempt of Damiens to assassinate Louis XV. of France this book was condemned by the Parliament of Paris as justifying the murder of princes by their subjects. The whole method and tendency of Jesuit morality were exposed with scathing irony by Blaise Pascal[4] in a series of letters which have

---

[1] See Carriere, *u. s.*, p. 365 ff.; Miss J. Frith, *Life of Giordano Bruno* (London, 1887).

[2] Philaréte Chasles, *Galileo, sa Vie*, etc. (Paris, 1862); Mary Allan-Olney, *Private Life of Galileo* (London, 1870); F. H. Reusch, *Der Process G.'s u. die Jesuiten* (Bonn, 1879); J. J. Fahie, *Galileo, his Life and Work* (London, 1903).

[3] On the history of casuistry see G. T. Meier, *Introductio in universum Theol. Moralis Studium* (Helmstadt, 1671); J. F. Mayer, *Bibliotheca Scriptorum Theol. Mor. et Conscientiariæ*, in his edition of Strauch's *Theol. Mor.* (1705); J. F. Buddeus, *Isagoge Historica*, p. 700 ff. (1730); C. E. Luthardt, *Geschichte d. Christl. Ethik*, vol. 2. See also H. Sidgwick, *Hist. of Ethics*, 148 ff.

[4] *La Vie de Pascal* par sa sœur Mad. Perier (1684); Bossut, *Discours sur la Vie et les Œuvres de P.* (1779); J. Tulloch, *Pascal* (Edinb. 1878); Emile Boutroux, *Pascal* (Paris, 1900); J. L. F. Bertrand, *Pascal* (Paris, 1891).

become one of the great French classics—the famous *Letters to a Friend in the Country*. The authors of casuistic treatises, he says, seeing that it was impossible to induce men and women living the ordinary life of the world to adopt the evangelic precepts in their integrity, modified the Gospel to suit them. They invented a modish religion which did not restrain men either from tricks of trade or immorality of life. And the root of this laxity he finds in "probabilism"; the theory, that is, which permits a man to perform an act which is commonly regarded as sinful if a "doctor probabilis," a teacher of repute, declares it to be innocent. The number of doctors being large and their opinions various, it was not generally very difficult for a man to find in the works of some "reputable" doctor a specious defence of anything which interest or pleasure might lead him to wish to do. This kind of casuistry was in fact the blight of morality, but it was too convenient to be cast aside, and probably has a certain vogue even to this day. *[margin: Lettres Provinciales, 1656—57. Probabilism.]*

The period from the beginning of the seventeenth to the middle of the eighteenth century is the great age of ecclesiastical learning[1]. The eager classicism of the early part of the sixteenth century, when the beauty and naturalness of ancient literature burst upon the world as something new, had passed away; but the scholarship which arose in those days remained, and was applied to the serious study of the voluminous literature of the Christian Church. Libraries were ransacked and manuscripts collated, so that there appeared in rapid succession editions of the Fathers and learned works founded on the study of original authorities, to which modern students and investigators are very deeply indebted. *[margin: Learning.]*

In this class of literature the Gallican Church was especially distinguished. The great impulse which all French literature received in the great outburst of prosperity and national life which marked the early years of Louis XIV. extended also to theology. The names of Petavius, Fronto le Duc, Sirmond, John and Julian *[margin: The learned works of the Gallican Church]*

[1] History of the literature of this period in Dupin's *Nouvelle Bibliothèque des Auteurs Ecclésiastique*, vols. 23–29 (Paris, 1714). The English translation includes only a part of the 17th cent. Werner, *Gesch. der Katholischen Theologie seit dem Trienter Concil* (Munich, 1866).

Garnier, Montfaucon, Mabillon, Massuet, Ruinart, De la Rue, Thomassin, Touttée, Martianay, Prudentius Maranus, Combefis, Vallarsi, Le Quien, Cotelier, Launoi, Baluze, Valesius, and many others, retain their places in the gratitude and the libraries of all serious students of theology. Du Pin and Ceillier produced admirable accounts of the lives and works of ecclesiastical authors. Natalis Alexander, Tillemont and Fleury wrote standard works on the history of the Church, while Labbé and Cossart, and somewhat later Hardouin, made collections of the documents necessary for the history of Councils which threw into the shade earlier works of the same kind. And the learned lawyer, the Sieur Du Fresne du Cange, to whose patient labours every student of mediæval history and archæology is so deeply indebted, is not to be passed over in silence. To this period also belong the great preachers of the Gallican Church, men such as Bossuet, Fénelon, Fléchier, Bourdaloue, Massillon, and Bridaine. In France, more than elsewhere, the great preachers rank among the classical authors of their country.

Italy. Italy also, though far behind France in literary activity, produced theologians of great ability and learning. In *Sarpi, 1619.* the year 1619 there appeared in London a pseudonymous history of the Council of Trent[1] in Italian, written in a spirit by no means favourable to Rome. The author was Paolo Sarpi, a Venetian, who encouraged his fellow-citizens in their resistance to papal claims. By way of *Pallavicino, 1664.* reply, a learned Jesuit, Pallavicino, who had access to the Vatican archives, spent twenty years in composing a rival history. Ranke[2], after examining them with much care, concludes that both are useful to the historian, but that if anyone were to undertake a new history of the Council he would have again to investigate the sources. Cardinal *Bona.* Bona published works on the liturgy and on the religious life which are distinguished by good sense and perspicuity *Muratori, 1672— 1750.* as well as learning and piety. Muratori, a man of the most extraordinary breadth of knowledge, not only made

[1] Ranke describes the edition of Geneva, 1629, as "the first free from extraneous additions." It was translated into English by N. Brent, 1675, and into French by Le Courayer.
[2] *Popes*, Appendix, sec. II.

contributions of the highest value to the history of his country, but also important researches in ancient liturgies, and introduced into theological controversy a moderation which had been too rare. Mamachi, Selvaggio, and Pelliccia investigated ecclesiastical archæology, while Dominic Mansi edited the most complete collection of Councils.

One of the most gigantic works which the Church has produced is the great collection of the Acts of the Saints of the whole Church, which was begun at Antwerp in 1643 and continues to be published even to the present day. The plan of the work was drawn up by Heribert Rosweyd, after whose death (1665) it was taken up by John Bolland, who brought together from all parts of Europe so rich a treasure of authorities that the eighteen volumes which were originally contemplated grew into an indefinite number. Many competent helpers joined in the work from time to time, among whom Godfrey Henschen and Daniel Papebroch are especially to be distinguished; but the whole is designated "Bollandist" from the name of him who exercised so important an influence over its beginning. The writers are by no means wholly uncritical, and frequently state the arguments for a historical view with much greater force than those which are suggested on behalf of pious tradition. The progress of the work was checked in 1773 by the suppression of the Company of Jesuits, to which most of its writers belonged, but was resumed when the change of times permitted its continuance[1].

The study of Scripture was by no means neglected and many commentaries appeared. Those of Maldonatus on the Gospels, and Estius on the Epistles of St Paul, for instance, are works of real learning and scholarship, and maintain a considerable reputation to this day, even among Protestants. But the commentary of Cornelius van den Steen (à Lapide) on all the books of Scripture, except the Psalms and the Book of Job, had for several generations a very wide circulation among the clergy. In regard to the Gospels and Epistles it is very inferior to the works just mentioned, and owed its immense popu-

CH. III.

Netherlands.

Bollandist Acta SS., begun 1643.

Henschen, 1600—1681. Papebroch, 1628—1714.

Scripture. Maldonatus, 1534 —1583. Estius, 1542—1613. Corn. a Lapide, 1566—1637.

---

[1] A list of the writers is given by Potthast, *Biblioth. Historica*, under *Acta Sanctorum*. See also Pitra, *Études sur la Collection des Actes des Saints publiés par les Bollandistes* (Paris, 1850).

Ch. III.

Freer tendency.

Ponce de Leon, d. 1591.

Less and Hamel, 1587.

Richard Simon, 1638—1712.

larity to its abundant patristic citations and its retention of allegoric interpretation[1].

It was natural that in the Roman Church, where faith was not held to depend wholly on Scripture, a somewhat freer treatment of Biblical questions should manifest itself than among Protestants. It was in Catholic Spain that Luis Ponce de Leon[2], professor of theology at Salamanca, but more poet than theologian, was imprisoned for five years by the Inquisition because he preferred the Hebrew text of Scripture to the Vulgate, and published a translation of the Song of Solomon, in which that book was treated as a pastoral poem describing the bliss and misery of love.

The Jesuits Less and Hamel[3] held and published theories of the inspiration of Scripture which certainly varied from those commonly current, even if they were not contrary to any authoritative decision of the Church. They maintained that for a book to be accepted as Scripture it is not necessary that its actual words, or even its thoughts and statements, should be directly inspired by the Holy Spirit. Such a book as the Second of Maccabees, for instance, written by human industry without the assistance of the Spirit, may be accepted as Scripture if the Spirit afterwards testifies that it is in fact free from error. These opinions were brought before the tribunal of Sixtus V., who delayed giving judgment in order that the heat of controversy about them might subside. The view of inspiration which ultimately prevailed in the Church, without being defined by authority, was that of the school of Antioch, of which St John Chrysostom is the most prominent example; a view which does not maintain the absolute infallibility of every line and every letter of Holy Scripture.

But by far the most notable contributions to Biblical science in the seventeenth century were those of the Oratorian, Richard Simon[4], who was, first and foremost,

---

[1] On the Roman Cath. commentators see G. W. Meyer, *Geschichte der Schrift-Erklärung*, III. 456 ff., IV. 358 ff., 464 ff. (Göttingen, 1802 ff.); F. W. Farrar, *History of Interpretation* (1886).

[2] C. Wilkens, *Fray L. de Leon* (Halle, 1866); F. Reusch, *L. de Leon* (Bonn, 1873).

[3] Gieseler, *K.-G.* III. ii. 612.

[4] Diestel, *Geschichte des Alten Test.*, 355 f.; H. Graf in *Strassburger Theol. Beiträge*, 1847, p. 158 ff.; G. Masson, *R. Simon* (London, 1867); A. Bernus, *R. Simon et son Hist. Critique du Vieux Test.* (Lausanne, 1869).

a philosopher and a critic. No prepossessions hindered his researches, but he frankly attempted to determine the age, the authenticity, and the integrity of the sacred books on the same principles which are applied to profane literature, from the best external testimony and from internal evidence. No one now would accept the whole of Simon's conclusions, but the germs of many of the theories which have found favour in modern times are in his work. He utterly ignored the allegories of mediæval commentators, and thought the expositions of the Port Royalists more pious than sound. As was natural, he was vigorously attacked both by Catholics and by Protestants.

Bernardo de Rossi devoted the industrious labour of a lifetime to the collation of MSS. of the Old Testament, and published a very full account of the various readings.

The Council of Trent had given a new character to theology by giving authoritative definition to many propositions which had before been loose and floating. Tradition was exalted to a place co-ordinate with Scripture, but it did not put an end to independent study of the latter. Michael de Bay (Baius[1]), a distinguished professor at Louvain, turned from the prevalent scholasticism to the Bible and St Augustine, and drew from them a doctrine of divine grace in which to some extent he anticipates the Jansenists. His denial that man could of his own strength do works acceptable to God was thought to savour of Protestantism. Pius V. (1567) published a Bull condemning seventy-two propositions said to be found in his works, but his own university disregarded it, maintained him in his office as professor, and even chose him Dean and Chancellor. Sixtus V. (1588) contented himself with attempting to impose silence on both the contending parties. At Louvain also Less and Hamel[2] were censured by the theological faculty for having maintained propositions thought to savour of Pelagianism. They maintained that God gives to all men sufficient help, after the Fall, to enable them to return to God; that Christ is the Redeemer of all men; that if men do what lies in their

[1] Duchesne, *Hist. du Baianisme* (Douay, 1731); F. X. Linsenmann, *M. Baius u. die Grundlegung des Jansenismus.*
[2] See above, p. 73.

Congregation on Grace, 1597. 1607.

power to serve God, with or without revelation, God will give them light; the doctrine that fallen man has no will to good they regarded as heretical. Similar opinions were expressed in Spain by the Jesuit Molina[1]. Clement VIII., bewildered by the charges and countercharges which came before him, instituted a Congregation to determine the orthodox view of the work of God's grace in the conversion of man. After the two parties had stated their case at great length, Paul V. dissolved the weary Congregation, and five years later attempted in vain to silence the dispute.

2. THE PAPACY.

It was mainly through the labours of the Jesuits that the theocratic policy of the Popes of the seventeenth century was defined and hardened[2]. The Church was (they held) related to the State as the soul to the body; the former must rule, and the latter, if need arose, be sacrificed to it. They did not contend that all regal authority was conferred by the Pope, or that in ordinary cases it was to be withdrawn by him; but they did maintain that where the salvation of souls required it princes might be deposed by the Pope, and their subjects freed from their allegiance. Princes have no rights against religion. The Jesuits also commonly maintained the theory hated by princes that the people was itself the source of all sovereign power. Not only did many Jesuits contend that it was permitted and acceptable to God to put to death a tyrannical King, but even the Sorbonne itself, the theological faculty of Paris, resolved (1589) that the French people might without scruple take arms against their King and that anyone might put him to death. These opinions of course had in view only those Kings who opposed the Catholic religion. But the majesty of Catholic Kings was supported by religion, and the Sorbonne when the French monarch was reconciled to the Pope retracted (1594) the doctrine which had by this time shed the blood of two Kings.

---

[1] Hardwick's *Reformation*, p. 310.
[2] On the Papacy of this period see Ranke's *Popes*, Book VI., Introduction (p. 175 ff. in Kelly's trans.; also p. 275 ff.); and Wessenberg's *Die Grossen Kirchenversammlungen*, IV. 263 ff.

The Papacy of the seventeenth century was by no means the same kind of power as it had been in the Middle Ages. It felt the need of support from the princes of this world, and sought to gain their favour by concessions and even in some instances by large gifts. Such subsidies, however, together with the provision which many Popes made for members of their families, very much increased the debt of the Roman States. The great families of Rome formed an aristocracy surrounding the Papacy, and from such families were generally drawn the 'Prelates'—dignitaries who without taking priests' Orders were eligible for many ecclesiastical offices. The Popes of this age scarcely professed to respect decrees of Councils; if they paid them any regard it was (they said) out of complaisance and not as of necessity. It was conceded almost everywhere that episcopal sees could not be filled without the consent of the Pope, but Popes were generally unwilling to quarrel with a temporal prince on the appointment to a bishopric, and were ready enough to favour the preferment of younger sons of royal Houses. In all capitals where the Court was Romish was an ambassador of the Pope called a nuncio, who conveyed the wishes of the See of Rome to the monarch to whom he was accredited, and informed the Curia of the course of events in the Church of his realm. The Curia began to require that the privilege of granting dispensations in matrimonial and other cases, which the German bishops had hitherto enjoyed in perpetuity, should be renewed at certain periods.

The imposing figure of Sixtus V.[1] fitly opens a new era in the history of the Papacy. So strongly did his extraordinary character impress the Roman world that it has been enveloped in a cloud of legend, through which however it is not difficult to discern the real traits. Felice Peretti rose to fame by his extraordinary ability as a

Sixtus V. Pope, 1585–1590.

---

[1] *Lives* of the Popes of this period are found in Guarnacci, *Vitæ et res gestæ Pontificum et Cardinalium a Clem. X. usque ad Clem. XI.* (1670 —1721); A. Bower, *Hist. of the Popes,* vol. VII. (to 1740); L. Ranke, *Die Römischen Päpste in den Letzten vier Jahrhunderte* (1889); on Sixtus V. see particularly pp. 111 ff., 177, 180 ff., and Appendix, p. 397 ff. (Kelly's trans.). Also Robardi, *Sixti V. Gesta* (Rome, 1590); Leti, *Vita di Sisto V.* (1669); J. Lorentz, *Sixtus V. und seine Zeit* (Mainz, 1852); A. de Hubner, *Sixte-Quint.* (Paris, 1870).

Ch. III.

His reforms.

leading Franciscan, a preacher of repentance, and an inquisitor. Chosen to the Papacy in 1585, he soon made himself felt in the administration of Church and State. The Roman Curia was completely transformed. The public scandals and lax discipline of an earlier time were heard of no more, and the nepotism which had been so baneful in the past came almost to an end. The Pope drew around him learned cardinals of respectable life, and gave to the arts a new impulse. Splendid buildings arose in Rome, including the great Vatican Library and the famous aqueduct called Acqua Felice. Unfortunately he destroyed many ancient monuments to provide material for his modern buildings. He put down with the utmost vigour the brigandage which under his predecessors had become a pest, while he encouraged agriculture in the country and trade in the towns. He left in the Castle of St Angelo an immense treasure, but as he had no means of raising money except by new taxes, sale of offices, and loans, his methods had in the end a very injurious effect on the finances of the State. Strong as he was at home, he shewed some weakness in foreign politics. He would gladly have made use of France as a counterpoise to the threatening power of Spain, but Henry IV. was not a monarch whom he could use to his purpose. Hence arose vacillation. His imaginative temperament led him to dream of expelling the Turks from Europe and conquering the East. Whatever his faults, Sixtus V. may be said to be the last Pope who stands out as a great figure in the history of the world.

Clement VIII., 1592— 1605.

The last Pope of the sixteenth century, Clement VIII.[1], (Aldobrandini) aptly typifies the gradual and cautious reassertion of the claims of Rome. Learned, able, and circumspect, zealous for the honour of God and the welfare of the Church, he has left a name free from reproach, except that of having fallen into the hands of favourites in his declining years. To his lot it fell to receive the submission of Henry IV. of France, which he did with all publicity and solemnity, gaining in the penitent whom he absolved a counterpoise for the too great power of Spain. The promised aid of the royal

---

[1] L. Wadding, *Vita Clementis VIII.* (Rome, 1723).

convert, added to the terrors of an interdict, enabled the Pope to take speedy possession of Ferrara, a papal fief which escheated to him on the failure of the ducal House of Este, its ancient lords. The brilliant court of that duchy, long the home of art and letters, passed away not unregretted, but the peasantry hailed the change of rulers as a deliverance from oppression. If the friendship of France was less burdensome than that of Spain, it still compelled the Pope to tolerate the Edict of Nantes, and to dissolve the marriage of Henry IV. with Marguerite of Valois.

Leo XI. passed in a few days from the throne to the grave, and was succeeded by Paul V. (Borghese)[1]. This pontiff, who had passed his life as a canonist and inquisitor, was in character not unlike our own Laud, uncorrupt, narrow, and bent upon asserting to the utmost the rights of the see to which he had been raised; nor was he hampered by any consideration of expediency or change of times; every letter of the decretals was sacred with him. Savoy, Genoa, Lucca, even Spain in her dependency of Naples, bowed before his imperious will; but the powerful republic of Venice stood firm. The Venetians had found it necessary to pass a law resembling the English Statute of Mortmain[2], forbidding spiritual persons to acquire real property without the license of the State; and had committed to the common prison certain ecclesiastics guilty of horrible crimes. The Pope demanded the repeal of the law, and the release of the clerical malefactors; he demanded in vain, for the Venetians were resolved to maintain their sovereignty in matters ecclesiastical as well as civil. In vain the Pope proceeded against the stiffnecked people with excommunication and interdict; his ban was disregarded, and the religious services in Venice proceeded as before; the dread weapon of older Popes had lost its power, and Paul was compelled at last to consent to a compromise with scarcely a show of submission on the part of Venice, who

---

[1] A. Bzovius, *Paulus V. Burghesius* (Rome, 1624).
[2] *Hist. of the Quarrels of Pope Paul V. with the State of Venice*, trans. from the Italian by Chr. Potter (London, 1626); *Interdicti Veneti Historia auctore Paulo Sarpi* (from the Italian, Cantabr. 1726); Italian original in Sarpi's *Opere* (Verona, 1761 ff.), vol. 3; T. A. Trollope, *Paul the Pope and Paul the Friar* (London, 1861).

Ch. III.

Paul V., 1605—1621.

Contest with Venice, 1606-7.

Ch. III.

Father Paul, 1552 —1623.

Gregory XV., 1621 —1623.

Urban VIII., 1623— 1644.

maintained her rights unimpaired. This contest excited the keenest interest in Europe, and even James I. of England so far forgot his usual caution as to promise to support the republic against the Pope. The great stay of the antipapal party in Venice was Paul Sarpi, the 'terrible friar,' who, living always the simple life of the Servite order, was the adviser of statesmen, the most powerful opponent of the extravagant claims of Popes; stabbed and left for dead, he recognized the "*stile* of the Roman Court," yet continued to plead for independence in Church and State. It was now clear that the old claims of the Papacy could not be maintained; henceforward the Popes had to content themselves with a mere show of deference in temporal matters, and to play one power against another as best they might.

Gregory XV. [Ludovisi], an old and feeble man at the time of his election, was governed by his nephew Cardinal Ludovisi. He prescribed the form which is still observed in the election of Popes, and canonized the founder and the greatest glory of the Jesuit order, Ignatius Loyola and Francis Xavier. In the great contest then raging in Germany, the Pope sided emphatically with the Catholic League, and received as his share of the spoil, after the conquest of the Palatinate, the excellent library of Heidelberg, a considerable part of which, having been carried off by Napoleon to Paris, was restored to Heidelberg in 1815[1].

To the feeble Gregory succeeded Cardinal Barberini, who took the title of Urban VIII.[2]; a man accomplished, vigorous, and deeply conscious of the leading part he had to play in Christendom. Yet his policy was mainly influenced by his desire to make himself a powerful Italian prince, and this consideration led him to fortify his territory, to carry on an inglorious war against the House of Farnese, and to cling to the friendship of France, even when that Power was allied with Protestants against the Empire. The Pope, it was said, remained cold and unmoved while churches and cloisters were blazing around him. Yet he protested against the extorted concessions

[1] A. Theiner, *Schenkung der Heidelb. Bibliothek* (München, 1844).
[2] S. Simonin, *Sylvæ Urbanianæ seu Gesta Urbani VIII.* (1637).

of the Treaty of Prague[1], and gave the final touches to the Bull *In cœna Domini*, a document not unworthy of the palmy days of the mediæval hierarchy, in which Saracens, pirates, wreckers, Wiclifists, Calvinists, and Lutherans, are consigned together to perdition. To him too is due a revision of the Roman Breviary.

Urban succeeded in taking possession of the duchy of Urbino, which lapsed to him, as Ferrara had done to Clement, by the failure of the line of feudatories. But the income from territories like Ferrara and Urbino did little to restore the Papal finances, which since the time of Sixtus V. had been falling more and more into confusion. Armaments, fortifications, subsidies to princes at war with Protestants or with Turks, improvements in the city of Rome, expenses of the Court, above all, the lavish provision made for the kinsmen of successive pontiffs, swallowed up the revenues of the See, and caused an ever-increasing load of debt. The funded debt amounted in the time of Urban VIII. to 30 million scudi, and the interest absorbed more than half the revenue; Papal stock, it is true, was in demand, successive loans were soon taken up, and possibly the interests of foreign capitalists tended to give a certain degree of stability to the Roman State; but the great amount of yearly interest to be paid forced the Government into most injudicious taxation, which gradually ruined agriculture and trade.

Innocent X. (Pamfili) was said by Contarini to have become Pope by talking little, dissembling much, and doing nothing[2]; yet he was a man of upright character, and even in old age patient and laborious; but falling, through feebleness of will, under the domination of his brother's widow, Donna Olimpia, he became a butt for the wits and caricaturists of Rome. In this reign the old quarrel with the Farnesi blazed up anew, and Odoardo Farnese, duke of Parma, deserted by the Italian princes, who did not fear Innocent as they had feared Urban, was compelled to cede to the Pope the territory of Castro, which was pledged for the debts of its lord. Innocent protested against the Treaty of

CH. III.

Escheat of Urbino.

Finance.

Innocent X., 1644—1655.

[1] See p. 20.
[2] *Relatione dell' ambasciatore Veneto*, in Ranke, App. No. 126.

Westphalia, and it is a sign of the times that he protested in vain; the days were past when the Pope could carry on a victorious struggle with the Emperor[1]; in the words of Alzog[2], 'the secular power was completely emancipated.' But never was the Papacy further from relinquishing its claims; Urban VIII. had intrusted to a special Congregation the task of watching over the encroachments of sovereigns, and the Curia guarded jealously every item of its ancient rights.

Alexander VII., 1655—1667.

Innocent was succeeded by Fabio Chigi, Alexander VII., whose pure life, noble character, and long experience as a statesman[3] raised the highest hopes of a prosperous reign, hopes which were not fully realised; for the energy which had distinguished him as a diplomatist deserted him as Pope, he was not free from the then common papal vice of nepotism, while his taste for building led to expenses which severely shook the credit of the Roman treasury. Moreover, he had to endure indignity such as has rarely fallen to the lot of a Pope. Louis XIV., displeased with the Spanish tendencies of the Roman Court, had interfered in the interminable dispute with the Farnesi, and sent to Rome, in his ambassador, the Duke of Créqui, an apt representative of his own unbounded arrogance. The French suite came into collision with the Corsican body-guard of the Pope, mortal wounds were given on both sides, and the ambassador himself was insulted and endangered[4]. The King at once expelled the nuncio from France, seized the papal possessions of Avignon and Venaissin, and marched troops towards Italy to demand satisfaction. The Pope was compelled to accept the humiliating Treaty of Pisa, by which he engaged never again to employ Corsicans in his service, and to have the terms of the treaty engraven on a pyramid in one of the most public places in Rome; a deep mortification to a pontiff who hoped that a renovated Rome should be his monument. Perhaps it was some compensation to him that he had received (1655) into the bosom of the Roman Church the daughter of the Protestant 'Lion of the

Treaty of Pisa, 1664.

---

[1] Ranke, 285 ff. and App. Nos. 122—128.
[2] II. 448.
[3] He had been one of the most distinguished negotiators of the Peace of Westphalia; Pfister, *Geschichte der Teutschen*, IV. 628.
[4] Hénault's *Abrégé Chronol.*, p. 778 f.

North,' Christina, Queen of Sweden, who, when her keen and restless intellect had led her to doubt all forms of faith, sought certainty in that Church which proclaims itself alone infallible. She lived long in the literary and artistic society of Rome, where her wit and self-will sometimes brought her into collision with the authorities, and at her death enriched the Vatican with her rare books and manuscripts. On the whole Alexander was found as trifling in great things as he was great in trifles; everyone would have thought him the fittest man for the Papacy had he not been Pope.

CH. III. *Christina of Sweden, d.* 1689.

The short reign of his successor, Clement IX. (Rospigliosi) was one of peace-making; he calmed the Jansenistic storm by the compromise which is known by his name[1], he mediated between France and Spain, and received Portugal, which for five-and-twenty years the Holy See had refused to recognize as an independent kingdom, into communion with Rome. His gentleness and beneficence won the hearts of the people, and no Pontiff died more regretted. For five months after his death the throne was vacant; at last the Conclave chose by 'inspiration,' Emilio Altieri, a hale old man of fourscore years, who took the name of Clement X. At such an age it is not wonderful that the Pope contented himself with giving the solemn benediction, while the real burden of government rested on Cardinal Paluzzi Altieri.

Clement IX., 1667–69.

Clement X., 1670—1676.

In the long line of Popes none have left a fairer name than Innocent XI.[2] (Odeschalchi), whose gentle and amiable character won the love of those about him, while it did not prevent him from being firm in his adherence to the right. He set himself in earnest to diminish the nepotism, the burdensome routine, the number of officials, and the debts which weighed down the papal administration, and both by precept and example set up a higher standard of morality among clergy and people. The Jansenist controversy slumbered, but the disputes with France on the subject of the 'Regale' and the Gallican liberties for some years troubled the papal see; and a dispute arose in which the King of France again displayed his haughty wilfulness. The ambassadors in Rome had

Innocent XI, 1676—1689.

[1] See p. 95.
[2] Bonamici, *De Vita Innocentii* XV. (Rome, 1776); *Vita d' Innocent XI.* (Venice, 1690).

CH. III.

The 'Franchise' of Ambassadors.

1687.

gradually extended the usual immunity of envoys not only to the precincts of their several embassies, but to the streets in which they lived, which thus became sanctuaries for all kinds of malefactors[1]. This immunity, which rendered all police regulations ineffectual, was relinquished at Innocent's request by all the great Powers, with the single exception of France; the French ambassador, with a regiment of cavalry for his suite, braved the Pope in his own capital, and was laid under the censure of the Church. In return, the papal nuncio in France was forcibly detained, and the papal territory of Avignon seized by the King; but Innocent, strong in the sense of right, did not yield, and the alienation continued until his death. Immediately afterwards Louis abandoned the right of asylum and restored Avignon. It was, no doubt, the intolerable insolence of the French monarch which impelled Innocent to support the Prince of Orange on the Rhine, and possibly even to favour his designs on England; certain it is that the papal court had early information of those intrigues which placed William on the throne, and put an end to the hopes then entertained of seeing a Romish dynasty in Great Britain. The latter years of this Pontiff's reign were cheered by the decided successes of his allies, the Poles and Imperialists, against the Turks, who from this time were no longer dreaded in Europe.

Alexander VIII., 1689—1691.

The reign of Alexander VIII. (Ottoboni) witnessed the restoration of much of the nepotism and venality which Innocent had repressed. Alexander remained however firm against the demands of France, and on his early death the French party exerted themselves to the utmost to procure the election of a more pliant successor. The choice fell on Antonio Pignatelli, who took the name of the Pope, Innocent, whom he intended to emulate, and of whose fair fame he was a not unworthy rival. By him the long dispute with the French King was at last ended by a compromise, which shewed a certain consciousness of weakness in the Holy See; and a vigorous attempt was made to abolish nepotism for ever by a special Bull on the subject, a measure which Innocent XI. had contemplated

Innocent XII., 1691—1700.

---

[1] Burnet's *Own Time*, i. 706.

without venturing to carry out. This Pontiff made the poor his 'nepotes,' the Lateran a hospital; and, in spite of his charities, his harbour-works, and his buildings, husbanded his resources so carefully that he left a considerable sum in the treasury at his death[1]. His successor, Clement XI.[2] (Albani), ascended the throne with a reluctance which seemed a presage of coming trouble, for his long reign was disquieted both by theological and political broils. The papal protest against the assumption by the Elector of Brandenburg of the royal crown of Prussia[3], once the possession of the Teutonic Order, was but laughed at in Germany[4]; but the war of the Spanish Succession produced much more important consequences to the Papacy. The Emperor, Joseph I., seeing that the Pope favoured Philip V., the French candidate for the Spanish throne, sent an army into the States of the Church; the Pope threatened excommunication and prepared for war, but as the Imperialists continued to advance he was compelled to accept a peace, to recognize the Austrian Charles III. as King of Spain, and to grant him investiture of Naples[5]. Fresh troubles followed. The Duke of Savoy, already at variance with the Pope, became by the Peace of Utrecht King of Sicily; there he asserted the peculiar spiritual rights of the 'Sicilian Monarchy' over certain refractory ecclesiastics of that country, upon which the Pope laid the kingdom under an Interdict, and had in consequence to maintain at Rome many hundreds of ecclesiastics who fled for refuge from Sicily to Rome. To these troubles the kindly and conscientious Innocent XIII. (Conti) succeeded, and put an end to the Neapolitan contest by granting enfeoffment to the Emperor Charles VI., while the duchies of Parma and Piacenza were treated, in spite of the Pontiff's protest, as feoffs of the Empire, and granted to the Spanish prince Don Carlos. This Pope, whose short reign was stained by only one act of unworthy compliance, the elevation of the infamous Dubois to the cardinalate,

Clement XI., 1700 —1721.

Spanish Succession.

1709.

Sicilian Monarchy. 1713.

Innocent XIII., 1721— 1724.

---

[1] Schröckh, VI. 350 ff.; Ranke, 319, and App. Nos. 153, 4.
[2] Buder, *Leben und Thaten Clement XI.* (Frankfurt, 1721); [P. Polidoro] *De Vita et Gestis Clem. XI.* (Urbino, 1727); S. Reboulet, *Hist. de Clément XI.* (Avignon, 1752).
[3] Carlyle, *Friedrich II.*, I. 52 ff.
[4] Schröckh, VI. 360 ff.
[5] Schröckh, VI. 363 ff.; Ranke, 321.

was succeeded by Benedict XIII.[1] (Orsini), who retained the views of his Dominican convent on the papal throne, which nothing but his own vow of obedience to the general had compelled him to accept. Good man as he was, his simple devoutness brought probably more ridicule than credit to the Holy See. His attempts to check the luxury of the clergy were unavailing, his Lateran Synod produced no permanent benefit to the Church, and his attempted canonization of Gregory VII. (1729) shewed that the great Catholic princes were by no means willing to venerate a saint whose principal glory was to have braved the temporal power. Affairs of state were managed by the hypocritical Cardinal Coscia, under whose management the dispute about the Sicilian Monarchy was ended (1728) by a compromise which permitted spiritual persons to be judged by Sicilian tribunals, except in certain extraordinary cases, the decision of which was reserved to the Pope. This well-meaning monk was succeeded by the able statesman Corsini, Clement XII., who still in old age loved magnificence and practised justice. He too, like so many of his predecessors, was made to feel that in this age even Roman Catholic princes were but undutiful sons of the Church, and he renewed the papal claims to the Duchies of Parma and Placencia in vain. He was succeeded, after a conclave which lasted six months, by the most learned of the Popes, the excellent Lambertini, who took the name of Benedict XIV.[2] In him the Church found at last a ruler who thoroughly knew how to adapt himself to the change of times, and gave up, in his dealing with foreign princes, the autocratic style of the older Popes. Finance, agriculture, and the internal administration of the State profited by his reforming hand; the relations of the Papacy with Spain, Portugal, and Naples were placed on a more satisfactory footing, and the disputes between Austria and Venice, on the subject of the Patriarchate of Aquileia, were ended by the division of that jurisdiction into the two Archbishoprics of Görz in Austria and Udine in the Venetian territory. The Pope could not, however, prevail upon the Venetians to repeal an edict of 1754, which forbade the execution of papal

---

[1] Alex. Borgia, *Benedicti XIII. Vita* (Rome, 1752).   [2] *Vie du Pape Bénédict XIV.* (Paris, 1783).

bulls, breves, and the like, within their territory until they had received the sanction of the temporal government; nor could he prevent Frederick the Great from regulating the ecclesiastical constitution of his new Silesian dominions after his own fashion[1]. At the request of the Empress Maria Theresa Benedict remitted the forced abstinence from labour on certain feast-days of the Church, a step which the famous Muratori defended and Quirini opposed. On the whole, few Popes have left a fairer name than Benedict: his ability, kindliness, and genial Bolognese humour won the hearts of all, and long after his death his reign was referred to as a period of almost unalloyed happiness and prosperity for the papal dominions.

During the seventeenth and eighteenth centuries a great change took place in the position of the Papacy. Henceforth the Italian prince is much more conspicuous in the Pope than the spiritual ruler of the world. There was probably no court in Europe in which there was more social enjoyment than in that of Rome. The Pope, generally a cultivated gentleman, was surrounded by great families, who in fact shared his power and splendour. But his relation to Western Europe in general was changed by the rise of great Protestant Powers and the discontent with the papal claims which shewed itself in many Catholic States. Every Pope was ready enough to claim universal dominion in the Church, but he no longer inspired the dread and awe which had enabled his mediæval predecessors to wield so tremendous a power. The movements of thought which characterised the eighteenth century were utterly beyond papal control.

3. NEW ORDERS AND SOCIETIES.

In nothing did the Church of Rome display better the fresh life which she had derived from the Reformation than in the new Orders which she brought forth during the seventeenth century. Childhood, poverty, sickness, learning, each found in some religious society its appropriate

[1] A. Theiner, *Zustände der Kath. Kirche in Selesien*, 1740—1758 (Regensburg, 1852); Carlyle, *Friedrich II*.

French Oratory, 1611.

Benedictines of St Maur, 1618.

Capuchins become independent, 1619.

patron and protector. Monasticism, which the Reformation had threatened with destruction, reappeared after the storm in shapes better adapted to the wants of the time[1].

After the model of the society which Philip of Neri had established at Rome in the sixteenth century Pierre de Berulle founded the 'Oratory of Jesus' in Paris, an association of clergy, free from the snare of perpetual vows, for the purpose of devotion and mutual edification. It not only attained this end, but fostered some of the most learned men of the age; many of the most distinguished men in France are among those whose names do honour to the Oratory of Paris[2].

The Council of Trent had decreed that independent monasteries should be associated, for the more ready prevention of irregularities, in 'Congregations' under a common rule. In accordance with this decree, through the unwearied efforts of the Prior of St Vannes, Didier de la Cour, and with the favour of Richelieu, a Congregation was formed from the French Benedictine abbeys which received the name of St Maur, a disciple of St Benedict. It devoted itself to the work of education and the study of antiquity, and the splendid names found among its members are an ample testimony to its success in cultivating piety and learning. Classical antiquity, the Fathers, the history of the Church and of France, especially profited by the unwearied labours of the Benedictines of St Maur[3].

Some of the older Orders received new forms and privileges. The Capuchins, the strictest of the Orders derived from St Francis, who had for nearly a century been subject to the general of the Conventual Franciscans, were now permitted to elect a general of their own, and acquired entire independence[4]. The sisters of the society

---

[1] On these Orders and Congregations see Holstenius, *Codex Regularum. Mon. et Canon*, edited with continuation by M. Brockie (Augsburg, 1759).

[2] Tabaraud, *Histoire de Pierre de Berulle* (Paris, 1817); Perraud, *L'Oratoire de France* (Paris, 1866); M. Houssaye, *Berulle et Richelieu* (Paris, 1875).

[3] Phil. de Cerf, *Bibliotheque Historique et Critique des Auteurs de la Congrégation de St Maur* (La Haye, 1726); Tassin, *Histoire Littéraire de la Congrégation de St Maur* (Paris, 1726); James Stephen, *Essays in Ecclesiastical Biography* (1849).

[4] Boverius, *Annales Fratrum Minorum qui Capuccini nuncupantur* (1632 ff.).

formed by the saintly Angela of Brescia (d. 1540) for works of Christian love, taking St Ursula as their patron saint, lived at first in their several families. These Ursulines however in 1604 adopted the conventual life, and devoted themselves to the education of their own sex. The instruction of boys was cared for by the Patres Piarum Scholarum, or Piarists, who, first formed into a society at Rome by a Spaniard, Joseph Calasanza, carried on their excellent work in most countries of Europe. Gregory XV. gave them all the privileges of a Mendicant Order in 1622. They were however deprived of these privileges in consequence of the hostility of the Jesuits, who regarded them as rivals, in 1646 by Innocent X., and did not recover them until in 1698 Innocent XII. gave them back. The care of the sick was undertaken by the Sisters of the Visitation, or 'Ordo de Visitatione Beatae Mariae Virginis,' a name thought to symbolize the longing of a virgin soul for the visit of the heavenly bridegroom. This sisterhood was first formed at Annécy by Madame de Chantal[1], under the influence of Francis of Sales (whence they were sometimes called Salesians) and was not at first placed under any set rule of life. After a few years, however, Francis gave it the rule of St Augustine, with certain peculiar constitutions, and Paul V. in 1618 raised it to the rank of an Order, committing to it, in addition to its earlier work, the care of the education of children[2]. A brotherhood, also for tending the sick, without distinction of creed, was founded by the surviving friends of a poor Portuguese, the saintly John di Dio (d. 1550), and under the names of Brothers of Hospitality, of Mercy, or of Christian Love, extended its work into Spain, Germany, and France. It was sanctioned in 1617 by Paul V.[3]

Among those who have carried on the work of Christ among the poor and needy there is perhaps no greater than Vincent de Paul. He himself in poverty and slavery learned to feel for the wretchedness of others, and devoted

Ch. III.
Ursuline Nuns, 1604.

Piarists, 1607, sanctioned by Paul V., 1617.

Visitationists, 1618.

Brothers of Christian Love, 1617.

---

[1] Daurignac, *Vie de Fr. Chantal* (Paris, 1858).
[2] *La Vie de S. François de Sales*, par Marsollier, 1747; Lady Herbert of Lea, *The Mission of St Francis in the Chablais* (1868); Henrietta L. Lear, *S. Francis de Sales* (1871).

[3] Besides the accounts in Holsten-Brockie (VI. 264 ff.) and Hélyot (*Ordres Monastiques* (IV. 156 ff.), see Villethierry, *Vie de S. Jean de Dieu* (Paris, 1691); J. W. Bowden, *Oratorian Lives of the Saints*, vol. IV. (London, 1875).

96 New Orders and Societies

Lazarists, 1624.

his life to alleviate it, both in body and soul. He founded the society of Mission-Priests, or (as they are frequently called from their house of St Lazare at Paris) Lazarists, who were to go forth to seek and to save that which was lost in the waste places of Christendom. That the sheep might not be lost from the carelessness of the shepherds, Vincent instituted, with the co-operation of several bishops, meetings and conferences for the spiritual edification of the clergy, which generally took place in the Mission-houses. His efforts, in fact, were directed to raise the secular clergy and not to promote monasticism.

Sisters of Charity, 1634.

To him too, with his friend Madame le Gras, is due the foundation of the Sisters of Charity, or Grey Sisters, whose gentle hands have nursed many generations of the sick poor in France. Societies of a similar character have been formed in several towns in Italy, the members of which, without wholly quitting domestic life, attend to the wants of pilgrims, to the sick, and to the dead[1].

English Ladies.

In 1607 a young English lady, Mary Ward (d. 1645), founded at Gravelingen in the Netherlands a sisterhood for the care of the sick, and for the education of her countrywomen, for whom no Catholic education was possible in England. This was shortly afterwards transferred to St Omer. The pious ladies soon fell under a suspicion of heresy, which, groundless as it was, sufficed to cause the closing of their houses by a papal Bull (1630) of Urban VIII. The Bull however was not everywhere carried into effect; the sisterhood continued to exist, and received a rule and formal authorization from Clement XI. in 1703. The work of the English Ladies has been by no means limited to the care of their countrywomen, but in many countries, without perpetual vows, they have carried on their work of love and mercy, and unobtrusively brought honour to their national name[2].

Trappists, 1662.

A strong contrast to the beneficent foundations of

---

[1] Abelly, *Vie de S. Vincent de Paule* (Paris, 1664); Gabillon, *Vie de Madame le Gras* (Paris, 1676); Feillet, *La Misère au Temps de la Fronde* (Paris, 1862); C. Butler, *Life of V. de P.*, appended to his *Life of Fénelon* (1819); P. Collet, *Vie de V. de P.* (Paris, 1818); Maria Wilson, *Life of V. de P.* (1873).

[2] J. Leitner, *Geschichte d. Engl. Fraülein* (Regensburg, 1869); *Life of Mary Ward* by Miss Chambers (1882); by E. Irving Carlyle in *Dict. Nat. Biog.*, Supplement III. 506.

Vincent de Paul is found in the Order of La Trappe[1]. The origin of this famous rule was as follows. Bouthillier de Rancé[2], a Frenchman of noble birth, though an ecclesiastic and richly beneficed, lived for several years the luxurious and self-indulgent life of a mere man of the world. At last, filled with horror at the unexpected sight of the corpse of his mistress, whom he had left in full health and beauty, he rushed from the world and buried himself in the melancholy abbey of La Trappe in Normandy, of which he had been abbot from his boyhood. There, not content with restoring the due observation of the Cistercian statutes, he instituted a rule of unexampled, nay, inhuman sternness. Continual silence, the coarsest food, the hardest labour lightened by no study or recreation, these were the lot of the Trappists; yet, such is the eagerness of a penitent to fly from himself, the order found recruits, principally among repentant debauchees, enough to support convents in several countries of Europe. De Rancé's objections to the pursuit of learning in monasteries were answered by the most learned of monks, Dom Mabillon. {Ch. III.}

For the promotion of schools for the poor, which were neglected at that time in France both by Church and State, Baptiste de la Salle founded the "Brothers of Christian Schools," or Ignorantins[3], sanctioned by Pope Benedict XIII. in 1725; and Nicholas Barré, a Franciscan, founded a similar female Order of "Sisters of Schools of the Children of Jesus," whose especial task it was to provide a succession of teachers for schools of elementary education. {Ignorantins, 1684. Sanctioned, 1725. Schoolsisters, 1681.}

The eighteenth century added another to the Orders which aimed at the revival of religion by means of missions. A noble Neapolitan, Alfonso Maria de Liguori, who had left the bar for the pulpit and the confessional, on a mission in the neighbourhood of Amalfi learned the crass ignorance and indifference of the peasantry. Moved {Redemptorists, 1732.}

---

[1] Holsten-Brockie, vi. 569; Gaillardin, *Les Trappistes...Hist. de la Trappe jusqu'à nos jours* (Paris, 1844).
[2] Marsollier, *Vie de l'Abbé de la Trappe* (Paris, 1703); P. de Maupeon, *Vie de P. A. J. de Rancé* (Paris, 1709); Chateaubriand, *Vie de Rancé* (Paris, 1844); Dubois, *Hist. de la Trappe* (Paris, 1824).
[3] Maria Wilson, *The Christian Brothers...with Life of J. B. de la Salle* (1883).

by a deep feeling of their need, he founded the order of Redemptorists (Congregatio Sanctissimi Redemptoris) or Liguorians[1], a society of secular priests who should follow in the steps of Jesus, strive after a higher tone of spiritual life, and preach the Gospel to the poor. The rule was fully established in 1742. The Liguorians, in spite of the nobleness and purity of their professed objects, fell into evil repute from their too great resemblance to the hated Jesuits.

The Sacred Heart. Margaret Alacoque.

One of the strangest phenomena of the seventeenth century was the rise of the practice of devotion to the Sacred Heart of Jesus. Margaret Alacoque[2] was a nun in a convent at Paray-le-Monial in Burgundy, sickly from her childhood, eager to mortify the flesh by the most extreme self-torture, and frequently visited by apparitions of the Virgin Mary. After a time however the visions of the Virgin no longer satisfied her; she began to regard the Saviour Himself as her lover, and to receive from Him tokens of affection and even an actual betrothal, though, to prove her love, He still left her a prey to the worst temptations of the devil. In 1675 the Jesuit La Columbière[3] became her spiritual adviser. In that year (June 16) she saw the side of her betrothed opened so as to expose His heart, glowing with a fire bright as the sun, into which He plunged her own. In another vision not only her own heart but that of her confessor was seen in the glow, and in a third the Saviour ordained the institution of a special "Devotion to the Sacred Heart" to be observed by all Christendom on the Friday following the octave of Corpus Christi Day, and on the first Friday in each month. The Jesuits did their utmost to promote the adoption of these forms of worship. They were opposed with equal ardour by the Dominicans, but spread notwithstanding into nearly all parts of the Church, and in 1765 Pope Clement XIII., under Jesuit influence, gave them formal sanction[4].

Vision, 1675.

---

[1] *Biographies* of Liguori, ed. by F. W. Faber (Lond. 1848-49); F. Meyrick, *Moral...Theology...according to S. Alfonso da Liguori* (1857).
[2] Languet, *Vie d'Alacoque* (1729).
[3] Eug. Seguin, *Storia del P. Claudio de la Colombière* (Bologna, 1877).
[4] J. B. Dalgairns, *The Devotion to the Sacred Heart* (Lond. 1853).

4. JANSENISM AND PORT-ROYAL.

There has hardly ever been a period when the Western Church has not been agitated more or less by controversies on the deep mystery of the Grace of God and the Free-will of man. This controversy is represented in the seventeenth and eighteenth centuries by the Jansenists and their opponents[1].

In the early part of the seventeenth century what would once have been called Pelagianism crept over the Church, and coloured the prevalent teaching of Christianity; much was said of the free-will of man, of his powers, of his duties; little of the all-sufficient grace of God. Some able and earnest theologians saw in doctrines such as these an attack on the sovereignty of Christ; they divined already, what the next century made plain, that the tendency of such doctrines was to do away with the necessity of a divine Redeemer, to make man himself sufficient for his own needs. They dimly foreboded a Rousseau in the teaching of Molina[2].

The theology of Augustine, which referred everything in the work of salvation to the grace of God and nothing to the free-will of man, though not openly impugned, had never been really accepted by the great body of Church teachers[3]. The Jesuits in particular in the latter part of the sixteenth century taught doctrines which were clearly opposed to it, and their teaching occasioned a strife which was in fact a renewal of the Pelagian controversy of an earlier age.

In 1638 died Cornelius Jansen[4], Bishop of Ypres, leaving in manuscript a work, the fruit of some twenty years' toil, on the theology of St Augustine. This work

Jansenism.

Jansen, 1585—1638.

---

[1] Leydecker, *Historia Jansenismi* (1695); [Gerberon], *Hist. Générale de Jansenisme* (Amsterdam, 1700); T. Bouvier, *Étude sur le Jansenisme* (Strassburg, 1864); S. P. Tregelles, *The Jansenists* (London, 1851). There is an Introduction on the Jansenists in J. B. Dalgairns' *Sacred Heart*. See also [Marguerite Tollemache] *The French Jansenists* (London, 1893).
[2] See Hardwick's *Reformation*, 310; Alzog, *K.-G.* II. 414.
[3] See S. Cheetham, *Ch. Hist. of First Six Centuries*, p. 321.
[4] A. Vandenpeereboom, *C. Jansenius, septième évêque d'Ypres* (Bruges, 1882).

was published in 1640 by the pious care of the bishop's friends, under the title *Augustinus*. It treated of the state of man after the Fall, of his natural helplessness, of the irresistibleness of God's grace; in all this representing the opinions of St Augustine, but perhaps with greater sharpness and less qualification than the great master himself had used. Yet this might probably have escaped censure had not Jansen distinctly asserted the identity of the conclusions of some of his contemporaries with those of the Pelagians, and controverted with equal plainness the morality taught by the Jesuits. To their too ingenious system of precepts and distinctions he opposed that "faith which worketh by love" which had been preached by St Paul and by his greatest disciple in the Latin Church. The grace of God, he says, looses that chain of our sins by which we are tied and bound; it infuses a spiritual delight, by which we are moved both to will and to do after God's good pleasure; man becomes good by having his thoughts and affections drawn to that supreme good, which is God Himself.

There is also a particular passage in Jansen's work which gave offence to the Roman See. He finds St Augustine at variance with a decision of the Roman Court; which shall he follow? He decides that the Holy See could never have deliberately pronounced a proposition of St Augustine's to be false, and resolves to follow the Father, though always professing submission to the Pope.

A vehement controversy followed the publication of *Augustinus*; Pope Urban forbade the reading of the book by the Bull *In eminenti*; but, not content with this, the Jesuits endeavoured to procure the distinct condemnation of certain tenets contained in it. With this view they submitted to the Theological Faculty of Paris seven points, which were reduced in the discussion which followed to these five. 1. There are some commandments of God which just men, though willing to obey them, are unable with their natural strength to fulfil; and the grace by which they might fulfil them is also wanting to them. 2. Inward grace is never resisted. 3. In order to have merit before God, a man does not need freedom from necessity, but only from actual constraint. 4. The Semi-Pelagians admitted the necessity of an inward prevenient grace, yet were heretical in that they maintained that the will of man was able either to resist or obey it. 5. It is Semi-Pelagian to say that Christ died, or shed His Blood, for all men without exception. These five the Faculty condemned, without however declaring that they were contained in *Augustinus*. In 1650 eighty-five French bishops laid the five propositions before Pope Innocent X., and called upon him to pronounce a decisive judgment. He had no taste for theological subtleties, and would willingly have avoided a decision; but at last, urged on by the energetic cardinal Chigi, he published the Bull *Cum occasione*, by which he condemned the five propositions as heretical, blasphemous, and damnable. He hoped to restore peace to the Church, while he had really brought it to the verge of a schism. For the views of Jansen were supported in France by a powerful party, especially by "Messieurs de Port-Royal." It is necessary to notice briefly the rise of this remarkable society.

Early in the seventeenth century the Cistercian nunnery of Port-Royal des Champs, near Paris, had risen to the highest repute under the presidency of "la Mère Angelique," a daughter of the famous family of Arnauld. The number of the nuns had indeed so increased that they occupied a second house, Port-Royal de Paris, in the suburbs of the capital. The Abbess and her nuns were much under the influence of Jean du Vergier de Hauranne, Abbé de St Cyran, the lifelong friend of Cornelius Jansen. In the neighbourhood of the country Port-Royal was gradually formed one of the most remarkable societies the world has ever seen[1]. The young advocate Le Maitre, Arnauld d'Andilly, Racine the poet, Antoine Arnauld, de Sacy, Nicole, Pascal, were among those who built themselves cottages near the nunnery, and lived almost like ancient anchorites in asceticism and devotion. The spirit of St Cyran animated them, and

CH. III.

Five Propositions laid before the Pope, 1650.

Bull "Cum occasione," 1653.

Port-Royal, 1639 ff.

Du Vergier de Hauranne, 1581—1643.

---

[1] J. Racine, *Histoire de Port-Royal* (1693); N. Fontaine, *Mém. pour l'Hist. de Port-Royal* (1736); H. Reuchlin, *Geschichte von Port-Royal* (1839-44); C. A. Ste Beuve, *Hist. de Port-Royal* (1840-48); M. A. Schimmelpenninck, *Memoirs of Port-Royal* (1835), *Port-Royal and its Saints* (1856); C. Beard, *Port-Royal* (1861).

they were all eager partizans of the doctrines of the *Augustinus*.

Renewed Discussion of the Five Propositions.

On the publication of Innocent's Bull the Jansenists at once submitted to the condemnation of the five propositions, but denied that they were contained in Jansen's work, at least in the sense in which they were condemned. This outlet Alexander VII. endeavoured to close by the Bull *Ad sacram*, in which he declared expressly that the five propositions were contained in Jansen's *Augustinus*, in the sense in which they were condemned; and in 1665, at the request of most of the French bishops, he drew up for the Gallican Church a formulary condemnatory of Jansen's views, which was to be subscribed without reservation by all spiritual persons whatever. This was accepted by the King, and registered by the Parliament of Paris.

Bull "Ad Sacram," 1656.

The resources of the Port-Royalists, who had now four bishops on their side, were however not exhausted. They took a distinction, which had already been maintained by Baronius and Bellarmine, between the question of law (*droit*) and the question of fact (*fait*). The Pope was empowered and inspired, they said, to declare the doctrine of the Church, but not to determine a matter of fact, which was a subject for simple historical investigation. They could heartily assent to the condemnation of the propositions, but as to the declaration that they were contained in *Augustinus* they could only promise a dutiful silence.

Persecution of Jansenists.

The ecclesiastical, reinforced by the secular power, now commenced a vigorous persecution of those who refused the formulary. The Port-Royalists fled or disguised themselves; the nuns of Port-Royal, who, in spite of Bossuet's eloquence, for the most part declined to subscribe, were treated with great harshness, and even at last deprived of the sacraments of the Church. Nothing in this unhappy persecution excited greater commiseration than the fate of those nuns who were expelled their convent because they could not declare that certain abstruse propositions in theology were contained in a large Latin work which most of them could not read.

Meantime, the recluses of Port-Royal pleaded their cause with extraordinary ability, learning, and literary skill; Pascal in particular, in his famous "Letters to a Friend in the Country," attacked the quibbles of the Dominicans and the casuistry of the Jesuits with a delicate wit and subtle irony which interested courtiers and men of letters as much as theologians. In spite of the severities of the Court the power of Jansenism increased, and things seemed tending towards a schism, when the "Peace of Clement IX." for a time put an end to the dispute. This Pontiff agreed, on the Jansenists declaring that they heartily condemned the five propositions, to be content with their "dutiful silence" on the question whether they were contained in *Augustinus*. This pacification was so far successful that the Jansenists continued for the most part unmolested for more than thirty years; but the recluses were driven from their hermitages around Port-Royal in 1678, the nuns were forbidden to receive pupils or novices, and half their revenues were taken from them.

In the beginning of the eighteenth century the contest was renewed. A confessor doubted whether he might absolve an ecclesiastic who had confessed that, with respect to the Church's decision on a matter of fact, he believed it sufficient to observe a respectful silence. A majority of the doctors of the Sorbonne decided for the absolution. The matter was however referred to Rome, and in 1705 Clement XI., by the Bull *Vineam Domini*, affirmed the principles of Alexander VII., requiring unfeigned assent on the point of fact, as well as of doctrine. This bull was accepted by the Parliament of Paris, and at once put into execution. The blow fell most heavily on Port-Royal des Champs; police-officers carried off the nuns and dispersed them in various convents; their abbey was destroyed and its very name abolished; nay, even the bodies of the dead were dug up and removed, and this by the enlightened government of Louis Quatorze.

The half-quenched flame was rekindled by Pasquier Quesnel, an Oratorian who lived, an exile, in the intimate friendship of Arnauld. His *Moral Reflexions on the New Testament*, a work full of earnest thought and true spirituality, was read and admired by thousands. Cardinal de Noailles recommended it in his diocese of Châlons, several prelates spoke favourably of it, and even Clement

XI. himself declared that no cleric in Italy could have produced such a work. It soon fell, however, under suspicion of Jansenism; the Jesuits were active against it, and the matter was referred to Rome. After long deliberation, the Pope published the famous Bull *Unigenitus*, by which 101 passages extracted from the *Moral Reflexions* were condemned; among them, several which were in fact Scriptural, and some taken verbally from St Augustine and other Fathers. A large part of the French clergy and people, with De Noailles, now Archbishop of Paris, at their head, were opposed to its reception; the King attempted to force it upon them without success, and the thought of the continued resistance to his will embittered his dying moments (1715). Under the Regent Orleans, who was indifferent alike to Pope and prelate, several bishops appealed against the papal decree to a future Council, whence their party received the name of "Appellants." In 1719, under the influence of the Abbé Dubois, who was intriguing for a cardinal's hat, the Regency decided against the Appellants; and when Louis XV. (1725) took the government into his own hands under the guidance of Cardinal Fleury, deposition, imprisonment and exile were freely employed to compel the withdrawal of the appeal. The registration of the Bull by the Parliament of Paris, as a law of the Church and kingdom, was only obtained by the most violent exercise of the royal prerogative, a *lit de justice*, and was after all disavowed by that powerful body. Cardinal De Noailles had himself received the Bull in 1728, and the party of the Appellants was much weakened; yet they might probably have held out against the persecution, had they not been discredited by the folly of some of their own body.

One of the Appellants, a deacon named François de Paris, died in 1727, and was buried in the churchyard of St Médard at Paris[1]. Rumours were soon spread that miracles were wrought at his tomb; convulsions, which commonly accompany fanatical excitement in all ages, certainly seized some of those who visited the cemetery.

---

[1] P. F. Mathieu, *Hist. des Miraculés et des Convulsionnaires de St Médard* (Paris, 1864).

Jansenism and Port-Royal

It was closed by order of Government; still the same effects were produced by particles of earth brought from the sacred precincts. The convulsionaries soon became ridiculous, and the party which had once been defended by the wit of Pascal was now laughed out of Paris through the extravagance of a few obscure fanatics.

Yet one more contest with Parliament arose out of the controversy. Archbishop Beaumont of Paris ordered his clergy to refuse the sacraments to any sick person who could not prove, by a certificate from his parish priest, that he accepted the Constitution *Unigenitus*, and the sacraments were accordingly refused to the Duke of Orleans. Complaint was made, by an *appel comme d'abus*, to the Parliament of Paris, and the Archbishop summoned to the bar (1752). In vain the King forbade the Parliament to interfere in spiritual matters, and even banished several of its members; those who remained still insisted on their privileges, and on their oath to maintain the rights of their countrymen. At last, Benedict XIV. closed the controversy by a moderate Brief (1756), in which, without repealing former ordinances, he recommended that they should be put in force only against open and notorious opponents of the Bull.

Sacraments refused to the Duke of Orleans, 1752.

Benedict XIV.'s Brief, 1756.

But the unwearied struggle of so many earnest and able men did not result merely in the folly and self-torture of the convulsionaries, nor in a factious opposition to ecclesiastical authority; in two ways the Jansenist movement produced lasting fruit.

In the United Provinces, on their separation from Spain, the religious foundations had been transferred to the Protestant community or secularized. Still, many Romanists remained in those districts, and the Popes exercised their pastoral superintendence over them by means of vicars-apostolic. In process of time, a Chapter was formed, or rather continued, at Utrecht. During the religious troubles in the neighbouring country of France, many Jansenists, including the great leaders Arnauld and Quesnel, sought refuge from persecution on the kindly soil of Holland, and the Church there was consequently leavened with Jansenist sentiments. In 1723, the Chapter of Utrecht elected to their archbishopric Cornelius

Jansenists in Holland.

CH. III.

Jansenist Church, 1723.

Steenoven[1], who was consecrated, in spite of the protest of Rome, by Dominic Varlet, bishop of Babylon "in partibus infidelium." On the death of Steenoven, Varlet consecrated his successor; and in 1742, by the restoration of the sees of Haarlem and Deventer, the episcopal succession in Holland was preserved from the danger of extinction. Archbishop Meindarts even held a Synod (1763) at Utrecht, and sent the Acts to Rome.

The Jansenist Church of Holland, in spite of numerous attempts at union, continues to this day separate from the Roman see, and steadily refuses to accept the Bull *Unigenitus.* It professes, however, submission to the primacy of Rome; every newly elected bishop applies to his Holiness for confirmation, and, on being rejected, appeals to a General Council. The Church also congratulates each successive Pope on his accession, and receives a kind of Bull of excommunication in return.

But far more important than the creation of a small independent Church was the effect of the Jansenist controversy in France. The spirited writings by which all classes had been interested in theological subtleties had an effect not contemplated by the Jansenists themselves; on the one hand, men of the world began to care little for the great truths which were for ever bandied about as party watchwords, or made the subject of humorous pamphlets; while, on the other, the able resistance of the Port-Royalists and their friends to political oppression tended, more than any other movement of this period, to keep alive the recollection of constitutional rights under the splendid tyranny of Louis Quatorze and his successor.

5. THE GALLICAN CHURCH AND ITS LIBERTIES.

Splendid Period of Gallicanism.

The period from the middle of the seventeenth to that of the eighteenth century is the golden age of the Gallican Church[2]. France was then, for the first time, united,

---

[1] Dupac de Bellegarde, *Hist. de l'Église Metrop. d'Utrecht* (Utrecht, 1784); C. W. F. Walch, *Neueste Religionsgeschichte,* vi. p. 82 ff.; J. M. Neale, *Hist. of the so-called Jansenist Church in Holland* (1858).

[2] [Picot], *Essai Historique sur l'Influence de Religion en France pendant le 17me Siècle* (1824); F. Huet, *Le Gallicanisme,* in *Révue des Deux Mondes,* Jan. 1, 1855; Bonnemère, *La France sous Louis XIV.* (1864).

powerful, and exulting in its strength; the troubles of the Reformation were over, a new generation of clergy sprang up under the fostering influence of the Court; arts and learning flourished as they never had done before; the stiff, quaint phrases of an older generation vanished, and religion was presented with a force and brilliancy of style which still command admiration wherever the French language is known.

In such a nation, eager, enterprising, and proud of its new-found strength, it is not wonderful that the sentiment of independence extended itself to matters ecclesiastical; indeed, a succession of French writers had already vindicated with much learning and ability the rights of national churches against the see of Rome. When Henry II. threatened to hold a national Council and to break with the Papacy, the jurist Charles du Moulin defended the King's proceedings in an able and learned work. Under Henry IV. arose a very distinguished champion of national rights, Pierre Pithou, whose well-known treatise gave a more definite shape to Gallican claims, claims which were supported with abundant learning by Pierre Dupuy; and in the beginning of the seventeenth century, while Sarpi in Venice was defending national governments against the Pope, his friend Richer with equal ability and courage maintained the same cause in France, and, though driven from the Sorbonne, left behind him a "Richerism" which was long the plague of the ultramontane party in the Church. After Richer's death similar principles were maintained by De Marca, the learned Archbishop of Paris, and by Launoy.

Under the powerful and self-willed Louis XIV. these theories of national liberty in spiritual matters received a practical development. Early in his reign the King shewed a disposition to humble the Papacy. It was an old claim of the French monarchy to receive the income of a bishopric during a vacancy, and to present to all simple benefices belonging to the see which fell vacant during that interval. This right, known as the Regale, which had long been exercised in the old provinces of the kingdom, Louis, in accordance with his usual policy, wished to extend to the four southern provinces, Guienne, Languedoc, Provence, and Dauphiné. The French clergy in general submitted

Du Moulin, 1500—1566.

Pithœus, 1539—1596.

Puteanus, 1582—1651.

Richer, 1559—1631.

Louis XIV., 1643—1715.

Regale.

in silence, but two Jansenist bishops, the saintly Pavillon of Alais and Caulet of Pamiers, refused their assent, deeming the attempt of Louis an unjust invasion of the spiritual rights of the Church. On the death of the Bishop of Pamiers in 1680, the Chapter elected a bishop of similar sentiments, a step which brought them into collision with their metropolitan, the Archbishop of Toulouse. Pope Innocent XI. supported the Chapter; the King, highly indignant, summoned an assembly of the Gallican clergy, which in 1682 produced the famous "Four Propositions," which embody the "Gallican Liberties[1]." These are (1) Jesus Christ did not commit to St Peter a secular, but only a spiritual power. (2) The Apostolic See has full power in spiritual matters, subject only to the decree of the Council of Constance that a General Council is superior to the Pope. (3) The exercise of this power is to be regulated by the Canons enacted under the influence of the Holy Spirit and hallowed by the veneration given to them by the whole world. (4) In the decision of matters of faith the Pope has the principal part; yet so that his decision is not irreformable until it has received the assent of the Church at large.

Bossuet, who took the lead in the Assembly, had no difficulty in shewing that these propositions were in harmony with Scripture and the ancient traditions of the Church, but they gave the highest offence at Rome; Innocent caused them to be burnt by the public executioner, and refused his Bull of confirmation to the prelates nominated by the French crown. This produced a highly inconvenient state of things; several French sees came to be occupied, so far as temporalities were concerned, by prelates who could neither ordain nor confirm, and as neither King nor people were prepared to declare France an independent patriarchate, it was necessary to seek reconciliation with Rome. This was at last brought about by the King tacitly allowing the bishops-designate to write, each for himself, a humble letter to the Pope, disclaiming the Four Propositions, and professing to regard them as null and void. Thus was the connexion

---

[1] E. du Pin, *Traité de l'Authorité Ecclésiastique et...la Declaration du Clergé de France en* 1682 (1707); Grégoire, *Les Libertés de l'Église Gallicane* (1817).

with Rome renewed without open humiliation to the government of France. The able work in which Bossuet[1] defended the Propositions was suppressed, but the spirit which had been aroused was not. A certain freedom of thought with regard to the Papacy continued to distinguish the French ecclesiastics. It was not, indeed, until after the Revolution that the French clergy in general exhibited that devotion to the Pope which has been designated Ultramontanism.

While the negotiations about the Gallican Liberties were going on, the relations between the French Court and the Papacy were embittered by the absurd conduct of the high and mighty King of France with regard to the immunity of the French embassy in Rome[2].

Immunity of French Embassy.

6. MYSTICISM AND QUIETISM.

There have ever been found in the Church tender souls, who have taken refuge from the strife of theologians and the corruptions of the outward community in the immediate intuition of things divine; falling often into delusion and extravagance, yet almost always diffusing around them a fresh glow of beneficence and love. Such was the noble Castilian, St Theresa, who in visions and raptures felt the nearness of the divinity, and whose soul was pierced through and through by the darts of divine love. Such too was John of the Cross, by whose help she brought back the female order of the Carmelites to their old severity of discipline.

Mysticism.

St Theresa, 1515— 1582.
John of the Cross, 1542— 1591.

In Spain, there continued to exist after St Theresa's days a sect of "Alombrados," or "enlightened," who have been called the Quakers of Catholicism; and in the seventeenth century, Mysticism received a remarkable development through the Spaniard Michael Molinos[3]. Born near Saragossa, he studied at Coimbra and Pampeluna, and came in 1669 to Rome, where he soon became famous as a Confessor and Director. Here he published his 'Spiritual Guide,' a book of mystical devotion, which was soon trans-

Molinos, 1640— 1697.

---

[1] *Defensio Declarationis quam... sanxit Clerus Gallicanus* (Luxemburg [really Geneva], 1730).
[2] See p. 89.

[3] H. Heppe, *Gesch. der Quietistischen Mystik* (Berlin, 1875); J. Bigelow, *Molinos the Quietist* (New York, 1882).

lated into several languages. He taught men to aspire to perfect stillness and quietness of human thought and feeling, to annihilate the sense of their own being so as to rest lovingly and entirely on God. This "Quietism" does not seem at once to have given offence, but rather to have received the approbation of several distinguished persons in the Church, including Pope Innocent XI. himself; when suddenly, at the request of Louis XIV., who was instigated by his confessor, the Jesuit Father la Chaise, Molinos was thrown into prison, his book examined, and sixty-eight passages in it condemned by the Pope. Molinos submissively abjured his errors, and died a prisoner in a Dominican convent a few years afterwards. It was thought by some that the fear of Spanish influence at the Court of Rome was a more powerful cause for Louis's persecution of Molinos than his zeal for orthodoxy.

Abjures, 1687.

Meantime, Quietism had found several adherents in France, especially Madame de Guyon[1], a lady of noble family, who, after an unhappy marriage, devoted herself in her widowhood to a contemplative life. Persecuted by the rulers of the Church in several cities, she came at last to Paris, where she found votaries even at Court. Her ecstatic fervour led her into expressions, in her devotional works, which were hardly compatible with orthodoxy; her doctrine, that the soul entranced in the love of God is indifferent even to its own salvation, was especially startling, and the keen-sighted Bossuet sounded the alarm. Mainly through his influence Madame de Guyon was confined in a convent; the Archbishop of Paris condemned her writings, and a commission (1694–5) attempted in 34 Articles to distinguish between true and false mysticism. The offender, on subscribing these articles, and declaring solemnly that she had never intended to write anything against the doctrines of the Catholic Church, was allowed to retire to Blois, where she ended her strange life in 1717.

Madame de Guyon, 1648–1717.

Imprisoned, 1688.

She had a disciple far greater than herself. Salignac

---

[1] *La Vie de Mad. Guyon par elle-même* [not wholly her own work] (Cologne, 1720), trans. by T. T. Allen (London, 1897); T. C. Upham, *Life etc. of Mad. Guyon* (New York, 1847, revised ed., London, 1854, 1859); L. Guerrier, *Mad. Guyon d'après les écrits orig.* (Orleans, 1881). See also St Cyres, *Life of Fénelon.*

de la Mothe Fénelon[1] had been attracted by her ecstatic reveries, and joined the ranks of her friends. In 1695 he became Archbishop of Cambray. Bossuet in vain endeavoured to induce him to concur in the condemnation of Madame de Guyon and her works; the only effect of his urgency was, that Fénelon wrote a book—"Maximes des Saints sur la Vie interieure,"—in which, without defending her views in all points, he sought to prove that her doctrine with regard to the pure love of God was in accordance with the principles held by many saints in all ages. This work, the most brilliant and popular defence of Quietism which had appeared, rekindled the controversy between its author and Bossuet; at last, for the sake of the peace of the Church, the Holy See was appealed to for a decision. Innocent XII. caused the 'Maximes' to be examined by a commission of ten theologians, who condemned the work in general terms, and specified twenty-three passages as dangerous and offensive. Fénelon received the news of this condemnation as he was preparing to ascend the pulpit of his own cathedral; he gave an earnest of his future submission by preaching on the obedience that Christians owe to their superiors. Bossuet was victor in the theological combat.

A Quietistic movement in the Netherlands found a leader in Antoinette Bourignon[2] of Ryssel, who taught a mysticism of a far less elevated character than that of Madame de Guyon, applying the terms of conjugal love with offensive freedom to the relations of the soul with its Maker. Believing herself to be the prophetess of a new dispensation, she was indifferent to the strife of Churches, and found eager adherents and opponents both among Romanists and Protestants.

Very different from Madame Bourignon was the pure, simple-hearted mystic, John Scheffler of Breslau, better known as Angelus Silesius[3]. Born a Protestant, educated

Ch. III.

Fénelon her disciple, 1687,

writes 'Maximes,' 1697,

book condemned, 1699.

Madame Bourignon, 1616 —1680.

Angelus Silesius, 1624— 1677.

---

[1] Bausset, *Hist. de Fénelon* (Paris, 1808; improved edition, 1850); C. Butler, *Life of Fénelon* (1810); J. Matter, *Le Mysticisme au France au temps de Fénelon* (1866); Mrs Follen, *Selections with Memoir of F.* (Boston, U.S.A., 1859); Mrs H. L. Lear, *Fénelon, Abp of Cambray* (Lond. 1877); Paul Janet, *Fénelon* (Paris, 1892); Viscount St Cyres, *François de Fénelon* (Lond. 1901).

[2] *Life* by P. Poiret, with her *Works* (Amsterdam, 1679 ff.).

[3] F. Kern, *J. Scheffler* (Leipzig, 1866); A. Creblin, *Angelus Silesius* (Breslau, 1877).

112 *Missions*

Ch. III.

Abraham a St Clara, 1707.

as a physician, he became in middle life a priest of the Roman Church, retaining still the passion for immediate communing with God which he had acquired in the Protestant Church under the influence of Jacob Böhme. His longing for absorption in the Divinity results in a kind of Pantheism, the deep philosophy of which he sets forth in such sweet, simple, childlike guise, that he has won the veneration of many thoughtful persons in all communions. Like Scheffler in popular power, though of a widely different spirit, is the famous preacher of Vienna, Ulric Megerle, known as Father Abraham a St Clara, who clothed in humorous form his longing for greater earnestness and purity than his own degenerate age could shew.

7. MISSIONS.

Roman Activity.

The revival of the Roman Church shewed itself in the increased activity of foreign missions[1] as well as in conquests nearer home. Jesuits and Mendicants engaged with equal ardour in the work, and a great institution in Rome became the centre of missionary enterprise. This was the Propaganda, or *Congregatio de Propaganda Fide*, a Board of prelates and learned men for the general direction and oversight of the Roman missions, with a College under its control for the training of missionaries, and a press for the printing of books in all languages. To the College of the Propaganda are sent promising youths from all parts of the world to be educated for the priesthood that they may serve in their own several countries. This native priesthood thoroughly imbued with Roman ideas has been the great support of Roman missions to the heathen.

Propaganda, Congregation, 1622,

College, 1627.

India. Nobili, 1606 ff.

The great work of Francis Xavier in India belongs to the previous period[2]. It was taken up by Father Nobili,

[1] J. A. Fabricius, *Lux Exoriens*, c. 33, where is also found a catalogue of the principal works relating to Roman Catholic Missions up to the date of publication, 1731. More recent information in M. R. A. Henrion, *Hist. Générale des Missions Catholiques*; F. E. Chassay, *Hist. de la Prédication de l'Evangile*; E. J. Durand, *Les Missions Catholiques Françaises*.

[2] Hardwick, *Reformation*, p. 403 ff. On Christianity in India, see La Croze, *Hist. du Christianisme des Indes* (La Haye, 1758); James Hough, *Hist. of Christianity in India* (Lond. 1839-45); J. W. Kaye, *Christianity in India* (Lond. 1859); J. C. Marshman, *Hist. of India* (Lond. 1867).

who, with the permission of his superiors, adopted the dress and bearing of a Brahman, and avoided intercourse with low-caste people. In this way he ingratiated himself with the Brahmans, of whom seventy are said to have become his disciples, and these were followed by a great number of the lower castes. In all one hundred thousand natives are said to have been won over by Nobili, who was able to set forth his position and teaching in Sanscrit. But the system of accommodation, or compliance with the prejudices of converts, did not meet with general approval. The "Malabar Usages" were vehemently attacked and brought before Gregory XV. without any decisive result. At last, in 1704, Cardinal de Tournon, touching at Pondicherry on his way to China, issued a decree suppressing the pagan usages, and this was some years later (1746) confirmed by a Bull of Benedict XIV. In Cochin-China and Annam the Jesuit Alexander Rhodez was a devoted missionary.

Ch. III.

Cochin-China, 1624 ff.

In Japan also the intrepid Xavier had planted a Christian Church[1], which is said to have numbered some 200,000 members, when in 1587 a fearful storm of persecution burst upon it. The Jesuits were supposed to have been driven from the country, though some few did in fact remain under the protection of friendly chiefs. The Church was beginning to recover from its misfortunes and to enjoy peace when fresh persecution (1596) arose, and the policy of the Japanese government was changed by the accession of a new dynasty. Converts to Catholicism were thought to have pledged their allegiance to a foreign power and to have acted offensively in Shinto and Buddhist temples. Hence in 1624 Christianity was forbidden, and in 1638 the Portuguese and their religion were finally expelled from the country. From this time until 1853 Japan had no intercourse with Europe except through the Dutch factory at Deshima, and even the Dutch were not allowed to visit the mainland.

Japan.

Persecutions, 1587, 1596 ff.

Christianity put down, 1638.

Xavier died in sight of the great empire of China, the

China.

[1] Hardwick, *Ref.* 406. See W. Adams, *Adventures in the Empire of Japan*, in Purchas's *Pilgrimes* and Harris's *Voyages*; *Early Documents on Japan*, ed. by T. Rundall (Hakluyt Soc. 1850); E. Kaempfer, *Hist. of Japan*, trans. by Schenckzer (London, 1728); P. Crasset, *Hist. de l'Église de Japon* (1719); Adams, F. O., *Hist. of Japan from the Earliest Period* (London, 1874).

conversion of which he was eager to attempt. The real founder of Catholicism in China, Matthew Ricci, landed on its coasts in 1582 and died there in 1610[1]. Ricci knew how to unite heavenly doctrine with earthly science, and by his scientific attainments very much diminished the contempt which the Chinese felt for Europeans. Even among the mandarins he made himself acceptable, and by their advice adopted their silk costume. His great object was to establish himself in Pekin, where he hoped to convert the emperor. His perseverance triumphed over all difficulties, and he did succeed at any rate in gaining some influence with the sovereign, and in bringing into the net some distinguished members of Chinese society. The success of Ricci at Pekin naturally rendered the carrying on of the work less difficult in other parts of the country. His most distinguished successor was Adam Schall, a German, who began his work in 1622. He also, like Ricci, gained influence with the learned class in China by his scientific attainments, and was permitted to build churches. During the minority of the young emperor Khanghi the regency caused the missionaries to be imprisoned, but when he himself assumed the government, the Jesuits came again into honour. Schall was succeeded by the Netherlander Ferdinand Verbiest, who rose greatly in Chinese estimation by instructing them in the forging of improved cannon; while Father Gerbillon gained credit by his skilful negotiation of a treaty between China and Russia. The result of the proceedings of a few able and earnest men was that in the latter part of the seventeenth century there were said to be 20,000 Christians in China, and in 1692 the preaching of Christianity was permitted by law.

The Catholic Church in China was largely supported, from the year 1663 onward, by the missionary seminary in Paris. But the contest about the "Chinese Usages" much interfered with the success of the mission. The principal worship of the Chinese is that of ancestors, and this the converts thought it impiety to discontinue. The Jesuits permitted them to retain their custom, as being analogous

---

[1] Hardwick, *Ref.* 408. For Roman Missions in China see Trigaut, *De Chr. Expéd. apud Sinas ex Comm. Riccii* (1625, often reprinted); Schall, *Relatio de Initio et Progressu Miss. Soc. Jesu ap. Chinenses* (Vienna, 1668); J. B. Du Halde, *General History of China* (Lond. 1736); E. R. Huc, *Christianity in China*, etc. (Eng. trans., London, 1857).

to prayers for the dead and invocation of saints, while the Dominicans utterly forbade it. And this was not all. The Chinese language supplied no adequate name for the One God, the Father Almighty, whom Christians worship, and the substitutes which the Jesuits employed, meaning properly "lord of heaven" or "chief ruler," seemed to their opponents inadequate. And other customs of minor importance were called in question. The controversy was referred to Rome for decision, and drew from Innocent X. (1645) and Alexander VII. judgments which can scarcely be reconciled. When the strife broke out afresh, Clement XI. in great perplexity sent out as his legate Cardinal Thomas de Tournon with full powers to investigate and decide the matter on the spot. Following the decree of the Roman Propaganda (1704) he disallowed the Jesuit rendering of the word "God," and a great number of rites and ceremonies which they had permitted as concessions to Chinese prejudice. The result was that Tournon was arrested by order of the emperor, who was under Jesuit influence, and died at Macao (1710) perhaps not a natural death. Clement however (1715), and even more emphatically Benedict XIV. (1745), condemned the mingling of Christian with pagan usages. Henceforward the Church in China was generally persecuted, though not exterminated. As its most active missions were those of the Jesuits, it was of course weakened by the abolition of that Order in 1773, and still further by the destruction of the Parisian Seminary in the French Revolution.

In Thibet[1], where Buddhism had become the dominant religion, the Roman missionaries met with a system not unlike their own—celibate priests, monks, monasteries, rosaries, pilgrimages, and the like. The early efforts of the Jesuits had no result, but a Capuchin mission, with Orazio della Penna at its head, was somewhat more successful. The Dalai-Lama, the Buddhist Pope, the nominal ruler of Thibet both in spiritual and civil matters, gave the missionaries a house of residence in the capital, Lhassa, and some remains of Roman Catholicism are said to exist there even to this day.

The east coast of Africa, where the colonists were for

[1] E. R. Huc, *Christianity in China, Tartary, and Thibet* (from the French), London, 1857.

CH. III.

Translation of "God."

Papal Judgments.

T. de Tournon.

Usages condemned, 1715, 1745.

Thibet.

Capuchins, 1707.

Missions in Africa, 1590 ff.

the most part Portuguese, was visited by Capuchin missionaries[1], who preached in Mozambique, Monomotapa, and elsewhere. On the west coast also preachers of Christianity found their way into Congo and Angola; but the degraded condition of the natives and the very unhealthy climate were unfavourable to the permanent establishment of Churches. The attempts to Christianize the Isle of France and Bourbon, under the dominion of France, were somewhat more successful. In the West Indies and South America the barbarities of the Spaniards towards the unfortunate inhabitants made the name of "Christian" hateful, but it was nevertheless a Spaniard, Bartholomew de Las Casas[2], whose noble labours brought some alleviation to their lot. Seven times he crossed the Atlantic in pursuit of his purpose, and did at last wring from the home government an edict which enacted that the natives were no longer to be reduced to slavery, while permitting the importation of negroes from the coast of Africa—a permission which Las Casas afterwards bitterly deplored. In South America the Jesuits and Capuchins won some of their greatest triumphs. The warm-hearted Jesuit, Pedro Claver[3], who called himself the slave of the negroes, did a wonderful work among them from the day when he landed at Carthagena to his death. In Father Sandoval he had a worthy yoke-fellow. A Dominican, Lewis Bertrand, also had some success in New Granada. On the west coast of South America the Jesuits founded the "Llanos-Missions," carried on mainly by German Fathers, and established themselves also on the higher branches of the Amazon. The apostles of Brazil early in the seventeenth century were also Jesuits, among them the famous Antonio Vieira, a Portuguese, the Las Casas of Brazil, who taught not only the knowledge of Christ, but arts and crafts, and contended against slavery. The Inquisition rewarded his zeal by two years' imprisonment. In Guiana too, where the Dominicans had begun a mission in 1560, the Jesuits extended their conquests after 1604, but a stop was put to their labours in 1762 by the French government.

---

[1] Külb, *Die Reisen der Missionäre nach Africa von 16 bis 18 Jahrhundert* (Regensburg, 1861).

[2] A. Helps, *Life of Las Casas* (Lond. 1868).

[3] F. X. Kraus, *Lehrbuch*, p. 509.

The missionaries found themselves so much hindered by the evil conduct of the nominal Christians towards the original inhabitants of conquered countries, that in 1610 the Jesuits persuaded the Spanish government to place in their hands the entire administration, civil as well as religious, of the province of Paraguay, and to give them the right of excluding all other Europeans from the colony. Their success was complete. The natives were converted, and were thenceforth treated as children, occupied in agricultural and pastoral work and in the practices of devotion, while they were carefully secluded from all knowledge which their masters considered unwholesome for them. The spectacle of the prolonged childhood of grown men and women is not perhaps altogether pleasant, but it must be confessed that this Jesuit settlement is probably the only instance in which European colonization in America has made the native population better and happier[1].

Paraguay, 1610 ff.

Jesuit rule.

In the peninsula of California also Christianity was first preached by the Jesuits from the year 1697, with enduring effect. Civilization was introduced together with Catholicism. When the Order of Jesuits was abolished the Dominicans and Franciscans continued their work, and it was by a Franciscan, Juniper Serva, that the town of San Francisco was founded. In Canada, French Jesuits began the work of founding a Church in 1611, and persevered under great difficulties, some of the most active among them being martyred by the Iroquois in the most barbarous fashion. In 1675 Louis XIV. caused a bishopric to be established at Quebec which received several excellent occupants and had many adherents among the Indian tribes.

California, 1697.

1776.
Canada, 1611.
1649.
See of Quebec, 1675.

The laws of the English colonies in North America were extremely unfavourable to Roman Catholics, and in 1700 all Roman priests were forbidden to enter New York on pain of death. Only in Maryland, founded by Lord Baltimore, a Roman Catholic, was toleration given, at first through the personal influence of the founder, afterwards by law[2].

English Colonies.

1632.
1649.

---

[1] Muratori, *Christianesimo...del Paraguay* (Ven. 1743); Nic. del Techo, *Hist. Provinciæ Paraguaciæ* (Liège, 1673); Charlevoix, *Hist. du Paraguay* (Paris, 1765); Echavarry, *Hist. du Paraguay sous les Jesuites* (Amst. 1780); C. A. Washburn, *Hist. of Paraguay* (Boston, U.S.A., 1871).
[2] *Dictionary of National Biography,* VIII. 271 f.

CHAPTER IV.

THE DEVELOPMENT OF PROTESTANTISM.

1. LUTHERAN ORTHODOXY.

Formula Concordiæ, 1577.

It had been hoped that the *Formula of Concord*[1] towards the end of the sixteenth century would put an end to the disputes between the disciples of Luther and Melancthon. But in fact these two names represent types of character and intellect which cannot regard serious questions in quite the same manner. The spirit which had led to endless disputations in the mediæval schools, the desire to formulate exact conclusions on mysterious points of theology, still led to infinite discussion. The relation of the Will of God to the will of man, the Two Natures in Christ Incarnate, the extent of the salvation by Christ, the manner in which the merits of Christ were to be appropriated by the individual believer—these points, and many others, supplied abundant matter for the exercise of subtle wits. Men believed that correct opinions on such points as these were essential to salvation, and they were not, for the most part, able to admit that some questions arising out of the Christian revelation are beyond the reach of human dialectic. The consequence was that controversy was too often conducted with little regard to Christian charity, and that mere correctness of belief came to be more regarded than the heartfelt faith or trust in God which had in earlier days animated the Reformers. How hot and uncharitable were the disputes of the early part of the seventeenth century may be

---

[1] Hardwick's *Reformation*, 163. See A. Tholuck, *Der Geist der Lutherischen Theologen im 17 Jahrhundert*; J. A. Dorner, *Hist. of Protestant Theology*, tr. by Robson and Taylor (Edinb., 1871).

seen in the case of Kepler, the great astronomer. He, a stedfast adherent of old-fashioned Lutherism, was attacked, and debarred from a Würtemberg professorship, because he disputed the dominant views on the ubiquity of the Lord's Body and the Holy Eucharist[1].

It was naturally in Luther's own university of Wittenberg that his opinions were most zealously defended. There it was, nevertheless, that a work appeared which by the breadth of its views scandalized the dominant party. Samuel Huber, who after many wanderings had become a professor of theology in Wittenberg, put forth a statement of his faith, in which he maintained that God through His only-begotten Son had not chosen only a remnant for salvation, but willed to save all sinners, that is to say, all men, and that it was only those who refused to accept the Saviour who were condemned to eternal punishment. This of course presumed that man has the power of choosing or rejecting. He was compelled to leave the university. His tract gave occasion to his colleague Ægidius Hunnius to produce a statement of doctrine which was afterwards generally adopted by his party, to the effect that only those souls experience the working of the grace of God who hear the Word with a certain readiness and eagerness. It is possible for the unregenerate man to dispose himself for or against the power of the Word and the inward operation of grace; nay, even a heathen may avoid sin and put away from him such things as oppose the entrance of the Spirit of God into his heart. Here was the theory of Melancthon without Melancthon's phrases[2].

Another controversy of this period recalls the spirit of the fifth rather than of the seventeenth century. Certain theologians of Giessen, especially Balthazar Mentzer, maintained that when the Son took our nature upon Him He "emptied Himself" ($\dot{\epsilon}\alpha\nu\tau\grave{o}\nu$ $\dot{\epsilon}\kappa\acute{\epsilon}\nu\omega\sigma\epsilon\nu$[3]) of His divine attributes; while the Tübingen theologians, particularly Matthias Hafenreffer and Theodore Thumm, maintained that in the humiliation of the Son there was but a hiding or veiling ($\kappa\rho\acute{\upsilon}\psi\iota\varsigma$) of the Divine omniscience

Ch. IV.

Kepler persecuted, 1611.

Huber, Professor 1592–94.

Hunnius "De Providentia," 1597.

Kenotic Controversy. 1619—1624.

---

[1] Zöckler's *Gottes Zeugen im Reich der Natur*, I. 164.
[2] Gieseler, *K.-G.* III. ii. 325;
Herzog, *K.-G.* II. 284.
[3] *Philippians* ii. 7.

and omnipotence. This dispute assumed so much importance that in 1623 the Elector of Saxony summoned at Dresden a conference of the principal theologians of his dominions with a view to put an end to it. This assembly produced in the following year a "Trustworthy Judgment" of the points in dispute which in all essential points favoured the views of the Giessen party[1]. The Tübingen party published a rejoinder, but the dispute sank out of sight in the troubles and disturbances of the Thirty-Years' War, and was not revived in the changed times which followed it.

More systematic treatises than those called forth by the heat of controversy were also produced. Leonard Hulfer, for instance, in the *Compendium* which he put forth in his lifetime, and the *Common-Places* which were published after his death, aimed at explaining or correcting Melancthon's theories where they deviated, or seemed to deviate, from Luther's. These books were then distinctly partisan, but as a clear statement and defence of the older Lutherism they retained a place in German theological teaching for several generations. But a work in every way superior to that of Hulfer was produced by John Gerhard[2], theological professor at Jena from 1615 to 1637, under the then common title of *Loci Communes*. This is a complete system of dogmatic theology, which is not only more learned, more complete, more methodical, and more acute than its predecessors, but is distinguished by a fairness and candour which are too rare in men who traverse the hot ashes of controversy. It soon rose into the highest repute, and even as late as 1876 a new edition was completed. The most complete statement of the extreme Lutherism of the seventeenth century is found in Calovius's *Systema Locorum Theologicorum*.

The excessive devotion to dogmatic minutiæ tended to pervert the interpretation of Scripture[3]. A man who is mainly engaged in searching for texts to support a foregone conclusion can hardly be a candid interpreter. Scripture, which according to Luther's principles ought to

---

[1] J. A. Dorner, *Person Christi*, vol. ii.; Gieseler, *K.-G.* III. ii. 327; Herzog, *K.-G.* ii. 285; Kurtz's *Lehrbuch*, ed. Tschackert, II. i. 248.

[2] E. R. Fischer, *Vita J. Gerhardi*, (Gotha, 1723).

[3] See G. W. Meyer's *Geschichte der Exegese*, vol. 3.

have supplied the basis alike for doctrine and discipline, became rather the servant than the mistress of dogma. The allegorical method of interpretation, which had for so many centuries made it possible to draw from Scripture any desired conclusion, was indeed generally rejected by the divines of the seventeenth century, but it can hardly be said that their own drier comments led to more solid edification.

Ch. IV.

The early Lutherists, engaged as they were in eagerly asserting the doctrine of justification by faith without the works of the law, did not contribute much to the theory of Christian morality[1]. It lay outside their region of thought. But Melancthon had vindicated against Luther the high claims of Aristotle to be regarded as an excellent moral teacher, and was himself one of the first among Lutherans to treat specially of morals. He conceded to the Greek moralists that they had rightly understood a great part of the moral law, but he held that without the Gospel they could not keep in view the true end for which man was made. At a later date George Calixtus, in the midst of the din of dogmatic controversy, turned his attention to ethical study. He at least saw the connexion between dogma and morals. For Calixtus it is not man, as man, that is to be treated of by Christian moralists, but man converted and born again, in whom the inward grace brings forth the outward fruit of a good life. He trod again, in fact, the path on which Melancthon had entered, but which had been since his time almost deserted.

Morality.

Melancthon's "Epitome Theol. Moral." 1538.

Calixtus' "Theol. Moral." 1634.

2. THE REVIVAL OF RELIGIOUS LIFE.

A. *Pietism.*

In the period succeeding the Reformation the dry orthodoxy, producing little effect upon heart and life, which prevailed in Germany, naturally provoked a reaction. There was never a time in which some at least

Orthodox dryness.

Pietism[2].

---

[1] See C. E. Luthardt, *Geschichte der Christl. Ethik*, vol. 2.
[2] P. J. Spener himself wrote a *Wahrhaft. Erzählung* of Pietism and the events connected with it (1697). See also J. G. Walch's *Die Streitigkeiten innerhalb der Lutherischen Kirche* (1733-36); H. Schmid, *Geschichte des Pietismus* (Nördlingen, 1863); A. Ritschl, *Ges. d. Pietism.* (Bonn, 1884).

were not conscious of the shortcomings of the system. "I have tried," said Balthazar Meisner[1], "to preach to the people, and therefore to guide men to heartfelt piety and good works, which are unfortunately passed over by so many. I see that not the man who knows much and teaches much is a theologian, but the man who leads a holy and godly life." Among those who earnestly desired to lead men from controversy to piety was John Arndt[2]. After studying in Wittenberg, Strassburg, and Basel, and holding a pastor's place in Anhalt, he became in 1599 minister of St Martin's church in Brunswick. He died in 1621, leaving behind him the remembrance of a pure and unselfish life, and a book the influence of which spread over all Germany. This was his *Four Books on True Christianity* (1605), the purpose of which he declares to be to turn the minds of students and preachers from constant and generally unprofitable controversy, and the people from a mere dead and formal belief to faith that worketh by love. The central idea of the book is Christ in us the hope of glory, and salvation by mystical union with Him. Another who laid more stress on the love of Christ than on mere dogmatic correctness was I. Valentine Andreä[3], grandson of Jacob Andreä who was known in the controversies of an earlier time[4]. It was in Calw, where he became Dean in 1620, that he began the career of practical piety which was so great a blessing to his country. His leading thought was to turn men's minds from the vain jangling of endless disputation, and to fix them on the encouragement of true religion in Christian households. This end was to be attained, he believed, mainly by winning the children through a teaching better adapted for their tender years than the almost wholly dogmatic catechisms which had for some years prevailed. His lot was cast in the miserable time of the Thirty Years' War. His own town of Calw was burnt, and the land was everywhere desolate. At the end of the war in a district which had contained

---

[1] Quoted by Herzog, *K.-G.*, 289.
[2] F. Arndt, *Johann Arndt* (Berlin 1838).
[3] See his *Autobiography*, ed. in Latin by Rheinwald, 1849; P. W. H. Hossbach, *J. V. Andreä und sein Zeitalter* (1819).
[4] See Hardwick's *Reformation*, 163.

more than a thousand clergy there were found little more than three hundred, and in the frightful calamities of the age many found it difficult to believe that God ruled the world. Andreä did his best to restore order and Christian teaching. A curious episode in his life is his supposed connexion with the Rosicrucians. In 1614 there appeared at Cassel an anonymous tract, with the title "The Fame of the laudable Order of Rosicrucians[1]," professing to describe an order of sages and alchemists in possession of secret knowledge founded by one Christian Rosenkreuz, probably an altogether imaginary person. As Andreä was known to have already written, without publishing, several ironical sketches to ridicule pretenders to occult science, this treatise was at once attributed to him, probably correctly. But he can never have anticipated the effect which was actually produced. It was taken seriously, and there arose a society of Rosicrucians, composed, no doubt, partly of impostors, partly of believers, which subsisted for several generations.

But the name which is most conspicuous in the history of the religious revival in Germany is that of Philip Jacob Spener[2], an Alsatian, who after a short experience as a pastor in Strassburg, became in 1666, still a young man, head of the Evangelical clergy in Frankfort-on-the-Main. Feeling strongly how little the ordinary preaching of his day, full of formal divisions and technical terms of theology, was adapted to win the hearts of the people, he set himself to preach rather in the spirit and the words of the Bible. He revived too the practice of catechising, which the preachers of that day had allowed to fall almost entirely into disuse. In 1670 he began to hold prayer-meetings (*collegia pietatis*) in his house, in which he expounded Scripture, and invited those who were present also to express their thoughts and to ask questions. Afterwards he published his views as to the need of a reform of clerical education in the Lutheran Church in the book called *Pia Desideria*, which, first appearing

---

[1] De Quincey, *The Rosicrucians and Freemasons*; H. Jennings, *The Rosicrucians, their Rites and Mysteries* (Lond. 1879); A. E. Waite, *The Real History of the Rosicrucians* (Lond. 1887); Gieseler, *K.-G.* iii. 2, 437 ff.

[2] P. W. H. Hossbach, *Leben Spener's*, 1827; Wildenhahn, *Life of Spener*, tr. by G. A. Wenzel (Philadelphia, 1881).

as the preface to a volume of John Arndt's sermons (1675), was frequently reprinted with large additions. In this work he insisted most on the need of a new spirit in the clergy. Most clergymen, he said, regarded religion from a purely intellectual standpoint, and were content to defend their dogmas against opponents, without greatly caring about their own spiritual life, and consequently without awaking spiritual life in those who heard them. He earnestly desired that the education of candidates for the ministry should be directed not merely to making them accurate in dogma and dexterous in polemics, but to instilling into them real and heartfelt piety. Without true piety a man might be a philosopher in things divine, but not in the true sense a theologian. But it was not only for the ministerial office that piety was required; every member of a Christian community was bound, so far as in him lay, to help and edify the brethren. In the spirit of Luther, he insisted that all Christians are priests, although within the Church certain functions are reserved to those who are set apart to the sacred ministry. This work caused much excitement. The evils which it combated could not be denied, nor the need for some change. Many of the clergy adopted Spener's views and attempted to give effect to them. Prayer-meetings were introduced in many places, and generally gave great offence to the older theologians. Perhaps, as commonly happens, the new fervour may really have given rise to some disorder.

Spener at Dresden, 1686.

Meantime, Spener's reputation continued to rise, and in 1686 he was called to Dresden as principal Court-chaplain. Here he found a wider sphere of influence, but also more opposition, for he was now in the very focus of Lutheran orthodoxy. His first care was the improvement of the teaching in the Saxon universities. In Leipzig things had come to such a pass that the theological students attended lectures only on dogmatics, polemics, philosophy, and homiletics; no lectures on the exposition of Scripture had been given for several years. Spener procured a Government order that such lectures should be resumed—an order which was very distasteful to the existing professors. Three young Leipzigers however, one of whom was August Hermann Francke[1], began

Movement at Leipzig.

---

[1] Kramer, *August Hermann Francke* (1880-82).

to give lectures in German on certain books of the Bible, with a view not to learned exposition but to the furthering of spiritual religion. These meetings, which were attended not only by students but also by many townspeople, were very much disliked by the clergy of the place. It was thought that the true Christian doctrine was much maimed in them, while the rather gloomy aspect of some of the votaries and their abstinence from all amusements gave rise to ridicule. The name "Pietists," originally given in scorn, was in the end—like that of Methodists in England—adopted by the party to whom it was given. This feeling against them became so strong that in 1691 the three young masters had to leave Leipzig. Spener could do nothing for them, as his stern insistence on purity of life had by this time alienated the Elector. He consequently accepted in 1691 an invitation to Berlin.

<small>CH. IV.</small>

Meantime Christian Thomasius[1], the ablest defender of Spenerism in Leipzig, finding his position there intolerable, had left the place (1690) and removed to Berlin, whence he passed on to Halle, where at his instance a university was founded by the Elector of Brandenburg. The Elector was the more ready to take this step as most of the Brandenburg candidates for the ministry had hitherto been educated at Leipzig or Wittenberg, where they acquired a vehement prejudice against the "Reformed" or Calvinistic community. Better results might be hoped for from a theological faculty under Spener's influence. The chairs were accordingly filled by his nominees, among whom were Francke and Paul Anton, who had left Leipzig with him. Halle accordingly became the great stronghold of the Pietists, and the object of constant attacks from Leipzig and Wittenberg—attacks which were all the more bitter as the number of students resorting thither was considerably diminished by the new foundation.

<small>Christian Thomasius, 1655—1728.</small>

<small>University of Halle founded, 1694.</small>

Francke may be regarded as a second founder of Pietism. From the time when he was appointed professor in Halle his active spirit found occupation in ever-increasing work of beneficence. He was unwearied in preaching and in conducting meetings for spiritual edification, and also wrought upon great numbers of

<small>Francke's work. 1692.</small>

[1] *Life* by Wagner (1872), and Nicoladini (1887).

sympathetic souls by his religious publications. As a teacher of divinity he held fast the principle that Holy Scripture is the source of theology, and therefore gave much of his energy to promoting the study of the Bible. He also endeavoured to prepare the students for the pastoral work in which they were to pass their lives. Theology was to him only the fuller and ampler development of heartfelt Christianity, Christ was to him the end and aim of all religious teaching. And he was active in good works as well as in teaching. Schools for the poor and an orphanage were the enduring fruit of his zealous labours. He met with constant opposition in his philanthropic schemes, but his earnest faith carried him onward to final success.

It was scarcely to be expected that a school which insisted almost exclusively on practical experience in religion would produce great names in theoretic divinity, but it did produce in J. F. Buddeus one who gave to Lutheran doctrine a form better adapted to the wants of the age, and wrote the history of the Old Testament with great skill and learning; and in J. A. Bengel one who, though time has overthrown his interpretation of the Apocalypse, produced a comment on the New Testament which is even now unrivalled for its close adherence to the text and its admirable terseness of expression. He was also the first who attempted to separate the "families" of New Testament manuscripts.

Spener's movement divided the religious world of Germany into Pietists and Orthodox. The Pietists were however, or at least intended to be, perfectly orthodox, but they attached less importance to the Lutheran standards of orthodoxy than their opponents did. They held that only one who had been consciously converted and had come to know the blessedness of the knowledge of God in Christ could be a true teacher of Christian doctrine or a competent expositor of Holy Scripture. Many wondrous things, they believed, were hidden from eyes which had not been opened by the Spirit of God; and, possessed with this idea, they did no doubt unduly disparage the religious attainments of many who were true servants of Christ, but had never passed through the ecstatic crisis which they regarded as the entrance to the higher life. They insisted so strongly on the necessity of faith working by love that their opponents reproached them with teaching salvation by good works; and their strictness of life, involving abstinence from balls, theatres, banquets, and entertainments of all kinds, did not conciliate those who were without their circle. Moreover, the opinion held by Spener and many of his followers, that a time would come when, the Jews being converted and the Papacy overthrown, Christ would reign for a thousand years on earth, was offensive to the orthodox, as having been condemned by the greatest of the early teachers of the Church. While the older preachers made the teaching of orthodoxy and the refutation of gainsayers their principal end and aim, from Pietist pulpits there was heard little besides the sinfulness of man, the need of repentance, and the merits of Christ. That tares were mingled with the wheat in the field of Pietism, that some Pietists held extravagant opinions and that others were little better than hypocrites, seems to admit of no doubt; but also it cannot be doubted that they infused a new life into the Lutheran community at a time when the lamp of Christian life burned very low.

B. *The Moravian Brotherhood*[1].

In the troubles which followed on the work of John Huss in Bohemia, a number of devout men from among the Hussites formed themselves into a brotherhood, which took definite shape in 1467[2], with a view of living in absolute obedience to the precepts of Christ. Their principles led them to reject all distinction of rank, military service, and oaths. These levelling ideas were however a good deal modified about 1494 by Lucas of Prague, a leading man among them; and from this time their tenets spread, so that at the beginning of the sixteenth

Bohemian Brethren.

---

[1] D. Crantz, *History of the [Moravian] Brethren,* translated by La Trobe (London, 1780); J. Holmes, *Hist. of the United Brethren* (London, 1825), and *Missions of the United Brethren* (1827); A. Bost, *Hist. de l'Église des Frères de Bohême et de Moravie jusqu'à 1741* (Geneva 1831), translated into English; A. Gindely, *Geschichte der Böhmischen Brüder* (Prag, 1857); Gotl, *Quellen und Studien zur Geschichte der Brüder* (Prag, 1880).

[2] Hardwick's *Ch. Hist. Middle Age,* p. 410.

*century more than three hundred communities belonged to the Unity of Bohemian Brethren, as they were called. The Brethren had many alternations of persecution and repose, but in the early part of the seventeenth century were reduced to extremity. Then arose their last and greatest bishop, Amos Comenius[1], the great educational reformer. Driven from Bohemia with his flock in 1624, he settled in 1627 at Lissa in Poland, and when compelled to leave that place also (1654) he found refuge in Amsterdam, where he died. Comenius was more famous for his admirable educational work, in which he anticipated much that was afterwards taken up by Rousseau and Pestalozzi, than for theology; but in this field also he was distinguished; he was the most eloquent preacher, the best writer of books of edification, and the ablest ruler that arose in the community, which after his death (1670) seems to have fallen to pieces.

But there remained in Bohemia and Moravia scattered families who clung to the remembrance of the days gone by, and these at the beginning of the eighteenth century longed to renew the ancient unity. This longing was promoted by Christian David, a Moravian carpenter, who, born a Roman Catholic, had passed through Lutheranism to the desire for a closer and purer brotherhood. Such a brotherhood he found in Görlitz, the town of Behmen. From Görlitz he several times visited the scattered communities in Moravia, and as he found among them a strong desire to emigrate, he undertook to search for a suitable place for their settlement in some Lutheran country. This he found on the estate of the young Count von Zinzendorf, in Saxony.

Nicholas Lewis von Zinzendorf[2] was born in 1700 in Dresden, in a family much influenced by Spener, who was his godfather. At the age of ten he was placed in a school founded by Francke at Halle, where he shewed*

---

[1] The reputation of Comenius in matters of education was such that he was invited not only to England by the Parliament (1642), to Sweden, and to Transylvania, but even to America, to succeed Henry Dunster as President of Harvard College. See Laurie, *The Life and Educational Works of Comenius* (London, 1881).

[2] Lives of Zinzendorf by Spangenberg (1773–75); Varnhagen von Ense (1846); Burkhardt (1866); Bovet (in French, Paris, 1860, in English, as *The Banished Count*, London, 1865).

much promise, and where a deep and sincere love of Christ became the great motive power of his life. From 1716 to 1719 he studied law in Wittenberg, and then—like other young men of good family in those days—he entered on his "grand tour," a tour which was destined to have great influence on his life. On it he made the acquaintance of men who widened his range of thought, as that of the Jansenist Cardinal de Noailles and of many Calvinists with whom he found a heartfelt sympathy. This experience led him to believe that in all communities was found the love of the sinner for his Saviour, and that in comparison with this dogmatic differences were of small importance. In 1722 he married a wife like-minded with himself, gave up his legal practice in Dresden, and devoted himself to a religious life, especially to aiding the fugitive Bohemian and Moravian Brethren. In the same year two families, under the guidance of Christian David, settled on his estate of Berthelsdorf, where they were joined in the course of the next seven years by about three hundred Brethren. A settlement was formed called Herrnhut ("Lord's-guard"), to which were admitted not only Bohemian and Moravian refugees, but Protestants from various districts in Germany. Zinzendorf hoped that they would all recognize his own principle, that the bond of Christian union was not so much identity of dogma as a common love for Christ. But even as early as 1725 differences arose on the Eucharist, on Grace, and on Discipline. Zinzendorf was however able to calm the excited spirits; in May 1727 statutes were agreed upon for the regulation of the society, and in August of the same year for the first time the whole body of Herrnhuters received the Holy Communion together. Zinzendorf and his friend Wattewille were chosen the first presidents of the society. Their rules of discipline were for the most part drawn from the *Ratio Disciplinae* of Comenius.

From the time of the settlement at Herrnhut Zinzendorf was the ruler and inspirer of the community. He was a Lutheran of the school of Spener, and in 1736 the Herrnhuters joined the Lutheran Church of the country in which they found themselves. But this union by no means excluded diversities of opinion on dogma; the formation of different ways of teaching (τρόποι παιδείας) was expressly permitted. Unity in variety was to be the end and aim of the brotherhood, not the founding of a new sect drawn together by common opinions. They wished to stand apart from the confessions of faith which divided men, not to insist specially on any one. Hence they laid more stress on edification and social discipline than on dogmatic teaching. Every morning and evening they assembled for prayer. The community was divided into groups; there were "choirs" of unmarried men and unmarried women, of widows and widowers, of married persons; and there were again smaller bodies, called "bands," which admitted of greater intimacy among the members. When separate settlements were formed, each was ruled by a council of elders, while the government of the whole Unity of Brethren was in the hands of a conference of elders representing the several settlements. From time to time a synod was summoned by which the members of the council of elders were appointed. For the settlement of disputes between brethren a domestic tribunal was instituted. In continuation of an old custom of the Bohemian Brethren the judgment of God was sometimes sought by an appeal to the casting of lots. In doctrine the Augsburg Confession received a general approbation. Like the Bohemian Brethren the Moravians retained the names and offices of bishop, presbyter, and deacon. In 1735 David Nitschmann was consecrated bishop of the Moravian Church by Jablonski, with the assistance of Christian Sitkovius, these two being survivors of the old episcopal succession. In 1737 Zinzendorf became himself bishop.

The Moravian society was not long confined within the bounds of Herrnhut. Zinzendorf himself undertook several journeys as a missionary of Moravian principles, and was in many places successful. In Jena many students were attracted by his teaching. And besides propagating the opinions of the Brotherhood he gave to the Lutheran Church its first impulse to undertake missions to the heathen. In Copenhagen the effect of his visit was that in 1732 the first Moravian missionaries to the heathen set forth from that city. After 1736, when he received from the Saxon government a notice to quit the country, he could continue his work only in places beyond its jurisdiction. The rulers however of his own land soon adopted a more favourable attitude towards him. The Brotherhood gradually spread in Saxony, Prussia, Denmark, Baden, Switzerland, and Russia. In 1735 the Moravians began their work in North America, in 1738 in England, the latter mainly through the labours of Peter Boehler, who had great influence on the religious development of John Wesley.

The years from 1743—1750 were what the Moravians themselves have called a "time of sifting." Great extravagance was displayed, both in doctrine and worship. Hymns were sung to Jesus of a tasteless, sentimental, and even offensive kind; the wounds of the Saviour, especially the wound in the side, became the objects of all kinds of far-fetched imagery. At the same time, under the influence of Zinzendorf himself, a strange fantastic doctrine of the Holy Trinity was taught. It was to Christ alone that service and worship were due; God the Father was virtually deposed; even in the first petition of the Lord's Prayer it was to Christ alone that the mind was to be directed. And this change in doctrine and worship was accompanied by a transformation of the social life, the former simplicity giving place to comfort and even luxury. The society seemed coming to utter ruin, but the means taken to stay the evil were crowned with success. Meantime, however, the attention of the outer world had been called to the excesses of the Brethren, who in consequence lost ground for the time in public opinion. They were attacked by several distinguished theologians, among whom Bengel, the well-known commentator, is the most important. When Zinzendorf went so far as to declare that the Lutheran Church was irredeemably lost it is scarcely wonderful that Lutheran theologians resented it. But from the middle of the eighteenth century the Herrnhut Society purged itself from its former extravagances, Zinzendorf removing from the hymn-book even his own hymns when they sinned against soberness or good taste. He died in 1760, living still in the memories of those who had known him as a man of singularly impressive and commanding personality, devout, earnest, and warm-hearted, who gave his great endowments with a single mind to the furtherance of the Gospel of Christ.

Death of Zinzendorf, 1760.

He himself admitted that his natural disposition was ill-balanced, but with all his faults he did a great work. He stirred up the missionary spirit in Protestantism, and his society became a witness for real and heartfelt piety in the midst of rationalism and indifference. Many were trained in Moravian schools who did not belong to the Brotherhood, but became a leaven to the Church at large. This success was in a great measure due to Zinzendorf's successor, Spangenberg (d. 1792), who was more cautious and prudent than the Count, and brought the community to accept as their belief a moderate form of Lutheranism.

3. MYSTICS AND THEOSOPHISTS.

Those of whom we have just spoken accepted the Lutheran standards and the Lutheran discipline. Pastors who adopted Pietistic views differed not at all in their status from their so-called orthodox brethren, and the Moravians held themselves to be Lutherans. But there were some earnest advocates of inward religion who cannot well be classed with any recognized religious community. Such was Valentine Weigel[1], the beloved pastor of Zschoppau, in the diocese of Chemnitz. Quiet and reserved in his teaching and conversation he escaped attack, though not suspicion, during his lifetime, but after his death his writings came to be regarded as heretical. He taught that scholastic and formal theology contributed little or nothing to vital religion; every man, he held, contained within himself, by divine grace, all that was necessary for a saving knowledge of God. It was the microcosm, himself, which man should study; all knowledge was to be found in self-knowledge. Weigel's attractive mysticism found many followers. A greater mystic of the same school was Jacob Boehme, or Behmen[2], the famous shoemaker of Görlitz, who in an inarticulate manner anticipated the Hegelism

[1] Hilliger, *Fata et Scripta M. Val. Weigelii* (Wittenberg, 1721); J. O. Opel, *Val. Weigel* (Leipzig, 1864); A. Israel, *Val. Weigeli Leben u. Scriften* (Zschoppau, 1888).

[2] C. Hotham, *Ad Philosophiam Teutonicam* (Lond., 1648); D. Hotham, *Mysterium Magnum* (Lond., 1654); E. Taylor, *J. Boehme's Teutonic Philosophy* (Lond., 1691); J. Pordage, *Metaphysica Vera* (Lond., 1698); J. Hamberger, *Die Lehre des Deutschen Philosophen J. Boehme* (Munich, 1844); H. Martensen, *J. Boehme* (Copenh., 1882; in German, Leipz., 1882).

of our own time. Interesting as are his philosophical theories, his theology is of more immediate importance in Church history. He too, like Weigel, set little store by the external institutions of Christianity. Humble as he was, he pronounced sharp sentence on what he thought mere formalism; the various sects were but children of the great Harlot of the Apocalypse, and must be put an end to—a consummation which he hoped to bring nearer by his own writings. Priests, who were but the elders of the community, were to be honoured so far forth as they ruled with love and gentleness, dealing with the lay-people as with children, but not as introducers of theological subtleties which were unprofitable and vain. But the central conception of his theology was that a divine and perfect universe underlies the gross and imperfect creation which we see and handle. This divine universe was visible to unfallen man in a paradisaical glory, but when he fell he saw the outward world, as he saw his own body, destitute of that original glory, with only such light as the material sun can cast upon it. At the same time the image of the Holy Trinity in Unity, which was within him, was marred and obscured. He came, like the beasts, under the elemental influences of matter. Each man carries with him his own hell, the devouring flame of his own passions and lusts. And as this is within us, our Redeemer or Regenerator must also be within us. The promised Seed of the woman, the Eternal Word, the Son of God made man, must kill this life of the serpent in us. The Trinity in the soul of man must be restored; the Son must again be born in us; the Spirit, proceeding from the Father and the Son, must again sanctify us. So may we be rescued from our disordered condition and born again to our first state of inward peace and love. Only by faith in the Son of God can we attain this; we can of our own selves do nothing; but saving faith is faith in the Son within us, not in a mere distant Christ whom we know only by the hearing of the ear.

Behmen's teaching, in spite of the uncouth ·form in which it was presented, found many followers in Germany, especially in Silesia, where a considerable body of "Silesian mystics" arose, mostly good, quiet laymen, indifferent to ecclesiastical forms, shrinking from the coldness of everyday Christianity, from politics and from public office, studying the older mystics as well as the works of Behmen himself, delighting in mystical hymnody and in the society of men like-minded. And these men propagated Behmen's leading thoughts so that they influenced many who were unconscious of the source of the teaching which moved them. In England many followers of Behmen have been found from the middle of the seventeenth century to the present day. Several of his works were translated into English; Charles Hotham expounded the "Teutonic Philosophy" in the school at Cambridge, and Henry More approved[1]. Jane Leade (1623—1704), the founder of the sect of Philadelphians, was deeply influenced by it. But by far the most important convert to Behmenism in England was William Law, the well-known author of the *Serious Call*. He not only prepared a complete edition of Behmen's works (published 1764), but expounded his views in a series of tracts[2] the clear and lively style of which is a great contrast to the obscurity and prolixity of Behmen himself and most of his followers. In England Behmen's theology, apart from his bewildered views on physical science, has had a considerable influence beyond the ranks of those who called themselves his disciples.

A very different man from Behmen, though like him earnestly recommending "inwardness" in religion, was Heinrich Müller[3], of Rostock, who inveighed against the four dumb idols, the font, the pulpit, the confessional, and the altar, which were to him simply marks of a worthless "outward" Christianity.

The author of a peculiar mysticism was Emmanuel Swedenborg, or Swedberg[4], who was born at Stockholm in

---

[1] See the list of English works on Behmenism, p. 132, n. 2.
[2] E.g. *The Spirit of Prayer*, 1749; *The Way to Divine Knowledge* and *The Spirit of Love*, 1752. Law's *Life* has been written by R. Tighe (1813) and J. H. Overton (1881).
[3] Herzog, *Kirchen-Geschichte*, ii. 290.
[4] J. J. Garth Wilkinson, *Emm. Swedenborg, a Biography* (London, 1849); William White, *Swedenborg, his Life and Writings* (London, 1856); R. L. Tafel, *Documents Concerning the Life and Writings of Em. Swedenborg* (London, 1875—77); B. Worcester, *The Life and Mission of Emm. Swedenborg* (Boston, U.S.A., 1883). A Society formed in London in 1820 for the printing and publishing of Swedenborg's works has diffused the knowledge of his opinions.

1688. His father was a distinguished Swedish clergyman who became Bishop of Skara. Emmanuel says of himself that even before he was twelve years old he delighted in conversing with clergymen about faith, insisting that the life of faith is love to our neighbour, and that God gives faith to everyone, though those only profit by it who practise love. In spite, however, of this early predilection the earlier portion of his life was passed as a member of the staff of the School of Mines, in which capacity he distinguished himself and produced many scientific works of practical utility. He was more than fifty years of age when he received, as he believed, a special revelation. To use his own words, "I was called to a holy office by the Lord Himself, Who most mercifully appeared before me His servant in the year 1743, when he opened my sight towards the spiritual world and enabled me to converse with spirits and angels; in which state I have continued to the present day. From that time I began to print and publish the various arcana that were seen by me, or revealed to me, concerning heaven and hell, the state of man after death, the true worship of God, the spiritual sense of the Word, and many other important matters conducive to salvation and wisdom." He did in fact from the date mentioned pour forth a long series of voluminous works. It was revealed to him that the Church founded by the coming of the Lord in the flesh came to an end in the eighteenth century, and in 1757 he witnessed its Last Judgment in the world of spirits. Then began a new dispensation, the New Jerusalem, of which Swedenborg was the precursor and his works the doctrine.

His Call, 1743.

Like most of the ancient fathers, Swedenborg found a spiritual sense underlying the literal sense of Scripture, with the exception of certain books, as the Acts and Epistles, which are good and edifying but have no inner sense. The real inner spiritual sense was revealed to the new prophet. But it is not in Scripture alone that the divine is concealed under the earthly; nature also is the product and the veil of the spiritual world. Inner evil is manifested in things hurtful and ugly, inner good in things useful and beautiful. All existence depends immediately upon God, so that if anything lost its connexion with Him it would instantly cease to be. The

Interpretation of Scripture.

"Correspondences" of visible and invisible.

good man is always in heaven, the bad man always in hell; it is only this mortal vesture of decay which prevents him from seeing his spiritual companions. When the veil of flesh is removed those who love God and man become conscious that they are in heaven, and the bad that they are in hell. There are three heavens and three orders of angels, those of love, of wisdom, and of obedience, all of whom began their existence as men. There are also three hells. There may be after death a short sojourn in the "world of spirits," where the good are healed of their infirmities and errors, and the evil are stripped of their seeming good. In theology proper Swedenborg seems to make no distinction between the Father and the Son; Christ is the one God and the only object of worship; from Him proceeds the Holy Spirit.

Swedenborg made no attempt to establish a sect, though he seems to have expected that from his teaching a new Church would rise to take the place of the obsolete Christian Church. It was in London that his *Arcana Cœlestia* (in Latin, like all his works) was published (1749—1756), and it was in London that Robert Hindmarsh (in 1788) first formed a separate sect or body of Swedenborgians under the title of "the New Church signified by the New Jerusalem in the Revelation." An active diffuser of Swedenborg's principles was John Clowes, Rector of St John's, Manchester, from 1769—1831, who translated the *Arcana Cœlestia* and many other of his works. There are many avowed Swedenborgians in England and America, and many—including several English clergymen—have accepted this teaching without joining their society. On the Continent Swedenborgians are few and scattered.

The same tendency to mysticism which in men like Jacob Böhme kindled a pure flame, gave rise when it encountered unstable or impure spirits to earthly fires. No impurity, but rather disordered reason, is to be attributed to Quirinus Kuhlmann[1], a follower of Böhme, "a poet who became himself a poem." He traversed the world full of eager desire to overthrow the modern Babylon, Rome, to establish the kingdom of Messiah, and to

---

[1] Schröckh's *Neuere K.-G.*, viii. 399; ix. 224.

make the princes of this world subject to Him. In Moscow he presented to the Patriarch a written account of his wild fancies, and in consequence was burnt at the stake. John George Gichtel[1], also a disciple of Böhme, originally a lawyer in Ratisbon, gave up his business and gathered round him a party of those likeminded in Holland. His aim was to found a priesthood after the order of Melchisedek, who like the angels should not marry, but should devote their lives wholly to prayer, so to avert the wrath of God from the world lying in sin. His disciples, under the name of "Angel-brethren," still existed in Holland and Germany some generations after the founder's death. Daniel Müller[2] looked upon Scripture as allegory, and the sacred books of all religions as alike Divine. He regarded himself as called to deliver men from the yoke of the letter, and traversed North Germany proclaiming the downfall of the outward and visible Church. Although he died in the belief that God had deceived him, his followers, who rejected the historical Christ, and believed that Müller would return to found His kingdom on earth, maintained their ground for some time after his death. The sect of "Hebrews," founded at Leyden about 1720 by one Verschooren[3], held that it was the duty of all Christians to read the Scriptures in the original tongues, and that the merits of Christ literally cleansed believers from all sin.

In troubled times the Counts of Witgenstein gave refuge in their little territory in the Wetterau to men of every faith or no faith on the simple condition that the settlers should lead decent lives and obey the civil authorities. Socinians and enthusiasts jostled each other in this strange community. It was this society which produced the Bible of Berleburg, a translation with annotations and extracts full of a theosophic mysticism appended to the text, which obtained a wide circulation. It was here that Hochmann[4], an uncalled preacher of repentance, whose pious heterodoxies brought him into

---

[1] Lipsius in Ersch u. Gruber's *Encyclop.*, vol. 66, *s.v. Gichtel*; C. G. A. Harless, *Life* of J. G. G. appended to his *Jacob Böhme* (2nd ed., 1882).

[2] Hase, *K.-G.* III. ii. 110.

[3] Schröckh's *Neuere K.-G.* viii. 730.

[4] C. W. F. Walch, *Religions-Streitigkeiten*, ii. 776 ff.; Hagenbach in Herzog's *Real-Encyc.* vi. 163.

trouble and sometimes into prison, found rest from outward annoyance. The Philadelphian Society, also, which took its rise from an English disciple of Böhme, Jane Leade, found adherents in Berleburg. And the "Instruments of the Holy Ghost[1]," believers in their own inspiration of the convulsionary kind, who had appeared in various parts of Germany, displayed their gifts here also. One of them, John Frederick Rock, though himself a convulsionary, had sufficient wisdom to attempt to moderate the extravagant displays of his brethren.

One of the most extraordinary products of emotional religion set free from the restraints of reason and morality was the "Buttler Gang." Eva von Buttler[2] or Buttlar with two of her lovers formed, under pretence of piety, an extraordinary society in Eisenach, and when driven thence by public feeling and ecclesiastical censure, transferred themselves to the Witgenstein territory. The three impostors sometimes gave themselves out to be Joseph, Mary, and Jesus; sometimes even to be the Holy Trinity itself. They found adherents, with whom it seems certain that they practised the grossest immorality. Their conduct was too bad for even the wide toleration of Witgenstein; the civil power interfered, and they had to leave the territory with the loss of the property which they had acquired. They fled to Paderborn, where the bishop caused them to be imprisoned. Nothing further is known of them after their release; they simply vanish from history.

The Ronsdorf sect, too, is a monstrous birth of Pietism. Elias Eller[3], a ribbon-weaver at Elberfeld, gave out to a circle of adherents that a certain girl, Anna, whom he seduced and afterwards married, was to be the mother of the Messiah, the apocalyptic woman clothed with the sun. When Elberfeld grew too hot to hold them Eller declared that town to be Babylon, and removed to Ronsdorf, then consisting of a few farmsteads, there to found the new Zion. There he built factories and shewed great power of organization; there the Elector Palatine granted

---

[1] M. Goebel in Herzog's *Real-Encyc.* vi. 700 ff.
[2] Goebel, *u.s.*, ii. 475 ff.
[3] J. A. Engels, *Gesch. d. religio-sen Schwärmerei im Herzogthum Berg* (Schwelm, 1826); G. H. Klippel in Herzog-Plitt, *s.v. Eller.*

a legal status to his colony, and permitted him to build a church and appoint a preacher. The preacher appointed was Daniel Schleiermacher, grandfather of the well-known theologian and philosopher, Frederick Schleiermacher. Mother Anna, strange to say, though her only man-child lived but a year, retained the respect of the community to the end of her days. Eller survived her seven years, and then the apocalyptic expectations began to fade and gradually died out.

Of a very different type was the sect which arose in Bruggeln[1] in canton Bern, which, if it began with delusion, continued with fraud. Here the brothers Kohler, whom in early days their parents had instructed to claim a power of divination, gave themselves out to be the two witnesses of the Apocalypse[2], and predicted the day of Christ's second coming, which however was deferred by their intercessory prayers. They slandered the Church, lived in debauchery on the alms of their followers, and seduced the females among them. Jerome Kohler at last, accused of blasphemy and child-murder, was hanged, to the astonishment of his adherents, who believed that death could not touch him, and who even after his execution believed that he gave spiritual signs of his presence with them. So tenacious of life is sensual superstition.

4. LITERARY ACTIVITY OF THE REFORMED.

The theological literature of the Reformed, or Calvinistic, Churches does not suffer by comparison with that of the Lutherans[3]. They produced indeed, in our period, no treatise of the first rank on dogmatic theology. Calvin's *Institutio* is, from his point of view, so clear, so complete, so logical, that nothing better could be desired. It long held its own as the great text-book, the almost infallible guide, wherever Reformed congregations were found. But

---

[1] *Das Entdeckte Geheimniss d. Bosheit in d. Brüggler-Secte* (Zurich, 1753); *Acta Historica Ecclesiæ*, vol. 17, pp. 906, 1031.
[2] xi. 3.
[3] J. Basnage, *Hist. de la Religion des Églises Reformées* (Rotterdam, 1725). Maimbourg's very prejudiced *Hist. du Calvinisme* (1682) was sharply criticised by Bayle, *Critique de l'Hist....de Maimbourg* (1683). In the early part of the seventeenth century the word "Reformed" was applied to the communities derived from Zwingli and Calvin, while the Lutherans were "Evangelical" or "Protestant."

on the other hand, they produced the most valuable contributions to Biblical criticism, exegesis and archæology. Even from the first the method of Scripture interpretation followed by Zwingli, Œcolampadius, Bucer, Calvin, and Beza was far more natural, more dependent on grammatical and historical considerations than that of their contemporaries. But it was in the study of the Oriental languages and their application to Biblical exegesis that the Calvinistic theologians were especially distinguished. Among these may be mentioned especially Thomas Erpenius (van Erpe)[1] and James Golius, both professors in Leyden; Samuel Bochart, minister of the Reformed congregation in Caen; and J. H. Hottinger, professor in Zürich. Here, too, may be mentioned Vitringa of Franeker, the famous investigator of the ancient history of the synagogue and commentator on Isaiah. The extraordinary family of the Buxtorfs did much to promote the study of Hebrew and Chaldee, though they were still so far under the influence of a worthless tradition as to contend for the primitive antiquity of the Hebrew vowel-points. Here they encountered a formidable opponent in Lewis Cappel[2], a professor at Saumur, who not only contended that the vowel-points were an invention of the seventh century after Christ, but ventured to doubt whether the current Masoretic text of the Hebrew Bible was absolutely pure from all corruption. In France also the family of Basnage supplied three famous names. Benjamin, the elder, though known rather as a practical teacher than a theologian, wrote an esteemed treatise on the Church; his grandson Samuel wrote against Baronius treatises distinguished by learning, acuteness, and literary merit; his relative James, driven from France by the Revocation of the Edict of Nantes, settled in Holland, where he was treated with great respect. His works are chiefly intended to shew the erroneousness of Bossuet's view of Church history. David Blondel, in a learned and able work, shewed decisively, against the Jesuit Torriano, the real character of the Pseudo-Isidorian Decretals; and when Du Perron wrote against King James I. of England a work in which he sought to prove

---

[1] P. Scriverius, *Manes Erpeniani* (Leyden, 1626).
[2] G. Schnedermann, *Die Controversie d. L. Capellus mit den Buxtorfen* (Leipzig, 1879).

the absolute supremacy of the Pope, he wrote in refutation of it a work on the authority of the Church the merit of which was generally recognised. He carefully examined and criticised the Sibylline books, which had been, he believed, a source of error in the Church. It is noteworthy that, following Jerome, he held that in primitive times the words "bishop" and "presbyter" were synonymous. Samuel Bochart, who was for a time entertained at the court of Queen Christina of Sweden, distinguished himself by his researches in sacred geography and in the natural history of the animals mentioned in Scripture. Bochart's learning in these subjects has probably not been surpassed, though the investigations of scientific naturalists have no doubt invalidated some of his statements.

A great man who entered the field of theology without being distinctively a theologian was the famous jurist, Hugo Grotius[1]. Master of the learning of his age, almost the founder of that system of international law which has done so much to facilitate the intercourse of nations, he brought to the consideration of theological problems a clear, cultivated, and well-balanced intellect, and a judgment practised and mature. His commentary on the Scriptures has been said to be written by a layman for laymen. It is brief and pointed, passing over dogmatic considerations in silence, and explaining the text in a style which had hitherto been applied to the Greek and Roman classics rather than to the sacred books. In this respect it is epoch-making. His manner of dealing with the Messianic prophecies without much regard to the common tradition brought upon him the suspicion of Socinianism, though in fact his theory of Satisfaction, if somewhat hard and juristic, is far removed from that of Socinus and his followers. As Grotius generally rejected the mystic or allegoric sense, he was said to find Christ nowhere in the Old Testament. Cocceius (John Kock)[2] found Him everywhere. Everywhere he finds behind the literal and historical meaning of the text a symbolical one of far deeper import. In every part of the Old Testa-

---

[1] Lévesque de Burigny, *Life of Grotius* (from the French, London, 1754); C. Butler, *Life of H. G.* (London, 1826).

[2] M. Leydecker, *Synopsis Controv. de Fœdere*, etc. (Utrecht, 1690); A. Ritschl, *Gesch. des Pietismus*, I. 101 ff.

142   *The Arminians*

Сн. IV.

Voet, 1589—1677.

Limborch, 1633—1712.

Clericus, 1657—1736.

Wetstein, 1693—1754.

ment he discovers a type of Christ or a foreshadowing of the fortunes of His kingdom. In his theology he gave so great prominence to the covenants which God has made with man that it came to be called federal theology. In spite of the eager opposition of Gisbert Voet, in his day leader of the party in the Netherlands which adhered to the views of Calvin, this school took root and grew, and trained some of the greatest of the Dutch divines, as the well-known writer on the Divine economy, Hermann Witsius, and the excellent commentators, Vitringa, Lampe, and Venema.

Among the disciples of Grotius we may reckon Philip van Limborch, the first among the Reformed who produced a system of dogmatic theology on principles not in harmony with Calvin's; and Jean le Clerc, who ranged over almost all fields of literature, and is a not unworthy successor of Grotius in the literal and historical exposition of Scripture. Here too we may reckon J. G. Wetstein, who, driven from Basel by the storm which was raised against him mainly because his research into the evidence for the text of the New Testament led him to prefer the reading ὅς to θεός in 1 Tim. iii. 16, took refuge in Holland, where he ultimately became Le Clerc's successor in his professorship. Wetstein's Greek Testament gives not only a large collection of various readings, but also numerous quotations of parallel passages from the classics, the fathers, and the rabbis, which have been constantly drawn upon by commentators ever since.

5. THE ARMINIANS.

United Provinces, 1579.

In 1579 the seven northern Provinces of the Netherlands formed themselves into a Confederation by the instrument known as the Utrecht Union, and after a long and gallant struggle compelled exhausted Spain to recognize them as an independent Power[1]. Scarcely had the young republic rested from outward enemies when it was torn by the quarrels of theologians.

Various streams of doctrine flowed into the Netherlands, derived from Erasmus, from Melancthon, and from Calvin; but the doctrines of the latter had received a sort

---

[1] J. L. Motley, *The Rise of the Dutch Republic.*

of sanction in the "Belgic Confession," which was generally accepted in the United Provinces[1]. It was not long, however, before it met with vigorous opponents. James van Harmin (Arminius)[2], who became in 1603 Professor of Theology in Leyden, found himself after long and earnest study unable to accept the rigid theories of unconditional Election and Reprobation which were held by the followers of Calvin. As his colleague, Francis Gomarus, vigorously defended the views of the Calvinists, "Arminians" and "Gomarists" soon spread themselves over the Republic[3]. On Arminius's death in 1609 Simon Episcopius[4] succeeded both to his professorship and to the guidance of the more liberal party; and in 1610 the Arminians presented to the Provinces of Holland and West-Friesland a declaration of their opinions in the shape of a "Remonstrance," whence they acquired the party-name of "Remonstrants." The distinctive tenets of Calvinism were summed up in five propositions: (1) God by an absolute decree has elected to salvation a very small number of men, without any regard to their faith or obedience; (2) Christ suffered death for these elect only; (3) By Adam's fall his posterity lost their free-will, so that whatever they do is done by an unavoidable necessity; (4) God, to save His elect, begets faith in them in such a way that they who have this grace cannot reject it, and the rest, being reprobate, cannot accept it; (5) Such as have once received that grace can never fall from it finally or totally, whatever sins they may commit[5]. To these the Remonstrants opposed the following: (1) God by an unchangeable decree ordained to save all those in Christ who by the assistance of the Holy Ghost persevere in faith and obedience to the very end; (2) Christ suffered death for all men, but with this condition, that none but true believers should have the benefit of the remission of sins; (3) Man cannot attain

Сн. IV.

Arminius, 1560—1609.

Gomarus.

Episcopius.

Remonstrants.

Five Articles, Calvinistic.

Arminian, 1610.

[1] Hardwick, *Reformation*, 148; in Niemeyer's *Collectio*, p. 360.
[2] Gerard Brandt, *Hist. of the Reformation in the Low Countries*, trans. by J. Chamberlayne (Lond. 1720–23); *Hist. Vitæ Arminii*, ed. Mosheim (Brunswick, 1725).
[3] Gieseler, III. ii. 333 ff.
[4] *Life*, by Limborch (Amsterdam, 1701); *Life and Death of J. Arminius and S. Episcopius* (London, 1672); Hartsoeker and Limborch, *Epistolæ Præstantium Virorum* (Amsterdam, 1660).
[5] P. Heylin, *Quinquarticular Hist.* in *Tracts*, p. 523 (London, 1681).

saving faith by the mere force of his own will, but must be regenerated and renewed by the working of the Holy Spirit; (4) The regenerate man can do no good thing without this grace preceding, stirring up, following, and co-operating; but it is not irresistible; (5) Those who have been grafted into Christ by faith have, by His grace, strength to resist the world, the flesh, and the devil, if they will avail themselves of it; but it is a matter to be anxiously weighed, in the light of Scripture, whether they may not fall from grace, and embrace again this present world. From these Five Articles[1] the controversy was often called "Quinquarticular."

In vain the civil power in the United Provinces endeavoured to secure toleration for Arminian teachers. The extreme Calvinists of course resented equally the interference of the State and the toleration of those opposed to them in doctrine. The quarrels of Remonstrants and Contraremonstrants agitated the whole republic, and became the more bitter because political was added to theological rancour; for while the republican leaders, the venerable Oldenbarneveld and the theologian and statesman Grotius, took the part of the Remonstrants, the Stadtholder, Maurice, Prince of Orange, who was thought to be aiming at the sovereignty, sided with the more numerous and popular Calvinists. To put an end to the controversy, the States General convoked a synod. The States of Holland, in a letter to King James[2], pointed out very clearly the inexpediency and futility of the course which it was proposed to pursue. "Is it to be expected," they ask his Majesty to consider, "that in those controversies in which the ancient fathers openly differ from each other, in which there is no agreement among the Reformers, nor even among the adherents of the Papacy, the ingenuity of our age can effect what hitherto no age has brought about? Is it to be expected that controversies which pervade all Churches can be settled by a synod of the United Provinces? How utterly did the Formula Concordiæ fail in Germany!" All the Reformed Churches, except Anhalt, were invited to send delegates. These foreigners, however, among whom one

---

[1] Heylin, *u. s.* 527; Gieseler, III. ii. 335, n. 11.

[2] In Gieseler, III. ii. 337, n. 14. This is of course Holland the province.

Scotch and four English commissioners attended by desire of King James, were but few in comparison with the numbers of the Netherlanders[1]. Before the assembling of the Synod a *coup d'état* of the Prince of Orange cast Oldenbarneveld and Grotius into prison, and disconcerted the Remonstrant party. Scarcely any but Calvinists were returned as deputies, and the fate of the Remonstrants was decided beforehand. The Synod met at Dordrecht, or Dort, on November 13, 1618, and sat until the end of May in the following year[2]. The Remonstrants, presenting themselves as to a conference[3], were introduced only as culprits to the assembly, and in spite of the vigour and eloquence with which Episcopius pleaded their cause, and contrary to the wishes of most of the foreign delegates, were declared incapable of any clerical or academical function until they should recant and return to the communion of the Church. In most of the provinces the Remonstrant preachers and professors, unless they consented to renounce all interference in Church matters, were banished the land[4]. On the death of Prince Maurice (1625), however, the republican party again rose to power, the Arminians were tolerated, and became a very learned and influential society.

Oldenbarneveld and Grotius imprisoned, Aug. 1618. Synod of Dort, 1618.

During the time of the exile of the Arminian ministers many of their flock, deprived of their accustomed teachers, formed prayer-meetings, "collegia," whence they received the name of "Collegiants." They rejected the separate order of ministers, and, while carefully enforcing the strictest morality, seem to have been nearly indifferent about forms of doctrine. In spite of differences among its members this society maintained itself until the beginning of the 19th century[5].

Collegiants, c. 1620.

[1] The list of those who signed the Canons in Niemeyer's *Collectio*, p. 700. The French Protestants were prevented by Louis XIII. from sending deputies. Gieseler, III. ii. 339, n. 17.
[2] The *Acta Synodi Nationalis Dortrechti habitæ*, and also the *Acta et Scripta Synodalia Dordracena Ministrorum Remonstrantium*, were published in 1620. The most graphic account of the Synod is in the letters of John Hales and Walter Balcanqual, Dean of Rochester, 1624, appended to Hales's *Golden Remains* (London, 1659). Canons of Dort in Niemeyer, 690 ff., and in the *Sylloge Confessionum* (Oxon.).
[3] Hales, Letter of Nov. 6, 1618, p. 24.
[4] *Sententia Synodi de Remonstrantibus*, in Niemeyer, 724 ff.; Gieseler, III. ii. 342, n. 21.
[5] Gieseler, III. ii. 345; Hase, *K.-G.* III. i. 293.

Amyrault (1596—1664) on Predestination, 1634.

In the Remonstrant contest, though its real grounds lay far deeper, the main issue had been joined on the question whether God predestinates a certain number absolutely to life eternal, or a certain number whose faith He foresees (*ex fide prævisâ*); the latter being held by the Arminians. The decisions of the Synod of Dort, though rejected by several Reformed Churches[1], became elsewhere a sort of standard of Calvinistic orthodoxy; but the moral sense of man inevitably revolted against the hard dogmas of the sterner predestinarians. In 1634, Moses Amyrault, Professor at Saumur, ventured to maintain a theory on the subject of Grace, derived from the teaching of his predecessor, Cameron[2]. This theory, known as Hypothetic Universalism, taught that God had decreed to save all men through Jesus Christ *hypothetically*, on the condition of their believing; to produce this faith in man, resistible grace was given to all, irresistible grace only to the elect. This seems but a futile attempt at reconciling opposing systems. Yet the opinion which Amyrault held, that even heathens might be saved by an implicit faith in the Christ not yet revealed to them in the flesh, shewed a far broader view of the extent of God's grace than had yet appeared in the Reformed Church. These doctrines were held to be allowable by the French Protestants in the Synods of Alençon and Charenton, but they long furnished matter for theological disputes; Blondel, Daillé, and Claude defending them, while other eminent men, as Dumoulin and Spanheim, attacked them with equal vigour and learning[3].

Synods of Alençon, 1637, and Charenton, 1644.

De la Place, 1596—1655.

The same Synods which admitted the views of Amyrault condemned those of his colleague De la Place (Placæus), who controverted the received opinions on Original Sin, maintaining that the sin of Adam was not imputed, except in case of actual sin[4]. Somewhat later, another Professor of Saumur, Claude Paion, raised another controversy, by maintaining that God's grace wrought mediately, through the motives and events of human life

Paion, 1626—1685.

---

[1] Gieseler, III. ii. 347.
[2] Schröckh, v. 352; De Félice, *Hist. des Protestants de France*, p. 347 ff.; C. E. Saigey, *Moïse Amyrault* (Strassburg, 1849).
[3] Gieseler, *u. s.* 350, nn. 9 and 10. De Félice, *u. s.* 347.
[4] Schröckh, v. 360; De Félice, 349. De la Place was one of the principal contributors to the once-famous *Theses Theologicæ* of Saumur.

The Arminians

and the threats and promises of the Word of God[1]. This was condemned by several Synods, which asserted the immediate as well as the mediate influence of the Holy Spirit.

Ch. IV.

These movements in theology occasioned the drawing up of a new formula of orthodoxy—the last of this kind—for the acceptance of the Swiss Churches[2], in which the new views as to the vowel-points, the investigations of those who held the Septuagint and other ancient versions to be co-ordinate authorities with the Masoretic Hebrew, and the doctrines of Amyrault and Paion on grace, were alike condemned.

Helvetic Consensus, 1675.

But the change which came over theology in the seventeenth century was deeper and more fundamental than appears in the discussion of particular points, even of matters so important as the relation of Divine grace to the human will. In the period between the Synod of Dort and the English Revolution a new mode of thought appeared which it is not easy briefly to describe. In England the school of Bancroft and Laud began to pale before that of Tillotson and Burnet; and a similar change also passed over continental theology. Up to the middle of the seventeenth century scholastic methods generally prevailed; dogmatic expression was hardened, and theologians followed their calling with an acuteness which a chancery barrister might envy. But after this time a great change, in harmony with a parallel movement in philosophy, came over theology. It began to be doubted whether the propositions over which divines fought with such eager acrimony were, after all, of the essence of Christianity. Moral considerations, drawn from the nature of man and of human society, began to assume a far greater prominence. Principles were drawn more directly from Scripture, less from systems and the traditions of the schools; and sometimes men of learning slid into indifference, and doubted whether in the endless war of sects truth were discoverable at all. The old weapons of controversy were dropped, and the combatants were perplexed to find themselves assailed from unexpected quarters and with unaccustomed arms. Arminianism

Real significance of Arminianism.

[1] Schröckh, VIII. 722.
[2] *Formula consensus Eccl. Helvet.* *Reformatorum*, in Niemeyer's *Collectio*, p. 729.

developed the humanism which had probably long been latent in the country of Erasmus. It was the moral side of Christianity on which it especially insisted. It aimed at abolishing or very much abbreviating the Articles of Faith and Systems of Doctrine in which the age of the Reformation was so extremely fertile. The excessive formulating of belief which prevailed in that age was seen to be an evil, and it seemed a more excellent way to limit the statement of the Christian Faith to a simple formula, such as the Apostles' Creed, which might be proved from Scripture. On abstract points, especially on the insoluble antinomies of fate and free-will, members of the same communion might differ without separating. The Arminians were in fact the apostles of toleration; they did not, like the Calvinists, attempt to annihilate their adversaries, nor did they, like them, attempt to shake off every shadow of State control. The result of their teaching was that for more than a generation Holland became the great refuge of men—especially of Frenchmen—who held opinions obnoxious to the dominant party in their own country.

6. PROJECTS FOR RELIGIOUS UNITY.

In the midst of controversy there are generally to be found men, more thoughtful than combative, who ask whether the battles which go on around them are not waged on mistaken issues and destined to lead to no good end[1]. Arminius himself, a man of gentle and amiable character, grieved over the divisions of his time, and would fain have persuaded men that all the points under discussion were not of equal importance[2]. Episcopius too, though he himself drew up a Confession of Faith, still contended that such documents were not to be regarded as standards of orthodoxy, and exalted the practical far above the speculative aspect of theology[3]. And in after-time there were not wanting excellent men who attempted to reconcile Roman Catholics with Protestants and

---

[1] C. W. Hering, *Gesch. d. Kirchl. Unionsversuche seit der Reformation* (Leipzig, 1836); C. G. Neudecker, *Die Hauptversuche zur Pacification der Evangel.-Protest. Kirche Deutschlands* (Ib. 1846).
[2] Gieseler, *K.-G.* III. ii. 334.
[3] Ibid, 344.

Lutherans with Calvinists. Among these reconcilers a conspicuous place is occupied by George Calixtus[1]. Born in 1586, he enlarged his knowledge of the various forms of religion by travels in England, France, and the Netherlands, and became Professor in 1605 at Helmstadt, where for many years he exercised a dominant influence, and became a confidential adviser of the Dukes of Brunswick. Full of admiration for primitive Christianity, he thought that the controversies of his own time were generally on points which it was not necessary to decide categorically; they were not of the essence of the faith. A man might be ignorant of all the modern Confessions of Faith, and yet be in the way of salvation if he sincerely believed all the articles of the Apostles' Creed. He distinguished primary or fundamental articles of faith from secondary or theological propositions. The Roman Catholics he would fain persuade to give up every article of belief which was not founded on Scripture and authorised by the Church of the first five centuries. So broad a theory in an age utterly unprepared for it naturally brought upon him condemnation from all quarters; Roman Catholics and Protestants alike attacked him. The former recognized in him a very keen critic of their modern corruptions, while the latter regarded him as at heart a Romanist. His system received the name of Syncretism, a name derived from a union of the warring parties in Crete against a common enemy[2]. A number of Roman Catholic and Protestant divines were invited by the King of Poland to meet in friendly conference at Thorn (1645), in the hope that better acquaintance might mitigate differences and increase agreement. Representatives of both the Lutheran and Calvinistic communities attended. The Calvinists proposed to the Lutherans to sink their differences in presence of a common foe, but the Lutherans of that time were too bitterly opposed to their rivals to consent to even a temporary truce. At the desire of the "Great Elector," Frederick William of Brandenburg,

Calixtus, 1586—1656.

---

[1] H. Schmid, *Geschichte der Synkretistischen Streitigkeiten* (Erlangen, 1846); E. L. T. Henke, *Georg Calixtus u. seine Zeit* (Halle, 1853); W. Gass, *Calixtus u. der Synkretismus* (Breslau, 1846); W. C. Dowding, *Life and Correspondence of G. Calixtus* (Oxf. 1863).

[2] See Plutarch, *De Fraterno Amore*, 490 B.

Calixtus presented himself at the Conference as a mediating influence between the parties. The uncompromising Lutherans, headed by Abraham Calovius, were by no means pleased with the arrival of Calixtus, whom they regarded as no true Lutheran, and his friendly attitude towards the Calvinistic theologians increased their suspicion. The Conference soon broke up, with no result except that of having increased the bitterness between the two Protestant parties. The Lutherans attacked Calixtus, whom they regarded as a traitor, with especial violence.

From this time began a Sycretistic controversy which lasted several years, in which Calovius, who in 1650 became Professor in Wittenberg, bore a leading part. He was unquestionably a man of great dialectic ability, and his "System" is one of the most remarkable works of the seventeenth century; but he was dominated by a burning zeal for Lutheran orthodoxy which occasioned outbreaks of unpardonable bitterness against all who deviated by a hair's-breadth from it. The theologians of Electoral Saxony even adopted as a standard of orthodoxy a document drawn up by him, the "Consensus Repetitus Fidei vere Lutheranæ," with the special view of excluding the Syncretists from their number. The opposition, however, of the divines of Jena prevented this from being adopted as one of the standards of the Lutherans generally. Syncretism found considerable favour among educated laymen, though little among theologians. But it foreshadowed much that was to come.

King James I. of England, who had a real interest in ecclesiastical affairs, made an attempt to heal the divisions of Protestantism, and both in France and Germany his proposals were received with much favour. On his invitation the famous theologian Du Moulin[1] came to England to take counsel with the King; while in France Du Plessis Mornay, whose distinguished services gave him great weight with his co-religionists, joined in promoting the King's views. But nothing came of it. The King wanted courage and energy to carry through

[1] J. Quick, *Synodicon*, II. 105 (Lond. 1692); W. Bates, *Vitae Select. Virorum* (*Ib.* 1681); D. C. A. Agnew, *Protestant Exiles from France* (2nd ed. Lond. 1871); *Dict. Nat. Biogr.* XXXIX. 201 f.

such a scheme, while the one point on which he was firm—episcopal government—was not acceptable to the Continental Protestants.

In 1631 a Synod of the French Reformed Church at Charenton[1] took a considerable step towards friendly relations with the Lutherans. Seeing that they accepted all the principal articles of the Augsburg Confession, they drew the inference that Lutherans who attended their services and lived decorously might be admitted, without any abjuration, to the Holy Communion. They were also permitted to marry members of the Reformed community, and the children of such marriages might be presented for baptism. Lutherans, however, could be admitted as sponsors only on making a solemn promise to teach their godchildren only such articles of faith as were common to the two communities. This well-meant attempt, however, met the usual fate of those who in quarrels interpose. Suspicious Calvinists saw in forbearance towards Lutherans an attempt to curry favour with Gustavus Adolphus, then in the full tide of victory. On the Roman Catholic side some thought that the conclusions of Charenton prepared the way for reunion, while others accused the synod of disloyalty, as acting without permission of the Crown. In short, the reconciliation of the contending parties was brought no nearer by the moderate counsels of Charenton.

A noteworthy man who laboured all his life to promote the union of Anglicans, Lutherans, and Calvinists was John Durie[2], a native of Edinburgh. Educated at Sedan under his cousin Andrew Melville, and at Leyden, where his father had settled, he was naturally acquainted with the state of continental Protestantism as few of his countrymen could be. In 1628 he was chaplain to the English merchants at Elbing, then in the hands of Gustavus Adolphus, who was sympathetic, and promised him letters to the Protestant princes of Germany. His hopes of help from this quarter were, however, cut short by the death of the King in 1632. For some fifty years he

Synod at Charenton, 1631.

Durie, 1596—1680.

Favoured by Gustavus Adolphus.

[1] De Félice, *Hist. des Protestants de France*, pp. 333 ff.; Schröckh, *Neuere K.-G.* v. 195.
[2] Scott's *Fasti*, I. 5, 103, 147, VI. 843; Calderwood's *History*; Knox's *Life of Melville*; *Dict. Nat. Biogr.* XVI. 261.

Spinola,
c. 1676.

Molanus,
1633—
1727.

travelled over a great part of the Continent, exhorting men to think more of their common faith in Christ and less of their differences in opinion, but he sadly confessed towards the end of his days, "the only fruit which I have reaped from all my toils is that I see the miserable condition of Christianity, and that I have no other comfort than the testimony of my conscience." His life had been an incessant round of journeyings, colloquies, correspondence, and publications.

Among those who exerted themselves to bring back the Lutherans of Germany to obedience to Rome one of the most conspicuous was Bishop Christopher Rojas de Spinola[1], who, beginning from the year 1676, under various names, quietly traversed various districts where he had reason to hope for a favourable reception from theologians, with a commission from the Emperor and probably the approval of the Pope. With the court of Hanover he had some success. In this country the leader among the clergy was Gerhard Wolter Molanus[2], a pupil of Calixtus, and devoted, like his master, to the discovery of real agreement amid apparent differences, while he was less cautious in dealing with opponents. He held union with Rome to be both possible and desirable, it was only necessary to agree on the essentials of the faith. Here he gave to Holy Scripture the first place, and to the traditional interpretations of the Church the second. These two points being granted, he thought that the parties might be convinced that neither side held damnable heresy. Differences in non-essential points might be mutually tolerated until a future Council should have decided upon them. The Eucharist should be administered to the laity in both kinds; marriage of priests should be allowed; and no recantation of former errors should be required. The next step was that the famous Bossuet was brought into the discussion. The Electress Sophia of Hanover, the granddaughter of James I. of England, and mother of George I., had a sister Louisa who had been converted to Catholicism in France. This lady, when she heard of the negotiations between Spinola

---

[1] Schröckh, *N. K.-G.* VII. 98 ff.; Herzog's *Real-Encycl.* XIV. 676; Gieseler, *K.-G.* IV. 181 ff.

[2] J. von Einen, *Das Leben des Theologi G. W. Molani* (1734).

and Molanus, persuaded her sister to admit Bossuet, with whom she was on very friendly terms, to the discussion. A secret correspondence then began between Molanus and Bossuet, in which after a short time the famous Leibnitz joined, but this, in spite of the ample concessions which Molanus was willing to make, in the end came to nothing. Bossuet would hear nothing of a union with Protestants unless they accepted the whole body of Roman doctrine, although he was willing to make the concessions which Molanus required as to communion, marriage of priests, and recantation. A few years later the correspondence between Bossuet and Leibnitz was renewed at the desire of Duke Anthony Ulrich of Brunswick-Wolfenbüttel, but again with no result except that Leibnitz was suspected of having been converted to Rome.

At the beginning of the eighteenth century great hopes were entertained both by statesmen and by theologians that the divisions of Protestantism might be healed. This was especially the case in Prussia, where the ruling House was of the Reformed community, while the great majority of its subjects were Lutheran. In 1701 the sovereign, who had hitherto borne the title of Elector of Brandenburg, assumed the title of King of Prussia, and at his coronation caused two of his chaplains to be named bishops—a step which was rightly believed to indicate a desire to draw nearer to the constitution of the English Church. Leibnitz, distinguished in theology as well as philosophy, was anxious for union, and the Queen of Prussia, who had great influence, followed his counsels. But stumblingblocks were soon found in the way. There was indeed complete agreement everywhere as to the supremacy of Scripture in matters of faith, and salvation by Christ alone; but the Reformed gave greater prominence than the Lutherans did to the doctrine of absolute predestination, while the latter insisted on a Real Presence in the Holy Eucharist and retained some of the ancient ceremonial and vestments. They also practised exorcism in Baptism. The matter was complicated by the publication, by a Reformed minister named Winkler, of a scheme of union which rested avowedly on the maxim that a territorial monarch was chief bishop within his dominions. This caused the

Margin notes: Ch. IV. 1691—1694. Leibnitz, 1699—1701. Prussian Kingdom, 1701. Bishops.

measures promoted by the King to be regarded with suspicion, and the scheme was opposed by so calm a judge as Leibnitz. The consequence was that the meeting for the promotion of mutual charity, which the King had contemplated, had to be abandoned. But hopes of union still lingered. Christopher Pfaff, chancellor of Tübingen and an eminent theologian, gave them vigorous expression in his pacific address to Protestants in the year 1720. He insisted that the different parties were in fact at one in the essentials of the faith, and severely blamed those who branded their opponents as heretics. Human passion and ambition occasioned, he thought, far more heated controversy than the sincere love of truth. Pfaff found a worthy supporter in Klemm, also a professor in Tübingen, whose book on the necessity for union among Protestants in matters of faith made a great impression both in Germany and elsewhere. His leading maxim was that union of Churches had been too much mixed up with union of pulpits; and he naturally condemned the narrow views of sectarian partisans. A long literary controversy followed, but no practical result, though in later times the difference between Luther and Zwingli came to be thought unimportant compared with those between Evangelicals and Rationalists.

7. PROTESTANT MISSIONS[1].

In the sixteenth century the time for Protestant missions was not yet. The Protestant communities were rather in the position of beleaguered garrisons, and were too much occupied in defending themselves to send forth distant expeditions. Then in the seventeenth century came the Thirty Years' War, which exhausted Germany for some generations, and this was succeeded by a period of barren theological conflicts, which did not warm men's hearts towards those who were without. And it is

---

[1] G. Plitt, *Kurze Gesch. d. Luther. Missionen* (Erlangen, 1871); G. Warneck, *Abriss einer Geschichte der Prot. Missionen* (Berlin, 1898); W. Grössel, *Die Mission u. die Evang. Kirche im 17ᵗᵉ Jahrhdt.* (Gotha, 1897); Newcombe's *Cyclopædia of Missions* (New York, 1856); Charlotte M. Yonge, *Pioneers and Founders in the Mission Field* (Lond. 1878); T. Christlieb, *Foreign Missions* (Boston, U.S.A., 1880).

remarkable that the first outburst of missionary zeal came not from any minister of religion, but from certain members of the law faculty at Lübeck. One of these, Peter Heiling[1], made his way to Abyssinia about 1634, and translated the New Testament into Amharic, the language of that country. Somewhat later, in 1664, Ernest von Welz made a most stirring appeal to his Lutheran fellow-countrymen to found a missionary society[2], and to establish in every university a college— Collegium de Propaganda Fide—for the special training of missionaries. Welz's own zeal never flagged, and he himself chose the Dutch territory on the Guinea coast for the scene of his operations; but there he soon died, and his efforts for the permanent establishment of missionary organizations came to nothing. Spener and his friends in the Pietistic revival earnestly pressed upon their co-religionists the thought of their duty towards the heathen. Towards the end of the century the philosopher and statesman Leibnitz propounded an ambitious design to unite all Christian states and princes in missionary enterprise. Francke also, as we shall see[3], was one of the first organizers of German missions, but it was not until a later period that mission-work enlisted the sympathy of a large body of supporters.

E. von Welz, 1664.

Leibnitz.

When the power of Portugal declined the Dutch superseded them in most of their East Indian possessions, where they shewed a decided missionary spirit. One of the avowed aims of the Dutch East India Company, chartered in 1602, was the conversion of the heathen. The history of the early Dutch mission is somewhat obscure, but we know that in Ceylon the Dutch governor admitted no one to any—even the lowest—position under government until he had signed the Helvetic Confession[4]. Baptism, however, was not refused to anyone who could repeat the Lord's Prayer and the Ten Commandments. Thousands came to be baptized, so that by the end of the seventeenth century there are said to have been 300,000 Cingalese Christians, and in 1722 more than 400,000—

Dutch East India Company, 1602.

---

[1] J. H. Michaelis, *Leben Pet. Heyling's* (Halle, 1724).
[2] Schaff's *Encyc.*, p. 1529.
[3] See p. 156.
[4] Kurtz's *Lehrbuch*, ed. Tschackert, II. 271; Schaff's *Encycl.* 1529.

probably rather vague estimates. The same methods were followed in Java, where 100,000 are said to have been baptized. A missionary college founded in Leyden in 1622 collapsed after sending out no more than twelve students. The Dutch also undertook mission work in connexion with their commercial establishment in Brazil. Some Indians were baptized, and schools established, but the whole scheme was brought to an end by the abandonment of the colony in 1667. Some good men were found among those who were employed by the Dutch, but it is to be feared that on the whole the Dutch method of offering temporal advantages to converts tended to produce nominal rather than genuine Christians.

Denmark did not seriously enter the mission field before the eighteenth century. In 1705 (four years after the foundation of our S. P. G.) Lütken, Court preacher at Copenhagen, who was in friendly relations with the German Pietists, was appointed by the Danish King, Frederick IV., to select men suitable for the work of missions to the heathen. Two young men, students of theology at Halle, Ziegenbalg and Plütschau[1], were recommended to him, and through him to the King. They were sent to the Danish settlement at Tranquebar in India, the King providing for their support. In 1714 a Danish Society for the Propagation of the Gospel was founded, but in spite of this the main direction of the mission was in the hands of the German Pietists at Halle, who were guided by August Hermann Francke. This excellent man seems to have received an impulse towards missions from Leibnitz, and wrote a remarkable tract, " The Lighthouse of Evangelical Missions," in which he urged the Prussian King, Frederick I., to take up the work of converting the heathen, especially the Chinese. He was eminently fitted by position and character to kindle among the students zeal for the spread of the Gospel, and to animate friends of the mission at home. Without him the Danish mission would perhaps have collapsed. He was the first to publish regular missionary reports, which he did from the year 1708 onwards. The missionaries seem to have been specially gifted for the

---

[1] W. Germann, *Ziegenbalg u. Plütschau* (Erlangen, 1867).

work in which they were engaged. Ziegenbalg soon learned to speak the most prevalent native language, Tamil, with perfect fluency, and made himself acquainted with the native literature. In 1708 he began a Tamil translation of the New Testament, which was completed in 1711. Plütschau was an admirable colleague, but Ziegenbalg was always the leading spirit of the mission. They taught wherever men most did congregate, and succeeded in reaching both Brahmins and Pariahs. Beginning with the works of creation as evidence of the being of God, they proceeded to point out man's consciousness of sin and longing for a Redeemer, so naturally leading to the great fact of the Incarnation. As early as 1707 they appointed native Catechists, the first step towards a native ministry. Ziegenbalg died in 1719, when he was no more than 36 years of age, but he had begun a great work which did not die.

Now it is to be observed that the number of converts made by these excellent missionaries is not to be compared with the numbers which are attributed to Xavier. They made converts at the rate of perhaps fifty in a year, while Xavier is said to have baptized his thousands. But those of the Germans were really instructed in the Christian religion, which can hardly be said of Xavier's; and the work was permanent. The Tranquebar mission flourished, and in 1778 had received 15,743 converts[1]. It also gave an impulse to Christian work beyond the limits of the Danish settlements.

Denmark also directed its attention to Lapland and Greenland. Thomas von Westen, a Norwegian preacher, thrice visited Lapland; while Greenland owes its Christianity to Hans Egede, a Norwegian educated at Copenhagen, who, after learning the language of the country, landed in Greenland in 1721, with wife, children, and several companions—in all forty-six persons. There he spent fifteen years, and by his earnest preaching and teaching established a Christian community which exists to this day. On his return to Copenhagen in 1736 he continued to serve the cause which he had at heart, and was named superintendent or bishop of the Greenland mission. He died in 1758. His son, Povel Egede, who

[1] Schröckh, *N. K.-G.* VII. 484.

Ch. IV.

Tamil New Testament, 1711.

Von Westen in Lapland, 1716–22.

Egede (b. 1686, d. 1758) *in Greenland*, 1721.

succeeded his father in Greenland, completed in 1766 the translation of the New Testament into the language of Greenland which his father had begun, and also produced a catechism and a prayer-book in the same tongue.

Meanwhile the conversion of the Eskimo in Greenland had become an object of interest to the Moravian Brethren. Zinzendorf, the head of that society, visited Copenhagen in 1731, and was induced by what he saw there to carry out the thoughts which had been suggested to his mind by a previous visit to Halle. In January, 1731, two of the brethren, Matthew and Christian Storch, set out for Greenland, where their first convert was baptized in 1739, and where their successors are at work even to this day.

Moravian Missions.

In the early part of the eighteenth century the Brotherhood of Herrnhut was by far the most active missionary society among the Protestants[1]. The thought of the salvation of the heathen pressed constantly upon the heart of Zinzendorf and animated the society. Men ready to make ventures of faith were always to be found among the Moravians. They were not highly educated, and were consequently unfit to influence the Brahmins of India, but among uncultured people their humility and earnest love of Christ drew men to join their worship and society. They lived simply and frugally and laboured with their hands, many of them having been drawn from the artisan class. The first Moravian missionaries, Leonard Dober and David Nitzschmann, went out in 1732 to the island of St Thomas in the West Indies, and in the fifty years which followed missionaries were sent to most of the other West Indian Islands, to Surinam, the Guinea Coast, the Cape of Good Hope, the North-American Indians, and Labrador. In fact, during these years the Moravians sent out more missionaries to the heathen than all the other Protestant communities together.

[1] J. Holmes, *Sketch of the Missions of the United Brethren* (Lond. 1827); A. C. Thompson, *Moravian Missions* (New York, 1882).

CHAPTER V.

THE EASTERN CHURCH.

THE Mohammedan conquests much curtailed the Eastern Church both in numbers and dignity, but by no means crushed it. The Patriarchs became the recognized heads of the faithful in their dioceses; much authority was given to them, and they were held responsible to the supreme government for the good behaviour of their people in civil as well as in religious matters. The position of an Eastern Patriarch under the Califs was in fact not very unlike that of the Jewish high-priest after the return from Captivity, under the Kings of Persia or Egypt.

The Church under the Califs[1].

The relations between the Church of the East and Western Christendom have not been happy. In the sixteenth century communications passed between some of the Lutheran Reformers and the Patriarch of Constantinople without any permanent result[2]. Another attempt of a similar kind was made in the seventeenth century. Cyril Lucaris[3], a native of Crete, then a Venetian possession, and influenced by Western ideas, entered

East and West.

Cyril Lucaris, 1572—1638.

---

[1] Paul Rycaut, *Present State of the Greek and Armenian Churches,* A.C. 1678 (London, 1679); J. Mason Neale, *Hist. of the Holy Eastern Church* (Lond. 1847—50); A. P. Stanley, *Lectures on the Eastern Church*; A. H. Hore, *Eighteen Centuries of the Orthodox Greek Church* (Lond. 1899).
[2] Hardwick's *Reformation,* 313 f.
[3] T. Smith, *De Græcæ Ecclesiæ Hodierno Statu* (Lond. 1678), translated by the author as *An Account of the Greek Church under Cyrillus Lucaris, etc.* (Ib. 1680), and *Collectanea de Cyrillo Lucare* (Ib. 1707); L. Aymon, *Lettres Anecdotes de Cyrille Lucaris* (Amst. 1718); A. Mettetal, *Cyr. Lucar* (Strassburg, 1869); P. Trivier, *Un Patriarche de Constantinople* (Paris, 1877).

160 The Eastern Church

Ch. V.

Patriarch of Alexandria, 1602.

Constantinople, 1621.

into communication with some of the Reformed ministers during a mission in Lithuania. When in 1602 he became Patriarch of Alexandria he was greatly troubled by the efforts of the Jesuits, under the protection of the French, to make converts among the Greeks, and again entered into communication with some of the Reformed through Cornelius de Haga, the Dutch ambassador at the Porte. Greek theology had undergone little or no change since the days of John of Damascus in the eighth century. Greek religion had tended more and more to become mere form and ceremony, and it was probably with a view of breathing new life into it, and making it more capable of resisting the attacks of Rome, that Cyril desired intercourse with the more active minds of the West. In 1616 he entered into correspondence with George Abbot, Archbishop of Canterbury, and sent Metrophanes Critopulus to Oxford for instruction in the principles of the English Church. Some years after (1628) he testified his goodwill towards England by his gift to Charles I. of the famous Alexandrine manuscript of the Bible in Greek, now in the British Museum. In 1621 Cyril became Patriarch of Constantinople, when the Jesuits attacked him with all the weapons of intrigue and bribery, and succeeded in bringing about his banishment to Rhodes. He was, however, soon permitted to return, and was supported by the ambassadors of England and Holland. When Cyril established a printing-press in Constantinople his enemies represented that this was intended to disseminate books hostile to the Koran, upon which the Grand Mufti, being consulted by the Vizier, gave the equitable judgment, that doctrines other than those of Mohammed were not of necessity blasphemies, and that as the Sultan permitted Christians to proclaim their doctrines by word of mouth, he must be taken to permit them to print and publish them. The Jesuits were shortly after expelled from the Turkish dominions (1628). But the Patriarch's troubles were by no means at an end. In 1629 a paper which he had written with a view of minimising the differences between the Greek Church and the Western Reformed communities was published in Latin by the Dutch ambassador, and excited great indignation among the Greeks. He was driven from his see and again restored, but at last, in 1638, was strangled by command of the Sultan, on the ground that he had conspired with the Cossacks against the Turkish government. The Eastern Patriarchs declared his remembrance accursed.

But the influence of Cyril Lucaris was not annihilated by his tragic death. Greek theology was found to be so much affected by his teaching that in 1643 all the Patriarchs adopted a Confession of Faith, drawn up by Peter Mogilas, Archbishop of Kieff, intended specially to guard the Church against Protestant innovations.

Confession of Mogilas, 1643.

The Negus of Abyssinia[1], where a Christianity strongly tinged with Judaism had maintained itself from early times, was moved by intercourse with the Portuguese to sever the connexion of his country with the Coptic Patriarch in Alexandria (1621) and to receive from Rome a Patriarch for itself. The discontent of the people, however, shewed itself in open revolt, the Jesuits were expelled from the country, and the submission to Rome broken off.

Abyssinia.

1621.

The Maronites[2] in the Lebanon and in many districts of Syria retained their connexion with the See of Rome, which conceded to them the choice of their own Patriarch, the marriage of priests, the use of Syriac in the Liturgy, and the administration of the Cup to the laity. The Maronite college at Rome has produced (since 1584) a number of Oriental, especially Syriac, scholars. A papal legate appeared at a Maronite council held in 1596 at Kannobin, at which, according to his account, an almost complete agreement with Rome was attained; but the Maronites retained their distinctive usages. To another council, held at Luweiza in 1736, the celebrated Maronite scholar, J. S. Assemani, was sent as legate, and had some success in the way of Romanizing. The Catechism of Trent, with its doctrine of transubstantiation, was introduced; the Gregorian Calendar was adopted; the marriage of the clergy was confined to the lower orders; the name of the Pope was introduced into the Liturgy.

Maronites.

Council in 1596;

in 1736.

---

[1] Ludolf, *Historia Æthiopica* (Frankfort, 1681-94); La Croze, *Hist. du Christianisme d'Éthiopie et d'Arménie* (La Haye, 1739).

[2] Schnurrer, *De Ecclesia Maronitica* (1810); Murad, *Notice Historique sur l'Origine de la Nation Maronite* (1844); Kunstmann, *Ueber die Maroniten* in *Tübinger Quartalschrift* (1845); Hardwick, *Middle Age*, pp. 71, 370.

162   *The Eastern Church*

CH. V.
Armenian Church.

Submission to Rome, 1624.

1652.

Polish Uniates, 1596.

Russian Church.

The relation of the ancient Armenian Church[1] to Rome was somewhat uncertain. The Armenian Patriarchs were often glad to seek help from Rome, and therefore paid much respect to the Pope, but without resigning their own doctrines and customs. The Armenians were, and are, a race of traders, and as such widely dispersed, but they notwithstanding clung to their own Church. It was not until the Propaganda, in the early part of the seventeenth century, began its work, that any considerable body of Armenians really adopted Roman doctrine and joined the Roman Church. In 1624 Archbishop Nicolas Torosowich, who was recognized as the ecclesiastical head of the numerous Armenian communities in South Russia, withdrew from the jurisdiction of the Armenian Patriarch in Etchmiadzin and made submission to the papal see. The Armenians in Poland did not give their adhesion until 1652, after which union with Rome was promoted by the foundation of a Roman college for the Armenians in Lemberg in 1664. The Patriarchs in Etchmiadzin, however, maintained friendly relations with Rome until the numerous conversions towards the end of the seventeenth century put an end to them, and caused a lasting breach between the United and non-United Armenians.

The attempts of the Roman Church to recoup itself by conquests in the East for its losses in the West were sometimes favoured by political circumstances. Thus in Poland, the mutual hatred of the Poles, recently the oppressors, and the Russians, recently the oppressed, was the principal reason why a large number of the Polish clergy, between 1590 and 1596, abandoned the Greek rite, entered into communion with the Latins, and acknowledged the supremacy of the Pope[2].

But any loss which the Greek Church sustained in Poland was more than made up to it by the splendid position which it acquired in Russia[3]. Already in 1588

---

[1] G. di Serpo, *Compendio Storico, &c.* (Venice, 1786); Chamick, *Hist. of Armenia*, tr. by Avdall (Calcutta, 1827); E. L. Cutts, *Christians under the Crescent* (London, 1877).
[2] Hardwick's *Reformation*, 316.
[3] A. N. Mouravieff, *Hist. of the Church of Russia to 1721*, tr. by Blackmore (Oxford, 1842); L. Boissard, *L'Église de Russie* (Paris, 1867); Schröckh, *N. K.-G.* IX. 156 ff.; Gieseler, *K.-G.* III. 2. 696 ff.; Hase, *K.-G.* III. 2. 940; [J. B. Mozley] in *Christian Remembrancer*, vol. x. p. 245.

the Czar Feodor I., with the assent of the then Patriarch, Jeremiah II. of Constantinople, had raised Moscow to the rank of a Patriarchate, a "third Rome." And in Russia the State was deeply indebted to the Church. It was mainly through the Church that the kingdom was organized after the Mongols were driven out; it was mainly the Church which repelled the Polish invasion in the early years of the seventeenth century. And when the reigning House of Ruric came to an end, it was to the clergy that the people looked to supply their future sovereign. In 1613 the nobles assembled to make their election. After three days of fasting and prayer they chose to fill the vacant throne Michael, son of Archbishop Philaret and grandson of Roman, from whom the present reigning house of Romanoff is descended. The Czar Michael and the Patriarch Philaret ruled together—probably the only instance in all history of a father as head of the Church and a son as head of the State governing a kingdom. It was a great epoch in the history of Russia. The nation was delivered from the Mongols and the Poles; the Church was freed from the Mussulmans and the Latins; both were free to follow their natural course of development.

One of the most extraordinary figures in all history is that of the Patriarch Nicon[1], who in the seventeenth century attempted to reform the Russian Church. With the support of the Czar Alexis he set himself with indomitable courage to root out the most crying evils in the Church and the priesthood. With a strong, often violent hand he waged war against the drunkenness which disgraced the clergy. The printing-press was set to work, Greek and Latin were taught in some of the schools. The harsh intonations of the Muscovites were superseded by the sweet chants of singers brought from Poland and Greece, who introduced that impressive music of men's voices which has become the glory of the Russian

---

[1] Contemporary authorities: *The Travels of Macarius in the 17th cent.* tr. from the Arabic by Belfour (Oriental Trans. Fund, 1827–36); W. Palmer, *The Patriarch and the Czar: Replies of Nicon, Patriarch*, &c. tr. from the Russian (1871–76); S. Collins, *Present State of Russia* (1671). See also Bachmeister, *Beiträge zur Lebensgeschichte des Patriarch. Nikon* (Riga, 1788); W. Palmer's *Dissertations*, c. 5; Stanley's *Eastern Church*, Lect. XI.

Church. He sought to exhibit in its purest form the Slavonic translation of the Bible, of which he was himself an eager student. He himself preached, and encouraged others to revive the sermon, which in Russia had long been obsolete. Sacred pictures to which he thought that idolatrous veneration had been paid he removed; and he hated the introduction of pictures painted after the European fashion into the houses of the wealthy. But perhaps the reforms by which he is best known are his correction of many traditional errors in the Liturgy, and his introduction of Byzantine forms differing from those to which the Russians were accustomed. He was a most munificent prelate, founding hospitals and almshouses, and in time of famine succouring the distressed with self-denying generosity. But in spite of his real nobility of character he retained all his life some of the traits of the peasantry from which he sprang. He was intolerant of opposition, he proceeded by violence where gentleness was required, and he was liable to fits of unreasoning fury. Probably nothing that he did gave so great offence as his corrections of the Liturgy—a region in which any deviation, however reasonable, from immemorial usage is highly offensive to the unlearned who form the great majority in every Church. His latter days were clouded. After nine years' withdrawal to a monastery he was in 1667 deposed from the patriarchal throne, and died fourteen years afterwards as he was returning from his exile. A great, noble, rude, and barbaric figure departed.

Rude and barbaric also, in spite of his earnest efforts to introduce into his kingdom the results of Western civilization, was the next great Russian reformer, Peter the Great[1]. On his journeys through Europe he investigated the doctrines and attended the worship of the countries through which he passed. He walked about London with Bishop Burnet, and dined at Lambeth with Archbishop Tenison. The Scottish Episcopalians and the English Nonjurors tried to secure through him an alliance with the Eastern Church. Wherever he went he caused a stir in ecclesiastical circles. But whatever he saw, whatever he admired, he was above all things a prince

---

[1] There are Lives of Peter by J. Mottley (1739), Voltaire (1759), Barrow (1883), Schuyler (1884), and others.

of the Orthodox Church, and his reforms were in harmony with the national spirit. He took measures for the increase of schools, restraints on the growth of monasteries, and regulations for the management of their property. But his greatest and most startling innovation was his abolition of the office of Patriarch, and the substitution for it of the Holy Governing Synod, consisting of prelates appointed and removed by the sovereign, and presided over by him or his deputy. Nothing shews more strikingly the awe with which Peter inspired his subjects than the fact that he was able to carry out this portentous change. Many of the clergy did for a time make a stiff resistance; some dissenters broke out into open rebellion, and even attempted the Czar's life; but in the end he carried with him the great mass of the nation. To the populace the Czar's changes in the Calendar were much more offensive than a change in the hierarchy, which scarcely touched them at all. The old Russian Calendar, like the Jewish, counted its years from the Creation, and began the year on the first of September. Peter ordained that the years should be counted from the Birth of Christ, and that the year should begin on the first of January. To the peasantry this seemed contrary to the laws of nature. The Gregorian reforms, by which the Calendar is brought into accurate correspondence with the solar year, have even now not been adopted in Russia. In one only of his innovations popular feeling was too strong for the mighty monarch. The period of his travels in Europe was one of shaven faces. When he returned home he ordered his subjects to shave their beards as a sign of civilization. The courtiers obeyed, but the clergy and the peasantry did not. Flowing beards are still distinctive of the Russian priests.

Ch. V.

Change in Calendar, 1700.

Beards.

The next great change in the status of the Russian Church was made by Catharine II., who by a simple decree did what in France was a consequence of the Revolution. She confiscated the property of the Church, and made the clergy and the monks stipendiaries of the State. They were not, however, ill-treated, having stipends sufficient to maintain them in their former social position, nor was the dignity of the services diminished[1].

Catharine II.'s confiscations, 1764.

[1] Schröckh, *N. K.-G.* IX. 184 ff.; Hase, *K.-G.* III. 2. 940.

Raskolniks or Starovers.

But it must not be supposed that reforms could be carried out in so conservative a country as Russia without irritation. There was a party in the Church which was provoked beyond endurance by the innovations of Nicon and Peter. Those who withdrew in consequence from the National Church received the name of Raskolniks—seceders or apostates—but the name which they themselves acknowledge, Starovers or "Old Believers," indicates the ground of their separation. They believe themselves to be the true Orthodox Church of Russia, from which the great majority have fallen away. But, once separated, they fell into fanaticism and peculiar superstitions of their own[1].

Duchoborzi.

Almost everywhere in Churches in which outward ceremonial is dominant, sects have appeared which rest on the sole and direct guidance of the Holy Spirit. Such a sect in Russia is that of the Duchoborzi[2], who reject the sacraments and the hierarchy, except that each community chooses for itself Elders. They have many peculiar customs, but are believed to lead pure lives. They form, in fact, a kind of Russian Quakerism. There are also several small fanatical sects.

[1] Schröckh, *N. K.-G.* ix. 240; Stanley, *Lect.* 12, p. 395.   [2] Hase, *K.-G.* iii. 2. 941.

CHAPTER VI.

THE AGE OF REASON.

1. ENGLISH FREE-THINKING.

THE seventeenth century was on the whole one of heated controversy. During the Civil War and the subsequent domination of Cromwell almost all traditions were called in question and the wildest new theories propounded. The early part of the century was agitated by the dissensions of Anglicans, Presbyterians, Independents, and a great variety of small sects, the votaries of which were generally violent in proportion to their insignificance. Nothing seemed fixed and sure. An immense impulse also was given to free inquiry into sacred things by the great results which were obtained from free inquiry into the physical universe. If, it was argued, so much truth was discovered in one field by disregarding traditional assumptions and explanations, why not in another? The self-reliant temper of the natural philosopher, appealing only to observed facts and logical deductions from them, was imported into theology. In short, it came to be acknowledged by the defenders and assailants of Christianity alike, that it was for right reason to decide what was true in matters of faith as well as of philosophy.

Reaction in 18th Century[1].

Physical Science.

---

[1] On the general characteristics of this period see Mark Pattison, *Tendencies of Religious Thought in England*, 1688–1750, in *Essays and Reviews* (1860), reprinted in *Essays*; J. Hunt, *Tendencies of Religious Thought in England* (London, 1870—73); Leslie Stephen, *English Thought in the Eighteenth Century* (London, 1876).

Ch. VI.

Locke, 1632—1704.

But that which gave the greatest impulse to the rational study of religion in England, and ultimately in all Europe, was no doubt the philosophy of John Locke[1]. He denied the existence of innate ideas and principles. The mind of man is at first a blank tablet, on which nothing is inscribed except impressions received from the senses, or from reflection on such impressions. Those are rational judgments, the truth of which we can discover by the investigation and development of conceptions which arise from sensation and reflection. Such a judgment he holds to be the belief in the existence of God; but there are judgments which transcend reason and rest only on faith. That which is actually contrary to sound reason can neither be revealed nor believed. Now Locke himself was a firm believer in Christianity, but it will readily be seen how great a shock was given by his teaching to the assumptions which underlie Christian theology, founded as it is on ideas which are not derived from the senses[2]. If Locke's teaching on the nature of the human mind was to be adopted a large portion of the existing theology would have to be abandoned. It was in fact for about a century almost superseded by systems which, if clearer than those of old time, were also less impressive and satisfying. The very title of Locke's famous essay on *The Reasonableness of Christianity as delivered in the Scriptures*[3] shews that in his view even propositions set forth in the Bible itself were to be brought to the touchstone of reason. He himself believed that they would endure this test, but it is obvious that others, on his own principles, might come to a different conclusion.

'Essay concerning the Human Understanding,' 1690.

'The Reasonableness of Christianity,' 1695.

Societies to promote morality.

The careless licentiousness brought in by the Restoration produced a number of societies " for the Reformation of Manners," which strove to check the open exhibition of vice and immorality mainly by putting in force the laws

---

[1] *Life* by Lord King (1829); H. R. Fox Bourne (1879); T. Fowler in Morley's *Men of Letters*; A. C. Fraser in Blackwood's *Philosophical Classics*. See also F. D. Maurice, *Moral and Metaph. Phil.* II. 433 ff. (ed. 1873).

[2] In 1697 E. Stillingfleet wrote an answer to Locke in which "his notion of ideas is proved to be inconsistent...with the Articles of the Christian faith."

[3] It is noteworthy that this treatise was published in the same year in which the censorship of the press was abolished.

against them¹. Many of these were in the habit of meeting for devotion and for mutual help in good works. Most of them have vanished, but two were founded in the later years of William III. which carry on their work to this day. Five good men, of whom Dr Bray was the chief mover, in 1698 formed a Society for the education of the poor, for providing at a cheap rate Bibles and other religious books, and for missionary work abroad. This society received a royal charter under the name of the Society for Promoting Christian Knowledge, and soon began to flourish. Three years after its commencement it formed a new society for missionary work, which also (1701) received a charter under the title of the Society for the Propagation of the Gospel in Foreign Parts, and did a great work, first among the British colonists in America, and afterwards in a larger sphere.

S.P.C.K., 1698.

S.P.G., 1701.

While these societies were pursuing the even tenor of their way, there arose vehement dissension between the two Houses of Convocation, the Lower House asserting an independence which the Upper, fortified by ancient precedents, refused to admit². The Bishops, generally of a more liberal school than the rest of the clergy, were even denounced, in Convocation and out of it, as enemies of the Church. The cry, "the Church in danger," was everywhere heard, and was even solemnly discussed in the House of Lords. The Queen herself censured the Lower House of Convocation and prorogued it. This of course exasperated the majority of the clergy, with whom the country generally sympathised. The Queen's ministers determined to make an example of one of the clamorous ecclesiastics with a view of silencing others.

Dissensions in Convocation, 1702 —1710.

25 *Feb.,* 1706.

The person whom they selected for prosecution was Dr Henry Sacheverell³, a man whom even his friends admitted to be vain and foolish, though he had great popularity as a preacher. He preached a sermon before the Lord Mayor

Sacheverell's Sermon, 1709.

---

¹ See *An Account of the Societies for Reformation of Manners* (London, 1699, several times reprinted); Josiah Woodward, *Account of...the Religious Societies in London* (London, 1701).
² Cardwell's *Synodalia,* 718 ff.;
Perry's *Student's Ch. Hist.* II. 567.
³ Howell's *State Trials,* xv. 1 ff.; Burnet's *Own Time,* II. 537 ff. References to the principal works relating to Sacheverell may be found in *Dict. Nat. Biogr.,* L. 83.

and aldermen on the 5th Nov. in which he represented those who had the management of public affairs as false brethren who would "admit a religious Trojan horse, big with arms and ruin, into our holy city...and are as destructive of our civil as of ecclesiastical rights[1]." For this and a previous sermon preached at the Assizes at Derby the House of Commons took the unusual step of impeaching the preacher before the House of Lords. He was found guilty of the misdemeanours charged against him, and suspended from preaching for three years. During the whole proceeding the doctor had been extraordinarily popular, and demonstrations were again made in his favour when, on the expiration of the inhibition, he took the earliest opportunity of shewing that he had not gained in wisdom or good taste[2].

One of the most conspicuous examples within the Church of the tendency to break loose from established traditions was William Whiston[3], Newton's successor at Cambridge, and a man of great though very ill-balanced ability. He came to the conclusion that the "Apostolical Constitutions"—a compilation of the fourth century containing matter possibly as old as the end of the second—was "the most sacred of the canonical books of the New Testament," and that the received doctrine of the Holy Trinity was erroneous. His own doctrine was thought to be Arian; he himself called his opinions Eusebian, meaning that they were those expressed by Eusebius of Cæsarea at the Council of Nicæa. The result of this publication was that he was deprived of his professorship[4]. Convocation censured his book, and in 1714 a Court of Delegates[5] was actually constituted for his trial, which was however brought to an end by the death of Queen Anne. Whiston continued all his life to propound unstable theories with a simple-minded honesty

---

[1] See Perry's *Student's Ch. Hist. Eng.* II. 573.
[2] Stanhope's *Hist. England*, I. 40 (ed. 1858).
[3] *Memoirs of Mr W. Whiston, written by himself* (1749); *Biographia Britannica*, VI. pt 2, p. 4202; L. Stephen in *Dict. Nat. Biog.*, LXI. 10.
[4] Cardwell's *Synodalia*, 753 ff.
[5] This was the Court through which the supremacy of the Crown in ecclesiastical cases was exercised until its powers were transferred to the Judicial Committee of the Privy Council by 2 and 3 William IV. c. 92.

which may have been in Goldsmith's mind when he drew the delightful character of the Vicar of Wakefield.

Samuel Clarke[1], who after the death of Locke was generally regarded as the first of English metaphysicians, rejected the sceptical conclusions of Locke's disciples, but was nevertheless condemned by orthodox divines for preaching a veiled deism. His *Scripture Doctrine of the Trinity* was held to savour of Arianism, and the Lower House of Convocation complained of it to the Upper House[2]. Clarke put in a reply, in which, without directly retracting, he made a declaration of his belief in which it is fully recognized "that the Son of God was eternally begotten by the eternal incomprehensible power and will of the Father, and that the Holy Spirit was likewise eternally derived from the Father by or through the Son, according to the eternal incomprehensible power and will of the Father[3]." The Upper House thereupon "thought fit to proceed no further," upon which the Lower House, dissatisfied, resolved that the inquiry ought not to have been dropped. The controversy which followed produced at least one book of permanent value, a *Vindication of Christ's Divinity* by Daniel Waterland, a man whose learning, orthodoxy and sound reasoning recall the best traditions of the English Church.

A few students like Whiston and Clarke may have persuaded themselves that Arianism represented an earlier phase of doctrine than the Nicene Creed, but it would be an error to suppose that Arian opinions were common in the eighteenth century. On the contrary, in no age of the Church did men's thoughts turn less to that speculation on the Being of the Son out of which Arianism arose. Their tendency was to regard the Incarnate Son as the great Teacher who gave authority to the moral precepts which all good men accept, and to drop out of sight the intercessory mediatorial office of the eternal Son of God, begotten before the worlds.

A controversy which stirred the Church of England to its depths, and brought innumerable pens into activity,

CH. VI.

S. Clarke, 1675—1729.
'Doctrine of the Trinity,' 1712.

Convocation, 1714.

Waterland's 'Vindication,' 1719.
Prevalent Christology.

---

[1] *Life* by Hoadley, prefixed to *Works*, 1738; Whiston's *Memoirs*; *Biographia Britannica*, II. 1356; Leslie Stephen in *Dict. Nat. Biog.*
x. 443.
[2] Cardwell's *Synodalia*, 785.
[3] *Synodalia*, 792.

was begun by Benjamin Hoadley[1], the absentee Bishop of Bangor, already known as an able controversialist. In March 1717 he preached a sermon on the Kingdom of Christ, in which he asserted that "Christ is Himself sole lawgiver to His subjects, and Himself the sole judge of their behaviour in the affairs of conscience and eternal salvation; that He hath, in these points, left behind Him no visible human authority; no vicegerents who can be said properly to supply His place; no interpretations upon which His subjects are absolutely to depend; no judges over the consciences or religion of His people[2]." It is probable that in saying this Hoadley did not intend to deny the right of the Church to decree rites and ceremonies, or to lay down points of order, but only its right to impose or define articles of faith, as necessary to salvation, which Christ had not imposed or defined. This was a matter, he held, between God and the conscience of the individual. But taking the whole sermon in conjunction with opinions which he had expressed elsewhere, many readers came to the conclusion that he altogether denied the existence of the visible Church of Christ. In this sense it was taken by the Lower House of Convocation of Canterbury, which presented (10th May) to the Upper House a "Representation about the Bishop of Bangor's Sermon[3]," criticising it at considerable length, and begging their Lordships to "enter upon some speedy and effectual method to vindicate the honour of God and religion that hath been so deeply wounded." What method the bishops would have adopted remains unknown, for Convocation was immediately prorogued by the ministers of the King, and was not permitted to assemble[4] for discussion of the affairs of the Church until 5 Nov., 1852. To put an end to the deliberation of a constitutional assembly by an exercise of the pre-

---

[1] *Life* prefixed to *Works*, ed. by J. Hoadley (1773); by G. G. Perry in *Dict. Nat. Biog.* xxvii. 16. See also J. Hunt, *Religious Thought in England*, vol. iii.; Leslie Stephen, *English Thought*, ii. 152; C. J. Abbey, *The English Church and its Bishops*, ii. 1.

[2] See W. Palin, *Hist. of Church of England*, p. 384.

[3] In Cardwell's *Synodalia*, p. 828.

[4] This is the usual statement, but a writer in *Notes and Queries* (viii. 465) has shewn that Convocation actually sat and passed resolutions in 1728 and 1742. The authority for this is *A Letter to Dr Lisle, Prolocutor*, by G. Reynolds, Archdeacon of Lincoln (*Choice Notes, History*, p. 227).

rogative of the Crown was no doubt a very harsh proceeding, but it may be doubted whether the Church would have gained if the divines of the eighteenth century had had an opportunity of discussing, and perhaps legislating upon, the doctrines and discipline of the Church. But if the discussion of the Bishop of Bangor's opinions was stopped in Convocation, it dragged its slow length along elsewhere in a series of pamphlets which have long lost any interest which they possessed. One work only among them retains its vitality, William Law's *Three Letters to the Bishop of Bangor*[1], in which the clearness, vigour and irony of the writer are as conspicuous as his devout conviction of the truth of what he maintains. He also attacked the Bishop for his views on the Eucharist[2], which the latter appeared to regard as a purely commemorative rite.

Immediately after the silencing of Convocation attention was drawn to the unsatisfactory position of Dissenters with regard to their civil rights. The Test Act still compelled those who held any office under the Crown or a Corporation to receive the Holy Communion according to the rite of the Church of England, while the Occasional Conformity Act of 1711 prevented their complying with this condition by one reception only before admission to office, and the Schism Act of 1714 prohibited any person from keeping a school without declaring that he conformed to the Church of England, and obtaining a license from the bishop of the diocese, which license was not to be granted without a certificate of the applicant's having communicated in the Church within the last year. Earl Stanhope, as first minister of the Crown, earnestly desired to give to the Dissenters perfect equality in civil rights, and to mitigate the penal laws against Roman Catholics. He succeeded, not without difficulty, in repealing the Occasional Conformity and the Schism Acts, but the Test Act remained in the Statute Book for more than a hundred years from this time[3], nor were the Roman Catholics materially relieved.

---

[1] Reprinted in *The Scholar Armed* (London, 1812), I. 249.
[2] In *A Demonstration of the Errors of [Hoadley's] Plain Account of the Sacrament*, 1737.
[3] Stanhope's *Hist. England*, I. 326.

Ch. VI.

Free-thinking Clergy.
Petition against Subscription to Formularies, 6 Feb., 1772.

During the eighteenth century many of the clergy in their ordinary teaching drifted away from the recognized standards of the Church, and were reluctant to bind themselves by its formularies. This feeling found expression in a petition to Parliament, signed by somewhat more than two hundred clergymen of no great distinction, in which it was prayed that the clergy should not be "required to acknowledge by subscription or declaration the truth of any formulary whatsoever beside Holy Scripture itself[1]." Its reception was opposed in a crushing speech by Edmund Burke[2] and negatived by a large majority. A still larger majority passed a Bill for relieving dissenting ministers from the necessity of subscribing to the dogmatic portion of the Thirty-nine Articles, but it was lost in the House of Lords, though supported by the high authority of the great Lord Chatham[3].

Natural Religion. Deism.

Those of whom we have just spoken at least acknowledged that we have in Holy Scripture a revelation of the Will of God. But as the spirit of purely rational inquiry gained force, the authority of Scripture itself came to be doubted. And when this point was reached, men began to ask themselves, if that which had for ages been recognized as the principal, perhaps the only, revelation of God to man, was set aside, what religion remained? The answer which some gave to this question was, that there remained natural religion, a religion independent of any special revelation, based on truths implanted by God in the mind of man as man[4].

Herbert of Cherbury, 1583—1648.
'De Religione Gentilium,' 1645.

The earliest English writer of distinction who taught a religious system independent of revelation was Edward Herbert, first Baron Herbert of Cherbury[5], who may be regarded as a pioneer of the modern study of Comparative Religion. He regards religion as the essential and dis-

[1] G. G. Perry, *Student's History*, III. 102 ff.
[2] *Works*, VI. 81 (ed. 1852).
[3] Stanhope's *Hist. of England*, V. 303 (ed. 1858).
[4] On this school generally, see J. Leland, *View of Deistical Writers* (1754–6); G. V. Lechler, *Geschichte des Englischen Deismus* (1841);
A. S. Farrar, *Critical Hist. of Free-Thought* (1862); J. H. Overton, *Eng. Ch. in 18th Cent.* I. 177.
[5] Herbert's *Autobiography* was edited by Sidney L. Lee (1886). See also C. de Remusat, *Lord Herbert de Cherbury* (1874); S. L. Lee in *Dict. Nat. Biog.* XXVI. 173.

tinguishing characteristic of the human race, and by comparing the various existing systems, he arrives at the idea of a universal religion, based on five truths which he believes to be everywhere recognized. These are, that there is a God; that God ought to be worshipped; that virtue and piety are necessary parts of worship; that men ought to repent of their sins and forsake them; that there are rewards and punishments in a future life. These great truths, which are (he holds) alone needful for the guidance of mankind to salvation, have been obscured by the artifices of priests and the growth of dogmatic systems. He did not deny the possibility of a revelation from God, and of systems claiming divine authority he thought Christianity the best; but he held that no revelation had received an assent so universal as to prove its truth.

In the year after the publication of Locke's *Reasonableness of Christianity* appeared a short treatise entitled *Christianity not Mysterious* by John Toland[1], which professed to defend revelation against deists and atheists; but the revelation which he defends contains nothing, in the popular sense of the word, "mysterious." The word "mystery" in the New Testament, he points out, denotes something once hidden but now revealed, not necessarily in itself obscure or hard to be understood. The "uncorrupted doctrines of Christianity" can be sufficiently understood by all; it is only "the gibberish of the divinity schools" which is "out of the reach of the vulgar." A book which spoke of the greater part of existing theology as "gibberish" could scarcely be popular with theologians. It raised in fact a furious outcry, which was increased when in a later work Toland discussed the question of the comparative evidence for the canonical and the uncanonical Gospels. In his contention that in the early Church there were two antagonistic parties, the Jewish and the Pauline, he anticipated the speculations of Semler and the Tübingen School. The invention of the word "Pantheism" is attributed to him[2].

John Toland, 1669—1722.
'Christianity not Mysterious,' 1696.

'Amyntor,' 1699.

'Nazarenus,' 1720.

---

[1] *Life* by Desmaizeaux, prefixed to *Works*, 1747; Berthold, *Toland u. der Monismus der Gegenwart*, 1876.

[2] See Traill's *Social England*, IV. 567.

Ch. VI.
Anthony Collins, 1676—1729.
'*Discourse of Free-thinking,*' 1713.
'*Grounds and Reasons of the Christian Religion,*' 1724.

'*Scheme of Literal Prophecy,*' 1727.

Shaftesbury, 1671—1713.

Tindal, 1656—1733.

In 1713 Anthony Collins[1], a friend and disciple of Locke and already known as an author, published anonymously a *Discourse of Free-thinking,* which is a bold vindication of the right of all men to think freely for themselves; a right which had been (he said) asserted by the Prophets of the Old Dispensation, by Christ and His Apostles, and by the wise and virtuous of all ages, from Socrates to Tillotson. In later works Collins, no longer content with asserting the freedom of thought and expression, came near to denying the authority of revealed religion altogether. He argues that the proof of the truth of the Christian revelation rests wholly, or almost wholly, on the correspondence of the facts of the Gospel with the Messianic prophecies of the Old Testament, and that as these latter can only be brought into harmony with the alleged facts by allegorical—that is, in his opinion, non-natural—interpretation, a great part of the evidence for Christianity loses its cogency.

Anthony Ashley Cooper, third Earl of Shaftesbury[2], though brought up under the influence of Locke, did not adopt his theories. He was rather influenced by Plato, and maintained the intuitive character of the moral sense, and the obligation of a virtue which is its own reward. In this respect he differs from the Deists generally; but in his invectives against fanaticism and priestcraft, his depreciation of mysteries and miracles, and his readiness to bring religious systems to the test not only of reason but of ridicule, he is at one with them. He exalts the natural affections of love and sympathy above the dogmas of positive religion, which have often led to inhumanity and the ascription of immoral qualities to the Deity. There is no doubt latent beneath Shaftesbury's irony the suggestion of a possible antagonism between Christianity and morality, though he was in the habit of attending the services of the Church, and thought Christianity the best form of religion.

That which was latent in Shaftesbury found full and

---

[1] *Life* by Birch in *Biogr. Britannica* (2nd ed.), from materials supplied by Desmaizeaux; Leslie Stephen in *Dict. Nat. Biog.* XI. 363.

[2] T. Fowler, *Shaftesbury and Hutcheson* (1882); James Martineau in *Types of Ethical Theory*, II. 449 ff. (ed. 1885); Leslie Stephen in *Dict. Nat. Biog.* XII. 130.

open expression in the works of Matthew Tindal[1], who, after oscillating for some time between Anglicanism and Romanism, became what he called a "Christian Deist." He published in 1730 the book by which he is best known, *Christianity as Old as the Creation, or the Gospel a Republication of the Religion of Nature*, in which he struck a note which echoed long. The religion of nature, he argues, as the law given by a perfect legislator, is itself perfect; no Revelation can increase or diminish its perfection. Christ came to restore natural religion to that original purity which had been corrupted in the course of ages; and all religious systems, including Christianity, are only true so far as they agree with natural religion, which consists in the promotion of the honour of God and the welfare of man. He inveighs against superstition and priestcraft, but the specific doctrines of the Christian religion are not directly attacked. Tindal was the ablest of the Deists, and his works produced great agitation both within and without the Church.

'Christianity as old as the Creation,' 1730.

A free-thinker who stands apart from the lines of thought generally taken by free-thinkers was Thomas Woolston[2], a Cambridge man of considerable learning and ability. He was one of the few who in those days studied Origen, from whom he adopted the allegorical interpretation of Scripture. This was no more than almost all the Fathers had done, but when Woolston carried his allegorizing to the extent of denying the historic reality of miracles, including the Lord's Birth from a virgin and His Resurrection, he was prosecuted for blasphemy, found guilty, and sentenced to fine and imprisonment. As he was unable to pay the fine he remained in the King's Bench prison until his death in 1733. Woolston wrote with great vigour, in an excellent style, and with a good deal of misplaced humour. Though he did not approach the subject from the same side, he may be said to have been a forerunner of Strauss.

Woolston, 1670— 1733.

His Trial, 1729.

---

[1] *Life* in *Biographia Britannica*, vi. 3960; by Leslie Stephen in *Dict. Nat. Biog.* LVI. 403. See also J. Hunt, *Religious Thought in England*, ii. 431 ff.

[2] *Life* by [J. Stackhouse?] (1733); Woog's *De Vita et Scriptis T. Woolstoni*, 1743; *Biogr. Britannica*, vi. pt 2, p. 4334; J. Hunt, *Religious Thought in England* (1871), ii. 400; A. Gordon in *Dict. Nat. Biog.* LXIII. 437.

Thomas Chubb[1], a Wiltshire glover and tallow-chandler, shews rather the effect of the deistic writings on an almost uneducated man of a speculative turn than any originality of opinion. He maintains, as others had done before him, that primitive Christianity was rather a rule of life than a system of dogmatic theology, and does not accept the common theory of the inspiration of the Bible. His life was blameless, and his writings are remarkably free from bitterness or violence.

The aristocratic Lord Bolingbroke[2] contributed nothing more original to deistic literature than the shopkeeper Chubb, but he supplied Pope with the superficial philosophy which is embodied in the *Essay on Man*, in its time a highly influential work; and he is said to have impressed Voltaire, who made his acquaintance during his visit to England. And there can be no doubt that the example of men like Shaftesbury and Bolingbroke helped to make free-thinking fashionable with the fops and would-be wits.

Among Deists is generally reckoned also Bernard Mandeville[3], a London physician, who published in 1705 a strange fable in verse called *The Grumbling Hive*, republished in 1714 under the title *The Fable of the Bees, or Private Vices Public Benefits*. In this book, which became extremely popular, he argued, as Hobbes had done, that society originated in the war of selfish and savage instincts, and repudiated anything like a moral sense. Moreover, he held that a society in which luxury, with its attendant vices, did not exist, would be a very poor one. The book was no doubt partly ironical, but it was generally understood to be an attack on morality. Mandeville's paradox naturally called forth many refutations, among which may be mentioned the lucid and forcible essay of the English Pascal, William Law[4], and the acute criticism of Bishop Berkeley[5].

[1] *Biographia Britannica*, Supplement, p. 29; Leslie Stephen, *English Thought in Eighteenth Cent.* I. 163, and *Dict. Nat. Biog.* x. 297.

[2] *Life* by Oliver Goldsmith (1770), T. Macknight (1863), J. Churton Collins (1886), A. Hassall (1889). See also C. de Rémusat, *L'Angleterre au Dix-huitième Siècle*, I. 111—452; Carrau, *La Philosophie Réligieuse en Angleterre* (1888), p. 64; Leslie Stephen in *Dict. Nat. Biog.* L. 129.

[3] Leslie Stephen, *English Thought*, II. 33 ff.; and *Dict. Nat. Biog.* XXXVI. 21.

[4] *Remarks on the Fable of the Bees* (1724), reprinted 1846 with Introduction by F. D. Maurice.

[5] *Alciphron* (1732), Dialogue 2.

While Christian apologists were still engaged in proving the reasonableness of Christianity, an eccentric person, Henry Dodwell[1] the younger, published a pamphlet entitled *Christianity not founded on Argument*, in which he sought to put reason out of court altogether. The irony of this tract may easily be misunderstood, and some thought it to be a serious defence of simple faith, but its real tendency no doubt is to shew that no man who is guided by the principles of reason can possibly be a Christian.

<small>Ch. VI.
Henry Dodwell, d. 1784. 1742.</small>

The one man among the British Deists who belongs to European literature is David Hume[2], who was not, as is sometimes said, an atheist. "The order of the universe," he says, "proves an omnipotent mind. The whole frame of nature bespeaks an intelligent author; and no rational enquirer can, after serious reflection, suspend his belief a moment with regard to the primary principles of genuine Theism and Religion[3]." But he concludes that no one type or form of religion has a claim to be universally accepted. When he looks at the opinions and practices of mankind with regard to religion, it seems to him "a riddle, an enigma, an inexplicable mystery." He was in fact what would now be called an Agnostic. But the point which was especially attacked in his writings was his objection to miracles, which is briefly this. It is much more probable that the narrator of an event which appears to be contrary to all our experience should have been deceived or untruthful, than that the event should have in reality occurred. It was soon pointed out[4] that, though we should be cautious in our acceptance of wonders, if we arbitrarily exclude an event alleged to have occurred simply because we think that our induction on that point is already complete, we violate the principle of the inductive philosophy. We must in each case take the evidence for what it is worth, even if it compel us to abandon or modify a preconceived theory.

<small>David Hume, 1711—1776.

Essays, 1750.</small>

---

[1] J. Hunt, *Religious Thought in England*; Abbey and Overton, *English Church in the Eighteenth Century*, 205 ff.
[2] *Life* by J. Hill Burton (1846), T. H. Huxley (1879), W. Knight (1886), L. Stephen in *Dict. Nat. Biog.* xxviii. 215.
[3] See Knight's *Hume*, p. 207.
[4] *E.g.* by George Campbell, *Dissertation on Miracles* (1762).

Within the Church also there were a few who incurred the suspicion of scepticism as regards important articles of the faith. Conyers Middleton[1], a distinguished scholar, but in ill repute as a plagiarist, published opinions on miracles which, though in terms he limited his criticisms to alleged ecclesiastical wonders later than the age of the Apostles, seemed scarcely compatible with belief in any miracles at all. Hume found that Middleton's book had eclipsed the volume which contained his own argument on the same point.

In the revolutionary period probably no English book directed against Christianity attained so great a vogue as Thomas Paine's *Age of Reason*[2], a blatant attack on the Bible by a man very incompetent to touch such a subject. "His ignorance," says Leslie Stephen, "was vast and his language brutal; but he had the gift of a true demagogue, the power of wielding a fine vigorous English, a fit vehicle for fanatical passion." His work was formidable because it gave outspoken utterance to current doubts; but as he was blind to the moral and spiritual truths of the Bible, he was really an utterly incompetent critic. He was not an atheist, but a Deist of the Voltairean school. In his will he speaks of reposing confidence in his Creator-God and in no other being.

Among the many replies which it called forth one may be mentioned, that of Richard Watson, Bishop of Llandaff[3], already known for an *Apology for Christianity* directed against Gibbon. Watson's *Apology for the Bible* is the work of a really able and clear-sighted man, sufficiently acquainted with the Biblical criticism of his day, and treating his opponent with fairness and courtesy. It was very widely read by the generation in which it was produced.

The attacks of the Deists on beliefs which had hitherto passed unquestioned among Christians called forth very

---

[1] *Biographia Britannica*, v. 3092; Leslie Stephen in *Dict. Nat. Biog.* XXXVII. 343.

[2] *Life* by F. Oldys [*i.e.* G. Chalmers] (1791); with additions by W. Cobbett (1796), James Cheetham (New York, 1809); T. C. Rickman (1814), C. Blanchard (New York, 1860), Moncure D. Conway (1892); Leslie Stephen, in *English Thought*, I. 458, II. 260; and in *Dict. Nat. Biog.* XLIII. 69.

[3] *Anecdotes of the Life of R. W.*, written by himself, published by his son Richard (1817).

numerous replies. In fact, during the first half of the eighteenth century every divine who wished to be known as a champion of established truth tried his hand on the Deists. Most of them are now forgotten, as their opponents are, by all except professed students, and but few can be mentioned here, though the now obsolete controversy called forth a great deal of ingenious reasoning.

First among the refuters may be mentioned Edward (afterwards Bishop) Stillingfleet[1], whose *Origines Sacræ*, a work of real learning and ability, is—as it claims to be—"a rational account of the grounds of natural and revealed religion." Richard Bentley[2], the first English scholar of that age, under the pseudonym of Phileleutherus Lipsiensis, attacked Anthony Collins in a pamphlet which is absolutely crushing in its exposure of the incompetence of his flimsy scholarship for such a work as that which he had attempted, but which gives the reader an impression that Collins has been treated rather unhandsomely by his overbearing antagonist. Addison bantered the Free-thinkers with his usual light and skilful touch in the *Spectator*, and also wrote a set book on the Evidences of Christianity, which, when it was published by an injudicious friend after his death, shewed very plainly that he had undertaken a task for which his studies had in no way fitted him. Thomas Sherlock[3] produced a work in defence of the Gospel history which exactly hit the contemporary feeling and was widely read for a generation. This was the *Trial of the Witnesses*, in which the Apostles are tried according to the forms of English law for having given false evidence in the case of the resurrection of Jesus, and are triumphantly acquitted by the jury. Sherlock's work shews a good deal of ability of a kind which is not acceptable to religious-minded people.

But a far greater man than Sherlock defended the faith in a spirit which left nothing to be desired. Bishop

Stillingfleet's 'Origines Sacræ,' 1662.

Bentley's 'Remarks,' 1713.

Addison's 'Spectator,' 1711, 1712.

T. Sherlock's 'Trial of the Witnesses,' 1729.

---

[1] Burnet's *Own Time*, I. 189; *Biographia Britannica*; T. Baker's *Hist. of St John's Coll.*, Camb., ed. J. E. B. Mayor, II. 698 ff.

[2] *Life* by J. H. Monk (2nd ed. 1833), and by R. C. Jebb (1882).

[3] *Life* by J. S. Hughes in *Divines of the Church of England*, vol. I.

Berkeley[1] regarded his famous dialogues between Hylas and Philonous, in which he is generally supposed to have maintained the non-existence of matter, as a contribution to the maintenance of truth against sceptics and atheists; and his *Alciphron, or the Minute Philosopher*, contains "an apology for the Christian Religion against those who are called Free-thinkers." It does, in fact, defend with great vigour and ingenuity the faith of Christians in all the points which were then most commonly impugned. He criticises the prejudices from which the so-called Free-thinkers are not free, shews the necessity of recognizing an authoritative moral law sanctioned by God Himself, and discusses the nature of revelation and the objections alleged against Scripture. If, he concludes, "our youth were really inured to thought and reflection...we should soon see that licentious humour, vulgarly called *free-thinking*, banished from the presence of gentlemen together with ignorance and ill-taste."

A still greater apologist, as pure in life and as fair in reasoning as Bishop Berkeley, but in all else a curious contrast, was Bishop Butler[2]. In the midst of the ignorant babble and groundless assertions which were current, he raises his quiet voice to shew that it is, after all, not quite so clear that there is nothing in the Christian revelation. What the Deists grant—the existence and power of God—he assumes, but he makes no further assumptions. The aim of his famous treatise is to shew that the current objections to religion are equally applicable to the whole constitution of nature; and that the principles of Divine government revealed to us in Scripture so strongly resemble those manifested in the course of nature that we may reasonably infer that they have the same author. The work is so cautious in its assumptions and so sound in its inferences that—with the most insignificant exceptions—it met with no attempt at reply. His friends did not think him vigorous enough;

---

[1] *Life* by Joseph Stock (1776), reprinted in *Biog. Britannica* (1780) and prefixed to *Works* (1784); A. C. Fraser (in *Works* 1871; 2nd ed. 1901), and in *Philosophical Classics* (1881).

[2] *Life* in Supplement to *Biog. Britannica* (1753), and by Kippis in his edition of the *B. B.* (1778); by Thomas Bartlett (1839); W. A. Spooner (1901); Leslie Stephen in *Dict. Nat. Biog.* VIII. 67. See also F. D. Maurice, *Moral and Metaphysical Philosophy*, II. 459 (ed. 1873).

his calmness is not what they expected from a Christian advocate; but this calmness is not that of the sceptical but of the judicial mind, and it is mainly this quality which has caused Butler's work to endure while the hasty effusions of heated champions have been utterly forgotten.

Far removed in spirit from the calm and candid Butler was the impetuous and arrogant William Warburton[1]. The Deists had alleged as a strange defect in the Mosaic legislation that it makes no mention of a future state. Warburton accepts this statement. The legislators and mystagogues of the pagan world had, he said, always attempted to check vice and encourage virtue by dwelling on the rewards and punishments of the life to come. If the promises were not fulfilled, the failure was not detected. Moses alone, conscious of his Divine commission, had ventured to say that his people were the special care of God, Who dealt out in this life rewards and punishments to the nation and to individuals. This could be brought to the test of fact. If Moses had not been divinely inspired he would long ago have been detected as an impostor. The maintenance of the thesis as to the pagan teaching on the judgment to come led him to produce a curious mass of multifarious learning.

By far the most learned of the apologetic works which appeared in the eighteenth century was Nathaniel Lardner's[2] *Credibility of the Gospel History*, in which he undertook to shew that all the facts related in the New Testament are not only credible, but free from essential discrepancies and largely confirmed by contemporary evidence. His collection of authorities for determining the date and authorship of the New Testament books is of the highest value, and has been constantly drawn upon, sometimes without acknowledgement, by subsequent writers. He may be regarded as the "father" of those

---

[1] *Life* by Hurd, prefixed to *Works* (1794); J. S. Watson (1863); Leslie Stephen in *Dict. Nat. Biog.* LIX. 301. See also J. Hunt's *Religious Thought*, III. 146; Mark Pattison's *Essays* (1889) II. 119.

[2] *Life* by Joseph Jennings (1769, published anonymously), A. Kippis, prefixed to *Works* (1788). See also J. Hunt, *Religious Thought*, III. 238; J. B. Lightfoot, *Essays on Supernatural Religion*, p. 40, note 1.

CH. VI.

W. Warburton's 'Divine Legation of Moses,' 1737—1741.

Lardner's 'Credibility,' 1727—1756.

who write "Introductions" to the New Testament. Lardner, like many of his contemporaries, regarded Christianity as a republication of the Law of Nature, with the addition of two positive institutions, Baptism and the Supper of the Lord.

Samuel Johnson, 1709—1784.

A man who, though he contributed no special work to the defence of the Christian faith, was in fact one of its ablest defenders, was Samuel Johnson[1]. His vigorous conversation was always on the side of religion and morality, and the most flippant of Free-thinkers could not treat with contempt a cause which found favour with that robust thinker who was universally recognized as the leading man of letters of his day.

Paley's 'Evidences,' 1794.

The series of Christian apologists may well close with the name of William Paley[2], certainly one of the ablest and by far the most popular of them all. He summed up, with incomparable vigour and lucidity, almost all that was worth preserving in the apologetic writings which had gone before him. If his premises are granted, it is hardly possible to find a flaw in his argument. To originality he scarcely makes any claim, though his manner of stating them often makes old reasons new. His main argument is, that it is grossly improbable that a body of men should face torture and death, as it is admitted that the Apostles and their disciples did, in preaching the Gospel, if they had not been absolutely convinced of its truth. The then current charge of forgery of documents is absurd, for what motive could there be for forging them? To the special objection against miracles, that it is contrary to experience that miracles should be true, but not so that testimony should be false, he retorts, that to say that a miracle is contrary to universal experience is to beg the question, for if the evidence for a miracle is adequate, the alleged event is not contrary to universal experience. If it is meant that it is contrary to ordinary experience, that is admitted, for if this were not so the occurrence would not be a wonder. For his learning Paley is greatly indebted to Lardner.

In Great Britain the defence of the Christian faith

---

[1] It is hardly necessary to refer to the *Life* by James Boswell (1791, often reprinted).

[2] *Life* by G. W. Meadley (1809), E. Paley (1825), Leslie Stephen in *Dict. Nat. Biog.* XLIII. 101.

against the Deists was completely successful. They were altogether overmatched by their able opponents, and from the middle of the eighteenth century we hear little of them. But they kindled a flame which burned much more fiercely in France than it had ever done in the land in which it originated.

2. METHODISM[1] AND EVANGELICALISM.

The coldness of the eighteenth century naturally brought about a reaction. Men could not be for ever content with proving the reasonableness of a Christianity which had no hold upon their hearts and lives. If the Gospel was true it must needs be a great force in the world, not merely a series of propositions.

Reaction against Rationalism.

The movement which was destined to revive real and heartfelt godliness in England began at Oxford. In the spring of the year 1729 a few young men, among whom was Charles Wesley[2], son of a Lincolnshire clergyman, formed a little society "to observe the method of study prescribed by the statutes of the University," from which they "gained the harmless nickname of Methodist[3]." Towards the end of the same year John Wesley[4], Charles's elder brother, who was a Fellow of Lincoln and in Holy Orders, joined the Methodists, and by natural force of character became their head. George Whitefield[5] of Pembroke was admitted to membership in 1735. These young men were not only assiduous in study, but met every night for mutual edification; they relieved the poor, and watched over the welfare of school-children;

The Wesleys at Oxford, 1729.
C. Wesley, 1708—1788.
Oxford Methodists, 1729.
Whitefield, 1714—1770.

---

[1] Isaac Taylor, *Wesley and Methodism* (1851); G. Smith, *Hist. of Methodism* (1857); Abel Stevens, *Hist. of Methodism* (New York and London, 1858); J. Porter, *Comprehensive Hist.* (Cincinnati, 1876).

[2] *Life* by Whitehead (1793), Moore (1824), T. Jackson (1841), J. Telford (1886).

[3] These are Charles Wesley's words. See *Dict. Nat. Biog.* LX. 298.

[4] Wesley's Journals and Correspondence in his *Works* (1829), vols. 12 and 13. *Life* by J. Hampson (1791); Coke and Moore (1792), amended by Moore (1824); Whitehead (1791); R. Southey (1820), R. Watson (1831); L. Tyerman (1870); J. H. Overton (1891). See also Julia Wedgwood, *Wesley and the Evangelical Reaction* (1870), D. Urlin, *Wesley's Place in Church Hist.* (1870).

[5] *Life* by Gillies (1771), R. Philip (1838), J. R. Andrews (1864), L. Tyerman (1876).

they visited the prison and read prayers there; they received the Holy Communion weekly, and observed the fasts and festivals of the Church. Law's *Serious Call to a Devout and Holy Life* and *Christian Perfection* greatly influenced them. They were not, however, so ascetic as to deny themselves recreation; Wesley's cheerful good sense and knowledge of human nature prevented their zeal from becoming morbid. In 1735 the society, so far as Oxford was concerned, was broken up, and the two Wesleys crossed the Atlantic with General Oglethorpe to help him in his work among the poor colonists of Georgia. John Wesley's stay in Georgia lasted not more than two years, but it had a highly important influence on his life. Both on the voyage and in Georgia he was brought into contact with Moravians, from whom he learned the doctrine that true faith is inseparably connected with constant peace arising from a sense of forgiveness, and that saving faith is given in a moment. This came to him, he believed, at a Moravian meeting in London, where he heard Luther's "Introduction to St Paul's Epistle to the Romans." This doctrine of "assurance" the Methodists always preached, but as time went on they so far modified it as not to consign to eternal perdition all who had it not.

Meantime, his friend Whitefield, who had also visited America, had returned to England, and entered on a new phase of evangelical work. At Kingswood, near Bristol, he preached in the open air to a large company of miners, who heard him gladly. Wesley, strongly attached to Church order, at first hesitated to follow his example, but he overcame his scruples, and in April of the same year preached in the open air near Bristol, and thenceforth never hesitated to preach in any place where an assembly could be got together. In unwearied preaching he spent fifty years, holding forth in churches, in the fields, in public halls and meeting-houses of all kinds, almost everywhere with remarkable success. Tears ran down the blackened cheeks of Kingswood colliers when they were humbled under a sense of sin and were told— for the first time—of God's redeeming mercy in Christ, through which they too might have access to the throne of grace. Sometimes convulsionary movements and exclamations followed, but Wesley, an eminently sane and orderly man, by no means encouraged them. The Methodist preachers were denounced as setters forth of strange doctrine, as deceiving the people and causing disturbance, as claiming miraculous gifts, and even as bringing in popery. Sometimes they were mobbed and treated with great violence. But no persecution induced Wesley and his friends to desist from preaching that Gospel which they believed God had commissioned them to preach. As societies were founded in various parts of the country, some kind of ministry was required. Wesley, therefore, with some reluctance, appointed the most promising of his converts to be lay-preachers—men generally without much education, but often eloquent from the living faith that was in them. By a rule passed in 1763 they were not allowed to remain more than two (afterwards three) years in the same place. Meeting-houses also had to be provided for the new societies. These were at first held in trust by Wesley himself, but were afterwards conveyed to a body of preachers called the "Legal Hundred." When it became manifest that unworthy persons attached themselves to the society he adopted the plan of giving tickets to members, which were renewed every three months. Those who proved objectionable did not receive new tickets, and thus ceased to be members. When building-debts came to be burdensome, it was arranged that one out of every twelve members should collect offerings from the other eleven. Out of this grew, under Wesley's care, the class-meetings, which were found of great advantage in promoting the feeling of brotherhood, and in giving opportunities to reprove, rebuke, and exhort. For the maintenance of order and discipline quarterly visitations were instituted, and in 1743 Wesley drew up a code of "General Rules" for the "United Societies." As the numbers increased, it was thought desirable that there should be some standard of the doctrine to be taught by the preachers, and a more definite arrangement of their fields of labour. Hence in 1744 the two Wesleys, with four other clergymen and four lay-preachers, meeting in London, agreed upon certain definitions of doctrine and rules for the conduct of the preachers. This was the first Methodist Conference. Two years later Wesley assigned to each of his helpers a definite "circuit," within which

Lay-preachers, c. 1740.

Chapels.

Class-Meetings, 1742.

First Conference, 1744.

Circuits, 1746.

he should itinerate, fearing that dulness would follow a stationary ministry. As his societies became more numerous and independent the question of separation from the Church became more and more pressing. Charles Wesley always strenuously opposed it. John wrote in 1745 that he and his friends would make any sacrifice to live in harmony with the clergy short of giving up their characteristic doctrine, their preaching in private houses or in the open air, and their lay-preachers. But, he said, "we dare not administer Baptism or the Lord's Supper without a commission from a bishop in the apostolic succession." In the following year, however, he became convinced that apostolical succession was not found in the bishops alone, but that he was himself "a scriptural *episcopos* as much as any man in England." From this it was a natural inference that ordination by presbyters was valid, though it was not until a much later date that he ordained his preachers by imposition of hands, and empowered them to administer the sacraments. A further step was taken when in 1787 he set apart, by laying on of hands, Dr Coke, a presbyter of the Church of England, to be superintendent or "bishop" in America, and a preacher, Alexander Mather, to a similar office in England. To both these he considered that he had committed the power of ordaining others. Thus what had been in its first intention an order or brotherhood for promoting spiritual life within the Church became a definitely schismatical body. Yet Wesley declared that he had not separated from the Church, nor ever intended to do so, and in fact he died in its communion.

While Wesley was building up the Methodist system, his early friend, George Whitefield, went on his own way. Wesley all his life held in horror the Calvinistic views of arbitrary election and reprobation, and expressed himself on the subject with outspoken vigour. Whitefield defended the decrees, and so fundamental a difference led in 1741 to separation. Whitefield, Harris, Cennick, and others became the founders of Calvinistic Methodism. Wesley and Whitefield soon renewed their personal friendship, but with others there arose a hot controversy.

Wesley died March 2, 1791, retaining much of his

activity to the last. He had preached at Leatherhead only nine days before his death. His life had been one of the most extraordinary vigour. He travelled unceasingly, generally on horseback, often preaching two or three times in a day. He supervised the business and the discipline of his numerous societies, he published a very large number of books on the most varied subjects, he entered zealously into controversies, and carried on an immense correspondence. Of the large sums which he received for his books he spent by far the greater part in furtherance of his work, and died poor. As the result of his lifelong labours he left 135,000 members and 541 itinerant preachers, bearing the name of "Wesleyan Methodist." Whether it would have been possible by gentler treatment to retain the Methodists within the Church of England is one of those questions which can never be determined. Several bishops treated Wesley with great respect and courtesy, but the feeling of the clergy generally was no doubt opposed to an enthusiasm which overleaped the bounds of ecclesiastical order and presented a startling contrast to their own inertness. In the end there can be no doubt that the indirect influence of Wesley produced a great effect upon the Church.

Ch. VI.
Wesley's death, 1791.

The career of George Whitefield differed widely from that of his friend Wesley. His extraordinary eloquence stirred great audiences not only in England, Scotland and Wales, but also in America, to which he paid seven visits. As to the effect of his preaching we have the testimony of hearers by no means prejudiced in his favour, such as Lord Chesterfield in England and Benjamin Franklin in America. But he preached a doctrine of election and reprobation which Wesley could not endure, and he had no genius for organization. His deficiencies in this respect were, however, to some extent compensated by his famous disciple, Selina, Countess of Huntingdon[1], who had it in a high degree. While Whitefield preached she built chapels, even selling her jewels for the purpose. She also opened her own house in London for religious meetings, to which her rank and social influence drew many of the upper class. In 1779 she left the Church,

Whitefield's Preaching.

Lady Huntingdon, 1707 —1791.

---

[1] Anon. *Life and Times of Selina, Countess of Huntingdon* (London, 1840); A. H. New, *Memorials* (1857).

finding that her chaplains could not preach without the consent of the clergyman in whose parish they desired to hold forth, and desiring that, as Dissenters, they should have the benefit of the Toleration Act. She exercised over her chapels much the same kind of authority which Wesley did over his, and at the time of her death there were sixty-four belonging to what was called "the Countess of Huntingdon's Connexion." In these the polity was Congregationalist, the doctrine Calvinistic, and the worship that of the Prayer-book of the Church. Such chapels subsist, in diminished number, even to this day

Evangelical Movement.

In consequence of the inertness of many of the clergy there arose from about the middle of the eighteenth century a movement which did not follow Wesley's lines, and was indeed in many cases distinctly hostile to him. Conspicuous among the leaders of this Evangelical revival was Augustus Toplady[1], author of the well-known hymn "Rock of Ages," whose very considerable powers and forcible style were devoted to the propagation of unmitigated Calvinism. He exalted the grace of God in the work of salvation to such an extent as to seem to deny free-will in man. Wesley he assailed, in his juvenile fervour and intolerance, with absolute scurrility. He was met by another clergyman of a very different spirit, a disciple of Wesley's, John Fletcher[2], vicar of Madeley, a man not only of saintly life but of real literary gifts, who pleaded, with good reason, that a "grey-haired minister of Christ, an old general in the armies of Emmanuel...should have met with more consideration." Another clergyman of the Calvinistic school was William Romaine[3], Lady Huntingdon's principal counsellor, whose doctrine of indefectible grace came perilously near to Antinomianism, though his personal holiness is unquestioned. A much more temperate advocate of Evangelical principles was Henry Venn[4], who, although influenced in early life by Wesley, adopted Calvinistic views, but without the arrogant assumption that all who rejected them must perish.

A. Toplady, 1740—1778.

Fletcher of Madeley, 1729—1785.

W. Romaine, 1714—1795.

H. Venn, 1725—1797.

---

[1] *Life* by W. Row (1794); W. Winters (1872). See also J. C. Ryle, *Christian Leaders of a Hundred Years ago* (1869).

[2] *Life* by J. Wesley (1786); J. C. Ryle, *Christian Leaders* (1869), p. 384 ff.

[3] *Life* by W. B. Cadogan (1796).

[4] *Life* by J. & H. Venn (1834).

Among Evangelical writers must be reckoned George Horne, Bishop of Norwich, who held that "whoever preaches and enforces moral duties, without justification and sanctification preceding, may as well declaim on the advantages of walking to a man that can neither stir hand nor foot." He fully recognized, however, the necessity of Church order, and complains that if a man spoke of the divine right of episcopacy and the danger of schism, he was said to be "just going over to Popery[1]." Likeminded with Horne was his friend William Jones of Nayland in whom so competent a judge as Bishop Horsley recognized an extraordinary power of making the deepest subjects plain to an ordinary understanding[2].

Of the bishops probably no man in the latter part of the century did more to promote truly Evangelical religion than Beilby Porteus[3], Bishop of London. He was in high repute as a preacher, and by his combination of firmness of principle with courtesy of manner did much to bring about a higher standard of conduct in the upper circles. Even the heir to the throne himself did not escape his reproof when he disregarded the sanctity of the Lord's Day. He did his best to put down the covert simony which was too often practised by the clergy, and refused to license men of doubtful character for foreign chaplaincies. He was also among the first to raise his voice for giving Christian teaching and better treatment to the slaves in the West Indies. But he was not tolerant of disorderly methods, and vigorously resisted the invasion of unauthorized preachers on parish churches. He approved of Sunday-schools, then looked upon by many with suspicion, and promoted their adoption in his diocese.

Probably the most learned men of the early Evangelical movement were the brothers Joseph[4] and Isaac Milner[5], the latter President of Queens' College, Cambridge, and a man of great influence in the University. Joseph wrote a Church History of an unusual kind. The terms "Church"

---

[1] See Perry's *History*, III. 38, 40. *Life* by W. Jones (1795).
[2] *Ib.* 39. *Life* by W. Stephens (1801).
[3] *Life* by R. Hodgson, prefixed to *Works* (1811).
[4] *Life* by Isaac Milner, prefixed to *Practical Sermons* (1800).
[5] *Life* by Mary Milner (1842); James Stephen, *Essays in Eccl. Biog.* II. 358 ff. (1849).

and "Christian," he says, in their proper use refer only to good men; his history is, consistently with this principle, mainly an account of those in each age whom the author held to be real followers of Christ. Joseph's work was edited and amplified by Isaac, who long survived his brother.

Cowper, the Poet, 1731—1800.

Among persons of taste and cultivation probably no man did so much to spread Evangelical teaching as William Cowper[1]. In his works religion is recommended by an admirable style and playful fancy, quick strokes of satire and genuine tenderness, while he shews a love of nature which is one of the first indications of the revolt against the smooth conventions of Pope and his school. He wrote many hymns, some of which are generally found in collections even unto this day—hymns as much distinguished from the coarser compositions of vulgar writers by their genuine feeling as by the scholarly grace and simplicity of their diction and rhythm. But the form of piety which Cowper had adopted, dwelling as it did too much on the condition of lost souls, unhinged a mind always over-sensitive and morbidly introspective. With all its humorousness Cowper's is one of the saddest of lives.

J. Newton, 1725—1807.

His principal adviser in matters of religion was John Newton[2], in his later days a very popular preacher in London, who had been in early life a seaman and—if we may trust his own account—a man of evil life. Newton, however, like many men who have been converted from carelessness to Calvinism, was much given to needless self-accusation, a tendency which had a disastrous effect on Cowper, whom he nevertheless tenderly loved and watched over. He was a moderate Calvinist compared with some of his contemporaries, and his spiritual letters, published under the title *Cardiphonia*, are the most remarkable writings of that kind produced by the Evangelical revival.

Thomas Scott, 1747—1821.

Another man distinguished for his advocacy of Evangelical principles was Thomas Scott[3], Newton's successor

---

[1] *Life* by W. Hayley (1803), J. Johnson (1815), R. Southey (1834), T. S. Grimshaw (1835), J. Bruce, prefixed to Aldine edition (1865), W. Benham, prefixed to Globe edition.

[2] *Life* by R. Cecil, prefixed to *Works*, 1816.

[3] *Life* by his son (1822).

as curate of Olney. He is probably best known as the author of a commentary on the whole Bible, once much read both by clergy and laity, now little used and, though not without merit, admitted to be overweighted with commonplace. But his great merit was his earnest protest against the teaching which made the doctrine of grace a cloak for want of holiness. It was this phase of his work which deeply influenced John Henry Newman in early life, and drew from him a strong expression of gratitude, for that to him, humanly speaking, he almost owed his own soul[1].

But towards the end of the eighteenth century the great leader of the Evangelical party within the Church was Charles Simeon[2], a Fellow of King's College, Cambridge. He began his ministerial career with a vehemence which frightened his congregation; he had not then learned, as he afterwards admitted, to consider not only what he was able to say, but what they were able to receive. But this phase of indiscreet juvenile dogmatism soon passed away; his character and his preaching won over the opponents in his parish, and he became the guide, adviser, and instructor of many generations of undergraduates, doing in fact much of the work which should have been done by the professors of theology. In this way his influence was diffused over the whole country, and countless disciples preached sermons founded on the outlines supplied in Simeon's *Horæ Homileticæ*. Throughout his long life he remained, as his letters shew, firmly attached to the doctrine and the liturgy of the Church of England. It would be a mistake to suppose that he was one of those who hold that, so long as the Gospel is preached, ecclesiastical forms are matters of indifference.

The teaching of the Evangelicals also roused many laymen to activity in the cause of Christ. William Wilberforce[3] devoted his remarkable powers almost entirely to religious and philanthropic objects, especially to the abolition of the slave-trade. John Thornton and

Charles Simeon, 1759—1836.

Influence at Cambridge, 1783—1836.

W. Wilberforce, 1759—1833.

J. Thornton, 1720—1790.

[1] Newman's *Hist. of my Religious Opinions*, p. 5 (1865).
[2] *Life* by W. Carus (1847), H. C. G. Moule (1892).
[3] *Life* by his sons, 5 vols. (1838), condensed by S. Wilberforce (1868).

See also James Stephen, in *Essays on Eccl. Biog.*; J. C. Colquhoun, *W. Wilberforce, his Friends, &c.* (1866); J. J. Gurney, *Familiar Sketch of W.* (1838); J. Stoughton, *W. Wilberforce* (1880).

his son Henry[1] were striking examples of men of business who regarded their wealth as held in trust for pious uses. Hannah More[2] set forth the principles of Christianity in a style acceptable to cultivated readers. The society of good Christian men and women which was formed round Wilberforce and the Thorntons, who lived at Clapham, came to be commonly known as the Clapham Sect[3].

3. FRENCH SCEPTICISM.

In the seventeenth century French society was dominated by three influences—Catholicism, the study of classical antiquity, and the monarchy of Louis XIV. The traits most conspicuous in the eighteenth were the sceptical philosophy, the assertion of the rights of man against despotism, and the sedulous cultivation of the literary style which has ever since prevailed in France[4]. Nothing can be more unlike than the two periods, but the passage from one to the other was not sudden or abrupt. The spirit of inquiry and innovation had precursors even before the days of Bossuet. The *Heptaplomeres*[5] of John Bodin, the famous publicist, shews the direction in which at any rate some thoughts were tending. It is a dialogue between a Jew, a Mohammedan, a Lutheran, a Zwinglian, a Roman Catholic, an Epicurean, and a Deist, who come to the conclusion that all positive religions are imperfect, and that it is well to be content with accepting those truths on which all are agreed.

But the ablest promoter of doubt in the seventeenth century was René Descartes[6]. He deliberately cleared

[1] M. Seeley, *Later Evangelical Fathers*, p. 20 (1879); Leslie Stephen in *Dict. Nat. Biog.* vol. LVI. p. 301.
[2] *Life* by H. Thompson (1838).
[3] James Stephen, *The Clapham Sect* in *Essays on Eccl. Biography*.
[4] The principal work on French philosophy in the 18th cent. is Ph. Damiron's *Mémoires pour servir à l'Histoire de la Philosophie au XVIIIme Siècle* (1858—1864). See also P. Lanfrey, *L'Église et les Philosophes au XVIIIme Siècle* (1879).

[5] This was first printed by Noack in 1857, but it seems to have circulated in MS. See H. Baudrillard, *Jean Bodin et son Temps* (1853) and R. Flint, *Philosophy of History in Europe*, vol. I.
[6] A. Baillet, *La Vie de M. des Cartes* (1691); Bordas-Demoulin, *Le Cartésianisme* (1874); Kuno Fischer, *Descartes and his School* (Eng. Trans, 1887); English works by W. Cunningham (1877), R. Lowndes (1878), J. P. Mahaffy (1880), and James Martineau (1885).

his mind, as far as possible, of all traditional prejudices, and started in pursuit of truth from the mere fact of personal existence. "I think, therefore I am," was his initial assumption—an assumption which was not accepted in the following century by Hume, who pointed out that the notion of personality is itself a hypothesis, all that we really know being present sensation. But even without Hume's corollary, it is evident that Descartes' rejection of all authority, and his assertion that all pursuit of truth must begin with doubt, while nothing was to be accepted which was not in accordance with right reason, could not be favourable to a religion which rests mainly on authority, even though he himself found, on his own principles, a demonstration of the being of God and of the universe. Moreover his explanation of the principal phenomena of the universe by the theory of vortices, or whirls of matter, had immense popularity, and tended in many minds to substitute purely physical conceptions for that of a personal creator and ruler.

The severity of the press-laws in France at once embittered the attacks on existing institutions and caused them to take covert forms. Thus one Vairesse, an otherwise unknown person, disguised an attack on the priesthood under the cloak of a history of an imaginary people called the Severambes, and Fontenelle introduced a similar attack into a history of Borneo[1]. But perhaps in the early part of the eighteenth century the man who did most to promote general scepticism was Peter Bayle, whose Dictionary—in many respects an excellent work— is pervaded by the doubting tone of a literary man of vast reading who has sought knowledge freely and frankly. It is sometimes said that the eighteenth century begins with Bayle. Montesquieu[2], under the disguise of a Persian visiting France, satirized many of her established institutions, not excluding those of the Church, and in his great work on Laws certainly favours the conception that natural causes may have produced all the phenomena of history, without recourse to the notion of supernatural intervention.

Ch. VI.
'*Disc. de la Méthode*,' 1637.

'*Principes de Philosophie*,' 1644.

1677.
1684.

Bayle, 1647— 1706. Dictionary, 1696.

Montesquieu,1689 —1755.

---

[1] Schröckh, *Neuere K.-G.* vi. 240.
[2] *Biographia Britannica*, s.v. Secondat (Supplement, 160); L. Vian, *Hist. de Montesquieu* (1878); A. Sorel, *Montesquieu* (Eng. by Masson, 1887).

Astruc,
1684—
1766.

1755.

Voltaire,
1694—
1778.

A remarkable critic may be mentioned here, though hardly to be included among sceptics, for he had no intention of promoting scepticism. This is Jean Astruc[1], surgeon to Louis XIV., who, it was said, applied his scalpel to the Pentateuch. A Hebrew scholar, and generally an accomplished and thoughtful man, he seems to have been the first to observe that in some portions of the book of Genesis the word " Jehovah " is used to designate the Most High, in others " Elohim," and to have drawn the conclusion that these belonged to different documents. He was far from denying the Mosaic authorship of the Pentateuch, as is manifest from the title of his book— *Conjectures on the Original Documents which Moses appears to have used in the Composition of the Book of Genesis.* His purpose seems in fact to have been apologetic; his hypothesis explained, he thought, the repetitions and inversions of chronological order which are found in Genesis. Whatever his intention, his unpretending book has been the fruitful parent of the various theories as to the documents which compose the Pentateuch, some of which in our own time have come to be generally accepted.

These were but sporadic attacks, but somewhat later so many of the most eminent men of letters in France joined in the attack on Christianity and the Church that they might almost seem to have entered into a conspiracy of irreligion. At the head of these was the most brilliant writer of his time, Francis Arouet, called Voltaire[2]. Voltaire was not an absolute atheist, but rather an agnostic, and he was accused by coarser minds of timidity and reticence, and of cherishing a prejudice in favour of the being of God. He undoubtedly did good service in defence of the oppressed, and that in days when opposition to a despotic government and a powerful Church involved real danger; but he put forth a series of writings in which the Bible and Christianity are assailed with most pungent wit and the most complete ignoring of the real nature of the institutions which are assailed. Whether he designed

---

[1] *Memoir* by Lorry (Montpellier, 1767). See Wellhausen in his ed. of Bleek's *Einleitung,* p. 654 f.

[2] G. Desnoiresterres, *Voltaire et la Société du XVIIIme Siecle*; D.F.

Strauss, *Voltaire* (six lectures, Eng. 1878); John Morley, *Voltaire* (1872); also sketches by E. B. Hamley (1877) and F. Espinasse (1892).

to crush Christianity itself, or only to put an end to the claims of sacerdotalism, remains doubtful. Diderot, a man of extraordinary ability and versatility, gave currency to the old Democritean theory that the world was formed by a fortuitous concurrence of atoms, producing, by their innate properties, an infinite number of creatures, of which only those survived which were adapted to their environment. D'Alembert, the famous mathematician, joined him for a time in the production of the famous *Encyclopédie*, but it was the courage and energy of Diderot which brought it to completion. This work, undertaken to give a systematic account of all the knowledge of the time, is hostile to all kinds of authority in matters of opinion, and nowhere refers any phenomenon to a supernatural origin[1].

But the anti-Christian spirit had by no means said its last word in Voltaire and his friends. There followed a more deliberate assault upon all religion and morality. In this second stage of the movement, aristocratic licentiousness passes into cynical defence of immorality, reasonable independence into defiance of all restraint, free inquiry into repudiation of all nobler principle. Condillac frankly announced that the object of his work was to shew how all our knowledge and all our faculties are derived from the senses; the soul thus sinks into nothingness. Helvetius also set himself to prove that sensation is the source of all intellectual activity, and that the great spring of human action is self-love. Such works as these prepared the way for the flat atheism and licentiousness of D'Holbach and his school, whose works are at once paltry and pernicious. Other writers indirectly contributed to the subversion of faith. Even Buffon's great work tends to regard a deified Nature as the cause of all things. Lalande treated of the laws which govern the heavenly bodies without thinking it necessary to mention God, while Dupuis seemed to regard the life of Christ as an astronomical myth.

Jean Jacques Rousseau[2] occupies a place apart. While

---

[1] See John Morley, *Diderot and the Encyclopaedists* (1878).
[2] *Life* by V. D. Musset-Pathay (1825); John Morley (1873). See also St Marc-Girardin, *J. J. Rousseau, Sa Vie et ses Ouvrages* (1875); C. Borgeaud, *J. J. Rousseau's Religionsphilosophie* (Jena, 1883); A. F. Villemain, *Litt. du XVIIIme Siècle*, pt I. Lectures 22—24.

Diderot, 1713—1784.

D'Alembert, 1717—1783. 1751—1772.

Coarser Atheism.

Condillac, 1715—1780.

Helvetius, 1715—1771.

D'Holbach's 'Système de la Nature,' 1770. *Buffon,* 1707—1788. *Lalande,* 1732—1807. '*Origine de tous les Cultes,*' 1795.

he admired the character of Christ, he did not accept historical Christianity. His book on the Social Contract begins with the words "Man is born free." If he has surrendered a portion of his natural liberty, it is in consequence of a definite contract with his fellows. All society, all morality is founded on contract; the people made it and may unmake it. From its decision there is no appeal. The theme of another famous book, *Émile*, is that man is born good; all the apparatus of education and civilization by which he is surrounded does but hamper and spoil his native goodness. Our great endeavour should be to strip ourselves of these mischievous accretions and return to the state of nature. These opinions Rousseau, a man of undoubted genius, maintained with a force, a clearness, a subdued passion, which gave them immense influence not only in France but in the rest of Europe and in America. Even now Voltaire and Rousseau exercise a large, though often unsuspected influence: in their own day they gave rise to an extraordinary enthusiasm, which contributed very largely to the overthrow of Church and State with which the century closed.

In Paris, in the latter part of the eighteenth century, scepticism came to have the authority and the intolerance of recognized dogma. Its doctrines, no longer merely negative, became a kind of creed. To sober doubts, to partial attacks, to raillery which respected at any rate certain great principles, there succeeded deliberate and systematic destruction of all belief in religion and morality. Materialistic opinions came to be asserted with lofty pretensions. There was a kind of apostolate of atheism. From such teaching it is naturally inferred that men should cease to occupy themselves with futile speculations about a First Cause, and devote themselves to the pursuit of their own well-being; as if man could reach his best state without cultivating his highest faculties, without the conception of God, of duty, and of virtue.

It must be confessed that in France the defenders of Christian truth were intellectually by no means on a level with those who attacked it. Many attempted to refute the destructive principles of the innovators, but their works have sunk into not unmerited oblivion. One only among them, the abbé Guénée, produced a work, *Letters of*

Certain Jews, which had some vogue. Superior to Voltaire in knowledge of the Hebrew language and history, he had a good style and a pleasant wit; but to defend the Bible and the foundations of the faith something more was needed. Yet there still existed in France men distinguished by good sense and purity of life who were not swept away by the current of infidelity, men who still maintained the tradition of Port-Royal, and presented a striking contrast to the sceptical and frivolous set which owned Voltaire as its king. To this group belonged the Chancellor D'Aguesseau, Rollin the historian, the younger Racine, and—greatest of them all—the Duc de St Simon, the keen-witted observer who has left us so vivid a picture of the latter days of Louis XIV. and the earlier portion of the reign of his successor. A Jansenist in such a court must have been a man of great steadfastness and force of character.

The assembly of the clergy directed the attention of King Louis XV. to the pernicious influence of the infidel writings, and proposed measures for checking their circulation. An advocate, Seguier, was commissioned to report to the King on the proposals of the clergy, and in the end the Parliament of Paris ordered certain offensive works to be publicly burnt; but it was impossible to annihilate the sympathy with the incriminated books which was so widely spread in France. Riches and power were on the side of the Church, but on the other side were the great multitude, including many of the nobles and even of the clergy themselves, who regarded the powers claimed by priests as founded on an illusion, and their riches as stolen from an over-burdened commonalty.

D'Aguesseau, 1668—1751.
Rollin, 1661—1741.
L. Racine, 1692—1763.
St Simon, 1675—1755.
Assemblies of 1765 *and* 1770.

4. GERMAN ENLIGHTENMENT[1].

In Germany, as in England, the tendency of the popular philosophy in the early part of the eighteenth century was towards the assertion of the supremacy of reason in all departments of human thought. Those who defended Christianity defended it on the ground

Philosophic movements.

---

[1] On the German religious literature of this period, see Joseph Gostwick, *German Culture and Christianity* (London, 1882).

B. Spinoza, 1632—1677.

that it was reasonable, those who attacked it attacked it on the ground that it was not reasonable.

Spinoza[1], a Jew and a recluse, was not a popular philosopher, but for more than two centuries he has been a power in the world, through the influence which he has had upon some of the foremost thinkers, such as Goethe. Spinoza was an ardent believer in God; outside of God nothing can exist. But his God is not the personal deity whom Christians worship, but only the substance or substratum of existing objects; and individual man is but a mode of the divine substance, moved by an infinite series of causes. If men seem to be free, it is because they are unconscious of the forces to which they are subject. Spinoza's system is thus incompatible with Christianity, or even with Judaism as commonly understood.

Leibnitz, 1646—1715.

G. W. Leibnitz[2], lawyer, mathematician, historian, metaphysician and theologian, had in his day immense influence in Germany and in Europe generally. His optimism is seen in his famous justification of the ways of God to man. All is for the best in the best of all possible worlds; evil is simply the necessary limitation of every created thing; something metaphysical, not moral. The course of events is regulated by a pre-established harmony which scarcely leaves room for the freedom of man's will. Christianity is no more than the best and purest of religions, natural religion made by Christ a law for all. His system hardly admitted the conception of supernatural revelation, though he was always regarded as a believer, and was even suspected of Romanism.

Wolf, 1679—1754.

But by far the most popular philosopher of Germany in the early part of the eighteenth century was Christian Wolf[3], who had the distinction of being banished from Prussia by the drill-sergeant king Frederick-William I.,

---

[1] Amand Saintes, *Hist. de la vie ...de Spinoza* (1842); Ginsberg, *Leben...Spinoza's* (1876); R. Willis, *B. de Spinoza* (1870); F. Pollock, *Spinoza, his Life and Philosophy* (1880); James Martineau, *Spinoza* (1882); M. Nourisson, *Spinoza et le Naturalisme Contemp.* (1866).

[2] *Life* by Guhrauer (1842-46), E. Pfleiderer (1870). On his philosophy, see A. Foucher de Careil, *Leibnitz, Descartes et Spinoza* (1863); M. Nourisson, *Philosophie de Leibnitz* (1860).

[3] *Autobiography* published by Wuttke (Leipzig, 1840). Ludovici, *Historie der Wolf. Philosophie* (Leipzig, 1737); Hartmann, *Historie der Leibnitz-Wolf. Phil.* (Leipzig, 1857).

and recalled with great triumph by his son Frederick II. He was in the main a disciple and interpreter of Leibnitz, not an original thinker. The great object of his life was to make all truth as binding on the reason as mathematical truth is; to give a mathematical demonstration of the mysteries of Christianity. His method was very favourably received, and had the effect that many of the clergy preached natural science instead of dogmatic theology. The weapons of sound reasoning were turned against those who assailed Christianity on what were thought to be scientific grounds. But gradually it became clear that reason, if it was to be the sole authority in the field of religion, might set to work to clear it of everything which rested on a supernatural basis. As natural religion rose, revealed religion sank. Hence there arose a strong anti-Wolfian reaction.

With Kant[1], the German Socrates, we enter on a new period in the history of philosophy, and consequently of theology. In the midst of the discussions which claimed to be founded on reason, Kant raised the preliminary question, What is reason? What are its powers in the search for truth? What are its limitations? Here he finds everything uncertain; even of the objects of sense we know only impressions, not what the objects are in themselves. What is certain is that the intellectual processes of all sane men are subject to certain laws which they cannot overleap. Moreover, man cannot emancipate himself from the inevitable laws which rule the universe, he cannot prove by pure reason that a God exists distinct from the world, that death does not await everything that has a birth or beginning. So far, the system seems to lead to universal scepticism or agnosticism. But Kant was very far from being a merely negative spirit. He saw in man not only reason, but will; a practical as well as a theoretical reason; a moral sense by which we recognize a moral law. Kant starts in this

Kant, 1724 —1804.

'Critique of Pure Reason,' 1781.

'Critique of Practical Reason,' 1787.

---

[1] Accounts of Kant's philosophy are found in all histories of modern philosophy, of which Kuno Fischer's may be specially mentioned. See also H. L. Mansel, *Lecture on the Philosophy of Kant* (1856), reprinted in *Letters, Lectures and Reviews*, p. 156 (1873); J. P. Mahaffy, *Kant's Critical Philosophy for English Readers* (1872 ff.). The *Kritik of Practical Reason* has been translated and edited by T. K. Abbott (2nd ed. 1879).

part of his investigation from the position that all true goodness depends on the will, and that that will is good which acts from a sense of duty, not from mere inclination. Duty is obedience to the moral law, and this law, recognized by the conscience or moral sense, is absolute in its authority; it is, to use his own term, a categorical imperative; its voice is "thou shalt." It is not dependent on antecedent principles or reasonings; it speaks as having authority to command man's actions. Hence it follows that man's will is free to act on the bidding of duty, for "thou shalt" can only be said where "thou canst" may also be said. And the true end of man's actions, thus guided by the moral law, is the highest good or blessedness. But this cannot be realized under the conditions of our sensuous existence. A frail and sinful being cannot realize moral perfection or holiness within the bounds of this mortal life. To realize this, man must be immortal; the law which requires perfection demands immortality as a condition for its realization. But all this presumes the existence of a just and almighty God; for only such a God could so order the course of the world that man may not be inevitably let and hindered in running the race that is set before him. Nature must serve the moral law if man's blessedness is to be complete, and only the Lord of heaven and earth can bring it so to serve. These then are the necessary postulates of the practical reason—the logical consequences of the categorical imperative—Freedom, Immortality, God[1]. These may be no objects of speculative knowledge, but they are objects of rational faith. Thus Kant is the prophet of duty and immortality, as well as the father of that critical philosophy which has so largely influenced the thoughts of men for more than a century.

Jacobi, 1743—1819.

Jacobi[2], agreeing with Kant as to the limited power of pure reason, preached faith as a philosophical principle. If we cannot attain by a mere process of reasoning to the knowledge of things divine and eternal, this incapacity is due to the use of the wrong instrument. Other

---

[1] A. M. Fairbairn, *The Philosophy of the Christian Religion*, pp. 87 ff. (1902).
[2] Ueberweg's *Hist. of Philosophy*, II. 198 ff. (Eng. Trans.), where J. Kuhn, *Jacobi u. die Philosophie seiner Zeit* (Mainz, 1834) and E. Zirngiebel, *F. H. Jacobi's Leben* (Wien, 1867), are referred to.

portions of man's nature, as well as reason, have their own powers and rights: there is still an organ for the apprehension of that which lies beyond understanding—feeling. In feeling, therefore, in intuition, in faith, Jacobi finds that certainty which Kant failed to find in mere discourse of reason. He said of himself that his understanding was pagan, but his heart was Christian. His works were popular rather than scholastic, and had much influence outside academic circles.

No one among the philosophers who followed Kant had greater influence on theology than Fichte[1]. He was driven from his professorship at Jena (1799) by a charge of atheism which had absolutely no justification. It was not the existence of God that he denied, but the existence of the external world. That which we call the world is merely assumed by the self-conscious being, the "ego"; it is only in and through the "ego" that it exists. In his later and more popular writings Fichte's philosophy assumes a distinctly religious character, the central point of the system being the absolute "ego," the one universal being or God, of whom all finite existence is but a manifestation, the vesture of the Eternal. Through Carlyle, Fichte has had an important influence on the formation of opinion in Great Britain and America. It is Fichte's conception of the universe which underlies Carlyle's most impressive teachings on human life and duty.

But outside the ranks of the more strictly philosophical writers, the poets and prose-writers of the greatest period of German literature received and diffused the spirit of their age, and their influence was not favourable to the Christian faith as it had been hitherto understood. Two men almost equally interesting in theology and in literature stand forth as the harbingers of the literary spring which was coming to Germany—Lessing and Herder.

Gotthold Ephraim Lessing[2], an admirable poet and still more admirable prose-writer and critic, said of himself that he was no theologian but an amateur in

[1] See W. Smith's *Memoir* prefixed to his translation of Fichte's *Popular Works* (1873); and *Fichte*, by Professor Adamson in Blackwood's *Philosophical Classics* (1881).

[2] *Life* by James Sime (1877), Helen Zimmern (1878), Rolleston (1889). On his theology, see Lichtenberger, *Idées Religieuses*, I. 69 ff.; Hase, *K.-G.* III. 2, 272 ff.

theology. No man however contributed more to the movement of thought which in the end changed the whole tone of theological studies in Germany. God, he held, educated and developed the race of man by His divine guidance of history, rather than by a revelation of His will in a series of documents of irrefragable authority[1]. The New Testament was the fruit, not the cause, of Christianity, and the tradition of the Church embodied in the Apostles' Creed was of no less authority than Scripture, though after all truth must prevail as truth, not by mere external testimony. The parable of the Three Rings[2] shews that he did not regard the claims of Christianity as absolutely and obviously superior to those of Judaism and Mohammedanism. In fact, it is clear that he regarded all religions claiming to rest on divine revelation as almost equally true and equally false.—John Gottfried Herder[3] was Chaplain to Duke Karl August at Weimar during the period when that court sheltered the greatest of German men of letters, among whom Herder is himself a not inconsiderable figure. Always rather a man of feeling than of definite opinions, and always inclining to faith rather than to doubt, his influence was yet, on the whole, favourable to a naturalistic view of Scripture and religion. If in writing on the "spirit of Hebrew Poetry" he found new beauties in psalms and prophecies, it was on the same principle on which he found them in Homer and Ossian. In the sketch which he put forth of the ideas which should preside over the study of mankind, the sacred history is presented as a part of universal history, not as altogether apart and miraculous.—The majestic figure of Goethe[4], great both in knowledge and in imaginative

---

[1] Temple's essay on the education of the world in *Essays and Reviews* is founded on Lessing's *Erziehung des Menschengeschlecht*.
[2] *Nathan der Weise*, act 3, sc. 7.
[3] *Life* by R. Haym (1880-85). See also Joret, *Herder et la Renaissance Littéraire en Allemagne* (1875), and H. Nevinson, *Herder and his Times* (1884). On his attitude towards theology, see A. Werner, *Herder als Theologe* (Berlin, 1871); Lichtenberger, *Hist. des Idées Rel. en Allemagne*, I. 179 ff.; Pfleiderer, *Development of Theology*, pp. 21 ff. (London, 1890); Hase, *K.-G.* III. 2. 280.
[4] *Life* by G. H. Lewes (1855), Düntzer (Eng. tr. 1883), James Sime (1888). On Goethe's religion, L. von Lancizolle, *Goethe's Verhältniss z. Religion u. Christenthum* (1855).

power, overtops all his contemporaries. In his youth he was deeply touched by Christian feeling, and to the end of his days he abhorred the dull and vulgar rationalism which brushes off the poetic bloom from the Scriptural narrative, psalm and prophecy; but, on the whole, in the fulness of his powers, he held no form of creed, but contemplated all, sitting in an enchanted palace amid all forms of beauty which appeal to the natural soul in its highest development. He was interested in Christian emotion, as in all emotion which was not violent enough to destroy his calm. Being, as he was, a keen and distinguished student of physical science, he was reluctant to admit any interference with natural law whether in the way of exceptional revelation or of physical wonders. On the whole, in the midst of a hard rationalism, he probably taught men to look more tenderly on Christianity than they would otherwise have done.—Schiller[1], perhaps the greatest of German dramatists, impresses us by the heroism of his struggle with narrow circumstances and enfeebled health. Not only had he a reverential feeling for moral beauty and nobleness of soul, but he honestly strove to live up to his ideal. He was conscious of the greatness of Christianity as one of the powers which have made the world what it is, but he can hardly be said to have favoured its progress. In fact, he sometimes seems to reject the conception of a personal God to Whom prayer may be addressed, and sometimes to look with greater delight on the old gods of Greece than on the God of the Christian. Of these great men it may be said that they accepted all the poetry of Christianity, little of its history, and nothing of its dogma.

The general movement in philosophy and literature could not fail to influence theology, and accordingly in the middle of the eighteenth century appeared a school of theologians and Biblical critics, who received the distinctive name of Rationalists, as using reason overmuch in what was regarded as the province of faith. Few terms are more difficult to define than Rationalism, for it represents tendencies rather than fixed opinions. We

[1] *Life* by T. Carlyle (1825), James Sime (1882), H. Nevinson (1889). On Schiller's religion, see R. Binder, *Schiller in Verhältniss zum Christenthum* (Stuttgart, 1839); Hase, *K.-G.* III. 2. 300 ff.

may say, however, that beneath its various phases lies the conviction that no system of religion has been so revealed and instituted by God that the human intellect, itself God's creation, may not examine it with perfect frankness and freedom, and admit or reject its claims. The Scriptures, which had hitherto been almost universally regarded as altogether different in kind from the general literature of the world, and interpreted with a constant view to Christian dogma, were to be subjected to the strictest examination, and their age, authorship and genuineness decided not by tradition, but by weighing all the available evidence, internal and external. And when these points were decided, they were to be interpreted like any other ancient books, by the aid of grammar, history and archæology. With regard to the Christian Scriptures in particular, the Rationalist held that it was his business to strip off the swaddling-clothes of Judaic traditions and prejudices in which Christianity was wrapped at its birth, and so to allow it to stand forth as it is indeed.

Spinoza's Tractatus, 1670.

In the seventeenth century appeared Spinoza's famous *Tractatus Theologico-Politicus*, which is an earnest plea for liberty of thought by one who had himself suffered for his opinions. In it he discusses the nature of prophecy and the special calling of the Hebrew race; the meaning and intent of the ceremonial law and of miracles; the interpretation of Scripture and the authorship of its several books, many of which he thinks are attributed to others than their real authors and are the work of several hands; the nature of the Apostolic office, and the authority of the Apostolic Epistles; the lessons to be derived from the Bible as a whole. In short, nearly all the biblical-critical problems which have occupied so many minds during the eighteenth and nineteenth centuries are found in germ in Spinoza's famous Tractate.

J. A. Ernesti, 1707—1781.

John Augustus Ernesti[1] ought perhaps scarcely to be reckoned among Rationalists, for his great distinction is that of a good and sober classical scholar who applied scholarly methods to the interpretation of Holy Scripture. But as he maintained that Scripture should be interpreted

---

[1] Ernesti's *Institutio Interpretis Novi Testamenti* was translated into English by C. A. Terrot (1833).

by the same methods as Thucydides or Livy, without regard to dogmatic prepossessions, he was looked upon with grave suspicion by the orthodox Lutherans, who saw that this kind of interpretation was not favourable to them. He defended, indeed, the Lutheran theory of the Eucharist, but as he allowed it to appear that he regarded existing dogma as, to some extent, a growth, and not a body of truths fixed once for all, this brought him little favour. He is the father in Germany of the scholarly interpretation of the New Testament, and he also broke ground in the history of dogma.

John David Michaelis[1] stands towards the Old Testament nearly in the same relation that Ernesti does to the New. On a visit in early life to England and Holland his attention was directed to the critical way of regarding Scripture, and for fifty years he taught it in Göttingen. While never consciously departing from the current Lutheran dogmatics he yet interpreted the Old Testament as a collection of Oriental documents by means of Oriental learning. The human side of the Bible is made more prominent in his writings than the divine, and he comments on the Law of Moses rather in the style of Montesquieu than of Augustine. He did not neglect the New Testament, but his fame rests on what he did for the Old.

A far more important figure than either of the two preceding is John Solomon Semler[2], in whom we see the principal tendencies of the following generation. Brought up under narrow pietistic influence, it was not until he was about thirty years of age that he became known as an independent inquirer, without abandoning the devotional exercises to which he had in early days been accustomed. He was a man of immense reading and great—too great—productivity. His treatise on the demoniacs of the New Testament gave great offence; in his dissertations on the history of the early Church he made

---

[1] Michaelis's *Autobiography* was published in 1793 by Hassencamp, his *Literary Correspondence* by Buhle in 1794 ff. His *Introductory Lectures on the N. T.* were translated into English (London, 1780); his *Introduction to the N.T.* by Herbert Marsh (1802); his *Law of Moses* by A. Smith (1814).

[2] Semler published an interesting *Autobiography* (1781–82). See also H. Schmid, *Die Theologie Semlers* (1858).

it evident that he regarded Nicene theology as the growth of various influences during the first three centuries, not as a part of aboriginal Christianity; in his *Free Investigation of the Canon* he dealt quite frankly with a question which had been left very much in the background—how did it come to pass that certain books were regarded in the Church with great—sometimes superstitious—veneration, and looked upon by the vast majority of Protestants as the only source of Christian doctrine? Semler's later days were saddened by the excesses of some who claimed to be of his school; he had kindled a flame which spread altogether beyond his control, and consumed some things which were dear to him.

Wolfenbüttel Fragments, 1774–78.

The Rationalistic movement in Germany entered on a new phase when in the years from 1774–78 Lessing published seven *Fragments of an Anonymous Writer*, which were described as having been found in the library at Wolfenbüttel. They were in fact portions of a *Defence of Reasonable Worshippers of God*, which had been left in manuscript by Hermann Samuel Reimarus[1], a man of unquestionable learning and ability, Hebrew professor in the Hamburg gymnasium. The work had been completed in 1744, but its author seems to have been engaged in its revision until his death in 1768. The fragments which Lessing published fluttered the thoughts of men in the dovecotes of German theology. These essays inveighed against the depreciation of human reason which was usual in the pulpit; they sharply criticised the accounts of miracles both in the Old and New Testaments, and even seemed to reject altogether the conception of a revelation made by God to man. The work of Jesus was described as mainly a moral reformation, and the subsequent immense extension of His name and influence was ascribed to the report that He had risen from the dead. Here was certainly matter for abundant controversy, and a book which bore the name of so brilliant a man of letters as Lessing could not be ignored. It is not too much to say that the *Fragments*, and the controversy which followed their publication, influenced most

Reimarus, 1694—1768.

---

[1] D. F. Strauss, *H. S. Reimarus* (1862). A sketch of Reimarus's life appears with the English translation of the *Fragments* (London, 1879).

powerfully the development of religion and philosophy in the next generation.

Frederick II.[1] of Prussia, with his want of faith, his hatred and contempt for everything that savoured of clericalism, and his scornful readiness to allow every man to be happy in his own way so long as he did not interfere with his neighbour, was no doubt a great power on the side of free thought. But he was by no means indifferent to the influence of Christianity on social life or to the power of ecclesiastical organization in the State. He wished to maintain the traditional Protestantism of Prussia, and men of all parties who frankly expressed honest convictions had no reason to complain of him.

A review, the *Allgemeine Deutsche Bibliothek*, published under the King's patronage by F. Nicolai, attained very considerable influence. It ridiculed, or damned with faint praise, everything that appeared on the side of faith, and accused of superstition or Jesuitism any work which rose above its own level of crude and narrow infidelity. This publication became towards the end of the century a target for the keen shafts of Goethe and Schiller[2].

The Rationalists lost their hold on historical Christianity, but were by no means disposed to give up their position in the Church which was founded on a divine history. And as they belonged for the most part to the ranks of academic theology, the considerations which must weigh heavily with a man engaged in pastoral work did not come home to them. So large a portion moreover of the self-styled "educated" class followed in their footsteps that they were practically secure from serious molestation.

While this movement in the direction of free thought went on among literary men and learned theologians, several doubters or deniers appeared, who, if insignificant in themselves, swelled the flood of popular scepticism. Strange forms struck out from the great army to explore for themselves new regions of thought, sometimes discovering tracks which were afterwards followed, sometimes perishing in the wilderness.

F. Nicolai, 'A. D. Bibliothek,' from 1765.

[1] *Life* by Lord Dover (1832); T. Campbell (1841); T. Carlyle (1885 ff.).

[2] See F. C. Baur, *Kirchengeschichte*, IV. 594; Hase, *K.-G.* III. 2. 257 ff.

Knutzen,
1645–
1700?

In the year 1674 there appeared in Jena a wanderer of about thirty years of age, a Holsteiner, who had been already admitted as preacher, but had been driven from office for lack of orthodoxy. In his knapsack he carried the manuscript of a letter in good Latin, purporting to be written from Rome, and of a dialogue on religion supposed to have taken place at Altona between an innkeeper and three guests. The latter was written in the vernacular, and was intended for popular use. This wanderer was Mathias Knutzen[1], who was destined to win an unhappy notoriety. He rejected the Bible as an authority, saying that it was neither more consistent nor more trustworthy than the Koran. Why, he asked, should not men trust to the light of reason and conscience as Enoch and Noah had done before Christ came? The conscience which mother Nature had implanted in man taught him to injure no one, and to render unto all their due. Here is a Bible written in the heart which no man can despise without despising himself. Heaven and hell are to be found in the conscience alone, marriage differs in nothing from fornication, priests and governors are altogether superfluous. Knutzen is said to have been influenced by Herbert of Cherbury, but, if so, he went far beyond his master. He set forth his views in a number of pamphlets, clearly and vigorously written, and claimed to have a considerable number of followers, but these seem to have existed mainly in his own imagination. He remains a solitary voice, not a leader of men.

Pietism, with its vigorous assertion of the necessity of individual conviction in religion, and its consequent disparagement of Church authority, naturally contained within itself the germs of rebellion. From Pietism sprang John Conrad Dippel[2], who, after studying theology in his youth, quarrelled with the Church, and became a physician of some distinction. It is said that in searching for a medium to turn base metal into gold he discovered Prussian-blue. Under the name of the Christian Demo-

Dippel,
1673–
1734.

---

[1] See J. Musäus, *Ablehnung der Verleumdung ob wäre in Jena eine neue Secte der Gewissene entstanden,* referred to by Hase, *K.-G.* III. ii. p. 81; H. Rossel in *Stud. u. Krit.,* 1844, heft 4; Lipsius in the Halle *Encyclop.,* vol. 66.

[2] Bruno Bauer, *Der Einfluss des Englischen Quäkerthums auf die Deutsche Kultur* (1878); W. Bender, *Dippel, der Freigeist aus dem Pietismus* (1882).

critus he inveighed against the Papism of Protestants, who virtually claimed infallibility in matters of faith, and he cast scorn upon the notion of a vicarious sacrifice. God, he said, requires only our love. The sacraments were mere ordinances of man, confession and absolution positive frauds. Jews, Turks, Infidels and Heretics might become members of the true Church simply by giving heed to the light which is in every man. After an adventurous life, part of which was passed in prison, he died in 1734.

Another notable man was John Christian Edelmann[1], who was for a time a member of Zinzendorf's society; as he himself in after life phrased it, he was one of the fools who were led astray by Brother Ludwig. His own theology was founded on the momentous words of St John's Gospel, "the Word was God[2]," which he took as equivalent to "God was pure Reason." The Church needed only one redemption, that from ecclesiastical Christianity. He declared that he had no wish to be a destroyer of religion, though in his numerous writings pulling down is more conspicuous than building up. Reason was, he said, the sole guide of his life, and according to reason he must judge even the Bible itself. Of the Gospels he held that they were the product of the mingling of a thousand voices in early days, and that there would be a terrible outcry in Christendom if one gathered from the several Gospels what were probably the genuine facts in the life of Jesus, and so formed a narrative which all might accept—a curious anticipation of Strauss. The Emperor caused his writings to be publicly burnt by the executioner, but he found protection in Berlin under Frederick the Great.

One of the strangest figures in the movement which claimed to be "enlightened" was Charles Frederick Bahrdt[3], a man utterly destitute of self-respect and self-restraint whether in morals or in intellect. Of his learning and ability there can be no question, but his irreverence

---

[1] J. Pratje, *Nachrichten von Edelmann* (Hamburg, 1755); *Autobiography* published by C. W. Klose (Berlin, 1840); K. Guden, *J. C. Edelmann* (Hanover, 1870); Mönckeberg, *Reimarus und Edelmann* (1867).

[2] In Luther's version, "Gott war das Wort."

[3] Bahrdt published an *Autobiography* (Berlin, 1790 f.). See also E. Frank, *Bahrdt*, in Raumer's *Hist. Taschenbuch*, 1867.

and immorality alienated many who might have given him a favourable hearing. Having gradually got free from the fetters, as he thought them, of the Christian faith, he set himself partly to destroy the credit of the Biblical records, partly to interpret them so as to suit the sickly sentimentality of his time. The higher classes in Germany, who were imbued with the polished scepticism of France, looked with scorn upon the rough and ready infidelity of Bahrdt, but it had nevertheless considerable influence on the lower classes, and was refuted not so much by the numerous controversial treatises which it called forth, as by the growth of a more truly enlightened theology.

The life of a people depends very largely upon the schools. This truth was keenly felt in the latter part of the eighteenth century by J. B. Basedow[1], a vigorous, if somewhat rough, disciple of Rousseau. The task of education was, he said, to form men who would lead virtuous, unselfish, and contented lives. The religion of sects was no business of the schools; theirs it was to teach natural religion and true morality. Nothing was to be taught in school which could give offence to the Christian, Jew, Mohammedan or Deist. It followed that in the textbooks used there could be no favouring of Christian or any other tenets, though a form of prayer was to be used which had been drawn up by a committee on which all forms of religion were represented. It was on this principle that in 1774 Basedow founded an institution which he called the Philanthropinum. In connexion with this certain educational dogmas soon came to be looked upon as articles of faith; still, it ought to be admitted that Basedow's efforts led to a warm interest in the training of the young, to more genial treatment of them, and to greater prominence being given to teaching from real objects as opposed to mere book-learning.

But if a large proportion of the literary men and the would-be wits were patrons of enlightenment, the lower classes remained firm adherents of the Protestant theology, utterly unaffected by the literary movement which went on about them. And educated men were

---

[1] [Meyer], *Basedow's Leben* (Hamburg, 1791); R. H. Quick, *Educational Reformers*, ch. xv. (1890).

not wanting to oppose what they naturally thought the dangerous tendencies of the age. John Urlsperger founded a society for the propagation of sound doctrine and the promotion of brotherly intercourse among all who reverenced Jesus Christ as their Lord and Saviour. Its centre was in Basel, but it had branches in all parts of Protestant Germany and gained considerable influence. The imminent danger caused Christians to ignore small differences and draw together to resist the common enemy. An able, if fanciful, combatant on the side of faith was the Swabian Christopher Frederick Oetinger, an independent and original thinker. Deeply influenced by Böhme and Zinzendorf, he studied physical science with a view to demonstrating the spiritual influence which underlies the material world—a part of philosophy which the Berliners had ignored. Every philosophy (he said) is unprofitable which does not adjust itself to Holy Scripture as a key fits a lock. In his own day his warmth and geniality had more influence than his opinions, but in the nineteenth century the admiration of a kindred spirit, R. Rothe, brought him again into notice. C. A. Crusius defended the free working of God in the universe against the Wolfian theory of necessity, and contended that the Lutheran theology should be a guide in the interpretation of Scripture, in opposition to the pure scholarship of Ernesti. He also found in prophecy predictions both of the present and the future. Melchior Goeze, a Hamburg pastor, whose name is preserved by his controversy with Lessing, revived the intolerance of the previous century, and severely censured a colleague who preached a religion of love and tenderness, and in public worship omitted a customary prayer, that God would pour out His indignation upon the heathen that had not known Him. For a student of theology to have written an innocent comedy seemed to him an almost inexpiable offence, and the reception given to Goethe's *Sorrows of Werther* irritated him beyond measure.

But there were wiser and gentler defenders of Christianity than Goeze. The extraordinary reverence paid to C. F. Gellert, a man of earnest Christian feeling but a second-rate writer, shewed how deep a sympathy could still be roused in many hearts by the expression of warm

CH. VI.
Christenthumsgesellschaft, 1779.

Oetinger, 1702—1782.

C. A. Crusius, 1775.

Goeze, 1717—1786.

Gellert, 1715—1769.

and genuine piety; and the enthusiastic reception given to the early cantos of Klopstock's Messiah would not have been possible without a deep-seated belief in the God who became Man and gave Himself a sacrifice for us. Both Gellert and Klopstock were writers of hymns which reflect rather the sentiment and polish of their own time than the vigour of Luther's.

John George Hamann[1], after a somewhat careless youth, underwent a spiritual crisis from which he came forth an ardent believer, eager to lead his brethren to the truth. His works are little more than pamphlets, but they have a touch of genius and found their way to many hearts. His style is peculiar, darkness and light, obscure allusions and striking thoughts succeeding each other with strange rapidity. These prophet-like utterances gave him the designation of "the Magus of the North," most of his works proceeding from Königsberg.

John Caspar Lavater[2] is best known for his work on physiognomy, which he wrote not with a merely scientific purpose but "to advance the knowledge and love of man." He was in fact one of the ablest and most influential evangelical leaders of his day, and in a time of spiritual dearth scattered the seeds of the Gospel with apostolic zeal and unfailing courage. His Christian life and character touched men who were little affected by argument. Among those who came under his influence were Goethe —who spoke of him with great respect and affection— Herder, Hamann, F. Stolberg, and Oberlin.

John Henry Jung, commonly known as Jung-Stilling[3], a mystic and theosophist, simple and pure-minded, was raised above his original rather narrow pietism by his friendship with Goethe and Herder, without abating anything of the warmth of his Christian feeling. His account of his own youth, in which facts appear through a golden haze of poetry, at once brought him into fame. His half-

---

[1] Gildemeister, *Hamanns Leben u. Schriften* (1857–68); J. Disselhof, *Wegweiser zu J. G. Hamann* (1871); J. Poel, *Georg Hamann* (1874–76).

[2] *Life* by Gessner (Zürich, 1802); Heisch (in English, 1842). See also Mörikofer, *Schweizerische Literatur d. 18. Jahrhunderts* (1861), p. 322 ff.

[3] Jung-Stilling's *Autobiography* was translated into English by S. Jackson in 1835. See Nessler, *Étude Théologique sur Johann Stilling* (Strassburg, 1860).

mystical, half-pietistic romances hit the taste of the age and had considerable influence on religious thought.

Matthias Claudius[1], who passed the greater part of his life at Wandsbeck near Hamburg, though neither theologian nor preacher, exercised a great influence over the religious life of his countrymen by poems and articles published in the "Wandsbeck Messenger" and other periodicals. His sincere Christian feeling is expressed in a style in which humour and irony are charmingly blended with warmth and earnestness.

The heart of the people retained much of its ancient piety, and in many a city manse and village parsonage there lived a kindly and helpful Christianity which, without any great profession of dogmatic accuracy, diffused a blessing and maintained a comely religious life in the community. As an example of the evangelical pastor of this period we may take Volkmar Reinhard[2], for many years the head of the Saxon clergy, one of the most learned theologians and one of the most eloquent preachers of his time. When in 1800 he preached the justification of man through the free grace of God as the foundation of Protestantism, some of his hearers were roused to wonder and some to anger. He was not a man however who was extremely anxious about conformity with strict Lutheran orthodoxy. He had felt the spirit of the time, and it was only after storm and stress that he had arrived at his strong convictions—an experience which led him to be tolerant of those who were still struggling. A contrast to the court-preacher in all outward circumstances is Pastor Oberlin[3], who in the Steinthal, a thinly-peopled glen in the Vosges mountains, not only instructed the rough inhabitants in the truths of the Gospel, but taught them to make waste places fruitful and altogether changed the aspect of the place.

A remarkable mystic, who helped to feed the lamp of faith, was Gerhard Tersteegen[4], by trade a ribbon-weaver, but whose real calling was that of a writer, preacher, and

---

[1] *Life* by Herbst (Gotha, 1857), Mönckeberg (Hamburg, 1870).
[2] R. Pölitz, *F. V. Reinhard* (Leipzig, 1813).
[3] Sarah Atkins, *Memoirs of Oberlin* (London, 1849); Josephine Butler, *Life of J. F. Oberlin* (London, 1882).
[4] *Life* by G. Kerlen (Mühlheim, 1851), P. Stursberg (Leipzig, 1869).

hymn-writer, under the influence of the French mystics, Madame de Guyon and Poiret. He worked principally in Mühlheim on the Ruhr, Elberfeld, and Barmen, but his influence spread over a wide region. To differences of religious communities he was indifferent; the one thing needful was to him that the believer should carry Christ in his heart. To preach this doctrine he felt himself called like a prophet of old.

Attack on Jena,1794. Efforts to set in motion the secular arm against rationalism produced little effect. An attempt to put an end to the freedom of teaching in Jena was quietly put aside by the Grand-Duke of Weimar, Karl August, the well-known patron of Goethe. It was in the very centre of enlightenment, Berlin, that the sharpest opposition to it arose. The Prussian king, Frederick William II., a man very unlike his great predecessor, fell into the hands of a religious party who had no scruple in using any kind of trickery or intrigue to influence him to their purpose. *Prussian Edict, 1788.* Under the guidance of Wöllner, he put forth an Edict which made any clergyman who deviated from the teaching of the authorized formularies liable to deprivation, or even more severe punishment, on the judgment of a secular court. But public opinion was so emphatically opposed to proceedings of this kind that, in spite of the unlimited authority of the Prussian Crown, very little effect was produced. Some weak men were made hypocrites, but the strong remained defiant. Even fines inflicted upon members of the High Court whose votes displeased the Government were of no avail; it became more and more evident that to fight moral and intellectual convictions by mere external pressure was a hopeless task. *Frederick William III., 1797.* With the accession of Frederick William III. the Edict came to an end, and the King declared that religious convictions were not proper objects for coercion, and that the kindred sciences, theology and philosophy, should both have free course in the Prussian dominions.

Scepticism common. But though there were still many who preached Christ and many who followed them, the general tendency of the educated, and still more of the half-educated, was to turn away from Christ. Even those who, like all truly noble spirits, felt an impulse to rise above the smoke and stir of this dim spot which men call earth, still congratulated themselves on having attained a wider and truer view of the universe than St Paul and St Peter. Instead of justification by faith, virtue was preached with a good deal of self-complacency and reiteration of cheap sentiment. The enlightened thought that the end of Christianity drew near, the pious the end of this wicked world altogether.

As was inevitable, the dying out in educated circles of any deep feeling for Christian doctrine and for Christian institutions brought about a great change in the ordinary life of Christians[1]. When Schiller[2] wrote that he had sacrificed all his opinions and burnt his ships, he expressed the thoughts of many minds which had not equal frankness or lucidity. Church-going came into disrepute. Why should men frequent services when all that was needed was a right disposition of the heart towards God? Why should not men cultivate piety at home? The man of letters and the man of business alike employed their Sundays in work or amusement. So the churches came to be deserted, and with the outward desertion came alienation of mind. Those who still maintained at heart their devotion to Christ were members rather of His invisible than His visible Church. "The Holy Communion was still administered, but with no belief in the Body and Blood of Christ; Christmas was kept, but without holding the Christmas Gospel of the Divine birth to be veritable history; Easter was celebrated with no real belief in the Lord's Resurrection; Ascension Day by men who acknowledged no throne of God above the heavens; Whitsuntide, without giving any credence to the tongues of flame or the gift of tongues; and Trinity Sunday with no belief in God Three in One; though no doubt a dim perception of eternal truths clung round these festivals without coming to definite expression[3]."

Christianity is the religion of the Cross; it teaches humility and self-renunciation, while rationalism rests on the pride of intellect. And as the belief in a future life grew weaker, the disposition to wring the utmost enjoyment from the present grew stronger. It shewed itself

Effect on society.

[1] On religious life in Germany during this period, see Sarah Austin, *Germany from* 1760—1814 (1854).
[2] Quoted by Hase, *K.-G.* III. 2. 337.
[3] Hase, *K.-G.* III. 2. 1, p. 337.

even in hymns used in public worship[1]. Christ had said "Blessed are the poor, blessed are they that mourn"; the old Greeks said, "The prosperous are the favourites of the gods." The two principles are hard to reconcile, and for some years the latter rather than the former was dominant in the greater part of Europe.

5. THE POPES AND THE PRINCES.

General rejection of papal Claims.

The general diffusion of liberty of thought among the educated classes, and the ever-increasing disbelief in the spiritual powers claimed by the Pope and the priesthood generally, occasioned almost everywhere a desire to put strict limits on the alien domination of the Papacy, and to give to domestic tribunals a large portion of the powers which it asserted as its right. The Gallican Church had vindicated its liberties towards the end of the seventeenth century, more, no doubt, from the pride of a powerful monarchy and an ancient Church than from any advance in liberality of thought; in the latter part of the eighteenth almost all the European Powers claimed to enjoy at least the Gallican liberties, and some much more.

Pope Clement XIII., 1758—1769.

In entering on his reign, Clement XIII. (Carlo Rezzonico)[2] seemed to give evidence of moderation in that he —himself a Venetian—begged as a favour from the Venetian Republic that which his predecessors had demanded as a right, the free publication of all papal Bulls, citations, and the like in the territory of the republic, without the express consent of the civil government. But his want of knowledge of affairs and his eagerness to vindicate the rights of his see soon brought him into collisions with several courts. One of the most troublesome of these arose out of his intervention in the affairs of the Duchy of Parma. The Grand-Duke had taken

Parma.

---

[1] Hase (*u. s.* 338) mentions that the song "Freut euch des Lebens," once well known in English as "Life let us cherish," was inserted in a collection of hymns, and that there was much opposition to its being struck out so late as 1861.

[2] *Life* in Rambach's Continuation of Bower's *Popes*, x. 2, p. 441 ff.; Schröckh, vi. 464 ff.; Wetzer and Welte, *Kirchen-lexicon*, ii. 613 ff. See also G. F. Ravignan, *Clément XIII. et Clément XIV.* (1854–56); A. Theiner, *Geschichte der Pontificat Clemens XIV.*, vol. i. pp. 1—127.

The Popes and the Princes

measures to prevent the increase of the property of the clergy by forbidding them to receive gifts or bequests above a certain amount, and ordering that any land which passed from lay into clerical hands should still remain liable to the same rates and taxes to which it was already subject. Moreover, appeals to any foreign potentate were not to be made, nor decrees of the Pope published in the Duchy, without the consent of the local authority. The Pope seems to have thought that he might safely assert his rights against so small a power as the Grand-Duke; but he was a Bourbon, and the Bourbon rulers of France, Spain, and Naples gave him their hearty support. The spiritual weapons of the Papacy were found to have lost their force, and the result of Clement's rashness was that France took possession of his territory at Avignon, and Naples of Benevento. But this was not the worst. Already in the time of Benedict XIV. it had become evident that various governments hardly tolerated the Society of Jesus, which was everywhere regarded as dangerous to their authority. The nature of the Jesuit state in Paraguay[1] was but imperfectly known in Europe when in 1750 Spain, the nominal sovereign, ceded a portion of its territory to Portugal. In 1753 the combined forces of Spain and Portugal were surprised to find themselves confronted by a regularly-organized Paraguayan army[2]. This event made a highly unfavourable impression in Portugal, where the King was no friend of the Jesuits, and where his minister, afterwards known as the Marquis of Pombal, a very despotic reformer, was their bitter enemy. An attempt to assassinate the King was attributed to the Jesuits. There was probably no ground for the accusation, but it served to rouse the popular fury against them, and on Sept. 3, 1759, they were banished from the country and their property confiscated. The Pope's intervention on their behalf was of no avail, and in 1760 his nuncio was conducted over the frontier and all relations with Rome broken off. This gave a proof to other Powers

CH. VI.

Papal Brief, 1768.

Cession of Paraguay.

Pombal against the Jesuits,

1759.

---

[1] See p. 117.
[2] The Jesuits represent this insurrection as a rising of the Indians on behalf of their benefactors; but it is at any rate certain that the organization and the arms (including artillery), which rendered the army formidable, were due to the Jesuits, who, in fact, ruled the territory.

that coercion could be applied to the Jesuits. Troubles arose in France from a different cause. The Jesuits used their wide-spread organization to favour commercial enterprise. Their missionary, La Valette, had established a flourishing house of business in Martinique, which practically monopolised all the traffic of the island, to the great discontent of those who found themselves outrivalled. Complaints to the government of the mother-country had little effect, but in consequence of the capture of two valuable ships by the English, La Valette became bankrupt with a very large indebtedness. The question then arose whether the whole society of Jesuits in France was liable to make good the loss. The case came on appeal before the Parliament of Paris, when the Advocate-General had no difficulty in shewing from their own constitutions that all the property which they held belonged to the whole Society in common, which must therefore be treated as a commercial association and made responsible for the debts of its members. The result of the trial was to make public the laws which regulated the life of the Jesuits, hitherto but little known, and the feeling aroused was so strong that in 1764 a Decree was issued banishing them from France as dangerous to the welfare of the State. A Brief in which the Pope attempted to defend them was utterly disregarded. A similar storm broke over the Jesuits in Spain, but there, though more than one Court of inquiry was held, as nothing was published the real causes of the proceedings remain in some doubt. Whatever may have been the immediate cause, the King declared his throne in danger, and issued a decree banishing the Society from the whole of the Spanish dominions. The minister, Count Aranda, who was entrusted with the execution of it, took his measures so effectually that in the night between the second and third of April, 1767, all the Jesuits in Spain, about five thousand in number, were arrested and conducted to the coast. All their property was confiscated, with the reservation of a small payment to the dispossessed fathers under certain conditions. The Pope's warm remonstrance simply brought a cool reply from Aranda. Similar proceedings were taken in the same year in Naples and Sicily. There the courts had decided that a society whose founder had intended them to live on alms ought not to possess property. This prepared the way for the catastrophe which followed, when in the night between the 20th and 21st of November the Jesuits of Naples were seized in their several houses, taken to seaports, and placed on shipboard for the States of the Church. Here also the general welfare of the kingdom was the only reason alleged for the expulsion; it was not held necessary to prove particular transgressions. Here too a pension was offered. Eight days later the Sicilian Jesuits were put on shipboard at Palermo, and in the following year the Grand-Duke of Parma followed the example of his kinsfolk. The Pope's remonstrance only called forth the most vigorous protests against his interference with the government of independent states. Clement XIII. died early in the year 1769, full of care, leaving to his successor many perplexities to unravel.

A dark cloud of intrigue hangs over the conclave which was to choose his successor, and prevents us from clearly distinguishing the actual events. What is clear is that there was a long struggle between the Powers and the Jesuits, but what were the considerations which finally gave a large majority of the cardinals to Lorenzo Ganganelli (Clement XIV.) is obscure[1]. It soon became clear, however, that he was no friend to the Jesuits, though he himself always insisted that he had given no pledge before his election. He was a man of vigorous character, and ruled with greater independence than most of his predecessors. His policy was so far as possible to transact important business by direct communication with the sovereigns of the several countries. Diplomatic relations were resumed with Portugal. With regard to Parma he practically repudiated his predecessor's injudicious Brief, and recovered the papal territories of Avignon and Benevento. He gave a taste of his quality when in the year after his accession (1770) he ceased to require the

[1] What is known of this Conclave as well as of the other events of Clement XIV.'s life may be found in A. Theiner's *Geschichte Clem. XIV.* See also Caraccioli, *Vie de P. Clément XIV.* (Paris, 1775); [Von Reumont], *Ganganelli, P. Clement XIV.* (Berlin, 1847); Cretineau-Joly, *Clément XIV. et les Jésuites* (Paris, 1847); *Clementis XIV. Epistolæ et Brevia Selectiora ex secretis Tabulis Vaticanis*, ed. A. Theiner (Paris, 1852). The authenticity of the letters published by Caraccioli is doubtful.

public reading of the famous Bull *In Cœna Domini*, which anathematises all forms of religion condemned by Rome. But the most important matter which pressed for decision was the relations between the European Powers and the Jesuits, and this the Pope was in no hurry to decide. Silently he waited and prepared his measures, in spite of the pressure of the Powers, especially that of Spain. At last, after various preliminary measures, on the 17th August, 1773, he formally and solemnly communicated to the General of the Jesuits at Rome a Brief (*Dominus ac Redemptor Noster*, dated 17th July) utterly abolishing and suppressing the Society of Jesus. In the preamble he gives at some length his reasons for this step, in which, he contends, he did but follow the method which his predecessors had adopted in dealing with Orders in the Church. As the Society had ceased to bring forth the fruits which its founder had looked for, and as its continued existence was injurious to the peace and well-being of the Church, he proceeds, in virtue of his Apostolic authority, utterly to suppress, abrogate and abolish the said Society, with all its statutes, usages, customs, decrees and constitutions, and also its houses, schools, colleges, hospices and other institutions. In the then disposition of the civil governments there was in general no difficulty in executing the provisions of the Brief in the several countries. But the Emperor was offended because Clement had caused the Brief to be communicated to the bishops within his dominions without reference to the Imperial government. This was however accommodated by an independent resolution of the Diet of the Empire that the Society of Jesus was abolished. Frederick II. of Prussia forbade the Brief to be published in his territory. He was bound, he said, by the Treaty of Breslau to maintain the existing state of things in Silesia with regard to religion, and as he was a heretic the Pope could not release him from the obligation to keep his word. This was of course his ironical way of saying that he claimed to be more independent than the Catholic princes. In Russia also the provisions of the Brief could not be carried out. Peter the Great had indeed in form not tolerated the Jesuits, but practically they were not disquieted. The Empress Catharine II. not only maintained the Jesuits in possession of their colleges in her dominions, but in 1782 permitted them to appoint a Vicar-General who, until it should be possible to restore the whole of their constitution, should have all the powers of a General of the Society. But it was impossible actually to annihilate the Jesuit organization. All public display of their functions could be put down, but no outward constraint could prevent the members from maintaining a secret understanding among themselves.

It is related that when Clement XIV. signed the Brief for the suppression of the Jesuits, he said that he had signed his death-warrant. He died in fact in the following year. Poison was of course suspected, but it seems probable that he died from natural causes, aggravated by constant anxiety lest his rancorous enemies should attack his life. They at least did their best to poison men's minds against him, not without success, though the calmer research of our own time has cleared his memory.

The Bourbon Powers sanctioned the elevation of Angelo Braschi (Pius VI.)[1] to the Papal throne, believing, rightly as it turned out, that he was neither so fanatical nor so heroic as to attempt to undo the past. In the early part of his reign, while affairs were comparatively peaceful, he spent large sums in stately buildings while the people were in want, and even to this day no name occurs so frequently as his in Roman inscriptions. He also lavished much money in an attempt to drain the Pontine marshes. In quiet times, he would probably simply have left the reputation of a splendid pontiff who provided handsomely for those of his own household, but he had the misfortune to live in days when old landmarks were disregarded, and to see at last Church and monarchy swept away in France.

The struggle between the Church of the Middle Ages, mitigated by the Jesuits, and the modern desire for political and intellectual freedom, still continued, not without some seeming successes of the former. In Portugal Pombal's anti-ecclesiastical proceedings came to an

Death of Clement XIV., 1774.

Pius VI., 1774— 1799.

Portugal.

---

[1] *Life* by [Ade] (Ulm 1781 ff.); P. P. Wolf (Zürich, 1793 ff.), Ferrari (Padua, 1802), Beccatini (Venice, 1801 ff.), Travanti (Florence, 1804), Schröckh, *N. K.-G.* VI. 486 ff., J. E. Bourgoing, *Memoirs of Pius VI.* (Eng. Trans. from the French, 1799).

224 The Popes and the Princes

Spain. end with the death of King Joseph (1777), when the all-powerful minister was glad to be allowed to go quietly into retirement. In Spain Count Aranda, who had put both Inquisition and schools under the management of the civil government, was driven from office (1772), and Don Olavides fell into the power of the Inquisition because he had endeavoured to make fruitful the waste places of the Sierra Morena by introducing Protestant colonists. The hills were restored to the brigands. Nevertheless throughout the Peninsula the seeds had been sown of discontent with the rulers both of Church and State.

Steinbühler, 1781. In Germany too there were signs of unrest. A young jurist, Steinbühler[1], in Salzburg, for some foolish jests on Catholic ceremonies, was sentenced to death, a sentence which was commuted to exile and penance. Lorenz Isenbiehl[2], who had been sent by the Prince-Archbishop of Mainz to Göttingen to study Oriental languages, brought back with him to Mainz from the lectures of Michaelis doubts as to the current interpretation of Messianic prophecy, which he published in an "Essay on the Prophecy of Immanuel." As the Pope, in accordance with many of the theological faculties, found that this book contained heretical teaching, Isenbiehl recanted, and received from his Archbishop, who had previously treated him with great harshness, some modest preferment. On the other hand, the Prince-Archbishop Emmerich (1763–74) withdrew the schools in his dominions from the management of the Jesuits, and his successor, Erthal, took much more pleasure in a splendid and cultivated court than in theological discussions, while his coadjutor, Dalberg, was well known in Weimar as a friend of the intellectual giants of his time. A curious phenomenon of a very different kind from the heretics was Father Gassner[3] of Ellwangen, an ex-Jesuit, who undertook to heal sicknesses and cast out devils in the name of Jesus. Crowds flocked to him, both Catholics and Protestants, most of whom came unhealed away, but some cures seem to indicate that the Father had a somewhat unusual magnetic power in nervous cases. Both

Isenbiehl.

1779—

1802.

Gassner, 1774.

---

[1] Hase, *Kirchen-Geschichte*, III. 2. 180.
[2] Schröckh, VII. 203 ff.
[3] Schröckh, VII. 330 ff.

Pope and Emperor were anxious to put an end to this untimely claim to miraculous power, but it does not appear that any harsh measures were taken. Another curiosity was the Order of Illuminati, founded by Adam Weishaupt[1], a pupil of the Jesuits, Professor of Law in Ingoldstadt. It aimed at forming a secret bond of union for free-thinking men of all conditions and religions, which was to reform and rule the world, and adopted partly the constitution of the Jesuits, partly (it was said) that of the Freemasons. Its avowed object was the perfecting of man's nature and the promotion of enlightened freedom in Church and State; but its secret teaching seems to have been anarchical. Differences among the leaders led to denunciation, a commission of inquiry was constituted, and Weishaupt fled to Gotha, where he was kindly received by the Grand-Duke, and where he remained until his death.

<small>Ch. VI.</small>

<small>Illuminati, 1777.</small>

<small>Inquiry, 1785.</small>

These occurrences shew the general unrest within the Church and the reluctance of the Roman Curia to allow any departure from traditional opinions. But meanwhile an agitation had been going on which involved the very foundations of Papalism. In the year 1763 appeared a book *De Statu Ecclesiae et legitima potestate Romani Pontificis* by Justinus Febronius[2], a name which was soon known to be the pseudonym of John Nicholas von Hontheim, the highly respected and influential coadjutor of the Archbishop of Treves. The question had been often asked by laymen, How are we to distinguish between the spiritual power of the Bishop of the Apostolic see and the claims of the existing Roman Curia? This book attempts to answer this question in the spirit of the Councils of Basel and Constance. The author declares his conclusions thus:—"The Church is strictly not a monarchy. The Power of the Keys is committed by Christ to the Church as a whole, and is to be exercised by all bishops alike; for the bishops are the successors of the Apostles, and the episcopal office is of divine

<small>Febronius, 1763.</small>

<small>Von Hontheim, 1701— 1790.</small>

<small>Febronius's Opinions.</small>

---

[1] Weishaupt himself published a *Geschichte der Verfolgung der Illuminaten* (1786) and an *Apologie* (1788). There is a good article on the Illuminati by Kluckhohn in Herzog's *Real-Encyclop.* 2nd ed.

[2] C. W. F. Walch, *Neueste Religionsgeschichte*, vi. 171; vii. 192, 455; viii. 529; O. Meier, *Febronius* (2nd ed. 1885); F. H. Reusch, *Der Index der Verbotenen Bücher*, ii. 110. Schröckh, vi. 533.

institution. The Pope is not, as the Curialists assert that he is, the universal bishop, and other bishops only his officials. The Pope is no doubt Primate, but the Church could, if it thought fit, confer the Primacy on some other see. The purpose of the Primacy is the maintenance of the unity of the Church; the Pope, as chief bishop, is bound to take measures for the maintenance of this unity and the due observance of the laws of the Church, but always by way of counsel and admonition. He has no right to issue mandates in other dioceses than his own, for there he has no jurisdiction. General laws can only be made by a general council, which alone can claim infallibility in matters of faith. It is not necessary that such councils should be convoked by the Pope, nor do their decrees require his confirmation[1]." Here was an attempt to abolish the modern Papacy and to return to the principles of Church government which St Cyprian had maintained in the third century. The Pope would, of course, not tolerate the publication of such opinions.

Clement XIII.'s condemnation.

Clement XIII., so soon as the book was brought under his notice, condemned it, and did his utmost to suppress it. This was however in the latter part of the eighteenth century impossible. The Pope's condemnation increased its notoriety; it was translated, and had a large circulation and great influence in almost every country in Europe. "Febronianism" became dangerous. It is not wonderful that the papal party put all possible pressure on the author to induce him to recant, and at last the old man, wearied with importunity, consented to retract the propositions which had given offence. His retractation was evidently extorted, though he was compelled to describe it as voluntary, and at any rate it did not refute his book. In 1781 he published a commentary on his retractation which made it tolerably evident that his opinions were unchanged.

Retractation, 1778.

Commentary, 1781.

Effects.

A hot controversy followed the publication of Febronius, the details of which are now forgotten; but a shock was given to the *prestige* of the Papacy from which it did not readily recover. The views of Febronius were

---

[1] Quoted by Herzog, *Kirchen-Geschichte*, II. 519 f.

adopted by many of the most cultivated and distinguished men of the time, and greatly influenced later treatises on the law and constitution of the Church.

Ch. VI.

The theories of Febronius are a fit prelude to the reforms which were attempted in the Austrian dominions. Joseph II.[1] had worn the shadow of an imperial crown for fifteen years when in 1780 the death of his autocratic mother, Maria Theresa, left him real and actual sovereign of his hereditary lands. He was a reformer of the most despotic kind, paying little heed to the will of his people or their capacity for receiving his decrees. Over-hasty in his measures, he had not the quiet perseverance which is necessary to carry out a great reform. Difficulties of course presented themselves which had not been foreseen, and these he attempted to meet by limitations and modifications which weakened his plans and satisfied no one. His ecclesiastical ordinances had two ends in view. In the first place, he wished to give to his non-Catholic subjects complete freedom in matters of religion. For this purpose he published an Edict of Toleration, in which he gave permission to his subjects to declare themselves members of the Roman Catholic or the Greek Orthodox Church, or of one of the Protestant societies, Lutheran or Calvinist. The latter also were allowed to build meeting-houses, which were not, however, to be open to the public, and to maintain preachers and schoolmasters. But no sooner was the Edict published than those Protestants who had outwardly conformed under the severe laws of previous reigns shewed themselves in their true colours. The number of these was so much greater than had been expected that the Roman Catholic clergy in alarm induced the Emperor to put several vexatious limitations on the freedom which he had granted. But in spite of all hindrances and impediments, and although the dissidents had to provide meeting-houses, ministers, and schoolmasters at their own cost, while they still had to pay certain dues to the Roman Catholic clergy, many

Reforms of Joseph II., 1780 ff.

Edict of Toleration, 1781.

---

[1] Of the *Lives* of Joseph II. may be mentioned those by Mensel (Leipzig, 1790), E. X. Huber (Vienna, 1792), Heyne (1848), Ramshorn (1861). On his reforms, Riehl und Reinöhl, *Kaiser Joseph II. als Reformator auf Kirchlich. Gebiete* (Vienna, 1881). See also Léger's *Hist. of Austro-Hungary* (English Trans. 1889).

Church Reform.

Protestant communities were formed in the Austrian territory and even in Vienna itself.

But even more important were the Emperor's ordinances for the Roman Catholic Church. His aim and intent was to put an end to any interference of the spiritual courts with the temporal jurisdiction, and in general to restrict the papal power in Austria to the limits laid down by Febronius. His intentions were, in fact, not very unlike those of our own Henry VIII. He shewed from the first the independent position which he wished to take in that he sought no papal confirmation for any of his ecclesiastical legislation, but issued his edicts purely and simply on his own authority as territorial sovereign. In the forefront was one which forbade the publication of Bulls and Briefs, or any document of a similar kind, without the consent of the civil power. In the same spirit it was strictly forbidden to recite publicly the damnatory Bull, *In Cœna Domini*, and newly-appointed archbishops and bishops were not permitted to take the oath which made them vassals of the Pope, but only the oath of canonical obedience in the older form. Without the permission of the sovereign no title or office conferred by the Pope could be borne or exercised, no subject of the Emperor would be allowed to study in Rome, monasteries were to be entirely independent of any foreign head or power, they were to send no portion of their revenues abroad, and they were to be under the jurisdiction of their own diocesan bishops. The number of members to be received in each monastery was limited, and monks were forbidden to lead a vagabond life. Further, all Orders were suppressed which did not occupy themselves with the cure of souls or with school-teaching, and their property formed a fund by the aid of which many new benefices and schools were founded and maintained. Among these schools were seminaries for the education of the clergy, and a strict scrutiny of all persons presented to benefices was instituted.

Opposition.

However well-intentioned and beneficial these measures may have been, they gave, as may be imagined, great offence to the majority of the clergy. When the news reached Rome the Pope determined to try what could be done by the immediate influence on the Emperor of his own handsome person and winning tongue. He resolved, contrary to all the traditions of the Papacy, to visit Vienna. The Emperor received him with all due ceremony and respect, but declined to discuss with him the affairs of the Church. For these he referred him to his minister, Kaunitz, who had already, even in the days of Maria Theresa, shewn himself unfriendly to the papal claims. The Pope obtained no concessions except in trifling details, and left Vienna dissatisfied and discouraged. He received, however, some comfort at the court of Bavaria, which he visited on his return journey, and where he found not only respect but obedience.

Ch. VI. The Pope in Vienna, 1782.

Bavaria.

After the Pope's departure the Emperor went eagerly forward in his course of reform, and seems almost to have resolved to free his dominions altogether from the papal yoke. But before he took this decisive step he suddenly made up his mind to take a journey to Rome, not so much to return the Pope's visit as to have an opportunity of conferring with the statesmen who represented various Powers in that city, especially Cardinal Bernis, the French ambassador, and Don Azara, the Spanish. These experienced men saw more plainly than the Emperor did the very serious consequences which might follow from forcing a measure of this kind upon a people altogether unprepared to receive it, and counselled delay. This counsel brought doubt and hesitation into the Emperor's mind, and the Pope gained more by the Emperor's visit to Rome than he had done by his own visit to Vienna.

Emperor at Rome, 1784.

Vacillation.

But if events at Rome were favourable to the Pope, there were elsewhere occurrences highly displeasing to him. The highest dignitaries of the German clergy, the archbishops of Mainz, Trier, Cöln, and Salzburg, joined in demanding from him the restoration of their ancient rights and privileges. The immediate occasion of this was the establishment by the Pope of a nuncio in the faithful city of Munich, through whom all communications from Bavaria were to pass to the Pope, instead of through the archbishop. To the latter the Emperor very readily promised his support. Relying on this promise, the archbishops arranged a meeting of their representatives at Ems, the result of which was a document known as the

Ems Agreement, 1786.

Ems Agreement (Punktation). Its principal provisions were these. While recognizing the Pope as Primate of the whole Church and the centre of unity, it pointed out that the claims which encroached on the jurisdiction of the bishops were not founded on primitive tradition but on the well-known forged Decretals, and ought to be abandoned now that the forgery was universally recognized. The bishops looked for the protection of the imperial authority in exercising the functions which God had entrusted to them. Bishops, as such, as successors of the Apostles, had the power of binding and loosing, and the Pope had no right to interfere with them in the exercise of such power. The Emperor approved these resolutions, and the bishops proceeded to act upon them. When the papal nuncio at Cologne protested, the Emperor at once declared the protest null and void. But these proceedings were altogether premature; the great majority of the bishops and other clergy were not prepared to follow their archbishops, who seemed to have rather their own interests in view than those of the Church at large; and the bishops had the support of the Bavarian authorities. Quarrels arose between the spiritual and the secular rulers, and when in 1788 the affair of the nunciature was brought before the Diet of the Empire the Bavarian representatives obtained the recognition of the principle, that it rested entirely with the civil government of a country to receive or reject a nuncio. The Pope had the courage to put forth a public reproof to the four archbishops. Thus the conflicting interests of archbishops and bishops, emperor and princes, brought to an end a movement which had seemed likely to bring about a great reformation.

Papal Admonition, 1789.

When the Emperor attempted to introduce in the Austrian Netherlands the same measures which he had introduced in his German territories serious disturbances arose. The suppression of the several episcopal seminaries and the institution of a general clergy-school at Louvain, with a subordinate establishment at Luxemburg, were vigorously opposed, especially by the Archbishop of Malines and the university of Louvain. In 1789 a revolt broke out which the imperial troops were unable to put down. It threatened to extend to the Austrian states

Proceedings in the Netherlands, 1786.

Revolt, 1789.

when in 1790 Joseph II. died suddenly, and all his plans for the future came to an end. What he had done was not unimportant, but it was lost sight of in the new order of things which was brought in by the French Revolution.

Ch. VI.
Joseph's death, 1790.

While Joseph was attempting to reform the Church in his own hereditary dominions, his brother Leopold was taking similar steps in Parma, of which he was Grand-Duke. He published several edicts with the intent not only of maintaining the rights of the sovereign against the Pope, but of introducing reforms in the Church of his realm. His principal supporter in these reforms was Scipio de' Ricci[1], Bishop of Pistoia, who in 1786, at the request of the Grand-Duke, held a synod of his diocese at Pistoia, at which not only were the four articles of the Gallican liberties[2] adopted, but also the following propositions. The Universal Church itself has no right to introduce new articles of faith or morals, but only to maintain in their original purity the truths committed to its charge by Christ and the Apostles. Further, it has no right to employ coercion in matters of religion, which depends on the mind and heart. The synod recommended that Divine service should be in the vernacular language, it rejected the "treasury of works of supererogation" and many other papal abuses. But though the synod of one diocese adopted these innovating resolutions, they were far from winning the assent of the whole Church in Parma. At a General Synod of the clergy of the Duchy held at Florence in 1787 all the acts of Pistoia were rejected, and it was expressly resolved that the territorial sovereign had no right to intervene between the Pope and his spiritual subjects. Leopold even still recommended to the clergy the principles of Pistoia, but nothing had really been effected when in 1790 he was called to assume the imperial crown.

Reforms in Parma, 1775 ff.

Ricci. Synod at Pistoia, 1786.

Synod at Florence, 1787.

While these things were enacted in the north of Italy, difficulties also arose on the southern frontier of the Papal States. The Kings of Naples and Sicily had long acknowledged that they were feudatories of the Pope,

Naples.

---

[1] The Life of de' Ricci was written by the Belgian statesman De Potter, *Vie et Mémoires de Scipion de Ricci* (Bruxelles, 1825).
[2] See p. 106.

Tribute to the Pope refused, 1788.

and had paid him a small annual tribute as acknowledgement. This payment in 1777 the King declared to be simply a token of respect for the Apostolic see, not tribute, and in 1788 it was refused altogether. In 1790, however, a compromise was arrived at by which each King should pay to the papal treasury 500,000 ducats on his accession, and no further tribute. But before this agreement was arrived at many monasteries had been despoiled of their estates and strong measures taken to defeat the papal claims in the Neapolitan territory[1].

[1] Schröckh, *Neuere K.-G.* vi. 513 ff.

CHAPTER VII.

THE SHAKING OF THE NATIONS.

1. THE FRENCH REVOLUTION.

AT the beginning of the year 1789 the Catholic Church, though everywhere threatened, still stood firm, if with privileges somewhat diminished. But in that year we enter on a period in which all the institutions of society, religious and civil, were greatly shaken, and many overthrown. It is sometimes represented that the errors and shortcomings of the clergy brought about the French Revolution. But in truth, whatever may have been the worldliness, luxury, and scepticism of many of the higher dignitaries, it can scarcely be doubted that the great majority of the country clergy led not unworthy lives, and sympathised with the sufferings of their flocks. The immense weight of public debt was borne wholly by the trading and agricultural population, and the latter was brought to the verge of starvation, while the nobles and the clergy were exempt from the payment of imposts to the State. The bulk of the population was thus prepared to break out furiously against the privileged classes so soon as they could find leaders.[1]

---

[1] For the general history of the French Revolution we may refer to the works of Lacretelle, Mignet, Thiers, Mortimer - Ternaux, H. von Sybel (Eng. trans. by W. C. Perry), H. Taine (Eng. by Durand). Carlyle's great work is rather an epic than a history, but should by all means be read. On the history of the Church during this period, see Barruel, *Collection Ecclésias-* *tique* and *Hist. du Clergé de France pendant la Révolution*; Jaeger, *Hist. de l'Église de France pendant la Rév.*; E. de Pressensé, *L'Égl. et la Révolution Française*; W. Henley Jervis, *The Gallican Church and the Revolution*; W. Milligan Sloane, *The French Revolution and Religious Reform* (New York and London, 1902).

The French Revolution

Ch. VII.
States General, 5 May, 1789.

The States General, summoned mainly to attempt to remedy the desperate state of the finances, met at Versailles on the 5th May, 1789. It had been intended by Necker, the principal minister of the Crown, that the three Orders—nobles, clergy, and commons or "Third Estate"—should sit and vote separately, and that the ultimate decision should be by the votes of the Orders. In this way the Commons would lose the advantage of their numerical superiority. But this was not to be. The Third Estate soon discovered its power; it was joined by many of the clergy and some of the nobles, and on the 17th June it declared itself a National Assembly, and proceeded to assume all the powers of government. Ten days later the King was compelled to yield to the logic of facts, and to recognize the clergy, the nobles, and the commons as forming one assembly, called the National or Constituent Assembly.

National Assembly, 17 June, 1789.

27 June.

In the great financial distress it is not surprising that the reformers cast covetous eyes on the large estates of the clergy. The tithes had already been suppressed when Talleyrand, Bishop of Autun, proposed that the property of the clergy, valued at many hundred millions of francs, should be given up to the State, which should then undertake to provide the expenses of public worship, and to devote the surplus to the payment of the public debt. The clergy resisted in vain. They were told that they were not owners, but trustees of the ecclesiastical lands, and that the State, so long as it provided for the duties charged on the estates, might lawfully reclaim its property. Bonds were at once issued on the security of these lands, which were called *assignats*, as representing lands assigned to the holder. This system relieved the government for the moment, but afterwards, being abused, brought about great financial instability. It caused, as was natural, great indignation among the clergy, and their alienation from the cause of the Revolution was completed by the enactment of a civil constitution of the clergy. Each of the departments, into which France had now been divided, was to be a diocese[1], and bishops and parish priests were to be chosen by popular election, the nation

Church Estates confiscated, 2 Nov. 1789.

14 Apr. 1790.

Civil Constitution, 12 July, 1790.

---

[1] This involved the reduction, without the consent of the clergy, of the 136 bishoprics of France to 83.

undertaking to provide salaries in lieu of those which had been derived from their own property. All sinecures were abolished. Every bishop was to be rector of his own cathedral, and in administration was to take the counsel of his clergy. The holding of diocesan and provincial synods was revived, and all interference of a foreign bishop in administration forbidden, though it was permitted to recognize the Pope as the visible Head of the Church in matters spiritual. Every parish priest was to receive a stipend of at least twelve hundred francs (£48) a year, with house and garden. The incomes assigned to the bishops were fairly adequate, though scanty compared with their former opulence. Monastic vows, as incompatible with the rights of man, were no longer recognized by law, but moderate pensions were assigned to monks of good character, and they were allowed, if they chose, to remain in their convents.

On the 14th July, the anniversary of the taking of the Bastille, there was an enormous assembly from all parts of France in the Champ de Mars. The Catholic Church being still recognized as representing the national religion, Talleyrand, Bishop of Autun, surrounded by a large number of conforming priests wearing the tricolour, celebrated a solemn mass at a high altar erected in the midst of the plain, after which the King and the deputies solemnly swore to observe and maintain the Constitution decreed by the National Assembly[1].

Champ de Mars, 14 July, 1790.

But the Pope, after some hesitation, refused to ratify the civil constitution of the clergy, which refusal rendered it difficult for a conscientious priest to accept it; and the Assembly aggravated the dissension by requiring from all priests actually exercising their vocation an oath of allegiance to the nation, the law, the King, and the civil Constitution. Deprivation was the penalty for refusal. This divided the clergy into two parties, those who accepted the oath and those who refused it, Jurors and Nonjurors (*assermentés* and *non-assermentés*). The Nonjurors refused to give up their offices at the bidding of a merely secular authority, and denounced those who were appointed by the same authority to succeed them. They

Oath of Allegiance, 27 Nov. 1790.

---

[1] Carlyle, *French Revolution*, I. 275 ff. (ed. 1857).

also employed all the influence which long tradition gave them over their flocks to attach them to their cause, and thus the ground was prepared for future outbreaks. In short, from this time, the clergy as a whole became the enemies of the Revolution which many of them had once welcomed. Compelled to choose between Church and country, they chose the former, and many withdrew into foreign lands from the coming danger.

Assembly dissolved, 29 Sept. 1791.

On the 29th September, 1791, the King declared the famous Assembly closed, having previously ratified its acts and decrees, the Assembly itself admitting that its task was accomplished. In two years it had wrought much good and much evil. It had recognized many just and right principles, but it had set loose forces which were destined for a time to sweep away all ancient landmarks in a sea of blood.

Legislative Assembly, 1 Oct. 1791. Convention, June, 1793.

It is not necessary here to give the history of the various assemblies which presided, or seemed to preside, over the destinies of France. Whether under Legislative Assembly or National Convention, from the autumn of 1791 to the spring of 1795, passion ruled, and idealists, who had no power to realize their ideal, struggled with rough and bloodthirsty fanatics who were eager to annihilate their enemies. Under the fermentation of new ideas among the populace, under the pressure of revolts and intrigues at home, and invasion from abroad encouraged by Frenchmen who had fled to foreign lands, a kind of frenzy seized France, and especially Paris, which led to appalling scenes of blood and terror. It is hardly too much to say that for a time the chief authority in the country was the rabble of Paris.

As regards the Church, the Legislative Assembly decreed that priests who refused the oath should be excluded from the churches and their incomes withdrawn. If they caused disturbances among the people, they were to be punished by imprisonment or banishment. The King refused assent to this decree so long as he could, and his own chapel was even served by Nonjurors; but he

Death of the King, Jan. 21, 1793.

was himself put to death, and under the Convention which succeeded the Legislative Assembly the noblest traditions of France were overwhelmed in a common ruin. The scepticism which had long been fashionable among the nobles and philosophers spread in a coarse form among the populace, and Christianity itself came to be thought unworthy of a free and enlightened people. The nobler spirits of the Revolution were rather antique Romans than Christians, while the ruder souls cast off religion and morality together. The Calendar was reformed in such a manner as to obliterate all traces of Christian influence, and to make the foundation of the Republic, Sept. 22, 1792, the epoch from which the years should thenceforward be numbered. The year which then began was reckoned the first year of Liberty[1]. Marriage was declared to be a dissoluble civil contract, and in the two years which followed this declaration more than five thousand marriages were dissolved in Paris alone. All the sacred vessels, ornaments, and vestments of the churches were declared national property and sold or broken up. A kind of idolatry took the place of the old religion. The goddess of Liberty, represented by a young English lady, appeared in the Convention, claiming to be the only deity worthy of adoration[2]: and the goddess of Reason, in the form of a ballet-girl, was actually enthroned on the high altar of Notre Dame[3]. Gobel, constitutional Bishop of Paris, appeared with some of his priests at the bar of the Convention, and declared that, as Liberty was now the true object of worship, he renounced his office as a servant of the Catholic Church. The Convention substituted the worship of Reason for that of the Church. The churches were closed or made temples of Reason, and in almost every town atheistic festivals were celebrated in which the common laws of decency were set at nought. The existence of God was publicly denied, and over the entrance to cemeteries was seen the inscription, "Death is an everlasting sleep." Robespierre, however, thinking that this absence of all belief would be destructive of civic virtue, induced the Convention to declare that the French nation recognizes the existence of a Supreme Being who is best served by the steadfast discharge of duty, and the Immortality of the Soul. In honour of this Supreme Being there was held, with the most absurd theatrical pomp,

Ch. VII.

Calendar reformed, 5 Oct. 1793.

7 *Nov.* 1793.

---

[1] The Republican Calendar may be found in Nicholas's *Chronology of History*, p. 173.
[2] Hase, *K.-G.* III. 2, 203.
[3] Carlyle, *F. R.* II. 302 ff.

a national festival[1]. When the Reign of Terror came to an end freedom was given for the practice of all kinds of religious worship. Then the Christianity which had never been uprooted from the hearts of the people was once more seen openly, and the old-fashioned week, with its Sunday, practically superseded the official or ten days' period.

Festival of Supreme Being, 8 June, 1794.
Freedom of Worship, 21 Feb. 1795.
Theophilanthropism, 1796—1802.

The freedom given by the State to every form of worship brought forth also a new sect. This was a system founded entirely on natural religion, which established itself in ten churches in Paris and in many provincial towns. The name given to it was Theophilanthropism[2]. It acknowledged the great Power which is manifested in the various phenomena of the universe as the true object of worship, it taught the immortality of the soul, and the obligation to lead a pure and honest life. But as this institution had no tradition to support its claims, and found no leader able to impress numbers by his personal character, it could hold its own neither against Christianity nor against indifference. Public opinion scoffed at it, and when in 1802 the First Consul withdrew from it the use of the churches, it sank at once out of sight.

2. NAPOLEON AND THE FRENCH CONQUESTS.

French Conquests.

In the early days of the Republic the wars of France were a struggle for existence; then came a period when it was the policy of those in power to distract the attention of the agitated people from internal affairs by external occupation; after this again the enthusiastic French desired to extend, even by force of arms, the blessings of republican government to the oppressed nations of Europe. In 1796 the young Napoleon Bonaparte led the French armies to victory after victory in Italy. Master of Italy, he required the Pope, Pius VI[3], to withdraw all the decrees which he had put forth against

---

[1] Carlyle, *F. R.* II. 333 ff.

[2] [Chemin] *Manuel des Théophilantropistes* (Paris, 1796); H. Grégoire, *Geschichte der Philanthropen*, translated from the MS. by Stäudlin (Hanover, 1806); Hagenbach in Herzog's *Real-Encylop.* XVI. 19 ff.

[3] On the events of this period see P. P. Wolf, *Geschichte der Kath. Kirche unter Pius VI* (Zürich and Leipzig, 1793—1802); [Bourgoing] *Mémoires Historiques...sur Pie VI* (Paris, 1801); P. Baldassari, *Relazione delle Avversità del Papa Pio VI* (reprint, 1889).

France, and on his refusal invaded the papal dominions. The Pope had no means of repelling one who set at nought his spiritual powers, and at Tolentino the papal legates had to accept such terms of peace as the victor would grant. These were hard enough. The discomfited Pontiff had to give up not only his ancient possessions in France, but the legations of Ferrara, Bologna, and Romagna; to pay an indemnity of thirty millions of francs (£1,200,000), and to permit the conquerors to carry off many of the precious works of art which are the glory of Italy. Northern Italy became the Cisalpine Republic, and a republican party appeared in Rome itself. In a riot which followed the French ambassador unfortunately lost his life, and General Berthier was ordered to enter the Papal States to demand satisfaction. Under the protection of French arms a Roman Republic was set up, and formal notice was given to the Pope that his temporal sovereignty was at an end. It was hardly possible that he should remain as a mere citizen of Rome; he was removed by his French masters, and died in captivity, bearing himself with constant patience and resignation, at Valence in Dauphiné. A strange fate for a Pope, to die in the hands of democrats who did not acknowledge the Christ whose vicegerent he claimed to be. He was indeed, according to the prophecy of Malachi[1], "peregrinus apostolicus moriens in exilio."

On the death of Pius VI, Rome being still in the possession of the French, thirty-five cardinals from various places of refuge assembled at Venice, then in the Austrian dominion, and formed a conclave in the monastery of San Giorgio Maggiore, which lasted for more than three months. At last Gregory Barnabas Chiaramonti, Bishop of Imola and Cardinal, was chosen, and took the name of Pius VII[2]. The scornful assertions that now at last the Papacy was at an end were refuted. The new Pope was a Benedictine, and on St Benedict's Day (21st March) he was crowned in St George's Church, and received the congratulations and homage of some of the Catholic

Ch. VII.

Treaty of 19 *Feb.* 1797.

Roman Republic, 15 *Feb.* 1798.

Death of Pius VI. 29 *Aug.* 1799.

Pius VII. elected, 14 *March,* 1800.

[1] One of the prophecies, probably written in the 16th century, attributed to Malachi, Archbishop of Armagh (1134—1148).

[2] Artaud de Montor, *Hist. du Pape Pie VII* (Paris, 1836); Berault-Bercastel, *Hist. de l'Église de* 1800—1833 (1833); H. Chotard, *Le Pape Pie VII à Savone* (1887).

Powers as if he had been enthroned in the Vatican. Nor was it long before he took his seat there. On the 3rd July, under the protection of the Powers allied against France, especially Austria, he entered Rome, in the midst of abundant signs of rejoicing. Meantime the battle of Marengo had placed all Northern Italy in the power of the French, and by the treaty of Luneville which followed the Pope lost, in addition to his previous losses, the legations of Forli and Ravenna.

Pius now thought it expedient to take steps for the reconciliation of France with the Apostolic see, and Bonaparte, who now ruled that country under the republican title of First Consul, was anxious to promote this. Little as he regarded the Catholic Church as a spiritual power, he was sensible of the great importance of having a stable belief at least in morality, and of placing the civil power in harmony with the religion to which in fact the greater number of Frenchmen belonged. He was therefore quite willing to enter into negotiations. These were difficult and prolonged. The civil Constitution of 1791 had annihilated many ancient dioceses by the mere fiat of the secular authority, and the property of the Church had come into the possession of laymen. Constitutional bishops held the dioceses, though in many cases the legitimate bishops were still living. A national Council of the constitutional clergy, convoked at the request of the First Consul, did not facilitate a solution. At last, after much discussion, a Concordat was concluded between Cardinal Gonsalvi, representing the Pope, and Bonaparte.

The principal provisions of the Concordat were these[1]. The Roman Catholic religion is recognized as that of the majority of the French nation, and is granted perfect freedom for all its public functions, subject always to the law of the land. The Holy See is permitted, in agreement with the civil government, to assign new boundaries to dioceses, the number of which is reduced to sixty, ten archbishoprics and fifty bishoprics. The nomination of

---

[1] The text of this Concordat is printed, together with the subsequent Organic Articles and the Concordat of Fontainebleau, in the original French by Walter, *Fontes Juris Canonici*, p. 143 ff.; in German by Alzog, II. 556 ff.

archbishops and bishops to the Pope for institution is given to the First Consul, and those nominated and instituted are to take the oath of fidelity, in a prescribed form, to the chief of the State before entering on office. The bishops undertake, with the sanction of the Government, to define the bounds of parishes in their several dioceses. The Pope undertakes to make no claim upon the actual possessors of alienated church-lands, in return for which concession the Government undertakes to provide suitable stipends for the clergy, and to permit Catholics to provide endowments for the service of the Church. The First Consul is to enjoy the same privileges with regard to ecclesiastical affairs which had been enjoyed by the head of the State before the Revolution. The Pope ratified this Concordat by a Brief in which he gave his reasons for this decision, and in a second Brief, dated two days later, he most earnestly besought the old legitimate bishops to endeavour to heal the wounds of the Church by resigning their sees. The greater part of them yielded to hard necessity and made the sacrifice, so as to permit new arrangements to be carried out. The constitutional bishops were required to resign not only by the Pope but by the Government of the country, and they chose to place their resignations in the hands of the latter.

Cardinal Caprara was sent to Paris as plenipotentiary to complete the transaction, and the ratification on the part of the French was duly given by the First Consul, in spite of much remonstrance from those about him. To mitigate the opposition, Napoleon put forth seventy-seven "Organic Articles," in some respects modifying the operation of the Concordat. They provided that no Bull, Brief, Mandate, or other document issued by the See of Rome, should be published in France without the sanction of the civil government. Offences of bishops should be subject to the judgment of the Council of State, which, after investigation, might issue a "déclaration d'abus." Teachers in seminaries were to subscribe to the four articles of the Gallican Liberties[1], and the bishops were to forward their subscriptions to the Ministry of Public Worship. No catechism was to be used in schools without the sanction

[1] See p. 108.

of the State. No council of the Church was to be held in France without the authorization of the secular power. During the vacancy of a metropolitan see the senior suffragan was to take charge of the administration of the diocese, and vicars-general were empowered to continue their functions in the interval between the removal of a bishop and the enthronement of his successor. Priests were forbidden to perform the marriage ceremony unless the parties had already been united in civil marriage. Church-registers were no longer to be accepted as evidence of the civil status of the persons registered.

Pius opposes the Articles.

The Pope in secret consistory from the first declared himself opposed to these Articles, and thenceforward made unceasing efforts to obtain their repeal, or at any rate some modification. An opportunity for doing so appeared to present itself when Napoleon, having become Emperor, desired the Pope to confer upon him the solemn unction at his coronation. He consented, and sought to obtain the revocation of the Articles and the restitution of the Romagna to the papal dominions. The Emperor, however, far from being in a mood for granting anything to the Pope, had it in his mind to require from him still further concessions, and so there arose a rift between the two parties which widened as time went on. When Napoleon had made himself master of all Italy he propounded his requirements to the Holy Father. He proposed to create a Patriarch of France, practically independent of Rome and nominated by the Emperor. The code of law which had already been introduced in Naples he proposed to introduce in Rome, to allow full religious liberty, to abolish the monasteries and the celibacy of the clergy. He further required the Pope to close his harbours against English ships. To all this the Pope firmly refused to agree, and further stated his objections to the recent ecclesiastical legislation in France. In particular, he urged that it was impossible for the Church of which he was Head to agree to regard all forms of religion as equal before the law. He found also great fault with the law of marriage contained in the French Code, which made the civil marriage alone valid before the courts, annulled some of the canonical impediments to marriage, and committed the decision of matrimonial causes to civil

Napoleon's Coronation, 2 Dec. 1804.

Napoleon's Proposals, 1808.

tribunals. He also declined to put himself in a state of war with England.

Upon this the French general Miollis entered on a military occupation of the States of the Church. And as the Pontiff still refused compliance with the Emperor's demands, an imperial decree in 1809 annexed the whole of the papal territory to the French Empire. Thereupon the Pope issued a Bull in which he excommunicated all who had taken part in infringing the rights of the Holy See, and in a Brief which immediately followed warned the Emperor expressly that he was included in the excommunication. The Bull did not become very widely known, as the Imperial Government sought in every way to prevent its attaining publicity. Pius, still protesting, was taken as a captive from the Quirinal and assigned a residence in Savona, on the Gulf of Genoa.

Miollis in Rome, 2 Feb. 1808.
Papal States annexed to France, 17 May, 1809.
Bull of 10 June, 1809.
Pius captive, 6 July, 1809.

But his resolution was by no means overcome, and he caused the Emperor no little perplexity by steadily refusing to give canonical institution to the priests nominated to vacant sees, so that there were at one time no less than twenty-seven unoccupied—a circumstance which naturally occasioned great discontent among the French Catholics. Napoleon attempted to bully the Pope into submission; all cardinals and officials, even his private secretary, were refused access to him, and he was not allowed to correspond freely with his friends. But all was in vain. The Pope simply declared that he could now do no official act, as he was in durance, and deprived of the presence of the cardinals, his lawful council.

Towards the end of the year 1809 the Emperor had constituted a commission of several bishops for matters ecclesiastical, from which he had obtained opinions on the points in dispute between himself and the Pope. At last, in 1811, he caused a national council to be summoned. But before it actually assembled he sent an embassy of bishops to the Pope, thinking that the latter, in his anxiety to prevent the council from taking independent action, would be ready to make concessions. The propositions which the ambassadors were authorised to make were, that he should have palaces provided at Paris and at Rome, with a yearly income of two million francs

(£80,000) and the honorary rank of a sovereign prince. In return, he was required to grant to the French clergy leave to subscribe to the Gallican Liberties, at once to institute those who had been nominated to the vacant sees, and for the future, if papal institution was not given within three months, to permit it to be given by the metropolitan or the senior bishop of the province in which the see was situated. The Pope gave a verbal promise that he would give canonical institution to the bishops already nominated, and for the future would empower the metropolitans to give institution if he himself did not give it within six months. As to the other points, the Holy Father declared that he could do nothing until his freedom and the presence of his council were restored.

Council, 1811.

The Council of the Church was opened immediately after the return of the ambassadors. Napoleon desired that the Council should independently make canons to the same effect as the papal agreement with regard to institutions, and submit them to him for approval, that they might become laws of the land. The Council was however not quite so submissive as had been expected. Voices were raised requiring that freedom should be granted to the Pope, and that his sanction should be given in form to any canons which were made. Napoleon therefore in a rage dissolved the Council, and even caused the three bishops who had been his chief opponents to be arrested. It was however soon recalled, a canon was made in the required form, and representations were sent to Savona to request the papal confirmation, which was given in a Brief in which the Holy Father styled the excommunicated Napoleon his beloved son. This concession, however, only led the Emperor to ask for more. In the summer of 1812 the Pontiff was brought to Fontainebleau, where negotiations were entered into during Napoleon's absence in Russia, and after his return continued by the imperious despot in person, in vain. The Pope resolutely maintained the same attitude. Certain preliminaries were however at last accepted on both sides, which the Emperor chose to regard as the conclusion of a Concordat, and published as such. The Pope thereupon declared that no Concordat had been concluded, and was in consequence treated with greater rigour. He was at last set free by the fall of Napoleon, and entered Rome on the 24th May, 1814.

Ch. VII. Pope returns to Rome, 24 May, 1814.

3. THE CHURCHES AND THE REVOLUTION.

As a consequence of the revolutionary wars the whole of the left bank of the Rhine was incorporated with the French Empire[1]. Not only were all the domains of ecclesiastical princes secularized, but secular princes whose dominions had been curtailed by the new arrangements were recompensed by additions from the territory of their ecclesiastical neighbours. The Diet of the expiring Empire in 1803 recognized, extended, and defined these arrangements. They were carried out by the secular princes generally in a selfish spirit, and with very little respect for the precious remains of antiquity found in the churches. The three spiritual electorates, Mayence, Cologne, and Treves, were altogether obliterated, the sees which had conferred the dignity of prince of the empire on their holders lost that privilege, and a considerable number of abbeys and monasteries were dissolved. The substitution of secular for ecclesiastical princes was, as may be supposed, by no means favourable to the Catholic Church in Germany. In the general wreck one conspicuous bishop was able to stand upright. Freiherr von Dalberg, after holding several distinguished positions, became Bishop of Ratisbon, to which see was annexed, with the consent of the Pope, the Primacy of Germany, which enabled him to exercise spiritual jurisdiction over the German territory on the right bank of the Rhine, with the exception of the dominions of Prussia and Bavaria. Dalberg was a man of distinguished character, acceptable to those in power from his tact and good sense, to artists and men of letters from his sympathy with their pursuits, and to Germany at large from his kindliness of disposition. He owed his exceptional treatment no doubt to the favour of Napoleon,

Peace of Luneville, 1801. Germany.

---

[1] On the events of this period in Germany see von Dalberg, *De la Paix de l'Église dans les États de la Confédération Rhénane* (Paris, 1810, and in German, Regensburg, 1810);
G. J. Planck, *Betrachtungen über die neuesten Veränderungen der Deutschen Katholischen Kirche* (Hanover, 1808).

and when the latter's power was annihilated by the battle of Leipzig, he resigned his dignities and possessions, retaining only the archbishopric of Ratisbon.

The promise had been given by those in authority, during the secularizing of the ecclesiastical property, that chapters should be provided with fixed incomes, and pensions given to dispossessed monks and friars. These were scanty and ill paid, and the permanent endowment of the cathedrals was constantly deferred. As, for want of maintenance, many canons ceased to reside, and many died, the sees had in some cases no chapters to elect a bishop, and consequently, as bishops died or resigned, many German dioceses came to be void, and were administered by Vicars-Apostolic, under the direct authority of the Pope. These, however, generally lacked the local knowledge necessary for a successful administration, and found themselves often hampered by the interference of the secular power, so that Catholicism tended to become cold and indifferent. There were, however, no doubt exceptions. In the diocese of Münster, for instance, Friedrich von Fürstenberg, encircled by many good Catholics, set an example of earnest devotion and successful administration.

In Italy and Spain, wherever the French power extended, the same measures were taken as in France; monasteries and religious societies were abolished, and the property of the Church confiscated. Bishoprics were reduced in number, and ecclesiastical courts placed under the control of the State. Even in the States of the Church seventeen sees were abolished. A Concordat concluded with the Italian Republic was somewhat more favourable to the sacerdotal party than that with France had been, but a decree of the civil government a few months later considerably diminished the power of the priesthood and increased that of the secular rulers. In Spain the anti-clerical measures converted most of the priests into ardent leaders of the movement for the expulsion of the French, and the King, Joseph Bonaparte, thereupon suppressed all the houses both of monks and friars, giving the dispossessed brothers a scanty maintenance. Bishops and chapters were required to declare their adhesion to the principles of the Gallican Church, a requirement to which few assented. This state of things naturally came to an end when the British army, in alliance with the Spaniards, drove the French over the Pyrenees.

CH. VII.

4. RELIGIOUS ROMANTICISM[1].

In the war of liberation all good Germans had come to feel the necessity of some guiding and moving power beyond the bare reason. Feeling was roused, patriotism and heroic devotion to duty gained the upper hand, and religion shared in the new life and brought forth new fruit. Men who had felt the oppression of the great conqueror, and made great sacrifices to shake off his yoke, turned to God with deep thankfulness for the hard-won victory. And the same struggle gave rise to a dislike of foreign, especially of French, influence. The younger men desired to return to old Teutonic ways and manners, so that even in speech and garb they aimed at an imitation of their forefathers. The students' associations at the universities were particularly eager to revive things old-fashioned. They attempted an impossible task, to bring back the years long gone by, and what they effected was for the most part artificial and fantastic. Nevertheless, the eighteenth century indifference to religion vanished. Orthodox and unorthodox alike recognized it as one of the great springs of human action and therefore a matter of the highest importance. It became more and more evident that the cold rationalism of the past century could not satisfy the longing of the soul after communion with God. Whatever may have been the defects of the older forms of religion, it was felt that they implied a real and ardent faith, and were capable of inspiring heroic deeds. The organization of mediæval society also, in which classes were distinctly marked and the subordination of one to another was easy and natural, seemed to many the true remedy for the evils of an age in which the old social principles were set at nought. This view was especially attractive to aristocrats and to students of constitutional law.

Germany.

Return to Old Teutonism.

[1] On the Romantic movement in Germany, see Julian Schmidt, *Gesch. der Romantik* (Leipzig, 1848); G. Brandes, *Main Currents in Nineteenth Cent. Literature* (Eng. tr., vol. I., published in 1901).

As was natural, the agitations of the past generation led many who longed for rest to seek it in the Church which offered them an infallible guide, the Roman. To those who were thus minded the Reformation presented itself as a break in the old beneficent order, as having introduced a destructive criticism in the place of devout obedience, doubt and unbelief in the place of childlike faith, sects in the place of unity. And the political solidity of Germany seemed to have been so shattered by religious differences that it had lost its great position among the States of Europe. This feeling was fostered from the beginning of the century by the Romanticist poets, such as Tieck and the brothers Augustus and Frederick von Schlegel. These writers aimed at bringing into vogue an idealized Middle Age, to display the noble qualities which they attributed to it under the glow of a warm and vivid imagination. They pressed the claims of the old Teutonic literature, art and architecture to be preferred, at least by Germans, to classical models. In this way the members of the Romantic School were drawn towards the Roman Church, which offered much to gratify them on the æsthetic side, and were disinclined to Protestantism, which offered a comparatively bald kind of worship. Protestantism appealed, they thought, too little to the emotional side of man. They forgot, perhaps, that there may be, that in fact there is, a deep religious feeling which is able to dispense with stimulants addressed to the senses, and this not in one community but in all.

One of the earliest and most notable proselytes was Count Frederick von Stolberg, who was received into the Roman Church in the year 1800, to the great wonderment of some of his friends. He was a man of real learning and ability, but one who looked at the past through the golden haze of poetic fancy rather than through the clear atmosphere of historic criticism. Frederick von Schlegel also went over to Rome. Tieck was suspected of having secretly done the same, a suspicion which was probably groundless, though he seems to have abandoned Protestantism. To the converts of Romanticism must be added Frederick von Hardenberg, known as Novalis, a sweet and devout, though not great, religious poet. To a very different class belongs Frederick Hurter, a minister of the Reformed Church in Schaffhausen, who was drawn to the Roman Church by the feeling that a man needs for religious guidance something more than the conclusions of his own individual reason, and that Christian society requires some recognized authority to put an end to the constant war of sects and parties. When he at last made up his mind to join the Roman Church, he received distinguished appointments in Vienna. Ch. VII.
Converted, 1844.

A religious movement distinct from Romanticism is that towards Mysticism, which seeks to attain the knowledge of God and union with Him rather through ecstatic feeling than by the use of external means of grace. Some pious mystics, who in their exalted devotion did not forget the claims of reason and authority, have won the love and admiration of all Christendom, but there have been others who have permitted the illusions of a troubled fancy to overpower the dictates of reason and authority alike. Times full of great and exciting events, and especially of great misfortunes, tend to produce this kind of mysticism; tender souls find in ecstasy a refuge from the miseries which surround them. Sometimes such mystics assume the prophetic office, declare God's will in what is actually occurring in the present, and even claim to foretell what His working will bring to pass in the future. *Mysticism.*

Such mysticism became rife in Germany during the troubles occasioned by the French invasion. Prophecies were circulated which sometimes claimed to rest on visions, sometimes on interpretations of the Apocalypse. A noteworthy mystic of this school was Frau von Krüdener, widow of a Russian diplomat, in early life a writer of novels, later a wandering seer and devotional leader. She gained great influence over Alexander I, Emperor of Russia, a man of sensitive nature and easily wrought upon by the personal magnetism of a religious enthusiast. She it was who suggested to the Czar the formation of a Holy Alliance among the Powers of Europe, who were to form one great family, acknowledging the law of Christ and promoting peace and all Christian virtues. The Powers did in fact adopt his proposal, with the exception of the King of England, the Sultan, and the Pope, but the Holy Alliance came to be regarded as a bond for the maintenance of absolutism, and was heard of no more after 1830. *Frau von Krüdener,* 1764—1824.

Holy Alliance, 1815.

In Switzerland her adherents formed a sect, nicknamed "Momiers," who interfered so much with the innocent amusements of their neighbours that disturbances arose, and the government attempted to put them down, not with entire success. In Germany she was regarded rather as a curious phenomenon than a religious force, and before her death she had dropped into obscurity.

A religious Romanticism[1], with characteristic differences from that in Germany, arose also in France when the storm of revolution was somewhat abated. Here the miseries of the period of unrest had stirred the deepest feelings of all hearts. Some returned from exile, some crept out of dungeons, all had lived lives overcrowded with sombre realities. The atmosphere was charged, so to speak, with sorrow, repentance, and disillusion. Souls just emerging from a conflict in which all earthly things seemed to be shaken and ready to vanish away sought some stable support. They turned to religion; they felt the need of faith.

The greatest exponent of the new feeling towards religion was François René de Chateaubriand, a scion of a noble family in Britanny. In his days of exile he had made acquaintance in the United States with some of the heroes of American independence, and with some of the remnants of Indian tribes, and had learned in a garret in London that he had brothers where poor men dwell. Returning to France when Napoleon opened the door to the emigrants, he published in 1802 the remarkable work, *Le Génie du Christianisme*, of which the striking, if somewhat florid, style departs widely from the classical models of the eighteenth century. The preachers and moralists of that time had sought to shew that Christianity is true and reasonable; Chateaubriand applies all his eloquence to shew that it is beautiful and comforting. It is, he contends, of all religions that have ever been, the most favourable to liberty, to humanity, to poetry, to arts, and letters. To it the modern world owes everything, its agriculture, its science, its hospitals, its noble buildings. Nothing can be more elevating than its morality, nothing

---

[1] On this, see Theophile Gautier, *Hist. du Romantisme* (2nd ed., 1874); Demogeot, *Hist. de la Littérature Française*, p. 558 ff. (ed. 1884).

more impressive than its doctrines and its worship. A few years later a visit to Rome brought vividly before his mind the great struggle which took place there between the old paganism and the infant Church. This visit produced "The Martyrs," an account of the sufferings of the Christians under Diocletian, in which the writer's very remarkable power of vivid description has full play. Such works as these brought forth in the midst of a highly sympathetic society, produced for the time an immense effect, though they were not sufficiently solid to endure when the emotional age which produced them passed away. That which Chateaubriand eulogised was the Catholic Church; his contemporary, the daughter of the former minister Necker, known to all the world as Madame de Staël, represents another aspect of the religious reaction against the philosopher. In her book on literature in its influence on society, and in her novel *Delphine*, if she does not insist on the absolutely unique glories of Christianity, she looks at the world with an eye for religion and poetry; she brings to light with great skill and eloquence the Divine government of the world and the constant presence of the Spirit of God with the spirit of man. These distinguished persons are but the most striking instances of a spirit which was widely diffused in France under the First Empire and the monarchy which succeeded it.

CH. VII.

'*Les Martyrs*,' 1809.

Madame de Staël, 1766— 1817.
'*Delphine*,' 1801.

5. SECTS OF THE REVOLUTIONARY PERIOD.

In Würtemberg, mainly through the influence of Bengel, Pietism was much occupied with Apocalyptic interpretation, and there was a general expectation that Christ would come again in the year 1836 and begin His thousand years' reign on earth. In this excited state of feeling it is not surprising that strange sects arose. From about the year 1785 a countryman, George Rapp[1], began to gather round him a knot of disciples who forsook the Lutheran Church of the country, looked for the speedy coming of the Lord, and had all their property in common. This communism, however, gave offence to the Würtem-

G. Rapp, 1757— 1847,

[1] C. Nordhoff, *Communistic Societies of the United States* (1875).

berg authorities, and in 1803 he migrated with a portion of his followers to the United States. They settled first in Pennsylvania, where they formed a village to which they gave the name of Harmony. Industrious and sober, they so prospered that in 1815 they were able to purchase a considerable tract on the Wabash in Indiana, to which they removed. This New Harmony was, however, purchased in 1824 by the well-known socialist Robert Owen; and the Rappists founded another settlement, called Economy, on the right bank of the Ohio.

Those of Rapp's followers who remained in Würtemberg fell into great extravagancies, rejected marriage and the eating of flesh, went about in strange clothing, railed against the regular ministers, refused obedience to the civil government, and held Bonaparte to be the Messiah. Another countryman, John Michael Hahn, whose teaching was a mixture of Pietism and Behmenism, also preached the near approach of the Second Advent, and drew round him many disciples. Under the name Michelians these sectaries are still found in various parts of the country[1]. A sect of a very different kind is that of the Pregizerians— so called from their leader C. A. Pregizer[2]—who believed themselves to be so completely made holy by faith that they had no need for confession of sin, and gave their meetings a very cheerful character, singing their hymns to popular tunes.

The multiplication of sects in Würtemberg in fact became such as to cause much anxiety to the civil government, which was ready consequently to welcome a proposed remedy. This came through G. W. Hoffmann[3], a much-respected citizen, who with certain associates bought the manor and village of Kornthal, near Ludwigsburg, where those whose conscience rendered it difficult for them to conform to the ordinary laws of the land should be permitted to live their own life. They were allowed to pay their taxes as a corporation and to buy exemption from conscription. The rulers consented to receive their word instead of an oath. There was conceded to them the

---

[1] Palmer, *Die Gemeinschaften und Sekten Württembergs* (1877).
[2] Palmer, *u.s.*; A. Ritschl, *Geschichte des Pietismus*.
[3] Palmer, *u.s.*; Kapff, *Die Württembergischen Brüdergemeinden Kornthals* (1839).

right to admit members to their body, and also to expel those who had been admitted, on condition that they provided for their reception into some other civil community. They did not practise community of goods, but no member was allowed to sell his portion, or to borrow money without the permission of the governing body. Even the reading of books was under control. In twenty years the society presented a highly prosperous appearance. It did not become a rallying-point for discontent, but rather came to a more friendly disposition towards the Established Church when its tenets and services were no longer pressed upon it.

In emotional communities there had always been a tendency to excess, and sometimes religious excitement leads to actual madness, as in the case of Margaret Peter[1] of Wildenspuch, in the canton Zürich. The conversation of religious people and the reading of tracts on the lost condition of human souls had so overpowering an effect upon her highly sensitive temperament that she became possessed with the idea of doing something great and extraordinary for the redemption of mankind. She and her adherents imagined that they had personal conflicts with a visible and palpable Satan, and at last her madness rose to such a pitch that she put to death her own sister as a sacrifice, and caused herself to be crucified as a renewal of the atoning death of Christ.

A very strange body of mystics were the so-called Muckers in Königsberg, who were indirectly called into existence by the teaching of J. H. Schönherr[2]. He taught a kind of Manichæan doctrine, that two great beings, a good and a bad, lay at the root of all existence, and that consequently there were two classes of men, those who belonged to light and those who belonged to darkness. Among the former were certain choice natures who were called and qualified to lead their brethren. One of his pupils, J. W. Ebel[3], withdrew from him in 1819, and founded a strange society of his own. He preached with

---

[1] Gieseler, v. 288.
[2] Gieseler, v. 198, who refers to Von Wegnern, *Zuverlässige Mittheilungen über Schönherr's Leben u.s.w.* in Illgen's *Zeitschrift*, 1838, Heft 2, p. 106 ff.
[3] W. Hepworth Dixon, *Spiritual Wives* (1868); Momberth, *Faith Victorious; an Account of the venerable Dr Johann Ebel* (1882).

great eloquence the need of repentance and sanctification, but, unlike the Pietists, he relied on the unaided powers of man and not on the grace of God. His followers were drawn, for the most part, from the upper classes, and ladies were especially attracted. To these he taught Schönherr's division of humanity, and claimed to be one of the choice spirits in union with whom alone the lower natures could find safety. He established in fact a tyranny of the most appalling kind, and it was believed that in the secret assemblies the most shameless indecorum was permitted and encouraged. So persistent were these rumours that in 1835 a criminal prosecution[1] put an end to Ebel's preaching.

[1] Graf Kanitz, *Aufklärung und Aktenquellen über den 1835—42... geführten Religionsprocess* (1862).

CHAPTER VIII.

THE ENGLISH SPEAKING CHURCHES.

1. THE OXFORD MOVEMENT[1].

THE early part of the nineteenth century in England is, as regards the Church, a period of quiet conservatism. The French Revolution, which on the Continent had caused so great changes, found an echo in this country also, and the French republicans had throughout the struggle sympathisers in England, but on the whole the upper classes and the clergy were reactionary, and very decidedly for maintaining the ancient constitution in Church and State. They hardly thought of the Church otherwise than as the "Establishment." The bishops were for the most part rather scholars and gentlemen than devout and earnest rulers of the Church. They had no opportunity of discussing the wants of the Church in Convocation, for Convocation was silenced. They did not hold diocesan synods, and the organization of the dioceses was mechanical and lifeless. The parochial clergy were generally respectable and respected, on good terms with their neighbours and kind to the poor, but with no very elevated views of their office and ministry and no very great fervour in the discharge of their duties. Their

State of the Church before the Movement.

General Conservatism.

The Bishops.

The parishes.

[1] Of the numerous books on this subject may be mentioned A. P. Perceval, *A Collection of Papers relating to the Movement of 1833* (London, 1842); W. Palmer, *Narrative of Events connected with Tracts for the Times* (*Ib.* 1883); E. G. Kirwan Browne (R.C.), *Annals of the Tractarian Movement*, 1842 —1860 (*Ib.* 1861); R. W. Church, *The Oxford Movement, 1833—1845* (*Ib.* 1891), an excellent book. But the best and fullest information is to be found in the biographies and letters of the several leaders, referred to under their names.

preaching was too often dull and perfunctory and their services slovenly and careless. The Evangelical clergy indeed paid much attention to preaching, but they do not appear to have been more assiduous in parochial visiting and the like than their less eloquent brethren. Non-residence and pluralities were as prevalent as they had been in the Middle Ages. The churches were kept in repair by church-rates and often retained interesting characteristics which have been since swept away by "restoration," but their fittings were generally in the worst possible taste, while cleanliness and neatness were too little attended to. Excepting on Sundays, they were for the most part closed. Where there was no educational foundation some kind of dame-school was generally found, but there were parishes in which even this was wanting, and many Englishmen never learned even the elements of reading and writing. The *Village* of the poet Crabbe gives a vivid and no doubt substantially true picture of a rural community of this period.

But if the thoughts of the clergy generally on ecclesiastical subjects strayed but little beyond the bounds of their parishes, there were still found here and there men who were conscious that the Church is a great spiritual society, having its own rights and its own laws. Whatever be its relation to the State, it retains the powers which were committed to it by its Founder. At Oriel College, Oxford, in particular, there arose under the provostship of Edward Copleston a very distinguished society of intellectual men, who were sometimes called Noetics. Two of these, Richard Whately[1] and Thomas Arnold[2], seized on the spiritual aspect of the Church, and endeavoured to raise it above the poor and mean conceptions which then prevailed. So far they agreed; but while Whately recognized the Church as an organized body, founded by Christ Himself, living its own life in the midst of an alien world, admitting to its fellowship whom it would, Arnold regarded no organization as specially divine; the faith of a Christian was a matter for his own intellect and conscience to determine; all were

---

[1] W. J. Fitzpatrick, *Memoirs of W.* (1864); E. Jane Whately, *Life and Correspondence of R. W.* (1866).

[2] A. P. Stanley, *Life and Correspondence of T. A.* (1844).

Christians who professed to acknowledge Christ as a divine person and to worship Him; and it was to be desired that the Church recognized by the law of the land should include all such persons. The State should make such arrangements as to render this inclusion possible. But neither Whately's views nor Arnold's gained much hold on the public mind. One was too abstract, the other too revolutionary. But others were found who had as eager and passionate a devotion to the old ideal of the Church as Arnold had for his new one. The Anglican theology of the seventeenth century had never entirely died out, and in the first half of the nineteenth it was to experience an extraordinary revival.

In 1811 there was elected to a Fellowship at Oriel a youth of nineteen who was destined to take—almost against his will—a great part in the ecclesiastical movements of his generation. This was John Keble[1], who, educated in a country vicarage by a religious and scholarly father, had won the highest honours of the University while still a boy. He was in no way elated by success, but remained to the end simple, earnest, unambitious. His mind expanded and his learning grew, he became known as a poet, a critic, a theologian and as one of the leaders of a great party; his perfect purity, devoutness, and sweetness of disposition caused him to be reverenced by those about him and consulted by many at a distance, but throughout his life he retained the impress of his early home. He was always by conviction and temperament a thorough English Churchman, leaning neither to Romanism nor Puritanism. As he said in his old age, "belief in the heroes of his youth had become part of him[2]." And the deep reverence which from boyhood he had felt for Holy Scripture had so imbued his mind, that when in later life a friend suggested to him that he should write something to relieve the trouble which was felt by many as to the inspiration of Scripture, he replied that "most of the men who had difficulties on this subject were too wicked to be reasoned with[3]." He had been in

---

[1] J. T. Coleridge, *Memoir of John Keble* (1869); Walter Lock, *J. Keble, a Biography* (1893); J. C. Shairp, *John Keble, an Essay* (1866).
[2] Coleridge's *Mem.*, p. 567.
[3] *Ib.* 568.

the habit of expressing in verse the thoughts of his heart on the festivals of the Church, and the series of poems which thus arose he published anonymously in 1827 under the title of *The Christian Year*. This little book has become familiar wherever English is read, and has had an enormous influence in promoting a sober and devout tone of mind with regard to the services of the English Church.

Keble had a pupil, Richard Hurrell Froude[1], "who was to be the mouthpiece and champion of his ideas, and who was to react on himself and carry him forward to larger enterprises and bolder resolutions than by himself he would have thought of....Froude's keenly-tempered intellect, and his determination and high courage, gave point and impulse to Keble's views and purposes[2]." From Keble he had lessons of self-distrust which at first moderated his natural impetuosity, but in the course of a few years he came to detest the Reformers, he accepted tradition as a guide in religious teaching, and was attracted to the mediæval, rather than to the primitive Church. His life was short, but it was long enough to enable him greatly to influence an Oriel colleague, somewhat his senior in age and standing, John Henry Newman[3].

This very remarkable man had been brought up under Evangelical influences, and his early impression of the weakness and depravity of fallen man, his need of divine help for his salvation and of right belief in order to obtain this help, never faded from his mind. His life was passed, at least so long as he remained in the English Church, in the search for a trustworthy guide. He was always supremely conscious of the nearness of the spiritual world; he believed in a divine guidance, an inner light, a call to special work, and was moved by what he regarded as out-

---

[1] *Life* prefixed to Froude's *Remains* (1838–9).
[2] R. W. Church, *Oxford Movement*, p. 24.
[3] J. H. Newman, *Apologia pro Vita sua* (1864), afterwards under the title *Hist. of My Religious Opinions*; Anne Mozley, *Letters of J. H. Newman during his Life in the English Church* (London, 1891);
E. A. Abbott, *Anglican Career of N.* (1892); R. H. Hutton, *Newman* (1891); F. W. Newman, *Contributions chiefly to the Early Hist. of N.* (1891); J. Oldcastle [*i.e.* Wilfrid Meynell], *Catholic Life and Letters of N.* (1881); L. F. Faure, *N. sa Vie et ses Œuvres* (1901); W. Barry, *Newman*, in *Literary Lives* series (1904).

ward signs and tokens. At the age of fifteen he passed through a crisis of conversion, "of which," he says[1], "I am still more certain than that I have hands or feet...I fell under the influence of a definite creed, and received into my intellect impressions of dogma which have never been effaced or obscured." After his election to a Fellowship at Oriel he became intimate with Whately, to whom he says that he owed, more than to anyone else, the development of his mind, and also the idea of the Christian Church as a divine appointment, a substantive body independent of the State, and endowed with rights, prerogatives, and powers of its own[2]. Then he fell under the influence of R. H. Froude, which he felt powerful beyond all others to which he had been subjected, and whom he described as "a man of high genius, brimful and overflowing with ideas and views[3]." As he had the temperament of a poet, and his convictions rested very much on his imagination and his affections, he distrusted and hated any use of reason which was likely to disturb them. Over and over again he declaims against "mere reason," "human reason," "usurping reason," "rebellious reason," and the like[4]. He was, he says, a rhetorician, not a philosopher[5]. His dislike for reason led him in later days (1870) to publish the curious essay in which he seeks to prove that our "assent" to a proposition is not due immediately to logical inference[6]. And the same feeling of the sacredness of his inward beliefs on religion led him sometimes to employ "economy" rather than withdraw the veil before persons whom he felt to be unsympathetic; to state a truth, that is, in the way which seemed least likely to provoke unfavourable or irritating comment, even at the expense of paring something from the truth itself. The more outspoken Froude[7] blamed his friend's "economizing," and pointed out that it led to misconceptions of his real meaning. Long after this period, in 1864, Charles Kingsley, much too hastily,

Conversion.

Oriel, 1822. Whately's influence.

R. H. Froude.

Hatred of reasoning.

---

[1] *Hist. of Rel. Opinions*, p. 4 (ed. 1865).
[2] *Ib.* p. 12.
[3] *Ib.* p. 24.
[4] See particularly *University Sermons*, p. 62 (ed. 1872).
[5] *Anglican Letters*, II. 156.
[6] *Essay in Aid of a Grammar of Assent* (1870).
[7] *Religious Opinions*, p. 45 (ed. 1865). See also R. F. Wilson in *Anglican Letters*, II. 207. For Newman's own view see *Rel. Opinions*, p. 343 ff.

declared in a magazine article that "truth for its own sake had never been a virtue with the Roman clergy. Father Newman informs us that it need not, and on the whole ought not to be." Newman was highly indignant, and, after some correspondence, published by way of defence a history of his religious opinions which is one of the most deeply interesting autobiographies ever written. He succeeded perfectly in convincing all but the most prejudiced that, whatever his theories, he was in his own person absolutely honest, that he had followed what he believed to be the truth through struggle and sacrifice. But the *Apologia* left it open to doubt whether he had in all cases dealt quite fairly with himself; whether, that is, he had not deliberately excluded from his mind some matters which ought to have been considered[1].

The Oxford Movement was the direct result of the searchings of heart and communings of Keble, Froude and Newman, but it was mainly Newman who gave it impulse and guidance. And certainly he was one of the purest and most attractive of the religious leaders of his time. He was a master of expression, both in verse and prose, he had a very magnetic personality, he gave his heart without reserve to further that which he believed to be right, he did not shrink from incurring obloquy which was most painful to his sensitive temperament, and throughout his life there never fell upon him any imputation of self-seeking.

While the new party was forming at Oxford great events were passing without. The cry for reform, choked during the great war, became more and more urgent, and the Utilitarian school of philosophy, guided by Jeremy Bentham and James Mill, constantly gained in importance. Statesmen of this school had of course no respect for the claims of the Church as a spiritual body. The Test and Corporation Acts[2], the effects of which had been already much mitigated by annual indemnity Acts, were repealed in 1828. In the following year was passed the Catholic

---

[1] It is significant that he never learned German, though as early as 1834 he was aware of the importance of that language for the study of theology. See *Anglican Letters*, II. 61.

[2] See p. 38.

Relief Bill, which allowed Roman Catholics to enter Parliament on taking an oath drawn in such terms as not to offend their consciences, and to hold any office except those of Regent, of Lord Chancellor, or Lord-Lieutenant of Ireland. In 1832 a Bill for the Reform of Parliament, which gave to the people an immensely extended representation, became law. In December of the same year Parliament was dissolved, and the new Parliament which met a month later contained a very large majority of Liberals. One of its first proceedings was to pass the Church Temporalities (Ireland) Act, by which two archbishoprics and eight bishoprics were suppressed, many ecclesiastical incomes were reduced, many sinecures swept away, and a commission appointed to administer surplus revenues.

It was very startling to those who were attempting to vindicate the independence of the Church in matters spiritual when ten sees were annihilated by the mere fiat of the State. Keble thereupon, preaching the Assize Sermon at Oxford, took for his theme "National Apostasy." When a nation which has for centuries felt itself bound to respect the laws and privileges of the Church throws off all such restraint, is Apostasy (he asked) too hard a word to describe the temper of such a nation? The sermon was a call to face in earnest a changed state of things, full of immediate and pressing danger. Newman always considered the day on which Keble preached this sermon in the University pulpit as the start of the religious movement of 1833.

A few days later a little party of friends—Arthur Perceval, R. H. Froude, and W. Palmer of Worcester College—met at Hadleigh Rectory in Suffolk, the home of Hugh James Rose, to deliberate on the measures to be taken to meet the dangers which threatened the Church. Mr Rose was a Cambridge man, who was, says Dean Church[1], "so far as could be seen at the time, the most accomplished divine and teacher in the English Church. He was a really learned man. He had the intellect and energy and literary skill to use his learning. He was a man of singularly elevated and religious character; he had something of the eye and temper of a statesman,

[1] *Oxford Movement*, p. 85 f.

and he had already a high position. He was profoundly loyal to the Church, and keenly interested in whatever affected its condition and its fortunes....He was certainly a person who might be expected to have a chief part in directing anything with which he was connected.... But his action in the movement was impeded by his failure in health, and cut short by his early death in January, 1839."

As a result of this meeting, an attempt was made to form an association for the defence of the Church. This came to nothing, but an address to the Archbishop of Canterbury, drawn up by Mr Palmer and embodying the views of the defenders of the Church, received the signatures of 7000 clergymen, and a similar lay address was signed by 230,000 heads of families. There can be little doubt that this agitation raised the spirits of Churchmen, and shewed that they were stronger and more resolute than their enemies thought. But more was needed to inform them what were the real claims of the Church, and the desire to supply this need led the three Oriel men to begin the publication of "that portentous birth of time, the *Tracts for the Times*[1]." Tract-distributing had long been a favourite method of propagating religious opinions, but the Tracts now produced were very different from those which well-meaning people sometimes pressed on chance passers-by. "They were clear, brief, stern appeals to conscience and reason, sparing of words, utterly without rhetoric, intense in purpose[2]." Newman wrote the first, as he himself says, "in an exuberant and joyous energy which he had never had before or since." The first three Tracts—all Newman's—are dated 9th September, 1833, and others, by him and his friends, appeared in rapid succession during the autumn and winter of that year. They were short, and treated in a plain and vigorous way the Apostolical Succession of the Christian ministry and its important consequences in doctrine, ritual, and discipline. These Tracts were intended to startle the Church of England, and they succeeded. They brought strange things to the ears of their generation. These things were in fact far from

[1] T. Morley, *Reminiscences*, I. 311. [2] Church's *Movement*, p. 98.

novelties, but their readers had for the most part forgotten some of the most obvious facts in Church History and some of the most certain of Church principles. The theological Liberals and the Evangelicals agreed in disliking them. They were "received with surprise, dismay, ridicule, and indignation. But they also at once called forth a response of eager sympathy from numbers to whom they brought unhoped-for relief in a day of gloom, of rebuke and blasphemy[1]." The teaching of the Tracts was powerfully reinforced by Newman's sermons at St Mary's. Clothed in a charmingly simple and flexible style, and animated by the quiet earnestness of the preacher, these discourses attracted many members of the University, who diffused their teaching throughout the country[2].

Towards the end of 1834 a new recruit of the highest importance joined the band of workers. This was Dr Pusey[3], the Professor of Hebrew, a learned and deeply religious man and a true son of the English Church. His position and high character gave the Movement a stability which without him it would probably not have attained. He had a hopeful mind and was not troubled by intellectual perplexities, but was always patient, resolute, and self-possessed. Such a man naturally became the chief of his party in the eyes of the world. He had before him a noble vision of a revived Church, earnest in purpose and strict in life, and of a great Christian University with a real sense of its powers and responsibilities. To him is due a great change in the character of the Tracts. He trusted more to learned argument than the earlier writers had done, and both by influence and example introduced a more solid and adequate treatment of important questions. To enable ordinary readers to see for themselves what was the theology of the early Church, a series of translations of the Fathers who lived before the separation of East and West—the *Library of the Fathers*—was projected, the volumes of which appeared at intervals from 1838

[1] Church's *Movement*, p. 106.
[2] On Newman's preaching, see Church's *Movement*, pp. 113 f., 121 ff.
[3] H. P. Liddon, J. O. Johnstone and R. J. Wilson, *Life of E. B. Pusey* (1893–4); [M. Trench] *The Story of Dr Pusey's Life* (1900).

to 1885, at first under the editorship of Pusey, Newman, Keble, and Charles Marriott.

From the beginning of the year 1836 the rapid spread of the Movement was observed both by friends and enemies, and as it spread it encountered more opposition. The excellent clergymen who became its advocates were of course not in all cases able and judicious, and, as is the manner of half-instructed disciples, they were apt to insist needlessly on unimportant matters. This brought upon them much odium, and a most inopportune Tract—the 80th of the series—on Reserve in communicating religious knowledge, greatly increased this. It was written in a thoroughly devout and reverent spirit by the blameless Isaac Williams, a scholar and poet, and was intended as a protest against the reckless way in which sacred words—especially on the great mystery of the atonement—were bandied about in popular declamation. The opponents of the Tracts raised a loud cry; here was the secret of the Tractarian party disclosed, its disingenuous professions, its holding doctrines which it dared not avow. The suspiciousness which this well-intended Tract awakened was never allayed. And an even greater outcry was occasioned by the publication of Froude's *Remains*. To have the faults and shortcomings of the English Church, for some of which the Reformation was held to be responsible, strongly insisted upon; to be taught that the Roman Church was more right than Englishmen had been led to suppose, and that our quarrel with it, in some points at any rate, was due to ignorance and prejudice; to have all this set forth in Froude's forcible style, with the frankness with which a man naturally writes to a friend, was extremely disquieting. And now the suspicion of a tendency to Rome was not altogether unreasonable. A change had in fact come over the minds of some of the leaders. The Tracts had begun by asserting the spiritual claims of the English Church, and to this ideal such men as Keble, Pusey, Isaac Williams and C. Marriott always remained faithful. But some of their associates began to ask themselves, Can we take the Church of England, with all its defects and anomalies, as a true and sufficient representative of the Catholic Church in England? To Newman in particular the

Church of Rome, which in earlier days he had looked upon as Antichrist, began to present itself in impressive grandeur. A period of doubt and mental struggle began which he has himself depicted with incomparable force and pathos in the *Apologia*.

In 1841 appeared a Tract, the 90th and last of the series, in which Newman endeavoured to shew that the Thirty-nine Articles, "the offspring of an uncatholic age, are through God's providence, to say the least, not uncatholic, and may be subscribed by those who aim at being catholic in heart and doctrine[1]." It may be imagined what horror and indignation were roused by a book which attempted to shew that the Articles by no means condemned every form of the doctrine of purgatory as a place of purification after death, nor every form of "sacrifices of Masses." To most men outside the Tractarian circle it seemed dishonest. The Oxford Heads of Houses censured it. The Bishops generally condemned it, none more strongly than that most staunch champion of High Church principles, Henry Phillpotts of Exeter[2]. "An epoch and a new point of departure had come into the movement;... it was the date from which a new set of conditions in men's thoughts and attitudes had to be reckoned[3]."

Among those who joined in the fray was William George Ward[4], Fellow of Balliol, a very clever and amusing person, who took a great interest in theological questions, was ready to argue, like a mediæval schoolman, on any imaginable subject, and was by no means afraid of his conclusions. He was not satisfied with Newman's explanations, and frankly admitted that he subscribed certain Articles "in a non-natural sense." In the remarkable volume which summed up his thoughts on theology— *The Ideal of a Christian Church*—the present-day teaching of the Latin Church is recognized as Catholic truth. "The Lutheran doctrine of justification and the principle of private judgment" are held to "sink below atheism itself[5]." As was to be expected, the Protestant party in Oxford was furious at this defiance of all its traditions. In

---

[1] *Tract no.* 90, p. 4.
[2] See Perry's *Ch. Hist.*, III. 233.
[3] Church's *Movement*, p. 255.
[4] Wilfrid Ward, *W. G. W. and the* *Oxford Movement* (1889); *W. G. W. and the Catholic Revival* (1893).
[5] *Ideal*, p. 587.

Ch. VIII.
Ward's 'Ideal' condemned, Feb. 1845.

February, 1845, two decrees were passed by Convocation, one condemning Ward's book, and a second depriving him of all his University degrees. A formal censure of the principles of Tract No. 90 was defeated by the veto of the Proctors, one of whom was R. W. Church. The shock was great, and was felt in all parts of the country. In the autumn of 1845 began a series of secessions. Ward went over to the Roman Church. On the 8th of October Newman was received into the same communion. These were followed by many friends and disciples, all respectable in character and intellect, some distinguished. Fellowships, benefices, curacies, intended careers, were given up. In almost all cases there was a surrender of some coveted social position. In this time of distress some almost despaired of the future, but the leaders—Keble, Pusey, Marriott—accepted the loss of their friends with unshaken faith in the Anglican Church. They had never so much as entertained the thought of submitting to the Roman claims. The Movement "was not killed, or even much arrested, by the shock of 1845; but after 1845 its field was at least as much out of Oxford as in it[1]." Whether men approved or condemned, the Oxford teaching lived, and in the last sixty years has changed the character of the English Church.

Jerusalem Bishopric, 1841.

Meanwhile a scheme for the establishment of a bishopric in Jerusalem by the Anglican Church and the Prussian Lutherans jointly, which received the sanction of Archbishop Howley in 1841, had given offence to many, as it seemed to imply an ignoring of the fundamental differences between the two communities. The suspension of Dr Pusey in 1843 by the Oxford Heads of Houses for preaching a sermon on the Eucharist, which was largely composed of quotations from the Fathers and Anglican theologians, naturally made his friends uneasy. In 1850 a new agitation arose. The Judicial Committee of the Privy Council decided in the case of the Rev. G. C. Gorham[2], who had

Dr Pusey suspended, 1843.

The Gorham Case, 1850.

---

[1] Church's *Movement*, p. 351.

[2] The case is reported in *Six Judgments of the Judicial Committee 1850—72*, by W. G. Brooke (Lond. 1874). Bishop Phillpotts (*Letter to the Archbishop; Letter to the Churchwardens of Brampton-Speke*, 1850), and Mr Gorham (*The Great Gorham Case; a Letter on the Recent Judgment*, 1850) both defended themselves before the public with great ability, and very numerous pamphlets followed.

been presented to a benefice in the diocese of Exeter, and to whom the bishop (Phillpotts) refused institution, that Mr Gorham's refusal to acknowledge that a baptized child is in every case regenerate by the grace given in baptism, was not a sufficient cause for the bishop to refuse him admission to the benefice. The Committee expressly stated that it "had no jurisdiction or authority to settle matters of faith, or to determine what ought in any particular to be the doctrine of the Church of England"; it only decided that Mr Gorham's language did not so directly contravene any formula of the Church of England as to disqualify him for preferment. But when men are under strong mental anxiety they are apt to look at tendencies rather than facts, and it was commonly said it was now apparent that the Church of England did not teach the doctrine of baptismal regeneration. At the same time, the fact that this momentous decision was given by a Court which could not possibly be regarded as "spiritual" led many good men to regard it as a proof that the Church of England was a mere State Church, and this caused fresh secessions. Within a year Archdeacon Manning, Mr W. Maskell, Mr Henry Wilberforce, and other distinguished men joined the Church of Rome. Archdeacon R. I. Wilberforce followed in 1854.

Secessions.

The early Tractarians had been too much occupied with the vindication of Catholic doctrine to take much thought for ritual. For the most part they accepted the Anglican services as they found them. But gradually changes crept in. About 1842 surplices began to be seen in the pulpit instead of the customary black gown, and surpliced choirs were introduced in parish churches where they had probably never appeared since the churches were built. Things which are actually seen are proverbially more exciting than those which are addressed to the ear alone, and these changes, however innocent in themselves, were thought to indicate a serious deviation from the recognized doctrine and practice of the Church of England. In some places they occasioned actual riots. Archbishop Howley very wisely recommended all to wait until some authoritative decision was given on the matters in dispute, but few followed his good counsel. Such men as Newman, while earnestly maintaining the Real Presence in the

Disputes on Ritual.

Surplice in pulpit and choir, c. 1842.

Eucharist, had seemingly not thought that additional impressiveness could be given to a purely spiritual doctrine by material splendour. But this abstinence from ritual innovation was not of long continuance. In the ten years which followed Newman's secession efforts were made in some churches to surround the celebration of the Holy Eucharist with more dignified accessories. Crosses, sometimes crucifixes, were introduced; credence tables were placed in the chancels; altar-frontals and stoles of different colours according to the ecclesiastical seasons came into use; the celebrating priest stood in front of the Holy Table with his face to the east. Then, in another ten years, the Eucharistic vestments, wafer-bread, and many of the ceremonies of the pre-Reformation period were adopted in numerous churches. All this, for which rubrical authority was claimed, was a breach of the Anglican tradition of two hundred years, and was done without the authority of the bishops, to whom the duty of interpreting rubrics was committed by the Church. A large number of sincere Churchmen were extremely indignant at the frank repudiation of Protestant principles which was brought both to their eyes and their ears. A number of cases of supposed illegality in the conduct of Divine service were brought before the courts of law, and the Judicial Committee of Privy Council, as the court of final appeal, decided most of the points in question against the Ritualists. Little regard was, however, paid to its decisions.

Meantime, in 1860, the English Church Union had been formed to defend and maintain what its supporters held to be Catholic doctrine and worship, and to aid those who should be attacked or persecuted for such doctrine or worship. There can be no objection to the formation of a society to maintain certain principles and to prevent individuals from being crushed for acts which are practised by many; yet it is to be feared that the English Church Union has tended to give a partizan aspect to the work of the High Anglicans. In its origin, Tractarianism was an influence; the Ritualists have become very decidedly a party. On the other hand, many excellent men deemed it their duty to contend for the maintenance of what they held to be the principles of the Reformation, and formed the Church Association, under the auspices and with the assistance of which many prosecutions of Ritualistic clergymen were undertaken.

A peculiar and highly important case was that of Bishop King of Lincoln, who was charged with illegal practices in Divine service, and whose case came before Archbishop Benson with four episcopal assessors. The result was a most able and weighty judgment[1] delivered by the Archbishop, in which the points raised are examined with great wealth of learning. By this judgment the use of the mixed chalice and the eastward position were declared to be not contrary to the law of the Church. The breaking of the bread and the blessing of the cup must be so performed as to be visible to communicants properly placed in the church. The law was not broken by the singing of "O Lamb of God" during the service of Holy Communion, nor by placing two lighted candles, not required for giving light, on the Holy Table. The making the sign of the cross at absolution or benediction is ordered to be discontinued. Some other points of ritual, such as vestments, were not before the Court, and were consequently not decided. The judgment concluded with the weighty words, little regarded: "The Court has not only felt deeply the incongruity of minute questionings and disputations in great and sacred subjects, but desires to express its sense that time and attention are diverted thereby from the Church's real contest with evil and building up of good, both by those who give and by those who take offence unadvisedly in such matters." This judgment has not been overruled by any court of law, but it can scarcely be said to have brought peace to the Church. Nor has the judgment or opinion given by the two Archbishops (Temple and Maclagan) some years later, as to the interpretation of certain rubrics, had much effect on the practice of clergymen who hold strong opinions on ritual matters. A Commission on Ecclesiastical Discipline, really on Ritual, is now sitting (1905).

Meantime, while High Anglicanism was acquiring great influence in the English Church, it must not be

[1] *Read and others v. the Bishop of Lincoln; Judgment Nov.* 21, 1890 (London, 1890).

supposed that Evangelicalism was obsolete or indifferent[1]. It continued to play a great part in the religious life of England. The traditions of Simeon and his friends were not lost, though no leader arose comparable to that excellent man. Evangelical religion has always, from the time of the Reformation, had many and steadfast adherents in the middle class, and such it has still. Nothing can shew this more clearly than the very generous support given to the Church Missionary Society, always faithful from its foundation to Evangelical principles.

Foremost among those who sided with the Evangelical cause in the nineteenth century was Antony Ashley Cooper, Earl of Shaftesbury, who during a long life gave himself with unwavering courage and patience to religious and philanthropic work. Evil report, contempt, and opposition did not turn him aside from the path on which he felt called to walk. He was conscious of the presence of the Saviour, and found in the Bible the sure oracle of divine truth. In every way, by legislation and by private endeavour, he sought to better the condition of the poor, and constantly used the influence of his rank and character to further what he held to be true Biblical Protestantism. In his opposition to Romanism and Rationalism he was not always judicious or well-informed, but the simplicity and earnestness of his nature impressed even those who had no sympathy with his views.

During the period in which Lord Shaftesbury was a conspicuous figure many able clergymen advanced the cause of Evangelicalism both by local effort and general influence. There were found in their ranks many pious, earnest, and able bishops, many eloquent preachers, and many devoted pastors, though the annals of the party do not supply any group of teachers comparable in character, learning, and power with the early Tractarians, and their influence has on the whole tended to decline. The strong adherents of Evangelical principles have as a whole been marked by much true piety, much strength of Christian principle and power of self-sacrifice, much solid philanthropy and splendid missionary zeal. To them, it ought to be remembered, is almost wholly due the forbidding

---

[1] See H. C. G. Moule, *The Evangelical School in the Church of England* (London, 1901).

of the slave trade in 1807, and the abolition of slavery throughout the British dominions in 1833. But in days when there was on all sides a great inrush of new ideas; when new views in politics, new schemes of philosophy, new discoveries in science, new theories, not only of the interpretation, but of the very nature, origin, and authority of the books of Holy Scripture, were struggling for the mastery over the minds and hearts of mankind, they supplied but little guidance. They stood too much aloof from the main currents of human thought.

2. LIBERAL TENDENCIES.

Some of the movements which have most influenced Christian thought had their origin outside the Church. The old adage, that nothing is found in theology which is not first found in philosophy, still holds good in the nineteenth century. It has never been possible for the Church to surround itself by an intellectual fence through which the thoughts of the world without cannot pass. In the period with which we are concerned the presuppositions upon which the Christian faith rests were examined by very able thinkers both within and without the Church. The being and nature of God and His relation to the universe were enquired into with no reference to revelation. The harmony of the orthodox creed with the Scriptures on which it professes to be founded; the authenticity and authority of the Bible itself, and its relations to the acknowledged results of science in astronomy, geology and the history of man upon earth; the compatibility of such doctrines as predestination and the everlasting torments of the condemned with what we believe of the goodness and mercy of God; all these vastly important matters came not only to be examined by philosophers but to be discussed freely by interested enquirers who were no philosophers at all.

Foremost among those who influenced Christian thought in the early part of the nineteenth century must be placed Samuel Taylor Coleridge, the first Englishman of distinction who was deeply influenced by German philosophy. He was, however, an original thinker, and did much to rescue religion from the

General Movement.

S. T. Coleridge, 1772—1834.

speculative systems under which it was becoming "a science of shadows under the name of theology," and to point out that "the heart, the moral nature, is the beginning and the end of religion." The poetry of Wordsworth too widened the thoughts of men on God and the world, and taught them to bring within the sphere of religion the works of nature, which in the previous century had come to be looked upon almost as a mechanism.

Thomas Carlyle, although in his eagerness to clear the truth from what seemed accretions he assailed many things of greater value than he supposed, still taught that there was in every man a God-given faculty enabling him to apprehend intuitively the Divine in the world and in human life, and to worship it in reverent obedience. Francis William Newman, younger brother of J. H. Newman, to whom he was not inferior in courage and intellect, described the process by which an active and enquiring mind may be compelled to resign one after another the articles of the creed in which he has been brought up. Religion, he held, is created by an instinct of the soul, its longing for true and heartfelt communion with God. But this instinct must be purified and chastened by the intellect or it becomes superstition, while intellect alone produces only a barren rationalism. The utilitarian philosophy of John Stuart Mill can hardly be considered favourable to Christianity, yet his experience led him to conclude that "those only are happy who have their mind fixed on some object other than their own happiness; on the happiness of others, on the improvement of mankind....Aiming thus at something else, they find happiness by the way." This is little else than the Divine paradox "Whosoever will save his life shall lose it." Sir William Hamilton, whom Mill criticized, taught a kind of agnosticism as regards the "absolute" of philosophers, but he believed his rejection of the arrogant claims of some of them to be favourable to revelation; and his disciple, H. L. Mansel, used his principles to shew that philosophy is not competent to criticize the subject-matter of revealed religion which is found in the Bible. His attempts to base faith on scepticism in some respects recall Pascal's.

The most eager opponent of Mansel's theory was Frederick Denison Maurice[1], already known to many disciples as the author of a thoughtful book on the Kingdom of Christ. The centre of his teaching may be said to be that Christ is in us as the Lord of our spirits, that we must yield ourselves to Him that He may work in us and through us. Christ, the ideal man, Who is in the whole race, is one eternal Person, Who by the Incarnation became the historical Saviour Jesus. It must be confessed that much of Maurice's work produces no very distinct impression on the mere intellect. "The key to his whole scheme of thought appears to be the really dazzling brightness of his own moral self-consciousness. The facts which he finds there are the only ones he really knows or at all apprehends, and his endeavour is to impose them in all their peculiar individuality on the history of mankind, which is so far more complete and comprehensive than the experience of any one man can be[2]." But whatever may have been his incapacity for impressing a set of propositions on the world—a task which indeed he utterly renounced—his earnestness and attractive personality, especially as expressed through his preaching, drew round him a body of disciples who again diffused his influence. Of these the most remarkable was Charles Kingsley[3], who expounded his master's views, together with his own, with warmth and clearness in a style which all the world could understand and admire. Another who connected the teaching of Christ with the thoughts of man and the history of the world in a broader and more intelligent way than had been done by most religious teachers was Frederick William Robertson[4], of Brighton, whose preaching acquired great influence among men of all parties. Matthew Arnold resembled Kingsley in being a poet and a distinguished man of letters, but in temperament and opinions differed very widely. To him Maurice was one who "beat the bush with emotion without starting the hare." In his own scheme religion has to do mainly with "conduct"; it is "ethics heightened, enkindled, lit

CH. VIII.

F. D. Maurice, 1805—1872.
'*Kingdom of Christ,*' 1838.

Charles Kingsley, 1819—1875.

F. W. Robertson, 1815—1853.
M. Arnold, 1822—1888.
'*Literature and Dogma,*' 1873.

[1] J. F. Maurice, *Life of F. D. Maurice, chiefly in his own Letters,* 2 vols., 1883-4.
[2] John Sterling, in *Letters etc. of R. C. Trench,* I. 247 (ed. 1888).
[3] Frances E. Kingsley, *Charles Kingsley, his Letters etc.* (London, 1877).
[4] Stopford A. Brooke, *Life and Letters of F. W. R.* (London, 1865).

up by feeling"; it is "morality touched by emotion." That which is the real object of religious faith is "the eternal, not ourselves, which makes for righteousness." Of this, and of the solidity of the precepts of Christ we may (he holds) be certain from experience, which alone compels assent. A man in relation to these matters more competent than Arnold, Professor J. R. Seeley, of Cambridge, set forth the ethical ideal of Christ with great force and eloquence, in a volume which attracted much attention, and also, after an interval of some years, treated with characteristic clearness and independence of natural religion. He too thinks that belief in the supernatural is waning, and inquires what is left when it is abandoned. He replies that men, scientific men at any rate, cannot but acknowledge the unity and regularity of the universe as inspiring awe and reverence; but in the conception of God we also include "whatever more awful forces stir within the human heart, whatever binds men in families and orders them in States." Such, in brief, is his conception of God present in nature and in man.

In 1859 a great impulse was given to the study of biology by the publication of Charles Darwin's[1] "Origin of Species by means of Natural Selection, or the Preservation of Favoured Races in the Struggle for Existence." Evolution, by which we are to understand (in Darwin's words) the belief that species "undergo modification, and that the existing forms of life are the descendants by true generation of preexisting forms," is an ancient cosmic speculation, and had been brought into modern philosophy by Kant and Lamarck. The theory of the latter was, that organs are modified in function, and so ultimately in structure, by change of environment, and also by use and disuse, and that these modifications are transmitted and increased from generation to generation. This theory, though after the excitement produced by its first publication it was neglected, is now generally admitted to have directed attention to true factors in evolution. In 1831 Patrick Matthew[2], an almost unknown naturalist, propounded the theory that the infinite varieties of plants and

---

[1] *Life and Letters*, by F. Darwin (London, 1887).

[2] In the appendix to a book on *Naval Timber*. See Grant Allen, *Charles Darwin*, pp. 18 and 82 (3rd ed.).

animals may have arisen from the survival of the fittest in the struggle for existence occasioned by the "extreme fecundity of nature." On this Darwin observes that "he gives precisely the same view on the origin of species as that propounded by Mr Wallace and myself. He clearly saw the full force of the principle of natural selection." To this natural selection occasioned by the struggle which results from the immense productiveness of plants and animals, Darwin added, perhaps as an afterthought, sexual selection, the theory that species are modified by the preference of individuals for certain individuals of the opposite sex rather than others. The whole theory depends on what Darwin called "spontaneous variations"; on the fact, that is, that the offspring of creatures of the same kind do not exactly resemble each other, but present "variations" from the common type. Those individuals, it is held, survive, whose variations give them an advantage in the struggle for existence, and they transmit to their offspring the characteristics which enabled themselves to survive. This process, continued over vast periods of time, has brought into existence the innumerable forms of life which we see on the face of the earth. The word "spontaneous" simply expresses the fact that we know nothing of the cause of these variations. It is to be noted, however, that Darwin himself did not attribute everything in the moulding of species to this potent factor. "I am convinced," he says, "that natural selection has been the main but not the exclusive means of modification." But his book gave an immense extension and importance to the general theory of evolution. That which had been before Darwin's time an obscure theory known only to a few students started into the full light of day, and "evolution" and "Darwinism" came to be regarded as equivalent terms. Herbert Spencer formulated it, and applied it to solve social and ethical problems which had not come within Darwin's view. Spencer is also regarded as the chief representative of Agnosticism; he holds, that is, that it is involved in the very nature of our consciousness that it can only know what is finite and limited, but he does not, like Hamilton, maintain that the "absolute" is a purely negative concept. The "absolute" is to him the necessary complement of the relative. When

Herbert Spencer, 'First Principles,' 1862.

he says that God is not cognisable by our natural powers, he agrees with many religious teachers. But while religious teachers hold that God may be revealed to us, the philosopher holds that the mystery which surrounds Him is absolute and impenetrable. The Spencerian agnosticism was forcibly criticized by two very acute thinkers, James Martineau and John Caird. The former pointed out[1] that Spencer's admissions as to the Great First Cause, while they are insufficient for religion, are too wide for nescience. The latter shewed[2] that the two propositions, that our intelligence is confined to the finite and relative, and that we have cognisance of an existence beyond the finite, are contradictory and cancel each other. Thomas Hill Green at Oxford taught an idealistic philosophy, founded on Hegel, which is antithetic to any system of materialism. There is, he holds[3], "one spiritual self-conscious being, of which all that is real is the activity or expression; that we are related to this spiritual being not merely as parts of the world which is its expression, but as partakers in some inchoate measure of the self-consciousness through which it at once constitutes and distinguishes itself from the world; that this participation is the source of morality and religion." But the general result was that the whole field of biology came to be regarded from an evolutionary point of view. Even man himself did not escape from the all-embracing theory, but was held to be descended from "more or less monkey-like animals, belonging to the great anthropoid group, and related to the progenitors of the orang-outang, the chimpanzee, and the gorilla[4]."

Effects of Darwinism.

It may readily be imagined how great a shock this was to the faith of Christians. It seemed not only to set at nought the Scriptural account of the Creation, but to exclude God from the universe. All the phenomena of life, including those of mind, appeared to arise from purely material causes. The theological world was greatly stirred, and replies to Darwin, of all degrees of merit, appeared in rapid succession; nor was criticism wanting from the

---

[1] *A Study of Religion*, I. 131 ff.
[2] *Introduction to Philosophy of Religion*, p. 10 ff.
[3] Quoted by Pfleiderer, *Development of Theology*, p. 345 (London, 1890).
[4] Grant Allen, *C. D.* 139.

scientific side. In the course of a generation, however, the alarm in a great measure subsided. Darwinism made its way among theologians also. It came to be felt by many that the quarrel between physical science and theology arose in great measure from the misconception that God is a great ruler, sitting apart from the created universe and only occasionally interfering with it. If it is once realized that God is immanent in His creation and that what we call laws of nature are indeed laws of God, His working out of His purposes through those laws from ages and generations gives a conception of the Almighty as worthy of awe and reverence and adoration as can possibly be. The doctrine of the immanence of God has been recalled from the old Greek Fathers for the service of our own day, but it is not possible at present to forecast its future amid the various streams of modern thought.

Ch. VIII. Change in Theology.

The man who did most to promote a candid and intelligent interpretation of Holy Scripture in the early part of the nineteenth century was Thomas Arnold. Before his time, though scholarly interpreters had not been wanting, those who interpreted with a view to edification had too little regarded scholarship, while those who looked mainly to scholarship had done little for edification, and exegesis was deeply influenced by the desire to harmonize Scripture with the prevalent theology of the day. Arnold "approached the human side of the Bible in the same real historical spirit, with the same methods, rules, and principles, as he did Thucydides. He recognized in the writers of the Scriptures the use of a human instrument, language; and the meaning of this he would ascertain and fix by the same philological rules as in other authors. But in the Bible he found and acknowledged also an oracle of God, a positive and supernatural revelation made to man, an immediate inspiration of the spirit[1]." Such were the principles which he impressed on several generations of pupils during the fourteen years of his head-mastership at Rugby; and the seeds which he sowed bore much fruit. He met with much opposition and denunciation, but this gradually died away, and to Arnold more than to any other man is due

Arnold on Interpretation of Scripture, 1831.

[1] Bonamy Price in Stanley's *Life of Arnold*, I. 216 (3rd ed.).

the more frank and vivid interpretation of Scripture in England in recent times. His distinguished pupil, Arthur Penrhyn Stanley, published in 1855 an edition of St Paul's Epistle to the Corinthians, in which scholarship and historical research are applied without reserve to the interpretation of the text. Simultaneously his friend Benjamin Jowett, shortly afterwards Professor of Greek at Oxford, produced an even more remarkable work in his edition of the Epistles to the Thessalonians, Galatians, and Romans, to which were appended a series of essays dealing with such matters as the Man of Sin, St Paul's Conversion, St Paul and the Twelve, conversion and changes of character, natural religion, and the doctrine of the Atonement, in a style to which British theologians were by no means accustomed. Both these works were fiercely attacked on their first appearance, but it is now evident that they made an epoch in the history of New Testament exegesis in England. Even those who did not accept the conclusions of Stanley and Jowett yet drew light from their methods.

A few years later appeared a book which occasioned a far deeper agitation than these had done. This was a collection of Essays and Reviews by seven writers, all men of some reputation, which is described in the short prefatory note as "an attempt to illustrate the advantages derivable to the cause of religious and moral truth from a free handling, in a becoming spirit, of subjects peculiarly liable to suffer by the repetition of conventional language, and from traditional methods of treatment." It answers fairly to this description, but it came before a society which was utterly unprepared to receive it. Jowett's essay on the interpretation of Scripture, which advocates in the main the same method of treatment which Arnold had done, was represented as denying its divine authority; and similar things were said of Rowland Williams' account of Bunsen. Baden Powell, in treating of the study of the evidences of Christianity, was thought to deny all miraculous intervention, and H. Bristow Wilson to represent that a National Church might very well dispense with statements of doctrine such as had been hitherto regarded as essential. The clergy were greatly alarmed. The matter was brought before the Convocation of Canterbury, and, after much discussion, both Houses in the end "synodically condemned" the volume as containing teaching contrary to the doctrine of the Church. Meantime, two of the essayists, Williams and Wilson, had been brought before a court of law on charges of maintaining unsound doctrine, which resulted in a very lucid judgment of the Judicial Committee of Privy Council, delivered by Lord Westbury as Chancellor, to the effect that the impugned statements did not so directly contradict any formulary of the Church of England as to constitute an ecclesiastical offence. The clergy generally received this judgment with great indignation, but the next generation saw reason to be grateful to the court which had vindicated their liberty.

Condemned by Convocation, 25 June, 1864,

acquitted by Judicial Committee, 8 Feb. 1864.

An even greater shock to the general belief as to Holy Scripture was Bishop Colenso's critical examination of the Pentateuch and the Book of Joshua. John William Colenso[1], a distinguished Cambridge man, had gone out in 1853 to Natal, where he gave himself with wholehearted devotion to teaching and tending his Zulu "children," whose language he learned. The childlike questioning of his Zulu disciples led him to reexamine the traditional views on the Bible which he had hitherto held, and brought him to the conclusion that the narrative portion of the Pentateuch contained much that was not historical, and that the extremely minute legislation of the books of Numbers and Leviticus was the work of an age many centuries later than that of Moses. These views he worked out and published in a book, the first volume of which appeared in 1862. There followed a cry of indignation and horror. Many Churchmen called upon him to resign his office as bishop, and indeed as a Christian teacher of any kind. Bishop Gray, as metropolitan of South Africa, sitting, with assessors, in judgment upon Colenso pronounced sentence of deposition against him, and when he disregarded this followed it up by excommunication. The Judicial Committee, on appeal, pronounced the whole of these proceedings null and void in law, and somewhat later Lord Romilly in the Rolls Court decided that in the eye of the law Dr Colenso was still Bishop of Natal and entitled to the temporalities

Colenso on the Pentateuch, 1862—1870.

Colenso deposed, 16 Dec. 1863.

Sentence declared null, 30 March, 1865.

Rolls' Court Judgment, 1866.

[1] G. W. Cox, *Life of J. W. Colenso* (London, 1888).

of the see. These decisions of course did not prevent Churchmen from holding that he had been canonically deposed. There were, however, many in Natal who eagerly supported him and continued to acknowledge his episcopal authority, and there he remained until his death in 1883, occupied in finishing his work, and in protecting, to the utmost of his power, the natives in his diocese.

Cambridge School.

While the Church was agitated by the controversies which began with the publication of *Essays and Reviews*, a school of thought was quickly rising at Cambridge which in the course of a few years produced very important work. Its leaders were Westcott[1], Hort[2] and Lightfoot[3], all Professors at Cambridge, and two of them successive Bishops of Durham. This school was characterized by frank and earnest inquiry into the history and value of the documents of the early Church, combined with a deep feeling of reverence for "the Christian faith committed to our charge." Westcott's careful and learned work on the Canon of the New Testament in the first four centuries was perhaps the first indication of the new spirit of investigation which was abroad, and this was followed by a series of works, critical and practical, which reveal the soul of a man who threw his whole mind and heart into the pursuit of truth, and was at the same time living an inner life in the closest communion with God in Christ. Lightfoot's edition of the *Epistle to the Galatians* a few years later was again a display of a method which was new in the history of English commentaries. Never before in England had such sound and thorough scholarship, such unwearied investigation, been brought to bear on the elucidation of a book of the New Testament. Even more epoch-making was his monumental edition of the Apostolic Fathers, in which an exhaustive acquaintance with the whole literature of their time, and with the writings dealing with the subject in more recent days, is applied to solve the many problems as to the meaning, the date, and the genuineness of the various treatises. With regard to the most controverted

---

[1] Arthur Westcott, *Life of B. F. Westcott.*
[2] Arthur F. Hort, *Life and Letters of F. J. A. H.* (London, 1896).
[3] Bishop *Lightfoot*, reprint from *Quarterly Rev.*, Pref. by Bishop Westcott; F. J. A. Hort in *Dict. Nat. Biog.*, XXXIII. 232.

question of all, he may almost be said to have definitely proved that seven Epistles attributed to St Ignatius are his actual work. While he lived, his force of character, his true devoutness, and the admirable force and lucidity of his exposition, made him the most conspicuous member of the school and its natural leader. Hort, a most able and thoughtful man, published little in his lifetime and was consequently less widely known, though he was an ardent student and left behind him much valuable matter which has seen the light since his death. But the work to which he gave the greater part of his time and energy for many years, in conjunction with his friend Westcott, was the production of a text of the New Testament in accordance with the most ancient authorities. In such a matter as an ancient text, where the opinions of critics differ both as to the value of the several authorities and the method of using them, there can be no absolute finality, but the text of Hort and Westcott is probably the nearest approach to that of the earliest times which has yet been made. The school of which these three may be regarded as founders continues to flourish, and has produced many works which have advanced Biblical Criticism and thrown much light on the history of the early Church. *[Ch. VIII.]* *[Westcott and Hort's N.T., 1881.]*

It is no doubt in a great degree due to this school that a great change has passed over the English clergy in regard to Biblical questions. High Churchmen, trusting to the voice of the Church for guidance in matters of faith, advanced in the way of inquiry with more courage than the Evangelicals had done. In 1889 a group of Oxford tutors put forth a volume of essays under the editorship of Charles Gore, entitled *Lux Mundi*, intended to shew how the doctrine of the Incarnation pervaded and influenced the various forms of modern thought. An essay in this volume by the editor on the Inspiration of Holy Scripture distinctly implied that some of the principal results of modern criticism might be admitted without injury to the Christian faith. This occasioned much agitation, but Convocation could not be induced to condemn it as it had condemned *Essays and Reviews*. This was a very significant indication of the change which had passed over the mind of the Church in twenty-five *[Change of Thought.]* *['Lux Mundi,' 1889.]*

years. The representatives of the clergy no longer took up a position of blind opposition to new views on the criticism of the Bible.

3. LIFE OF THE CHURCH.

Religious Revival.

In spite of the evils occasioned by party-spirit, there was from the middle of the nineteenth century an immense revival of the religious spirit in the Church. The clergy had higher aims and led a more devout life, and the same may be said of a large number of lay-people. Bishops are no longer the stately prelates of a former age, taking little part in the actual work of the diocese and often scarcely known by face to their clergy. They are now the active promoters of every organization for the moral and spiritual good of the people committed to their charge, and are seen in all parts of their dioceses, stimulating, advising, guiding. Under the pressure of the increased work it became necessary in many cases for the bishop of a diocese to seek help in his episcopal functions. This was afforded by the provisions of the Act 26 Henry VIII., c. 14, which authorised the bishop of a diocese to petition the king to appoint one of two clerks named as a suffragan bishop[1]. In this way suffragans have been appointed in many of the more important dioceses.

First Bishop Suffragan, 2 Feb., 1870.

The first of these was Bishop Mackenzie of Nottingham in the diocese of Lincoln, then presided over by Bishop Christopher Wordsworth. Confirmations became more frequent and more solemn, and greater attention was paid to preparation for them. The clergy frequently met for devotion and edification. Communions became more frequent and communicants more numerous.

Missions.

"Missions," conducted by clergymen specially gifted with the power of moving the people, often led by the bishop, were held with the view of raising the spiritual life of a district above the religious routine into which even good men are apt to fall. Efforts were constantly made to relieve the spiritual destitution of large towns, of which the population is constantly increased by the flocking-in of country-people. New churches were built and new parishes created. Societies

[1] The word "suffragan" is here used in a peculiar sense. All the diocesan bishops of a province are suffragans of their metropolitan.

were set on foot for promoting the work of the Church. In particular, sisterhoods, communities of women for the double purpose of fostering the inner life of their members and of working for the good of the Church, were formed in several places. A few years later the primitive order of deaconesses, who should visit and relieve the sick and poor, and generally undertake such ministrations as can best be discharged by women, was revived, when the first English deaconess of modern times was duly invested with her office by Bishop Tait of London.

With the renewal of energy in the Church, it is not wonderful that there went a demand for the revival of its ancient constitutional legislatures, the Convocations of Canterbury and York. They had indeed always been summoned together with each new Parliament, but their business had never gone beyond the passing of an Address to the Crown. In 1847, however, an amendment was moved on the Address in the Convocation of Canterbury and a discussion took place, with the result that the Address as presented contained an "earnest prayer" that her Majesty would call on the Convocations for advice in ecclesiastical matters. This was a step towards the revival of the right of debate, and in 1852 the Convocations were permitted to meet to discuss questions of interest to the Church and to frame resolutions. To give validity to a canon the sanction of the Crown was still necessary, and it rested with the law officers of the Crown to say whether a given canon fell within the authority of the license which had been granted. Under these restrictions there has been but little valid legislation, but the suggestions made in debates, and perhaps still more the reports of committees, have often been of great value.

As the feeling grew that the Church is a living Body with a corporate life, a desire naturally arose that this life should have a broader representation than that in Convocation. By the exertions of W. (afterwards Archdeacon) Emery and W. J. Beamont a Church Congress, open to all Church people, lay and clerical, was organized, and held its first meeting at Cambridge in 1861. The attendance was small compared with the vast numbers which have since been gathered together, but the success attained was so considerable that it was determined to repeat the experiment in the following year at Oxford, and from that time its meetings have been annual, and have been held in almost every large town in England. At first, the Evangelicals were reluctant to take part in conferences which admitted men who confessed their sympathy with pre-Reformation teaching and worship; but about ten years after the foundation of the Congress, Edward Hoare, J. C. Ryle, and others, gave the weight of their influence to the cause of attendance on its meetings, and thenceforward there can be little doubt that the gathering together of clergy and laity of all shades of opinion has tended to soften animosities and produce a more forbearing tone in dealing with opponents.

A further step in the direction of Christian intercourse and counsel was made in the institution of Diocesan Conferences, composed of duly elected representatives of the clergy and laity of a diocese, meeting under the presidency of its bishop. These Conferences have given admirable opportunities to the bishop of addressing his people on matters of common interest, and also of learning from a really representative diocesan body the thoughts by which their hearts are stirred. In these also, as in the larger assemblies, the meeting face to face has tended to soften the asperity of men's thoughts towards those from whom they differ in opinion. The first Diocesan Conference was held in 1864 in the Diocese of Ely under Bishop Harold Browne, and they have since extended to every diocese in England.

Somewhat later, Bishop Christopher Wordsworth of Lincoln summoned a synod of the whole of the clergy of his diocese. They met, to the number of more than 500, in the cathedral church of Lincoln on Sept. 20, 1871. This example has been occasionally followed in other dioceses.

Since 1845, the year in which the secession of Dr Newman had appalled timid souls with the fear that the end of the Church of England had come, several new sees have been created in England, while many bishops had availed themselves of the services of suffragans or assistants. But the change in the missionary enterprises of the Church was quite as remarkable. The missions of the Church in earlier days were too isolated; missionaries too often worked without cooperation or superintendence. Now it came to be felt that, wherever the Anglican Church existed, it ought to be with its due hierarchy of bishops, priests, and deacons. An immense impetus to the true missionary spirit was given by George Augustus Selwyn[1], who in 1841 became Bishop of New Zealand and Melanesia. Endowed with extraordinary energy, both physical and moral, he first visited every portion of his huge diocese, now divided into seven sees, and then set himself to organize it, a work which he accomplished with great success. He may in truth be regarded as the Anglican Apostle of the South Sea Islands. Visiting England in 1854, he brought back with him John Coleridge Patteson[2], afterwards Bishop of Melanesia, who shewed remarkable power of acquiring languages and of bringing the natives to abandon their savage customs and adopt the decencies of Christian society. He was killed at Nukapu in 1871 by natives who had become hostile to all Europeans in consequence of the fraud and cruelty of traders who had carried off many of their brethren to serve as labourers, almost as slaves, in distant lands. His life and death were fruitful. At the present time it may be said that wherever the English race is found some effort is made to provide them with the means of grace, and that the numerous tribes in whose midst or on whose borders our countrymen have settled are the objects of anxious care, while many missionaries have gone forth into lands whose sole claim upon us is that the dwellers in them are partakers of that humanity for which Christ died.

The Archbishop of Canterbury had grown from being the head of an isolated communion to be the centre of the organization of a world-wide Church, to whom, as to a Patriarch, flowed in appeals of various kinds from every quarter of the globe. It was natural to give to this vast network of authorities opportunities for mutual help and counsel. To this end in 1867 a Conference of the whole English-speaking episcopate was held at Lambeth Palace under the presidency of Archbishop Longley, which was

CH. VIII.

G. A. Selwyn, bishop of New Zealand, 1841—1867.

J. C. Patteson, missionary, 1855, bishop, 1861—71.

First Pan-anglican Conference, 1867.

[1] *Life* by H. W. Tucker (1879); by G. H. Curteis (1889).
[2] *Life* by Charlotte M. Yonge (1874); *Sketch* published by S.P.C.K. (1872).

attended by 76 prelates. Resolutions were passed on matters of interest to the Church at large, and at the conclusion of the sitting an "Address to the Faithful" was issued, giving them counsel and exhortation on the errors and perils of the time. A similar assembly was held under Archbishop Tait in 1878, and thenceforth the "Pan-anglican" Conference may be considered an institution of the Church. There have been probably in the whole history of the Church few more impressive assemblies than these great gatherings of prelates of one blood and one speech from every nation under heaven.

4. CHURCH AND STATE.

While great changes, some of which were hardly perceived, were taking place in philosophy and theology, changes were also occurring in the more obvious and visible field, where Church and State came into contact and sometimes into hostile collision. The old theory of Hooker and his followers that Church and State consist of identical persons, differently organized for different ends, could no longer be maintained when men of all kinds of belief or non-belief were found in the nation and in Parliament. The Church not unnaturally grew uneasy under the dominion of an assembly largely alien, and Parliament undertook reluctantly, and discharged ill, the duty of ecclesiastical legislation.

When the reforming spirit was in the air it was natural that attention should be directed to the many anomalies which existed in the temporal affairs of the Church. A Commission constituted for the purpose of "suggesting such measures as might be conducive to the efficiency of the Church by providing for the cure of souls and by preventing pluralism" issued a very important Report in 1836, the leading provisions of which were embodied in an Act of Parliament[1] in the same year. This Act regulated the incomes of the several sees, raising some and diminishing others. Another Act[2] four years later dealt in a similar manner with deans and chapters, reducing the number of canons residentiary in many cathedrals, and

---

[1] 6 and 7 William IV. c. 77.   [2] 3 and 4 Victoria, c. 113.

assigning definite incomes, varying in amount, to deans and canons. The duty of carrying out these provisions was entrusted to a permanent body of Ecclesiastical Commissioners, in whom for the time being the whole of the episcopal and capitular property throughout England was vested, from which they provided the incomes allotted by Parliament to the several bishops and chapters. The Commissioners, after providing for these re-endowments, wisely retained in their own hands property likely to increase largely in value, such as mines, and lands in the vicinity of large towns, and from this source they were for many years able to endow churches in populous neighbourhoods, and in many ways to benefit the Church. They are also able, with the assent of the Crown in Council, to make regulations in such matters as the creation of archdeaconries and rural deaneries, and the assignment of their boundaries.

An ancient and crying evil in the Church of England was that of pluralities. There was nothing to prevent a spiritual person, whether bishop or priest, from holding several benefices at the same time, and possibly not residing in one of them, so that many parishes were served by ill-paid curates, while the vicars or rectors took their ease at a distance. This state of things was put an end to by the Pluralities Act of 1837[1], which forbade a clerk to hold more than two benefices, and that only with the licence or dispensation of the archbishop. The law against pluralities was made more strict by an Act of 1850[2], which forbade the holding of two benefices together unless the two churches were within three miles of each other and the annual income of one of the parishes was less than one hundred pounds a year. By a later Act (1885)[3] the distance was extended to four miles and the maximum value to two hundred pounds.

The constitution of the ecclesiastical courts, once brought into prominence by the numerous cases brought before them, occasioned much trouble. It has generally been recognized that "in accordance with the constitution of this Church and realm the right of appeal for the maintenance of justice in all ecclesiastical causes lies to the

Pluralities restricted, 1837.

1850.

1885.

Ecclesiastical Courts.

---

[1] 1 and 2 Vict. c. 106.   [3] 48 and 49 Vict. c. 54, s. 14.
[2] 13 and 14 Vict. c. 98.

Judicial Committee, 1833.

Crown[1]." From the time of Henry VIII. to that of William IV. this appellate jurisdiction was exercised through the Court of Delegates, a body of persons named for the particular case under review, who sat by virtue of the king's commission issued under the Great Seal. A court named simply for the time being to try a case was obviously objectionable, but it nevertheless endured for three centuries, at the end of which appellate jurisdiction in ecclesiastical and admiralty cases was transferred by Parliament to the Judicial Committee of the Privy Council[2]. As, however, litigation in ecclesiastical cases increased in consequence of the changes in ritual, the whole system of ecclesiastical courts was found to be cumbrous, expensive, and unsatisfactory. As a partial remedy for this state of things a "Public Worship Regulation Act[3]" was passed through Parliament, which introduced a simpler and more expeditious manner of proceeding against clerks accused of making unlawful additions to the fabric, ornaments, or furniture of the Church, of using unlawful ornaments of the minister, or of making unlawful additions to, omissions from, or alterations of, the services of the Church. A single judge superseded the judges who had presided over the courts of the two archbishops, and the archdeacon or three parishioners may bring before him, through the bishop, any clerk charged with misconduct in relation to the matters specified above. The bishop may, in his discretion, refuse to bring the case before the judge. There were several points in this Act to which Churchmen might fairly take exception, and it was in fact received with a storm of disapprobation, which was increased by the fact that Lord Penzance, who was the first judge appointed under the Act, a man of great distinction and high character, had been judge of the Divorce Court. Many of the clergy felt unable to recognize the judge or his decisions, and five were actually imprisoned for disobedience. This not unnaturally brought about a considerable change of feeling, and when bishops refused to pass on to the court cases which had been brought before them, moderate men of all parties generally ap-

Public Worship Regulation Act, 1874.

---

[1] Resolution of the Lower House of Convocation, quoted by Perry, III. 531.
[2] 3 and 4 William IV. c. 41.
[3] 37 and 38 Vict. c. 85.

proved their conduct. Nor was the Judicial Committee thought to be either specially competent in matters ecclesiastical, or to have such an authority that its decrees should bind the consciences of the clergy.

This widely spread feeling led to the appointment in 1881 of a Royal Commission to consider and report upon the whole subject of ecclesiastical courts. The names of the commissioners were such as to inspire complete confidence in the minds of Churchmen, and included at least one of the first historians and antiquarians of the day, Bishop Stubbs. This Commission, after exhaustive inquiry and research, reported unfavourably to the existing system, and proposed to revive, with some changes, the old Courts of the archbishops and bishops, in which it desired to make the prelates personally more prominent than they had been for many generations. The clergy would, it was thought, be more ready to pay respect to a decision pronounced by a bishop in person than to one which seemed to be the work of an official principal or a chancellor only. The difficulty of constituting a court to represent the Crown in ecclesiastical appeals, which should satisfy both clergy and laity, has hitherto been found insuperable. A considerable change was however made by the Clergy Discipline Act (1892), which greatly modified the constitution of bishops' courts, and gave them increased authority in regard to immorality and other grave misdemeanors of the clergy, while expressly excluding from their jurisdiction any question of doctrine or ritual.

In 1868 Mr Gladstone introduced and carried a Bill for the abolition of compulsory Church-rates, which was in fact nearly equivalent to abolishing them altogether; for though Church-rates may still be made, those who pay them are not discharging a legal impost, but voluntarily contributing to the expenses of the Church. In 1880 an Act was passed which deprived the clergy of the Church of England of their exclusive right of conducting burials in consecrated ground, and made it lawful for burials to take place with any "Christian and orderly religious service," or without any service at all.

The ancient universities of England had been regarded from their foundation until the year 1877 as places of education for members of the Church; but by an Act of Parliament of that year all official connexion with the Church was abolished, except as regards the Professors of Theology, and the obligation laid upon colleges to maintain divine service in their chapels according to the use of the Church of England. No religious test was henceforth to be applied as a condition of membership of the University, or to Scholars or Fellows, or to any of the officers of the University or of a College. The influence of the Church, however, continues to be dominant, and the graduates who present themselves as candidates for Holy Orders are certainly as well prepared as their predecessors under the more exclusive system.

Elementary Education.

The Church has always recognized the duty of instructing the young, especially in the articles of the Christian Faith; but, in fact, in the early part of the nineteenth century this duty was very ill performed, and great ignorance prevailed almost everywhere even of its most essential truths. So far back as 1698 the Society for the Promotion of Christian Knowledge had founded elementary schools, and within about twenty years charity schools had been established in most of the great centres of population. Still, it became more and more evident to thoughtful observers that the people were destroyed for lack of knowledge, and in 1812 the National Society was founded, to secure, as is expressed in its charter, "that the poorer members of the Church shall have their children duly instructed in suitable learning and the principles of the Christian religion according to the Established Church." This Society has ever since done a great work in guiding and aiding elementary education throughout the country. After some years it came to be recognized that an object of such vast importance as national education claimed the direct assistance of the State[1], and in 1833 a small grant, £20,000, was voted by Parliament in aid of elementary schools, the greater part of which was administered through the National Society. Such was the feeble beginning of a public system of elementary education in England. In 1839 the annual vote was increased to £30,000, and a new Board was created to superintend and control its expenditure. This was a special Committee of the Privy Council,

National Society, 1812.

Parliamentary Grant, 1833.

Committee on Education, 1839.

[1] See H. Craik, *The State in Relation to Education* (London, 1884; new ed. 1896).

assisted by inspectors and other officers, and in 1856 this was organized so as to become an Education Department, of which the Lord President of the Council was head, assisted by a Vice-President of the Committee of Privy Council on Education.

<small>Ch. VIII. Vice-President created, 1856.</small>

This system, with several modifications in detail under the various "codes" issued by the Committee, continued in force for many years. Under it schools were in almost all cases provided and maintained, with help from the Government grant, by the Church or some other religious body, and definite religious instruction was given in accordance with the principles of that body, exemption from this being granted to children whose parents desired it. Only in schools connected with the British and Foreign School Society, which was largely supported by Nonconformists, the religious teaching was indefinite. This system had many merits, but in time it became evident that the voluntary efforts of religious bodies were not providing adequately for the education of the country, and that the existing system must be changed or supplemented. A powerful party advocated the establishment of free and unsectarian schools throughout the country by means of local rates, and the enforcement by law of the attendance of all children of school age. This was resisted by many of the leading promoters of education, who advocated an extension of the system already existing, under which grants were made to efficient schools of any religious body, the children belonging to other sects than that of the managers being allowed to claim exemption from religious instruction. The effect was that such children might possibly receive no religious instruction at all. In 1870 an Education Act was passed by Parliament which was to some extent a compromise between these opposing views. Its object, as stated by Mr W. E. Forster, who introduced it, was "to complete the voluntary system and to fill up gaps." The whole country was divided into school districts, and each district was required to have sufficient accommodation in its schools for the children within its borders who required elementary education. Wherever it was found that this was deficient, a School Board was elected, which provided out of the rates, aided, like the voluntary schools, by Government grants, for establishing

<small>Voluntary System inadequate.

Education Act, 1870.</small>

and maintaining undenominational schools sufficient, with the existing schools, to supply the requisite number of school places. Great efforts were made by Church-people and others interested in religious education to cover the ground so as to render Board-schools unnecessary, and these were in many cases successful. But in very many districts School Boards were formed, and it was found that these, far from limiting themselves to supplementing the voluntary system, tended, having greater and more certain resources, to annihilate it, as was perhaps inevitable. When this system had been nearly thirty years in operation it was seen that the strain upon voluntary schools was becoming intolerable, and as at the same time attention was directed to the defects of secondary education, the whole school system of the country came before Parliament, where it was discussed at great length and with much animation. The result was Mr Balfour's Act of 1902, which abolished the School Boards, and gave the control of educational institutions, whether elementary or secondary, to the County Councils or Municipal Corporations. The religious character of every denominational school was to be maintained according to the terms of its trust-deed, but a certain number of elected managers were to be added to those appointed under the trust. Only on the head-teacher in such a school was any religious test to be imposed. All schools equally were to be provided for out of the rates, except as regards the buildings of the denominational schools. This Act made provision for the support of schools of any denomination in districts where schools were required, and aimed at a complete organization of national education. It has, however, encountered the liveliest opposition, and most of the religious sects are united with the irreligious against it. What will be the future of religious education in this country is now (1905) highly uncertain.

5. NON-ANGLICAN RELIGIOUS BODIES.

A. The lot of the Roman Catholics in Great Britain and Ireland was for some generations a hard one, although when nothing occurred to rouse the populace against them the penalties to which they were liable were not strictly enforced. William was averse to persecution and desired to deal gently with the adherents of the Pope, but the national feeling was too much excited by the proceedings of James II. to permit of any substantial relief being given. The dread of the adherents of a foreign power; the belief, which was commonly held all over Europe, that the Jesuits were an intriguing and dangerous body; the suspicion that Roman Catholics generally were in favour of the restoration of the House of Stuart; the plots, or rumours of plots, against the reigning sovereign—all these things prevented the Roman Catholics from receiving favourable, or even equitable, consideration. It was penal for a priest to celebrate Mass, and the lay-people were deprived of almost all the rights and liberties of English citizens. The penalties to which they were liable were not always enforced, but both clergy and laity were in constant dread of common informers or mob violence. Under such circumstances it was naturally their interest to make no stir. Their chapels were as unobtrusive as possible and their clergy did not court observation by any peculiarity of dress. Earl Stanhope[1] in 1718 designed to repeal, or at all events greatly to mitigate, the penal laws which pressed so hardly upon them, but the first negotiations for that purpose failed, and Stanhope's life was too short to permit him to carry the design any further. Probably no one could have succeeded at that time against the strong current of public opinion. In 1778 the leading Roman Catholics presented an Address to the King in which they assured His Majesty that they held no opinions repugnant to the duties of good citizens, as they had shewn by their irreproachable conduct for many years past[2]. A few days afterwards Sir George Savile, seconded by the well-known lawyer John Dunning, brought in a Bill to render the celebration of Mass no longer penal, and to repeal the statutes which affected the succession to, or acquisition of, landed property by Romanists. Some of the penalties which it was proposed to repeal were, said Dunning, no longer necessary, and others had always been a disgrace to their enactors. Thurlow, then Attorney-General, gave the measure his

Proposal for Repeal, 1718.

Address, 1 May, 1778.

[1] Stanhope's *Hist. Eng.* I. 326 (ed. 1853).
[2] Stanhope's *Hist. Eng.* VI. 237 ff.

support. With such advocacy the Bill was readily passed through both Houses. This Act did not apply to Scotland, but the Lord Advocate, Henry Dundas, promised to introduce a Bill to abolish the similar pains and penalties in Scotland in another session.

Outcry against Papists.

It was in Scotland that the earliest and the loudest outcry arose against any relief to Papists[1]. Protestant Associations were formed in Edinburgh and some other Scottish towns to defend the religious principles which were thought to be in peril, and the press and the pulpit vied in denunciation of the proposed measure. From Scotland the ferment spread to England. But though the disturbers were many it was not easy to find a head, for no statesman of any distinction would give them the slightest countenance. At length they found a leader, or perhaps rather a tool, who had at any rate rank and rashness to recommend him. This was Lord George Gordon, who was at that time a Christian, though he died a Jew. Henceforth the foolish speeches of this young nobleman in the House of Commons acquired some importance, as he boasted to have tens of thousands of followers at his beck and call. These followers soon shewed of what metal they were made. On June 2, 1780, while the Duke of Richmond was speaking in the House of Lords in favour of manhood suffrage and annual Parliaments, a mob led by Lord George poured tumultuously to Westminster with a petition for the repeal of Savile's Act[2]. Members of both Houses were hustled and ill-treated, and for some time the mob endeavoured to burst into the House of Commons. Failing in this, they rushed off in a dangerous mass and plundered the Roman Catholic chapels. Sir George Savile's house was also sacked and his life placed in jeopardy. Reinforced by the scum of London, they attacked and burned Newgate prison and liberated the prisoners. They fell also with especial eagerness on the houses of those enemies of evil-doers, the magistrates. For six days a large part of London was in possession of a mob composed for the most part of scoundrels whose only objects were riot and plunder, nor was the rabble dispersed until the Guards were called out and ordered to

Gordon Riots, 1780.

---

[1] Stanhope, *ut supra*, VI. 260 ff.   [2] *Ibid.* VII. 17 ff.

attack them. Then at last order was restored, but many had to lament peaceful homes ruined and destroyed.

Emancipation. Mr Pitt's attempt, 1800.

The Roman Catholics in Ireland in the beginning of the nineteenth century had a special grievance. Mr Pitt, when negotiating with them the preliminaries of the union with Great Britain, had pledged his word to introduce into the Parliament of the United Kingdom a measure to relieve them of their many political disabilities. He was very ready to redeem his pledge, but on consulting the King he found that he had made up his mind to refuse his assent to any such measure. His Coronation oath bound him "to defend the Protestant Church as by law established," and he persuaded himself, as did many of his subjects, that to place the Roman Catholics in a position of equality, as citizens, with their fellow-subjects would be an act of hostility to the Established Church. The result of the refusal was Mr Pitt's resignation early in 1801. From this time for many years strenuous efforts were made to induce the Parliament of the United Kingdom to take Roman Catholic claims into serious consideration, especially by the great orator and true Irish patriot, Henry Grattan, himself a Protestant[1]. In 1813 he even carried a motion for a Committee of Inquiry, and the second reading of a Relief Bill, but nothing effectual was done. After 1820 there was a king, George IV., whom no one suspected of conscientious objections. But the Tory party, with the exception of Canning and his friends, declined to take up Pitt's abortive pledge, and the Duke of Wellington, himself an Anglo-Irish Protestant, who became Prime Minister in 1828, seemed as unbending as any of them.

The King's refusal.

Henry Grattan, d. 1820.

Meantime, in 1823, Daniel O'Connell, an Irishman of splendid eloquence, endowed with every quality to endear him to his countrymen, and capable of leadership, had founded a league called the Catholic Association to put pressure on the English Government. It was a powerful organization, and its proclamations and monster meetings produced a widespread agitation. It even collected an

---

[1] An account of these efforts, up to 1820, may be found in W. J. Amherst's *Hist. of Cath. Emancipation* (Lond. 1886). See also R. Dunlop, *Life of Grattan* (1889), and W. E. H. Lecky, *Leaders of Public Opinion in Ireland* (1861).

impost called the "Catholic Rent," which was paid by its members with much more regularity than the King's taxes. O'Connell was absolute master of the Association, but he set his face against any outbreak of armed force, believing—rightly—that he would attain his end more speedily and effectually by peaceful means. With the support of all the Roman Catholics in Ireland and all the Whigs in England, he was a very formidable power. Nevertheless, Wellington for some time refused to listen to any proposal for Emancipation. Suddenly, in the spring of 1829, he gave way, to the surprise and disgust of his most strenuous supporters, the old Tory party, and declared himself fully persuaded that further resistance to Roman Catholic claims would lead to civil war in Ireland. A Catholic Relief Bill passed the House of Commons in March, and the House of Lords in the following month, in both cases by large majorities composed of Whigs and Canningites. Roman Catholics were put in possession of the ordinary civil and political rights, and were henceforth eligible for offices under the Crown, with only three exceptions, on the same conditions as members of other religious bodies.

As was natural, under these circumstances the Roman Church became much more conspicuous. In many of the large towns stately churches superseded the old meeting-houses, and both its teaching and its ceremonies began to attract more attention from those who were without. Proselytes became more numerous, and the horror and dread which the Protestants of an earlier generation had felt towards Papists were much diminished when there was no longer any secrecy.

In 1840 Pope Gregory XVI. divided the Roman Church in England into eight districts, over each of which presided a bishop *in partibus*[1] as Vicar Apostolic, appointed directly by the Pope. This excited but little attention, but when, ten years later, a Bull was promulgated dividing the whole of England into twelve dioceses,

---

[1] A bishop *in partibus infidelium* is one who is consecrated to a see where there are no faithful for him to superintend, and who can be sent by the Pope at his pleasure to discharge episcopal functions as need may arise in any part of the Church. Wiseman (*e.g.*) when Vicar Apostolic was Bishop of Melipotamus.

with bishops bearing territorial titles under an Archbishop of Westminster, a cry of rage burst out from all quarters. This was increased when Wiseman, the new Archbishop, put forth a pastoral, dated from the Flaminian Gate, in which he spoke of restoring "Catholic England to its place in the ecclesiastical firmament." The Premier, Lord John Russell, in a published letter, designated the action of the Pope as "insolent and insidious," and all sorts and conditions of men protested against it. The result was the Ecclesiastical Titles Act, which prohibited a Roman Catholic bishop from assuming the title of a see in England under a penalty of £100. Many English Churchmen were opposed, to use Mr Gladstone's words, "to all attempts to meet the spiritual dangers of the Church by temporal legislation of a penal character." The Act proved a complete failure, and was repealed in 1872[1].

B. Without any avowed alteration of formularies, a great change crept over the great societies of Protestant Dissenters[2] during the eighteenth and nineteenth centuries. They grew both in numbers and importance. Their ministers received an excellent training in the colleges of the various denominations, and the abolition of theological tests has now given them access to the older universities. Many of them became distinguished both in theological and general literature. Their preaching also often attained a high degree of excellence. The shabby chapels of a former generation in almost all the large towns have been swept away, and large and dignified structures have taken their place.

The oldest form of English Dissent is the Congregational or Independent[3]. Its members hold that every Christian congregation is entitled to elect its own officers and to manage its own affairs, in entire independence of any authority but that of the Supreme Head of the Church, the Lord Jesus Christ. They regard Holy

---

[1] For the events of this period see Wilfrid Ward, *Life and Times of Wiseman* (London, 1897).
[2] Herbert Skeats, *Hist. of the Free Churches of England* (1868), new edition by Miall, 1892; John Stoughton, *Religion in England 1702—1800* (1878); D. Bogue and J. Bennett, *Hist. of Dissenters* (1808–12).
[3] Hardwick, *Reformation*, 271. For more recent history, J. Waddington, *Congregational History* (London,1869–80); Joseph Fletcher, *Hist. of Independency* (1847–49).

Scripture as their only standard. Practically, however, the early Independents differed little in their doctrinal views from others who were called Puritans, and accepted generally the standards of the Westminster Assembly, while denying the right of that or any other assembly to make their Confession binding upon the whole kingdom for all time. This early Puritanism has, however, yielded to the influence of a later age, and Independents generally now recognize, as involved in their principles, the freedom to interpret Scripture, not according to any scheme or system, but as loyalty to truth and the spirit of Christianity may require. They find in Scripture no authority for uniting the Churches of a nation or province into one polity, whether under episcopal or synodal rule. But they do not so rigorously hold to the principle of the independence of congregations as to condemn union for the promotion of common ends, or fraternal aid and counsel among the different societies in cases of variance or other difficulty. On this principle is founded the "Congregational Union for England and Wales," which is careful to lay down that "it shall not in any case assume legislative authority or become a court of appeal." Each congregation is of course at liberty to choose any man for its minister whom it may consider qualified for the office, but institution to a chapel has to be sought from the neighbouring ministers, who would no doubt refuse it to one whom they deemed unworthy. The Independents look back with a natural pride to the learned and able men, such as Howe and Owen, who were their leaders in the seventeenth century, and, as soon as the Act of Toleration of 1689 allowed, took measures for securing a succession of educated ministers.

The distinctive tenet of the Baptists[1] is, that the validity of baptism depends on an intelligent faith in the recipient. It follows that infants are not proper subjects of baptism. They also hold that for a valid baptism actual immersion in water is necessary. Their form of Church government is congregational. Each Church is held to be possessed of the power of self-government, and

[1] T. Crosby, *Hist. of English Baptists* (London, 1738–40); Joseph Tirmey, *Hist. of English Baptists* (London, 1811–23); J. M. Cramp, *Baptist Hist.*, ed. J. Angus (1871).

within it discipline is to be exercised by the rulers in presence and with the consent of the members, whose voice decides on the reception or exclusion of those submitted to their judgment. They maintain that, since the days of the Apostles, the only orders of the ministry are pastors—sometimes called elders or bishops—deacons, and evangelists. The Baptists also have their internal divisions. The "General" Baptists maintain that Christ died for all men, while the "Particular" Baptists hold that He died only for an elect number. At the present day, however, the general feeling is against any arbitrary limitation of the Atonement. They are also divided on the terms of communion, one section admitting to communion those who recognize the validity of infant baptism, while another section refuses it to any but Baptists in the strict sense. The former are called open, the latter strict, communionists. They were early in the field of missions, the Baptist Missionary Society having been founded in 1792, and their emissaries have displayed the utmost zeal and courage in their perilous enterprises. The names of such men as Carey and Marshman stand out brightly in the roll of missionaries. They have excellent schools for training candidates for the pastoral office, and there has never been wanting to them a supply of earnest and excellent pastors and preachers.

English Presbyterianism[1], though earlier attempts were made to establish presbyteries, may be said to date from 1647[2]. In that year the Long Parliament abolished Prelacy and enacted a Presbyterian system for the whole nation. It was, however, almost wholly abortive; only in London and in Lancashire was the legal system brought into being, for it did not suit Cromwell and his soldiers, who preferred Independency. Some of the ministers ejected in 1662 were Presbyterian, but they shewed none of the vigour and enthusiasm of their Scottish brethren, and when they gained liberty of worship at the Revolution, they soon fell under the influence of the chilling atmosphere of the eighteenth century, so that many lapsed into Socinianism. But during the nineteenth

[1] T. McCrie, the younger, *Annals of English Presbyterianism* (London, 1872); A. H. Drysdale, *Hist. of the Presbyterians in England* (Lond. 1889).
[2] See above, p. 35.

century there was a revival. There sprang up in England several congregations connected with the Presbyterians of Scotland. At the time of the Scottish Disruption the greater part of the Presbyterian congregations in England sympathised with the Free Church, and organized themselves separately as the Presbyterian Church of England, but there are still a few congregations in England which retain their connexion with the Scottish ecclesiastical system.

Society of Friends. The Society of Friends, commonly called Quakers[1], held on the even tenor of their way. The outward peculiarities of dress and speech which once made them conspicuous have almost wholly disappeared, but their steadfast assertion of the constant guidance of the faithful by the Holy Spirit, and of love as the binding influence of Christian society, with their constant protest against war and against social vanities and follies, have had some influence, none the less because they are—unlike their predecessors in the seventeenth century—unobtrusive.

Methodism. Wesleyan Methodism[2] was originally founded as a society to raise the standard of spiritual attainment among the members of the Church of England[3], but during the nineteenth century it ran its own course with a very vigorous and successful independent organization. The annual assembly which governs the whole Connexion is called the Conference. Down to the year 1784 it consisted of such of Wesley's preachers as he chose to call together to take counsel with himself. In that year he gave it a definite constitution, defining its rights over chapels, and over the appointment and control of ministers. Until 1877 the Conference was composed of ministers only, but in that year a scheme of lay representation was adopted, and brought into operation in the following year.

The 'Legal Hundred.' The "Legal Conference," or "Hundred," is a body of one hundred ministers constituted and perpetuated by Wesley's Deed of Declaration, the assent of which is necessary to give legal validity to the acts of the General Conference.

---

[1] J. S. Rowntree, *Quakerism Past and Present* (1859); F. Storrs Turner, *The Quakers, a Study* (1889). See above, p. 66.

[2] W. H. Daniels, *Short Hist. of Methodists* (Lond. 1882); W. C. Holden, *Brief Hist. of Methodism* (1877); G. S. Smith, *A Hist. of Wesleyan Methodism* (1865); Abel Stevens, *Hist. of Methodism* (1875).

[3] See above, p. 185.

Under the Conference is an elaborate constitution of circuits and classes, so arranged that every member of the Society is led to feel that he is taking part in its religious work, as well in administration as in worship.

Like other voluntary societies, that of the Methodists has not been able to avoid schisms. The "Methodist New Connexion" detached itself so early as 1796 from the original one, from which it differed only in giving to the lay members an equal share in the transaction of all the business of the society, secular and spiritual. The "Primitive Methodists," vulgarly called "Ranters," were first formed into a society in 1810, the principal cause of secession being differences of opinion as to the propriety of holding religious camp-meetings and of allowing women to preach. They also gave great power to the lay element. "Independent" Methodists reject a paid ministry. The "Bible Christians" were formed by a local preacher named Bryan, who seceded in 1815. They appear to differ from the body from which they seceded principally in receiving the Holy Communion in a sitting posture. The society of "United Free Church Methodists" was formed in 1857 by the amalgamation of two bodies which had seceded earlier—1836 and 1849—on similar grounds, grievances against the existing authorities in regard to the removal of ministers. Independency of Churches and freedom of representation in the general assembly are its most distinctive traits. The Welsh "Calvinistic Methodists" sprang from the preaching of George Whitefield[1] and his disciple, the famous Welshman, Howel Harris. These have an organization similar to that of the Wesleyans, but are in doctrine wide as the poles asunder.

A curious offshoot of Methodism is the Salvation Army. From the year 1865, William Booth, a Methodist Preacher, engaged in efforts to evangelize one of the most disreputable districts in East London[2]. Finding no success from work on the old-fashioned methods, he determined to adopt a quasi-military organization, of which he would

---

[1] See p. 189.
[2] W. Booth, *Aggressive Christianity* (1882); *In Darkest England* (1890); "Commissioner" Railton, *Twenty-one Years' Salvation Army*; Josephine Butler, *The Salvation Army in Switzerland* (1884); L. Pilatte, *Un Coup d'œil dans le Salutisme* (Paris, 1885); J. Fehr, *Die Heilsarmee* (1891).

himself be general, for the war against evil. In this he was much assisted by his excellent wife. The formation of the army on its present lines dates from 1878. Its officers, male and female, in uniform, and its bands of music, at once attracted attention, and drew many to listen to the message which its preachers had to deliver, which was of the usual Methodistic type. It made many converts, and among those regarded as most hopeless, drunkards and gaol-birds, it had noteworthy success. It is not only diffused into all parts of England, but in almost every foreign land its barracks and its officers are found. Besides its directly religious influence, it has done much in providing homes of refuge for the destitute and work for the unemployed.

One of the most remarkable sects of the nineteenth century was that which gave itself the name of the Catholic Apostolic Church, but which is commonly known to the outer world as Irvingite[1]. Edward Irving[2], who had been assistant to Dr Chalmers in Glasgow, in 1822 became the minister of a Presbyterian Church in London. There his fervent eloquence, contrasting strongly with the tame and commonplace preaching around him, drew crowds of hearers, among them several men of cultivation and distinction. Canning referred to him in terms of praise in the House of Commons, but Walter Scott[3] found his "*outré* flourishes and extravagant metaphors" unsuited for the eloquence of the pulpit. In the fervour of his religious teaching Irving turned his thoughts especially to the interpretation of prophecy and the coming of the Kingdom of God. A turning point in his career was his becoming acquainted with Henry Drummond[4], a rich banker deeply interested in religious subjects, in whose house at Albury in Surrey, in 1826, and in many following years, Irving, Joseph Wolff and others met for the discussion of unfulfilled prophecy. Irving taught, in opposition to the Scottish Presbyterianism from which he sprang, that Christ died for all men, and that He so completely

[1] E. Miller, *Hist. and Doctrines of Irvingism* (1878).
[2] Margaret Oliphant, *Life of Edward Irving* (1862); W. Wilks, *Edward Irving, an Ecclesiastical and Literary Biography* (1854).
[3] Lockhart's *Life of Scott*, p. 677 (ed. 1842).
[4] Memoir in Lord Lovaine's edition of his *Speeches etc.* (1860).

took our nature upon Him that He was capable of sin, though in fact the Spirit which was given without measure to Him preserved him from actual sin. He also attributed a sacerdotal character to the ministers of Christ—a trait in which we find the mode of thought which a few years later became conspicuous in the Oxford Movement. He longed for the spiritual gifts of the early Church, and in 1830 the tidings came from Scotland that a female disciple had spoken in an unknown tongue. In 1831 the public service in Irving's church in London was interrupted by an outbreak of unintelligible discourse from a female worshipper, and such occurrences soon became habitual. In 1826 Irving had given offence to a large portion of the religious world by a sermon before the London Missionary Society, in which he denounced hireling missionaries, and called for men who would go forth in the spirit of the Lord, trusting to Him for support. His views on the Person of Christ were also regarded by many as heretical. The result of the growing dislike and distrust was that in 1832 he was removed from the pulpit round which he had drawn so many admirers, and in the following year the presbytery of Annan, which had ordained him, deprived him of his status as a minister. This was a blow from which he never recovered. He, who had never been favoured with supernatural gifts, gave place to those who claimed to have them. His health declined rapidly, and on the 7th Dec. 1834 he died at Glasgow. Irving no doubt overestimated his own powers, and was too ready to believe himself set apart for extraordinary works; yet he often gave evidence of a touching humility. His intellect was by no means of the first order, and the influence which he obtained was mainly due to his eloquence and earnestness of character. His discourses attracted hearers much more by their manner than their matter, which, stripped of its sonorous diction, is too often commonplace.

Irving's life ended in sadness, but he had kindled a fire in other hearts. John Bate Cardale, a man in whom was found a remarkable union of enthusiasm with capacity for the management of affairs, in 1830 became deeply interested in the reports which reached him of the speaking with tongues. His own wife in the following year

CH. VIII.

The Tongues begin, 1830.

Irving's views on the Person of Christ.

Irving deprived, 1833.

J. B. Cardale, 1802— 1877.

"spoke with great solemnity in a tongue and prophesied." Cardale soon after became a regular attendant on Irving's ministrations, and defended him before the London Presbytery. Towards the end of 1832 a considerable number of those who regarded the tongues as a true spiritual gift became convinced that it was the will of God that the Apostolic office should be restored. God Himself was believed to indicate who should fill this office. Cardale was himself the first apostle, and, as such, ordained Irving himself to be the "angel" of a newly-formed Church. By the middle of 1835 the full number, twelve, was completed, and they entered on their work of organizing a Church, to which they gave the name of the Catholic Apostolic Church. As one apostle after another died, while the mystic number twelve could not be increased, coadjutor-apostles were appointed. Mr Drummond was one of the apostles, and in 1835 the twelve, accompanied by seven prophets, retired to Albury, where they remained long in consultation and in seeking to learn the divine will. It was now revealed through their prophets that the Church should comprise a fourfold ministry—Apostles, Prophets, Evangelists, and Pastors. It is through the apostles only that the gifts of the Spirit can be conferred on the ministers and the mysteries of God unfolded to the Church; prophetic utterances do not acquire authority without their sanction; they decide on all matters of order and discipline. Through the prophets the will of God is made known, whether in the way of interpretation of Scripture or of direct revelation. The work of an evangelist is to declare and enforce the truths of the Gospel, of a pastor to help and comfort the various members of the flock. The principal minister of a Church receives the name of "angel," in supposed conformity with the Apocalyptic angels of Churches. In 1838 the parts of the world in which they proposed to proclaim their faith were divided into sections named after the twelve tribes of Israel. England was recognized as the tribe of Judah, and was assigned to Cardale, the pillar of the apostles. In 1842 a liturgy, in great part the work of Cardale, was adopted. This was brought together principally from the service-books of the Greek, Latin and Anglican Churches, but was considerably modified by the belief that the Jewish Tabernacle was a type of the worship of the Christian Church. The Holy Eucharist is regarded as a sacrifice, and the consecrated elements are displayed upon the Holy Table, as in the old days the holy bread was placed on a table before the Lord. Holy water and incense are also used, and the sick are anointed with oil. In their desire for beauty and dignity of service the Irvingites were the forerunners of the modern Ritualists. The characteristic note of the Church is that it believes the organization, the wonders, and the spiritual gifts of the Apostolic Age to be, not temporary, but intended for the Church of all time, and that through these a people is being prepared for the Second Coming of Christ.

CH. VIII.

In 1847 a new ceremony was introduced, the "sealing" of a believer by the laying on of the hands of an apostle and anointing with holy oil. This was believed to be equivalent to the Apocalyptic sealing[1] of the servants of God in preparation for the great tribulation.

'Sealing,' 1847.

Thomas Carlyle[2], as ninth apostle, received as his sphere of action North Germany, the tribe of Simeon, and had considerable success in extending the faith and forming societies. The political agitations of the year 1848 led many to believe that the Coming of the Lord drew nigh, and to join the society which was specially preparing for it. By far the most important convert was H. W. J. Thiersch, then a theological professor in Marburg. He received the imposition of hands from Carlyle, and became "the Tertullian of the New Montanism."

Carlyle in Germany, 1838.

Thiersch converted, 1849.

The Lord comes not in the way that the early followers of Irving had fondly hoped, but the sect still subsists and numbers many excellent men among its members. Of late years it has probably increased but little in England, but in Germany, where there is a literary propaganda, a slight accession of numbers is said to continue[3]. There are also Irvingite congregations in the United States of America.

[1] Apocalypse vii. 3 ff.
[2] This Carlyle, who was a schoolfellow of Irving, is referred to in the *Reminiscences* (I. 312) of his more famous namesake. There is however no reason whatever to suppose that the "apostle" designedly contributed to any mistake of identity. See *Dict. of National Biog.* IX. 110.
[3] Herzog, *Kirchengeschichte*, II. 706.

Ch. VIII. Plymouth Brethren.

The society of Plymouth Brethren or Darbyites[1] originated in a feeling of deep dissatisfaction with the spiritual deadness which had crept over both the Church and the Nonconformists in the early part of the nineteenth century. The very same feeling, which found vent at Oxford in earnest efforts to give new life to the Church, was at the same time giving rise to a society outside the Church founded wholly on the inward convictions of believers without any regard to authority. John Nelson Darby, a clergyman, left the Church in 1827 under deep religious convictions, and set himself to do the work of an evangelist without connexion with any Church. In 1830 he founded at Plymouth, where there were congenial spirits, the congregation of "Plymouth Brethren," the name now given to the whole community. Darby was certainly one of the most extraordinary religious leaders of his time. While he had the most untiring energy and bodily strength, he was capable of very severe asceticism and of the highest flights of mystical devotion. He was also a man of considerable learning. His great fault was that he never seemed capable of believing that he might be mistaken—a fault which no doubt contributed to his success. He and his disciples believe the visible Church to have fallen away from the truth and to be rejected of God. The Church, in their view, consists of all truly regenerate persons wherever they may be found, and the test of regeneration is simply the individual's own inmost conviction that he is regenerate or born anew of the Spirit. It follows that they do not recognize any form of church government or official ministry as of special authority; every individual is permitted to minister according to his gift for the edification of the whole. But while they disown anything of the nature of ordination to the ministerial office, they hold it right to acknowledge those in whom the gifts of the Spirit are in fact displayed, and practically there are but few who are found fit publicly to teach or minister in the congregation. Ordinances are of course of little importance, but those who are recognized as believers are

J. N. Darby, 1800—1882,

at Plymouth, 1830.

---

[1] E. Herzog, *Les Frères de Plymouth et J. Darby* (Lausanne, 1845); J. S. Teulon, *The Hist. and Teaching of the Plymouth Brethren* (S.P.C.K. 1883); W. Blair Neatby, *A Hist. of the Plymouth Brethren* (Lond. 1902).

usually baptized, without regard to previous infant baptism; and the Supper of the Lord is celebrated. The interpretation of unfulfilled prophecy occupies a large space in the literature of the Darbyites, and they commonly look for a Coming of the Lord before the final millennium. In a society where individual conviction is all-important, schism is inevitable. Two parties, which regarded each other with mutual acrimony, were formed before Darby's death, and the Darbyite section has since been more than once divided on points of doctrine and discipline. But the warmth of faith in the society has great influence, and has caused it to spread widely in Great Britain and Ireland, in the United States and Canada, in Germany, France and Switzerland.

By the word "Unitarians" we are to understand those who not only maintain the unity of God, as all orthodox Christians do, but regard the doctrine that "the Son is God" as incompatible with the oneness of the Eternal Father. Lælius and Faustus Socinus were conspicuous asserters of this opinion in the latter half of the sixteenth century[2]. From whatever source derived, opinions resembling those of the Socini were rife in England in the seventeenth century. In 1665 Dr John Owen wrote that "the evil is at the door, so that there is not a city, a town, scarce a village, in England wherein some of this poison is not poured forth." Many of the English Presbyterian congregations after 1689 became Unitarian, and many preachers proclaimed very low views of the Person of Christ without exciting controversy. In the latter half of the eighteenth century, Dr Priestley[3], a man of the highest distinction in physical science, maintained the humanitarian view of Christ's nature, and by his great influence caused that doctrine to be more openly avowed. In 1773 Theophilus Lindsey, a Cambridge man of some distinction, having adopted Unitarian opinions, withdrew from his position in the Church and became the first pastor of the Chapel in Essex Street which was long a centre of London

CH. VIII.

Schisms.

Unitarianism[1].

Priestley,
1733—
1804.

Lindsey,
1723—
1808.
Essex Street Chapel,
1774.

---

[1] Bonet-Maury, *Early Sources of English Unitarianism* (trans. 1884); John Orr, *Unitarianism in the Present Time* (1863); James Martineau, *Essays, Reviews and Addresses* (1891); W. Turner, *Lives of Eminent Unitarians* (1840–43).
[2] Hardwick's *Reformation*, p. 264.
[3] *Memoirs*, by himself and his son (1809).

Unitarianism. Until the year 1813 to maintain that Jesus Christ was not God was a penal offence, though penalties had long ceased to be enforced. The Unitarian organization is purely congregational, but the various congregations are drawn together for common action by the British and Foreign Unitarian Association. At the present time Unitarian congregations, not generally very numerous, but reaching a high standard of general culture, are found in all the large towns in England.

But the Unitarianism of our own time is by no means identical with that of the seventeenth century. The theology of the Unitarians, like that of all religious bodies, has been deeply affected by the general trend of thought. The older race of Unitarians had acknowledged, if not the infallibility, at any rate the authority of the New Testament; but as criticism more and more shook the old foundations, it came to be felt that the authority of Scripture was not what an earlier generation had supposed[1]. The more progressive Unitarians, "far from regarding man as entirely dependent upon his reasoning powers for his knowledge of religion, rather look upon him as standing in a living relationship with the one infinite source of all truth, and as having within his own nature the germs of the highest religious faith. Christianity, accordingly, they regard not as a *message*, or a system of truth communicated from without, but as the highest expression of the Divine in humanity—an expression not necessarily preternatural, but connected with the previous history of mankind by the natural laws of moral and spiritual development[2]." From this point of view the question of the reality of the miracles recorded in the Gospels is not vital, and many Unitarians reject them altogether. They have no definite confession of faith, but all agree in rejecting the doctrines of the Holy Trinity, original sin, vicarious atonement, and everlasting punishment. They generally baptize infants, and celebrate the Lord's Supper as commemorative of the death of Christ, and symbolic of spiritual communion with Him.

---

[1] See James Martineau, *The Seat of Authority in Religion* (Lond. 1890).
[2] R. B. Drummond.

6. SCOTLAND.

When William III. landed in England, Episcopal clergymen still had possession of all the sees and parsonages in Scotland, and in many places the people were content to have it so; but many had been raised to fury by the cruelties of James II.'s reign. No sooner was the heavy hand of the Stuart king removed than their pent-up wrath burst forth[1]. In many cases priests were laid hold of by the rabble, carried about in mock procession, told to be off and never to shew themselves in the parish again. The furniture of the manse was often tumbled out at the windows. These rabblings went on for two or three months, until almost every parish in the south and west was cleared of its Episcopal incumbent. About two hundred clergymen, with their wives and children, were thus rendered homeless, some of whom had no means of subsistence. In July, 1689, an Act was passed by the Scottish Parliament abolishing Episcopacy; then, as nothing was for the time put in its place, there followed a time of chaotic disorder. On the one hand, bishops still ordained; on the other, kirk-sessions again met. The Parliament of 1690 gave to the Presbyterians full possession of the property of the Church, and the free exercise of their ecclesiastical constitution under the protection of law. With the clergy of the despoiled Church it was far otherwise. They were very generally disaffected to the new dynasty; many refused to take the oath of allegiance; some continued to pray for King James. Some, taking the oath and accepting the Presbyterian polity, were protected in their livings, and even some who had not done so continued to occupy their manses and their pulpits. For in some districts it was no easy matter to dispossess the Episcopal incumbents. Where the people had become attached to them, they would not allow them to be turned out of their churches to make room for intruders, and sometimes the patrons defied the presbyteries.

'Rabbling' of Clergy, 1689.

Episcopacy abolished, 1689.

---

[1] De Foe, *Memoirs of the Ch. of Scotland* (Lond. 1717); G. Grub, *Eccl. Hist. of Scotland*, vol. IV.; J. Skinner, II. 516 ff.; T. Stephen, *Hist. of Ch. of Scotland*, vol. IV.; John Cunningham, *The Ch. Hist. of Scotland*, II. 259 ff. (Edinb. 1859).

Nor was it possible at once to find qualified Presbyterian ministers to fill vacant churches; during the long prevalence of Episcopacy few had been ordained. At the time of the Union, eighteen years after the Revolution, there were a hundred and sixty-five Episcopal clergymen living in the manses, preaching in the pulpits and drawing the stipends. Soon after the accession of Queen Anne the Episcopalians petitioned her for permission to be admitted to benefices where a majority of the heritors and inhabitants were Episcopalian. No attention seems to have been paid to this, and the following year they besought the Queen of her clemency to compassionate their starving condition, which she was very willing to relieve so far as she could, but her power was of course small. An Act of the Queen's reign however (10 Anne, c. 7) did grant toleration to the Episcopalian clergy, on condition of their praying for the existing sovereign. Many of the Episcopal clergy were implicated in the rising of 1745, and after Culloden the whole of the clergy, guilty or not, suffered[1]. They were treated as if they were belligerents or outlaws by the Duke of Cumberland's soldiery. They "were obliged to leave their houses, which sometimes were plundered, and to skulk where they best could that they might not fall into the soldiers' hands. Their hearers stood aghast between pity for their ministers and fears for themselves." Their chapels were burned, pulled down, or closed. In the panic which arose it is not wonderful that Parliament passed severe laws against those who were as a body suspected of treason. That the clergy should be required to profess allegiance to the existing sovereign was not unreasonable, but the Act went much further. Every house in which five or more persons besides its usual occupants assembled for worship was declared to be a meeting-house. No letters of orders were henceforth to be registered but such as had been given by some bishop of the Church of England or Ireland—a clause which disqualified almost the whole of the Scottish clergy. Nor did the laity escape. Any one who attended an illegal Episcopal meeting, and did not give information within five days, was to be fined or imprisoned. If any peer was twice guilty of this offence he could neither be chosen a

Cunningham, 312, 328.

[1] See Walker's *Life of J. Skinner*, p. 28 ff.

representative peer nor vote at the election of another; and if any commoner was so guilty, he could not sit in Parliament[1]. The clergy who remained in Scotland commonly exercised their functions in private assemblies of less than five persons. An Act of two years later was yet more severe; a priest could now neither preach, nor baptize, nor celebrate the Eucharist without incurring the risk of being cast into prison. Bishops Sherlock and Secker strenuously opposed this measure in the House of Lords, and the whole Episcopal bench refused to support it. Under these laws the Church languished. It was not extinguished, but it sought to escape notice. The death of Prince Charles Edward, however, in 1788, changed the feeling of many Jacobites towards the reigning house. Most of the clergy were now disposed to abandon their attitude of stubborn resistance, and to pray in church for King George by name. A synod of the diocese of Aberdeen, presided over by Bishop Skinner, in the same year recommended this course to all its members. In a short time the whole Church, with insignificant exceptions, had followed the example of Aberdeen, and thus at last the way was prepared for the repeal of the penal laws. Bishop Skinner, who was Primus of the Scottish episcopate, went to London, with two other bishops, early in 1789 to promote this object. They were courteously received by Archbishop Moore, but the man who gave them really zealous help was Horsley, Bishop of St David's. A Bill was introduced which passed the Commons, but was rejected in the House of Lords through the opposition of Lord Chancellor Thurlow, who would own no bishops not appointed by the Crown. In 1792 a Relief Bill was introduced into the House of Lords, passed the Commons with some difficulty, and received the Royal Assent, 15 June, 1792. The Act, however, did not give universal satisfaction, as it required the clergy to subscribe the Thirty-nine Articles of the English Church, thus, as they thought, diminishing the liberty they had hitherto enjoyed of treating theological questions freely within the limits imposed by the Creed of the Catholic Church. Subscription to the Articles was in fact not accepted by any Scottish ecclesiastical authority until the year 1804.

[1] T. Stephen, *Hist. of Ch. of Scotland*, IV.

During the period of oppression, a considerable number of priests in English or Irish Orders, encouraged by the advantage which the Act gave them over the native clergy, formed congregations in the great towns. These clergymen ignored the Scottish bishops, and were of course regarded by them as intruders and schismatics. This state of things Bishop Skinner earnestly desired to put an end to by bringing the Anglican congregation into the communion and discipline of the Scottish Church. In 1804 a synod at Laurencekirk, mainly through the influence of the venerable Bishop Jolly, proposed terms of union embodied in six articles; and in 1806 the vacant see of Edinburgh was filled by the unanimous election of Dr Daniel Sandford, one of the English clergy. Thus the rent in the Church seemed to be happily closed, but there have in fact been many congregations since that time in which the authority of the Scottish episcopate was not acknowledged. Scottish Orders were not admitted to qualify for English preferment until a much later date.

The Scottish Church enjoys full inter-communion with the Anglican, but it is not identical with it. The difference of position of necessity brought with it differences of administration. Every minister of the Church holds his office on terms of a voluntary contract which he makes at the time of his entry, and these terms may vary according to the views of patrons and congregations. In Scotland the clergy of each diocese are accustomed to meet in synod and to pass resolutions affecting the diocese. The Scottish bishops are chosen by the clergy and representative laymen of the vacant diocese, but their choice requires the confirmation of the College of Bishops in order to be valid. Nor is the liturgy of the Scottish Church absolutely the same as that of the Anglican[1]. A Prayer-Book for Scotland had been sanctioned by Charles I. in 1637[2], but had scarcely been used when the Church was for the time swept away. In the period between the Restoration and the Revolution, the Church, though Episcopal in constitution, had no liturgical forms. After the disesta-

---

[1] On the "Usages" of the Scottish Church, see *Life of Skinner*, p. 105 ff.; Skinner's *Hist.* II. p. 165 ff.; J. Dowden, *Historical Account of the Scottish Communion Office*; W. H. Frere, *Hist. of Common Prayer*, p. 226 ff.

[2] See above, p. 45.

blishment of 1688 a desire for such forms sprang up among the faithful, and, as copies of the Scottish Book were scarcely to be had, the English Book was commonly used. The Communion Office of 1637, however, began to come into use, and in the early part of the eighteenth century the English Non-jurors, among whom were found several learned ritualists, had much influence on their Scottish brethren. In 1755 Bishop Gerard of Aberdeen issued an edition of the Communion Office, which in 1764 was revised and published under the authority of Bishop Falconar, as Primus, and Bishop Forbes of Ross. The synod of Aberdeen in 1811 declared this to be the Office of primary authority, while liberty was given to retain the English Office in all congregations where it was in use, and where its continuance was desired. But the general use of the English Common Prayer tended to bring with it the English form of Communion, and by the Canons of 1863 it was declared to be the Service-book of the Church, to be used in all new congregations, unless a certain number of the communicants should declare their desire to use the Scottish Office. The result has been that it is used (1905), either solely, or alternately with the English, in about half the churches. The Scottish formularies were much influenced by Bishop Rattray's reconstruction of the *Ancient Liturgy of the Church of Jerusalem* (published 1744), and contain specific directions for mixing Water with the Wine, Prayer for the Dead, Prayer for the Descent of the Holy Spirit upon the Elements, and the Prayer of Oblation. These revivals of ancient ritual were of course not acceptable to all, and when in 1857 Alexander Penrose Forbes, Bishop of Brechin, addressing his synod for the first time, took occasion to vindicate the Scottish Office and to inculcate the doctrine of the Real Presence, a great stir was made. The College of Bishops issued a Pastoral letter declaring that they felt bound to resist the teaching of the Bishop of Brechin, and somewhat later he was formally charged with erroneous teaching before the bishops sitting as a court. The result of this trial was that Forbes was censured and admonished not to offend again in this matter.

The Church of Scotland since 1688 has never been a numerous society, but it has exercised an influence out of

CH. VIII.

Forbes's Charge, 1857.

1858.

May, 1860.

all proportion to its numbers. Its adherents include many of the most cultivated of the Scottish nation, and its freedom from state control has attracted many devout, able, and learned men to serve in its ministry. It is found flourishing in all large towns, and its small, often beautiful, churches are objects of interest in many a remote district.

Presbyterianism re-established, 1690.

In the year 1690 Presbyterianism was re-established in Scotland, with its orderly succession of governing bodies, presbytery, kirk-session, and general assembly[1]. The latter is the supreme power in ecclesiastical legislation and also the highest court of appeal in ecclesiastical cases. The Westminster Confession of Faith was ratified as the national standard of belief, and the right of patrons to nominate to benefices was taken away. An Act of the British Parliament, however, in 1712, restored their former rights to patrons in Scotland. This Act was destined to have momentous consequences in after time.

Act for settling of Schools, 1696.

The Scottish Parliament in its short session of 1696 passed a memorable law by which it was "statuted and ordained" that every parish in the realm should provide a commodious school-house and should pay a sufficient stipend to a schoolmaster. The effect was not of course immediately evident, but as generation succeeded generation it became clear that to whatever land the Scotchman might wander the advantage which he derived from his early education raised him above his competitors.

The persecuting spirit.

It is sad to turn from an Act which shews an enlightenment in advance of the rest of Europe to transactions which shew how deeply engrained, even on the verge of the eighteenth century, was the spirit of fanaticism and persecution. Hardly had the Schools Act been touched with the sceptre when the rulers of Church and State in Scotland began to persecute witches. A crowd of wretches, guilty only of being old and miserable, were accused of trafficking with the devil. The shops of the booksellers were searched for heretical works, and one of the condemned books was Thomas Burnet's *Sacred Theory of the Earth*[2]. But worse was to come. A student of eighteen, named Thomas Aikenhead, a youth of blameless life, had in the course of his reading met with writings

---

[1] Hardwick, *Reformation*, 352 ff.
[2] Macaulay's *Hist. of England*, IV. 781 (ed. 1855).

hostile to Christianity, and proclaimed his discovery to four or five of his companions. Trinity in unity was, he said, a contradiction in terms; Ezra was the author of the Pentateuch; Moses had learned magic in Egypt, and the like. For this wild talk of a youngster intoxicated with a supposed new discovery he was prosecuted by the Lord Advocate, convicted, and sentenced to be hanged. The ministers of Edinburgh, who might have obtained from the Privy Council a respite of the sentence, demanded not only the poor boy's death, but his speedy death. He heartily repented his folly and recanted what he had said, but he was hanged nevertheless[1].

Ch. VIII.

During the whole period from 1712 to 1843 the question of patronage occasioned much uneasiness in the Presbyterian Church. Those who held that a congregation had an absolute right to choose its minister, unhindered by rights of patronage conferred by the State, were of course discontented. The leader of the dissatisfied party was a minister named Ebenezer Erskine, who with his adherents separated from the Kirk as by law established, and formed a society which took the title of the Associate Presbytery, though its members were popularly known as Seceders. The Seceders themselves were soon divided into two bodies, called Burghers and Antiburghers, by a dispute as to the lawfulness of taking the Burgher's oath of allegiance[2]. In 1761 another body seceded in consequence of objections to the system of Patronage, and called itself the Presbytery of Relief, or Relief Church. Still further divisions arose, of which space does not allow an account to be given here, but, as time went on, the two bodies, divided on no question of principle, felt a desire for union. Committees were appointed and conferences held; and at length, in 1847, the union of the Secession and Relief Churches was formally accomplished, and they became one body under the

Seceders, 1733.

Relief Church, 1761.

---

[1] Howell's *State Trials*, xiii. 917; Macaulay, *ut supra*, 782; Cunningham's *Church Hist. of Scotland*, ii. 313; J. Hill Burton, *Hist. of Scotland from 1689 to 1748*, i. 256 f.; Arnot's *Celebrated Scotch Trials*, p. 326.

[2] A burgher, or burgess, of a Scottish burgh had to take, on admission to his privileges, an oath in which he accepted the religion established in the country and professed allegiance to the sovereign and to the provost and baillies of the burgh.

CH. VIII.
United Presbyterian Church formed, 13 May, 1847.
Moderates and Evangelicals.

name of the United Presbyterian Church, which has had a career of great prosperity.

During the eighteenth century the Established Church was divided into two parties, the Moderates, among whom were found most of the clergy who were distinguished for general culture, and who were comparatively indifferent to the dogmatic controversies of the time; and the Evangelicals, who retained much of the old Scottish fervour for purity of doctrine. These parties differed, in fact, much as the bulk of the parochial clergy differed from the Evangelicals in England. The Moderates were, as was perhaps natural, generally in favour of the law of patronage, which was looked upon by the Evangelicals with no friendly eyes. By the Evangelicals their opponents were generally represented as having a merely intellectual knowledge of Christianity, as teachers of bare morality, as Rationalists, or even as unbelievers. In the later years of George III. however, and during the reign of George IV., the ascendancy which the Moderates had hitherto held in the General Assembly and throughout the country began to decrease. In the early part of William IV.'s reign the Reform agitation deeply moved the leaders on both sides, and the two parties in the General Assembly engaged in a struggle fiercer than any in which they had yet met. The main subject of dispute was, as before, the law of patronage.

The system of patronage up to 1834 was this. A patron selected one from among those whom the Church had already licensed to preach, and presented him to the vacant living. After he had preached in the parish the congregation might sign a "Call," after which the presbytery of the district proceeded to the "Trials," or examination of the candidate. During these trials, and again on the day of "ordination," or institution to the parish, the people might object in writing to the candidate on moral or doctrinal grounds. If such objections were not made, or not substantiated, the presentee was ordained and settled. The people's right of objection had, however, in the period of which we are speaking, almost fallen into disuse.

But the General Assembly of 1834 passed what was known as the Veto Act, which provided that "if the people declared the presentee unacceptable, the presbytery should on that ground reject him." That is, a presentee might be rejected simply because the people, with no reason assigned, refused to have him. This went far beyond the ancient right of the people to reject a presentee on the definite ground of faulty life or doctrine. The Moderates contended that the presentee should be rejected only in case the people's objections should be, in the opinion of the Church Courts, well-founded. Equity seems to require this; but in any case the Veto Act was an ill-conceived measure. It would surely have been better to give the initiative at once to the people than to give them a free veto. Another Act of 1834 gave to ministers of chapels—places of worship, that is, without parishes—a seat in the Church Courts. Both these Acts were of doubtful legality. A collision between Church and State soon followed.

In 1834 the Earl of Kinnoul presented Mr R. Young to the parish of Auchterarder[1]. He was vetoed by the people, and in July, 1835, rejected by the presbytery. Young appealed, with the concurrence of the patron, to the Court of Session, the supreme civil court in Scotland. The Court decided that the conduct of the presbytery in rejecting the presentee was illegal, and this judgment was affirmed on appeal by the House of Lords. Other cases of a like nature followed, and there ensued a conflict between the civil and ecclesiastical courts, the former enforcing their decision by civil penalties, the latter suspending and deposing the ministers who obeyed the Court of Session. In the General Assembly of 1841 the differences were seen to be irreconcileable. Attempts to meet the difficulty by legislation had failed, and vigorous attacks were made on the existing system of patronage. These were renewed in 1842 when a distinguished clergyman, Robertson of Ellon, and other ministers who had maintained communion with seven members of the Strathbogie presbytery, deposed by the Assembly for obeying the Court of Session in defiance of the Assembly's sentence, were suspended from all their judicial functions for nine months. Under these circumstances the meeting of the Assembly of 1843

May,1839.

[1] C. Robertson, *Report of the Auchterarder Case*, 3 vols. (Edinburgh, 1838–9).

was big with fate. The defenders of the people's rights had discovered that even if Chapel-ministers were admitted, contrary to the decision of the Court of Session, they could not command a majority. They resolved to leave a body in which, as they believed, the rights of Christian men were infringed by the secular power. After the usual levee at Holyrood the procession went in order to the High Church and thence to the Assembly Hall. The customary opening formalities were observed, and then the non-intrusionist party read their protest and left the Hall. Gravely they marched through a multitude of spectators to another hall which had been prepared for this emergency, and constituted themselves the Assembly of the Free Church of Scotland. Dr Chalmers, by general consent the most distinguished minister of the Church, was chosen Moderator. A great secession had been accomplished. Of the whole number of ministers of the Kirk 752 remained, 451 seceded[1]. Many, probably most, of those who seceded gave up, for the time being, all the living that they had for conscience' sake. It was not without reason that Lord Jeffrey, a man not enthusiastic in matters of religion, exclaimed, "there is not another country upon earth where such a deed could have been done." And the hearts of many went with them. Even men whose calm judgment disapproved their defiance of the law of the land were moved by their conscientious self-sacrifice. In every class of life over all Scotland the people shared in the movement. Funds flowed in with a liberality beyond precedent. Churches were built, and it was arranged that the seceding ministers should be mainly supported from a common fund, so that the poor districts might be aided by the rich. The bitterness of the first conflict has passed away for the present generation. Patronage has been abolished in the Established Church, and a minister is elected by the congregation. The original cause of difference has thus ceased to exist: the two

[1] Ample information on this Disruption may be found in W. Hanna's *Life and Writings of T. Chalmers* (Edinb. 1849-52), and in A. H. Charteris's *Life of James Robertson of Ellon* (Edinb. 1863). See also Robertson's *Observations on the Veto Act* (Edinb. 1840); James Bryce, *Ten Years of the Church of Scotland* (Edinb. 1850); R. Buchanan, *The Ten Years' Conflict* (Glasgow, 1849); W. Wilson, *Memorials of R. S. Candlish* (Edinb. 1880).

communities are identical in doctrine and discipline; but the cleft remains.

And another has shewn itself. In 1903 the Free Church formed a union with the United Presbyterian, under the title of the United Free Church of Scotland. A small minority, however, of the members of the Free Church refused to accept this union and contended that the change which it involved was so considerable that the United Church could not be considered to represent the Free Church, and that consequently all the property of the latter belonged to the minority who were faithful to the original standards. This contention was rejected by the Scottish Courts, but the House of Lords, on appeal, overruled their decision, and assigned the property of the Free Church to the small minority. Thus this insignificant body was placed in possession of a very large number of churches, colleges, and other institutions, of which they were utterly unable to make use. This state of things was evidently intolerable, and recourse was had to legislation. A Commission was named by an Act of Parliament which should make an equitable distribution of the property in question. Their labours are not yet (1905) concluded.

United Free Church, 1903.

Judgment of the House of Lords, 1 Aug., 1904.

7. IRELAND.

No Englishman can look back upon the state of the Irish Church in the eighteenth century without a sense of shame. The appointments which were in the patronage of the Crown, especially bishoprics, were made almost entirely with a view to maintaining English influence. The majority of the persons appointed were Englishmen, sometimes, it is to be feared, men whom public opinion would not have permitted to obtain preferment at home. Nevertheless, something was done for the benefit of the Church. During the reigns of William and Anne Acts were passed to facilitate the building of churches and parsonages, many of which had been destroyed or allowed

Irish Church in 18th Century[1].

---

[1] R. Murray, *Ireland and her Church* (1845); T. Olden, *The Church of Ireland* (1892); J. Macbeth, *The Story of Ireland and her Church* (Dublin, 1899); J. A. Froude, *The English in Ireland in the Eighteenth Century* (1872–4); W. D. Killen, *Ecclesiastical Hist. of Ireland* (1875).

to fall into ruin. Queen Anne also, in Ireland as in England, surrendered the Firstfruits which were paid to the Crown by every incumbent on institution to a benefice, and caused them to be paid to a board of trustees, to be applied towards providing parsonages and buying back impropriate tithes. A few efforts were made to enlighten the Irish people through their own language, but these were not vigorously seconded by those in authority, and were not long kept up. There was no copy of the Bible in Irish printed during the whole of the eighteenth century.

Yet the prospect was not all dark. Archbishop King, who for nearly half a century was a prominent figure in the Irish Church, was a man equally admirable in character and intellect. He not only gave freely of his own to promote the material prosperity of his diocese, but was most earnest in the discharge of his spiritual duties. But he was saddened by the state of things about him. In 1714 he declares that there were only two resident bishops in the province of Armagh. Primate Boulter is especially conspicuous as a zealous upholder of the English ascendancy, but he did much for the material welfare of the Irish clergy. The income which he received as Primate he freely distributed in various ways during his life, and at his death left more than £30,000 towards the purchase of glebes and the augmentation of poor livings. Bishop Stearne of Clogher was another munificent prelate. George Berkeley[1], for nineteen years Bishop of Cloyne, to whom Pope attributed "every virtue under heaven," sheds an undying lustre on the Irish Church. Dean Swift, though of English blood, had the interests of Ireland at heart, and exerted his great powers for what he believed to be the benefit of the land in which he was born. And many others struggled against the influence of base politics and lukewarm religion.

The Irish Parliament, up to 1782, was restrained by Poynings' Law of 1495, which required that any Bill introduced into it should be approved by the English Council. In 1782, however, legislative independence was conceded, and for eighteen years the Irish Parliament, composed wholly of Protestants, had the power of making laws for the nation. But there was much disaffection in the

---

[1] See p. 182.

kingdom, which at last, stimulated by the hope of aid from Revolutionary France, broke out into the Rebellion of 1798. Political though it was in origin, it was carried out in a spirit of hostility to the Church. Some of the clergy were put to death, many Protestants were massacred and some abjured. The Roman Catholic priests frequently did their best to mitigate the fury of the rebels. It was felt that the experiment of an independent Parliament had not been successful, and on Jan. 1, 1801, Ireland was merged in the United Kingdom of Great Britain and Ireland, with the sanction of the Parliament of each nation. By the same authority, without the consultation of any synod or convocation—though the bishops with one exception approved—the national Churches were united, and became the United Church of England and Ireland. The continuance of this United Church was to be deemed and taken to be an essential and fundamental part of the Union.

Ch. VIII.
Rebellion of 1798.

Union with Great Britain, 1801.

The condition of the Church at the time of the Union was somewhat more satisfactory than it had been fifty years before, though it was still too much infected by worldliness and apathy, and had its own special disadvantages. The refusal of the Parliament in 1735 to allow tithe to be taken of the rent paid for the grazing of cattle very much impoverished the clergy in a country where the greater part of the land was pasture. But to get tithe paid at all to Protestant clergy in a country where almost all the cultivators were Roman Catholic was difficult. The tithes were paid in kind, and the clergy had to employ "proctors[1]" to collect them. As this collecting was extremely unpopular, it was undertaken only by men who were indifferent to the esteem of their neighbours and often took harsh measures. Combinations against the payment of tithe were organized throughout the country, and riots and even murders were of frequent occurrence. Several Acts of Parliament attempted to put an end to the tithe riots, and in 1838 the tithe was made a rent-charge payable by the owners of property. As a large proportion of the landowners were Protestants, this measure made for peace. For many generations the cost of

State of the Church.

Tithe riots.

Tithe Act, 1838.

---

[1] A proctor (=procurator) is one who holds letters of procuration to act on behalf of another person.

Vestry Cess abolished, 1833.

Abolition of Ten Sees, 1833.

Progress.

Disestablishment, 1869.

the Church services, and of the maintenance of the fabrics, was provided for by a rate, called a vestry cess, levied on all householders alike—Churchmen, Roman Catholics and Dissenters. This was abolished in 1833, and a fund was formed by taxing all bishops and clergy whose incomes exceeded £300 a year, for the building and repairing of churches, augmenting small livings, and other ecclesiastical purposes. In the same Parliament of 1833 the Irish episcopate was greatly reduced. As vacancies occurred, no further appointments were to be made to the archbishoprics of Tuam and Cashel, and to eight bishoprics, and their incomes were to be transferred to a body of Ecclesiastical Commissioners, to be used in various ways for the benefit of the Church. This Act seems to have produced more agitation in England than in Ireland[1], where the period which followed was one of quiet progress. Excellent appointments were generally made to the Episcopal Bench, and increased earnestness in matters of religion was shewn both by clergy and laity. Many bishops and other clergymen were distinguished as theologians and men of letters. The Church, by the diligence of the clergy, the spread of education, and the cooperation of the laity in various voluntary associations, gradually extended its influence over the masses of the people.

But it had long been felt by thoughtful men that it was an anomaly hardly to be defended that a Church whose adherents formed but a small part of the population should be in possession of all the ecclesiastical endowments throughout Ireland. Many statesmen had wished to change this condition of things and make a more equitable distribution of the temporalities. But it was not until the session of 1868 that the great influence of Mr Gladstone with the country and Parliament rendered it possible to pass a Bill depriving the Irish Church of its ancient possessions. The Act by which it was disestablished and disendowed received the Royal Assent on the 26th July, 1869, and came into force on the 1st Jan. 1871. Mr Gladstone himself testified that disestablishment was not brought about by the shortcomings of the Irish Church. "We must all accord to that Church," he said, "the praise that her clergy are a body of zealous and

---

[1] See p. 261.

devoted ministers, who give themselves to their sacerdotal functions in a degree not inferior to any other Christian Church." The principal effects of this measure were as follows. The Church of Ireland was separated from that of England, and became a free Episcopal Church. The Irish Bishops no longer had representatives in the House of Lords, and the old ecclesiastical courts were abolished. The fabrics of the churches, with the adjacent graveyards and parochial schoolhouses, with all private endowments given since 1660, were retained by the Church, while the parsonages, with a portion of the land connected with them, might be purchased back on easy terms for the benefit of the parishes. It was also arranged that a capital sum should be paid out of the Church funds to the College of Maynooth and to the Presbyterian body in lieu of the annual payments at that time made to them from public funds. The clergy and officials of the Church were to have their life-interests respected. Any portion of the Church property which remained after all these claims were satisfied was to be given to the relief of "unavoidable calamity or suffering," as Parliament should determine. The Church Act authorized the creation of a "Representative Body" which should receive and manage any property entrusted to it on behalf of the Church. The constitution which the liberated Church formed for itself was as follows. The "General Synod" consists of the House of Bishops, twelve in number, and the House of Representatives, composed of 208 clergy and 416 laymen, elected by the several Diocesan Synods. The "Representative Body," incorporated in 1870 as the official trustee of the property of the Church, consists of the Archbishops and Bishops, of twelve clergy, one for each diocese, elected by the clerical representatives of that diocese in the General Synod, of twenty-four laymen, similarly elected by the lay diocesan representatives, and of twelve co-opted members. The General Synod is the supreme governing body of the Church. It may alter or abrogate canon or rubrics, and may vary, repeal or supersede acts of Diocesan Synods. The Representative Body soon had highly important functions to discharge in respect of finance. The Church Act permitted every ecclesiastical life annuity due under the Act to be capitalized at its

Pecuniary arrangements.

The Representative Body, 1870.

Commutation.

calculated value, and such capital to be paid to the Representative Body. Further, it offered a bonus of twelve per cent. on this sum, if within a certain time three-fourths at least of the clergy consented to commute their annuities for capital. More than the required proportion did consent, and the result was that a sum of over £7,500,000 was paid into the hands of the Representative Body, charged of course with the sums payable annually to the existing clergy so long as they lived. In the course of a few years the annuitants were removed by death, and the interest on this large sum became available for the general purposes of the Church. Provision was made meanwhile for forming sustentation funds in the several dioceses, and the laity shewed their attachment to the Church by their liberal contributions to the maintenance of the clergy.

Lectionary, 1873.
Prayer-Book, 1878.

A Lectionary, which excluded all lessons taken from the Apocrypha, was adopted in 1873, and in 1878 a revised Prayer-Book was agreed upon, after much discussion in the Synod, in which laymen as well as clerics took an active part. It differs in several points from the English Book, but there is no change of such a nature as to make it difficult for an English churchman to worship and communicate in an Irish church.

The loss of its ancient endowments was of course a great shock to the Irish Church, but it rose out of its troubles with great courage and force. It may in truth be doubted whether the Church of Ireland has ever been in a more healthy and vigorous condition since the days of Henry VIII. than it is at present.

Roman Catholics.

The Treaty of Limerick put an end to the war between the adherents of James II. and of William III. in Ireland. In this treaty it was not stipulated that the Irish Roman Catholics should be competent to hold any civil or military office, or that they should be admitted to any corporation. But a promise was given that they should enjoy such privileges in the exercise of their religion as were not forbidden by the law, or as they had enjoyed in the reign of Charles II., when the Roman Catholic worship had not been interfered with, so long as it was not obtrusive. When the English Parliament met in October, the treaty was discussed in both Houses. The result

1691.

was a Bill drawn by Chief Justice Holt, which was supposed to be in accordance with the terms of the capitulation, and which in due course became law. It attracted little notice at the time of its enactment, but in the discussions which preceded Catholic Emancipation it was alleged that the treaty had been violated. It is difficult to admit that the treaty was violated by this particular Act, but it is only too certain that the Roman Catholics had good reason for complaining of its violation at a later date. The Irish Parliament, seven years after the treaty was made, passed a law for banishing from the kingdom Roman Catholic bishops, dignitaries, and clergy who were members of any Order. The celebration of Roman Catholic rites was not interfered with, and an ordinary secular priest was allowed to remain in each parish[1]. For a century there was peace in Ireland. The Irish of the native race were too completely broken in spirit to rebel. They were still the same people who had sprung to arms at the call of Shane O'Neill, but the men who might have been their leaders were to be found everywhere but in Ireland, at Versailles and Madrid, in the armies of Frederic and Maria Theresa. For a century the history of the Roman Catholic Church in Ireland is uneventful. There is only to record the devotion of the people and the priests who kept their faith alive under all possible discouragement. When the time came for the Union with Great Britain, the Roman Catholics were generally in its favour, thinking it possible that they might gain something by it, and they had nothing to lose. From this time the treatment of the Roman Catholics in Ireland does not differ from that of their brethren in Great Britain.

In the beginning of the eighteenth century Cromwell's Baptists and Independents had almost disappeared, but the Presbyterians in the North of Ireland, constantly recruited from Scotland, were more enduring. It was not however without some difficulty that the Irish Parliament, Protestant as it was, granted them toleration. In 1727 the Presbyterian body was weakened by the secession of the Synod of Antrim, in which low views of the Divinity

Presbyterianism[2].

Toleration, 1719. *Antrim secedes*, 1727.

[1] Macbeth, p. 235.
[2] J. S. Reid, *Hist. of the Presbyterian Church in Ireland*, with notes by W. D. Killen (Belfast, 1867).

of Christ had become so rife as to make subscription to the Westminster standards hardly possible for its ministers. And it was still further weakened by the emigration of many of its members to America. The secession which took place in the Scottish Kirk propagated itself in Ireland. In 1746 the first seceding minister settled in Ireland, and in 1750 the first presbytery of Seceders was established. The system of lay patronage, which gave occasion for the Scottish secession, had never existed in Ulster, but the rigidly orthodox Seceders found in the prevalent Socinianism a reason for existence. In the early years of the nineteenth century, the state of religion among the Presbyterians was not satisfactory, but a better day soon dawned. In 1827 the Synod of Ulster, under the leadership of Henry Cooke, required from all its members a declaration of belief in the Holy Trinity, and so excluded all Socinians. As a result of this, those ministers who were excluded formed a Remonstrant synod. From this time much more zeal was shewn. Many new congregations arose, and those already existing shewed new life. In 1840 the Secession Synod was absorbed into the regular Synod of Ulster, and the union formed the Presbyterian Church of Ireland, which remains a flourishing community to this day.

8. NORTH AMERICA[1].

It is to be feared that Bacon's words of the Spaniard's discoveries in the Western World are to some extent true of all European colonization. "It cannot be affirmed," he says, "if one speak ingenuously, that it was the propagation of the Christian faith that was the adamant [loadstone] of that discovery, entry, and plantation, but gold and silver and temporal profit and glory; so that what was first in God's providence was but second in man's appetite and intention[2]." Yet it cannot be said that the

---

[1] S. Wilberforce, *Hist. of the Episcopal Church in America* (1844); J. S. M. Anderson, *Hist. of the Ch. of England in the Colonies*, etc. (1845-56); White, *Memoirs of the Prot.-Episc. Ch. in U.S.A.* (3rd ed. by B. F. De Costa, New York, 1880); W. Perry, *Hist. of the Amer. Episc. Ch.* (1885).

[2] Quoted by Tucker, *Eng. Ch. in other Lands*, p. 7.

early English colonists[1] were indifferent to the spiritual welfare of those among whom they came, however much in some cases their conduct may have belied their avowed intentions. Some, as the Puritans in New England and the Roman Catholics in Maryland, had left their homes expressly for the sake of their religion.

When the great federation of the United States was formed, the Constitution adopted under Washington in 1787 provided[2] that no religious tests should ever be required as a qualification for any public office in the United States. And even more emphatically the first Congress laid down that "Congress shall make no law respecting an establishment of religion, or prohibiting the free exercise thereof, or abridging the freedom of speech or of the press, or the rights of the people peaceably to assemble, and to petition the government for the redress of grievances[3]." Thus, so far as the Federal law of the States was concerned, the most absolute freedom was given to every form of religious organization. The State was no further concerned with Churches than with any other corporations existing within its limits. So long as they observed the laws of the land they were protected, and assisted, in case of necessity, to enforce their own regulations upon their own members. But when the State proclaimed its indifference to ecclesiastical organizations, it is not to be understood that the nation repudiated Christianity. There is probably no country on which the religion of Christ has a firmer hold than the United States of America. And even the State, as such, acknowledges that it is not a society without religion. Congress nominates chaplains, of different confessions, and opens every sitting with prayer. The President appoints chaplains for the army and navy. A Thanksgiving-Day is yearly celebrated in all the States on the proclamation of the President and the concurrent action of the several governors. Fast-days have not unfrequently been ordered by the civil power on great emergencies. The perfect equality of religions before the law has no doubt had a considerable social effect. To belong to a small and little-

CH. VIII.

Freedom of Religion in the United States, 1787. 1789.

The State Christian.

Social Equality.

[1] See p. 78.
[2] Art. VI. § 3.
[3] Gale's *Debates and Proceedings of Congress,* I. 729, quoted in the Herzog-Schaff *Encycl.* 2424.

known community is not necessarily to be excluded from society. Many settlers in America have left their old homes in Europe in consequence of the social discomfort which they incurred from adopting some strange form of faith in the midst of ancient and settled institutions. The States allow the older forms of religion, such as are known in Europe, to flourish greatly, but also they afford a fertile soil for the growth of new and strange denominations, a growth which does not seem to be checked by the wide diffusion of education. In spite of the general aptitude of the Americans for practical life, there is in them a strong under-current of emotionalism which enables a new prophet, or sometimes a new impostor, to draw followers after him. By far the greater portion of the population belongs to some form of Protestantism. The most distinguished Americans—the great philanthropists, the great thinkers, the great statesmen, the great scholars, inventors, writers, professors, and teachers, have been and are, with rare exceptions, Protestants, though often of no very pronounced religious opinions. Some prominent politicians and eloquent orators have been Roman Catholics of Irish origin. Ministers of the Gospel are for the most part dependent on their congregations for support, but probably nowhere are they held in higher honour, and nowhere is the example of a pious and consistent life more influential. The free-will offerings of the lay-people are large and generous.

In the various States of the Union, Church and State are now separated, but each State has in this respect its own history. In only three colonies, before the Declaration of Independence, were differing forms of religion tolerated. These were Maryland, where the Roman Catholics were dominant; Rhode Island, settled by Baptists under the influence of Roger Williams; and Pennsylvania, which was an asylum not only for the persecuted Quakers but for all Christian brethren. In the other colonies, Church and State were very closely connected. In New England, with the exception of Rhode Island, a Puritan Congregationalism was the State religion, and civil rights depended on adherence to the dominant form of belief. Baptists were expelled, Quakers were condemned to public scourging, ear-slitting, and even to the gallows. As a more enlightened and humane spirit crept over the colonists these things ceased to be, but traces of the old laws remained in Massachusetts until 1833. In Virginia, as in the southern colonies generally, the Church of England was the State Church, and all other denominations were nearly in the same position as Dissenters in England. As however they increased in numbers and power, they naturally became discontented with their religious and political inferiority, and presented petitions for relief to the Virginian Legislature. They found a powerful advocate in Thomas Jefferson, who, if he had no love for Dissenters, was an eager advocate of equal rights for all. The result was that the principle of the independence of Church and State was carried in the Legislature in 1776, and was embodied in various Acts of the ten following years. Soon after the adoption of the Federal Constitution by the several States, the connexion between Church and State in New York, Maryland, South Carolina, and the other colonies where the Anglican Church was dominant, was broken, and complete religious freedom proclaimed. The conception of the duty of enforcing religious tenets by State sanction clung longest, as we have seen, to the Puritans of New England.

In 1784, Samuel Seabury was consecrated by Scottish bishops as bishop of the Church in North America[1]. The American Church has however a direct succession of Anglican Orders, for on Feb. 4, 1787, Samuel Provoost and William White were consecrated as bishops in Lambeth Chapel by John Moore, Archbishop of Canterbury. Subsequently James Madison was consecrated, and the succession thus made canonical. At a Convention of the Church in 1789 the American Book of Common Prayer, differing in some points from the Anglican, was adopted, and the Church entered on her independent career, under the judicious guidance of Bishop White, who for forty years took the lead in her councils. The Church is governed in accordance with a constitution and a body of canons drawn up by conventions which included bishops, other clergy, and laity. Its supreme authority, the General Convention, is composed of the House of Bishops, and the House of Deputies, clerical and lay. The assent of both Houses is required to give validity to any Act. The

[1] p. 71.

House of Bishops is composed of all the bishops of the Church, whether diocesan or missionary; and the House of Deputies consists of an equal number of clergy and laity, elected by regularly organized diocesan conventions. It also admits representatives of missionary jurisdictions. The Upper House is presided over by the bishop senior in consecration, who also has charge of various matters of administration. The Lower House elects its President by ballot. The General Convention meets triennially. In each diocese a Convention, composed of the parochial clergy with three lay delegates from each parish, meets annually. In some cases two or more dioceses have entered into a confederation for the purpose of dealing with special objects which affect those dioceses, but cannot conveniently be brought within the range of General or Diocesan Conventions.

The doctrine of the Church is to be found in the Apostles' and Nicene Creeds. The Athanasian Creed is not used, and in the Apostles' Creed, the recitation of the clause "He descended into Hell" is optional, as is also the use of the sign of the Cross in Baptism. The direct indicative form of absolution—"I absolve thee"—is not used in the office for the Visitation of the Sick, or elsewhere. The office for Holy Communion, which bears traces of the influence of the Scottish office, is generally regarded as having been modified by Bishop Seabury. In several other respects the American Prayer-Book differs from the Anglican Common Prayer, but not in any essential point.

Some dispute having arisen as to the use of the word "regeneration" in regard to Holy Baptism, the bishops of the Church in 1870 put forth a "Declaration" that the word "regenerate" is not so used in the Baptismal Office "as to determine that a moral change in the subject of baptism is wrought in the sacrament." Thirty-eight of the Articles of the Church of England are retained, with such modifications as are required to meet the new conditions under which they exist. These are not by any means universally approved, and their admission among the formularies was strongly opposed by Bishop Seabury, who had seen that the Scottish Church was reluctant to admit them.

All the phases of theological opinion which exist in the English Church, Evangelical, High, and Broad, are reflected in the American, but modified by national character and varying schools of thought. The *Tracts for the Times* were not without influence in the Church of the United States. As early as 1843 protests were made against the ordination of a young man, Arthur Carey, who considered the separation from Rome unjustifiable, and declared that he received the Articles of the Creed of Pius IV. so far as they were repetitions of the decrees of the Council of Trent. The protest was disregarded, and the High Church party continued to gain ground, while the Evangelical opposition to it acquired greater intensity. A clergyman in the diocese of Illinois went so far as to omit the word "regenerate" in the baptismal office. A movement was quietly set on foot for the revision of the Prayer-Book, which was seen to be of the nature of a compromise, and to contain some things which seemed to support views and practices of which the Evangelicals disapproved. Many remonstrances and suggestions were addressed to the General Convention of the Church. The feeling of unrest was brought to more vigorous expression by the following act of a conspicuous ecclesiastic. During a meeting of the Evangelical Alliance at New York in October, 1873, Bishop G. D. Cummins officiated at a communion of the various denominations represented in the Alliance. This gave much pain and offence to High Churchmen, and Bishop Cummins became aware that his views were not in harmony with those of his brethren generally. He came to the conclusion that he could no longer serve in the ministry of a Church in which the great majority were intolerant of such fraternizing with Christians outside the Church as that which he had practised, and he accordingly withdrew from it. The result was the formation of a "Reformed Episcopal Church[1]," to which, in the first instance, eight clergymen and twenty laymen gave their adhesion. Its distinctive features are that it does not recognize episcopacy as a distinct order, but only as an office; a bishop

Ch. VIII.
Church Parties.

Tractarian views.

Bishop Cummins.

Reformed Episcopal Church, 1873.

[1] *Memoir of G. D. Cummins*, by his Wife (New York, 1878); B. Ayerigg, *Memoirs of the Reformed Episcopal Church* (2nd ed., New York, 1882).

is simply a presiding presbyter. It expressly repudiates the doctrines that the Church of Christ exists only in one form or polity; that Christian ministers are "priests," except in the sense that all believers are "a royal priesthood"; that the Lord's Table is an altar; that in the Lord's Supper Christ is present in the elements of bread and wine; that regeneration is inseparably connected with Baptism. This Reformed Church soon found many adherents, and has now congregations in all the chief cities of the United States.

Congregationalists. The Congregationalists[1] are the natural successors of the religious emigrants who landed on American shores in 1620. The principle of the independence of congregations is so completely in harmony with the spirit of a people with whom religious observances are absolutely free, that it is not wonderful that it has a wide extension. The American Independents are not now fettered by the narrow views of their seventeenth-century predecessors, and differ little in doctrine from their English brethren.

Presbyterians. The Presbyterians[2] in America are of Scottish origin, and retain much of the deep interest in dogma and the practical energy of those from whom they sprang. They do not differ much in dogmatic views from the Congregationalists, but hold fast to their ancient organization and discipline through presbyteries composed of clerical and lay representatives. Doctrinal differences have however divided them into several parties.

Baptists. The Baptists[3] in America are very numerous, and active both in home-work and foreign missions. They are divided into many sects, of which it may suffice here to mention the most important, the Calvinistic or "Regular" Baptists, and the Arminian or "Free-Will" Baptists.

Methodists. Methodism[4] flourishes in America. We have seen[5] that,

[1] J. Punchard, *Congregationalism in America* (1880 f.); H. M. Dexter, *The Congregationalism of the Last 300 Years* (Lond. 1879).
[2] Roberts, *Hist. of the Presbyterian Church in the United States* (1888); Glasgow, *Hist. of the Reformed Presbyterian Church in America* (1888).
[3] T. Armitage, *Hist. of the Baptists* (St Louis, 1887); D. C. Haynes, *Hist. of the Baptist Denomination* (New York, 1875); G. H. Orchard, *Hist. of Foreign Baptists* (Nashville, 1858).
[4] Abel Stevens, *History of Methodism* (New York, 1858-9); P. D. Gorrie, *Hist. of the Methodist Episcopal Church in the United States* (N. Y. 1881).
[5] p. 188.

in 1784, John Wesley appointed Thomas Coke "bishop" or superintendent of the Wesleyan societies on that continent. This episcopacy however is not diocesan, but an "itinerant general superintendency," and the bishops are amenable to the body of ministers and preachers, who may divest them of their office. They are not regarded as a distinct order, but only as presbyters set apart for special functions. But many members of the Wesleyan society were dissatisfied with the episcopal form of government, and this feeling of dissatisfaction led at length, in 1830, to a secession, and to the formation of a new organization, called the "Methodist Protestant Church." The question of slavery again divided the Methodists, as many among them pronounced all slave-holding unlawful, and excluded slave-owners from Church membership and Christian fellowship. This led to a secession in 1843 which did not acquire any great importance; but in 1844 a far larger and more important secession took place, when the whole of the Methodist societies in the then slave-holding states, aggrieved by the treatment of one of their bishops by the General Conference, resolved to break off connexion with their Northern brethren. Hence originated the Methodist Episcopal Church of the South. A movement to reunite North and South after the abolition of slavery was unsuccessful.

Colour divides the Methodist body, as it does most American institutions. The conversion of the negroes born in America was largely due to the Methodists, but so strong is the prejudice of the white race against social intercourse with "niggers" that from an early date it was found expedient to provide for the black Methodists an organization of their own with separate places of worship. About a fourth part of the American Methodist congregations are said to be black.

The decorous and prosperous Quakers of North America have nothing in common with the fanatics of the seventeenth century except their doctrine of the inward light. Their principle of love to mankind naturally brought them to take a leading part in the struggle against slavery. Their reliance on the guidance of every man by

---

[1] For the literature, see pp. 66, n. 2, and 300, n. 1. Add Samuel J. Jauncey, *History of Friends* (New York, 1859 ff.).

the direct influence of the Holy Spirit led to the disparagement of outward authority, even that of Scripture itself. A Rationalist of a startling kind was Elias Hicks[1], who rejected the supreme authority of Scripture, and held that Jesus Christ, however filled with the Spirit, was still a natural man. The Yearly Meetings of London and Philadelphia in 1829 maintained the authority of Holy Scripture and disowned Hicks, upon which his followers formed a society of their own, commonly called Hicksites. On the other hand, the Society of "Evangelical Friends" maintained expressly that the inner light of individuals was to be tried by the standard of Scriptural revelation.

In America, as in England, many of the congregations which were in their origin Puritan and Calvinistic fell in later days under Unitarian influence. Unitarianism in America has also passed through a change not very different in character from that which has influenced it in England[2]. This change is very largely due to the influence of two very distinguished men. William Ellery Channing[3] was brought up among cultivated people of the ordinary Puritan type of that day, and himself became the pastor of a Calvinistic congregation in Boston. Here however he forsook Calvinism and joined the more liberal party of which in no long time he became the leader. But he distrusted sectarianism, he had no sympathy with the sharp dogmatism of Priestley, and "stood aloof from all but those who strive and pray for clearer light, who look for a purer and more effectual manifestation of Christian truth[4]." He found in Christ a perfect revealer of God to man, speaking with divine authority, and at the same time the ideal of humanity. He was a man of the most attractive character, and his influence has extended far beyond the society to which, though he said he was "little of a Unitarian," he outwardly belonged. He has been

---

[1] Hicks's *Journal* (New York, 1832), *Letters* (N.Y. 1834).
[2] J. H. Allen, *Our Liberal Movement in Theology* (Boston, 1882); J. F. Clarke, *Events and Epochs in Religious History* (Ib. 1881); O. B. Frothingham, *Boston Unitarianism, 1820—1850* (1890). See above, p. 307.
[3] *Memoir*, by W. H. Channing (London and Boston, 1848); Ch. de Remusat, *Channing, sa Vie, etc.* (1857); Renan, *Études d'Histoire Religieuse*, p. 357.
[4] *Memoir*, II. 380.

styled, with some appropriateness, the American Fénelon. Theodore Parker[1], who also began his career in Boston, while maintaining that Christ's teaching was that of the absolute and eternal religion, and that His character was the ideal of humanity, swept aside as exaggeration, myth, or fable all that claims to be supernatural in the Gospel narrative. To most of the Unitarian ministers in Boston these views appeared to transcend the bounds of permitted speculation, and their attitude led to his withdrawal from their body. He soon however made arrangements for an independent pastorate and drew round him numerous and earnest followers. At the present day it may be said that all American Unitarians are, consciously or unconsciously, disciples of Channing or of Parker. They are a very powerful body in Massachusetts, and especially in Boston, and exercise a dominant influence in the Harvard University.

Theod. Parker, 1810—1860.

1845.

The "United Society of Believers in Christ's Second Appearing" are commonly called "Shakers[2]" from the convulsive quivering which sometimes accompanies their devotional exercises. This was founded by an Englishwoman, Ann Lee, who received her first impulse towards an ecstatic form of religion from a small sect at Bolton in Lancashire, said to have originated from a party of French refugees from the Cevennes[3], about 1705. Ann joined this society, of which she became the leader, in 1758. Cruelly treated in England, she had a revelation that the foundations of Christ's Kingdom were to be laid in America, whither she went in 1774 with thirty believers. Here too the sect was not free from persecution, but about 1780 several Shaker Communities had been formed, of which the principal was that at New Lebanon in the state of New York, which still exists. Ann died in 1784, but the prophets of the society proclaimed that she had but put off the earthly and put on the heavenly, and "Mother Ann" became a kind of deity. In her life-time she had declared herself "the Bride, the Lamb's wife[4]." Her belief was developed by her followers. As Christ

The Shakers.

Ann Lee.

In America, 1774.

New Lebanon, 1780.

---

[1] *Life*, by Weiss (Boston, 1864); by Frothingham (New York, 1874).
[2] F. W. Evans, *The Shakers* (New York, 1859); and *Autobiography of a Shaker* (London, 1869).
[3] See above, p. 11.
[4] Rev. xxi. 9.

is the Son of the Eternal Father and Mother, so is she the daughter; as Christ is the second Adam, so is she the second Eve, and the spiritual mother of all believers. Mother Ann, herself a wife and mother, taught, and her followers maintain, that the strictest celibacy is essential to the perfect life. Only worldlings enter into the state of matrimony. They live together in communities of men and women as brothers and sisters, nor is any charge of impurity brought against them. They employ themselves generally in cultivating their gardens, from which they produce for sale flower-seeds and medicinal herbs. Their worship consists of music and song, dancing and making merry, followed by silent communion, and sermons. As no children are born to them, their communities are kept up solely by proselytes, whom they do not seek, and by waif and stray children whom they bring up. Their numbers do in fact diminish, but they retain their faith that the first heaven and earth are passing away, and a new heaven and a new earth being evolved out of the now chaotic elements.

Adventists, from 1833.

Reckoning the 2300 days of Daniel viii. 14 as so many years, William Miller[1] began in 1833 to proclaim that the coming of the Lord to judgment would take place in the night of Oct. 23, 1847. Many thousands accepted the message and awaited in the open air to hear the sound of the trumpet and to be caught up into the air to meet the Lord. In spite of the failure of their hopes the sect did not come to an end, but rather increased in numbers. An offshoot of it founded in Michigan by James White added to its belief in a speedy Advent the observance of a seventh-day Sabbath.

Seventh-Day Adventists.

Oneida Community. Noyes.

One of the strange phenomena of religious life in America was the Oneida Community. John H. Noyes, being present at a "Revival" meeting, was moved to the study of the Bible and to serious thought on religion. He came to the conclusion that Churches are of the devil, and that the only true Church is found in the hearts of individual believers, who are no more under the law, which is intended only for sinners. Such faithful

---

[1] Herzog, *Kirchengeschichte*, II. 704; Kurtz, *Lehrbuch der K.-G.*, II. ii. 292.

ones he felt himself called to gather into a Biblical family[1]. He made his attempt near Oneida, in the state of New York, where he acquired a tract of fertile land, and where the family abode in one large building, having every kind of possession, including wives and children, in common. Noyes however saw after a time that a community cannot exist without some law, and became aware that the community of wives was a cause of grievous offence to the outer world. He issued therefore a supplementary declaration, that, although the perfectionists are above law, yet it behoves the individual to submit to the sympathetic influence of the whole family. On the ground of "sympathy" monogamy was restored. They have always remained a very small community of industrious and skilful farmers.

One of the strange products of a time of mental and spiritual unrest is the so-called Christian Science[2]. In 1867 Mary Baker Eddy, a prominent lady in Boston, announced that she had re-discovered the true method of healing, as it had been practised by Jesus Himself. She renounced all medical treatment, for Jesus alone is the true physician. Full knowledge of God, communion with him in prayer, and acceptance of His guidance, will heal us of whatsoever disease we may have. God is holy, omnipotent and omnipresent; He wills no evil, consequently He wills not disease. Evil has no real existence; the only real existence is God. Whoever therefore lives in God recognizes the true nothingness of evil and so is freed from it. Further, such a person can again heal others, provided that they do not resist the divine influence. All this is wrought through Christ, who was manifested that He might destroy sin, sickness and death. In 1879 Mrs Eddy opened a meeting-house in Boston with a special form of worship, and so became the foundress of a sect. In accordance with her conception of religion, in the Sunday assemblies prayer is not generally in an audible voice, but passages are read from

Ch. VIII.
1847.

Christian Science.
Mrs Eddy, 1867.

Sect formed, 1879.

---

[1] J. H. Noyes, *Hist. of American Socialism* (Philadelphia, 1870); C. Nordhoff, *Communistic Societies of the U.S.A.* (London, 1875).
[2] The doctrines of this sect are to be found in Mrs Eddy's book, *Science and Health*, of which the first edition was published in 1875, the 114th in 1896.

the Bible and from Mrs Eddy's book, and hymns of praise are sung. It is not perhaps wonderful that the sect has many votaries in Europe as well as in America. The healing influence of the spirit on the body has been too much neglected, and the proclamation of it was grateful to the numerous souls who desired to rest in God and find all in Him; the souls who have in all ages delighted in some form of mysticism. Nor can it be doubted that many victims of over-excited nerves have been freed, by the soothing of inward tumult, from the real or imaginary disorders under which they laboured. The teaching that evil is not something real and positive, but only a privation, is of great antiquity; but that which was to such philosophers as Plato, Augustine, and Leibnitz, a metaphysical and abstract theory, is with Mrs Eddy physical and concrete. In this shape it is absurd, but its absurdity is not evident to the thousands of her votaries. Logical contradictions have never hindered the spread of teaching which appeals to feeling and imagination.

One of the most astonishing phenomena to be found in all history is the rise of the Mormon sect, in the full light of the nineteenth century. Joseph Smith, its founder, was born in the state of Vermont in 1805. In 1823, while still a boy, he claimed to have received an angelic visit, and thenceforth to have been guided by visions, voices, and angels. He may have been subject to hallucinations, but the fact that in 1826 he was convicted of fraud in connexion with treasure-seeking[2] casts suspicion upon his claim to divine guidance. In 1830 he printed a romance called the *Book of Mormon*, which tells a wonderful story of things before unheard of. In a remote antiquity a portion of the Ten Tribes of Israel landed

---

[1] Jules Remy and J. Brenchley, *Journey to the Great-Salt-Lake City, with Hist. of the Mormons* (London, 1861); R. F. Burton, *The City of the Saints* (London, 1861); H. Caswell, *The Prophet of the Nineteenth Century* (London, 1843); Pomeroy Tucker, *The Origin and Progress of the Mormons* (New York, 1867); [C. Mackay], *The Mormons or Latter-Day Saints* (London, n.d.). Of Mormon publications may be mentioned—Lucy Smith, *Biogr. of Joseph Smith* (Liverpool, 1853); Orson Pratt, *A Series of Pamphlets* (Liverpool, 1851); Parley Pratt, *Key to the Science of Theology* (Ib. 1877); Franklin D. Richards, *Compendium of Faith* (Ib. 1857).

[2] The depositions of the witnesses in this case are given in the Herzog-Schaff *Encyclop.*, p. 1576.

on the shores of America, where they divided into a pious and a godless tribe. About four hundred years after Christ the godless annihilated the pious, with the exception of the prophet Mormon and his son Moroni. These men before their death hid in a cave the record of the history of this people, and of the revelation which they had received, graven on plates of gold, for a testimony to the pious or "saints" who should arise in the latter day. These plates Smith claimed to have discovered in 1827, together with two transparent stones of magical power[1] which enabled him to read and translate the unknown language of the inscription on the plates. The plates themselves vanished and were seen no more. That all this is pure fiction admits of no doubt, but it is probably not an original invention of Smith's, who seems to have been an illiterate person. It appears to have been taken almost entirely from an unpublished romance by one Solomon Spaulding[2], a Presbyterian preacher of Western Pennsylvania. How this came into Smith's possession is unknown, but it seems probable that it was through the intervention of Sidney Rigdon, a printer turned preacher, who joined him and became his right-hand man. Rigdon was older, abler, and better educated than Smith, and played a great part in the early history of Mormonism. A later publication, the *Book of Doctrine and Covenants*, contains the multifarious revelations which Smith claimed to have received, with one put forth by Brigham Young in 1847 to encourage the saints in their painful pilgrimage to the West. From the time of the publication of the *Book of Mormon* followers came round the new prophets in ever-increasing numbers. Driven from their first settlement in Ohio by the hostility of their neighbours, who resented the claim of the Saints to inherit the earth in a literal sense, they emigrated into Missouri, and thence again into Illinois, where they built a large town, called Nauvoo, with a splendid temple. They prospered, but they were still pursued by the hatred of the surrounding

Spaulding's Romance.

'Book of Doctrine and Covenants.'

Nauvoo, 1838.

---

[1] It may be observed that he used a stone, through which he professed to see things not visible to ordinary sight, in his treasure-seeking.

[2] This rests mainly on the testimony of Spaulding's widow. The question, however, whether Smith and Rigdon were plagiarists is not of much importance.

Ch. VIII.

Murder of Smith, 1844.

Brigham Young, 1801—1877.
1847.

Salt Lake City.

population, who charged them with all kinds of crime and immorality. There Joseph Smith and his brother Hiram were placed by the civil authority in custody at Carthage, near Nauvoo, pending an investigation; the gaol was broken open by a furious mob and the brothers were shot dead. The martyr-like death of Smith threw a halo round his character and history which gave a great impulse to the spread of his teaching. The guidance of the sect fell into the hands of Brigham Young, a man of great ability and force of character, who determined to settle the Saints in some spot where an uninhabited country should afford them space for peaceful development. In 1847, with a band of one hundred and forty-two pioneers, he pushed resolutely westward, and on July 24 arrived in the valley of the Great Salt Lake, in the district called Utah. In the following year he led four thousand of the faithful to the same spot. There arose a large and prosperous community, and there a city was built where Brigham Young reigned for nearly thirty years, with the authority of king and priest. The fundamental doctrines of the Mormon society, as given by Joseph Smith, are as follows. " We believe in God the eternal Father, and his Son Jesus Christ, and in the Holy Ghost. We believe that men will be punished for their own sins and not for Adam's transgression. We believe that through the atonement of Christ all men may be saved, by obedience to the laws and ordinances of the Gospel. We believe that these ordinances are (1) Faith in the Lord Jesus Christ, (2) Repentance, (3) Baptism by immersion for the remission of sins, (4) Laying on of hands for the gift of the Holy Ghost[1]." There is much more on the subject of the orders of the ministry, the gifts of the Spirit, and the like, in which the prophet claims to have maintained those of the primitive Church. On the face of it, this creed is one which many Christians would accept. In fact, the Mormon belief is materialistic and polytheistic. " The Father has a body of flesh and bones as tangible as man's; the Son also; but the Holy Ghost has not a body of flesh and

---

[1] This is given as it is printed by Remy, II. 20, but it is found in numerous Mormon publications.

bones." These are Joseph Smith's words[1]. His disciples have developed a curious polytheism. There exists an infinity of gods with a chief god at their head. The gods have a body like our own, and wives as we have. These are the queens of heaven, who have existed from all eternity, and are mothers of gods by a process quite unlike human procreation of children. Since the Head of the gods has begotten Jesus Christ and other gods, he must have had wives. The Holy Spirit is a subtle form of matter, which penetrates the pores of the most solid substances, and moves through space with inconceivable rapidity.

There are two orders of priesthood. To the order of Melchizedek belongs the right of presidency, that is, power and authority in spiritual things over the Mormon community in all parts of the world. It may also exercise the functions of the inferior order, the Aaronic or Levitical priesthood, which has the right and the power to execute temporal ordinances. The Presidency of the society consists of a prophet-president with two counsellors. Under the Presidency are the Twelve, or council of travelling officers, to whom it belongs to build up and establish the society in all parts of the world; the Seventy, whose duty it is to preach and testify to those who are without, called Gentiles; and a council of high-priests. The orders recognized as essential to the well-being of the sect are bishops, elders, teachers, and deacons. But during the reign of Brigham Young, all orders and all officials bent to his imperious will. Certain mystic rites are practised, called "endowments," of the real nature of which nothing is authentically known, and which are therefore said to be irreverent and blasphemous. Funds for public purposes are obtained by a tithe of all property and income.

Endowments.

An unavowed engine of the central power was a secret band of "Danites" or "Destroying Angels," who at the beck and call of the prophet were ready to crush the smallest symptom of disaffection by removing the offender, and to prevent the entrance into the territory of those who were unacceptable to him. To these fanatics is attributed

Danites.

---

[1] Quoted by Remy, II. 25, from Smith's sermon of 2 April, 1843.

the atrocious massacre in 1857 of a caravan of emigrants on their way to California[1], and also the dastardly murder of Dr J. K. Robinson in Salt Lake City in 1866.

Polygamy avowed, 1852.

The relations of the Mormon community with the government of the United States do not here concern us, except so far as they relate to the sanction of polygamy. In 1852 the permission of polygamy, given by a supplemental revelation to Smith in 1843, but hitherto concealed from the Gentiles, was avowed. Only a woman who had been "sealed" to a Latter-Day Saint could hope for felicity in the world to come. Up to the year 1862 it may be said that polygamy was not a direct violation of any statute, but in that year Congress passed a law prohibiting polygamy in all Territories of the United States, including, of course, Utah. This law had however little effect, and in 1882 an Act, the Edmunds Act, was passed, making it an offence punishable by fine and imprisonment for a man to marry more than one wife, and this was vigorously enforced. It was no doubt a consequence of this that in 1887 a convention of Mormons, of whom the vast majority were monogamic, adopted a constitution for Utah which contained a clause prohibiting and punishing polygamy. Following this, the Mormon president Woodruff in 1890 issued a proclamation declaring that the Mormon society no longer teaches the doctrine of polygamy or plural marriages. Congress had steadfastly rejected the repeated applications of Utah to be admitted as one of the United States, on the ground that in its secret assemblies engagements were entered into incompatible with a true allegiance to the central government. At last, having convinced the authorities of its loyalty, the Territory of Utah was admitted, 4 July, 1896, as the forty-fifth State of the great Republic.

Polygamy forbidden, 1862, again, 1882,

abandoned by Mormons, 1890.

Utah admitted as a State, 1896.

Missionaries.

The Mormons soon began to send out missionaries far and wide, who had considerable success on the continent of Europe, and even more in Great Britain and the Scandinavian countries. The promise of new social conditions was alluring to those who attributed the hardships of their toilsome life to the evil customs of an old society;

[1] The evidence for this was produced on the trial in 1877 of John D. Lee, who was convicted and executed for participation in this massacre.

the Mormons offered the means of emigration to the discontented, and crowds of serviceable workers emigrated to Utah. *Ch. VIII.*

With all their fanaticism, the Mormons seem to be a very prosperous community. They have their schisms, of which the world knows little, but these do not seriously shake the firm constitution of their society. The settlement, with its peculiar laws, has now been so long established that probably few of its members look back to the strange transactions in which the society began. *Prosperity.*

Roman Catholics have been found in the United States since the early years of the seventeenth century, often under considerable oppression in consequence of the generally Puritan sentiment of the population. After the Declaration of Independence, the Vicar Apostolic of London virtually ceased to exercise the control over American Roman Catholics which had previously belonged to his office. Their number was constantly increased by immigration from Europe, and with the immigrants came priests, not always of the highest character. There was, in fact, a period of ecclesiastical chaos. When John Carroll was appointed Prefect Apostolic in 1786 order began to be established. Three years later he was consecrated, in England, Bishop of Baltimore, and in that capacity held the synod of Baltimore, which enacted the first body of canons for the Church in the United States. This code, supplemented by certain rules of the bishops in 1810, remained in force until the assembling of the first Provincial Council of Baltimore by Archbishop Whitfield in 1829, under the sanction of Pope Leo XII. Several Councils have since been held, many sees created, and the organization of the Church extended as it has grown in numbers and importance. The immigrants from Ireland, from Italy, and from South Germany, belong almost wholly to the Roman Communion. It is probable that Roman Catholics form about a ninth part of the whole population of the States, and their unity and common action in matters relating to religion and education give *Roman Catholic Church [1]. / J. Carroll, Prefect, 1786. / Synod of Baltimore, 1791.*

---

[1] De Courcy, *The Catholic Church in the United States* (1879); Le Clercq, *The Establishment of the Faith* (New York, 1881). There is a list of works on particular portions of the R. C. Church in the U. S. in the Herzog-Schaff *Encyclop.*, p. 2067.

them a political influence even greater than their millions could claim. In almost every large town splendid churches testify to the devotion of a community which consists to a great extent of the poor.

But even the Roman Catholic Church feels the disintegrating effect of the moral and intellectual atmosphere in the midst of which it exists[1]. Large as are its numbers in the States, if all the Roman Catholic immigrants and their descendants had continued in the faith of their fathers they would have been much larger. And within the Church intellectual movements arise indicating a longing for greater freedom of thought and action than it has generally conceded. For example, Isaac Thomas Hecker, an earnest and religious man born in America of German parents, after searching for truth among the various Christian sects, believed that he had found it in the Roman Church. But he was still restless; he was unable to accept without question an archaic and perhaps obsolete type of religion; he protested against what he considered the undue suppression of individuality by the Roman Church, and believed that the only hope for the growth of that Church in a free community was to adapt its teaching to the spirit of the age. The direct effect of Hecker's teaching was not great, nor did any great result follow the labours of the Paulists, an order which he founded; but they are nevertheless important as indicating a trend of thought among devout well-wishers of the Church. But when such men as Cardinal Gibbons, Archbishop Ireland, and Bishop Spalding, frankly endeavoured to get rid of a past which is out of harmony with the present; when they made known their disapproval of acts and words of popes and prelates of the Middle Ages, and acknowledged that, though the essential articles of the faith are immutable, yet "the thoughts of men are widened with the process of the suns"; it was evident that the modern spirit wrought on the minds even of men in high place. At last, the progress of "Americanism" attracted the notice of the Papal Curia, and Leo XIII. addressed a letter to Cardinal Gibbons in which it was explicitly condemned. No ignoring or softening of

---

[1] Abbé Houtin, *L'Américanisme* (Paris, 1904); John A. Bain, *The New Reformation*, ch. xxv. (Edinburgh, 1906).

mediæval dogma, no insistence on the sufficiency for individuals of the guidance of the Holy Spirit, or on natural rather than supernatural virtues as fitted for the time, was to be tolerated. No sooner had this Encyclical reached America than the heads of the Church there submitted, and protested that they had never taught the errors which it condemned. Much discussion followed the decision of the Pope, with the inevitable result that the conservatives triumphed. Romanism and aspiration after spiritual liberty cannot exist together.

CHAPTER IX.

THE PAPACY AND THE VATICAN COUNCIL.

Pius VII. returns to Rome, 1814.

1. THE cessation of the Napoleonic despotism was naturally the signal for attempts at the restoration of the Catholic Church everywhere to the position which it occupied before the French Empire arose. Pius VII.[1] not only regained his throne on the Vatican as an independent ruler, but also received back from the Congress of Vienna the ancient possessions of the See, with the exception of Avignon and a narrow strip of territory beyond the Po. Consalvi, the Pope's all-powerful minister, publicly expressed his thankfulness that the French rule had introduced into the Papal States unity of administration. The feudal rights of the nobles, and exemptions and privileges of various kinds, remained abolished, and the centralized system was continued, but with prelates instead of laymen for its chief officials. The inhabitants of the States of the Church, however, preferred the rule of the marshal's baton to that of the pastoral staff. The lay-people found themselves thrust into the background, and the government of priests supported by police was harsh and inquisitorial. This was so deeply felt that in 1816 and 1817 there were attempts at insurrection. The secret society of "Carbonari," formed about 1808 to oppose despotic government of any kind, grew in numbers and importance, and those who cherished patriotic views saw in the temporal power of the Pope a greater hindrance

Feudalism not restored.

Carbonari, 1808.

[1] B. Pacca, *Memorie* (1833), trans. by G. Head (London, 1850); E. Cipoletta, *Memorie di Conclavi di Pio VII. a Pio IX.*; G. Giucci, *Storia di Pio VII.* (Rome, 1857); E. Henke, *Pius VII.* (Stuttg. 1862); B. Gams, *Geschichte der Kirche im 19 Jahrhdt* (1853); F. Nippold, *Handbuch der Neuesten K. Geschichte*, Band II. (Elberfeld, 1883); L. C. Farini, *Lo Stato Romano* (Firenze, 1850-1), trans. by W. E. Gladstone, *The Roman State*, 1815— 1850 (London, 1851-4).

to Italian unity than even in the Austrian dominion. Meantime, the friends of the Pope were not altogether of one mind, but were divided into two parties. The Zelanti were for restoring the old state of things exactly as it existed before the time of Napoleon. The Liberals, following Consalvi, did not wish to bring back the Middle Ages. *Ch. IX.* *Zelanti.*

The Pope was no doubt at heart very well satisfied with the concessions of Vienna, which were much more favourable to him than could have been expected; but the traditional policy of the Papal See nevertheless compelled him to protest, not only against the withholding of the territory on the Po and the occupation of the fortress of Ferrara by Austria, but also against the dissolution of the Roman Empire. The assembled representatives at Vienna did not, however, extend their complaisance so far as to comply with the Pope's wishes. He had enough to occupy his mind in the restoration of the old hierarchical institutions and the status of the Pontiff. To bring back the Church into a stable order after the tremendous shocks which it had everywhere experienced was indeed a task which might well appal him. He soon made it plain in what spirit he intended to set about his vast undertaking. His first important act after his return to Rome was the restoration of the Jesuits. *Papal Protest.*

2. On the 7th of August, 1814, the Pope proceeded with great pomp to the Church of the Jesuits, said a Mass there at the altar of St Ignatius, and afterwards caused to be read in the presence of many cardinals and bishops, and about fifty Jesuits who had come over with their Provincial from Sicily, the Bull *Sollicitudo omnium ecclesiarum*[1], by which the Order was restored to its former constitution and to all the privileges which it had enjoyed under earlier Popes. His Holiness declared in the Bull that he believed that he would commit a grievous sin if, in the midst of the storms which raged round the Bark of St Peter, he failed to bring back to it the powerful and experienced rowers who were capable of bringing it successfully through the waves which every instant threatened its destruction. The Catholic world (he said) with one voice demanded the restoration of the Society of Jesus, *Jesuits Restored 1814.*

[1] 2 Cor. xi. 28 Vulgate.

and almost daily he received letters from archbishops, bishops, and other distinguished persons imploring him to take steps for this end. On the very day of their restoration the Jesuits received back the three palaces which they had possessed in Rome, and in the following years very liberal subventions were granted to them for the founding of colleges in the principal cities of the papal territory.

Indignation at the Restoration.

That which the infallible Clement XIV. had dissolved, and declared for ever incapable of restoration, the infallible Pius VII. nevertheless restored. How eagerly the Christian world desired the restoration of the Jesuits was soon evident in the anger and indignation with which the tidings of it were received in Austria, Germany, France, and the Netherlands. Portugal and Brazil protested. But the thing was done, and those who guided the policy of Rome knew very well that while an act remains, the indignation which it has at first caused dies out. In the States of the Church, in Modena, in Naples and in Spain the houses of the Order were re-opened in 1815. It was comparatively unimportant that the nation which had given the Jesuits a refuge in their time of trial now refused it.

Russia.

Russia had received them, and had not interfered with their efforts to convert Jews and Protestants; but when they attempted the conversion of orthodox Russians, and actually converted the young Princess Galitzin; when they carried on their propaganda in the army and reviled the Bible Society; an edict in 1820 banished them from all parts of the Empire.

Effects of restored Jesuitism.

The revival of the Company of Jesus was soon felt throughout the Roman Church. As in former days, they took charge, wherever it was possible, of education. "Freedom of Catholic instruction" was the watchword which they everywhere opposed to the claims of the civil government to regulate both primary and secondary teaching. They succeeded in possessing themselves of many seminaries and theological colleges. The sons of the higher classes were attracted into their boarding-schools, where they were sedulously imbued with ultramontane principles, while sisterhoods under Jesuit influence undertook the education of girls. The Order did not perhaps produce many men of original genius, but it had among its members many distinguished in the exact sciences, such as astronomy, whose high repute gave a certain lustre to their more commonplace brethren. In the region of history, they continued the great work, the *Acta Sanctorum*, which was begun so far back as 1643, and found industrious successors of the old Bollandists to give their strenuous labour to it. Jesuit morality seems to be in this later period the same as it had ever been. Father Gury published a *Compendium of Moral Theology*[1] for the use of confessors which again brought into prominence the casuistry, especially the probabilism, against which Pascal had inveighed[2], and treated at length and in detail subjects on which modest men are silent. Giovanni Perrone, in his *Theological Lectures*, produced a work covering the whole field of dogma, of which it may be said, as Bossuet said of Bellarmine, that it had more weight at Rome than the whole of Apostolic tradition. Perrone was a man of great ability and learning, and in one respect is unsurpassed—his power of expressing contempt for the Reformers and the Reformation. The very word "Reformation," he says, ought to cause a good Catholic to shudder as at the mention of a great crime; Protestantism he calls a pestilence and its adherents a pack of scoundrels. The freedom of scientific research in Germany was seriously hampered by the Jesuits, and the theological faculties found it difficult to resist their attacks.

But it was not through learned treatises that the influence of the Jesuits made itself most felt. They everywhere sought, and often gained, influence over the princes and rulers of the world. On missions—efforts made by a band of chosen men to revive the spiritual life in a particular district—Jesuits were commonly prominent and successful workers, and Jesuit preachers were found who could attract not only the people at large, but even the careless denizens of the fashionable quarters.

They were not now commonly in opposition to other Orders; rather, they may almost be said to have subdued them. The Redemptorists after 1773 had received many Jesuits into their ranks, and now that the Jesuits were

---

[1] On this book, see Döllinger and Reusch, *Geschichte der Moral-Streitigkeiten in der R. K. Kirche*, vol. I. (1889).
[2] See above, p. 77.

renewing their youth, became almost dependent upon them. Their old opponents, the Dominicans, were reconciled, walking thenceforth in the ways of the Jesuits; and new allies were found in the Congregations of the Sacred Heart and the Tertiaries of the Franciscans. The Benedictines, indeed, were too great and powerful a body to fall openly under Jesuit sway, but even they were quietly influenced. There were some houses of the Order of St Basil in Galicia, and the Ruthenian monks were greatly respected by the members of the Orthodox Greek Church in that district. Here skilful management brought it about that in 1882 the Basilian monasteries were handed over to the Jesuits. The result of their energetic work has been that the history of modern Romanism is the history of the Jesuits. The "Black Pope," the General of the Order, stands at the right hand of the actual occupant of the Papal throne, and his ten thousand subordinates are everywhere active.

3. Pius VII. died in 1823, after a reign of twenty-three years, the troubles of which he had borne with exemplary patience. His successor, Annibale Della Genga, the candidate of the Zelanti, who had been as cardinal a declared enemy of the Jesuits, became, as Pope, their supporter. To them he entrusted the charge of the Collegium Romanum, and therewith an immense influence on the education of the clergy. The work of Consalvi, who was a liberal in the Roman sense, was so far as possible undone under Leo XII., who even wished to restore the abolished feudalism. He called upon Catholics to celebrate in 1825 a solemn jubilee, and to make pilgrimages to Rome, not only to pray for the extermination of heresies, but to give thanks to God for the victory which He had given them over the conspiracies of recent times against truth and right—a thanksgiving which was, perhaps, premature. In the same year he beatified the Spanish Minorite Julian, on whose behalf miracles were brought forward by his advocate which even good Catholics thought childish. More important matters were that he brought the Church in the South American Republics, which had shaken off the yoke of Spain, into connexion with the See of St Peter,

[1] Artaud de Montor, *Hist. de Léon XII.* (Paris, 1843).

and that he concluded, by the Bull of 1827, the negotiations for Concordats with the smaller German States, which had been long under discussion. He remonstrated with the French Government because Protestant temples and worshippers received privileges which, he thought, ought to be reserved for Catholics; and from the King of Naples he demanded the renewal of the tribute of a palfrey, by which in former days he had acknowledged the Pope his feudal suzerain. The condemnation of Bible Societies, and of philosophers who taught tolerance in matters of faith, marked the spirit of his reign. He seems to have been a well-meaning man without much tact or ability, out of harmony with the age in which he lived. His enforcing of religious duties by the aid of the police was disliked by all classes, and he became a very unpopular ruler.

4. On the death of Leo XII., the choice of the Conclave fell on Francesco Castiglione, the candidate favoured by Austria and France. He, like other Pontiffs, condemned secret societies, which were commonly supposed to be republican and atheistic. He also declared Bible Societies impious and heretical. The proceeding which reflects most credit on his short reign is his wish to check nepotism, which led him to forbid his own kindred to come to Rome. He had nearly attained the age of threescore-and-ten when he ascended the Papal throne, and the labours and anxieties of his high office, to which he devoted himself with conscientious assiduity, soon exhausted his failing strength.

The Conclave which followed the death of Leo took place in the midst of the agitation which followed on the French Revolution of July, when Charles X. was driven from his throne. The choice of the cardinals fell on Mauro Cappellari, who in time of trouble and darkness had prophesied the triumph of the Holy See, and now as Gregory XVI.[2] saw it, outwardly at least, triumphant. He had been Prefect of the Propaganda, and as Pope he did not forget his old experience, but promoted its

Ch. IX.

Pius VIII.[1], 31 *March*, 1829, *to* 1 *Dec.* 1830.

Gregory XVI. elected, *Feb.* 2, 1831.

---

[1] Artaud de Montor, *Hist. du Pape Pie VIII.* (Paris, 1844).
[2] N. Wiseman, *Recollections of the Last Four Popes* [*Leo XII.,* *Pius VIII., Gregory XVI., Pius IX.*]; Wagner, *Gregor XVI.* (Sulzburg, 1846).

work by every means in his power. In his reign of fifteen years he founded thirty new sees, presided over by Vicars Apostolic, and fifteen missionary bishoprics. In his relations with kings and rulers he asserted the claims of the Papacy vigorously and often successfully. In France, Louis Philippe, the King of the barricades, was as anxious as Napoleon had been to secure the support of the Church. In Prussia the Pope gained his point in the question of mixed marriages. To the freedom of the press and of scientific teaching he was an inveterate enemy, but to repress the thoughts of men was a task beyond his powers. His reign as a temporal prince was a disturbed one. In the very year of his accession insurrections broke out in the Legations and the March of Ancona, which were not put down without the help of Austrian troops, while in the following year the French, uninvited and against the Pope's protest, seized Ancona, which they did not relinquish until 1838, Austria vacating Bologna at the same time. But the fiery desire for liberty still glowed under the ashes; a guerilla warfare went on from 1843 to 1845, when it was quenched in blood by the Swiss troops in the Pope's service, aided by a band of truculent volunteers. Meantime, secret societies, especially the Carbonari, honeycombed all Italy, filling the minds of the young Italians with hatred for the foreign yoke which held in subjection so large a portion of their country, and for the temporal sovereignty of the Pope. A memorandum of the European Powers had in 1831 requested the Pope to reform his administration, and some of the suggested reforms had been carried out; but the Secretary of State, Lambruschini, positively refused to entertain the notion of liberal institutions, and the Pope himself declared that constitutional government was incompatible with the existence of the Papacy. The situation grew more and more critical, and the most distinguished Catholic laymen saw the need of reform. In 1846, the year of Gregory's death, there were in the Papal prisons two thousand political prisoners, the public debt had been doubled, and there was an annual deficit in the revenue. But however poor the State might be, the Pope's kindred and favourites had grown rich. When the Pope died, no signs of popular mourning accompanied his funeral.

5. After a Conclave which lasted only two days, Mastai Ferretti, Bishop of Imola, was chosen Pope in the room of Gregory, and took the title of Pius IX.[1] Rarely has the choice of a Pope been greeted with so hearty a popular approval. He was known as a man of genial disposition and courteous manners, with adequate firmness of character, and it was hoped that he was sufficiently in sympathy with the wants of the time to join the party of progress. His handsome and still vigorous person, for he was but fifty-four years of age, helped to make him a popular favourite. And in the early years of his reign he deserved the favour with which he was received. His kindly and familiar bearing and his aversion from needless pomp and formality won for him general acceptance, all the more as he let it be seen that he was by no means averse to all reform. Every one looked forward with confidence to a general amnesty for the political offenders whom his predecessor had left in captivity or banishment, and when on the 16th July the decree of amnesty was published, there broke out a general cry of joy. It produced an excellent state of feeling among the people, but it made a very different impression on persons in high place, and in Rome itself the ecclesiastical conservative party thought such a beginning of the reign highly dangerous. But the Pope went on in the way of reform, beginning with a considerable reduction in the expenses of his own household. He gave the press greater freedom, strengthened the already existing commission on law and law-courts by the addition of experienced and trustworthy members, favoured the introduction of railways, made the higher offices of State tenable by laymen, resolved to raise a contribution to the State from the monasteries within his territory, made a beginning in municipal reform by giving to the city of Rome a liberal constitution, and even put arms in the hands of the Romans by the formation of a civic guard; he sum-

Ch. IX. Pius IX. elected, 16 June, 1846.

Amnesty, 16 July, 1846.

Reforms of Pius IX.

---

[1] Legge, A. O., *Pius IX., his Life to* 1850 (Lond. 1875); J. F. Maguire, *Rome, its Ruler, etc.* (Lond. 1857; new ed. 1878); C. de Montalembert, *Pius IX. and France* (Eng. trans. 1859); F. Clavé, *Vie et Portrait de Pie IX.* (1848); Godde de Liancourt, *Pius IX.* (1847); A. Gallenga, *The Pope and the King* (1879); T. A. Trollope, *Story of the Life of Pius IX.* (Lond. 1877); W. Arthur, *The Modern Jove* (Lond. 1873); *The Pope, the King, and the People* (1877).

moned from the provinces men in whom the people had confidence to be members of the Council of State, contemplated disbanding the Swiss troops, and began to take measures for the formation of a confederacy of the Italian States. He wished to abolish the restriction of the Jews to the hateful Ghetto, but here the opposition of the Christian population was so vehement that his intentions could not be carried out. A number of the clergy frankly were on the side of the Holy Father, and the eloquent preacher, Joachim Ventura, proclaimed the reconciliation of Catholic piety with political liberty. Even the Jesuits declared themselves friends of progress. The ideal of the banished Gioberti, the Pope as the head of a federation of the Italian princes, with national independence and civil freedom, seemed on the point of being realized.

Discontent in Rome.

But it was impossible that the Pope's schemes of reform should satisfy all parties. The old officials, especially those whose offices were abolished, were of course angry, and formed, either openly or covertly, a powerful opposition. On the other hand, those eager patriots who had been liberated from prison or brought back from exile, found the Pope's concessions altogether inadequate. The leader of this party was Mazzini, an honest enthusiast who his whole life long laboured for the creation of a free, independent, and united nation of Italians. The French Revolution of February, 1848, gave a great impetus to revolutionary movements in Italy. Risings took place in almost all the Italian States from Lombardy to Sicily, and the Roman Liberals judged that the time was come for them also to take action. They roused the people by their fiery oratory, and turbulent mobs pressed the Pope to make further concessions. In particular, they urged him to summon all Italy to a crusade against the Austrian domination. It was to no purpose that the Pope granted a constitution, including a nominated and an elected Chamber, which should have authority over legislation and taxation, and appointed a ministry favourable to reform; new disturbances arose, and his refusal to engage in war with Austria was made the pretext for forcing upon him the revolutionary ministry of Mamiani. This, however, did not endure long. The Pope dismissed Mamiani, and entrusted the conduct of the government

Democratic Movements.

Constitution of 14 March, 1848.

to Count Pellegrino Rossi, who was prepared to employ vigorous measures for the restoration of order, and at the same time to proceed steadily with constitutional reforms. But Rossi was assassinated as he ascended the steps of the Capitol to open the Chamber of Deputies, and there followed threatening deputations to the Pope, demanding a democratic ministry, recognition of a united Italy, war against Austria, and the summoning of a national Constituent Assembly. The Pope, who had become virtually a prisoner, deeply mortified and disillusioned, fled in disguise to the small fortress of Gaeta, in the Neapolitan territory. *Rossi assassinated, 15 Nov. 1848.*

The Pope flies to Gaeta, 24 Nov. 1848.

The Mazzinists now formed a Provisional Government and summoned a National Assembly, which on Feb. 9, 1849, declared the temporal sovereignty of the Pope at an end, and a few days later passed a law declaring all ecclesiastical lands to be the property of the State. A period of great disturbance followed. The victory of the Austrian troops over the Piedmontese at Novara put an end for the present to all hopes of Italian unity; the Pope from Gaeta called upon the Catholic powers to intervene; the French Republic sent an overwhelming force which took possession of Rome, bravely defended by Garibaldi, on July 3, while the Austrians invaded the Legations. From this time a Commission of three Cardinals, named by the Pope, administered the city and territory of Rome under the protection of the French. On Sept. 12 the Pope, still in Gaeta, issued a letter promising reform in finance and administration, and a few days later an amnesty, which was, however, so clogged with exceptions as to leave ample room for the persecution of those who had taken part in the rebellion. When at last Pius returned to Rome, the diplomatic corps assured him that the various governments which they represented hailed the return of His Holiness to his States as a happy omen and an important step towards the restoration of order, which was so important for the welfare of the nations and the maintenance of peace. The old state of things was soon resumed in Rome and its dependencies. A regular ministry was named, of which Cardinal Antonelli, as Secretary of State, was the ruling spirit. Public instruction was again put into the hands of the Jesuits. *Mazzinist Government.*

French in Rome.

Pope's return to Rome, 12 Apr. 1850.

6. Meantime, the thoughts of the friends of Italian unity were directed towards Piedmont, where King Victor Emmanuel[1], under the influence of Gioberti, entered on a path of reform which satisfied the leading men not only of his own territories but of all Italy. The Jesuits were expelled with the hearty assent of the people. The equality of all citizens before the law was made a fundamental principle, and this involved the abolition of the privilege of the clergy to be tried by their own courts even in civil and criminal cases. Civil marriage was instituted. Religious foundations lost their exemption and the right of asylum. The Archbishop of Turin, Fransoni, who in a Pastoral Letter had violently protested against the diminution of the privileges of the Church, was summoned before a civil tribunal, and when he refused to appear was found guilty of contempt of court and sent into exile. The Pope commended him as a martyr for conscience' sake, and denounced the legislation which violated the rights of the Church as set forth in many Concordats. The Piedmontese replied that Concordats were not of the nature of treaties made between two sovereign powers, but concessions made by the State to the Church within its own territories, which might at any time be recalled by the supreme legislative authority of the country. An Act of 1854 abolished all Orders which did not justify their existence by preaching, education, or care of the sick, and generally confiscated sinecures. The surplus which remained after providing for the Orders and Institutions which were left was paid into an ecclesiastical treasury for the improvement of small benefices. The Pope pronounced his anathema on such laws, and the agitation of the clergy against the recent legislation, especially against civil marriage; against the courts of justice which, in consequence of their proceedings against the clergy, had been excommunicated; against professors in the University who were not members of the Church; against those clergymen who ventured to obey the Government; and against what they called

---

[1] C. Arrivabene, *Italy under Victor Emmanuel* (Lond. 1862); A. Gallenga, *The Pope and the King* (1879); Georgina S. Godkin, *Life of Victor Emm.* (1879); E. Dicey, *Cavour, a Memoir* (Camb. 1861), *Victor Emm.* (Lond. 1882).

the Protestantizing and Unchristianizing of the State, kept up a constant disturbance, which sometimes broke out into armed violence.

At Rome, during the time when the French and Austrians were in possession of the country, some improvements were undoubtedly made in the papal administration. Still, the prisons were filled, the press was subject to a very severe censorship, moderate counsels were rejected, and, in short, the States were subject to an unmerciful despotism. It is not wonderful that the old complaints of the incapacity and unscrupulousness of sacerdotal rule were renewed. The agitation became more intense when Count Cavour, the very able minister of the King of Sardinia, declared himself on the side of constitutional government and against the Austrian dominion in Italy. He concluded a secret treaty with the French Emperor, who, on New Year's Day, 1859, made the famous speech to the Austrian Ambassador, which informed Europe that war between France and Austria was impending. The Austrians were defeated at Magenta and at Solferino by the combined forces of France and Sardinia. Still, Napoleon and Cavour desired to preserve the temporal sovereignty of the Pope, though the Romagna, Umbria, and the Marches were taken from him, and his territory reduced to about a third of its former magnitude, while even this was only retained by the aid of French bayonets. The Pope anathematized the sacrilegious invaders of his territory, and declared that he could in no case resign any portion of the Patrimony of St Peter. It is perhaps not surprising that, after his very ill success as a reformer, he refused to countenance any further reforms. A swarm of pamphlets directed attention to the wretched condition of the States of the Church, and urged the necessity of satisfying the aspirations of the Italians for the unity of Italy. Cavour attempted to come to an understanding with the Pope on the principle of "a free Church in a free State." But Antonelli declared that the Papal Government could hold no intercourse with robbers, and the Pope steadily maintained his "non possumus" attitude. By a Convention in September, 1864, Italy bound herself to leave the remainder of the Papal States intact, and France to withdraw the army of occupation

Ch. IX.

Oppression at Rome.

War between France and Austria, 1859.

Convention of 1864.

within two years. The Pope had no voice in all this. After the withdrawal of the French, Garibaldi again summoned his volunteers to his standard, and an insurrection took place in the States of the Church. Napoleon declared the Convention broken, and again sent troops to the assistance of the Pope. The Italian volunteers were routed at Mentana, mainly because the French had a very superior weapon in the Chassepot rifle, and Garibaldi was wounded. The Franco-Prussian war of 1870, however, compelled the Emperor to recall his troops to their own country, when not only did the Garibaldian volunteers at once reappear, but after the great disaster to the French at Sedan, Victor Emmanuel, the King of Italy, set his troops in motion towards Rome. The papal troops everywhere fell back before the superior forces of the enemy, and Rome after a short cannonade surrendered. The Romans greeted the Italian army as their deliverers, and a plébiscite in the papal territory gave 133,000 votes for annexation to the kingdom of Italy and only 1500 against. A law of the following year secured to the Pope an income of three million lire (£120,000), with the possession of the Vatican, the Lateran, and Castel Gandolfo. Within these limits he was to enjoy the full rights of a sovereign prince, and in spiritual matters was to be absolutely free to exercise his authority as in times past, except that bishops were not to enter on office in Italy without the sanction of the Crown. The Pope, or his minister Antonelli, professed to regard this arrangement as untrustworthy and refused to accept it. He thenceforth never left the Vatican, but in a series of allocutions and documents protested against the changes brought about by the series of events since 1860, which had reduced him to a position which he considered to be utterly incompatible with the dignity and liberty of the Supreme Head of the Church. He forbade his former subjects to take part in elections or to hold office under the new Government. No Catholic power intervened to deliver the Pope from what he called his imprisonment, but the contributions of the faithful in all parts of the world, the so-called Peter's Pence, supplied His Holiness with an ample income. And there were many occasions, especially the completion of the twenty-fifth year of his reign, when he overpassed the traditional years of St Peter, which brought to Rome crowds of devoted pilgrims and many rich presents. It was perhaps the experience of so much devotion to him in the Catholic Church which encouraged him from time to time to issue protests which were neither dignified nor effectual. Pius died Feb. 7th, 1878, having outlived both his friend Antonelli and his enemy Victor Emmanuel.

Ch. IX.

Pius died, 7 *Feb.* 1878.

Probably no Pope had ever assumed the tiara with a more hearty desire to do good both as a spiritual and a temporal ruler; and probably no Pope, not even Gregory VII. dying in exile, had experienced more bitter disappointment at the failure of schemes certainly well-intentioned. And yet he left the Papacy with far greater moral and spiritual weight than it had at his accession. The spiritual leader of the Catholic Church was no longer overclouded by the follies and misgovernment of a petty prince, and the various rulers of Europe treated him with a respect which it had often been impossible to give under previous circumstances.

7. During the troubles which so closely pressed upon him in respect of his temporal sovereignty, the Pope by no means forgot that he was the spiritual ruler of the Roman Church. He gave earnest attention both to organization and dogma.

The Vatican Council.

The doctrine that the Virgin Mary had been, even from the time that she was conceived in her mother's womb, miraculously preserved from the taint of sin, had been a subject of hot discussion between Franciscans and Dominicans in the Middle Ages. It had not gained formal recognition in the Council of Trent, but had nevertheless come to be regarded, especially in Spain and Italy, as a pious opinion, and was strongly defended by the Jesuits. The Popes had avoided giving any decision on the subject, but Pius, always an earnest advocate of it, after his return to Rome in sorrow and bitterness of spirit, yielded to the urgency of the Jesuits who surrounded him to give definiteness and authority to the dogma. The replies of the bishops who were consulted were not wholly favourable; several thought the time inopportune; but as a commission of three theologians, Perrone, Passaglia and A. Theiner, reported

*Immaculate Conception of the Virgin.*

Decree of 8 Dec. 1854.

favourably, the Pope, after consultation with a number of bishops, proceeded on Dec. 8 (the Festival of the Conception of the Virgin), 1854, to St Peter's, and there in the presence of fifty-four cardinals and about one hundred and forty bishops, read aloud a decree, laying down definitely as a dogma of the Church, that the Blessed Virgin was conceived without stain (macula) of original sin. This decree was given without the decision of a council, so that by it the Pope implicitly asserted his own infallibility.

Syllabus, 8 Dec. 1864.

Ten years later he summed up the protests, which he had made from time to time in various allocutions and official documents against what he took to be the fatal errors of the age, in a Syllabus[1] which was appended to an encyclical letter, dated 8 Dec. 1864. In this famous document eighty errors are pointed out which every good Catholic is bound to abhor, detest and abjure. Some of these are in fact abhorred by good Christians everywhere; but among the condemned errors are Rationalism of every kind, every claim to freedom of faith and worship or of the press, the placing of the clergy on an equality with the laity in civil status, all secret societies and Bible societies; and—most important of all—the opinion that the Holy Father can by any possibility be reconciled with what modern civilization regards as progress and liberalism. The world saw with astonishment that papal immobility had declared war with human thought. France forbade the publication of the Syllabus within her dominions.

The year 1866, when Prussia's victory over Austria weakened the principal Catholic State, can hardly have been considered favourable to papal enterprise, but the undaunted Pope nevertheless turned his thoughts to a fresh display of spiritual power. On the supposed eighteenth centenary of the death of St Peter in the

The Pope's Canonizations, 1867.

summer of 1867, when more than four hundred bishops were assembled in Rome, he canonized twenty-five holy men, among them Peter Arbues, a Spanish inquisitor who served under Torquemada with at least equal cruelty. On the same occasion in a consistory the Pope announced

[1] Given in the *Offizielle Aktenstücke zu dem Œkumen. Concil* (Berlin, 1869).

that he had long had it in his mind to call, so soon as a favourable moment presented itself, an œcumenical and general Council, to apply remedies to the various evils under which the Church suffered. The assembled bishops replied that such a Council would bring new glory to the Church. A year later Pius, as Supreme Bishop of the Catholic Church, called a Council of all the bishops of the Roman communion for 8 December, 1869, at the Vatican. Somewhat later he invited also the bishops of the Eastern Church and Protestants to return to the only fold of Christ. To this some polite and some offensive refusals were returned. Among those who replied in a dignified and courteous manner was Dr Pusey. Only one government, that of Russia, absolutely forbade its subjects to attend the Council. France, which hesitated, was pacified by Antonelli's assurance that no proposal relating to infallibility would be brought forward.

Council summoned.

The objects of the Council[1] were at first set forth in general terms. The Bull convoking the Council followed in form that by which Paul III. convoked the Council of Trent, and described the objects of the Council as being to consider most carefully what, in the difficult circumstances of the time, would most contribute to the honour of God, the purity of the faith, the dignified celebration of divine service, the salvation of souls, the discipline, and the sound and thorough education, of the clergy, both regular and secular; the observance of the precepts of the Church, the improvement of morals, the Christian training of children, and the peace and concord of all. Further, with God's help, it was to

Objects of Council.

---

[1] The principal documents relating to the Vatican Council are to be found in the *Aktenstücke*, already referred to, in J. Friedrich, *Documenta ad illustrandum Concilium Vaticanum* (Nördlingen, 1871), and in *Acta et Decreta Sacrosancti Œcumen. Concil. Vatic.*, ed. Th. Grandrath, S.J. (Freiburg, 1891). Of the numerous books relating to the Council may be mentioned—F. Bungener, *Pape et Concile* (Paris, 1870; trans. Edinb. 1870); Janus [Döllinger and Friedrich], *Der Papst und das Concil* (Leipzig, 1869), Eng. trans. (1869); J. Friedrich, *Tagebuch während d. Vatican. Concil* (Nördl. 1873); *Geschichte des Vatikan. Concil.* (Bonn, 1872–87); E. Pressensé, *Le Concile du Vatican* (Paris, 1872); H. E. Manning, *The True Story of the Vatican Council* (London, 1877); Quirinus, *Letters from Rome on the Council* (trans. by H. N. Oxenham, Lond. 1870); W. E. Gladstone, *Rome and the Newest Fashions in Religion* (Lond. 1875); T. Mozley, *Letters from Rome on the Occasion of the Œcumenical Council* (Lond. 1891).

endeavour to remove abuses from the Church and civil society, to bring back into the way of truth those who have erred and strayed from the right way, so that righteousness and charity may everywhere flourish and abound.

Infalli-bility of the Pope.

In all this, it will be observed, there is no mention of papal infallibility. But on 6 February, 1869, just at the time when the theologians of the dogmatic commission appointed by the Pope were discussing that doctrine, there appeared in the *Civiltà Cattolica*, the organ of the Jesuits, the anticipation that the coming Council would last but a short time, inasmuch as it was intended that it should simply confirm the doctrines of the Syllabus and proclaim the Infallibility of the Pope. This, it was hoped, would be accomplished by acclamation. Such a statement, from such a source, attracted universal attention, and gave rise to animated controversy in almost every country of Europe. In Germany a large number of the most distinguished Catholic laymen presented a respectful address on the subject to the bishops assembled in Fulda, who in reply issued a pastoral letter intended to calm men's minds. It was absolutely impossible, they thought, for a General Council to enact a dogma which was not found in Scripture or in Apostolical Tradition. The Church does not proclaim new doctrines, but sets forth old truths in new light as the circumstances of the time may require. Equally groundless, they believed, was the fear that restraint would be placed on the deliberations of the assembled prelates. Bishop Dupanloup also attempted to soothe popular feeling in France, which, he said, for the present shewed no enthusiasm for the centre of unity.

Address of German Laymen.

Preparations for Council.

Meanwhile, a committee of cardinals was making preparations for the Council, a difficult task. In the first place, a "congregatio cardinalicia directrix" scrutinized the claims of those who desired to present themselves as members. An order of proceeding was drawn up. The commission on dogma decided that the definition of infallibility should not be brought forward unless some of the bishops should propose it. One member of the commission, Professor Alzog, the Church-historian, had the courage to declare that such a proposal would be in any case inopportune. All these proceedings were secret. At the opening of the Council, of 1037 who were qualified to sit 719 were present, a number which was increased by late arrivals to 764, but afterwards sank to 535. Of those present 276—considerably more than a third—were Italians, 84 French, only 19 German, while more than 100 came from North and South America. The place of assembly was the southern transept of St Peter's, the acoustic properties of which turned out extremely bad. In the plenary sessions under the presidency of the Pope only decrees already prepared were read, and received with *placet* or *non-placet* by the assembled bishops. Business was prepared (1) by committees of 24 members, each under the presidency of a cardinal; and (2) in general "congregations" under the presidency of five cardinals to which all members of the Council were admitted. All these proceedings were supposed to be secret; the members were forbidden to take notes, or even to see the formal minutes. Nevertheless, the keenness and ingenuity of correspondents were not to be defeated, and trustworthy accounts did in fact appear, of which the most remarkable was a series of letters, attributed to Lord Acton, in the Augsburg *Allgemeine Zeitung*, which were afterwards published under the name of "Quirinus." The debates took place in the general congregations, which were held almost daily, but the hindrance occasioned by the bad acoustic properties of the hall, and the difficulty of speaking and understanding a language, like the Latin, no longer in common use in public speech or in conversation, prevented any real discussion. Speeches were generally read from a complete copy.

A quarter of a year was passed in drawing up a general statement of admitted Catholic doctrine, "Constitutio dogmatica de Fide Catholica," which, after considerable concessions to the opposition, was accepted unanimously in the session of April 26, 1870. The opposition, which was strong enough to preclude the hope that the Infallibility of the Pope would be accepted by acclamation, found itself much hampered by the order of proceeding and always formed a small minority. It was composed however of representatives of the great civilized states with important dioceses, while in the

Ch. IX.
Numbers.

Committees.
Congregations.

Debates.

Constitutio Dogmatica, 26 Apr. 1870.

majority were hundreds of missionary or titular bishops, some of whom were actually dependent on the Pope for maintenance during their stay in Rome. By the Archbishops of Vienna and of Prague, and by the Bishop of Mainz, treatises were distributed in the Council and in the city shewing that the infallibility of the Bishop of Rome was unknown to the ancient Church, and that in stress of controversy on matters of faith he was never appealed to as an infallible judge. Further, that when the dogma was first propounded it was rejected, that it had always been a subject of controversy, and down to the most recent times had been no more than an opinion which a Catholic was free to accept or reject. The Bishop of Rottenburg (Hefele) directed attention to the case of Pope Honorius I., who was condemned as a heretic by the Fifth Œcumenical Council, and had always been regarded as heretical by his successors. The other party rejoined that even historical facts must yield to the supreme authority of divine revelation. If the Holy Father is the Vicar of Christ on earth, he must share in Christ's infallibility as the ever-present channel of divine truth. The acceptance of this doctrine is the only deliverance from the abyss which lies before us in the fearful errors and uncertainties of the age. To this it was replied that the doctrine in question, far from giving certitude to Catholics, would, if it were forced upon their unprepared minds, occasion suspicion and division, as many decrees of mediæval Popes, which it was at present permitted to doubt, would be surrounded with a halo of infallibility. So they fought, within and without the hall, until they came to the hot Roman summer.

Preliminary Voting.

The heat brought with it weariness and sickness, so that almost every one was eager to make an end. In a preliminary voting, 451 of the members voted for the Infallibility, 88 against, while 62 were ready to accept the decree with modifications. The minority was larger than had been expected; if the dioceses followed their bishops, a schism seemed imminent. On the 13th July the minority sent a deputation of six bishops to the Holy Father, who was, in appearance at least, surprised that any one should feel his conscience wounded by what was proposed, as the Church in all ages had taught the infallibility of the Supreme Pontiff. Then Bishop Ketteler of Mainz, the protagonist of the ultramontane party in Germany, falling at the Pope's feet, besought him to give peace to the Church by withdrawing the proposed definition. He seemed moved, but the leaders of the infallibilist party, Manning and Senestrey of Ratisbon, found means to change his mind. On the 18th of July the great decision was made. Fifty-six bishops had made it known to the Pope in an address, that although they adhered to their *non-placet*, yet out of reverence for the Holy Father they would prefer to absent themselves from the session and return to their dioceses. In the final voting there were but two dissentients, Ricci of Cajazzo and Fitzgerald of Little Rock in Arkansas. In the midst of a thunderstorm—like Moses on Sinai, said the infallibilists—the Pope declared the result and confirmed the decree. The essential portion of it is, that the Roman Pontiff when he speaks *ex cathedra*, that is, when, executing his office of pastor and doctor of all Christians, by his supreme apostolic authority he defines a doctrine relating to faith or morals to be held by the whole Church, by the divine assistance promised to him in St Peter he is endued with that infallibility with which the Holy Redeemer willed His Church to be supplied in defining doctrine relating to faith or morals, and that consequently such definitions of the Roman Pontiff are irreformable of their own nature, not as a consequence of the consent of the Church[1]. He who teaches otherwise is anathematized. Some other matters were after this formulated in the Council, but the unhealthiness of Rome at that season and the outbreak of the great war drew away one bishop after another, and on Oct. 20 the First Council of the Vatican was dissolved.

CH. IX.

Infallibility decreed, 18 July, 1870.

That the decrees of the Vatican Council have in

Effect of the new Dogma.

[1] The original Latin of this (Cap. IV, can. iv) is as follows: "Approbante Concilio docemus et divinitus revelatum esse dogma definimus, Romanum Pontificem cum ex cathedra loquitur, i.e. cum omnium Christianorum pastoris et doctoris munere fungens pro suprema sua apostolica auctoritate doctrinam de fide vel moribus ab universa Ecclesia tenendam definit, per assistentiam divinam ipsi in B. Petro promissam ea infallibilitate pollere qua Sanctus Redemptor Ecclesiam suam in definienda doctrina de fide et moribus instructam esse voluit, ideoque ejusmodi Romani Pontificis definitiones esse ex sese non autem ex consensu Ecclesiæ irreformabiles." This was embodied in the Bull *Pastor Æternus.*

ecclesiastical law the same weight as those of other Councils claiming to be Œcumenical need not be doubted. As to their moral weight, probably few great assemblies have been altogether free from the influence of trickery, intrigue, and brow-beating. Certainly this was not. The result of its action was that the conception of the Papacy which had been in the minds of many theologians for some generations past was stereotyped in its extreme form, and received the highest authority. Many states in their Concordats had already recognized the Papacy as the final court of appeal in ecclesiastical cases; to this was now added that what the Pope decreed as dogma was also final. He could make law under the guise of declaring it. Pius IX. had declared even before the momentous decision of the Council, when the traditions of the Church were appealed to, that he was himself the traditions. It was now affirmed by a great gathering of Catholic dignitaries from all parts of the world that he was right.

Attitude of the Nations.

The civil powers were for the most part indifferent to the new definition, though Austria repudiated its Concordat and forbade the publication of the dogma within its territory. Saxony, Bavaria, Hesse, Würtemberg and Baden did not admit it as of legal validity. But no government gave open support to the bishops who had joined in the opposition. Some among them, including even Ketteler of Mainz, had in vain entreated their several sovereigns to declare what kind of protection they would grant them. The minority found themselves hampered by the fact, that they had not opposed the dogma of infallibility frankly as an error, but only its definition as inopportune. Now that Rome had spoken, and the opposition threatened to become a schism, most Catholics felt it their duty to submit.

Attitude of German Bishops.

So far back as August, 1870, while the Council was still sitting, the opposition-bishops in Germany, with a much less numerous body of infallibilist colleagues, had assembled in Fulda, and declared in a common Pastoral Letter, that the faithful must, as they valued the salvation of their souls, submit unconditionally to the decrees of the Council. With the usual zeal of a recent convert, each bishop in his own diocese proceeded to require all clerics and all Professors and teachers of theology to give their assent to the dogma of Papal Infallibility under pain of excommunication. The last to surrender were Haneberg of Speyer and Hefele of Rottenburg. The latter, after a long struggle with his conscience, stated his view to be, that the infallibility extended only to propositions on faith or morals actually revealed, and in relation to them it was only the bare definition which was infallible, not any introduction, confirmation, or consequences by which it might be accompanied. This was not considered satisfactory, and he did at last, under severe pressure from the government of the country (1872), fall into line with his fellow-bishops, though he still did not require from his clergy and the theological faculty of Tübingen the strict acceptance of the Vatican decrees. In Austria, Strossmayer long held out, but at last yielded to the threats and blandishments of Rome. As to the Catholic laity, many of the educated class disliked the new decree, but were not generally sufficiently in earnest to take any action which would set them at variance with the ecclesiastical authorities or with the society in which they moved. The lower classes, or at any rate the devout among them, had long looked upon the Holy Father with a vague reverence which could neither be increased nor diminished by the assertion of his infallibility. Historical proofs were of course nothing to them; that which the actually existing Church taught they were satisfied to accept.

Hefele.

Laity.

8. The bishops who had opposed the new decree, hard pressed by the ecclesiastical authorities and unsupported by the civil, had stifled the voice of reason to accept the repugnant dogma. Among the lower clergy few were found who did not bow their necks to the yoke. But an opposition of great importance sprang up in the ranks of the German theologians. They were as far as possible from wishing to form a schism; they desired to remain within the Catholic Church and to protest against innovations. The decrees of the Vatican Council, they held, were passed in such a manner as not to have full conciliar authority. Further, even an œcumenical Council had no power to invent or declare new dogmas; it could only give its testimony to doctrines already current in the Church from primitive times. To reject the decrees of a Council was by no means the same thing

OLD CATHOLICISM. *Opposition of German Theologians.*

as to repudiate Catholicism; in fact, several Councils summoned as œcumenical had been rejected by the Church in consequence of their decrees being afterwards found to be unsound. The Catholic Church, from the moment when it accepted the infallibility and the universal episcopate of the Pope, became a different Church; those who loved true Catholicity should take their stand on the firm ground of the ancient traditions. As was to be expected, the principles by which they sought to obtain a *locus standi* naturally led the "Old Catholics[1]"—as they soon came to be called—beyond the mere controverting of the infallibility dogma. Many other points in the papal system came to be attacked, so that we may regard the Old-Catholic movement on the one hand as a protest against doctrinal innovation, on the other as a prolongation of the characteristic national life of a Church, which Rome had long endeavoured to suppress. The leaders of the movement were among the most able and learned men in Germany, and always sought support not merely in Holy Scripture, as the Lutheran Reformers had done, but in the genuine ancient traditions of the Church. Church History and Ecclesiastical Law were therefore constantly appealed to. Moreover, the Old Catholics soon shewed that spiritual life had by no means degenerated among them.

Many of the most distinguished professors of theology and philosophy in Germany were agreed in refusing to accept the Vatican Council as œcumenical and its decrees as Catholic. In Munich the Archbishop, instigated by the Papal nuncio, required from those under his jurisdiction express submission to the Vatican requirements. To this J. Ignaz von Döllinger, by far the ablest and most respected of the professors, and a man of noble character, who during the sitting of the Council had never ceased to raise a warning voice and to expose the unsoundness of the papalist reasoning, replied, that as Christian, as

[1] J. F. von Schulte, Die Berechtigung der Altkatholischen (Bonn, 1873); E. Friedberg, Aktenstücke die Altkathol. Bewegung betrachtend (Tübingen, 1876); F. Meyrick, The Old-Catholic Movement (Lond. 1877); A. M. Scarth, The Story of the Old-Catholic and Kindred Movements (Lond. 1883); Theodorus [J. Bass Mullinger], The New Reformation (Lond. 1875); R. S. Oldham, Old Catholicism in Religions of the World (Lond. 1893).

theologian, as historian, and as citizen, he was compelled to reject the dogma of infallibility. He was ready to prove before an assembly of bishops and theologians that it was contradictory to Holy Scripture, the Fathers, tradition and history. Addresses of sympathy came to him from the Catholics of Germany; from Rome came excommunication. Many learned men had the courage to protest against it.

In September, 1871, some five hundred representatives from all parts of Germany came together at Munich, forming the first Old-Catholic Congress. Over this assembly presided J. F. von Schulte, the canonist of highest repute in Germany. The Congress was of one mind as to the continued recognition of the earlier Councils, including that of Trent, and as to the retention of the faith, worship and institutions of the Catholic Church as they were understood before the Vatican decrees. It recognized the independent, the so-called Jansenist, Church of the Netherlands, and expressed a hope that they might have union with the Greek Church and a friendly understanding with the Evangelical Churches. But when the President proposed that they should have independent worship, pastorate and episcopate, Döllinger pointed out the danger of this course; to adopt it would be to leave the firm ground of simple opposition and become a protesting sect. This advice was not followed, but Döllinger continued to devote his vast learning to the service of the Old-Catholics to the day of his death (1890). They did in fact find it a serious disadvantage that when they claimed the privileges of Catholics, their opponents were able to reply that they had now deliberately separated from the Catholic Church. It is to their credit that in the midst of difficulties and controversies they did not cease to care for the spiritual edification of the little flocks of adherents. At the second Congress, at Cologne in September, 1872, a Committee was named to prepare a scheme for the election of bishops. When this was settled, twenty-two priests and fifty-five laymen met in Cologne (4 June, 1873), as representatives of the Old-Catholic communities in Prussia, Hesse, Baden, and Bavaria, and chose Dr J. Hubert Reinkens of Breslau as their bishop. He was consecrated (11 Aug.) by Bishop

Heykamp of Deventer, a prelate of the Hollandish Catholic Church. He chose Bonn, where the theological faculty was friendly to the movement, as the seat of his bishopric, and published as an indication of the principles which guided him a treatise on St Cyprian, who in his lifetime had stoutly resisted the claims of the Bishop of Rome to authority over the whole Church. The Prussian government, seeing in the Old-Catholic party, which included some of its most respected ecclesiastics, a possible ally against the Papacy, and holding the principle that the State was not called upon to decide in the internal dissensions of a religious body, recognized the Old-Catholic community within its dominions as an integral part of the Church, and Dr Reinkens as a Catholic bishop. Further, it gave the bishop an endowment, and caused a law to be passed to the effect that in any parish where a considerable number of Old-Catholics existed they should be allowed to use at suitable times the church, the churchyard, and the church-buildings generally. They were also to share in the enjoyment of the income of the parish in proportion to their numbers, and an incumbent who became an Old-Catholic was secured in the possession of his benefice. Baden and Hesse in like manner recognized the Bishop. Bavaria declined to take such a step, holding that it would be contrary to the provisions of an existing Concordat, but did not in any way oppose the exercise of spiritual functions by the Old-Catholic clergy within its dominions.

Recognised by Prussian Government, 19 Sept. 1873.

Old-Catholic Synod, May, 1874.

In the Old-Catholic Synod, held at Bonn[1] under the presidency of the Bishop, a constitution for the Church was adopted. The Synod, to be convoked annually, was to be the legislature of the Church and also the highest court of appeal. It was to consist of the whole of the clergy of the community, and lay representatives from each congregation, according to its numbers. The Bishop was to be assisted, and his power in some respects limited, by a Council of two clergymen and three laymen chosen by the Synod. It was declared, in harmony with the teaching of the best theologians in the past, that the

---

[1] *Beschlüsse der 1 Synode der Altkath.*, 27—29 *Mai* (Bonn, 1874); *Report of the Conference at Bonn* 1874, trans. from F. Reusch by E. M. B. (Lond. 1875).

absolution of the priest avails nothing where there is no true inward repentance for sin. The practice of auricular confession was left to the discretion of individuals. It was recommended that the vernacular should be employed in divine service, with the exception of the Mass. A proposal to abolish the compulsory celibacy of the clergy, made in the Synod of 1876, was rejected as inopportune. At this time the Old-Catholic Church was reckoned to include about 60 clergymen, 100 congregations of 50,000 souls in all, within the German empire. Döllinger found consolation in his sorrow for his breach with the past in the hope of union with the Greek and with the Anglican Church. Some English dignitaries did in fact attend the Synods, but with no authority to represent the English Church[1].

The religious atmosphere in Switzerland was not favourable to the Infallibilists. As a result of conferences of liberal Catholics, and popular meetings relatively more numerously attended than those in Germany, a Christian-Catholic community was formed, which, through a meeting of representatives at Olten (June, 1876), assembled with the sanction of the Council of the Swiss Confederation, chose Professor Herzog of Bern to be Bishop of the Christian-Catholics in Switzerland. He was consecrated in the church of St Martin at Rheinfelden by Bishop Reinkens, amid circumstances which made the occasion seem almost a national festival. Here too the bishop had the co-operation of a council, and the theological faculty of Bern was designated as the training-school of the clergy.

In France but few were found to maintain the old Gallican liberties against Papal absolutism. No bishop emulated the courage and patriotism of Bossuet. But the Abbé Michaud, rather than accept a dogma which he thought foolish and obey what he called "a council of sacristans," forsook his splendid position at the Madeleine in Paris and took refuge in Switzerland. There he did excellent service as a teacher in the Christian-Catholic Faculty at Bern, and became the faithful coadjutor of Bishop Herzog for the French-speaking part of his diocese.

[1] The Old Catholics, whom Döllinger organized, number now [1905] from 180,000 to 200,000; F. Meyrick's *Memories*, p. 268.

Loyson.

In Geneva.

In Paris.

Conversions to Rome checked.

Old-Catholic Difficulties.

Father Hyacinth, who at Notre Dame had been the favourite preacher of the fashionable world in Paris, stripped of his Carmelite habit, became M. Loyson. In 1872 he formed a committee in Rome for the reform of the Church by returning to the laws and usages of the first eight centuries. He afterwards became pastor of a church in Geneva which had joined the Old-Catholic movement, but his peculiar opinions soon led to differences with the Church, and his temperament to a want of harmony with the Swiss. His marriage also, before any authoritative sanction had been given to the marriage of priests, was an offence to many. In 1879 he opened a "national" church in Paris, where, though he drew round him by his eloquence many admirers, he simply formed a congregation and produced no permanent effect.

One effect of the decree of Infallibility in Germany was to check the stream of conversions to the Roman Church, and even to produce a current in the opposite direction. Some of those who were driven by conscience to join the Old-Catholics did not find themselves at ease in their new position. Some joined the Old-Lutheran party. Some pastors passed through a double conversion, and the Old-Catholic Church saw many of its members pass over to the Evangelical. In truth the Old-Catholics, regarding, as they still professed to do, the Bishop of Rome as the Patriarch of Western Christendom, and yet setting at nought his denunciations, had to tread a narrow path with precipices on each side. The mere denial of the Pope's infallibility was a purely negative proposition which afforded no ground on which to build a Church, while to go further, to put forth a new statement of doctrine and frame an independent constitution, was very like falling into Protestantism.

LEO XIII. 1878— 1903.

9. When Pius IX. died, a two-days' conclave sufficed for the election of his successor, Joachim Pecci, Cardinal and Archbishop of Perugia, who took the title of Leo XIII.[1]

---

[1] Bernard O'Reilly, *Life of Leo XIII.* (Lond. 1887); J. Oldcastle [*i.e.* Wilfrid Meynell], *Life of Leo XIII.* (1887); Justin MacCarthy, *Leo XIII.* (1896); Julien de Narfon, *Pope Leo XIII.* (trans. by G. A. Raper, 1890); J. de Witte, *Rome et l'Italie sous Léon XIII.* (Paris, 1892).

By nature and training a diplomatist, the new Pope was much more disposed than his predecessor had been to enter into negotiations to try what could be won by diplomatic skill, and in matters not of the highest importance could accept a compromise; but he was firm in his maintenance both of the ancient claims of the Papacy and of those which had been occasioned by recent events. He made courteous advances for a reconciliation with those states which he found at variance with the Holy See, but he abated nothing of the claims of the Papacy for the restoration of the States of the Church, nor would he enter into any friendly relations with the kingdom of Italy. He remained a "prisoner" in the Vatican. In his first encyclic he condemned all the errors in religion and philosophy which his predecessors had condemned, and claimed by implication the infallibility which the Vatican Council had decreed. He was however anxious to raise the standard of education for the clergy, and strongly recommended the study of Thomas Aquinas instead of the often misleading manuals which were commonly used in seminaries. His denial of the validity of the Orders of the English Church called forth a vigorous defence of the Anglican position from the Archbishops of Canterbury and York. In 1888 the Pope celebrated with great pomp the fiftieth anniversary of his ordination to the priesthood, when he received congratulations and valuable presents from almost every country in which Roman-Catholics are found, while thousands of pilgrims streamed into Rome. Presents or good wishes from the Italian government he refused to receive. In the year following this Jubilee the friends of free thought celebrated an anti-papal demonstration, attended by representatives of almost every civilized country, in the unveiling in Rome of a statue of Giordano Bruno, who in 1600 had been burnt to death by the papal authorities for holding that God manifests Himself in and through the universe, a doctrine maintained in aftertime by Spinoza and many others of high repute. The Pope's reputation for acuteness and knowledge of the world was considerably impaired by his sending his blessing to an unscrupulous impostor called Léon Taxil, who professed to have evidence for the devil-worship of the Freemasons, who were, in

Ch. IX.

Claims States of the Church.

Encyclic.

Jubilee, 1888.

Statue of Giordano Bruno, 1889.

Italy, supposed to be very strongly anti-papal. In 1897, on occasion of the 400th anniversary of the death of Canisius, the first German Jesuit, the Pope described the Lutheran Reformation as a revolt, which had brought in its train the utmost deterioration of morals and social life.

Question of removing the Papacy.

During the life of this Pope many of his friends thought the actual position of the Papacy no longer tenable, and there was talk of removing the seat of it to some foreign country, probably to Malta, a central spot where he would have been safe, and free in all spiritual matters, under the British government. Even a Jesuit, one of the founders of the *Civiltà Cattolica*, Father Curci, published his opinion that the restoration of the Temporal Power was no longer possible. For this he was expelled from the Order, and soon after recanted. He continued however to treat the same theme in the same spirit in various works up to 1883, but again submitted to his superiors. Leo XIII. died in 1903. His successor, Sarto, Patriarch of Venice, who took the title of Pius X., found the ecclesiastical atmosphere troubled by the legislation in France respecting the Religious Orders and education, and afterwards by the annulling of the Concordat made with Napoleon I. and the abolition of the Budget of Public Worship. There were also in Austria murmurs of a withdrawal from the papal domination.

Curci.

Pius X., 1903.

CHAPTER X.

FRANCE AND THE LATIN NATIONS.

1. THE ROMAN CATHOLIC CHURCH IN FRANCE.

THE principal centres of Catholic movement in the nineteenth century were France and Germany, where the new opinions were most sharply opposed to the old and found their ablest opponents and defenders. It was in France that questions bearing on the relations of the Church and the civil government, of national Churches to the Pope, were most eagerly discussed[1].

When Louis XVIII. was placed by the Allies on the throne of France[2], there returned with him from exile many nobles and many priests who, as Napoleon said, had learned nothing and forgotten nothing in the days of their banishment. Bishops who had spent twenty-one years in poverty and obscurity naturally expected to be raised to high positions as a reward for their sacrifices. And the government of the restoration was not indisposed to gratify them. Catholics could not but be conscious of the great need there was of a restoration of religion, for a whole generation had grown up unbaptized and unacquainted with even the elementary truths of Christianity.

Louis XVIII. had been a free-thinker before the Revolution, and even in later days had probably no strong convictions on the subject of religion. His leading principle was to keep himself on the throne. Like our Charles II. he did not wish to go on his travels again. But the extreme Papalist party gained great influence. To this belonged the King's brother Charles, who after

---

[1] R. F. Guettée, *Mémoires pour servir à l'Hist. de l'Église de France pendant le 19ᵉ Siècle* (1881).

[2] A. F. Nettement, *Hist. de la Restauration* (Paris, 1860-72).

a dissolute youth became devout and an eager partisan of the Pope; and his sister, the Duchess of Angoulême. She could never forget that her father and mother had died on the scaffold, and looked on the French people as a mob of murderers who were bound to make atonement for the innocent blood which they had shed.

Many of the clergy, renouncing their former independent spirit, became Ultramontane. To these the Concordat made by Napoleon[1], which asserted all the old liberties of the Gallican Church, and more, was of course offensive. Consalvi, who was still in power at the Papal court, had no mind to destroy his own handiwork, but in spite of his reluctance in 1817 a new Concordat was drawn up, the first article of which ran—"the Concordat made between our Sovereign Lord Pope Leo X. and the Most Christian King Francis I. is restored." It was proposed, that is, to ignore all that had passed in the last three hundred years, and to go back almost to Mediævalism. An additional article seemed to threaten to oust the bishops and priests of the Napoleonic *régime* from their position and property. Bishops were named to bring up the number of sees to that which existed before the Revolution. But the money for their stipends and the repeal of the existing law which established the Concordat of Napoleon, could only be obtained by an appeal to the Legislative Chambers, and the Chamber of Deputies utterly refused to accept the Concordat *en bloc*; they would discuss its terms; and throughout France there was an outcry against what was proposed. The result was that the proposal was abortive.

In the period of which we are speaking, in spite of the efforts of what we should now call the Ultramontanes, a considerable party in France paid little regard to the lofty spiritual claims of the Church, and seemed to regard it as little more than a department of the civil service. The Bourbon government recognized the institutions of the Revolution too much to satisfy one party and too little to satisfy the other. The revolutionary and the reactionary party soon displayed their mutual hostility, and as the clergy almost universally sided with the latter, they bore a large share of the ill-will of the former. The King's

[1] See above, p. 240.

brother came to the throne as Charles X. in September, 1824, and in 1828 his government found itself compelled by the Liberal opposition to close the schools of the Jesuits. But the storm rose higher, and in July, 1830, in consequence of the ordinances of the minister Polignac limiting the freedom of election and of the press, the King was driven from the throne by a Revolution, and the head of the younger branch of the Bourbon family, Louis Philippe[1] of Orleans, made constitutional King of the French. In these "days of July" the hatred of at least a portion of the Parisian populace for the Church broke bounds. The palace of Archbishop Quélen of Paris was levelled with the ground and the church of St Germain l'Auxerrois sacked. *[Ch. X. Charles X., Sept. 1824. July Revolution, 1830.]*

In the general unrest occasioned by the July Revolution, the Abbé Chatel attempted to revive the almost forgotten sect of Theo-philanthropists, and when this failed set up an Anti-Roman French-Catholic Church, which in the disturbed condition of the time found some adherents. It soon however rejected the Divinity of Jesus Christ, and declared all doctrines not written in the hearts of all men superstition and mysticism. Its resistance to Papal tyranny gave it a short vogue, but a Church founded on mere liberalism cannot endure. After a feeble existence of twelve years it was suppressed by the police, and passed away unregarded and unregretted. *[French-Catholic Church, 1830.]*

The new dynasty was by the Pope's desire recognized by the clergy, but it was felt that the political change materially altered the position of the Catholics in France. It was under these circumstances that the Abbé Félicité de la Mennais[2], already known as an eloquent and vigorous writer, with a little party of like-minded friends, became prominent in the politico-ecclesiastical struggles of the time. The great danger of the Church was, he thought, the indifference of a large portion of the cultivated class to *[La Mennais, 1782—1854.]*

---

[1] Cretineau-Joly, *Hist. de Louis-Philippe* (1862); A. F. Nettement, *Hist. du Gouvernement de Juillet* (1855); F. Guizot, *France under Louis-Philippe* (London, 1865); J. F. Michaud, *Biographie de Louis-Philippe* (1849); V. de Nouvion, *Hist. du règne de L.-P.* (1857–61).

[2] P. Janet, *La Philosophie de Lamennais* (1890); G. E. Spuller, *Lamennais* (1892); Lacordaire, *Conferences* (1850), vol. IV. contains *Considérations sur le Système de la Mennais*; A. Ricard, *L'École Mennaisienne* (Leipzig, 1882).

margin notes:
- Ch. X.
- 'Essai sur l'Indifférence,' 1817.
- The Church should be Liberal.
- 'L'Avenir.'

Catholicism, and to these he endeavoured to point out that it was of the very highest importance. In his famous essay on "Indifference in regard to Religion" he treats with the utmost scorn and contempt those cultivated persons who, themselves sceptics, nevertheless think religion necessary for the populace, and those who hold that God is to be worshipped, but that He has not given to man any special revelation of Himself. And he pours forth hardly less scathing invectives on those who believe that God has given a divine revelation in a book, but has left men without any authority divinely commissioned to interpret it. What man needs is unity and certitude. If society is to be preserved, it must be by adhering to the Roman Church and to its Head, the divinely appointed expositor of the truth. He held moreover that the Church reaped far more harm than good from its connexion with the State, and that it would be wise if it leaned for support solely on the love of the people. But other dreams than that of a pure theocracy enthroned in the Vatican soon began to fill his mind, and he became eager that the Church, headed by the Pope, should take the lead in the struggle for political liberty. He wished to bring the Papacy into a close alliance with democracy and free thought, and to make the Pope the centre and guide of the popular reaction against existing misgovernment and tyranny. Soon after the Revolution of July, with the help of an illustrious group of friends—Montalembert, a man of distinguished family, an attractive writer, and a most devout man; Lacordaire, soon to be known as the greatest preacher in France; Gerbet, afterwards Bishop of Perpignan, and others—he founded the journal called *L'Avenir*, to serve as the organ of those New-Catholics who fought—to use their own phrase—" for God and Liberty, for Pope and People." The great talent of the writers and the boldness with which they maintained their views deeply moved the minds of men, and caused great alarm to all who wished to maintain the current opinions against all innovation. In 1831 the publication of *L'Avenir* was suspended. The word "Avenir" expressed the reliance of its editors on the future, and their readiness to abandon tradition when they thought it evil. A tricolour episcopate was, they said, just as good as one that adopted the Bourbon lilies. Napoleon had given the Church that which it would in any case have gained—bread—but had kept back from it what it most of all had need of, freedom. The clergy of the day had, they thought, lost their influence with the people by their too great devotion to the restored Bourbons. In making common cause with the rulers, the Church had made itself an accomplice with despotism—a fatal error. Let the clergy renounce the State, live on the alms of the faithful, and be free. Let them not ask from the public treasury a maintenance which is always grudgingly given. Let them raise their eyes to Him who sent forth His disciples with cloak and staff, ready to give the gospel of peace in return for the hospitality of a day. Let them, poor themselves, throw themselves with confidence into the arms of the poor. Gregory VII. (Hildebrand) was invoked as the patron of this new Catholicism, the great Pope who to his last breath upheld the supremacy of intellect over brute force, the inherent superiority of right over might.

Opposition to innovation.

These bold thoughts, expressed in eloquent language, soon gained great influence in France and Belgium; but the clergy in general had no great taste for apostolic poverty; it required apostolic earnestness to adopt it. Conservatives of all schools were against these daring innovators. They were censured by the French ecclesiastical authorities, and Lamennais, Lacordaire and Montalembert set out for Rome, full of hope, to plead their cause before the Pope himself. They were coldly received, and shortly afterwards Gregory XVI. condemned *L'Avenir* in an encyclical letter. Lacordaire and Montalembert humbly accepted the decision of the Holy See. So, to all appearance, did Lamennais, but that ardent soul was not conquered. His reception at Rome had left behind a bitterness which his friends in vain attempted to mitigate, and which found vent in the famous book called "Words of a Believer," in which, in the style of a Biblical prophecy, he sets before the imagination an ideal society, hampered and spoiled indeed for a while by the tyranny of despots, but destined ultimately to triumph in perfect love and perfect liberty. In this book he no longer refers to the Church or the Pope as a teacher

Lamennais at Rome, 1832.

'Paroles d'un Croyant,' 1833.

of the truth, but founds his reasoning on the nature of man, as man, of which he takes an optimistic view. Henceforward, though all his works are pervaded by a certain religious mysticism, he was scarcely regarded as a Christian.

There was now a complete breach between him and his former friends, who set themselves to heal the wounds of the Church by quite other methods. Already in 1830 an association had been formed, under the honoured name of St Vincent de Paul, to give help and Christian teaching to the poor. Over this society, a natural outcome of the task committed to the Church by her Lord, presided with kindly zeal Frederic Ozanam[1], afterwards well known as an admirable Church-historian and archæologist, and under him were enlisted some of the choicest spirits of the Catholic revival. A new flame was kindled in men's hearts when Lacordaire[2] defended Christianity and the Church in his famous Conferences, productions very different from the ordinary sermon. France heard with delight the burning words of this new Bossuet, from whose lips, as from the rock smitten by the staff of power divine, poured forth an irresistible stream of the noblest eloquence. For some time after 1836 he withdrew from public notice in order to devote himself to study, but in 1841 he reappeared in Notre Dame in the habit of the Dominican Order, which he had joined in the previous year, and preached with even greater power than before. During his absence the Conferences at Notre Dame had been kept up by the Jesuit Father Xavier de Ravignan, who, if less original and less forcible than Lacordaire, was his equal in reasoning and in nobleness of aim. The Count of Montalembert[3] at the same time powerfully contributed, both as a politician and as a man of letters, to encourage the revival of Catholic feeling. These men, and the like-minded friends who gathered round them—the "Sons of the Crusaders," as they were sometimes

[1] Kathleen O'Meara, *F. Ozanam, his Life and Works* (Edinb. 1876); A. Coates, *Ozanam's Letters, with Sketch of Life* (1886).
[2] Dora Greenwell, *Lacordaire* (1867); Henriett L. Lear, *Lacordaire, a Biog. Sketch* (1882); Montalembert, *Memoir of L.* (1863); B. Chocarne, *L. sa Vie intime* (Eng. translation, 1895).
[3] Margaret Oliphant, *Memoirs of Montalembert* (1872); Vicomte de Meaux, *Montalembert* (1897); Lecanuet, *M. d'apres son Journal et sa Correspondance* (1898 ff.); Perrand, *Le Comte de Montalembert* (1870).

called—sought to bring again into honour the great Catholic past, and to give to the theology, the philosophy and the art of the Middle Ages their due place in public opinion. Still, they hailed with joy the progress of modern science, and thought a return to the intellectual and social conditions of by-gone ages neither practicable nor desirable. They rejected the use of compulsion in matters of opinion, and looked to the increase of true enlightenment for the furthering of Catholic principles.

Perhaps there has never been in France a party more truly Catholic, more devout, more refined, more tolerant, than that which included, and to some extent was guided by, Montalembert—the party to which the first impulse was given by the eager Lamennais, who had the power of moving, but hardly that of guiding. But the great mass of the nation were not greatly influenced by such men as these, men too much withdrawn from common life,to have much influence with common people. With such,coarse and vigorous denunciation of opponents was much more influential.

Party of Montalembert:

Meantime, the subject of popular education had become prominent. Guizot, a Protestant, wished to introduce a system which should place every kind of education in France under State control, with the exception of seminaries intended for the education of the clergy only. The clergy required, as the price of their support, freedom of teaching, a provision which would have given them control of by far the greater number of French schools. A very unprofitable controversy sprang up, the clerical party accusing their opponents of materialistic atheism, to which the latter retorted by charging clerical, especially Jesuit, teachers with false morality and even indecency. As a compromise, the clergy were allowed to open colleges for general education as well as seminaries, on complying with the conditions imposed by law. But this was not final. After the Revolution of 1848, during the Presidency of Louis Napoleon, a new Law of Public Education abolished the educational monopoly of the University of France[1] and gave freedom to found and carry on schools

Guizot's Educational Measures, 1833.

Villemain's Measures, 1844.

Loi Falloux.

---

[1] It should be borne in mind that in France the word "University" does not mean a place of education, but is the name given to the whole organization of secondary and superior education under public authority throughout France.

independently. This law was due mainly to the strenuous efforts of Count Falloux, a member of the government, and is commonly known by his name. As Emperor, Napoleon III. did not abolish the Organic Articles, which were thought to hamper the life of the Church, but he did in fact give the Church greater freedom of action. The Pantheon, the scene of so many vicissitudes, was made once more a Christian church; many of the ancient churches which are the glory of France were restored, and some new ones built at the public expense.

Anti-Jesuit Movement, 1844.

In 1844 Eugenie Sue's famous romance, *The Wandering Jew*, excited public feeling against the Jesuits, and to some extent against the Church generally; but on the whole the more solid portion of the nation, terrified by the spread of communistic opinions, became year by year more favourable to the Church. The revolutionaries of 1830

Revolution of 1848.

had dragged the crucifix in the mud, those of 1848 bore that which they had taken from the Tuileries reverently to the nearest church. And the Republic which was founded in the tumults of that year was not hostile. Lacordaire and Ozanam, true to their principles, advocated the alliance of Christianity with democracy, but the dread of socialism drove France into the arms of Imperialism. Louis Napoleon, nephew of the first Napoleon, was elected President of the Republic mainly through the magic influence of his name, and conciliated the clergy by the restoration of the Papal authority in Rome, the improvement of the pecuniary position of the French clergy, and considerable concessions in their favour with regard to education and religious congregations. The *coup d'état* of December 2, 1851, which gave immense power to the President and practically annihilated French liberty, was heartily approved by many of the clergy, who also readily acquiesced in his assumption of the imperial title, as

Napoleon III. Emperor, 1852.

Napoleon III. in the following year. In vain Dupanloup, Bishop of Orleans and a distinguished man of letters, reminded his countrymen that the First Empire, after making a pretence of restoring the Church, had failed to give it freedom and even persecuted it. The great majority of the clergy, fearing the return of an anarchy hostile to the Church, threw themselves into the arms of the Emperor. If he would further their interests, they were ready to further his. But the real intellectual leaders of the Church joined the liberal opposition. Montalembert, who for a while had trusted the Emperor, Lacordaire, the philosophic Gratry, Berryer, the great defender of legitimate monarchy, and many other Churchmen, boldly made head against the new despotism. Lacordaire, in his last sermon, preached at St Roche, declared that the man who employs villainous means, even with a view to good, is himself a villain; and he affirmed that political servitude corrupts the souls of men. Even in religion it enfeebles them. It gives rise to an episcopate which is a cowardly worshipper of the powers that be, and which again infects the clergy with timidity mingled with self-seeking. "A free Church in a free State" now became the watchword of the liberal Catholics, especially of Montalembert. Against him and his friends Louis Veuillot, who had been converted from unbelief to liberal Catholicism and from this again to extreme Ultramontanism, advocated with great literary power and unscrupulous vigour the alliance of the Church with the man of the 2nd December, and indeed with any power which seemed able to combat Liberalism in Church and State. Veuillot, said Ozanam[1], does his best to make the Church unpopular by depreciating all that is popular within it. There are two schools, he continues, which aim at serving God in literature. One is ready to put forth the most startling paradoxes, the most hazardous statements, if only they are contrary to the modern spirit. It presents the truth to men not in an attractive, but in a repellent guise. It does not set itself to bring back unbelievers into the fold, but to rouse the worst passions of believers. The other, once that of Chateaubriand, now that of Lacordaire, has for its aim to seek in the human heart the secret ties which may bind it to Christianity, to awaken in it the love of truth, goodness and beauty, to shew it, in the revealed faith, the ideal towards which every noble soul aspires; in short, to bring back wandering souls into the fold of Christ and swell the number of true disciples.

Lacordaire's sermon, 10 Feb. 1858.

L. Veuillot.

The friendship between the Ultramontanes and the Emperor lasted just so long as the Emperor felt the need

[1] Quoted by Kraus, *Lehrbuch*, 562.

of the support of the Church. The Italian campaign of 1859[1] ended in a great reduction of the territories subject to the Pope as a temporal sovereign, to the great indignation of many of the French clergy. Napoleon replied to the attacks of some of the disillusioned bishops by suppressing the Society of St Vincent de Paul, expelling the Redemptorists, and reviving the Organic Articles of 1801[2].

Catholicism depressed.

Meantime, Catholicism had almost lost control of public opinion and feeling. The hydra of materialism, with its attendant communism, reared its heads. Novels of the most shameless kind became popular and ribald plays were represented before the Court. The Empire, deserted by all the nobler spirits, could maintain itself only by the grossest corruption. So alarming was the state of things that Dupanloup in 1870 declared that all that had been gained by the Catholic revival was in danger of being lost. France was ripe for the great catastrophe of 1870 which drove the Emperor from his throne.

The best and purest leaders of French Catholicism, Berryer, Lacordaire and Montalembert, had been taken away from the evil to come before the fatal year 1870, but the society in which the ideas of these excellent spirits were preserved formed a charming oasis of true and refined religion in the midst of heated partisanship. How attractive and ennobling this society was may be seen in the correspondence of Madame Swetchine, whose salon was its point of union, and of Eugénie de Guérin. The same traits are found in the *Sister's Story* of Mrs Craven, a daughter of the family of La Ferronays, whose book was warmly praised by Montalembert.

Ernest Renan, 1823.

In 1863, a portent sprang from the bosom of the French Church. Ernest Renan[3] was born in the religious

[1] Laguerronière, *La France, Rome, et l'Italie* (1860).
[2] See above, p. 241.
[3] Renan's early life is depicted by himself in his *Souvenirs d'Enfance et de Jeunesse* (1883); Madame J. Darmesteter, *Life of Renan* (1897); F. Espinasse, *Life of R.* (1895); G. Monod, *Les Maitres d'Histoire: Renan*, etc. (1894); Jules Simon, *Quatre Portraits: Renan*, etc. (1896); M. E. Grant Duff, *L. Renan* (1893); H. Lasserre, *L'Évangile selon Renan* (17th ed. 1883); E. de Pressensé, *L'École Critique et Jésus Christ* (1863); A. Reville, *La Vie de Jésus devant les Orthodoxies*, etc. (1864); John Young, *The Christ of History* (4th ed. with criticism of R. 1868).

and imaginative atmosphere of Brittany, and was educated for the priesthood through the usual course, ending with the Seminary of St Sulpice. Here however he was overcome with doubts, left the Seminary, and abandoned all thoughts of the priesthood. He had become distinguished in linguistic, and had been employed by the government on an exploration of Syria and Phœnicia in the interests of archæology, when he published the *Life of Jesus* which almost immediately leaped into notoriety. He was prepared for this work by a thorough knowledge of what had been done by previous enquirers, by critical study of the New Testament and of other early authorities, and by an acquaintance with the Holy Land which enabled him to give to his descriptions of scenery a great impression of reality. And he was master of a style not surpassed by that of any other French writer in vividness and charm. In his narrative he rejects wholly every supernatural event related in the Gospels. History is to be found in them, but only after diligent sifting and divining. The Jesus who issues from this process is a young Galilæan peasant, educated so far as education could be had in a village of Northern Palestine, religious with the earnest piety of the heart, and hating the load of tradition which had been heaped upon the Law and the Prophets. In the end, he is swept away by the fierce current of Messianic expectation which was in flood in his time, he is beset by the illusion that he is himself the Messiah and the Son of God, is brought before the Jewish tribunal as a blasphemer, and finally executed by the Roman procurator as a rebel. He who founded the Church which after almost nineteen centuries still venerates His Name in every quarter of the globe, was different in kind from Renan's amiable enthusiast. But the book in fact made an immense impression. Previous biographies of the Lord had scarcely attracted notice beyond the circle of professed students, but here was a book which found its way into drawing-rooms wherever the French language was known. Among religious-minded people the alarm was great. Refutations and official condemnations appeared in rapid succession, but the book continued for some years to be very widely read. It is thought in some instances to

Margin notes: Ch. X. | 1846. | 'Vie de Jésus,' 1863. | Renan's Jesus.

Religious revival after 1870.

National Assembly, 1871.

Thiers President.

Bishops' Petition.

have brought men who were indifferent to religion to see at any rate something to revere in the man Christ Jesus, but on the whole it tended to shake men's faith in the Divine Nature of the Son of God.

The disastrous war with Germany and the Parisian insurrection which followed brought about a readiness to recognize the intervention of powers higher than man in human affairs. The Virgin Mary was thought to be especially the protectress of France and her worship greatly increased. A stately church was raised by popular subscription on Montmartre, dedicated to the Sacred Heart of Jesus, in order that, as one of the hymns of the time ran, that Heart might deliver Rome and France. Crowds of devotees, including many of high rank, joined in pilgrimages, especially to Lourdes, where the waters were believed to have wrought miraculous cures.

The government came in February, 1871, into the hands of a National Assembly chosen by the whole nation, which placed at the head of affairs the old Minister of Louis Philippe, Adolphe Thiers[1], as President of the Republic. Thiers was far from friendly to the Roman Church from the point of view of religion, but as a political power he knew that it must be reckoned with. That France should be recognized as the protector of Roman-Catholics throughout the world, and that the French clergy should be heartily in sympathy with the civil government, he saw were necessary conditions for reclaiming from Germany what she had lost, an object which every Frenchman had deeply at heart. A petition of five bishops to the National Assembly, supplicating that France should join with other great powers in restoring the States of the Church to the Pope, was rejected as inopportune; but Archbishop Guibert of Paris published the Vatican decree of Papal Infallibility without requesting the permission of the government, and the Minister, Jules Simon, contented himself with a friendly admonition to the bishops not to offend in like sort again. The influence of the clergy also caused the rejection of an Education Bill which would have placed

[1] P. de Remusat, *Thiers* (1889, trans. 1892); Jules Simon, *Le Gouvernement de Thiers* (1878, tr. 1879); E. Michaud, *L'État actuel de l'Église Cath. en France* (1875).

all schools under the supervision of the State, and have compelled all the children in France to attend them. In May, 1873, however, Thiers was compelled to abdicate the Presidency, and was succeeded by Marshal MacMahon, under whom, with the Duc de Broglie as Prime Minister, the clerical party felt itself safe, and the restoration of the older line of the Bourbons was nearly accomplished. Nor was the clerical influence diminished under the Ministry of Buffet. To it is due the important concession of liberty to found Catholic universities, with the privilege of conferring degrees. When however the general election of 1876 produced a large anti-clerical majority in the Chamber of Deputies, Buffet was driven from office. The new Ministry, in which the Minister of Education was W. H. Waddington, a man of English family and English education, declared itself friendly to free education, but prepared to oppose the granting of degrees by the Catholic universities. The Bill however embodying these principles, after passing in the Chamber of Deputies, was rejected, by a small majority, in the Senate. The founding of universities thereupon proceeded, but they succeeded in attracting only a small number of students.

On Jan. 30, 1879, MacMahon was driven from office, and from this time begins a more active phase of the struggle between anti-clerical Ministers and an ultramontane clergy. He was succeeded as President by Grévy, who entrusted the formation of a new Ministry to W. H. Waddington. Jules Ferry became Minister of Education, and introduced a Bill by which the representatives of the bishops were to be removed from the Council of Higher Education. The Catholic universities were allowed to remain, but their students were to enter themselves on the register of the State university, to pass its examinations and receive its degrees. Further legislation was proposed affecting Orders and Congregations.

Napoleon I. had interdicted all religious associations which he had not authorized, and he authorized only three—the Orders of St Lazare, of the Saint Esprit, and of the Missions Étrangères. The Brothers of Christian Doctrine were also recognized, not as a religious Congregation, but as a teaching body, under the jurisdiction of the Minister of Education. The Sulpicians, the

MacMahon President, 1873.

1875.

Grévy President, 1879.

Authorized Congregations.

teachers and managers of the famous Parisian seminary for the education of the secular clergy, received authorization in 1816. These five communities alone were authorized. The great historical Orders, Benedictines, Carthusians, Franciscans, Dominicans, Jesuits and Trappists, existed in France only on sufferance, having no legal corporate existence. Still, they flourished, so that after thirty years of anti-clerical government, the religious in France were very much more numerous than they had been under the old monarchy. Ferry's Bill proposed to forbid members of the unauthorized Orders and Congregations to teach in schools. It passed through the Chamber of Deputies without amendment, but the Senate threw out the clause which disqualified members of Orders for teaching. The President now put forth two decrees, which, on the authority of statutes never repealed though regarded as obsolete, (1) required the dissolution of all the Jesuit houses in France within three months, and (2) obliged all Orders and Congregations not already authorized to apply for recognition within six months, or to dissolve their establishments. These decrees naturally called forth a storm of protests. Even the Pope caused an autograph letter to be handed to the President, in which he declared that he must needs defend the Jesuits and the threatened Orders, as they were absolutely indispensable for the wellbeing of the Church. When the police entered on their work of expelling the Jesuits from their houses, the Fathers brought actions against them in the courts of law for violation of domicile and interference with personal freedom. When the time came for closing their schools, it was found that they had been transferred to owners who were under no legal disabilities. The provisions of the second decree relating to unauthorized Orders were not at once put in force. During the period of suspense, an attempted compromise, that, instead of seeking authorization, the Orders should make a solemn declaration that they would not interfere in matters political nor take any step against the established system of government, brought about the fall of the Ministry of Freycinet, who had succeeded Waddington. At the head of the next was Ferry, still retaining the portfolio of Education, who proceeded to carry out the second of the March decrees.

Up to the time of the meeting of the Chambers in November, 261 houses of male Orders had been emptied of their inhabitants. All this had not been done without much difficulty and disturbance, the police being often resisted in the execution of their duty. But still more threatening was the attitude of the jurists. A declaration that the March decrees were unconstitutional and therefore invalid received the signatures of some 2000 advocates; a large number of the legal officials of the State gave in their resignations, as did also several officers of the army, to avoid participation in the execution of the decrees. As it was expected that some at least of the courts would favour the appeal of the Jesuits, the government took steps to declare the ordinary courts incompetent to try such matters. There were also propounded other decrees unfriendly to the Church. Military chaplaincies were abolished, and students in priestly seminaries were made liable to military service in the ranks. The burial of non-Catholics in Catholic cemeteries, without Catholic rites, was sanctioned. Boarding-schools of higher education for girls were set up, with State subventions, as rivals to the convent schools.

The most severe blow to religious instruction was given in 1882, when Paul Bert, an uncompromising enemy of religion, carried an Education Bill which compelled the attendance of all children in elementary schools, abolished all religious instruction, which was to be the care of Churches and families, and strictly forbade the clergy to take part in any way in the instruction given in schools supported by the State. At the same time all crucifixes, religious symbols, and pictures of sacred subjects were ordered to be removed from the walls of class-rooms. In December, 1884, a tax was laid on the property of all clerical Orders, the subvention given to the Catholic universities was withdrawn, and many important reductions were made in the budget for Catholic worship. After several attempts, a Bill permitting divorce by the decree of a civil court, and authorizing re-marriage, passed both Chambers of the Legislature in July, 1884. During this anxious period the Court of Rome had been, in its public conduct at least, remarkably quiescent. Certainly in 1883 the Pope addressed to President Grévy a solemn

Paul Bert's Law, Oct. 1882.

Divorce permitted, July, 1884.

Pope's Letter, July, 1883.

remonstrance against the proceedings of the Republic in matters of religion, but this the President chose to regard as a private letter. Without officially communicating it to his Ministers, he replied, that he and his government were most anxious to avoid any conflict with the Holy See. They did in fact succeed in throwing out many proposals for extremely radical measures against the Church which were made after the fall of Gambetta in 1882[1].

Loubet's Visit to Italy, 1904. In 1904 President Loubet paid a visit to the King of Italy. This was highly distasteful to the Catholic party, as the King was in possession of the territory which was once Papal, and the Pope, far from receiving M. Loubet, entered a protest against his action, a protest which was resented by the French government. And graver complications arose[2]. Geay, Bishop of Laval, and Le Nordez,

Case of the Bishops of Laval and Dijon. Bishop of Dijon, both in favour with the government, were summoned to Rome to answer to charges of irregular conduct which had been preferred against them. The French Ministry protested against this, holding that it was a violation of the Concordat, under which the Papacy could not in any way diminish the powers and prerogatives of a bishop without their approval. Cardinal Vanutelli replied, on behalf of the Pope, that the bishops were dependent on the Holy See in the exercise of their spiritual functions. The French government was not satisfied.

Quarrel with Rome. On July 30, 1904, diplomatic relations with Rome were broken off, a preliminary to legislation which put an end to the relations of France with the Papacy, which had existed for more than a century. The final step

Bill for separation of Church and State, Feb. 9, 1905. was taken when on Feb. 9, 1905, M. Rouvier's Ministry laid on the table of the Chamber of Deputies a Bill for the separation of Church and State[3]. This became law in December of the same year, and applies to Protestant and Jewish Congregations as well as to Roman-Catholic churches. It begins with the declaration that the State guarantees liberty of conscience and of religious observance, but in no way recognizes or subsidizes any form of religion. Within

[1] Kurtz, *Kirchengeschichte*, II. ii. 240 ff.
[2] For this period, see J. E. C. Bodley, *The Church in France* (1906), and *Quarterly Review*, July, 1906; Aristide Briand, *La Séparation des Églises et de l'État* (Paris, 1905).
[3] The text is given by Bodley, 145 ff.

a year from the passing of this Act all movable and immovable property of the several churches are to be conveyed to "Associations Cultuelles," associations for the maintenance of public worship. That property which had belonged in time past to the State or to public bodies is to be restored to its original owners, but pious endowments created since the date of the Concordat are not interfered with. Ministers of religion who are sixty years of age, and have received for thirty years the State salary, are to receive for life three-fourths of its amount, while those who are forty-five years of age, and have received pay for twenty years, are to receive a life-pension of half their salaries, but no pension is to exceed £60 a year, the sum hitherto paid to an ordinary parish priest. The churches and chapels are left at the disposal of the Associations; but episcopal palaces, parsonages, and seminaries are to be granted rent-free for two years only, on the expiration of which some arrangement must be made with the authorities concerned. The "Associations Cultuelles" are to consist of residents in the parish, in number from seven to twenty-five according to population. These may raise funds by subscriptions, collections, and fees, and may give any surplus which they possess to other Associations. Libellous or provocative utterances in churches may be punished by fine and imprisonment. The transference of ecclesiastical property naturally required an inventory of it, the taking of which caused agitation and often riot throughout France. Thus the old Gallicanism, long declining, received its death-blow. The Pope is now free to rule the French clergy after his own devices, so far as he can enforce his decrees by purely spiritual penalties.

Ch. X.

Ultramontanism Triumphant.

2. PROTESTANTISM IN FRANCE.

The "Reformed," the successors of the old Huguenots, shared in the Napoleonic Establishment of religion. On the restoration of the Bourbons the Roman-Catholic mob

Reformed Church[1].

Riots in 1815.

---

[1] G. De Félice, *Hist. des Protestants de France* (Paris, 1850); *Les Œuvres de Protestantisme Français en 19ᵐᵉ Siècle* (Paris, 1893), an official publication; S. Smiles, *The Huguenots in France* (London, 1876); E. Smedley, *Hist. of the Reformed Religion in France* (London, 1832-4).

in Nismes and its neighbourhood broke out into various atrocities against their Protestant neighbours, which continued for some three months unhindered by the civil authorities[1]. When at last the indignation of France and Europe made itself heard, a stop was put to the riots, but rioters were not punished, nor did the persecuted people recover their rights until the Revolution of 1830 removed their oppressors from power. Even then they were prevented from holding a General Synod, and a decision of the Court of Cassation brought Evangelical communities under the Law of Associations, so that it rested with the government of the day, or some local official, to give or withhold authorization. They were however permitted to hold a General Synod at Paris in 1848 to consider as to changes in their ancient constitution rendered necessary by the new position. As this assembly, anxious to maintain at least an outward appearance of unity, refused to enact dogmatic conditions of membership which would have caused division, Frederick Monod and Count Gasparin protested against what they considered a desertion of true Christian principles, and in 1849 founded a Union of Evangelical Churches to maintain Protestant doctrine, in complete independence of the State. Louis Napoleon sanctioned in 1852 a Central Council of the Reformed, having under it consistories and presbyteries. At this time Adolphe Monod was regarded as the leader of the Evangelical party, while the elder Coquerel was the champion of a more liberal school of thought. The latter was opposed to dogmatic tests, holding that considerable differences of doctrine were not inconsistent with a true union in Christian life. The number of the Reformed steadily increased, and new congregations were formed almost every year, in spite of the many hindrances occasioned by the action of Roman-Catholic prefects and other local magnates. In his speech at the opening of the year 1858 the Emperor repeated the declaration that full liberty of worship was granted to all Protestants. Still, he reminded his hearers that Catholicism was the religion of the great majority of Frenchmen. The prefects generally took this to mean that they were not to favour

[1] M. Wilks, *Persecution of Protestants in South of France* (London, 1821).

Protestantism, and shortly afterwards General Espinasse, who had been made Minister of the Interior, expressly warned them to extend to Protestant Societies the same vigilance which they gave to political suspects, and to forbid altogether the colportage of Protestant Bibles. This latter clause was however withdrawn when Espinasse left office, and licenses were refused only to agents of foreign Societies. An Imperial Decree of 1859 withdrew from local boards the power of authorizing or refusing to authorize the opening of new Protestant places of worship, and committed it to the Council of State. At the same time the State salary was given to the minister of any Protestant community which consisted of not less than four hundred souls. Under the Third Republic, in the Presidency of Thiers, a General Synod was held in Paris, with the sanction of the government, to reconstitute the Church, at which Guizot, Louis Philippe's unfortunate minister, appeared as the champion of the old Evangelical orthodoxy, while the younger Coquerel, with Colani, lately a Professor at Strasburg, represented a more liberal tendency. The former supported the statement of doctrine proposed by Professor Bois, which recognized Holy Scripture as the supreme authority in matters of doctrine, and made the acknowledgement of Christ as the Son of God, and the justifier of all who have faith in Him, the foundation of education, worship, and discipline. The latter objected to making any formula of man's device absolutely and legally binding upon the Church. The Orthodox party had a majority, and passed a resolution rendering those who refused their formula incapable of sitting in the Synod. This resolution the Council of State declared to be null and void, and Ferry, as Minister of Worship, reinstated the deprived members. His successor, Paul Bert, with the full assent of the Liberal party, but against the wish of the Orthodox, legalized the separation of the Synod into two independent Consistories, those of Paris and Versailles. But as, contrary to expectation, the first elections to the Paris Consistory gave a large majority to the Orthodox, the newly-formed body entered a formal protest against the decree to which it owed its existence. Under these circumstances the government declined to sanction a General Synod, and both parties held assemblies

Synod of June, 1872.

Bois' Resolution.

Division of Synod, 25 March, 1882.

Lutherans. for their own purposes without any legal authorization and, of course, without any legal force.

The Lutherans in France, largely composed of German immigrants or their descendants, were naturally looked upon with some suspicion during the war with Prussia. After the peace, however, the prudent government of Thiers restrained any fanatical movement against them, and their former position was maintained. As French Lutheranism had lost through the war its theological Faculty in the university of Strasburg, Waddington established a Protestant Faculty at Paris, which was to serve however for the Calvinists as well as the Lutherans. The number of Lutheran consistories in France was reduced by the cession of Alsace and Lorraine from 44 to 6.

Paris Synod, July, 1872. At a General Synod in Paris, called by the government for the re-organization of the Church, it was decided that it should have henceforth two separate organizations, representing respectively the Evangelical and the Liberal party. The General Synod was to be formed of delegacies from both. Each of these bodies, in matters requiring the intervention of government, was to communicate direct with the Minister of Public Instruction, but in matters of doctrine, worship and discipline the General Synod was to be supreme. Both parties maintained Scripture to be the ultimate authority in matters of faith, and the Augsburg Confession to be the foundation of the constitution of the Church, without requiring an explicit and formal assent to it from the clergy. It was not until May, 1881, that the first General Synod actually held a regular session in Paris, when the two parties shewed a mutually friendly disposition.

General Synod, 1881.

Disestablishment, 1905. By the disestablishing Act of 1905 the State salary is of course withdrawn from ministers of the Lutheran and Reformed Churches alike, but as some compensation they gain greater freedom from State interference.

3. SOCIALISTIC MOVEMENTS.

It is impossible to leave altogether out of sight any waves of thought which have a tendency to change the conditions of existence of a society which is built on a foundation of principles derived from Christianity. And the movements which we call socialistic have a special claim to be regarded as a part of the history of the Church, inasmuch as some of their leaders have believed the teaching of the Lord to be favourable to a social system very different from that which has for many centuries prevailed.

The spread of a materialistic philosophy, with its denial of another and better world, tended to concentrate men's thoughts on the present. Those who looked for no future life were eager to make the most of that in which they actually moved, and to resent social arrangements which, as they thought, shut out a large portion of the race from the advantages and enjoyments of which they ought to be partakers.

In France, C. H. St Simon[2], a man of aristocratic family, influenced by the French Revolution, was the first to advocate such a reconstitution of society as would put an end to the glaring inequalities which are found in human life. The man who laboured with his hands should have his due share in the profit which arose from his productions, and none should have more than his just portion. The advantage of the individual must not be sought when it is antagonistic to the good of the whole society. This is

SOCIAL-
ISM[1].

St Simon,
1760—
1825.

---

[1] E. Belfort Bax, *The Religion of Socialism* (1887); L. Gronland, *The Co-operative Commonwealth* (1886); H. M. Hyndman, *The Historical Basis of Socialism* (1883); Rev. M. Kauffman, *Socialism and Communism* (1883), and *Christian Socialism* (1888); E. de Laveleye, *The Socialism of To-day*, trans. by G. H. Orpen (1884); R. T. Ely, *French and German Socialism* (New York, 1886); John Rae, *Contemporary Socialism*; Alfred Barry, *Lectures on Christianity and Socialism* (1890); R. Flint, *Socialism* (1894); T. Kirkup, *Enquiry into Socialism* (2nd ed. 1900); W. Graham, *Socialism, New and Old* (1891).

[2] A. J. Booth, *St Simon and St Simonism* (1871); Paul Janet, *Saint-Simon et le Saint-Simonisme* (1878); G. Weill, *Saint-Simon et son Œuvre* (1894), and *L'École Saint-Simonienne* (1896); articles on *St Simon* and *Socialism* by Robert Owen in *Encyclop. Brit.*, 8th edition.

of course a part of Christian teaching. St Simon[1] held that modern Christian teaching had been in practice too much confined to spiritual precepts and to the prospect of future blessedness, whereas it ought to have brought about a better organization, a nobler brotherhood, here on earth. It was to realize this that he set himself, no doubt with great sincerity, though with many errors. Neither the efforts of St Simon in France, nor those of his disciple Robert Owen in Scotland and America, permanently succeeded in maintaining communities on socialistic principles. But Socialism was almost eclipsed for a time by a system which offered a more radical cure for existing inequalities. In 1840, P. J. Proudhon frankly proclaimed[2] that all property is robbery, and waged war against existing institutions in Church and State. In the Revolution of 1848 he gained a certain influence, but the attempts which were made to carry some of his principles into practice had no good result. In Proudhon's system, anarchy is the culmination of social progress inasmuch as he teaches that the moral improvement of man would in the end render external law unnecessary; in the perfect society, order would be maintained through the individual's self-control and respect for the rights of others —an ideal which has many advocates, but which at present is a dream. Man is not yet fit to be freed from the restraint of positive law. Auguste Comte, in early days a disciple of St Simon, founded a philosophy, called Positive, which renounced all theology and idealism, and taught that we can know nothing except observed phenomena and the logical inferences from observation. Comte's philosophic system was expounded by his disciple Littré much more clearly than by himself. To his philosophy Comte added in his later days a Positive religion[3], which consists in the worship of the abstract conception of Humanity, and has been said to be Catholicism without God.

---

[1] In *Le Nouveau Christianisme* (1825).
[2] In his book, *Qu'est-ce que La Propriété?* (1840).
[3] In *Le Culte Systématique de l'Humanité* (1850). See R. Congreve, *Essays* (1874) and *Human Catholicism* (1876); Frederic Harrison, *Politics and a Human Religion* (1885); J. S. Mill, *Comte and Positivism* (1865).

4. BELGIUM.

The Congress of Vienna in 1815 welded Holland and Belgium into one kingdom, called the United Netherlands[1]—an unnatural union of peoples differing in race, speech, character and religion. In Belgium, the sacerdotal party which had resisted the proposed reforms of the Emperor Joseph II.[2] had lost but little of its fanaticism under the French domination. No sooner was the new constitution made known than episcopal opposition arose against the proposed equality in the eye of the State of all forms of religion, and an invading army of Jesuits waged war on the same side. The government now, in spite of its theoretical indifference, closed the theological seminaries and drove out the brothers of teaching Orders who had charge of them, while founding under their own control a college at Louvain, in which the course of philosophy was to be made obligatory on all candidates for the priesthood. This provoked the ultramontane party to join the advanced Liberals in defence of freedom of education. In their perplexity the government sought the help of the Prefect of the Propaganda, Capellari, afterwards Pope Gregory XVI., with a view to a Concordat, and ceased to insist on the attendance of candidates for holy orders on the lectures in the State college at Louvain. The college was speedily deserted, but the unwise conduct of those in authority soon gave plenty of openings for the attacks of the extreme clerical party.

In 1830 a revolt in Belgium brought to an end the uneasy union of that country with its uncongenial neighbour Holland[3]. It was fortunate enough to receive as King of the Belgians Leopold of Saxe-Coburg[4], who, though a Protestant reigning over mainly Roman-Catholic

---

[1] Théodore Juste, *Le Soulèvement de la Hollande en* 1813, etc. (Brux. 1870); P. H. Ditchfield, *The Church in the Netherlands* (1893).
[2] See above, p. 230.
[3] G. Oppelt, *Hist. de la Belgique de* 1830–60 (Bruxelles, 1861); C. V. de Bavary, *Hist. de la Révolution Belge de* 1830 (*Ib.* 1873); H. Heugh, *Religion in Geneva and Belgium* (Edinb. 1844); J. Thonissen, *La Belgique sous la Règne de Leopold I.* (Liège, 1855–9).
[4] T. Juste, *Memoirs of Leopold I.*, translated by Black (1870).

subjects, was a thoroughly constitutional king, a statesman, not a partisan. The temporary alliance between the Clericals and the Radicals was transformed into fierce hostility, and the struggle between these two parties has been since their severance the dominant factor in Belgian politics. The Moderates were soon absorbed by one or other of the extremes. Under the new constitution complete freedom of worship and education was established; the State undertook to provide stipends for the clergy, but otherwise stood aloof from the affairs of the Church. The emancipated Church founded a university in Louvain entirely under its own control, to which the Liberals responded by setting up a scientific and non-religious university in Brussels. Religious houses rapidly increased in number. When in 1878 the Radicals came into power under the leadership of Frère-Orban, and the teaching in elementary schools was taken out of the hands of the brothers and sisters of the teaching Orders and State schools were set up, the clergy founded Church schools in opposition to these, and refused absolution to the teachers and to the parents of pupils in them. The effect was that all Catholic children were withdrawn from the greater number of the State schools. Leo XIII., on the complaint of the Belgian government, expressed his disapproval of the proceedings of the bishops, but privately encouraged them to continue their resistance. The Prime Minister publicly denounced this duplicity and broke off diplomatic relations with Rome. The general election of 1884, however, gave the clericals a majority, the consequence of which was that the Church schools were encouraged while the non-religious were starved.

5. SPAIN[1] AND PORTUGAL.

No country in Europe during the nineteenth century suffered so severely as Spain from revolution, insurrection, and civil war. Governments have changed, ministries have fallen, constitutions have been given and revoked;

---

[1] P. B. Gams, *Kirchengeschichte von Spanien*, vol. III. pt. 2, from 1492–1879 (Regensburg, 1879); H. Baumgarten, *Geschichte Spaniens von d. Franz. Revol. bis auf unserer Tage* (3 vols., Leipzig, 1867 ff.); W. Lauser, *Geschichte Spaniens vom Sturze Isabellas an* (Leipzig, 1877).

sometimes clerical absolutism has prevailed, sometimes democratic radicalism; and nowhere has the party of revolution shewn more unsparing hostility to the clergy and the monks.

Ferdinand VII. had been nominally king of Spain from the time of his father's abdication in 1808, but he was of course unable to assert his regal authority during the French occupation of his kingdom. When in 1814 he became actual king, the Jesuits were re-admitted, the clerical party became again dominant, and even the Inquisition was restored. The discontent of the people broke out in the insurrection of 1820, and when this was put down by the help of a French army, a renewal of despotism followed. In the civil war which raged under the regency of the Queen-Dowager Christine, the national government gained sufficient power to abolish all monastic Orders, to confiscate their buildings, to declare all the estates of the clergy public property, and to abolish tithes. A threatening allocution of Gregory XVI. caused great indignation in the Cortes, and when in the following year he ventured to declare all their acts null and void, the assembly replied by making any intercourse with Rome a criminal offence. In 1843, Queen Isabella, a girl of thirteen, was declared by the Cortes to be of age, and after many delays and difficulties arising from the constant change of ministries a Concordat was arranged with the Pope, which provided that monastic and ecclesiastical property which had not been sold should be restored to its former owners, and an indemnity paid for such as had been sold; the number of dioceses was diminished by six, public instruction and the censorship of books were placed under the supervision of the bishops, and the Roman-Catholic religion was declared to be the only one tolerated by the State. By the Constitution of 1855 the nation bound itself to protect and maintain Catholic worship, but no Spaniard was to be persecuted on account of his religion so long as he abstained from overt acts of hostility to the established Church. Clerical influence however soon gained the upper hand with the Queen, but the instability of the various ministries prevented a settlement of ecclesiastical matters until in 1859 a new Concordat was sanctioned, giving further advantages to the

CH. X.

Ferdinand VII. 1814, *reactionary.*

Insurrection, 1820.

1833–37. *Anticlerical legislation.*
1841.
1842.

Isabella Queen, 1843.

Concordat, 1851.

Constitution of 1855.

Concordat of 1859.

Church. The Queen found herself at liberty to indulge in the persecution of Protestants, and expressed tender, if unavailing, sympathy with the Pope in his differences with the Italians. The Pope requited the kindly feeling of his affectionate daughter by sending to her the Golden Rose, the reward of virtue, at a time when her shameless life was destroying the last remnants of respect for the representative of the ancient Spanish monarchy. Eight months later her reign came to an end. The Provisional Government expelled the Jesuits, and abolished all monasteries and religious associations generally. The Cortes in 1869 sanctioned the draft of a new Constitution, under which Catholic worship was to be maintained, but foreigners, and even natives under certain circumstances, were to be allowed to practise other forms. All political and municipal rights were to be entirely independent of religious profession. The son of Isabella, Alphonso XII., returned to Spain as king in 1875, and was succeeded in 1886 by his posthumous son, Alphonso XIII., under the guardianship of his mother, Queen Maria Christina, an Austrian Archduchess. Under these sovereigns the struggles of clericals and radicals still continued, in which, on the whole, the clericals have maintained their advantage. Under these monarchs no very material change took place in the legal position of religious bodies.

Under the Constitution which was enacted after the expulsion of Queen Isabella, Protestantism was no longer a crime, though the scattered bodies of Protestants were obliged to conduct their worship in the most unobtrusive manner and were subject to annoyance from the fanatical spirit of the people. Of more importance than the scattered congregations of Protestants was the "Spanish Church," an attempt at the formation of a really reformed national Church of Spain. A priest of the Roman Church, Cabrera, was moved to leave it in consequence of what he believed to be its errors and corruptions, and from the year 1868 onwards preached and formed congregations in Seville and Madrid. This movement found a warm and

---

[1] J. A. Wylie, *Daybreak in Spain* (London, 1870); Mrs Peddie, *The Dawn of the Second Reformation in Spain*; J. A. Bain, *The New Reformation*, p. 169 ff. (London, 1906); F. Meyrick, *The Church in Spain* (London, 1891).

disinterested champion in Lord Plunket, Archbishop of Dublin[1]. His exertions in its favour extended over eighteen years; he thrice visited Spain to satisfy himself of the reality of the reformation, and freely gave of his substance for its support. In 1894 he had satisfied himself that the time had arrived for giving the detached congregations a complete hierarchy. In spite of much opposition from his brethren in England and Ireland, he paid a visit to Spain in the autumn of 1894, accompanied by the bishops of Clogher and Down, and on the 23rd Sept. in that year consecrated Cabrera as bishop of the "Iglesia Española." The Church thus formed is not to be regarded as an Anglican Church in Spain, but as a Reformed branch of the ancient Spanish Church, and in forming its vernacular offices and liturgy much has been drawn from the old Mozarabic, once the common use in Spain. *Archbishop Plunket consecrates bishop, 1894.*

Portugal, like Spain, suffered for some years from revolutions and changes of government. Donna Maria, who was recognized as Queen in 1834, devoted herself to promoting friendly relations with Rome. In 1841 she entered into negotiations for a Concordat, but the terms proposed were vigorously opposed by the Cortes, who desired to maintain the obligation of seeking the sanction of the State for all ecclesiastical enactments, and other constitutional limitations of the hierarchy. The Penal Code of 1852 made the clergy liable to heavy fines and imprisonment for any misuse of their spiritual privileges or any contravention of the law of the land. At last, in 1857, a Concordat was arranged, though it was not accepted by the civil government until 1859. It relates principally to the exercise by the Crown of the patronage of bishoprics, and by no means put an end to the strained relations of the Portuguese government with the Roman Curia. The civil Constitution declares the Roman-Catholic Church to be the national form of religion, and a Portuguese who passes to any other forfeits his civil rights. But it forbids persecution on religious grounds, PORTUGAL[2].

Concordat attempted, 1841,

arranged, 1857.

---

[1] *Memoir* by F. D. How (London, 1900); *Dict. Nat. Biogr.* Supplement, III. 275 ff.

[2] H. Morse Stephens, *Portugal* (London, 1891); F. Nippold, *Handbuch der Neuesten Kirchengeschichte*, II. 497 (ed. 1883); H. Kurtz, *Lehrbuch*, II. ii. 252 (ed. 1899).

and allows Protestant meeting-houses to be erected, provided that they are not made to resemble Churches. Protestantism has however made little progress in Portugal, and the Protestant congregations which exist are almost wholly composed of foreigners.

6. THE SOUTH-AMERICAN REPUBLICS.

General traits.

The South-American Republics[1] were shaken by the same instability of government, the same constant hostility between clericals and radicals, as the States in Europe from which they sprang. The Catholic Church, to which the populace are fanatically devoted, became stiffer and less amenable to outward influences, its ceremonies more practices of magical virtue here than elsewhere, while many of its opponents were not men who were earnestly seeking the truth, but denouncers of all religion as a priestly fraud.

Mexico,

1823.

Of all the South-American States none suffered more from revolutions and civil wars than Mexico[2]. From the beginning of its existence as an independent State, the government leaned for support mainly on the clergy, who were extremely rich and powerful. This state of things, however, came to an end with the accession to the Presidency, by the help of the Liberals, of Benito Juarez, a man of extraordinary ability and force of character. He proclaimed absolute freedom of religion, introduced civil marriage, declared estates of the clergy to be the property of the nation, and exiled the bishops who opposed him. The early years of Juarez's rule were, however, disturbed by a rebellion promoted by the clerical party, and during this chaotic period wanton aggressions on foreigners and an Act suspending all payments due to them for two years, drew on Mexico the hostility of England, Spain and France. With the two former powers, however, arrangements were made before actual hostilities commenced, and France alone in 1862 formally declared war against the government of Juarez. An Austrian Archduke,

Juarez President, 1859.

Anti-clerical measures.

War with France, 1862.

---

[1] R. G. Watson, *Spanish and Portuguese South America* (London, 1884).

[2] H. H. Bancroft, *Mexico*, vols. v. and vi. (San Francisco); W. Butler, *Mexico in Transition* (New York, 1892); Susan Hale, *Mexico* (London, 1891).

Maximilian, with the support of the French emperor, received the title of Emperor of Mexico and the benediction of the Pope. There was, however, no enthusiasm in favour of an Austrian supported by France. Maximilian found himself utterly unable to satisfy the monstrous demands of his clerical allies, Napoleon, alarmed by the attitude of the United States government, withdrew his troops, and the unlucky prince, deserted by almost every one, was taken prisoner and shot as a rebel by the sentence of a court-martial. From this time Juarez maintained his position, and carried out his anti-clerical laws, until his death in 1872. After this clericalism again raised its head, but Congress in 1873 nevertheless gave constitutional validity to the reforms of Juarez. Religious instruction in elementary schools was abolished and the Church generally was in many ways placed in an inferior position compared with that which it had previously enjoyed. Evangelical principles, when they were no longer forbidden by law, made considerable progress, though not without violent opposition from the fanatical populace. A Church—"Iglesia de Jesus"—formed by a converted priest, Francisco Aguilar, and an ex-Dominican, Manual Aguas, with evangelical doctrine and episcopal constitution, found many adherents, and in 1879 a clergyman named Riley, who had been the minister of a Spanish-speaking congregation in New York, became their bishop. Besides this, North-American missionaries of various denominations steadily carried on the work of evangelization.

In Brazil[1] up to 1884 the Roman-Catholic was the recognized religion of the State, but foreigners were not debarred from having their own places of worship and their own pastors. Protestant marriages were not recognized until in 1851 a law was passed which gave them legal validity, though it did not change the attitude of the Roman clergy towards them. After the year 1870, however, the government proceeded with more energy to curb the arrogant claims of the hierarchy. Protestant marriages were expressly declared to be on the same

---

[1] M. G. and E. T. Mulhall, *Handbook of Brazil* (Buenos Ayres, 1877); Sellin, *Das Kaiserreich Brasilien* (1882); Kurtz, *Lehrbuch*, II. 2, p. 274.

footing as Catholic, excommunication ceased to have any effect on a man's civil status, papal Bulls were not to be published in Brazil without the authorization of the government, and ecclesiastical appointments were to be notified to the civil officials. These liberal measures were not tamely submitted to by the clergy. Oliveira, Bishop of Olinda, published, without asking the sanction of the government, a Breve which the Pope had issued against Freemasonry, and himself excommunicated all Freemasons within his jurisdiction. The consequence was that he was brought before the highest civil tribunal on a charge of contravening the public law, and sentenced to four years' penal servitude. This was, however, commuted to imprisonment in a fortress, and after a year and a half remitted altogether. Seeing the constant influx of monks and nuns from abroad, the government in 1884 constituted a commission to put in force the already existing laws for the secularization of all monastic estates, compensating the actual holders by pensions. In the same year naturalized immigrants, and non-Catholics generally, were made eligible to the Imperial and Provincial parliaments. In 1888 the emancipation of the slaves was carried out with the hearty assent and coöperation of the bishops. The reign of the emperor Pedro II. was, with slight exceptions, peaceful and prosperous, but in November, 1889, a sudden revolution drove him from the throne, and proclaimed the conversion of the empire into a republic with the style and title of "the United States of Brazil."

In Argentina[1] toleration of all forms of religion was granted by the Constitution of 1865. In 1875 the proposal of the Archbishop of Buenos Ayres to restore to the Jesuits the chuches, houses, and properties of which they had been deprived, followed by other unpopular acts, caused a tumult in which the Jesuit College was sacked. In 1884 the papal nuncio received his passport, and formal communication with the Court of Rome was broken off. The diplomatist Pope, however, Leo XIII., found means of reestablishing friendly relations with the government.

---

[1] M. G. and E. T. Mulhall, *Handbook of the River Plate* (1884); Kurtz, *Lehrbuch*, II. 2, p. 273; Herzog, *Abriss*, II. 582.

The South-American Republics

In Chili[1] the episcopate excommunicated (1874) the authors of the Code which gave full freedom of worship to all sects alike. The President of the Republic himself was included in the bann, which was in fact however wholly disregarded. When in 1878 the archiepiscopal see of St Iago became vacant, the Pope, under flimsy pretexts, refused to accept the President's nominee. After the victory of Chili over Peru and Bolivia the nomination was pressed upon the Pope more emphatically than ever. The result was that the Curia sent out, with a view to an agreement, an apostolic delegate, who however, forgetting his position, made himself so vehement a political agitator that the government required his recall. In the end, he was removed from the territory of the Republic, and Congress decreed the complete separation of Church from State, with all its consequences of civil marriage and the freeing a man's civil status from all dependence on the Church. Guatemala[2] expelled the Jesuits, who had become both rich and powerful, in 1872. Two years later, President Borrias annoyed the clergy by forbidding them to wear clerical dress, unless in actually executing some clerical function. He also abolished all convents of nuns. In Venezuela, Guevara, Archbishop of Caracas, in 1872 forbade his clergy to take part in a national festival, and being then deprived and banished by the civil government, kept up an agitation from Trinidad, in British territory. The President, Guzman Blanco, after long and ineffectual negotiations with the papal nuncio, in 1876 submitted to Congress the draft of a law declaring the national Church independent of Rome. Congress not only accepted it, but intensified it by abolishing the territorial status of the bishops and assigning their incomes to the subvention of popular education. At last the Curia acquiesced in the deposition of Guevara and accepted as his successor the person who had previously been nominated. The anti-clerical laws were thereupon repealed.

In Ecuador[3] President Moreno concluded a Concordat with Rome, which provided that no form of religion but the Roman-Catholic was to be tolerated, education was to be put in the hands of the Jesuits, the bishops were to be

CH. X.
*Chili.
The Church against the State,* 1874.

*Guatemala.
Jesuits expelled,* 1872.

*Venezuela.
Archbishop Guevara banished,* 1872.

Church to be independent of Rome, 1876.

*Ecuador.
Concordat,* 1862.

---
[1] Kurtz, *u.s.* 272 ; Herzog, *u.s.* 582.
[2] Kurtz, *u.s.* 273.
[3] Kurtz, *u.s.* 272.

entrusted with the censorship of books, and all heresies to be put down by the State. Observance of the rites of the Church was to be enforced by the police. The State was in pecuniary difficulties, but nevertheless a tenth part of the annual revenue was to be handed over to the Pope. Moreno was however assassinated in 1875, and the Jesuits thereupon fled from Quito. The tenth paid to the Pope was forthwith abolished, and in 1877 an end was put to the Concordat.

CHAPTER XI.

THE TEUTONIC AND SCANDINAVIAN NATIONS.

I. THE ROMAN-CATHOLIC CHURCH.

1. CHURCH AND STATE[1].

THE conclusion of the great struggles, intellectual and material, which followed the French Revolution, found the Catholic Church in Germany enfeebled and disorganized. When the Peace of Paris in 1814 seemed to promise greater stability in matters ecclesiastical, there were left in Germany, outside Austria, only five bishops, mostly men in extreme old age.

But imperative as was the necessity to reorganize the dioceses and to provide them with bishops, the negotiations with the Papacy for this end lingered long. The Pope was reluctant to enter into treaties for ecclesiastical organization with princes who were in possession of secularized Church property, lest he should seem to acquiesce in the secularization, and the state of affairs after the Peace seemed at first so unstable that he was disposed to wait on events. On the other hand, the secular princes were anxious in any settlement to secure themselves against future encroachments of the spiritual power. It

The Church disorganized.

Negotiations with the Pope.

---

[1] H. v. Treitschke, *Deutsche Geschichte im 19 Jhdt.* (Leipzig, 1879 ff.); G. Gervinus, *Geschichte des 19 Jhdt.* (Leipzig, 1855 ff.); H. v. Sybel, *Cler. Politik im 19 Jhdt.* (Bonn, 1874); H. Schmid, *Gesch. d. Kath. Kirche Deutschland v. d. Mitte d. 18 Jhdt.* (Munich, 1874); E. Friedberg, *Der Staat und d. Bischofwahl in Deutschland* (Leipzig, 1873); H. Brück, *Gesch. d. Kath. Kirche im 19 Jhdt.*, vol. 3 (Mainz, 1896); *Akten-Stücke zur Gesch. d. Verhältnisse zwischen Staat u. Kirche im 19 Jhdt., mit Anmerkungen von H. v. Kremer-Auenrode* (Leipzig, 1880); J. J. v. Görres, *Germany and the Revolution*, trans. by J. Black (London, 1820).

would have seemed natural for the princes to make common cause in defence of their interests, but the circumstances of the several states were so various as to render such a course difficult if not impossible. Only some of the minor princes of South Germany took common action. Pius VII. entered into negotiations with the several states of Germany for the reorganization of ecclesiastical order.

PRUSSIA.

The negotiations with Prussia, which by the conquest of Silesia and the partition of Poland had acquired considerable Catholic territory in the East, and now in the recent settlement an addition in the West, led to a Convention between Pius VII. and King Frederick William III., the results of which appeared in a papal Bull of 1821. To the archbishopric of Cologne were made subject the sees of Treves, Münster, and Paderborn, to Gnesen-Posen that of Kulm. The dioceses of Breslau and Ermeland were "exempt," subject, that is, only to the direct authority of the Pope. The election of the bishops was assigned to the chapters, who were recommended by a papal Breve to choose only such persons as they had reason to believe would be acceptable to the king. But it was long before the Roman-Catholics came to a good understanding with the State. The former discovered many grievances in their relations with the latter. An actual conflict broke out on the question of marriages between Catholics and Protestants[1]. From the year 1803 a state-regulation had been recognized in the Eastern Provinces that the children of a mixed marriage should be brought up in the religion of the father, and such marriages had received the benediction of the priest. But when, in 1825, this regulation was extended to the Western Provinces, it encountered vehement opposition. Under the authority of a papal Breve of 1830, the priests in the Rhine Province and Westphalia refused to give their blessing to mixed marriages unless an undertaking was given that the children should be brought up in the Catholic faith. They were permitted to be present while

Bull of 1821.

Mixed Marriages.

Breve of 1830.

---

[1] J. Rutschker, *Die gemischte Ehen vom Kath. Standpunkt* (Wien, 1837); G. Jacobson, *Über die gemischte Ehen in Deutschland* (Leipzig, 1838); E. v. Ammon, *Die gemischte Ehen* (Dresden, 1839).

the essentials of the marriage were gone through, so as to make it valid, but they could not pronounce the matrimonial blessing. The Prussian government however did not withdraw its regulation, and the bishops seemed at first disposed to give way. Archbishop Von Spiegel of Cologne entered into an agreement with the government which, under colour of explaining the Breve, practically sanctioned the old practice. At this critical time Von Spiegel died, and was succeeded by Clemens August Von Droste-Vischering[1], an ardent and uncompromising supporter of the claims of the Church. He first gave a taste of his quality by silencing those Professors in the Roman-Catholic Faculty at Bonn who were suspected of liberal opinions in theology. In regard to the mixed marriages, he resolutely refused to yield to the requirements of the State, and was in consequence sentenced to imprisonment in a fortress. Archbishop Von Dunin, of Gnesen-Posen, shared his fate. Their suffragans recanted their acceptance of the agreement, and the bishops of the Eastern Province now declared, with one exception, that they would be guided strictly by the Breve of 1830. But in the end the authorities of the State did not find it expedient to proceed to extremities. Even Frederick William III. shewed some inclination to give in to the opposition, and his son and successor, Frederick William IV., a religious man and tolerant of Roman-Catholic views, went still further to meet the wishes of the Catholic clergy. He released the imprisoned archbishops, and ceased to insist on requirements the fulfilment of which might be contrary to the rights of conscience. Further, from and after Jan. 1, 1841, he sanctioned the direct intercourse of the bishops with Rome, and in the same year instituted a Catholic Department in the Ministry of Public Worship. Droste-Vischering resigned the see of Cologne, and was succeeded by Johann von Geissel[2], who had the happiness of seeing the work of completing Cologne Cathedral begun under the auspices

CH. XI.

Agreement of 1834.

Droste-Vischering and Dunin imprisoned, 1837.

Geissel, Archbishop, 1846.

[1] Irenæus [*i.e.* Gieseler], *Über die Kölnische Angelegenheit* (Leipzig, 1838); K. Hase, *Die beiden Erzbischöfe* (Leipzig, 1839); W. Maurenbrecher, *Die Preuss. Politik u. d. Kölner Kirchenstreit* (Stuttgart, 1881); C. Mirbt, art. *Droste-Vischering* in *Real-Encyclopädie*, v. 23 ff. (3rd ed.).

[2] Baudri, *Kardinal v. Geissel u. seine Zeit* (Köln, 1882).

of the king. After the revolutionary year 1848 the right of the Roman-Catholic Church in Prussia to manage its own affairs was recognized, and the German bishops in conference at Würzburg declared that they would not stand aloof from the renewed life of their country; that they welcomed the declaration of the Frankfort Parliament in favour of absolute freedom of religion; that they claimed the inalienable right of the Church to control its schools; that they looked to the renewal of Christian life through the raising of the standard of scientific teaching, through reform of discipline, and the reintroduction of synods of the Church. From this time the Church party became an important political factor in the Prussian state.

Bavaria had already accepted a Concordat[1]. This secured to the Church throughout the kingdom the maintenance of all its spiritual and canonical privileges and powers. The country was divided into two provinces; to the archbishopric of Munich-Freising the sees of Augsburg, Regensburg, and Passau were made suffragan, to Bamberg those of Würzburg, Eichstätt, and Speyer. The nomination of persons to fill vacant sees was given to the sovereign, their canonical institution to the Apostolic See. Bishops were to have a free hand in the administration of their dioceses so far as regards spiritual matters. The business was however not yet concluded. The supremacy of the State had to be safeguarded, and the Protestant discontent with the revival of episcopal privileges in a somewhat indefinite form to be taken account of. This was done in an Edict, which granted complete liberty of conscience in matters of religion, and placed the Protestant communities in a position of civil and political equality with the Roman-Catholic. This excited great dissatisfaction in Rome, and caused many of the Bavarian clergy to refuse to take the oath of allegiance to the Constitution unconditionally. After a time however the Roman authorities came to the conclusion that the Bavarian attitude towards the Church, if not approved, might at any rate be tolerated. The feeling of security was increased by the royal declaration of Tegernsee, that the government would strain no man's conscience, and

---

[1] H. v. Sicherer, *Staat u. Kirche in Baiern v.* 1798—1821 (Munich, 1873).

that the oath of allegiance to the Constitution was to be understood to refer to civil matters only.

In Hanover by a papal Bull of 1824 the ancient bishoprics of Hildesheim and Osnabrück were restored and declared "exempt." In elections of bishops the so-called "Irish Veto"—the right, that is, of striking out of the list of candidates unacceptable persons—was reserved to the Crown.

In South-western Germany, Würtemberg, Baden, and Hesse-Darmstadt, together with the state which had lately been electoral Hesse, the Grand-Duchy of Nassau, the principalities of Hohenzollern-Sigmaringen and Hechingen, and the free city of Frankfort, were formed by a Bull into a Province of the Upper Rhine, with Freiburg as its metropolis, and four bishoprics, Mainz, Rottenburg, Fulda, and Limburg. In the Province the chapters received the same rights in episcopal elections which had already been given to those in Prussia.

In Baden a fierce conflict between Church and State arose when on the death of the Grand-Duke Leopold the Archbishop, Hermann von Vicari, forbade the saying of a solemn mass, as not recognizing him for a Catholic. In 1853 the bishops of the Province of the Upper Rhine petitioned for the liberties needful for the due administration of the Church; freedom of education for the clergy and of their appointment to benefices; freedom to erect and hold possession of Catholic schools; the pastoral superintendence of the life of the people and the admission of religious orders to work in their dioceses; the management by the Church itself of the property guaranteed to it by the Peace of Westphalia or subsequent decrees of the Diet of the Empire. The refusal of these requests by the civil government led to the excommunication of the president of the Church Council by the archbishop, to which the government replied by bringing the archbishop as an offender against the law before a court of criminal jurisdiction. During the trial the archbishop was placed under arrest in his palace. These events led to negotiations with Rome, which resulted in a Concordat; but the vehement opposition of Liberal Catholics and Protestants induced the Second Chamber to refuse its sanction. The archbishop never-

Marginalia: Ch. XI. — Hanover. Bull of 1824. — South-western States. — Baden. Death of Leopold, 1852. — Bishops' Petition, 1853. — Concordat, 1859.

theless recognized the Concordat as legally binding, but found it expedient in 1860 to agree to a legislative compromise which gave him greater freedom in the institution to benefices. Fresh differences between Church and State arose when in 1862 the government declared all schools to be state-schools and placed them under the authority of an undenominational school-board, while the Catholic educational and charitable endowments were placed under the administration of the State. The Roman Curia forbade the clergy to become members of school-boards, but this order after some time, when the injurious effects of it became manifest, was withdrawn. On the death of Archbishop Vicari a dead-lock ensued, as the government and the chapter could not agree as to the choice of a successor, and the diocese was administered by a vicar-general, who maintained the same attitude which the archbishop had done.

Würtemberg entered into a convention with the Pope in 1857, Hesse-Darmstadt and Nassau with the bishops of Mainz and Limburg in 1854 and 1861.

In Austria the edicts of Joseph II. for the regulation of the Church[1] were in some respects modified by his successor Leopold II. In particular, episcopal seminaries were substituted for the general seminaries, to which the clergy were for the most part hostile. The Emperor Francis Joseph did away with the "placet," the necessity for obtaining the sanction of the civil government for any ecclesiastical edicts, allowed free intercourse with Rome, and gave to the bishops the right to administer discipline and regulate divine worship. In 1855 a Concordat was concluded with the See of Rome, which gave to the hierarchy both privilege and power, but the unfortunate issue of the war with Italy in 1859 induced the government to enter on a more liberal course, and to grant a real parity before the law to all forms of religion. The Concordat, after being in many respects limited by law, was utterly shattered on the proclamation of the dogma of Papal Infallibility in 1870, as it was evident that the position of one of the contracting parties, the Papacy, was materially changed. In 1874 three laws of the Austrian Diet provided, that all pastoral letters and other circulars

[1] See above, p. 228.

of the bishops, all appointments to ecclesiastical benefices, and all ordinances which made any considerable change in divine service, must be subject to the approval of the civil government. All abuses of ecclesiastical authority were to be made liable to punishment by the secular courts; the incomes of all benefices and monasteries were to be taxed to increase the incomes of the poorer clergy, and conditions were laid down for the formation of new religious societies. The bishops declared that they could only obey these laws so far as they were, in substance, in harmony with the Concordat; but no actual conflict occurred as both parties desired to avoid it. About 1899 a movement began, partly religious, partly political, to declare the Church in Austria independent of Rome—"los von Rom[1]"—which if it should find a leader of commanding character may perhaps turn out to be important.

In the revolutionary year 1848, when changes of all kinds seemed to be impending, the bishops saw that isolated efforts were insufficient, and that they must make common cause to gain what they believed to be their rights. In the autumn of that year the whole episcopate of Germany met in conference at Würzburg, under the presidency of Archbishop Geissel of Cologne. In 1850 a conference of the bishops of the Rhine Province took place at Freiburg, which addressed a memorial to the several governments, in which the right of the bishops to regulate the education and discipline of the clergy and their appointment to benefices, to erect and maintain their own schools, to have the pastoral superintendence of the people and to manage Church property, was insisted on. As the reply of the governments was not satisfactory, a new memorial was presented by a second assembly in Freiburg, and meanwhile the bishops proceeded to put into practice the more important of the rights which they claimed, a proceeding which naturally brought them into conflict with the State authorities. The Archbishop of Freiburg was even for a short time placed under arrest. Nevertheless, an impression was made, and after a time the several governments consented to treat with the Church.

[1] J. A. Bain, *The New Reformation*, p. 98 ff., who refers to P. Braeunlich, *Berichte über den Fortgang der Los-von-Rom Bewegung*.

In Switzerland[1] was presented the singular spectacle of a religious war in the midst of the nineteenth century. The Napoleonic period had thrown into confusion both the civil and ecclesiastical organization of the Confederation, and it was not until after long negotiations with Pius VII. and Leo XII. that an arrangement with Rome was arrived at, which was embodied in a papal Bull in 1828. This Bull, supplemented by agreements in 1841 and 1845, divided the country into the dioceses of Chur, Basel, Sion, St Gallen and Lausanne with Geneva. Ticino was placed under the jurisdiction of the Bishop of Como. No archbishopric was created for Switzerland, but a papal nuncio resided in Lucerne. From the year 1830 onward strained relations arose between the Protestant and the Catholic cantons, in consequence of which several monasteries were abolished, while Lucerne, on the other hand, readmitted the Jesuits. In the end, the Catholic cantons resolved to withdraw from the Swiss Confederation, and to form a Separate Confederation (Sonderbund) of their own. The question, whether their withdrawal could be acquiesced in, came to the arbitrament of war (1845). The Catholic alliance was defeated and fell to pieces. As a result, it was compelled to pay a heavy indemnity, most of the monasteries were dissolved, restrictions were placed on the actions of the Roman-Catholic hierarchy, and Marilley, Bishop of Lausanne, who protested against such legislation, was banished from the territories of the Republic. The Vatican Council occasioned further trouble, especially in the dioceses of Geneva and Basel. When the former was separated from the diocese of Lausanne and put in charge of a Vicar-Apostolic, that dignitary, Bishop Mermillod, was at once exiled from Geneva, and the churches were gradually put into the possession of the Old-Catholics. Bishop Lachat of Basel, as he visited with ecclesiastical censure those of his clergy who did not accept the Vatican decrees, was disowned by the several cantons of his diocese, with the exception of Lucerne and Zug, and ordered to quit Solothurn. Those of the clergy

---

[1] C. Gareis u. Ph. Zorn, *Staat u. Kirche in der Schweitz* (Zürich, 1877); A. Kelber, *In rei Memoriam, Aktenstücke* (Aarau, 1882); Nippold, *Neueste Kirchengeschichte*, II. 33; Kurtz, *Lehrbuch*, II. 2, 202; Hase, *Kirchengeschichte*, III. 2, 333.

who adhered to the bishop shared his fate. The proceedings of the State pressed with special hardness on the Catholics of the Bernese Jura. Their churches were everywhere given over to the Old-Catholics, and the clergy not only deprived of their benefices but in many cases banished. This banishment lasted only three years, but divine service had to be celebrated in barns and suchlike makeshifts, as some years passed before the churches were given back to their original possessors. The see of Basel was restored in 1884. In connexion with this, Canton Ticino had been separated from the diocese of Como, and placed in charge of an Apostolic Administrator, to which office Bishop Lachat was appointed, so that a personal union was created between Ticino and Basel— an arrangement which was further regularized in 1888. Geneva was again united to Lausanne on a vacancy of the see, but when Mermillod was nominated Bishop of Lausanne, the government resumed its unfriendly attitude. Mermillod's successor was, however, recognized.

Though Holland[1] may be considered on the whole a Protestant country, a considerable portion of its population is Roman-Catholic. In Brabant, Limburg and Luxemburg they are both numerous and zealous. When the Constitution of 1848 laid down the principle of absolute religious equality, there was a large influx of Jesuits, and Pius IX. reorganized the Roman-Catholic hierarchy under an archbishop and four bishops. Thereupon arose a great agitation among the Protestants, both in and out of Parliament. In the end, however, the papal ordinances were allowed to stand, with certain safeguards against abuses. The Hollandish Old-Catholics—the so-called "Jansenist" Church—in consequence of their rejection of the doctrine of the Immaculate Conception of the Virgin Mary, were excommunicated anew, and on the enacting by the Vatican Council of the Infallibility of the Pope joined the Old-Catholics of other countries in refusing to accept the innovation.

[1] F. Nippold, *Die Römisch-Kath. Kirche im Königreich der Niederlande* (Leipzig, 1877).

2. LITERATURE AND LIFE.

Condition of the Church.

The Roman-Catholic clergy in Germany had fallen in the later years of the eighteenth century under the influence of a new spirit which had thawed much of the old rigidity of dogma. On the one hand, many had drifted into a spiritual dulness and indifference resembling that which prevailed in the English Church in the same period. On the other, some of the best spirits had come to insist so strongly on the truly evangelical side of their faith, the teaching of Christ Himself, that the distinctive doctrines of the Church had been much obscured. This state of things made for quietness, for neither the indifferent nor the pious were disposed to quarrel with their Protestant neighbours or with the laws of the kingdom in which they lived.

Sailer, 1751—1832, Bishop, 1829.

One of those whose life was pervaded by the true spirit of Christ was John Michael Sailer[1], the German Fénelon, who after a varied career became in 1829 Bishop of Ratisbon, and was in word and deed the model of a Christian teacher, so that Görres[2] describes him as one who had kept touch with the spirit of the age in all its forms; one who had the courage of his opinions, had thoroughly examined the claims of science and had not shrunk from any depth of research. In the higher regions of thought he had boldly held the Cross on high, winning hearts and minds by simplicity and love. To his training is due a school of priests abreast of the requirements of the time, capable of undertaking the charge of the people and the education of the young; of restoring the true conception of God to the schools, and sowing good seed which will bring forth an hundred-fold. With Sailer should be associated his friend von Wessenberg[3], who, like him, was eager to raise the education of the clergy above the dull level of routine into which it had fallen, and who went further in the direction of liturgical reform

Wessenberg, 1774—1860.

---

[1] F. W. Bodemann, *J. M. Sailer* (Gotha, 1856); J. Aichinger, *J. M. S.* (Freiburg, 1865); Mesner, *J. M. S.* (Mannheim, 1876); A. Buchner, *Zur Verständigung über S.'s Priesterschule* (Augsburg, 1870).

[2] Quoted by Kraus, *Lehrbuch*, 564.

[3] His life has been written by J. Beck (1862); see *Saturday Rev.* Dec. 20, 1862; and by Friedrich, in *Badische Biographien* (1875).

than any of his contemporaries, even ordering the Mass to be said in German within his diocese of Constance. Another remarkable figure was George Hermes[1], Professor at Münster and afterwards at Bonn. Like Descartes, he was for shaking off all preconceptions, and starting on a career of philosophy from the bare fact of existence; like Kant, he found in the practical reason a demonstration that God is a necessary hypothesis; but further, he believed that reason, duly used, led to the very same truths which are presented to the Catholic in Scripture and Tradition. Through his public teaching he attracted a large number of admiring followers, who came to occupy most of the professorial chairs in the Catholic universities or faculties of Westphalia and the Rhine provinces. In 1835, however, the Holy Father condemned Hermesianism, which thenceforth dropped gradually out of sight, though much of its influence remained.

Hermes, 1775—1831.

Anton Günther[2], a secular priest in Vienna, set himself to defend Christianity. Starting from the Cartesian premiss, that the thinking subject must certainly exist, he endeavoured to shew that correct reasoning from this premiss must result in the acknowledgement of the creation of the world by God and the Incarnation of the Saviour. In fact, the whole of Catholic theology might thus be logically proved. Günther found disciples who popularized and propagated his views. But a defence of Christian dogma which rested on reason was by no means to the taste of the Ultramontanes; the cry was raised that Günther contradicted the traditional theology. Early in 1857 his works were placed in the Index of prohibited books, and the Pope declared that the philosopher was heretical with regard to the Trinity, to anthropology and to Christology; that he over-valued reason and undervalued the Fathers. Günther at once submitted. His adherents were silent, but his influence continued to work quietly among the Catholics of Germany, and contributed much to form the theology of the Old-Catholics.

Günther, 1783—1863,

declared heretical, 1857.

---

[1] Elvenich, *Acta Hermesiana* (Göttingen, 1836); C. G. Niedner, *Philosophiae Hermesii Explicatio* (Leipzig, 1838).

[2] P. Knoodt, *Anton Günther* (Wien, 1881); F. Michelis, *Die Günthersche Philosophie* (1854).

Franz von Baader[1], a physician and man of science, who had been drawn to theology by writings of Böhme, and much influenced by Schelling, shared the lot of the Hermesians. His teaching on the feasibility of an emancipation from the dictatorship of Rome was naturally not acceptable to the Papalists, who had sufficient influence to procure the suppression of his public lectures, though he did not cease to express his opinions in writing. Akin to Baader is Joseph von Görres, a physicist who was also a mystic. He was accused of pantheism, but in his great work on Christian Mysticism, while still maintaining his opinions on physiology and psychology, he was careful to shew that he held unimpaired the faith of the Church.

A remarkable group of men is known as the Tübingen school, though that university was not in all cases the principal scene of their activity. Franz Anton Staudenmaier, Professor in Giessen, afterwards at Freiburg-in-Breisgau, like Günther attempted to build a philosophical system on the bare fact of consciousness. He never departed, however, from the principles of the Christian revelation; the substance of his doctrine rests wholly on faith, philosophy only gives form to that which faith has accepted. In Tübingen itself taught for many years John Sebastian v. Drey, who, in his earlier days influenced by the writings of Kant, Fichte, and Schelling, became in his mature years perhaps the ablest defender of Christianity among Catholic theologians. A kindred spirit was John Baptist v. Hirscher, author of a standard book on Christian morality, pervaded by a warmth of Christian feeling which had not been found in the dry and formal treatises of his predecessors in the region of ethics. The very able man who came to be recognized as the head of the Tübingen school, John v. Kuhn, was influenced both by Drey and Hirscher. In his earlier days he gained a high reputation as a metaphysician, and was also a distinguished figure in the politics of his native country, Würtemberg, but his fame rests mainly on his great work on Christian Dogmatics. Probably no theological work of this period shews a more remarkable union of philosophic thought with

[1] Kuno Fischer, *Zur 100-jährigen Geburtsfeier F. v. Baader* (Erlangen, 1865).

theological learning. Like Kant, he was opposed to the notion that everything worth knowing could be proved by logical demonstration, like a proposition in geometry, but he believed that philosophy had a great task before it in the wide region of Christian thought. He regarded Thomas Aquinas as his master and guide, and held, as many of his contemporaries in Germany held, the strong conviction that modern divines had undervalued and too hastily cast aside the treasures of ancient and mediæval theology. More than one controversy arose out of his dogmatic work, especially as to the teaching of Aquinas on nature and grace; and again on the subject of predestination and election. This discussion was thought of sufficient importance to be referred to Rome for investigation, the result of which was not unfavourable to Kuhn. [1869.]

Among those whom it is difficult to assign to any school may be mentioned Jacob Frohschammer[1], a Professor in Munich, who in treating of the origin of the human soul defended traducianism—the theory that a man's soul as well as his body is derived from his parents—against creatianism—the theory that the soul is in all cases a special creation—and by his work on the freedom of science incurred the censure of Rome. In the end he forsook the definite Roman-Catholic standpoint, while continuing his contest against what he held to be fatal error in D. F. Strauss and Darwin. Of a very different stamp was F. Michelis, a Professor in Braunsberg, who, after giving his great scientific attainments to the defence of the Christian faith, devoted many years to the study of the relations between Platonic philosophy and Christian theology. [Frohschammer, b. 1821. 1862. F. Michelis, 1815—1856.]

At the head of the great historical school of Catholics in Germany we must place John Adam Möhler[2]. This remarkable man was an alumnus of Tübingen, who had enlarged his knowledge and field of research by visits to Austria and North Germany, where he was influenced by the teaching of Schleiermacher. Returning to Tübingen in 1823 as tutor in theology he devoted himself to the [J. A. Möhler, 1796—1838, at Tübingen, 1823.]

[1] Autobiography in Heinrichsen's *Deutsche Denker und ihre Geistesschöpfungen*, 2nd and 3rd Heft (2nd ed. 1888).

[2] Wörner, *J. A. Möhler* (Regensburg, 1866); Reithmayer in Wetzer and Welte's *Kirchen-Lexicon*, VII. 189 ff.

Ch. XI.

'Athanasius,' 1827.
'Symbolik,' 1832.

study of the Fathers. His great work on "Athanasius and the Church of his Time" shewed him to be not only full of knowledge, but a master of thought and expression. He is probably best known by his "Symbolik," a treatise on the differences between Catholics and Protestants as shewn in their public Confessions of Faith, a work which convinced his opponents at any rate that a Roman-Catholic might be a fair-minded man and a good reasoner. This work was vigorously attacked from the Protestant side by F. C. Baur and K. I. Nitzsch; and Möhler, finding his position in Tübingen uneasy, accepted

Munich, 1835.

a call to Munich. There, however, after three years he passed away, worn out by ill-health and constant toil. In no one of modern German theologians is there found a more remarkable union of critical keenness with heart-felt enthusiasm, or greater charm and personal influence. When Möhler arrived in Munich, he found there as Professor of History a singularly impressive figure,

Döllinger, 1799— 1890, Professor at Munich, 1827.

J. J. Ignaz v. Döllinger[1], who in numerous writings shewed the extraordinary breadth of his knowledge, his critical acumen, and his deep interest in the welfare of the Church. His personality was impressive and attractive. In the controversies about the temporal power of the Pope, which preceded and followed the Vatican Council, he rises superior in a certain stateliness of character above the general throng of excited combatants, and when the Council decreed the Infallibility of the Pope he could not receive the innovation, but became the principal guide of the Old-Catholics. Probably no other German theologian has had so much influence in the Anglican Church. By the side of Döllinger may be

Hefele, Prof. 1840, Bishop 1869, d. 1893.

set his younger contemporary, Karl Joseph v. Hefele, for nearly thirty years Professor of Church History in Tübingen, afterwards Bishop of Rottenburg. He took a conspicuous part in the Vatican Council, and was with much difficulty persuaded to accept its decree as to Papal Infallibility. His works, of which the best known is his History of Councils, are distinguished by thorough and unprejudiced research, mastery of the subject, and literary

---

[1] J. Friedrich, *J. von Döllinger* (München, 1899—1901); Luise v. Kobell, *J. von Döllinger, Erinnerungen* (München, 1891).

skill. His equal, or probably his superior, in mere learning, was Augustin Theiner, who passed the greater part of his life at Rome, from the year 1833 onwards as Prefect of the Vatican Archives, where he used his position to publish a series of learned works of the highest value. During the Vatican Council the intrigues of the Jesuits brought him into disfavour with Pius IX., and caused his removal from the office which he so well filled. In 1874 he died.

The lives of many eminent German Catholic theologians have shewn the prevalence of an independence of thought which was by no means satisfied with mere current tradition, and when in 1844 Archbishop Arnoldi exhibited to public view the "Holy Seamless Coat" preserved in the treasury at Treves[1] as the actual vesture worn by the Lord Himself, this discontent manifested itself in several quarters. Many men who had held all the articles of the Catholic faith were still reluctant to have a mediæval superstition revived with great pomp and ceremony. A Silesian priest, Johannes Ronge, who was under suspension in consequence of his free opinions, but was otherwise of unimpeached character, gave voice to this feeling in a published letter to Archbishop Arnoldi, in which he protested strongly against this particular act of fanaticism, and against many similar superstitions elsewhere. Ronge was deprived of his orders, but his letter was approved by many thousands of Catholics and Protestants. Meantime, a little band of thoughtful people in Schneidemühl, in Silesia, without leaving the Church, had arrived at the conviction that some of the doctrines reputed Catholic rested on no sure foundation. To these came in 1844 a like-minded priest, Johann Czerski, whom they recognized as their leader. Czerski was suspended

Ch. XI.

A. Theiner at Rome, 1833,

removed from office, 1870.
d. 1874.

The Holy Coat of Treves, 1844.

J. Ronge, 1813— 1887,

his letter, 1844.

J. Czerski, 1813—?.

---

[1] A. J. Binterim, *Zeugnisse für die Aechtheit d. Heil. Rockes zu Trier* (Düsseldorf, 1845); J. Marx, *Ausstellung d. Heil. Rocks* (Trier, 1845); V. Hansen, *Aktenmässige Darstellung...d. Heil. Rocks* (Regensburg, 1845); J. v. Görres, *Die Wallfahrt v. Trier* (Regensburg, 1845); J. Gildemeister u. H. von Sybel, *Der Heil. Rock zu Trier u. die 20 andern Heil. ungenähten Röcke* (Düsseldorf, 1844); J. N. v. Wilmowsky, *Der Heil. Rock, eine Archäol. Prüfung* (Trier, 1876). The Coat was again exhibited in 1891; see F. Korum, *Wunder...bei der Ausstellung d. Heil. Rockes, im J.* 1891 (Trier, 1894); Clarke, *A Pilgrimage to the Holy Coat of Trèves* (1892).

by his ecclesiastical superiors, when he and his supporters formed a separate body and petitioned the government for authorization, which was granted. Ronge joined them, and formed a congregation in Breslau. The society in Schneidemühl put forth a declaration in favour of Communion in both kinds, against the invocation of saints and the devotion before images, against sacramental absolution and indulgences, against the use of Latin in the Churchservices, against the forced celibacy of priests, against the refusal of benediction to mixed marriages, and against the claim of the Pope to be the Vicar of Christ on earth. On this basis a "German-Catholic" society[1] was founded, which at first, as it fell in with a great body of religious opinion hitherto obscure, seemed to promise a great future, and in fact for a few years had followers in many of the large towns; but their views were too wholly negative to hold together a permanent society; no standard of positive doctrine was attained; many of the members denied the Divinity of Christ, and the pale light of the German-Catholic Church vanished in the telluric fires of the Revolution of 1848. This stormy period gave to the Church freedom in the formation of associations for various purposes, which was freely used. Everywhere arose societies for the promotion of Christian beneficence, for the defence of the faith, and for its extension by means of Christian missions. In particular, the various ultramontane "Pius Associations" in the Rhine district united themselves in a great "General Assembly of Catholic Associations," to which both the bishops assembled in Würzburg and Pius IX. himself gave their blessing. The plan formed by this body of founding a free Catholic University, opposed by the various governments and very feebly supported by the public, came to nothing.

[1] S. Laing, *Notes on the Prospects of a Schism from Rome, called the German-Catholic Church* (London, 1845); W. A. Lampadius, *Die Deutschkath. Bewegung* (Leipzig, 1846); Eduin Bauer, *Geschichte d. Deutsch-Kath. Kirche* (Meissen, 1845).

3. THE CONTEST FOR CULTURE[1].

The liberal movement in Germany in 1848, though it gave greater freedom to the Church to regulate its own concerns, caused great alarm to an important section of the clergy. From that time came into prominence a school of theologians who wished to make the Church supreme in every part of civil and religious life. They were therefore deadly enemies of liberalism of every kind; they denounced constitutions, parliaments, and civic privileges as irreconcilable with the majesty of the Crown and injurious to the rights of the Church. It naturally followed that they looked with dread on the education given in the German universities, the tendency of which was to produce inquirers and patriots, rather than devoted Roman-Catholics. The future clergy, at any rate, should, they urged, be educated wholly in episcopal seminaries or in schools managed by members of regular Orders. This party was sometimes spoken of as that of the "New Scholastics"; its principal champions were Jesuits. It was scarcely to be expected that the accession of a Protestant to the Imperial throne of Germany would be pleasing to the Roman-Catholics of this school. In fact, the enthusiasts among them seem to have felt that the Emperor's Protestantism could be condoned only on his entering on a crusade for the restoration of the temporal power to the Pope—a romantic imagining which could hardly commend itself to a king of Prussia who was also an ally of the king of Italy.

For some years after 1848 the relations between Church and State in Prussia had been, if not cordial, at any rate not openly hostile. The feeling of the Protestants towards their Roman-Catholic neighbours was however much changed by the Papal Syllabus of

[1] L. Hahn, *Geschichte des Kulturkampfes in Preussen, in Aktenstücken dargestellt* (Berlin, 1881); A. Mücke, *Der Kirchenpolitische Kampf u. Sieg in Preussen* (1878); R. Schlottmann, *Der Deutsche Gewissenskampf* (Halle, 1882); R. A. Lipsius, *Zehn Jahre Preuss.-Deutsches Kirchenpolitik* (Halle, 1887); F. X. Schulte, *Geschichte des Preuss. Kulturkampfes in Aktenstücke* (Essen, 1882); P. Majunke, *Gesch. d. Kulturkampfes* (Paderborn, 1886).

1864[1], in which war was declared against even the most moderate liberalism, and still more by the Vatican Decree of Papal Infallibility. The consequence was that when Prince Bismarck returned in 1871 from the victorious campaign against France, if, on the one hand, he found a compact army of clerics who took the word of command from Rome, he found, on the other, a state of feeling in Parliament and in the country at large which rendered it easy to carry enactments which would much hamper their obedience to the behests of their foreign Head. In fact, the mediæval war of Papacy against Empire was on the point of being renewed. On the one hand, the state claimed, when it clashed with the Church, itself to define the extent of its authority; on the other, the Church asserted a divine right to be allowed to carry out unhindered its canon law and its great mass of traditional customs and observances. The principles of Pope Hildebrand, who claimed the feudal sovereignty of all the kingdoms of the West, were doubtless held also, if not avowed, by Pius, and it was with this in his mind that Bismarck uttered his famous saying, "we are not going to Canossa[2]."

The first proceeding in Prussia was to abolish the Catholic Department of the Ministry of Public Worship, which was thought to have become Ultramontane. The favour which the government shewed to the Old-Catholics led to conflicts with those ecclesiastics who refused to grant to them such use of church buildings as the civil authorities required. To break the power of the clergy over elementary education, which in Prussian-Poland at least was thought a political danger, a Law on School-Inspection was passed, which gave to the state the power of inspecting all public schools. Soon after, members of religious Orders were excluded from taking part in elementary education, and the congregations which had been formed for work in the higher schools (gymnasia) were dissolved. As the pulpits were thought to be too often unpatriotic, a law of the Empire made preachers who abused the privilege of free speech liable to imprisonment. The Prussian Parliament asserted the right of the

---

[1] See above, p. 360.   [2] See Hardwick, *Middle Ages*, 245.

government to regulate the schools, and to nominate school-inspectors at its own discretion. An Imperial law expelled the Jesuits and several kindred Orders from the territory of the Empire. This was taken to be an open declaration that the Church was to be persecuted. To clear the field for the general action, two articles of the Prussian Constitution, 15 and 18, which gave complete independence to all religious societies, were so modified as to assert subjection of such societies to the laws of the state and to the superintendence of the government. Thereon followed the famous "Laws of May," introduced by Falk, the Minister of Public Worship, and passed by large majorities. These were as follows. (1) No Church is empowered to inflict on its members any other than purely spiritual penalties, such as the withdrawal of religious privileges. (2) Discipline over officials of a Church can be maintained only through German tribunals and by a regular process. An appeal was in all cases to be allowed to a King's Court for ecclesiastical affairs, to which authority was given to dismiss any official who had so offended against the law in the exercise of his office that his continuance in it was incompatible with the maintenance of order in the state. (3) Every candidate for the ministry must have been educated in a German high-school (gymnasium) and have passed three years in a university recognized by the state, or some other place of education admitted to be equivalent by the Minister of Public Worship. Candidates must also satisfy the state as to their attainments in general culture. All ecclesiastical seminaries are to be subject to state inspection. Every appointment to an office in the Church is to be notified to the governor of the province, who within thirty days may object to it, such objection to be subject to an appeal to the King's Court. Every benefice with cure of souls must be filled within a year after the occurrence of a vacancy. (4) Withdrawal from a Church is free to all its members, and those who have withdrawn are thenceforth free from all payments or services to it.

The attempt in the third law to secure for the clergy a better and more liberal education than they could receive in episcopal seminaries caused the whole struggle to receive the name of the "Contest for Culture" (Kultur-

CH. XI.

May-Laws, 21 May, 1874.

Kultur-Kampf.

Kampf) which very imperfectly describes the great battle between Papacy and Empire, between civil and ecclesiastical authority.

Resistance to May-Laws.

On the first introduction of the "May-laws," as they came to be called, the bishops had represented in a memorial that they were in conscience bound to take no part in carrying out these un-Catholic measures. These laws did in fact hamper them in almost every function, and they could hardly be faithful to their duty to the Church without disregarding them. The most frequent cause of collision was the requirement which bound the bishop to submit the name of a clerk to the governor of the province before appointing him to a benefice—a requirement which had existed in Prussia up to 1850, as well as in Bavaria, Würtemberg, and Baden, and had been carried out in practice, though lacking the sanction of the Roman Curia. Cases of disobedience multiplied from day to day, and as fines, distraint on goods, and suspension of stipend were found ineffective, a long series of bishops had to submit to periods of imprisonment, and, when they remained contumacious, to deprivation of office. The Imperial authority reinforced the Prussian legislation by the Law of Expatriation, which empowered a state of the Empire to banish a contumacious clerk from the whole Imperial territory. An Imperial enactment in 1875 made civil marriage obligatory in all cases. In 1875 the Pope made himself a party to the strife by an Encyclical to the Prussian bishops in which he declared the Prussian laws relating to the Church to be null and void. Prussia replied by increased severity towards the clergy. All state aid to bishops and incumbents was now suspended until they should make a formal declaration of their ready obedience to the law of the land; those articles of the Constitution of 1850 which guaranteed the right of self-government to Catholic and Protestant communities alike were repealed, religious Orders and Congregations were abolished, and their various institutions were ordered to be dissolved within six months. With the accession of Leo XIII. to the See of Rome hopes of peace began to dawn on the disturbed Church, as he entered into negotiations which in the end led to his giving the long-refused permission to the bishops to notify to the civil

Pope's Intervention, 1875.

authorities their appointments to benefices; but nine years elapsed before a definite peace was concluded with the Prussian government. At last, terms were agreed upon, and the Parliament passed five amending Acts in which it gave up in succession almost all the positions for which it had fought. Of the whole of the May-laws there remained in the end only the law restraining the abuse of the pulpit, the anti-Jesuit legislation, and the repeal of the three articles of the Constitution. The law against the Jesuits, however, was so modified as to permit them to pass freely through all parts of the Empire. The obligation laid upon the bishops to notify their appointments, and the possible veto of the civil magistrate, remained indeed, but so pared down as to be of little importance.

Of the other German states Baden and Hesse-Darmstadt took the most active part in the contest with Ultramontanism, taking measures against the claims of the Church in some respects more severe than the Prussian May-laws. In Baden all theologians were required to pass an examination in general culture before a Commission named by the state, or they were excluded from every ecclesiastical office. The Archbishop of Freiburg forbade candidates in his province not only to sit for this examination, but even to acknowledge it by seeking exemption from it. After six years' defiance however the archbishop ceased to insist on the last requirement, and the government requited him by ceasing to require the examination. After the example of Prussia, the government of Hesse-Darmstadt also made its peace with the Roman Curia. On the whole, the Church gained more than the state from the unsatisfactory contest.

4. THE EVANGELICAL UNION[1].

In the early part of the nineteenth century the state of theology was favourable to an attempt to unite the long-separated Protestant Churches. In face of the ever-

---

[1] J. G. Scheibel, *Aktenmässige Geschichte der Neuesten Union* (Leipzig, 1834); A. G. Rudelbach, *Reformirte Lutherthum und Union* (Leipzig, 1839); C. J. Nitzsch, *Urkundenbuch der Evang. Union* (Bonn, 1853); F. Brandes, *Geschichte der Kirchl. Politik d.Hauses Brandenburg* (Hamburg, 1873); Gieseler, v. 209 ff.; Hase, *K. Geschichte*, v. 528 ff., 595 ff.; Kurtz, II. ii. 34 ff.

advancing Rationalism the differences between Lutheran and Reformed seemed insignificant compared with those which divided them from their common enemy. Theologians could not but be aware, that the doctrines which had occasioned separation were not revealed with such absolute clearness and certainty in Holy Scripture that no deviation from them could be admitted. Forms and customs the two Churches agreed in thinking non-essential. These views were accepted by the people generally with the more readiness as the value attached to the speculative development of revealed truth declined. In fact, the wall of partition between Lutheran and Calvinist had to a great extent crumbled away under the influence of a disintegrating atmosphere, and all that was needed seemed to be a formal recognition of the fact that it was no more. In the amalgamation of the different ecclesiastical organizations it would not be necessary to introduce everywhere identical forms of divine service. Mutual acknowledgement that in each Church the pure Word of God was preached and the sacrament duly administered would suffice to form the basis of one community for the two. When the third centenary of the Lutheran Reformation came round, in 1817, there was in fact general readiness to welcome proposals for unity.

Frederick William III.'s measures.

On the 27th Sept. in that year King Frederick William III. of Prussia made a request to the ecclesiastical authorities of his kingdom that they would use their influence, in this year of Jubilee, to bring together the two existing Churches into one Evangelical Church. It met with very general acceptance, and in many places on the day of Jubilee, 31st Oct., a common Eucharist was celebrated by Lutherans and Calvinists. In Prussia so overwhelming a majority accepted it that the national Church was described in legal documents as the "Evangelical Church," no distinction of Lutheran and Reformed being recognized. But difficulties and divisions arose when a new liturgy was introduced.

Royal Commission on Liturgy, 1814.

The King had, so far back as 1814, constituted a Commission to draw up an amended liturgy for the Protestant Churches in his dominions. Of the labours of this Commission nothing is known, but in 1816 there was put forth a new liturgy for the Court and Garrison Churches in Berlin and Potsdam, and for the military everywhere. The author's name was not avowed, but it soon became known that it was the work of the King himself. It was taken principally from old liturgical forms of the Reformation period, and included versicles to be sung antiphonally by the priest and choir. The congregational singing, which had been so marked a feature of Lutheran worship, was much abridged.

Ch. XI.
New Service-book, 1816.

Many objections were raised to this form of worship, which became louder when, in 1821, a still more elaborate liturgy was put forth, which it was the King's desire to introduce into all the Evangelical Churches of the kingdom. It was still derived from old Lutheran documents, and the King hoped that an orthodox liturgy would be to some extent an antidote to Rationalistic doctrine. As however the old formularies were generally translated or adapted from the previously existing Missals and Breviaries, the rumour ran that an attempt was being made to restore Romanism. It was an offence too that the sermon was to be limited to half-an-hour, and was not to be prefaced by any introductory prayer. When the question was addressed to all the clergy in the kingdom, whether they would adopt the liturgy, the response was generally negative. Not only was the liturgy itself found fault with, but the right of the territorial lord to make changes in public worship without consulting the authorities of the Church was disputed in a series of pamphlets. Still, as the King continued to press the point, most of the clergy in the end gave way. Thereupon it was intimated to the whole body that they must either accept the new Form (*Agenda*) or recur to the old Agenda which was still binding upon them in law. Further, in 1826, candidates for orders were required to enter into an engagement to use the new formularies. Still, things did not work smoothly, and many unauthorised changes and abridgements were made which materially altered the character of the liturgy without giving complete satisfaction to the congregations. There were many recalcitrants. In particular, Professor Scheibel of Breslau refused either to acknowledge the Union or to adopt the new liturgy, sharing the old Lutheran objection to enter into communion with Calvinists, who were (it was held) in grievous error with regard to the faith. To join with

Service-book of 1821.

Scheibel's resistance.

them would be to open the door to indifferentism. Scheibel at first stood alone, but when he was suspended by the civic authorities, he was joined by some two thousand members of the Church who announced their intention of abiding by unchanged Lutheranism. Scheibel was deposed, but the movement spread, and in many places the Old-Lutherans held separate meetings for worship. The government then had recourse to force, and in one case soldiers were called in to expel the Old-Lutheran pastor favoured by the people and install his successor.

So long as Frederick William III. reigned, these Old-Lutherans were not tolerated in Prussia. Doubtless they were somewhat fanatical, but they had good reason to complain that they were deprived of the religious liberty which was the right of every subject of the Prussian Crown. The violent proceedings of the Prussian government occasioned a re-action in favour of strict Lutheranism even in territories where the Union had not been introduced. Some even emigrated to America in order to enjoy the freedom of worship which was denied them in their native land. When Frederick William IV. came to the throne, just one hundred years after the accession of Frederick the Great, there came a change. The new king took a real interest in matters of religion, rather perhaps from the emotional and imaginative side than from strong reasoned conviction, and his presence at the Anglican ceremony of the baptism of the Prince of Wales and at the Roman-Catholic ceremony on the beginning of the new work at Cologne Cathedral, left his subjects in some doubt as to his tendencies. His love of old fashions, as well as his desire to be equitable, led him at once to release the Old-Lutheran pastors who were in prison for disobeying the orders of the government, and in 1841 a General Synod constituted a Lutheran Church in Prussia entirely independent of the Established United Evangelical Church, and this in 1845 received the royal sanction. It was again divided by a schism on a point of church-government in 1861, which was however healed in 1904. In 1847 the King issued a Charter on religion, which, recognizing and authorising the existing state of things, permitted all who found themselves out of harmony with the Established Church to form societies of their own. The year of the Revolution (1848) threatened to unchristianize the Prussian state altogether. After the restoration of 1850 this dread vanished, but it was felt that there was a pressing necessity for the remoulding of the Protestant organization, a task which presented considerable difficulties, the more so as several Lutheran territories were annexed to Prussia after the war of 1866.

The Rhenish and Westphalian provinces had received in 1835 a Constitution which was in the main satisfactory to them. A similar Constitution was given in 1873 by William I. to the Eastern provinces, the details of which were to be elaborated, without touching standards of faith, by an Extraordinary General Synod in 1875. In accordance with its provisions, a High Ecclesiastical Council was to be the head of the administration. The legislative power was given to an elective General Synod sitting every sixth year. In the interim between its sessions this was represented by a Synodal Council sitting in conjunction with the High Council, and a Standing Committee of the Synod. There were also Synods for the various provinces and divisions of the kingdom, two-thirds of the members of which were laymen. The General Synod of 1894 introduced a revised Form of Service.

In Saxony the reigning house has been since 1697 Roman-Catholic, but the population is almost wholly Protestant. A constitutional law commits the administration of the affairs of the Evangelical Church, so long as the royal family is Catholic, to a special minister *in evangelicis*. The first Synod of the newly-formed Lutheran-Evangelical Church substituted for the oath imposed on all church-teachers to accept the symbolical books, a simple promise to teach the pure doctrine of the Gospel according to the Scriptures and the Confession of the Church. The other North-German states for the most part sanctioned the election of representative Synods for the Protestant Church within their borders.

Bavaria, in spite of its repute as a champion of Romanism, had also a vigorous and active Protestant population, and a distinguished centre of Protestant teaching in the university of Erlangen. Under Maximilian II. (1848-64), a man who wished to deal fairly with all classes of his

Marginalia: CH. XI. | Church in Eastern Provinces. | SAXONY. | Subscription changed, 1871. | BAVARIA.

subjects, the Protestant Church attained full enjoyment of equal rights with the Catholic. King Ludwig II., in spite of the opposition of the Ultramontanes among his subjects, powerfully assisted in the foundation of the new German Empire under a Prussian and Protestant Emperor.

In Baden, which had a "United" Evangelical Church since 1821, endless contests arose between the defenders of the old orthodoxy on the one hand, and the advocates of liberal views on the other. After the abolition (1860) of the orthodox High Ecclesiastical Council, the liberals gained the upper hand in Parliament and Synod. In Hesse-Darmstadt as early as 1819 the government had desired a union of all the Protestant communities in the country, but this had been carried into effect only in the Rhenish district (1822). The General Synod called in 1873 submitted to the government a draft of a representative synodal constitution for the Church, which should include all the Protestants, without prejudice to the dogmatic standards of the several communities. This was ultimately adopted, but in spite of the saving clause, fifteen Lutheran pastors withdrew from the United Church for conscience sake. Würtemberg is essentially a Protestant country, and full of religious activity. Probably in no part of Germany is there so much Pietism, or so many meeting-houses of various sects. But it must not be supposed that Würtemberg is wanting in the higher Christian training. In its university of Tübingen are found distinguished Roman-Catholic, as well as Protestant, Professors, and the latter, mostly of the school of F. C. Baur, have considerably influenced the views of the clergy of the country. The first General Representative Synod met in 1869.

In Switzerland the canton of Basel was long the great stronghold of Evangelical religion against the assaults of liberalism and rationalism. But even here at last so great a change came over public opinion, that in 1883 Basel and Zürich declared that baptism was no longer indispensable for membership of the Established Protestant

---

[1] Hug and Stead, *Switzerland* (London, 1890); Boyd Winchester, *The Swiss Republic* (Philadelphia, 1891); Adams and Cunningham, *The Swiss Confederation* (London, 1889); Theresa Lee, *The Story of Switzerland* (London, 1885).

Church. In the other cantons the laws and regulations with regard to religion are various, but generally lean towards vagueness of doctrine and wide tolerance of opinions. In most cantons the appointment of a pastor is made for only six years, though he is capable of re-election for another similar period. In Geneva the old Calvinism had given way in the eighteenth century to Voltairean enlightenment, but in the early part of the nineteenth century an Evangelical revival had begun, stimulated by Frau von Krüdener and Robert Haldane[1], a Scottish layman, under whose influence Cæsar Malan[2], a Genevese preacher, became a powerful advocate of the old teaching of the Reformation period. This occasioned divisions, which the "Venerable Company" of preachers, the chief ecclesiastical authority in Geneva, thought to put an end to by requiring from candidates for ordination a pledge that they would not preach on the Natures in Christ, on Original Sin, or on Predestination. This brought on a crisis; the adherents of the forbidden doctrine separated from the Established Church; some were imprisoned or banished by the liberal and enlightened government, and almost all were subjected to various kinds of annoyance for which they could obtain no redress. It was not until 1830 that a Free Church was allowed to be formed and to carry on its work in peace. The revival in Geneva spread into the neighbouring Canton Vaud, where, especially in Lausanne, it met with still rougher treatment. It was however after 1845, having parted with some of its sectarian harshness, absorbed in the thriving Free Church of Vaux. The extreme point of ecclesiastical radicalism was reached when in 1874 the Protestant law of Public Worship for Geneva threw overboard all definite profession of faith, all dogma, all liturgical forms and all ceremony of ordination.

In the beginning of the nineteenth century the dogmatic fire which had once burned so fiercely in Holland

---

[1] Alex. Haldane, *Memoirs of R. and J. A. Haldane* (London, 1852).
[2] C. Malan, *Vie et Travaux de César Malan* (Genève, 1869).
[3] Chantepie de la Saussaye, *La Crise Religieuse en Hollande* (Leyden, 1860); *Die Unruhen in der Niederländischen Reformirten Kirche*, 1833–39, ed. by Gieseler (Hamburg, 1840); Hofstede de Groot, *Die moderne Theologie in den Niederlanden* (Bonn, 1870); P. H. Ditchfield, *The Church in the Netherlands* (London, 1893).

was almost quenched by the rising tide of Rationalism. Liberal principles in theology were everywhere dominant, and were supported, from 1873 onwards, by a yearly Congress of Protestants (Protestantentag). How far this liberalism had gone was manifested in 1853, when the National Synod declared expressly that it did not require from its ministers absolute and literal agreement with all the recognized formularies, but only the acceptance of their spirit and essence. In 1877 the Synod decided by a majority that no definite profession of faith should be required from candidates for confirmation. The School-law of 1856 banished from all elementary schools which received State support every kind of religious formulary; and in 1876 an Act of the legislature substituted for the old theological chairs in the universities professorships of religious philosophy from which dogmatic teaching was expressly excluded. The Synod of the Church was however permitted to found professorships for definite doctrinal teaching, nor was it forbidden to establish denominational schools for the instruction of the lower classes. The adherents of the old Dutch Calvinism, who were still numerous, were permitted in 1880 to found a University of their own at Amsterdam, but as in 1885 the National Synod declined to admit students from this university as candidates for the ministry, the concession was of little value, and a vehement controversy ensued, which at one time threatened to rend the Hollandish Church, though ultimately actual schism was averted. The Liberal school of theology in Holland has produced men like Scholten and Kuenen of European reputation.

In Norway a simple uneducated farmer, Hans Nielsen Hauge, raised his voice against the Rationalism which began to prevail in the pulpits, and traversed the whole country as a preacher of Evangelical truth with a spirit and activity which reminds us of Wesley. He was very harshly treated by the civil government, imprisoned and fined, so that at last his strength failed and he retired to his farm; but a numerous body of preachers of his own class carried on his work, the effects of which continue to this day.

[1] H. H. Boyesen, *History of Norway* (new edition with addition by C. F. Keary, London, 1890).

In Sweden from the year 1803 onward there existed a body of earnest pietists, who, without any heretical views, were dissatisfied with the "high and dry" Established Church. As their most obvious characteristic was that they were devoted to the reading of the Bible and Luther's writings, rather than to church-going, they received the name of "Readers" (Läsare). They suffered much from mob violence, and from fine and imprisonment under the harsh laws of an earlier period, but their influence continued to spread. It was not until the year 1870 that the old laws which denied toleration and civil rights to all except Lutherans were completely repealed.

In Denmark, Rationalism made considerable advances in the early part of the nineteenth century, under the leadership of H. N. Clausen, a man of varied culture, much influenced by Schleiermacher. On the side of faith rose up a strong champion in the person of Nicolas Grundtvig, a patriotic Dane, and an ardent student of the ancient literature of his country, who attacked Clausen with an inconsiderate vehemence which unfortunately rendered him liable to the penalties of the law of libel. The war of Germany against Denmark in 1848-9 not only inflamed his mind against the Germans generally, but rendered him bitterly hostile to Lutheranism as the religion of the enemy He was for putting an end to the Lutheran Church in Denmark, and substituting one founded on the Apostles' Creed, which he called the "Little Word from the Lord's own lips," and believed to have been used by the Apostles in the baptism of the three thousand at the first Christian Pentecost; the words of institution of the Eucharist; and the Lord's Prayer. He also recognized in the old Scandinavian mythology a preparation for the Gospel, as the Alexandrian fathers had done in the Greek. Grundtvig's party, by untiring activity, brought it to pass that all forms of religion were admitted to be civilly on an equality (1849); that baptism was no longer compulsory (1857); and that a body of not less than twenty householders might form a religious society, with the right of

---

[1] Otte, *u. s.*; Berggren, *Ueberblick ü. d. Kirchl. Verhältnissen Schwedens* (Leipzig, 1884).

[2] Elise C. Otte, *Scandinavian History* (London, 1874).

nominating their own minister (1868-73). The Grundtvigian movement as time went on spread into Sweden and Norway.

5. THEOLOGY AND BIBLICAL CRITICISM.

The speculative theology of German Protestantism[1] in the nineteenth century was developed under influences very different from those which brought about the rationalism of the eighteenth. The antithesis of mind and matter, subject and object, which lay at the base of the older philosophy, was no longer recognized; the wider study of the religions of the world gave rise to new views of religion; and the theory of evolution which prevailed in natural science had its counterpart in moral philosophy and theology.

The early part of the nineteenth century was dominated by the philosophy of Schelling and Hegel[2], of whom the latter exercised by far the most important influence. Hegel taught that the actual is rational and the rational actual. If reason is everywhere the foundation and guiding law of reality, our thoughts are turned to the actual history of man, and we are shewn how at all times and in every nation the sovereign reason works towards its own lofty ends, though each end, so soon as reached, is seen to be but a stepping-stone to higher things. We are taught to reverence the heroic figures in history, in whom is embodied the genius of nations and ages, who have brought into light and life the thoughts slumbering in the souls of all. The religions of the world are necessary creations of the peculiar spirit inherent in each nation, but Christianity rises above the rest, in that

[1] Karl Schwartz, *Zur Geschichte der Neuesten Theologie* (Leipzig, 1856); Amand Saintes, *Hist. Crit. du Rationalisme en Allemagne* (Paris, 1843); F. Lichtenberger, *Hist. des Idées Religieuses en Allemagne* (Paris, 1873); J. A. Dorner, *Hist. of Protestant Theology*, trans. by G. Robson and S. Taylor (Edinburgh, 1871); O. Pfleiderer, *The Development of Theology in Germany*, trans. by J. F. Smith (London, 1890).

[2] Rosenkranz, *Leben Hegels* (Berlin, 1844); Haym, *Hegel und seine Zeit* (Berlin, 1857); Köstlin, *Hegel in Philosophischer ... Beziehung* (Tübingen, 1870); J. Stirling, *The Secret of Hegel* (London, 1865); E. Scherer, *Mélanges d'Histoire Religieuse*, p. 283 ff. (Paris, 1863); O. Pfleiderer, *Development* etc., p. 68 ff. Hegel's *Logic* has been translated, with valuable Prolegomena, by W. Wallace (Oxford, 1874).

in it the spirit, not of a single nation but of mankind as a whole, becomes conscious of its essential relation to God, and is thus the absolute religion; though even this, regarded on the human side, is clothed in conceptions more or less inadequate to the idea which it embodies. It was not unnatural that when Hegel's philosophy was first published it was hailed by many as the long-sought reconciliation between faith and science, though in the end it came to be felt that Hegel's deity was rather an intellectual abstraction than the living God.

Among those who sought to defend and expound the old faith on Hegelian principles was Carl Daub, who in the strange book on the theology of his contemporaries, which Strauss[1] called a veritable Inferno, in which dogmatists and commentators, naturalists and supernaturalists, suffer torture side by side, is guided by Hegel as Dante of old by Virgil. Philip Conrad Marheineke, an able man of varied learning, in his treatise on Christian doctrine regarded as science, claims to have relinquished no jot of Christian verity, but to have established it in all its fulness by the application of the Hegelian method, by which alone it can be freed from the contradictions which have enveloped it. Karl Friedrich Goeschel, a jurisconsult, endeavoured to shew that Hegelian principles were in perfect accord with every part of the Lutheran Catechism. He ended, however, as a defender of the strictest Lutheranism, and even as a persecutor of its enemies. And several others, notable in their day, though now forgotten, fought, as they believed, for Christianity under the banner of Hegel.

A reaction from Hegelism appears in Ludwig Feuerbach[2], who attacked all religion. Rejecting altogether the Hegelian "absolute" being, he regarded religion as a product simply of man's own faculties. The deities which man has worshipped are simply illusions of his own imagination, the projection of his own longings, excellencies and defects, outside himself, so as to form an imposing, but cloudy and unsubstantial, image. And this belief in supernatural beings, and especially the faith of Christians, is in his view by no means innocuous, but

Daub, 1765—1836.

Marheineke, 1780—1846.

Goeschel, 1784—1861.

Feuerbach, 1804—1872.

---
[1] Quoted by Lichtenberger, *Idées Relig.* II. 321.
[2] E. Beyer, *Leben und Geist L. Feuerbachs* (1873).

is the chief cause of man's aversion to a reasonable theory of the universe, of hatred to free thought, and of all kinds of fanaticism. In the spirit of Lucretius, he regarded the religion which led to so much evil as a thing to be rooted out and destroyed.

Schleiermacher, 1768—1834.

The most powerful influence in the formation of modern German theology is no doubt that of Schleiermacher[1]. This very remarkable man was in his youth placed under the influence of the Moravians, but their theology did not satisfy a young man of extraordinary activity of mind and deep religious feeling. Their doctrine of everlasting punishment, their teaching on the divinity of Christ and His vicarious suffering for man, their insistence on the total corruption of human nature, were repugnant to him. Nor was he able to sympathise with the religious "experiences" of his Moravian teachers. Passing away from this influence, he plunged eagerly into the study, not only of theology, but of art, literature, philosophy, and modern culture generally. In all he pursued noble ideals, and was especially influenced by Plato and Spinoza. In 1810 his vivid personal influence found an adequate field in a theological professorship in the newly-founded university of Berlin. There his eager mind, stimulated by congenial society, ranged over almost all branches of human knowledge. He was interested in everything. But in the midst of this intellectual whirl the centre of his thought was always religion. Faith was essential to his life, and he felt that a true and living faith could not be grounded on mere historical testimony or mere authority. Religion is the sense of absolute dependence on God, and genuine theology is founded on the inner life of the soul in its relation to God. By founding religion and theology on faculties found in man, as man, he hoped to free them from their dependence on schools of thought and the ever-changing systems of

---

[1] W. Dilthey, *Aus Schleiermacher's Leben in Briefen* (Berlin, 1835–64), Eng. trans. by Rowan (London, 1860); *Leben Schleiermacher's* (Berlin, 1870); D. Schenkel, *F. Schleiermacher, Ein Lebensbild* (Elberfeld, 1868); W. Bender, *Schleiermacher's Theologie* (Nordlingen, 1876–78), A. Twesten, *Zur Erinnerung an S.* (1869); J. F. Smith in *Encycl. Brit.* XXI. 409 ff. E. Zeller's warm eulogy of Schleiermacher (*Vorträge u. Abhand.*, pp. 179 and 200) is printed in Ueberweg, *Philosophy*, II. 247 f.

philosophy. But he was far from recognizing the mere individual consciousness as the sole and adequate guide of the believer. Religion implies a body of worshippers; it everywhere forms churches, which are the necessary instruments and organs of the highest life. The members of the Christian Church are conscious of having been delivered by Christ from a condition in which the true spiritual life was overridden by the world of sense, and brought into one in which the spirit is dominant. The appearance of the Saviour in the world is a divine revelation, but neither absolutely supernatural nor absolutely beyond reason. Such doctrines as are not founded on the Christian consciousness form no part of true evangelical theology. Here it must be admitted that he rejected some doctrines which the Catholic Church regards as necessary truths. His idea of religion is defective; his conception of the Deity savours of Spinozism; his exegesis of Scripture is often fanciful. Yet, with all his faults, in the midst of a society generally indifferent to religion, he brought into vivid light the forgotten or misunderstood truths of the Gospel; he loved, and brought others to love the Person of Christ, as the very central fire of faith and spiritual life; he shewed that the true type of humanity is to be found only in Him who called Himself the Son of Man. There is scarcely a German theologian in the generation which followed Schleiermacher who does not shew traces of his influence.

Schleiermacher's Defects.

The greatest perhaps among the disciples of Schleiermacher was the Jew, David Mendel, who when he acknowledged Jesus as the Messiah became Neander, a new man. He too loved Plato, in whom he found a constant aspiration towards a noble ideal, above the clouds of sense. He had, from the time when he was moved by Schleiermacher's famous Discourses to receive baptism, an earnest and heart-felt faith, which did not prevent his being a candid enquirer. The history of the Church soon presented itself to him as the field to the cultivation of which he should devote his life. Schleiermacher had turned men's thoughts to the immense importance of the Christian community, the development in a concrete form of the truths of Christian revelation; Neander set himself to trace its history in the various

Neander, 1789— 1850.

forms which it has assumed throughout the ages. His vivid conception of the divine power embodied in the Church has given to his History a life and an organic unity which raise it above the often excellent works of his predecessors. All his writings, which are numerous, have some relation to Church History. They were widely read, discussed and controverted. But the influence which he exercised through his lecture-rooms and the more private teaching in his study was perhaps even greater than that of his writings. Those who met him face to face were conscious of his earnest wish, not merely to communicate knowledge, but to bring his hearers to the feet of the Master, and to enable them to taste the secrets of life in Him which he himself enjoyed. Rarely have faith and knowledge been more admirably blended than they were in Neander.

It is impossible to enumerate here all the distinguished men in whom we may trace the influence of Schleiermacher. It must suffice to say that nearly all those who have striven to reconcile the claims of science with a sincere and heart-felt faith in Christ, and who have favoured the union of Lutheran and Calvinist in one body, have been more or less directly his pupils.

Richard Rothe[1] stands almost alone among theologians and cannot be classed as any man's disciple. With devout heart and eager active mind he thought out in solitude the problems presented by the Incarnation and the Church of Christ. No one of his contemporaries surpassed him in power and originality. On the Church his view is that its proper task is the regeneration of the State. It is not intended to give authority to a powerful priesthood, but to transform and ennoble all those relations, political and social, in which man finds himself by the necessity of his nature. Every action of man is religious and moral, or the reverse, and it is an evil that he should make an unnatural division of himself, and owe allegiance in one respect to the Church, in another to the State. When the State becomes truly Christian, the Church is destined to be absorbed in it. The great work which Rothe called "Theological Ethics" deals not only with good and evil, virtue and vice, but with the whole field

[1] E. Achelis, *Richard Rothe* (Gotha, 1869).

of Christian doctrine, the idea of God and the Creation, sin, salvation, and things to come. We have in it, as was natural from the author's point of view, a fusion of dogma and morality. The notions of orthodoxy and heterodoxy have scarcely any place in his mind[1].

At a later date Albrecht Ritschl[2] may also be reckoned among those who felt the influence of Schleiermacher. A deserter from the school of Baur, he devoted himself for many years to the study of Christian doctrine. In this he attempted to keep theology entirely apart from metaphysical speculation, and to shew that the dogmas of the schools were quite distinct from true religion. His own teaching he regarded as resting on Luther and the old Evangelical formularies. The Scriptures, recognized as they are by the primitive Church as of the highest authority, supply, even without any special theory of inspiration, sufficient support for the great Christian verities. Christ, according to His own testimony, had the charge to preach on earth the love of God for man, and to found the Kingdom of God. To Him belongs of right the title of "Only-begotten Son of God," since He alone among men continued in life and death in perfect harmony with the will of His Father. To Him worship is rightly paid. The Kingdom, the society on earth in which God's love and truth reign, is the redeemed or reconciled community. The individual attains redemption as a member of this community. Ritschl does not deny that conversions take place as the result of a spiritual struggle, but he regards them as abnormal; normally, the believer is by degrees transformed through the consciousness of redemption which prevails around him; his relation to God depends on his relation to the Church. Ritschl's theories, especially what was thought his too great dependence on the Christian community, were vigorously attacked and

A. Ritschl, 1822–89.

---

[1] Rothe's views on Church and State are practically identical with those of Thomas Arnold, who had read Rothe's *Anfänge der Christl. Kirche*, with entire assent to his views, though he rejected his history. See his letter to Bunsen, Jan. 27, 1838.

[2] James Orr, *The Ritschlian Theology and the Evangelical Faith* (London, 1899); A. E. Garvie, *The Ritschlian Theology* (Edinburgh, 1899); Otto Ritschl, *Albrecht Ritschl's Leben* (Freiburg, 1892–96); Otto Pfleiderer, *The Development of Theology in Germany*, p. 183 ff. (London, 1890).

vigorously defended. It may perhaps be said that they are more important for the impulse which they gave to Christian thought than in themselves, but they have certainly had a wide influence.

Controversy on Apostles' Creed, 1892.

Quite recently a controversy on the use of the Apostles' Creed[1] has occasioned much agitation. Pastor Chr. Schrempf in Würtemberg refused to make use of that Creed in Baptism or in the ordinary services of the Church, and was consequently deposed from his office by the Church-board which had authority in the matter. Thereupon Professor Adolf Harnack, being appealed to by some of those who attended his lectures, published an opinion on the matter, in which, while fully acknowledging the venerable antiquity and great value of the document, he deprecated the enforcing of its use by Church authority[2]. This declaration of so distinguished a man gave rise to a lively controversy, and many conferences of the clergy declared themselves against Harnack's views. An edict of the Highest Church Council of the Evangelical Church in Prussia, declaring that any attempts by the clergy within its jurisdiction to reject the Apostles' Creed were not to be tolerated, tended to clear the atmosphere, and the disturbance gradually died out, but not without leaving behind it a somewhat embittered feeling on the part of the evangelical against the scientific theologians.

BIBLICAL CRITICISM.

Nothing is more remarkable in the ecclesiastical history of the nineteenth century than the development of Biblical criticism in Germany. It deserted the sober paths of such men as Ernesti and Michaelis, and followed rather the ways opened by the Wolfenbüttel Fragments[3]. Not only the interpretation, but the origin and authority of the sacred books were called in question. Conjectures were freely made, and when they ceased to be novelties were sometimes regarded as authentic history.

De Wette, 1780— 1849.

We may regard De Wette, who was much influenced by his friend of early days, Schleiermacher, as a link between the old and the new criticism. He approached the great problems of the age and authorship of the books

---

[1] Kurtz, *Lehrbuch*, II. ii. p. 76.
[2] In *Das Apostolische Glaubensbekenntniss* (Berlin, 1892); controverted by H. Barclay Swete, in *The Apostles' Creed, its relation to Primitive Christianity* (Cambridge, 1894).
[3] See above, p. 208.

of Scripture in the spirit of a scholar and a candid investigator. But the man who may be most emphatically described as the leader of the new school of Old Testament criticism is Heinrich Ewald[1], who was recognized in his day as one of the greatest of Oriental scholars. Arbitrary, intolerant, violent as he was, he is still the man to whom, more than to any other, is due the new life infused into the study of Hebrew history and literature. Under his touch the Prophets fall into their true place as the inspired preachers and counsellors of their native land, and the poets of Israel recover their poetry, while the historical books are seen to be the work of many minds and many ages. Ewald's special theories on the Pentateuch are probably now accepted by none, but no labourer in the field of Old Testament exegesis has failed to receive something of his influence.

During Ewald's lifetime a school had arisen which reversed the traditional relation of the Law and the Prophets. The Law, as we have it, came to be regarded as having received its form in the period subsequent to the Exile; as the end, not the beginning of Israelitish history. The germs of this theory are found in Edward Reuss[2], who mentioned it in his lectures at Strasburg so far back as 1834, though it was not until 1882 that he at last gave publicity to his views in his admirable history of the sacred writings of the Old Testament. But meanwhile a pupil, R. J. Graf, had published (1866) a treatise on the historical books of the Old Testament in which the views of Reuss were expounded, whence the theory came to be commonly known as the Graf hypothesis. A much greater impression was, however, made when Julius Wellhausen maintained, as the result of his own investigation, a similar theory, with great acuteness and true historical sense, in a vigorous and interesting style. Reuss and his followers fully admit that the prophetic must have been preceded by a priestly period, though they hold that it was the priests after the Exile who by their codifying and amplifying of the Law gave to Judaism the characteristics which it has retained for so many centuries. They do

[1] T. K. Cheyne, *Founders of Old Testament Criticism*, p. 66 ff. (London, 1893).

[2] T. K. Cheyne, *Founders*, p. 175 ff.

CH. XI.

Ewald, 1803–75.

'Die Poetischen Bücher,' 1839.

Reuss, 1804– 1891.

Graf, 1866.

Wellhausen, b. 1841.

not doubt that under the kings there existed a ritual the origin of which was referred to Moses; but they do not admit that it was at this time regulated by a formal written code entering into every detail. And certainly we are to regard Moses not only as a historical person, but as one who wrought great things for his people by the power of the Divine Spirit which was in him, and was recognized as sent from God by his contemporaries and their descendants. These views have generally been the starting-point for subsequent investigators, and many differing theories arising out of them have been propounded by capable independent authorities. Eduard Rupprecht, with considerable learning and acuteness, rejects them altogether, and maintains the traditional view of the authority of Scripture and of the religion of the Old Testament. To speak generally, two views of Israelitish history and religion now stand opposed to each other, the evolutionist and the supernaturalist. According to the evolutionist theory, the primitive religion of Israel was a natural religion, distinguished from that of the surrounding nations by the worship of Jehovah as a national deity. The prophets, conscious of a divine commission and a divine revelation, raised this conception of Jehovah to that of the one all-ruling power, and gave to Judaism the more lofty ideal which has given it enduring influence in the world of thought and religion. According to the supernaturalists, a religion practically identical with that which we find in the law and the prophets existed in Israel from the time of the Exodus and the Sinaitic law-giving.

While the exegesis of the older Scriptures was passing through this great change, an even greater transformation came over the interpretation of the books of the New Testament. David Friedrich Strauss[1] treated the Gospels,

---

[1] There are Lives of Strauss by L. Zeller, *D. F. Strauss in seinen Leben u. seinen Schriften* (Bonn, 1874; trans. into English 1874); A. Hausrath, *D. F. Strauss u. die Theologie seiner Zeit* (Heidelberg, 1876-78). Among the numerous works called forth by Strauss's may be mentioned W. H. Mill, *Application of Pantheistic Principles to the Gospels* (Cambridge, 1840); J. R. Beard, *Voices of the Church* (1845); P. Harwood, *German Anti-supernaturalism* (1841); E. Quinet, *Examen de la Vie de Jésus* (in *Œuvres*, vol. 8, Paris, 1895); F. A. Tholuck, *Glaubwürdigkeit der Evangel. Geschichte* (2nd ed. 1838). See also F. C. Cook in *Aids to Faith*, ed. W. Thomson, p. 147 ff. (3rd ed., London, 1862).

which had hitherto been considered, even by Rationalists, to be in the main historical, as little more than collections of myths. It was no new thing to find myths, stories with which the imagination of subsequent generations had glorified the life of a great man, or which had been invented to account for existing institutions; but these had originated in those primitive times of which no written record existed; it was hardly contemplated that myths would be found among the Jews, to whom written records were familiar, in the days of the early Roman Empire. But Strauss essayed this very thing. In his *Life of Jesus* he rejected utterly the Christian tradition of eighteen centuries, and regarded the Saviour as a simple Jewish teacher around whom the unconscious poetry of succeeding generations had woven a tissue of legend through which the original form shewed in gigantic proportions. Everything miraculous belonged to this mythical veil. He saw, however, that a myth would scarcely be formed about a person while men were actually living who had seen and lived in familiar intercourse with him. No one of the existing Gospels therefore could have been the work of the Master's immediate disciples; they must be removed to a much later date. But he did not at this time admit that his resolution of the Gospel history into myth was necessarily destructive of Christianity. That which is untrue historically may have a high value ideally. He is aware, he says, "that the essence of the Christian faith is perfectly independent of his criticism. The supernatural birth of Christ, his miracles, his resurrection and ascension, remain eternal truths whatever doubts may be cast on their reality as historical facts.... A dissertation at the close of the work shews that the dogmatic significance of the life of Jesus remains inviolable[1]." The book made an immense impression. The application of the mythical hypothesis to the Gospel history was not indeed absolutely new, but it had hitherto remained comparatively insignificant in the flood of theories and conjectures. It was now set forth with great lucidity by a master of style, who was also gifted with a vivid imagination, and who practised no shifts or

Myths.

'*Life of Jesus*,' 1835.

'*Ideal*' Christianity.

[1] *Life of Jesus*, trans. by "George Eliot," p. xxx., ed. 1906.

evasions to disguise his real meaning from the crowd. The book was read not only by theologians, but by clergy and laity everywhere. It is not too much to say that for a whole generation no theological treatise was published in Germany which did not contain some reference to Strauss. Veteran theologians attacked the daring innovator, and young aspirants sought to win their spurs by entering the lists against him. Before the end of his life however Strauss definitely renounced Christianity, and adopted purely materialistic theories on the creation and maintenance of the universe[1].

Bruno Bauer, in his youth an ardent champion of speculative orthodoxy, in later life converted to extreme scepticism, complained that even Strauss conceded too much to the old theory of inspiration, and himself regarded the Gospels as purely and simply works of fiction. For a time he made some noise in the theological world, but his assertions were so utterly unsupported by proof, his aiming at notoriety so evident, and even his statement of truth so distorted, that his influence was transitory.

Of a very different stamp was Ferdinand Christian Baur[2], the famous founder of the Tübingen school[3] of Biblical criticism. He applied his great learning and acuteness to the investigation of the rise and progress of Christianity, and of the origin of the canonical Gospels. Strauss had shaken the existing conceptions of the age and authenticity of these writings, but he had not put forward any definite theory of his own to account for their existence and their characteristics. This vacant space in his system Baur undertook to fill, and for this end gave his vigorous mind to an exhaustive research into the earliest documents of the primitive Church. He sees in the early Christian writers manifest traces of a struggle going on between the Judaizing and the Pauline party, the fusion of which in the second century gave rise to the Catholic Church and Catholic dogma. Of this struggle he finds clear indications in St Paul's Epistles, of which

[1] In *Der Alte und der Neue Glaube*; Eng. trans. by M. Blind (London, 1873).
[2] See *Worte der Erinnerung an F. C. Baur* (Tübingen, 1861), and Zeller's *Vorträge u. Abhandlungen*, 1te Sammlung (2nd ed. 1875).
[3] K. Hase, *Die Tübinger Schule* (Leipzig, 1855); F. C. Baur, *Die Tüb. Sch.* (Tübingen, 1859); R. W. Mackay, *The Tübingen School and its Antecedents* (London, 1863).

those to the Romans, Galatians and Corinthians are admitted to be genuine letters of the Apostle. Further, he regards the Acts of the Apostles not as a purely historical narrative, but as a work written—with a basis, no doubt, of fact—to promote the union of the Petrine and Pauline parties. The Fourth Gospel was written in the second century for the purpose of setting forth a view of the Person of Christ different from that which is found in the three which from their use of common documents are called Synoptic. But these also are written with a purpose, are "Tendenz-schriften"; each representing one of the forms of thought which strove for the mastery in the Church of the first century.

No one probably now holds Baur's theories as a whole, but they have influenced the discussions on the origin of the Catholic Church, on the dates of the Gospels, and on their relations to each other, up to the present time. A very large number of works on these subjects has been published of all degrees of merit, from the really important productions of learned scholars to the ingenious fatuities of men who wish to win renown by saying what had not been said before. Really solid works, such as those of Theodor Zahn on the Canon of the New Testament, and of Adolf Harnack on the literature of the Early Church, have tended to give a more fixed ground for subsequent inquirers.

In the midst of the eager movement which drew into its vortex so many of the German theologians, there was still a large number of earnest men who were for treading the old paths of Protestant orthodoxy, rejecting alike extreme Rationalism and the indefinite belief which was a legacy from the eighteenth century. In the year of Jubilee of the Reformation (1817), Klaus Harms[1], a much respected clergyman in Kiel, published, in emulation of Luther, ninety-five new Theses, which were to hold up Luther's teaching before the eyes of a generation which had almost forgotten him. In 1827 Augustus Hahn in an academic discourse at Leipzig contended that Rationalists ought to be dismissed from the service of the

[1] Baumgarten, *Ein Denkmal für Kl. Harms* (1855); Kaftan, *Kl. Harms* (1875); Lüdemann, *Erinnerung an Kl. Harms u. seine Zeit* (1878).

Church, and three years later the dismissal of Gesenius and Wegscheider from their professorships in Halle was in fact demanded. The Prussian government, however, more anxious to keep things quiet than to side with a party, took no action. And in almost all the Protestant States of Germany Pietism waged an active war with Rationalism and gave occasion to much controversy. For some time matters seemed to go so ill for the latter that some sanguine Pietists thought it almost time to celebrate its funeral. But a large portion of the educated middle-class, who had been brought up under the influence of eighteenth century liberalism, were opposed to persecution. When in 1840, W. F. Sintenis, a clergyman in Magdeburg, declared that in his opinion the invocation of Christ in prayers was heterodox, he was censured by the consistory to which he belonged. Thereupon, to defend the liberty of the clergy, a society was formed, called "The Friends of Light," which was soon joined by thousands of the clergy and the laity. As was natural however in a society founded rather on negation than on positive truth, dissensions soon appeared. The more radical party fraternized with the German-Catholics and formed societies in several towns, gradually degenerating into democratic clubs, which after 1848 were placed under the control of the police, and in some cases suppressed. The few that remained sank almost into ignominy. Through all this period the Evangelical party was supported by Ernest William Hengstenberg[1], who fought for it with unfailing courage and energy. He was a man of real learning and ability, and his numerous works on Biblical subjects, though decried as narrow and antiquated by the "advanced" party, are by no means without merit. As a journalist he took a leading part in defence of evangelical truth, with perhaps rather too strong a tendency to speak harshly of his adversaries.

During the eager controversies which agitated Germany in the nineteenth century the needs of practical Christian life by no means dropped out of sight. From about the year 1816 various institutions were formed for the rescue of the weak, especially of the young, from vice and im-

---

[1] Bachmann, *E. W. Hengstenberg* (1876–80).

morality, or from degrading surroundings. Here J. H. Wichern[1] deserves special mention. Beginning with a Sunday-School in Hamburg, his native place, in which he drew round him five hundred of the most destitute and vicious children in the city, he founded in 1833 a house for the correction of juvenile offenders, to which he gave the name of "the Rough House" (*das Rauhe Haus*). Here weak and evil-minded children are received and often made useful members of society. With unwearied activity Wichern traversed Germany for the purpose of rousing his countrymen to the necessity of a revival of spiritual life among them, and its natural consequence, the care for those who had erred and strayed from the right way. In 1849, at the Church Congress held that year in Wittenberg, he originated a Congress for Home Missions, to be held yearly, at which all who were engaged in isolated efforts for the good of the submerged classes might meet for mutual counsel and encouragement. In 1836 Pastor Fliedner[2] founded the famous Deaconesses-Institution at Kaiserswerth on the Rhine. This was devoted at first to supplying trained nurses for hospitals; but there was soon added to it a class who gave themselves up to teaching, and yet another, the parochial deaconesses, who aided clergymen in their parish work. The Kaiserswerth House has been the parent of similar institutions in almost all parts of the world. Pastor Löhe[3], an earnest and eloquent preacher of the strict Lutheran party, founded at Neuendettelsau in Bavaria in 1840 a college for the training of missionaries to the Germans in foreign lands, and in 1853 a Deaconesses-Institution, which became one of the most important in Germany. Round this there grew up asylums for the weak-minded and for fallen women, as well as hospitals for the sick. He also founded in 1849 the Lutheran Society for Home Missions. In 1854 Professor Clemens Perthes founded, at Bonn, a Rest-house for poor travellers, especially

---

[1] *Lives* by F. Oldenburg (Hamburg, 1882) and by Hermann Krummacher (Gotha, 1882).
[2] Florence Nightingale, *Account of the Institution for Deaconesses* (London, 1851); Catherine Winkworth, *Life of Pastor Fliedner*, from the German (London, 1867); T. Fliedner, *Kurze Geschichte der Entstehung der ersten Evang. Liebesanstalten zu Kaiserswerth* (1856).
[3] Deinzer, *Wilhelm Löhe's Leben* (Gütersloh, 1873 ff.).

journeymen in search of work, which soon led to the foundation of others, so that similar houses are now found on all the great roads in Germany. They are a means of diffusing Christian influence, as well as of giving temporal help to the weary. Pastor von Bodelschwingh, after founding in 1867 a "Bethel" at Bielefeld, principally for the reception of epileptic patients, established in 1882 the first Labour-colony with the view of bringing into wholesome and active life the numerous class of idle vagabonds who are everywhere to be found. The experiment was so successful that it has been very widely followed. The excellent Amalie Sieveking[1] in 1832 formed the female Society for the Care of the Sick and Poor in Hamburg, which gave attention to their spiritual as well as their bodily needs. Similar societies were soon formed in other large towns.

Important Missionary Societies, generally in connexion with the United Church, are found in the principal cities of Germany. Strictly Lutheran are the Societies of Dresden and Hermannsburg, the latter of which labours especially to cause colonization and Christianity to go hand in hand. A Free-Protestant Association founded in 1884 in Weimar has sent missionaries to Japan and China.

Many leading Protestants looked with sadness on the disunion of Churches which all alike professed Evangelical principles, and it occurred to some of them that men might undertake work in common even where formal agreement in dogma and organization was impossible. Such a union for common work, composed of Evangelicals of all sects and parties, was founded in 1832, the second centenary of the death of the Protestant hero, Gustavus Adolphus, under the name of the "Gustavus Adolphus Union[3]." This was intended chiefly to assist struggling

---

[1] *Denkwürdigkeiten aus d. Leben von A. Sieveking, von einer Freundin* (Hamburg, 1860).

[2] G. E. Burckhardt, *Kleine Missionsbibliothek*, 2nd ed. by R. Grundemann (Bielefeld, 1877); R. Grundemann, *Die Entwick. d. Evang. Mission* 1878-88 (H. 1890); G. Plitt, *Gesch. d. Luth. Mission*, fortgeführt von O. Hardeland (Leipzig, 1894); G. Warneck, *Abriss einer Gesch. d. Prot. Missionen* (4th ed., Berlin, 1898); T. Christlieb, *Foreign Missions* (Boston, 1880); Robert Young, *Modern Missions* (London, 1882); Charlotte M. Yonge, *Pioneers and Founders in the Mission Field* (London, 1878).

[3] K. Zimmermann, *Der Gustav-Adolf Verein* (Darmstadt, 1878); H. F. v. Criegern, *Der G.-A. V.* (Leipzig, 1882).

Protestant communities which had need of extraneous help to maintain themselves in unfavourable surroundings, especially in Roman-Catholic countries. It soon appeared, however, that even such practical work as this might occasion division. The Old-Lutherans refused to acknowledge that bodies which did not conform to the Lutheran standards were Protestants worthy of help, and founded a Fund of their own, which did not greatly prosper.

The Evangelical Alliance[1], which, though founded in England, is largely a German society, was intended to bring together in brotherly union Evangelical Christians of all countries and of all sects, and to strengthen, defend, and promote Protestantism everywhere against the encroachments of Popery and Puseyism. The membership is limited to those who hold "the views commonly called Evangelical," which are defined in a Creed or Confession of Faith consisting of nine articles. General conferences of the Alliance have been held in London, Paris, Berlin, Geneva, and other large towns, and it is believed to have done good work in diffusing more accurate information about the different Churches, and in raising its voice against persecution of Protestants.

In the stormy year 1848 there assembled at Wittenberg a number of religious men, clerical and lay, to take counsel how best to serve the Church in so trying a crisis. It was arranged that this body should hold a meeting (Kirchentag) yearly to deliberate on current events. The strict Lutherans, however, soon ceased to take part in these assemblies, and those who belonged to the United Churches grew lukewarm. The result was that after the meeting at Halle in 1872 the attempt at an annual meeting was given up. In opposition to this conservative movement, there were formed in Southern Germany local "Protestant Unions," which, uniting with those of like opinions in the North, held the first general Protestant Congress in 1865 at Eisenach, and this Congress became annual, meeting in various places. This body announced its aims to be. unlimited freedom of scientific research in matters of religion, the union of all German Protestants, freed from the bonds of dogmatic standards, and utter disregard of the distinctive peculiarities of existing Churches.

[1] *Proceedings of Evang. Alliance*, 1846 (Partridge, London, 1847).

The agitation which was caused by the Prussian "Culture-Combat" gave occasion in 1887 to the foundation of the German "Evangelical League" (Bund), composed of moderate representatives of different theological schools. It was intended to include all who believed in the Only-begotten Son of God as the Redeemer, and who accepted the principles of the Reformation. The work which it set itself to do was generally to defend Evangelicalism against the growing power of Rome, and to give it a higher tone above the mean conflicts of party, religious indifference, and aggressive materialism. In 1903 the various Evangelical Churches of Germany formed an association, which is represented by a standing Committee, the "Deutscher Evangelischer Kirchenausschuss."

Marginalia: Ch. XI. — Evangelical League, 1887. — Evang. Kirchenausschuss, 1903.

CHAPTER XII.

THE EASTERN CHURCH[1].

THE nineteenth century has been a time of awakening in the Eastern Church. Hostile as it is for the most part to the theology and the culture of the West, it has yet not been able altogether to withdraw itself from their influence.

The position of Christians in the early part of the century in the Ottoman Empire was strange and anomalous. The Patriarch of Constantinople was in theory the responsible organ of the Sultan for the government of the Orthodox Church both in spiritual and temporal matters, but the Sultan was his absolute master. The Church formed a state within the state, with considerable privileges, but as against Islam it had no rights. A Christian was free to exercise his religion, to obtain education, to accumulate wealth, to rise to power; but he was liable at the caprice of his master to be hurled from wealth and power into penury or death. And the corruption of official life extended even to the Church, the Patriarch of which was commonly believed to have obtained with a great sum the privilege of exercising his office. Under pressure from Russia, and feeling his existence imperilled, the Sultan could not avoid some concessions to his Christian subjects. In 1839 he issued the Hatti-sherif of Gulhane which placed Moslim and Christians on a footing of political equality; but this decree remained a dead letter. The quarrels of Christians and Turks about the Holy Sepulchre at Jerusalem, where

TURKEY[2]. *The Patriarch of Constantinople.*

Hatti-Sherif of 1839.

---

[1] H. F. Tozer, *The Church and the Eastern Empire* (London, 1888).
[2] Joseph von Hammer-Purgstall, *Geschichte des Osmanischen Reiches* (2nd ed., Pesth, 1834–5); J. W. Zinkeisen, *Osmanisches Reich in Europa* (Hamburg, 1840 ff.); E. S. Creasy, *Hist. of the Ottoman Turks* (London, 1854); Stanley Lane Poole, *Turkey* (London, 1888); Sutherland Menzies, *Turkey, Old and New* (London, 1880); A. de Lusignan, *The Twelve Years' Reign of Abdul Hamid II.* (London, 1889).

454   The Eastern Church

Ch. XII.

Russia claims Protectorate, 1853.

Hatti-Humayum of 1856.

Druses and Maronites, 1860.

Clergy in Turkish Empire.

Greece[1].

since 1847 there had been a Latin Patriarch, introduced a new confusion into the religious question. When in 1853 Russia formally claimed a protectorate over the Christians in the Ottoman Empire, the Sultan refused to admit it. He was supported by England and France and the question was fought out in the Crimean war. The Treaty of Paris, which concluded the war, obliged the Ottoman government to grant political equality to all its subjects, and this was supposed to be accomplished in the Hatti-humayum of Feb. 18, 1856, which was very imperfectly brought into practice. A Turk is, however, now permitted to leave the faith of Islam without punishment. But the painful and dangerous position of Christians was made evident in 1860, when the Turkish authorities failed to put an end to the savage warfare of Druses and Maronites, which desolated a considerable portion of Syria and caused the loss of thousands of Christian lives. And again in 1864 the Turkish government could not, or would not, protect the Christian converts in Constantinople from an attack of Moslem fanaticism.

It could hardly be expected that the Christian clergy in Turkey, living a precarious life in the midst of enemies, for the most part in poverty, should be distinguished for culture or learning. Nevertheless, the higher clergy in recent times have received a tincture from Western literature. The name of Archbishop Bryennios, to whom we owe the first editions of the complete Epistles of Clement of Rome, and of the Teaching of the Twelve Apostles, stands on an equality with those of European scholars. Two theological schools have been founded for the Orthodox Church in Turkey, and it is understood that in future no one is to be elected bishop who has not passed through a course of study in one of them.

In Greece the Church was closely connected with the

---

[1] G. Finlay, *Hist. of Greece from B.C. 146—A.D. 1864* (new ed., ed. H. F. Tozer, Oxford, 1877); G. F. Herzberg, *Gesch. Griechenlands*, vol. IV. (Gotha, 1879); R. C. Jebb, *Modern Greece* (London, 1880); T. T. Timayenis, *Hist. of Greece to present time* (New York, 1881); W. Alison Phillips, *The War of Greek Independence* (London and New York, 1897); G. L. von Maurer, *Das griechische Volk in öffentlicher, kirchlicher...Beziehung* (Heidelberg, 1835); D. Bikelas, *Seven Essays on Christian Greece*, trans. by John, Marquess of Bute (Paisley and London, 1890).

national movement for freedom from the Turkish yoke. The clergy had for many generations set themselves to keep alive the love of liberty in the hearts of the Hellenes, and it was Archbishop Germann who raised the standard of the cross at Patras on April 2, 1821. A few days later, the Sultan Mahmoud, in a paroxysm of rage on hearing of a massacre of Mussulmans in the Morea, ordered the venerable Patriarch, Gregory, to be seized, and, with two of his bishops, all three in their sacerdotal vestments, to be hanged before the gate of the patriarchal palace. The effect of this outrage was to rouse the indignation of all Christendom, especially of Russia, against the barbarous infidel. During the years of war against Turkish oppression, the tie which bound the Church in Greece to the Patriarchate of Constantinople was gradually weakened, and in 1833 the Greek bishops in Synod at Syra declared Jesus Christ to be the only Head of their Church, which was independent of all foreign authority. The internal regulation of ecclesiastical affairs was committed to a permanent Synod consisting of five spiritual and two secular members nominated by the King. In this way, and by the transference of a portion of the episcopal jurisdiction to the State, the Church was brought more completely under the secular arm than it had been before. Under these circumstances it is not perhaps wonderful that a party among the clergy pressed for reunion with Constantinople. The Patriarch however in 1850 recognized the independence of the Orthodox Church in Greece. In 1837 arose the University of Athens, and the modern Greeks, not unmindful of their past, were eager to attain a higher level in theological as well as secular studies. The former were cared for by a special faculty in the university as well as by seminaries elsewhere. In the present generation Hellenic theologians have been in touch with the theology and criticism of Western Europe, and have produced treatises of much merit. But only a small portion of the clergy can give themselves to learning and culture. The parish priests are for the most part not sufficiently educated to take the lead among a people of very quick intelligence and eager to acquire knowledge.

The Bulgarians suffered severely from their ecclesias-

[1] James Samuelson, *Bulgaria, past and present* (London, 1888).

tical dependence on Constantinople. Bishoprics and archbishoprics were objects of traffic, the Greek clergy seldom understood the speech of the country, and the liturgy was celebrated in a language not understood of the people. But the Church-dues were exacted with great rigour. When the Crimean war roused the national feeling in the Balkan provinces, the Bulgarians struggled both for political and ecclesiastical emancipation. They succeeded in obtaining the latter before the former. In 1870 the Sultan permitted the formation of a Province of Bulgaria independent of the Patriarchate of Constantinople, to which the Orthodox Church of the other Slav principalities might be annexed on the request of two-thirds of their members. Against this Bulgarian Exarchate the Patriarch protested in vain; in 1872 Anthimus was chosen Exarch of Bulgaria and his appointment confirmed by the Sultan. Thereupon the Patriarch and his Synod condemned this assertion of national independence as schism, and excommunicated the Exarch with his whole Church. From this decision dissented only Cyril, the Patriarch of Jerusalem, who thereupon fell into great disgrace in his own diocese and was in the end deposed. Even after this diminution of territory the Patriarch still counts under his jurisdiction eighty sees in Europe, Asia Minor, and the islands of the Levant. The provinces of the Patriarchs of Antioch and Jerusalem are much smaller, and the once great and powerful see of Alexandria has sunk into insignificance. The Greek is the growing and advancing element in the Churches, and has probably still a considerable part to play in Christendom.

The ancient Armenian Church had long been divided[2], and fresh divisions arose in 1866 and were not terminated until, in 1877, Hassun, the archbishop of the Church of the Roman obedience, was recognized by the Porte as Patriarch of the whole Armenian Church. Hassun was made a Cardinal by Leo XIII. In Armenia itself in 1895, the Christians were horribly maltreated by the savage

---

[1] See above, p. 162.
[2] S. C. Malan, *The Differences between the Armenian and Greek Churches*, trans. from the Russian (London, 1871); F. C. Conybeare, *The Armenian Church* in *Religious Systems of the World* (London, 1893); A special Correspondent [A. Fraser Macdonald], *The Land of Ararat* (London, 1893).

Kurds, encouraged, as was generally believed, by the Turkish authorities. About one hundred thousand men are said to have been murdered, besides the ruthless slaughter of women and children. In 1896 an attempt by some Armenian revolutionaries to rob the Ottoman bank caused an outbreak against the Armenians in Constantinople generally, in which large numbers suffered. There was great sympathy in Europe for the unfortunate Armenians, and much private help was given to the sufferers, but no security exists against the repetition of such outrages.

In spite of the great traditions of Constantinople, the comparatively modern Church in Russia has come to be the most important member of the Eastern Church. The Emperor Alexander I.[2], a sincerely religious and earnest man, was anxious to raise the spiritual and intellectual tone of the clergy. To this end he founded seminaries for theological training and favoured the study of the Bible. With his successor Nicholas I.[3] came a change. All foreign influences, whether on the State or the Church, now came to be regarded as modern, liberal, and dangerous. The circle of ideas in the Church was narrowed, but it became more distinctly national and popular. Under Alexander II., a liberal and humane monarch, the Church, as well as the State, entered on a way of reform which was to bring it more into harmony with the spirit of the age. Count Tolstoy, who was both Minister of Education and Procurator of the Holy Synod, freed the clergy from the caste-system into which they had virtually fallen, so that it became no longer the invariable practice for a parish priest to be the son or the son-in-law of a parish priest, but the ranks of the clergy might be recruited from all conditions of men. At the same time a higher standard of culture was required from candidates for the

CH. XII.

RUSSIA[1].

Alexander I., Tzar, 1801—1825.

Nicholas I. 1826—1855.

Alexander II., 1855—1881.

---

[1] A. Leroy-Beaulieu, *L'Empire des Tsars et les Russes* (Paris, 1881–9; trans. by Ragozin, New York, 1893–6; vol. III. contains the hist. of religion); D. Mackenzie Wallace, *Russia* (London, 1877); W. Palmer, *The Patriarch and the Tzar*, from the Russian (London, 1871); "Stepniak," *The Russian Peasantry* (London, 1888 : vol. II. treats fully of the Russian Church); A. F. Heard, *The Russian Church and Russian Dissent* (London, 1887).
[2] C. Joyneville, *Life and Times of Alexander I.* (London, 1875).
[3] Paul Lacroix, *Hist. de la Vie et du Règne de Nicholas I.* (Paris, 1864).

458   *The Eastern Church*

Ch. XII.

Dissenters.

Pobiedo-nostzeff.

Poland.

Union with Orthodox Church, 1839.

sacred ministry. In 1860 a Missionary Society was formed for the conversion of the peoples of the Caucasus, and in 1866 another to work among the Mohammedans and Pagans within the bounds of the Empire itself. In 1872 some of the more earnest and thoughtful members of the Church formed a union for spiritual improvement as a means of exciting greater interest in Church matters among the educated class, and in particular of bringing to their notice the peculiarities of other forms of faith. Alexander was anxious also to place the various Dissenting bodies in a more favourable position, though in this attempt he had to encounter the strenuous opposition of the clergy. In the latter part of this emperor's reign, the outrages of the Nihilists produced the inevitable reaction, and checked all liberal tendencies in Church and State. The Procurator of the Holy Synod, Pobiedonostzeff, was of opinion that the Orthodox Church was capable of producing from its own bosom the powers necessary for the regeneration of the nation, and that foreign influence would be only prejudicial. He consequently did his best to suppress the Evangelical movement. The Procurator was not blind to the faults of the national Church, but he was anxious that it should retain its ancient type, even at the expense of falling behind the culture of other Churches.

In the partition of Poland in 1772 the provinces which had been acquired by the successful war under Stephen Bathori in 1585 were restored to Russia. The Church in these provinces belonged to the Roman communion[1], and its clergy, stimulated both by patriotism and by a dread of being forcibly united to the Russian Church, took an active part on the side of the Poles in the insurrection of 1830. When peace was restored the religious freedom which they had enjoyed was considerably restricted, and great efforts were made to induce them to join the Orthodox Church, which under Nicholas I. to a large

---

[1] A. Theiner, *Vicissitudes de l'Église Catholique des deux Rites en Pologne et Russie* (Paris, 1843); E. Likovski, *Geschichte des allmäligen Verfalls der Unirten Kirche in dem XVIII^ten und XIX^ten Jahrhundert* (Posen, 1885–7); Lescœur, *L'Église Catholique en Pologne sous le Gouvernement Russe* (Paris, 1860; new ed. 1903); W. R. Morfill, *Poland* (London, 1893); W. A. Day, *Russian Government in Poland* (London, 1867).

extent succeeded, and in 1839 a Synod at Poloczk declared for union with it. By this decision Rome lost two million adherents. There still remained however a large number of "Uniates," but almost the whole of these renounced their allegiance to Rome in 1875, alleging among their reasons for separation the new Roman dogmas of the Immaculate Conception and the Infallibility of the Pope. In the disturbances of 1861 and the following years the Roman-Catholic clergy again sided with the unfortunate Poles and suffered with them. In 1865 their property was seized by the State, they became stipendiaries of the government, and were generally harshly treated. Pope Leo XIII., however, soon after his accession (1878) succeeded in regaining for them some of their lost privileges.

CH. XII.

In the Baltic Provinces, in many of the large towns of the Empire, and among the German colonists of Southern and Eastern Russia, the Lutherans are numerous, and are much superior in general culture to the great mass of Russian population. Alexander I., who favoured Evangelical teaching, founded for them the University of Dorpat. Under Nicholas I., the national feeling in the country was unfriendly to a form of religion which was regarded as foreign, and in 1845 and the following year some sixty thousand country-people in Lithuania and Esthonia went over to the Russian Church in hope of receiving grants of fertile land. When they were undeceived and wished to return to Lutheranism, they found their wishes treated as criminal. Alexander II., however, would not countenance proceedings so undignified, and also repealed by an Order in Council, so far as regards the Baltic Provinces, the edict which compelled the children of a marriage between Orthodox and Lutheran to be brought up as Orthodox. But Alexander III., with Pobiedonostzeff as his minister, was less friendly disposed. The use of Russian was enforced in the schools and extraneous managers forced upon them. The children of mixed marriages were again ordered to be brought up as members of the Russian Church. Converts to the National Church received favourable treatment, and some Lutheran

LUTHER-
ANISM[1].

Conver-
sions to
Orthodox
Church,
1845.

---

[1] Berkholz, *Die Evang. Kirche in Russland* (Berlin, 1857); H. Dalton, *Gesch. d. Reform. Kirche in Russland* (Gotha, 1865), and *Die Evang. K. in Russland* (Leipzig, 1890).

Lutherans in Cherson.

pastors, for having received into their communion persons who wished to return to the Church which they had left, were sentenced to banishment. In the province of Cherson the Lutheran community founded in 1817 by colonists from Würtemberg still exists. Recently the Russian government has taken the first step towards freedom of conscience, for in 1905 a manifesto of the Czar exempted from punishment those who left the National Church, and granted a larger measure of freedom to the Starovers[1], and to the Bible and prayer meetings of the "Stundists[2]."

Conclusion.

These pages have traced the history of the Church from the turmoils, dogmatic and warlike, which followed the Reformation; through the naturalistic morality of the eighteenth century; through the great removal of ancient landmarks which accompanied the French Revolution and the outburst of renewed devotion to religious ideals which followed it; to the rationalism which arose as the romanticism of the early years of the century died away and the general questioning of traditional opinions which is characteristic of the age in which we live. If, on the one hand, the feeling of the powerlessness of human reason to explain the mysteries which surround the life of man leads many to agnosticism, the same feeling draws the more earnest and devout spirits to seek rest for their souls in the Church of Christ. If, even within the Church, it is felt by many that the eternal doctrines of the faith may perhaps receive a new expression to meet new intellectual wants, this does not hinder the true worshippers from holding fast their faith that God in Christ is with us alway, even unto the end of the world.

---

[1] See p. 166.
[2] A sect which arose among the German colonists in Southern Russia, called "Stundists" from the name "Stunde" (hour) which they gave to their meetings.

INDEX.

Abraham a Sta Clara 112
Abyssinian Church 161
Acta Sanctorum, the Bollandist 79
Addison's *Spectator* 181
Ad Sacram, Bull of Alexander VII. 102
Africa, Missions in 115
Aguesseau, Chancellor de 199
Aguilar, Francisco 403
Aikenhead, Thomas, hanged for blasphemy 315
Alacoque, Margaret 98
Alais, Peace of 8
Alençon, Protestant Synod of 146
Alexander VII., Pope 88
Alexander VIII., Pope 90
Allegiance, Oath of (1606-7) 42
Allgemeine Deutsche Bibliothek 209
"Alombrados," Sect of 109
Altranstadt, Treaty of 27
Ambassadors, immunity of 90
America, Roman Catholic Church in 343
America, Church Convention in (1789) 329; Prayer-Book and Canons 329; Church Parties in 329; Reformed Episcopal Church in 331; Dissenters in 332
"Americanism" in Roman Catholic Church 342
Amyrault, Moses 146
Andreä, Valentine 122
Andrewes, Lancelot 57
Angela of Brescia 95
Angelus Silesius, mystic 111
Anglicanism 55
Antrim, Synod of, Secession 325
Apostles' Creed, Controversy on, in Germany 442
Appellants against Bull *Unigenitus* 104

Aranda, Count 220
Argentina, Church in 404
Arianism in eighteenth century 171
Armenian Church 162; divisions in 456
Arminian party 142; significance of 147
Arminius (James van Harmin) 143
Arndt, John 122
Arnold, Matthew 273
Arnold, Thomas 256, 277
Arnoldi, Archbishop 421
Assemani, J. S. 161
"Associations Cultuelles" in France 391
Astruc, John, on the Pentateuch 196
Auchterarder case 317
Augsburg, Peace of 15, 21
Austria, Protestantism assailed in 17; Duchy of 27; Church Reform in 227; Concordat with, 1855 412
Avenir, L', the newspaper 378

Baader, Franz von 418
Baden, Church and State in 411; contests with the Church authorities 427; contests among Protestants 432
Bahrdt, Charles Frederick 211
Baius, Michael 81
Baltic Provinces of Russia, Lutherans in 459
Baltimore, Synod and Provincial Council of 343
Bangorian Controversy 173
Baptists 65, 298
Barbadoes 72
Barclay, Robert 67

Barré, Nicholas, founder of School-sisters 97
Barrow, Isaac 61
Basedow, J. B. 212
Basnage, family of 140
Bauer, Bruno 446
Baur, Ferdinand Christian 446
Bavaria, Concordat with 410; Protestantism in 431
Baxter, Richard 62
Bayle, Peter 195
Beards in Russia 165
Bedell, Bishop of Kilmore and Ardagh 50
Behmenists 66
Belgium, Church in 397
Bell, Philip, Governor of Barbadoes 72
Benedict XIII., Pope 92
Benedict XIV., Pope 92; closes Jansenist controversy 105
Bengel, J. A. 126
Benson, Archbishop, Judgment 269
Bentley's, Richard, *Remarks* 181
Berchtesgaden exiles 27
Berkeley, George, in America 71; Bishop 182, 320
Berleburg, Bible of 137
Bert, Paul, Education Bill (1882) 389
Bertrand, Lewis 116
Berulle, Pierre de 94
Berwick, Pacification of (1639) 46
Bethlen, Gabriel 14
Bible, Authorised Version of 30; translated into Algonquin 70
Bible Christians 301
Bismarck, Prince, against Ultramontanism 424
Blondel, David 140
Bochart, Samuel 140, 141
Bodelschwingh, Pastor von, founds Labour-colony 450
Bodin, John, sceptical 194
Boehler, Peter 131
Boehme, Jacob (Behmen) 132
Bohemia, Protestants oppressed in 17
Bohemian Brethren 127
Bolingbroke, Henry St John, Lord 178
Bollandist *Acta SS.*, begun 1643 79
Bona, Cardinal 78
Booth, William 301

Botskai, Stephen 14
Boulter, H., Primate of Ireland 320
Bourbons, Restoration of, in France 375
Bourignon, Antoinette, Quietist 111
Boyne, Battle of the 53
Bramhall, John, Primate of Ireland 52
Bray, Dr 70
Brazil, Dutch Missions in 156; Church in 403
Breslau, Peace of 27
Brüggler Sect 139
Bruno, Giordano, burnt 1600 76
Brunswick-Wolfenbüttel, Church system of 25
Bryennios, Archbishop 454
Buddeus, J. F. 126
Buffon, the naturalist 197
Bulgarian Exarchate (1870) 456
Bull, George 62
Burial Law (1880) in England 289
Busenbaum, casuist 76
Butler's, Bishop, *Analogy* 182
"Buttler Gang," the 138
Buxtorfs, the 140

Caird, John 276
Calasanza, Joseph 95
California, R.C. Missions in 117
Calixtus, George 121, 149
Calovius, Abraham 120, 150
Calvinism in England 55
Cambridge Platonists 63; Theologians and Critics 280
Camisards 11
Canada, R.C. Missions in 117
Canonization by the Pope (1867) 360
Canons of 1604, Anglican 30; of 1640 33
Cappel, Lewis 140
Capuchin Missions 115
Capuchins, independence of 94
Caraffa, Count 14
"Carbonari" in Italy 346
Cardale, John Bate, Irvingite 303
Carlyle, Thomas, Historian 272
Carlyle, Thomas, Irvingite 305
Carroll, J., Bishop of Baltimore 343
Casuistry 76

Index 463

Catechisms, Longer and Shorter, in Scotland 47
Catherine II. of Russia, confiscates Church property 165
"Catholic Apostolic Church" of Irvingites 302
Catholic Association 295
"Catholic League" (1609) 17
Catholic Relief Bill passed 261, 296
Caulet, Bishop of Pamiers 108
Cavour, Count 357
Ceremonies, objected to in England 28
Cevennes, revolt in 10
Channing, William Ellery 334
Chantal, Madame de 95
Charenton, Protestant Synod at (1631) 151; (1644) 146; (1673) 9
Charity, Sisters of (Grey Sisters) 96
Charles X., King of France 377
Charles XII., of Sweden 27
Chateaubriand, F. R. de 250
Chatel and the French-Catholic Church 377
Cherson, Lutherans in 460
Chili, Church in 405
Chillingworth, William 60
China, Catholic Church in 114
"Christenthumsgesellschaft" 213
Christian Knowledge, Society for Promotion of 71
Christian Science 337
Christian-Catholics in Switzerland 371
Christina, Queen of Sweden, in Rome 89
Chubb, Thomas 178
Church and State in England 286
Church Association 268
Church Congress organized (1861) 283
Church Missionary Society founded 74
Church of England in early nineteenth century 255
Church Rates abolished 289
Circuits, Wesleyan 187
Clarke, Samuel, on the Trinity 171
Claudius, Matthias 215
Clausen, H. H., in Denmark 435
Claver, Pedro 116
Clement VIII., Pope 84
Clement IX., Pope 89; pacifies Jansenists 103

Clement X., Pope 89
Clement XI., Pope 91
Clement XII., Pope 92
Clement XIII. elected 218; died 221
Clement XIV. elected 221
Clergy, Freethinking 174
Clergy Discipline Act (1892) 289
Clericus (Jéan le Clerc) 142
Cleves, Church system of 26
Clowes, John 136
Coke, Dr, Methodist bishop for America 188
Colenso, J. W. 279
Coleridge, S. T. 271
Collegial system 23
"Collegiants" 145
Collins, Anthony 176
Colonies, care for religion in 68
Comenius, Amos 128
Comprehension Bill rejected 40
Comte, Auguste, Positivist 396
Condillac 197
Congregational Union 298
Constantinople, Patriarch of 453
Conventicle Act 38
Convocation of 1689 40
Convocation, dissensions in 169; suppressed (1717) 172; meets for business 283
Copernicus 6
Copleston, Edward 256
Coquerel, A. L. C. 392
Corpus Catholicorum 22; *Evangelicorum* 22
Covenant, the, drawn up at Edinburgh (1638) 45
Cowper, William 192
Créqui, the Duke of, in Rome 88
Cromwell, Protector 36
Crusius, C. A. 213
Cudworth, Ralph 64
Cummins, Bishop, in America 331
Cum occasione, Bull against Jansenism 100
Curci, Father 374
Czerski, Johann 421

Dalberg, Freiherr von 224, 245
D'Alembert 197
"Danites," Mormon 341
Darby, J. N. 306
Darwin, Charles, *Origin of Species* 274
Daub, Carl 437
David, Christian 128

Deaconesses, Order of, revived in England 283
De la Cour, Didier 94
Denmark, Rationalism in 435
Descartes, René 194
De Wette, W. M. L. 442
Diderot 197
Dio, John di 95
Diocesan Conferences instituted (1864) 284
Dippel, John Conrad 210
Directory for Public Worship 35
Divines, Assembly of 34
Divorce permitted in France (1884) 389
Dober, Leonard 158
Dodwell, Henry 179
Döllinger, J. J. Ignaz von 368, 420
Donauwerth, under ban 17
Donne, John 58
Dorpat, University of 459
Dort, Synod of (1618) 144
Drey, J. Sebastian von 418
Droste-Vischering, C. A. von 409
Drummond, Henry 302
Druses and Maronites (1860) 454
Duchoborzi in Russia 166
Dumoulin, Pierre 150
Dunin, Archbishop von 409
Dupuis, *Origine des Cultes* 197
Dupuy, Pierre (Puteanus) 107
Durie, John 151
Dutch methods of promoting Christianity 155

Eastern Church, relations to Western 159
Eastward Position, Anglican 268
Ebel, J. W. 253
Ecclesiastical Commission (1836) 286
Ecclesiastical Courts 287; Royal Commission on 289
Ecclesiastical Titles Act 297
Ecuador, Concordat with (1862) 405
Eddy, Mary B., Christian Scientist 337
Edelmann, John Christian 211
Education, Elementary, in England 290
Education Act (1870) 291; (1902) 292
Egede, Hans and Povel 157
Eliot, John, missionary to American Indians 69

Eller, Elias 138
Emmerich, Prince - Archbishop, withdraws schools from Jesuits 224
Ems Agreement of German Archbishops 229
Encyclopédie, French 197
English Church Union 268
English Ladies, sisterhood 96
Eperies, atrocities at 14
Episcopius, Simon 143
Erasmus 5
Ernesti, J. A. 206
Erpenius, Thomas (van Erpe) 140
Erskine, Ebenezer 315
Erthal, Archbishop 224
Escobar, casuist 76
Essays and Reviews 278; condemned by Convocation 279; two authors of acquitted by Judicial Committee 279
Estius, commentator 79
Evangelical Alliance 451
Evangelical Party in England 190, 269
"Evangelical Union" (1608) 17
Ewald, Heinrich 443

Falloux, Comte, law of, on Education 381
Familists 66
Febronius, Justinus (J. von Hontheim) 225; condemned by the Pope 226
Fénelon, Salignac de la Mothe 111
Feoffees, Puritan, put down 32
Ferrar, Nicholas 69
Ferrara added to Papal dominions 85
Feuerbach, Ludwig 437
Fichte, J. G. 203
Field, Richard 57
Field-preaching, 186
Fifth-Monarchy Men 65
Firmian, Count 26
Five Mile Act 38
Fletcher, John, of Madeley 190
Fliedner, Pastor, founds Deaconess' Institution 449
Florence, Synod at (1787) 231
Fontanelle, covertly attacks priesthood 195
Forbes, Alexander P., Bishop of Brechin 313
Formula Concordiae (1577) 118

Index 465

Fox, George 66
France, States General of, meet 234; National Assembly recognized 234; Church Estates confiscated 234; Civil Constitution of clergy 234; Oath of Allegiance 235; National Assembly dissolved 236; Legislative Assembly 236; Calendar reformed 237; National Council in 1811 244; Roman Catholic Church in 375; new Concordat attempted in 376; July Revolution of 1830 in 377; Religious revival in (1871) 386; Catholic Universities in 387; Religious Associations interdicted in, by Napoleon III. 387; further regulations 388; Quarrel with Rome (1904) 390; Church and State Separation Bill (1905) 390
Francke, August Hermann 124; on missions 155, 156
Fransoni, Archbishop of Turin, exiled 356
Frederick II. of Prussia 222
Frederick IV., Elector-Palatine 17
Frederick V., Elector-Palatine, made king of Bohemia 18
Free Presbyterian Church of Scotland formed 318
Free-thinking, English 167
Freiburg, Conference at (1850) 413
French Lutherans 394
French National Assembly, 1871, relation with the Church 386
French Protestantism 391
French Reformed Church, position of 392
French Revolution, the 233
French Revolution of 1848 382
French Scepticism 194
Frère-Orban, Belgian minister 398
Friends, Society of 66, 300
"Friends of Light" 448
Frohschammer, Jacob 419
Froude, R. Hurrell 257; his *Remains* 264

Galileo abjures 76
Gallican Church, Literature of 77; Preachers 78; Liberties of 108
Garibaldi 355, 358
Gassner, Father, undertakes to heal sickness 224
Geay, Bishop of Laval 390

Gebhard, Archbishop of Cologne, becomes Protestant 16
Geissel, J. von, Archbishop of Cologne 409
Gellert, C. F. 213
General Assembly in Scotland dispersed (1653) 47
Geneva, religious movement in 433
Gerbet, O. Phil. 378
Gerbillon, Father 114
Gerhard, John 120
"German-Catholics" 422
German Clergy, anti-liberal 423
German Enlightenment 199
German Missionary Societies 450
Germann, Archbishop, in Greece 455
Germany, Church and State in Revolutionary period 245; Concordat of 1803 246; Roman Catholic Church in 407; South Western States 411; Roman Catholic Clergy in 416; Evangelical Union in 427; Protestant Church in Eastern Provinces 431; Speculative Theology in 436; Biblical Criticism in 436, 442; Christian Institutions in 448; Protestant Congress in 451; Evangelical League in 452; Evangelical Standing Committee in 452
Gichtel, John George 137
Giordano, Bruno, Statue of, at Rome 373
Glamorgan, Earl of, treaty of 1645 52
Glasgow Synod (1638), revives Presbyterianism 46
Gobel, Bishop of Paris 237
Goeschel, Karl Friedrich 437
Goethe, J. W. von 205
Goeze, Melchior 213
Golius, James 140
Gomarus, Francis 143
Gordon Riots 294
Gore, Charles 281
Gorham Case, the 266
Görres, Joseph von 418
Grace, Congregation on 82
Grace, Edict of (1629) 8
Graf, R. J. 443
Grattan, Henry 295
Gray, Bishop of Capetown 279
Greece, Church in 455; separates from Constantinople 455

C. 30

Greek clergy, their education and theology 455
Green, Thomas Hill 276
Gregory XV., Pope 86
Gregory XVI., Pope 351
Gregory, Greek Patriarch, murdered 455
Grotius, Hugo 23, 141
Grundtvig, Nicholas, in Denmark 435
Guatemala, Jesuits expelled (1872) 405
Guénée, Abbé 198
Guevara, Archbishop of Caracas, banished 405
Guizot, his educational measures 381; in Reformed Synod 393
Gunpowder Plot (1605) 42
Günther, Anton 417
Gury's *Compendium* 349
Gustavus Adolphus 19
"Gustavus Adolphus Union" 450
Guyon, Madame de 110

Hadleigh Meeting of Tractarians 261
Haffenreffer, Matthias 119
Hahn, Augustus 447
Hahn, John Michael 252
Haldane, Robert, in Geneva 433
Halle University founded (1694) 125
Hamann, John George 214
Hamel, his views on Scripture 80
Hamilton, Sir William 272
Hammond, Henry 60
Hampton Court Conference 29
Hanover, Bull restoring bishoprics in 411
Harms, Klaus 447
Harnack, Adolf 442
Harriot, Thomas, missionary 68
Hassun, Patriarch of Roman-Armenian Church 456
Hauge, Hans Nielsen 434
"Hebrews," Sect of 137
Hecker, Isaac Thomas 344
Hefele, Bishop 367, 420
Hegel, G. W. F. 436
Heiling, Peter 155
Helvetic Consensus 147
Helvetius 197
Hengstenberg, Ernest William 448
Henry IV. of France 17
Henschen, Godfrey 79
Herbert of Cherbury 174

Herder, John Gottfried 204
Hermes, George 417
Herrnhut, Community at 129
Herzog, Bishop of Christian-Catholics in Switzerland 371
Hesse-Cassel, Church system of 25
Hesse Darmstadt, Protestantism in 432
Hicks, Elias, American Quaker 334
High Commission Court, in England 28
Hindmarsh, Robert 136
Hirscher, John Baptist von 418
Hoadley, Benjamin 172
Hobbes, Thomas 23, 63
Hochman 137
Hoffmann, G. W. 252
Holbach, Baron de 197
Holland, Jansenist Church in 105, 415; Roman Catholic Church in 415; Protestants in 434
Holy Alliance 249
Holy Coat of Treves 421
Holy Ghost, Instruments of the 138
Holy Table, set altar-wise 32
Hontheim, John Nicholas von 225
Hooker, Richard 56
Horne, Bishop 191
Hort, F. J. A. 280
Hotham, C., Behmenist 134
Hottinger, J. H. 140
Huber, Samuel 119
Hulfen, Leonard 120
Hume, David 179
Hungary, persecution of Protestants in 13
Hunnius, Ægidius 119
Hunt, Robert, in Virginia 68
Huntingdon, Countess of 189
Hurter, F., romanizes 248
Hyacinth, Father 372

Ignorantins 97
Illuminati, Order of, founded 225
Immaculate Conception, dogma of 359
In Cœna Domini, Bull 87
Independency 70, 297
Independent Party in 1645 35
Indulgence, Declaration of (1672) 38; (1687) 39
In eminenti, Bull 100
Infallibility of the Pope 362; decreed 365; opposition to 366

Innocent X., Pope 87
Innocent XI., Pope 89
Innocent XII., Pope 90
Innocent XIII., Pope 91
Ireland, state of Church in 49
Ireland, Union with Great Britain 321
Irish Act of Uniformity 52
Irish Articles (1615) 51
Irish Church, Temporalities Act 261; in eighteenth century 319; disestablished (1869) 322; Representative Body 323; Protestants under English Parliament 52; Rebellion (1641) 51
Irish Laws against Roman Catholic Orders 325; Parliament 320; Prayer-book 324; Presbyterianism 325; Rebellion (1798) 321; Sees, ten abolished (1833) 322; Tithe Act (1838) 321; Vestry Cess abolished 322
Irving, Edward, and Irvingites 302
Isenbiehl, Lorenz, doubts on prophecy 224
Italian Insurrections (1831 ff.) 352

Jacobi, F. H. 202
Jamaica, an English possession 72
James I. of England, attitude towards the Church 28
James II. of England 38; abdicates 42
Jansen, Cornelius, author of *Augustinus* 99
Jansenism, Five Propositions of, condemned 101
Jansenist Church in Holland 105
Jansenists distinguish between law and fact 102
Japan, Christian Church in 113
Jerusalem Bishopric 266
Jesuit Influence on Society, and on other Orders 349
Jesuit schools 348
Jesuit trading 220
Jesuits banished from France, Spain, Naples, Sicily, and Parma 220, 221; suppression of, by Papal Brief 222; restoration of (1814) 347
John of the Cross 109
Johnson, Samuel 184
Jones, William, of Nayland 191

Joseph II., Emperor, Church reforms of 227; receives Pius VI. at Vienna 229
Jowett, Benjamin 278
Juarez, Benito, President of Mexico 402
Jubilee, Lutheran, of 1817 428; Roman, of 1825 350; of 1888 373
Jung-Stilling (J. H. Jung) 214

Kaiserswerth, House for Deaconesses 449
Kant, Immanuel 201
Kaunitz, Austrian minister 229
Keble, John 257; his sermon in 1833 261
Kenotic Controversy (1619-1624) 119
Kepler, astronomer 119
King, Archbishop 320
King, Bishop of Lincoln, his case 269
Kingsley, Charles 273
Klemm, Professor 154
Klopstock 214
Knutzen, Mathias 210
Kock, John (Cocceius) 141
Kohler, the brothers 139
Kornthal Settlement 252
Krüdener, Frau von 249; in Geneva 433
Kuhlmann, Quirinus 136
Kuhn, John von 418
"Kultur-Kampf" 425; Papal Intervention in 426

Labour-Colonies established in Germany 450
Lacordaire, H. D. 378, 380, 383
Lalande, J. J. 197
Lamarck's Philosophy 274
Lamennais, H. F. R. de 377; at Rome 379
Lampe 142
Lapide, Cornelius a (Van den Steen) 79
Lardner, Nathaniel 183
Las Casas, Bartholomew de 116
Lateran Synod (1725) 92
Laud, William, Archbishop 31; impeached 33; executed 35; as theologian 59; his revision of Liturgy for Scottish Church 45
Launoy, J. de 107
Lavater, John Caspar 214

Law, W., edits Behmen's Works 134; writes against Hoadley 173; against Mandeville 178
Layman, casuist 76
Lay-Preachers 187
Lazarists 96
Leade, Jane, Philadelphian 134
Lee, Ann, foundress of the "Shakers" 335
Le Gras, Madame 96
Leibnitz, G. W. 153, 155, 200
Leighton, Robert, Bishop of Dunblane 47
Le Nordez, Bishop of Dijon 390
Leo XII., Pope 350
Leo XIII., Pope 372
Lesley, Alexander 46
Less, his views on Scripture 80
Lessing, Gotthold Ephraim 203
Liberal tendencies in England 271
Library of the Fathers 263
Lightfoot, John 62
Lightfoot, Joseph B. 280
Liguori, Alfonso Maria de 97
Limborch, Philip van 142
Limerick, Treaty of 324
Lindsey, Theophilus 307
Locke, John 168
Löhe, Pastor, founds Missionary College 449
Long Parliament 33
Loubet, President, in Italy 390
Loudun, Assembly of 7
Loyson (Father Hyacinth) 372
Lubeck, Peace of 19
Lucaris, Cyril 159; corresponds with Archbishop Abbot 160
Lucas of Prague 127
Luneville, Treaty of 240
Lutheran Orthodoxy in seventeenth century 118
Lux Mundi 281

Malabar Usages 113
Malan, Caesar 433
Maldonatus, commentator 79
Mandeville, Bernard 178
Mansel, H. L. 272
Marca, Pierre de, Archbishop of Paris 107
Marheineke, Philip Conrad 437
Maronites 161
Martineau, James 275
Maryland, toleration in 117
Massachusetts, Charter of, 1628 69

Matthew, Patrick, naturalist 274
Maurice, F. D. 273
Maximilian of Bavaria 17
Mazarin, Cardinal, not hostile to Protestants 9
Melville, Andrew, exiled (1606) 43
Mentzer, Balthazar 119
Mercy, Brothers of 95
"Mère Angelique" of Port Royal 101
Methodism, organization of 300; divisions of 301
Methodist bishop ordained 188
Methodist Conference, the first 187
Methodists 185
Methodists, Episcopal, in America 333
Mexico, Church in 402; "Iglesia de Jesus" 403
Michaelis, J. D. 207
Michaud, Abbé 371
Michelis, F. 419
Middleton, Conyers 180
Milan, Peace of 12
Mill, John Stuart 272
Millenary Petition 29
Miller, William, Adventist 336
Milner, Joseph and Isaac 191
Missions, English, work in foreign parts 284
"Missions" in England 282
Missions, Protestant 154
Missions, Roman Catholic 112
Moderates and Evangelicals in Scotland 315
Mogilas, Peter 161
Möhler, J. A. 419
Molanus, Gerhard Wolter 152
Molinos, Michael 109
Momiers in Switzerland 250
Monod, Adolphe 392
Montalembert, C. Forbes de Tryon 378, 380
Montesquieu's satire 195
Montpellier, Peace of 8
Moravian Brotherhood 127; extravagances in 131
More, Hannah 194
More, Henry 64
Morland, Samuel 13
Mormonism 338
Mornay, Philippe de 150
Moscow a Patriarchate 163
Mosheim, J. L. 23
Moulin, Charles du 107
Muckers in Königsberg 253

Index 469

Müller, Daniel 137
Müller, Heinrich 134
Muratori, Ludovico 78
Mysticism in Roman Church 109; German 249
Mystics, Protestant 132

Nantes, Edict of, revoked (1685) 10
Naples refuses tribute to the Pope 232
Napoleon I., his Concordat 240; proposes to create a French Patriarchate 242
Napoleon III., Emperor (1852) 382
National Society founded (1812) 290
Natural Religion 174
Natural Selection 275
Nauvoo, Mormonites at 339
Neander (David Mendel) 439
Nepomuk, John 18
Netherlands, Revolt in (1789) 230
Newburn, Battle of (1640) 46
New England, intolerance in 328
New Jerusalem, Church of the 136
Newman, F. W. 272
Newman, J. H. 257
Newton, John 192
Nicolai, F. 209
Nicon, Patriarch 163
Nismes, Riots in 391
Nitzschmann, David, Moravian Bishop 130
Nobili, Father, missionary 112
Noetics at Oxford 256
Nonjurors, schism of 41
"Normal Year" 21
North America, Church in 326
Norway, Religion in 434
Novalis (F. von Hardenberg) 248
Noyes, John H. 336

Oates, Titus, perjuries of 42
Oberlin, J. F. 215
O'Connell, Daniel 295
Oetinger, Christopher Frederick 213
Old-Catholic Congresses 379; Synod (1874) 370
"Old-Catholics" 367; recognized by Prussia 370
Oldenbarneveld 144
Old-Lutherans 430
Oliveira, Bishop of Olinda 404
Oneida Community 337
Orange, William of, Landing of 39
Oratoire, the French 94

Organic Articles of Napoleon I. 241
Osnaburg, Treaty of (1648) 20
Oxenstierna, Chancellor 20
Oxford Movement 255
Owen, John 62
Ozanam, Frederic 380

Paine, Thomas 180
Paion, Claude 146
Paley, W., *Evidences* 184
Pallavicino 78
Pan-Anglican Conference, the first 285
Papacy, the, in nineteenth century 346
Papal Aggression 297
Papal claims questioned 218
Papal States annexed to France 243
Papebroch, Daniel 79
Paraguay, Cession of 219
Paraguay, Jesuit rule in 117
Paris, François de, deacon 104
Parker, Theodore 335
Parma and the Papacy 218; Reforms in 231
Paroles d'un Croyant (1833) 379
Pascal, Blaise, *Lettres Provinciales* 77, 103
Patronage question in Scotland 316
Patteson, John Coleridge 285
Paul V., Pope, Briefs against Oath of Allegiance 42; his reign 85
Pavillon, Bishop of Alais 108
Pearson, John 61
Penn, William 67
Penna, Orazio della, Capuchin missionary 115
Perrone's *Prælectiones* 349
Perth, Articles of (1618) 44; no longer to be insisted upon 46
Perthes, Professor Clemens, founds Rest-houses 449
Peter, Margaret 253
Peter the Great 164; institutes the Holy Governing Synod 165
Pfaff, Christopher Matthew 23, 154
Philadelphians in Berleburg 138
"Philanthropinum,"Basedow's 212
Philosophic Movement 3
Piarists 95
Piedmont, Waldensians in 12; Reforms in 356

30—3

Pietism, German 121
Pisa, Treaty of (1664) 88
Pistoia, Synod of 231
Pithou, Pierre (Pithœus) 107
Pius VI. (Angelo Braschi) elected 223
Pius VII., elected at Venice 239; captive at Savona 243; returns to Rome 245
Pius VIII., Pope 351
Pius IX., Pope 353
Pius X., Pope 374
Placæus (De la Place) 146
Pluralities Act (1837) 287
Plütschau, H. 156
Plymouth Brethren 306
Pobiedonostzeff, Procurator of Holy Synod in Russia 458
Poland, Protestants oppressed in 14; partition of 15; Church in 45; Union with Orthodox Church (1839) 458
Polignac, French minister 377
Polish Uniates 162
Polygamy, Mormonite 342
Pombal, Marquis of, in Portugal 219
Ponce de Leon, Luis, commentator 80
Popish Plot 42
Porteus, Bishop 191
Port Royal, society of 101; destroyed 103
Portugal, Church in 401
Prague, Peace of 20
Prayer-book revised 37
Pregizer, C. A. 252
Presbyterians in England 28, 299
Priestley, Dr 307
Propaganda, Congregation instituted 112
Propagation of the Gospel, Society for (1649) 70; (1701) 71
Protestant Dissenters 297
Protestant dogma 3
Proudhon, P. J., Communist 396
Prussia, movement in, for unity (1701) 153; Mixed Marriages 408; Bull of 1821 408; Church and State in 423; State regulation of Church schools and discipline of Clergy 424; "Laws of May" (1874) 425; revised 426; Service-Books of 1816 and 1821 429; Lutheran Free Church constituted 430

Public Worship Regulation Act (1874) 288
Pusey, E. B. 263; suspended 266

Quakers 66, 300
Quesnel, Pasquier 103
Quietism 110
Quinquarticular Controversy 143

"Rabbling" of Clergy in Scotland 309
Racine, L. 199
Rakoczy, George 14
Raleigh's, Walter, Gift to promote Christianity 68
Rancé, Bouthillier de 97
Ranters 66
Rapp, George 251
Raskolniks or Starovers in Russia 166
Rationalism in Germany 205; attempts of the civil power to restrain 216; its effect on society 217
Ravignan, Father Xavier de 380
Reason, goddess of, in France 237
Redemptorists 97
Reformation, its character and consequences 1; Political problems of 2
Regale, right of 107
Reimarus, Hermann Samuel 208
Reinhard, Volkmar 215
Reinkens, Dr J. Hubert, Bishop 369
Relief Church in Scotland 315
Religious Revivals in England 282
Religious Societies in England 168
Remonstrants in Holland 143
Renan, Ernest 384
"Reservatum Ecclesiasticum" 16
Reserve, Tract on, by Isaac Williams 264
Restitution, Edict of (1629) 19
Reuss, Eduard 443
Reynolds, Edward, Bishop of Norwich 62
Rhodez, Alexander, missionary 113
Ricci, Matthew 114
Ricci, Scipio de, Bishop of Pistoia 231
Richelieu, Cardinal, intervenes in Germany 19; not unfavourable to Protestants 9
Richer, Edmond 107
Ritschl, Albrecht 441

Ritual, disputes on, in English Church 267
Robertson, F. W. 273
Robertson of Ellon 317
Robespierre's State religion 237
Rochelle, Protestant assembly at 7; siege of 8
Rock, John Frederick 138
Rollin, against Scepticism 199
Romaine, William 190
Roman Catholic disabilities (1604) 41
Roman Catholics address the King of England (1778) 293; in Ireland 295
Roman Church, characteristics of 75
Roman Republic 239
Romanoff, Michael, Czar 163
Romanticism, French 250; German 247
Rome, oppression in 357; taken (1870) by the Italian army 358
Ronge, Johannes 421
Ronsdorf Sect 138
Rose, Hugh James 261
Rosicrucians 123
Rossi, Bernardo de 81
Rosweyd, Heribert 79
Rothe, Richard 440
Rousseau, Jean Jacques 197
Rupprecht, Eduard 444
Russia, Church in 162, 457
Russia, Dissenters in 458
Russian Calendar, change in 165
Ryswick, Treaty of 24

Sacheverell, Dr 169
Sacred Heart, Devotion to the 98
Sailer, John Michael 416
St Maur, Congregation of 94
St Simon, C. H., Socialist 395
St Simon, Duc de 199
Sales, Francis of 12
Salle, Baptiste de la 97
Salt Lake City 340
Salvation Army 301
Salzburg exiles 26
Sanchez, casuist 76
Sancroft, Archbishop 39
Sanderson, Robert 61
Sandoval, Father 116
Sarpi, Paolo 78, 86
Savoy Conference 37
Saxony, Church system of 25; Protestantism in 431

Schall, Adam 114
Scheibel, Professor, resists Union 429
Schelling, F. W. J. 436
Schiller, J. C. F. 205
Schlegel, A. and F. 248
Schleiermacher, F. L. D. 438
Schönherr, J. H. 253
Schrempf, Pastor Chr. 442
Schulte, J. F. von 369
Schwartz, Christian Frederick, missionary 73
Scotland, independent spirit of 43; General Assembly in, forbidden 43; titular Bishops 43; consecrated (1610) 44; Bishops restored in 1661 47; Episcopacy disestablished in 309; Presbyterianism re-established in (1690) 314; Anglican Congregations in 312
Scott, Thomas, commentator 192
Scottish Church in 1689 309; persecuted 310; Relief Bill (1792) 311; organization of 312; Liturgy of 312
Scottish Presbyterians, persecuting spirit of 314
Scottish Schools Act 314
Scottish Secession of 1843 317
Seabury, Bishop of Connecticut 71, 329
Seceders in Scotland 315
Secessions, Anglican, to Rome, in 1845 266; in 1850 267
Sects in Revolutionary Period 251
Seekers 66
Seeley, J. R. 274
Sees, new, in England 282
Sees, Roman Catholic, founded in England 296
Selwyn, George Augustus 285
Selwyn, William, Governor of Jamaica 73
Semler, John Solomon 207
Sequier, reports on offensive books 199
Serva, Juniper 117
Seven Bishops' Petition 39; trial of 39
Shaftesbury, third Earl of 176; seventh Earl of 270
Shakers, American 335
Sharp, Archbishop, murdered 48
Sherlock's, T., *Trial of the Witnesses* 181
Sicilian Monarchy, spiritual claims of 91

Sieveking, Amalie, cares for sick and poor 450
Sigismund III. 14
Silesia, Reformation in 27
Simeon, Charles 193
Simon, Richard, Oratorian 80
Sintenis, W. F. 448
Sisterhood at Devonport 283
Sixtus V., Pope 83
Skinner, Bishop 311
Smith, John, Platonist 64
Smith, Joseph, Mormon leader 338
Socialistic Movements in France 395
Solemn League and Covenant 34, 47
Solida Decisio of Dresden (1624) 120
South American Republics 402
South, Robert 62
Spain, Church affairs in nineteenth century 398; Protestants in 400
Spangenberg 132
Spanish Succession and Clement XI. 91
Spaulding, Solomon, his Romance 339
Spinola, Bishop 152
Spinoza, B., influence on theology 200, 206
Spencer, Herbert 275
Spener, Philip Jacob 123; on missions 155
Staël, Madame de 251
Stanhope, Lord, desires to relieve Dissenters 173
Stanley, Arthur Penrhyn 278
Star Chamber 33; abolished 34
Staudenmaier, Franz Anton 418
Stearne, J., Bishop of Clogher 320
Steenoven, Cornelius, Archbishop of Utrecht 106
Steinbühler sentenced for blasphemy 224
Stillingfleet's *Origines Sacræ* 181
Stolberg, Count F. von, Romanizes 248
Storch, Matthew and Christian 158
Strathbogie Presbytery 317
Strauss, D. F. 444
Suarez, casuist 76
Subscription to Formularies, petition against (1772) 174
Suffragan Bishops appointed (1870) 282

Sunday Sports 32
Supreme Being, festival of, in France 237
Sweden, Pietists in 435
Swedenborg, Emmanuel 131
Swift, Dean 320
Switzerland, Protestants in 11; Church and State in 414; Sonderbund of Catholic Cantons 414
Syllabus, Papal (1864) 360
Syncretism 149
Synod at Lincoln (1871) 284

"Tables," Committees formed at Edinburgh to oppose liturgy 45
Tamil New Testament 156
Taylor, Jeremy 61
Tegernsee, Declaration of 410
Teinds (tithes) Commission on 44
Territorial System 23
Tersteegen, Gerhard 215
Test Act 38; repealed 248
Theiner, A., at Rome 421
Theophilanthropism in France 238
Theosophists 132
Theresa, St, 109
Thibet, missions in 115
Thiersch, H. W. J., Irvingite 305
Thomasius, Christian 23, 125
Thorn, Conference of 15, 149
Thornton, John and Henry 193
Thumm, Theodore 119
Tieck, Ludwig 248
Tillotson, John, Archbishop of Canterbury 64
Tindal, Matthew 177
Titular Bishops in Scotland 43; consecrated 44
Toland, John 175
Tolentino, Peace of 239
Toleration Act (1689) 40
Tolstoy, Count 457
Toplady, Augustus 190
Tournon, Thomas de, Cardinal 115
Tracts for the Times 262; no. 90 265
Tranquebar, Danish mission in 156
Trappists 97
Triers, the 36
Tübingen School, Protestant Critical 446
Tübingen School, Roman Catholic 418
Turkey, Russia claims Protectorate over Christians in 454; Hatti-Sherif of Gulhane (1839) 453; Hatti-Humayum (1856) 454

Index 473

Turkish Empire, Clergy in 454

Ulster, Presbyterian Synod of 326
Uniformity, Act of (1662) 37
Unigenitus, Bull 104
Unitarianism 307; in America 334
United Free Church, Scottish (1903) 319
United Presbyterian Church, Scottish 315
United States of America, Religious Freedom in 326
Unity, Projects for 148
Universalism, Hypothetic 146
Universities, Religious Tests in, abolished 1877, in England 289
Urban VIII., Pope 19, 86
Urbino lapses to the Pope 87
Urlsperger, John 213
Ursuline Nuns 95
"Usages" in Malabar 113; in China 114
Ussher, Archbishop 50
Utah, admitted as State of U.S.A. 342
Utrecht, Archbishopric of 106

Vairesse attacks priesthood 195
Vanini burnt (1619) 75
Vatican Council, the 359
Vaud, Canton, Free Church in 433
Venema, H. 142
Venezuela, Church in 405
Venice, contest with Papacy 85
Venn, Henry 190
Verbiest, Ferdinand 114
Vergier de Hauranne, Jean du 101
Verschooren 137
Vestments, Anglican 268
Veto Act, Scottish 316
Veuillot, Louis 383
Vicari, Hermann von, Archbishop 411
Vicars Apostolic of the Pope in England 296
Victor Emmanuel, King 356
Vieira, Antonio 116
Vienna, Peace of (1606) 14
Villemain's Educational Measures 381
Vincent de Paul, Society of 95, 380
Vineam Domini, Bull 103
Virginia, provision for religion in 68; Church in 329
Visitationists 95

Vitringa, C. 140
Voet, Gisbert 142
Voltaire, François Arouet de 196

Waldensians, persecution of 12
Warburton, William 183
Ward, Mary 96
Ward, W. G. 265; his *Ideal* condemned 266
Waterland, Daniel 171
Watson's *Apology for the Bible* 180
Weigel, Valentine 132
Weimar, Bernard of 20
Weishaupt, Adam, founds "Illuminati" 225
Wellhausen, Julius 443
Welz, Ernest von 155
Wesley, Charles, joins "Methodist" society at Oxford 185; in Georgia 186; opposed to separation from the Church 188
Wesley, John, joins the Oxford society 185; in Georgia 186; receives "assurance" 186; preaches in the open air 186; appoints lay-preachers 187; founds classmeetings 187; Methodist Conference 187; circuits 187; ordains preachers and bishops 188
Wessenberg, I. H. K. von 416
West Indies, Roman Catholic missions in 116
Westcott, B. F. 280
Westen, Thomas von 157
Westminster Assembly of Divines 34; Confession accepted in Scotland 47, 48
Westphalia, Peace of 20
Wetstein, J. G. 142
Whately, Richard 256
Whichcote, Benjamin 64
Whiston, William 170
Whitaker, Alexander, in Virginia 69
White Mountain, Battle of 18
Whitefield, George, joins Oxford Methodists 185; visits America 72; returns to England and preaches in the open air 186; separates from Wesleyans 188; produces extraordinary effects by his preaching 189; aided by Selina, Countess of Huntingdon 189
Whitgift, Archbishop 28

Wichern, J. H., founds Das Rauhe Haus 449
Wilberforce, William 193
Wilkins, John, Bishop of Chester 64
Williams, Bishop 34
Winkler, A. 153
Witches persecuted in Scotland 314
Witgenstein Settlement 137
Witsius, Hermann 142
Wladislav IV. 15
Wolf, Christian 200
Wolfenbüttel Fragments 208
Woolston, Thomas 177
Wordsworth, Bishop Christopher 284

Wordsworth, W., the poet 272
Würtemberg, Church system of 24; Convention with Pope (1857) 412; Protestantism in 432
Würzburg, Protestants expelled from 17; Conference at (1848) 410, 413

Young, Brigham, Mormon leader 340

Zelanti at Rome 347
Ziegenbalg, missionary 156
Zinzendorf, Nicholas Lewis von 123

www.ingramcontent.com/pod-product-compliance
Lightning Source LLC
Chambersburg PA
CBHW070300010526
44108CB00039B/1255